American Standards of Living
1918–1988

This book is dedicated to the memory of my father Norman S. Brown and my sister Baird Brown Hays. Their love and wisdom nurtured me through the years. Their wit and humor made life fun.

AMERICAN STANDARDS OF LIVING

1918–1988

Clair Brown

BLACKWELL
Oxford UK & Cambridge USA

First published 1994

Blackwell Publishers, the publishing imprint of
Basil Blackwell Inc.
238 Main Street
Cambridge, Massachusetts 02142
USA

Basil Blackwell Ltd
108 Cowley Road
Oxford OX4 1JF
UK

Library of Congress Cataloging-in-Publication Data
Brown, Clair, 1946–
  American standards of living, 1918-1988 / Clair Brown.
    p. cm.
    Includes index.
    ISBN 1-55786-371-7
    1. Cost and standard of living—United States—History—20th century.
  I. Title.
  HD6983.B79 1994   94–14113
  339.4'7'09730904—dc20   CIP

British Library Cataloguing in Publication Data
A CIP catalogue record for this book is available from the British Library.

Typeset in 10 on 12 pt Times
by Pure Tech Corporation, Pondicherry, India
Printed in Great Britain by T. J. Press Ltd, Padstow, Cornwall

This book is printed on acid-free paper

Contents

List of Figures and Tables

Acknowledgments

This book, which I began over a decade ago, reflects the changing economy and society in which it was written. As a labor economist, I began investigating the American standard of living to answer the question posed earlier by the Lynds – why do we work so hard? I thought the answer to this would give us an understanding of the theory of labor supply. It would also reveal how differences in occupation and earnings translate into differences in daily life.

The answers, as well as the data, were much more complex than I had assumed they would be a decade ago. The project stretched out over many years. Perhaps the perspective of the years was fortuitous, since the changes we have been experiencing in the 1980s and 1990s presented new insights into the evolution of the American standard of living and how we evaluate it. This study did not reveal the standard economic answers I had expected. Instead, institutions and consumerism turned out to provide important parts of the answer as to why people work so hard, even after living standards have risen dramatically.

The person who has influenced me most, and provided the most support for this project, is Lloyd Ulman. His comments, both to me and to others, through many years of the Graduate Labor Economics Seminar at the University of California at Berkeley, are echoed throughout this book. As director of the Institute of Industrial Relations, Lloyd provided support for the research assistants who made this book possible. His support never wavered, even when others thought the topic was not of sufficient interest to economists. Lloyd Ulman has also served as mentor and role model for me, and I hope to continue his legacy of providing unfailing support and deep insight into projects students and colleagues choose to pursue.

Other colleagues have also provided important support and intellectual stimulation. David Matza made sure that I did not ignore important sociological concepts, and his input influenced my thinking throughout the project. He also was generous in his willingness to read various versions of the manuscript. Michael Reich provided a continual sounding board and was a constant source of encouragement. The manuscript was considerably improved by critical reading and suggestions from Carolyn Shaw Bell, Sam Bowles, Juliet Schor, and Myra Strober. I am also grateful to Bill Dickens, Theresa Ghilarducci, Sandy Jacoby, the late Joseph Pechman, Tibor Scitovsky, and Richard Sutch for their interest and comments at various points in the project. Special thanks go to Suzanne Murphy for teaching me about nutrition studies; to Siobhan Reilly for helping me learn about Food Stamp regulations; and to my mother, Mary Wolfe, for serving as a font of information on nutrition. In addition, I would like to thank editor Susan Milmoe, formerly of Blackwell's, for her interest and faith in this book.

Since this project is based on data collection and manipulation, I am deeply indebted to many excellent research assistants, who worked long hours with great dedication. Early on, Deborah Armida, Sean Flaherty, and Julie Hansen worked with me on evaluating the data, especially from the pre-war years, in order to decide how the data might be analyzed. After deciding on an approach that followed specified family types, the data collection and manipulation began in earnest, for several years done by David Brauer, Anna Cook, and Amelia Preece, who displayed particular insight into the idiosyncrasies of lifestyles historically. Then we reached the 1970s, when computerized microdata became available. Lars Arriola worked with the data during this period. Meanwhile, I became involved in a new project on comparing the employment, training, and wage structures of American and Japanese companies and began traveling. I am grateful to Ruth Given for her tireless work and intellectual focus that renewed this project and brought it to completion. Dennis Toseland took over the final stages of the data analysis. Finally, Wendy Williams' unflagging efforts, patience, and intellectual input were invaluable in verifying and correcting the tables and making the manuscript ready for publication.

Kathey Mooney did an excellent job of editing the early chapters, and Barbara Porter typed them. Amrei Kieschke performed a great service when she computerized the text, which brought a new look to the manuscript and made the editing process much easier. Janice Cripe and Teresa Ojeda performed the difficult task of computerizing the tables. Judy Greenspan performed numerous tasks in the final stages. Diane Leite made sure all these activities were accomplished. I am deeply grateful to these wonderful people, who never complained about my sloppiness or unending requests.

The Institute of Industrial Relations at Berkeley generously provided funding for the graduate student research assistants and support staff who worked on this project.

My husband, Richard Katz has been an important part of this project. I am fortunate that he has provided intellectual and emotional support. He has a gift with language that he is always ready to share, and I am indebted to him for his inexhaustible help with matters both of usage and of text. Richard and our sons Daniel and Jason enrich my life; they provide me with a reason to care about the American standard of living.

Clair Brown
Point Richmond, California
August 1994

1 Economic Growth, Living Standards and Social Welfare

Living standards in the United States have improved dramatically during the twentieth century as the country completed a transformation from an economy based on agriculture to an economy based on industry. The economic forces behind the improved living standards include mass production of goods with continuous automation of production; introduction of new goods and services as a result of technological innovation; development of credit and mass marketing systems; development of worldwide communication and information systems; and integration of the global economy.

Our documentation and analysis of living standards begins in 1918 at the end of World War I, an event which marked the beginning of the automobile era. Living standards were high compared to those of the previous century, which had in turn experienced much growth, however sporadic. Even though industrialization had already been well under way by the turn of the century, mass production characterized the first half of the twentieth century, as the assembly line techniques begun by Ford in 1909 spread rapidly. Computerization has characterized the second half of our century, as access to information and a diversity of products shaped consumption decisions and production processes.[1]

The economic lot of working-class families had improved considerably as a result of the high demand generated by World War I, but monotony and drudgery still characterized everyday life. The urban working-class family tended to live in cramped, dark apartments; ate large amounts of bread with little jam or butter; wore remade and mended clothing; stayed mostly within walking distance of home except perhaps for going to work; attended church or temple as their main social activity; and had little money to spend on treats or gifts. Severe economizing was required to attain even this austere life-style. Any economic mistakes, such as buying uncomfortable shoes or a cut of spoiled meat, meant temporary deprivation for the family since their budgets could not accommodate the replacement of these items. The bleakness of everyday material life provided little relief from the difficult physical labor of husbands and the exhausting housework of wives.

By the late 1980s, daily material life had improved in ways that could not have been imagined in 1918. Working-class families had a richer material life in 1988 than the salaried class had in 1918. Their food, transportation, medical care, and home comforts provided a material quality of life that was not attainable even by the elite in any previous era. Their meals featured a dazzling variety of foods, including fresh fruits and vegetables and store-bought baked goods; their private automobiles provided comfortable and speedy transportation; leisure time activities became an important part of life. Working-class families owned sports equipment and toys, attended sporting and cultural events, and even took vacation trips. In addition, their economic security had been vastly improved with the promise of retirement income. Their homes had central heating and cooling systems, flush toilets, hot running water, and a wide array of machines for cooking and cleaning; they faced a longer life span and received much more sophisticated health care.

The material richness of life brought with it new concerns, however. People now worried about consuming *too many* calories as well as too much fat or salt. Having sufficient space to store clothes and consumer goods became a problem. Finding time to buy and maintain all the goods the family wanted to consume became one more demand in a society already feeling the stress of work and family commitments. In addition, economic growth brought with it congested roadways; environmental concerns about air and water pollution and global warming; and renewed interest in the possibility of inadequate supplies of natural resources and food. Population growth, coupled with demands for more equal access to the world's resources and productive capacity had become the number one global problem.

Paid work and housework had both become less physically demanding, so parents had more energy to enjoy life at the end of the day and on weekends. Yet families were spending *more* total hours at paid work in 1988 than in 1918; wives now had jobs, and the standard workweek had not declined since 1935.[2] The drudgery and austerity of 1918 had been replaced by modern-day pressures stemming from affluence – the need to buy and use a wide array of goods and services in everyday activities, which were now much less likely to take place at home.

American Standards of Living, 1918–1988 documents the family's expenditures that form the material basis of everyday life for laborer, working, and salaried classes in the urban United States from 1918 to 1988. A central goal here is to understand how economic growth has affected the ways people live in the United States and how differences in income, or economic distance, have translated into differences in daily life. We also want to understand how a higher standard of living has changed the social valuation of money and its distribution, and our valuation of time and its use. This chapter provides an overview of the tools for analysis, the hypothesized patterns governing consumption norms, an overview of income distribution, work roles, and consumption norms during 1918–88, and the major findings. The second chapter discusses the methodological approach used in analyzing the standard of living and economic inequality across classes. A chapter is then devoted to the description and analysis of each of five selected years (1918, 1935, 1950, 1973, and 1988). On the basis of these empirical findings, the last chapter draws conclusions about the standard of living in the United States during the twentieth century.

Basics, Variety, and Status

The tools for analysis used in this volume include a standard of living index, a measure of economic distance between classes, and measures of the dynamics of consumption norms, all developed by the author. Here living standards are described in terms of the social norms that govern expenditures within a given class, since consumption is assumed to be governed by these norms and to be motivated by a desire for social differentiation, and not by a desire for basic provisioning.

The standard of living index used here breaks down expenditures into three functional categories: basics, variety, and status.[3] Each of these three components represents the use of expenditures to accomplish different goals of consumption.

The basics component includes expenditures made to meet fundamental physical needs and minimum requirements for social integration, which includes holding a job and sustaining a family. This level of consumption reflects social norms and is assumed to be required for physical welfare and social functioning. Operationally, basics are determined by the laborer family's consumption coupled with 'scientific' evidence about health requirements. How the standard itself changes over time is analyzed whenever possible in terms of scientific criteria, such as nutritional allowances and shelter standards. Specific standards, then, are used with social practice to identify purchases for socially-required basics in food, clothing, shelter, and other categories.

The basics standard represents the fundamental material requirements for a working-class family to function economically and socially. It was not developed to serve as a poverty benchmark. Another benchmark is required for families who are dependent upon the state but are not employed. For this group, a 'dependency' benchmark is calculated.

Once the basics standard is met, improvements in consumption provided by higher expenditures are broken down into variety or status components according to whether they reflect greater diversity (i.e., quantity) or higher quality (i.e., price) for the same, previously specified items (e.g., protein, or street dresses, or dining tables). This enables us to distinguish between improvement in the standard of living that reflects more of the same goods (variety), versus improvement that reflects the purchase of higher-priced goods (status). The former makes life more interesting and comfortable, since it allows more variety and less drudgery as well as more room for errors in consumption activities. The latter provides status markings of one's social position through decoration or showiness or exclusion. Variety is differentiated from status by the characteristic of usefulness. Variety measures the usefulness of commodities above the minimum required level; status measures increments in social differentiation or markings. Operationally, these three components of the standard of living form the basis for measuring economic distance across classes at a point in time as well as economic improvements over time.

Economic Distance

Economic distance measures how the actual difference in spending between two classes is translated into improvements in consumption norms and daily activities. The increment in each expenditure category is calculated as a percentage increase, and how families actually spend more money to separate themselves from the class below is described in detail for each category.

Economic distance is tangible. It marks people by their clothing and belongings; it spatially separates people by their housing and their activities; and it defines the control people have over their own lives.

Economic distance, which is a measure of income inequality, provides a way to examine how material possessions directly influence living standards across classes. In particular, the standard of living index breaks down economic distance into basics, variety, and status. The economic distance created through purchases of basics results in fundamental differences in people's well-being. Economic distance produced through purchases of variety and status create only subtle differences among classes.

The economic distance categorized across classes is a good indicator of the actual differences in living conditions achieved by most families in each class. Interclass comparisons can be made, although interpersonal comparisons are ignored. The distinction between basics, variety, and status provides a foundation for making policy judgments about the living standards and well-being produced by the national income and its distribution.

Emulation and Innovation

The process of incorporating economic growth, including technological change, into the material basis of daily life is long term and includes transformations in consumption, in family composition, in the work roles of family members, and in government policy. Here, the transformation of consumption norms is described through a process of emulation, innovation, and dis-emulation. *Emulation*[4] is the imitation of the norms of a higher class as income rises and is here used as the benchmark for the family's acclimatization to a modified economic structure. Deviations from emulation require a departure from the traditional ways of consuming as income rises. A pattern of higher expenditures for a category than that predicted by emulation is termed *innovation*, one of lower expenditures is termed *dis-emulation* or economizing.[5] The assumption is made that, in the absence of technological change, increases in real expenditures are made according to traditional norms. However, when technological change alters the market goods and services available and introduces new ones, the process of emulation is disrupted and adaptation to market innovation occurs. Innovation is paid for by economizing in another category or by reducing savings.[6] For example, when a laborer family's income increases 20 percent between generations, the laborer family who emulates would adjust meals, automobile purchases, and leisure time activities to copy the consumption of wage-earner families in the previous generation who had 20 percent higher budgets. But if technological change had made new goods and services available, such as television or long-distance telephoning or fast-food restaurants or computers, then the laborer family's consumption of these would be innovation, since these expenditures do not replicate past consumption patterns.

Sometimes, the innovation itself causes dis-emulation when technological change relegates some goods to the attic or some activities to reminiscing. Nylons replaced silk stockings; automobiles replaced horses and streetcars; television cut into reading and moviegoing. In the future, computer networks can be expected to further change leisure time activities and access to information.

Families at the top of the income ladder are constantly innovating in terms of breaking new ground in spending money as their incomes rise. For our employed classes, which represent approximately the middle three quintiles of the income distribution, the amount of innovation versus emulation occurring depends upon the length of time between periods. We would expect more innovation to occur between 1950 and 1973 (23 years) than between 1973 and 1988 (15 years), all else equal, but many other forces are constantly at work.

Emulation was the main force governing the dynamics of consumption during the growth of mass consumption in the first half of this century when working-class families were still struggling to procure basics. Innovation became the main force during computerization and rapid technological change in the second half of the century when basics had been largely met and working-class families were purchasing variety and status.

Emulation requires a family to adapt to a new structure of daily activities as its income rises, but this adaptation process is not considered socially disruptive because the family is adjusting to a life-style already practiced by others. In contrast, when innovation occurs, economic growth must be accompanied by adaptation to a changing structure of material goods. The process is socially disruptive in the sense that social conventions and norms must be reshaped to accommodate the innovations.

Consumption carries no individual psychological component in this analysis, which focuses on social patterns of averages and ignores deviance.[7] It is a collective action of families in their consumption patterns that determines whether emulation is occurring; the bold or timid spirits of individuals play no role. Emulation reflects the extent to which the social norms governing consumption are maintained, and innovation the extent to which they are changed. Together, they represent the ways in which technological change, along with economic growth, affects material life across class.

Hypothesized Patterns

Absolute change in total expenditures, shifts in income inequality across classes, and technological innovation affect consumption norms. In practice, at least part of economic growth occurs through innovations in market goods and services, and innovation becomes a more significant ingredient in growth as the economy matures. Even when real expenditure growth is slow or negative, families want to appear modern by keeping apace with market innovations, so some dis-emulation occurs in order to allow innovation (i.e., one economizes here to innovate there). Moderate real expenditure growth is accomplished to a large extent through innovation. Only when expenditures grow rapidly can families realize emulation as well as innovation. Their rising expectations are met, traditional patterns are less disrupted, and they are more likely to be aware of their improved living standards.

Periods of economic growth traditionally are characterized by greater equality of classes. Consequently, the growth in real expenditures across classes deviates from the growth in total output, as families in a lower class experience greater growth in consumption than families in a higher class. A class with higher expenditure growth is hypothesized to experience more emulation than a class with lower expenditure growth; the latter class will experience relatively more innovation and dis-emulation, which leads to dissatisfaction. Since government policies heavily influence total output and relative incomes, and because each class will try to maintain its relative position, shifts in income inequality tend to have a cyclical nature, as a class that loses out relatively in one period tries to improve its position in the next period. A period of increasing inequality usually follows a period of decreasing inequality.

The qualitative transformation in consumption norms first allowed, and then required, the labor market participation of women to increase. Specifically, economic growth has caused a shift in the family's budget from expenditures related to home life and housework to expenditures related to social life and economic security. As the family's budget shifted away from food and clothing towards transportation, recreation, and personal insurance, the work roles of women shifted from mainly housework to a combination of housework and paid work. As a growing proportion of the family's budget is spent on market goods and services that are not directly related to housework activities, the family's ability to consume those items depends primarily on its money income, not on its time available for housework or other unpaid activities.

With rising incomes, families spend a growing part of their budgets on variety and status. Although the maturing economy requires an increase in the basics for the individual family, this appears to be fairly small. Growth in the required infrastructure occurs primarily in public goods, including transportation, communication, and educational systems, provision of public health and safety, environmental protection, and coordination with other countries. These must be at least partially provided by the government and paid through taxation.

The rate of economic growth and society's beliefs about what opportunities should be, and are, available to people form the struggle over the distribution of income. In a mature economy with rapid technological change, innovation drives consumption norms. When the economy is growing steadily at a moderate rate, families are able to improve their absolute standard of living by buying innovative goods and services without decreasing purchases of traditional goods and services. If economic growth is low and sporadic, families can only buy innovative goods and services by economizing in traditional areas.

If society believes that basics are available to everyone who is willing to work and function within the society, then the public is unwilling to support income support programs for the economically disadvantaged. These two forces of economic growth and social beliefs do not necessarily work in a rational manner. For example, if the economy is performing poorly, families feel economically pinched and political leaders may take advantage of the poor economy to blame the unemployed for their poor work habits. When the economy is performing well, families face rising incomes and political leaders may take advantage of the growing incomes to create programs for those at the bottom of the income distribution. Overall, however, rising affluence intensifies the struggle over variety and status once society believes that basics are available to employed families or through social programs. Instead, the struggle over income distribution becomes focused on the level of variety and status marking economic distance across the employed classes. Hard work is viewed as being rewarded by vacations, fancy cars, and second homes. Status markings reinforce the notion that the unequal outcomes are fair rewards.

Perhaps the struggle over income to buy variety and status with a callous disregard for some people's inability to buy basics is the inevitable outcome in a free market culture that uses 'the measuring rod of money' to determine the value of an individual's contribution and in a society that values individual rights over social order.[8] The forces behind the bias in the United States in favor of private goods and against public goods has created a similar bias toward money-earning activities and away from unpaid activities.[9] Thus the irony of twentieth-century America: growth has intensified the need for paid work, and affluence has increased the desire for economic distance across classes.[10]

Overview of Income Distribution, Work Roles, and Consumption Norms

The empirical basis of this study is household expenditure data from the Consumer Expenditure Surveys (CES) taken in 1918–19, 1934–35, 1950, 1972–73, and 1988.[11] The years available for analysis fortuitously represent important points in US economic history:

- the end of the Great War in Europe and the beginning of massive industrialization with assembly-line production in the United States (1918);
- the beginning of the recovery from the depths of the Depression and the end of the period without national social security programs (1935);
- the beginning of reconstruction in Europe and Japan after World War II and of US supremacy in the world economy (1950);
- the beginning of the period of major restructuring of the economy, both domestic and international, in response to large increases in energy prices and the desire to promote world trade (1973); and
- the end of the period of deregulation and lower taxes, vigorous international competition for markets, and with a massive military build-up continuing (1988).

There are three classes of employed families and one poor class in this study. The three employed white classes are defined by husbands' occupation and by the median urban family income for each occupational group. The three occupational groups, which are distinguished by type of payment of earnings, are:

1. Salaried managers and professionals (termed 'salaried'), who are paid by the year rather than by the hour and who suffer relatively little job insecurity;
2. Skilled and semi-skilled workers (termed 'wage earners'), also known as craft and operative workers, who are paid by the hour and suffer cyclical unemployment; and
3. Unskilled workers, laborers, and service workers (termed 'laborers'), who are paid by the hour and have insecure jobs.

Urban black families represent the poor, or underclass, in 1918 and 1935, since some data are available by race. Otherwise no data were collected for low income families. By 1950, black intact families were at the twenty-fifth percentile for urban families and had incomes one-tenth lower than laborer families. No government poverty benchmark existed, so we do not know if the typical black family were poor, but we do know that their spending was 15 percent below the BLS standard for city workers. Black urban families were in transition from the underclass to the lower working class, and the 1950 data documents their dramatic material improvements. In the 1950 CES, data are available by race, and data on low income families is problematic; therefore, black families continue to represent lower income families in 1950. In 1973 and 1988, poor families can be directly included with available data. Black single-mother families are represented by the poor or underclass class, and black intact families by the working class in 1973 and 1988.

Data are also available to include seniors in 1973 and 1988. Seniors represent the typical household with a head over 64 years old.

The occupational distribution of family heads changed dramatically over this period as family incomes grew (see table 1.1). In 1920, 30% of employed family heads worked on farms, while 12% were professionals and managers. By 1988, only 4% of employed heads worked on farms, while 30% were professionals and managers. As the economy matured, jobs were created in relatively high-paying, white-collar occupations, while relatively low-paying farm work almost disappeared. But economic growth, interacting with social norms, affected families in other ways. Families without employed heads grew from about one-fifth of the families during the Depression and after World War II to over one-fourth since the early 1970s. Increasingly, low-income families were headed by single women. Fewer families were low income during retirement years because Social Security and private pensions prevented a substantial decline in retirees' standard of living.

Table 1.1 Occupational shifts and family incomes, 1918–88[a]

	1918 %	1918 Annual median income ($)	1918 To total median	1935 %	1935 Annual median income ($)	1935 To total median	1950 %	1950 Annual median income ($)	1950 To total median	1973 %	1973 Annual median income ($)	1973 To total median	1988 %	1988 Annual median income ($)	1988 To total median
Employed heads:															
Professional and managerial															
Salaried	12	1,765	1.55	9	2,280	1.97	12	4,930	1.48	25	18,639	1.55	30	51,074	1.59
Self-employed	b	1,830	1.61	11	1,650	1.42	b	4,380	1.32	4	17,015	1.41	b	36,871	1.15
Clerical and sales	10	1,160	1.02	15	1,710	1.47	10	3,950	1.19	16	13,474	1.12	20	34,108	1.06
Craft and operative workers	30	1,290	1.13	29	1,330	1.15	30	3,800	1.14	37	12,686	1.05	32	23,227	0.72
Laborers and service workers	18	990	0.87	10	1,070	0.92	18	2,730	0.82	14	9,467	0.79	14	22,155	0.69
Farmers and farm managers	18	912	0.80	26	965	0.83	18	2,000	0.60	3	9,812	0.81	4		
Farm laborers and foremen	12	660	0.58	b	b	0.00	12	1,580	0.48	1	5,669	0.47	b		
Black urban families[c]	7	NA	NA	8	680	NA	7	2,270	NA	11	7,779	0.65	12	20,509	0.64
Retired, not employed or armed forces (% of employed head)	NA			22[d]	685	0.59	0.2	1,835	0.59	28	6,250	0.519	25	17,516[e]	0.54
Median income (all families)		1,140			1,160			3,320			12,051			32,191	
Median income[f]–1992 $		10,615			11,856			19,349			38,054			28,786	
Unemployment[g]	1.4			20.1			5.3			5.6			5.5		

[a] Income is annual median family income (current dollars), estimated from distributions and rounded to the nearest $10; 1918 is not comparable to the other years since income is average earnings (including all workers) calculated from Kuznets, since occupational distribution is for all males 10+ years from 1920 census, and since only selected occupations were used in the estimates. 1935 data are from the National Resource Committee Survey. The data since 1935 are from the Current Population Surveys and income is associated with occupational status in March or April 1936.

[b] These data are not distinguished from above data (e.g., self-employed professionals are included with salaried professionals in 1918).

[c] The population percentages represent urban population that was Black for 1918 (1920 Census), 1935 (NRPB Survey), and 1950 (Census) and the urban families that were Black for 1973 (CPS) and 1988 (CPS).

[d] Of these, 84% were on relief.

[e] Calculation of median income of families whose head did not work.

[f] CPI Source: Historical Abstract of the US Series E135-166 and Economic Report of the President 1992, Table B-56.

[g] Sources: Historical Abstract, Series D85-86; Economic Report of the President 1992, Table B-37.

Meanwhile, the number of workers per family grew until 1973 and then declined – from 1.2 (1918) to 1.3 (1988) for laborers. Salaried families steadily increased their number of earners from 1.3 during the Depression (1935) to 2.2 (1988) (see table 1.2). These changes reflect the continued rise in the participation rate of adult women over the entire period, the increased participation rate of teenaged girls since 1940, and a decline in the participation rate of men as they retired earlier.[12] The proportion of salaried families with only one worker fell by more than one-half between 1950 and 1988, while the proportion with more than two workers tripled between 1950 and 1973, and then declined between 1973 and 1988. Changes for the other classes are in the same direction, but they are less dramatic.

Table 1.2 Earners per family and sources of income, 1918–88[a]

	1918	1935[b] CES	Adjusted	1950	1973	1988
Average number of earners per family						
Laborer	1.20	1.23	1.00	1.31	1.51	1.33
Wage earner	1.21	1.29	1.17	1.39	1.76	1.65
Salaried	1.57	1.35	1.31	1.40	2.06	2.20
Black		1.41				
Proportion of income from earnings[c]						
Laborer	0.97	0.96	0.82	0.85	0.77	0.89
Wage earner	0.96	0.96	0.91	0.91	0.87	0.95
Salaried	0.95	0.96	0.96	0.91	0.90	0.96
Black		0.98			0.38	0.45

[a] The income proportions are from the CES. The earners per family are from the CES in 1918 and 1935 and from the Current Population Survey for the other years.

[b] The 1935 CES data on earners and income sources include only non-relief families. The adjusted figures include urban relief families. The estimates were made using the average income for the relief population, and the relief percentages by occupation (39% of laborers, 19% of wage earners, and 5% of salaried workers). Works Progress Administration, 'Source of Income of Former Urban Relief Cases,' *Research Bulletin*, Series I, No. 22, 1936 and 'The 1935 Relief Population in 13 Cities,' *Research Bulletin*, Series I, No. 23, 1936.

[c] Excludes self-employed income.

Relative income by occupation shifted somewhat during the Depression, as the earnings of salaried professionals and managers continued to rise while the earnings of production workers in manufacturing and services fell.[13] Black families made substantial gains during World War II, and the earnings distribution across occupations has remained fairly stable since then. Retired people, however, made substantial gains during the 1960s as a result of government income-support programs.

Between the Depression and 1988, the proportion of family income from earnings did not rise, although the number of paid family workers

Table 1.3 Family budgets and social norms[a] (all figures are percent)

				Social life						Security			
		Home life		Presentability			Integration						
Total		*Food-at-home*[c]	*Shelter*[d]	*Medical care*	*Personal appearance*[e]	*Gifts and contributions*	*Activities*[f]	*Transportation*	*Auto owner*	*Personal insurance*	*Home owner*	*Spending rate*[b]	*Tax/gross income*
Laborers													
1918	100	42	26	4	16	2	3	2	9	3	20	100	0.1
1935	100	32	0	4	11	2	7	6	33	4	24	109	0.1
1950	100	27	26	5	11	3	12	11	49	4	37	116	5.0
1973	100	16	29	5	7	4	12	18	89	8	52	101	12.8
1988	100	11	31	4	5	7	13	18	95	9	55	112	7.3
Wage earners													
1918	100	40	28	4	17	2	4	2	13	3	24	97	0.1
1935	100	31	31	4	11	3	8	7	43	5	26	107	0.1
1950	100	26	25	5	12	3	11	13	68	4	47	111	5.9
1973	100	15	29	5	7	4	13	18	95	9	69	95	13.9
1988	100	10	28	3	6	7	13	20	99	10	71	106	9.2
Salaried													
1918	100	35	25	4	20	3	5	5	31	3	36	90	0.2
1935	100	23	29	4	13	3	11	11	80	5	31	101	0.3
1950	100	24	24	5	12	3	13	13	78	4	54	108	7.1
1973	100	14	27	4	8	5	15	17	97	11	76	88	16.4
1988	100	9	28	3	6	7	15	17	100	12	86	94	10.1
Blacks													
1918	100	48	22	NA	13	NA	NA	NA	NA	NA	NA	99	NA
1935	100	35	33	4	11	2	7	4	11	3	19	104	0
1950	100	30	27	4	15	2	10	8	24	4	27	110	3

		Home life		Presentability		Social life — Integration			Security				
	Total	Food-at-home[c]	Shelter[d]	Medical care	Personal appearance[e]	Gifts and contributions	Activities[f]	Transportation	Auto owner	Personal insurance	Home owner	Spending rate[b]	Tax/gross income
Seniors													
1973	100	20	33	10	8	6	9	10		2		111	2
1988	100	13	30	13	5	8	11	15	82	2	59	114	
Low income													
1973	100	22	37	6	7	3	9	12		4		132	4
Poor													
1988	100	18	35	5	6	4	12	15	66	3	29	235	3

[a] Percentage shown (unless otherwise indicated) are expenditures in category/total expenditures; i.e. for Laborers 1950 food-at-home $786/$2,947.
[b] Spending rate = expenditures/net income.
[c] Alcoholic beverages have been included here; for each class this constituted 1%–2% of total expenditures.
[d] Shelter consists of the housing, fuel and light, furnishings, and household operations categories combined.
[e] Personal appearance includes clothing and personal care.
[f] Activities include recreation, education, and food away-from-home.

did. As one moves up the class structure, earnings become a larger part of income, the family has more earners, and the relative importance of government benefits falls. Although the average age of the family head is the same for the three employed classes, the number of children under 18 increases with class, and the probability of receiving Social Security benefits or unemployment compensation decreases with class.

Access to market work is the primary determinant of family income. Higher class families were able to improve their relative income position because of their greater access to paid work with higher earnings. The laborer family's earnings per worker averaged 75% of the earnings per worker for the wage earner family. Government support payments partially made up for the lack of access to market work and for the lower wages paid to laborer families.

Consumption norms changed dramatically as real incomes grew, as can be seen in the budgets for the wage earner family (see table 1.3). The most remarkable changes in the daily structure of economic life occurred with the offsetting shifts in food and the automobile: food at home declined from 40% of the wage-earner family's 1918 budget to only 10% of its 1988 budget, and automobile-related expenditures rose from 2% of the 1918 budget to 20% of the 1988 budget. By 1950, transportation had replaced clothing in the 'basic three' of food, clothing, and shelter. Car ownership had become almost universal among wage-earner families by 1960. Ownership of a second car then became an important consumption goal. By 1988, wage earner families averaged 1.4 vehicles.

Less dramatic but still fundamental changes occurred in the relative positions of clothing, recreation, and personal insurance (including Social Security payroll tax). Recreation and food away-from-home (social activities) had become as important as clothing and personal care (appearance) by 1950. Insurance, recreation, and clothing formed the second-ranked group, after food, shelter, and transportation. The family budget was shifting away from being dominated by items related to home life and toward items related to social integration and security. The rise in taxes paid by wage earners from less than 1% of gross income in 1918 to 18% in 1988 occurred with the vast change in the role of government in the economy and society.

These budgetary changes reflect substantial improvements in well-being for the employed classes: adequate nutrition and mobility needs (i.e., car ownership) were attained by 1950. The more stringent requirement of homeownership was met by over two-thirds of the wage-earner and salaried families in 1960. Laborers did not hit the half-way mark in homeownership until 1973, however, and blacks lagged considerably behind white laborers. As basic needs in food, transportation, and housing were being met, other needs were being created such as more flexible transportation provided by a second car, greater security through savings and retirement income, housing amenities such as air-conditioning, restaurant meals, vacations, and paid recreation activities.

Classes differ according to the decade in which they finally meet basic needs and according to how much they exceed these basics. Although ability to buy basics is important in determining physical well-being, a family's sense of well-being is also influenced by how its income (and thus its life-style) compares to others. To offset shifts in relative and absolute income over time, families can use two tactics – a change in family size or a change in their spending rate (i.e., expenditures divided by net income) and an increase in work hours.

In 1918, economic distance between two classes was established by more and better food and clothing (per person), nicer homes in a better location, and larger families. Between the black and white laborer classes, the basics of food, clothing, and housing were more important components of economic distance than was larger family size. For the wage earner and salaried classes, additional family members were as important in creating economic distance as purchases of the three basics. By 1935, transportation replaced clothing in defining distance across classes; food, housing, and transportation accounted for about one-half of the economic distance; and larger family size became much less important. This pattern continued to form at least one-half of the economic distance from 1950 through the 1980s.

Overall, up to 1950, movements in family size across classes reinforced trends in inequality. Salaried families, especially, seemed able to protect their class position from shifts in relative and absolute income by varying family size. After 1950, the shifts in inequality were less dramatic and family size differences were fairly constant across employed classes.

The role of economic security in defining economic distance across classes was also affected by trends in inequality. In general, changes in the spending rate across employed classes reinforced changes in their relative expenditures. Not only did the salaried class spend more on variety and status, savings provided them with greater economic security. Higher incomes provided more economic security in terms of assets, since expenditures did not rise as rapidly across class as did income. Since 1935, the spending rate of the laborer class compared to the salaried class has steadily increased. The black spending rate relative to the white employed families' rates reinforced the rising inequality between 1918 and 1935.

Spending rates rose between 1918 and 1950 for all classes, largely because of the improved availability of credit. Spending rates fell for the employed classes. By 1973, the laborer class was at the break-even point, with expenditures equal to net income, and the wage earner and salaried classes were accumulating assets. With real family incomes growing less than expected between 1973 and 1988, spending rates rose once again for all families.

Overall, the family's economic security increased dramatically between 1950 and 1973, as the ratio of expenditures to income declined and as the expenditures for personal insurance increased. These improvements in security reflect the continued growth of income even after basic nutrition, housing, and transportation needs had been met. They also reflect the need for planned retirement income as life expectancy increased. Between 1918 and 1988, the expected age at death for a 20-year-old increased eight years for white males – from 65 years old to 73; and it increased 13 years for white females – from 67 years old to 80. White men at the beginning of their working lives could expect almost no years of retirement in 1918, but they could expect at least eight years of retirement in the 1980s. The need for life insurance to provide an income to the family in case of the head's pre-retirement death diminished sharply, while the need for retirement income for both spouses increased.

Major Findings

The material basis of everyday life has changed dramatically since 1918. An orientation towards home and concerns about physical needs have given way to an orientation towards the larger society and concerns about social integration, security, and individual autonomy. This transformation occurred as the shares of the family's budget devoted to food and clothing shrank and those devoted to recreation, transportation, and personal insurance rose. Security also grew with improvements in Social Security and the rapid increase in homeownership rates.

Economic growth has been accomplished through the establishment of a larger, more complex economy that requires integration of the family into the economy and community through the spread of the marketplace in work and consumption activities. As the society has become more dependent on the marketplace rather than on work at home to procure goods and services, the need for economic interdependence within the family has declined. This change has both required and allowed the development of the norm of individual economic autonomy at the expense of the economic well-being of the community and the traditional family. With most adults expecting to work for pay, the economic basis for family ties has eroded further. Economic security is now tied to the acquisition of education and to income support programs, both of which are provided or regulated by government.

Between 1918 and 1988, changes in the consumption norms for food, housing, transportation, and family size had a substantial impact on women's work roles. Between 1918 and 1950, major improvements in meals, in nutritional value as well as in variety, lessened the family's reliance on the wife's cooking skills. Economic growth pulled women into the paid labor force in the United States only after growth had fulfilled basic needs, first in food, and then in transportation and housing. Further material improvements could only come through the family's increased consumption of market goods and services. More reliable birth control and reduced childbearing after 1960 were accompanied by women devoting more years to paid work, and the growth of the service economy created more jobs open to women.

How economic development affects work roles depends on the cultural importance of money versus other measuring rods (e.g., artistic endeavors or community life). Because ours is a society in which money is the primary measure of social position, once wives with older children began increasing their labor force participation in the 1940s, and once basic needs associated with housework were being met, it became inevitable that more and more wives would work for pay. Since a wife's employment can raise her family's income to the level of the next higher class, the income distinction between classes is blurred during the transitional period in which some wives work and some do not. A full-time homemaker cannot use her housework to bridge the economic distance between her family and the family of an employed wife since her homemaker's efforts provide very different consumption items from those bought with the wife's wages, and families perform essentially the same housework whether or not the wife is employed.[14] Each class's consumption standard shifts to include the earnings of both husband and wife.

With our particular culture and institutions, economic growth has affected individuals' everyday social functioning in special ways. Earlier, it was materially restricted by basics – lack of nutrition affected health and vitality; clothing had mainly a practical use; the need to bathe affected social presentability; and poor sleep resulting from crowded housing affected work. Today, it is materially restricted by variety and status items – travel and entertainment mark one's life-style, and clothing, the automobile, and an address mark one's place in society, in addition to filling utilitarian needs. Moreover, social and economic functioning is now circumscribed by one's access to information and contacts as well as by one's opportunities in the labor market. Effective functioning is improved by the allowance for economic mistakes (i.e., purchase of 'wrong' clothing or purchase of a gadget no one uses), which have no consequence for the family's standard of living. Although the amount of time devoted to shopping has increased, an income buffer makes fulfilling everyday consumption tasks easier than before.

In summary, the importance of food and clothing in the family budget declined as that of transportation, recreation, and personal insurance increased. Items that allow building a broader social life and greater financial security have gained ascendancy over items related to the provision of family life. Status has become relatively much more important, variety somewhat more important, and basics less important as incomes have grown. Class differences became more visible in everyday life as they became centered on variety and status items, especially those related to social activities, rather than on basics, especially those related to home activities.

The integration of the family into the marketplace seems to have reinforced the need for economic distance between classes. Since 1973, as national economic performance and income growth have lagged, the combination of having basic needs met for employed families and of having consumption made more public seems to have increased the conflict over income and fanned people's desire to widen the distance between themselves and the class below. As the rising standard of living has encompassed more items for variety and status, the desire to differentiate oneself seems to have intensified during a period of economic stagnation. This is especially true in a society such as ours where the great majority of members have their basic needs met and where those with inadequate incomes are disproportionately minorities. Employed classes can believe that the struggle over income shares no longer *necessarily* means that the attainment of greater variety and status by one class comes at the expense of decreased consumption of basics in a lower class.

NOTES

1. See Michael J. Piore and Charles F. Sabel, *The Second Industrial Divide* (New York: Basic Books, 1984).
2. For an analytical insight of time use and why Americans still work so hard, see Juliet Schor, *The Overworked American: The Unexpected Decline in Leisure* (NY: Basic Books, 1991). Stanley Lebergott in *Pursuing Happiness: American Consumers in the Twentieth Century* (Princeton, NJ: Princeton University Press, 1993) questions whether Americans are 'overworked.' He emphasizes the decline in hours of work and the rise in real wages over the century (Ch. 9). He argues that economic growth has allowed people to extend 'lifetime hours of worthwhile experience,' including medical expenditures to extend life; artificial lighting to extend day; automobile to speed travel; telephone to speed communication; prepared foods, finished clothing, and household devices for cleaning (Ch. 6).
3. The components of basics, variety, and status correspond to Marshall's notions of necessaries, comforts, and luxuries. The tripartite division was widely used to make policy prescriptions. For example, Paul Douglas (later a US senator) termed luxuries (i.e., those goods and services above necessities and comforts) as 'evil seeds,' in Paul Douglas, 'The Economic Waste of Luxury,' in Thomas D. Eliot, ed., *American Standards and Planes of Living* (Boston: Ginn & Co., 1931),

pp. 449–54. Keynes distinguished between absolute needs that are universally shared and relative needs that make people feel superior, in J. M. Keynes, 'Economic Possibilities for Our Grandchildren,' *Collective Writings* (London: St Martin, 1971–3), IX, p. 326. Harrod also used a two-way classification between 'democratic wealth' (available to all through economic growth) and 'oligarchic wealth' (possible only for a select few); see Roy Harrod, 'Possibility of Economic Satiety-Use of Economic Growth for Improving the Quality of Education and Leisure,' in *Problems of United States Economic Development* (New York: Committee for Economic Development, 1958). Fred Hirsch developed this two-way division in a provocative and important book, *Social Limits to Growth* (Cambridge, MA: Harvard University Press, 1976).

4. The concept of emulation, or 'the pecuniary classification of one's self as compared with one's neighbors' is Thorstein Veblen's; see *The Theory of the Leisure Class* (1899; reprint ed., Boston: Houghton Mifflin, 1973). This concept is used here in conjunction with the relative income approach developed by James S. Duesenberry, *Income, Saving, and the Theory of Consumer Behavior* (Cambridge, MA: Harvard University Press, 1952). In Duesenberry's framework, quantity differences are assumed to translate into quality differences rather than increased amounts of the same goods. His four propositions, which assume culturally-required consumption and general agreement about the best way to satisfy any particular requirement, underlie the definition of emulation used here and the assumption of a socially-determined structure of daily life. Neither Veblen's nor Duesenberry's theories mention the concept of innovation, since neither of these authors specifically distinguishes between old and new goods. For Veblen, the problem was to explain the motivation behind ownership; technological change, however, was considered a major factor behind institutional change. Duesenberry did not address new products because he did not think they were important in short-run consumption versus savings decisions. However, Simon Kuznets in 'Quantitative Aspects of the Economic Growth of Nations: VII The Share and Structure of Consumption,' *Economic Development and Cultural Change*, 10, 2, Part 2 (Jan. 1962), discusses how changes in technology require modification of economic organization and values in order to assure proper assimilation of the changes. In turn, values affect the conditions under which technology and organization emerge.

5. Empirically, predicted emulation (PE) for a given consumption category equals the increase in expenditures made by the higher income group (in the same period) that corresponds to the income earned in the next period (deflated back to the base period). Innova-

tion (IN) equals the actual change in expenditures (ΔE) above predicted emulation. The amount by which expenditures fall short of predicted emulation is dis-emulation (DE). In the few instances when income growth is low (or negative), predicted emulation may be less than the expenditure in the base year, which is viewed as a reduced standard (RS). Then the following holds: if $0 \geqslant \Delta E \geqslant PE$, $RE = \Delta E$, $IN = 0$, $DE = \Delta E - PE$; if $0 > PE > \Delta E$, $RE = PE$, $IN = 0$, $DE = \Delta E - PE$; if $\Delta E > 0 > PE$, $RE = 0$, $IN = \Delta E$, $DE = -PE$, where actual change in expenditures is ΔE. Assets change more or less than predicted by the total dis-emulation minus total innovation. Realized emulation (RE) equals predicted emulation minus dis-emulation. The following identities hold:

$$
\begin{aligned}
&(1) \quad \text{If } \Delta E \geqslant PE > 0, \qquad IN = \Delta E - PE, \\
& \qquad\qquad\qquad\qquad DE = 0, \\
& \qquad\qquad\qquad\qquad RE = PE \\
& \text{If } 0 \leqslant \Delta E \leqslant PE, \qquad IN = 0 \\
& \qquad\qquad\qquad\qquad DE = PE - \Delta E, \\
& \qquad\qquad\qquad\qquad RE = \Delta E. \\
&(2) \quad RE = PE - DE \\
&(3) \quad \Delta E = PE + IN - DE.
\end{aligned}
$$

When expenditures fall below the initial level, realized emulation is zero and dis-emulation exceeds predicted emulation. This special case of dis-emulation (reduced standard) is noted separately in the documentation of data, since this process indicates that the disruption to traditional consumption norms is so great that families cannot even replicate their previous expenditures in some categories.

6. In addition to the long-run adjustment process, short-run adjustments to cyclical downswings are made through economizing. Economizing patterns are culturally governed – convention determines the appropriate expenditures and activities to cut back. See, for example, David Caplovitz, *Making Ends Meet: How Families Cope with Inflation and Recession* (Beverly Hills, CA: Sage, 1979).

7. Tibor Scitovsky, in *The Joyless Economy* (New York: Oxford University Press, 1976), emphasizes the negative aspects of the 'conformity and established life-style' that result from the mass (homogeneous) consumption required by mass production. Scitovsky argues persuasively that people seek pleasure from novelty and stimulation (Chs 1, 4). Alternatively, Carolyn Shaw Bell, in *Consumer Choice in the American Economy* (New York: Random House, 1967), emphasizes the two-way relationship between consumers and sellers and the independence of consumer choice ('business does not control consumers and . . . no basis for the belief that consumers are controlled by

other consumers) (Ch. 10). In our model, such 'novel' pursuits could become part of a class's life-style among status items once income levels are sufficiently high. As discussed above, ability to make individualistic pursuits, which are seen as synonymous with individual freedom, increase with relative income.

8. John Kenneth Galbraith, *The Affluent Society* (Boston: Houghton Mifflin, 1958) eloquently analyzes the distortions that occur in a privatized economy that measures value by price and social standing by income. He discusses how the public sector, which nurtures artistic and intellectual growth, protects health and the environment, builds the infrastructure necessary for economic growth, and develops community, will languish while individuals collect gadgets and buy items that are never used. See also Scitovsky, *The Joyless Economy*; Staffan Linder, *The Harried Leisure Class* (New York: Columbia University Press, 1970); and Richard A. Easterlin, 'Does Economic Growth Improve the Human Lot?' in Paul A. David and Melvin W. Reder, eds, *Nations and Households in Economic Growth: Essays in Honor of Moses Abramovitz* (New York: Academic Press, 1974), pp. 89–125. Lebergott's *Pursuing Happiness* argues that consumers are not overly influenced by advertising to have false values rather than inherent and natural ones. Lebergott questions economists (including Veblen, Galbraith, Scitovsky, and Mishan) who have criticized American materialism, and he praises the increase in consumption. However, he joins these institutional economists in assuming that consumption is influenced by social norms, 'The social environment has always shaped human values, and wants' (p. 19).

9. See Schor, *The Overworked American . . .*, (1991).

10. Hirsch, *Social Limits to Growth* (1976), attributes the heightened struggle over income distribution that accompanies economic growth to the importance of positional goods, which deteriorate in quality when consumed by more people. Either their price will rise as the demand increases or the satisfaction gained from their consumption will decline. He assumes that positional goods (or oligarchic wealth) is static and the positional economy is zero sum. However, status consumption is created by social norms and therefore can expand. In addition, innovation allowed basics and variety consumption, which would form his material economy, to expand. His cogent argument illuminates the limits to emulation and the importance of innovation in a mature economy. It also underscores why ecological concerns will increase the distributional struggle as well as decrease social concern over the disadvantaged both at home and abroad. Lebergott (*Pursuing Happiness*) questions the importance of Hirsch's concept of unavailability as well as Veblen's

emphasis on waste. Lebergott argues that congestion and pollution reflect rising living standards for the majority of workers.

11. Data sources are discussed in the Appendix.

12. For a thorough study of women in the US labor market, see Claudia Goldin, *Understanding the Gender Gap* (New York: Oxford University Press, 1989). Goldin documents a decline in wives' paid labor throughout the nineteenth century with its nadir about 1920 (Ch. 2). This book opens at a time when wives were beginning another long rise in participation. Goldin also gives an excellent discussion of 'marriage bars' (Ch. 6) and emphasizes the importance of cohort effects and period or contemporaneous factors in women's longterm increase in labor force participation (Ch. 5).

13. See Simon Kuznets, *National Income and Its Composition, 1919–1938*, 2 vols. (New York: National Bureau of Economic Research, 1941).

14. Myra H. Strober, 'Wives' Labor Force Behavior and Family Consumption Patterns,' *American Economic Review*, 67 (Feb. 1977), pp. 410–17; Myra H. Strober and Charles B. Weinberg, 'Strategies Used by Working and Nonworking Wives to Reduce Time Pressures,' *Journal of Consumer Research*, 6 (March 1980), pp. 338–48; Richard A. Berk and Sarah F. Berk, *Labor and Leisure at Home: Content and Organization of the Household Day* (Beverly Hills, CA: Sage, 1979); and Clair Brown, 'An Institutional Model of Wives' Work Decisions,' *Industrial Relations*, 24, 2 (Spring 1985), pp. 182–204.

2 Modeling and Measuring the Standard of Living

Every society's view of its standard of living necessarily reflects an underlying web of social values, which include equity, maintenance of class structure, cohesiveness, well-being of the poorest, individual rights, competitiveness, global power, and growth.

Since the structure within which the economy functions and the values by which it is judged are socially determined, any set of numbers is meaningless without its social interpretation. Over time, society's interpretation of its standard of living regularly undergoes modifications as underlying values change. In the span of a single lifetime, an individual is affected by several shifts in societal values. In the United States, for example, judgments about the fruits of economic growth have changed to reflect the economic and political realities present in each new decade. The roaring 1920s reflected the alluring promise of a consumer society liberated by the automobile. The depressed 1930s were characterized by a thrifty, small-expectations, security-seeking orientation; the warring 1940s, by a self-sacrifice-to-overcome-world-evil view. The reconstructing 1950s touted rugged individualism with a strong work ethic, while the culture became more homogeneous as people spent hours watching network television. The full-employment 1960s emphasized the role of government to promote racial and gender equality and reduce material suffering; the transitional 1970s, a re-examination of the state's role with a scaling down of economic expectations. The deregulated 1980s proclaimed the glorification of individual achievements amidst market competition.

In the global 1990s, conflict over income distribution, including government provision of education and other social welfare services, intensified as it expanded to encompass the threat of 'have-not' countries to US and western European living standards. With economies integrated by lowering trade and financial barriers and with societies integrated by permeable borders, low-wage countries are attracting capital while high-wage countries are attracting immigrants.

Social rules and customs (i.e., institutions) provide the general framework within which the world is evaluated; at the same time, they provide the guidelines by which we live.[1] Since institutions structure our conceptions, we often have difficulty even describing the institutional structure itself. We tend to think of our own institutional structure as natural and unique (i.e., as literally the only possible one). Thus, many economists have no compunction about divorcing social structure from economic value. The resulting model of idiosyncratic individuals functioning in abstract free markets to determine prices and wages that can then be assumed to be socially optimal, is not, from a market perspective, problematic. If, however, the social structure that creates and guides the markets is in a continual and dynamic process, then social optimality is not merely a bloodless abstraction by economists, but rather the result of a ceaseless battle between social groups with conflicting needs and goals.[2] These struggles directly affect the marketplace and are registered by it. The outcomes can be traced in the economy's performance, especially the standard of living across classes.

To evaluate class differences in the standard of living requires a familiarity with the institutions that govern the wage distribution and the consumption norms by which wages are translated into a family's standard of living. In an institutional model,[3] underemployment (including unemployment) is assumed to be a basic characteristic of the labor market: absence of the full utilization of all workers' potential requires that workers be allocated into unequal positions in the labor market. This process is governed by the institutional structure within which the labor market functions; it is through social rules and customs that jobs are rationed. The wage rate of any given job reflects its underlying bargaining power and designates its societal valuation.

This chapter discusses the role of institutions in structuring the labor market and sustaining economic distance across classes in an orderly fashion. How society defines economic inequality, which shapes the policies that affect the distribution of income and the standard of living, is also discussed. The standard of living has both relative and absolute dimensions irrespective of the level of economic development or the rate of economic growth.

Social Order and Social Reproduction

A basic requirement for any society is stability with reproduction over time. This occurs neither inevitably nor automatically. Members of a society must be prepared for their positions and must be taught to willingly carry out the roles associated with these positions. This process –

which sociologists refer to as 'socialization' – requires institutions that define and shape the individual. Observed personality traits (e.g., behavior differences by gender) grow out of the social structure that prepares the child and places the adult. Each person has a social role as well as a work role. These two must be well integrated in order for the individual and the system to function properly. Consequently, both private (within the family) and public (within the school) efforts are made to prepare children for the social and work roles deemed appropriate for their sex and their class background. This learned behavior helps ensure that social roles and work roles are compatible.[4]

Two additional functions of a society's basic institutions are to help maintain harmonious social relations and to allow gradual accommodation to new social and economic realities. Here, role compatibility is important – so much so that if social and work roles are in conflict, the structure must change to reintegrate the two. This type of conflict is exemplified by today's demands being made on women and men to be full-time paid workers, while they continue their responsibilities for child-rearing and family life. The institutional response to this 'role strain' has taken two forms, each producing a vastly different outcome.

In one scenario, women and men are trying to restructure work life and family life so that gender roles are more equal at work and at home. The parents must find sufficient time to create and sustain family life and to earn incomes adequate for their class. In another scenario, the labor market pressure on women is alleviated through 'special treatment' (e.g., part-time work, working at home, unpaid maternity leave) in order both to retain them as lower paid workers and to ensure that they continue to provide family life. These policies, which are usually not available to men, provide a safety valve. They make the woman's dual role more manageable, and they keep pressure on the man to maintain his primary attachment to the employer rather than shifting some of his commitment and energy from work to family life. Which scenario will dominate will depend on whether the 'egalitarian' or the 'traditionalist' forces have the sociopolitical power to form new rules governing work and family life. Although the egalitarian forces seemed to have forced changes in the 1970s, the traditionalist forces seem to have regained control in the 1980s.

As with gender relations, class relations are governed by institutions. In our society, social and work roles provide the basis for defining and dividing classes. Incomes are directly tied to these roles, and the goods and services commanded by income outwardly mark each class in the society.[5] In this way, placement in the labor market simultaneously determines the individual's earnings, standard of living, and status. By experience, these have not been the same for all members of society. The unequal access to resources is the source of ongoing conflict over the rules and customs that recreate that inequality (with some minor deviations). Conflict can take place directly at the workplace, in the form of hierarchical wage rates and working conditions; it can take place in society at large, in the form of disagreements over norms governing the standard of living; or it can take place in the political process, in the form of different policy agendas for governmental action.

In most cases, however, established institutions successfully diffuse the potential impact of conflict over resource distribution. The government plays an important role in reconciling the changing social and economic needs that reflect minor shifts in power among the unequal classes. This is usually accomplished through legislative changes that accommodate newly legitimated claims made by one or more classes to certain social, economic, or political resources. The labor market also assists in the maintenance of social order and stability. Its function is to ration people into the unequal job structure in such a way that workers remain productive and the structure is recreated over time.

The function of the standard of living is somewhat different.[6] It provides the economic separation or distance between classes by determining where they live, how they appear in public, with whom they interact, and in which activities they engage. Although policy concerns about the standard of living typically are motivated by a concern about the well-being of various classes, the people themselves are more concerned about relative position.[7] A family's standard of living provides its reference point within society while defining the family's control over the lives of family members, including their physical mobility and their access to activities. Command over resources determines freedom to choose among options, to make mistakes, or to change one's mind as well as to decide the education, experiences, and networks available to one's children.

Defining Economic Inequality

Class conflict is centered around *relative* differences in income, and an integral part of the conflict itself is deciding whether relative or absolute standards of well-being should be the basis for making policy. The managerial/professional class, which resists improvements toward equality, argues that absolute standards are the appropriate benchmark for judgment. Their relatively advantageous position is justified by a meritocratic world view, such as human capital theory,[8] that rationalizes unequal labor market outcomes. The welfare class, whose standard of living would be improved by greater income equality, argues that relative standards are the appropriate benchmark for judgment; poor people experience daily the social exclusion that accompanies a standard of living below the norms achieved by the working class.

Since concern with income distribution has been tied historically to concern with income inadequacy,[9] we might expect that a society would tolerate more income inequality during a period of economic growth if growth raised the absolute standard of living of the lowest class above some socially defined standards. However, as economic growth allows unskilled workers' wages to rise above subsistence, the class conflict over whether relative or absolute standards of well-being should be the basis for judging economic performance becomes both more salient and more public. In the first part of the twentieth century, economists prepared quantity budgets for various standards or planes of living, ranging from 'poverty' to 'comfort.' This needs-based appraisal was an absolute one, used in an economy where a large part of the working class was not even earning above-subsistence wages. Until workers' wages rose above subsistence levels, the needs-based approach provided a useful guide to policy.[10] Although the needs-based approach expanded to incorporate the idea of 'a living wage' that covered many items other than those required for basic nutrition and shelter, the conflict over income distribution became centered around *relative* income differences and income inequality.[11] Since relative income differences materially differentiate and separate classes, this focus posed a threat to class position.

In contrast, Friedman's powerful permanent income approach allowed the possibility that everyone was economically equal, regardless of how unequal their measured incomes appeared.[12] Unequal incomes at any point in time could be explained by differences in the timing (including investments) of the income stream, differences in the labor/leisure choices made, and differences in endowments, constraints, and abilities. This approach, however, left economists without an objective standard for evaluating the distribution of income and economic well-being. The criterion for judging economic performance was growth within the ideology of individual freedom of choice. Attempts to redistribute income through taxation or in-kind programs were discredited because of the assumed negative impact they would have on freedom and incentives, an influence which would adversely affect economic growth.

The permanent income approach replaced the relative income approach at about the same time the majority of working-class families were receiving incomes above the minimum required to meet nutrition and shelter standards. This was no accident. The permanent approach – with its emphasis on personal choice providing optimal outcomes within a free market setting – was not politically feasible in an economy where the working-class majority clearly had inadequate nutrition and shelter. Once the permanent income approach became the mainstream theory of consumption, attempts to develop measures to evaluate relative standards of living became irrelevant, even though relative standards were now the socially-relevant measure in inequality.

Evaluating the Fruits of Economic Growth

Growth requires change to occur both in the process of growth itself and in the process of integrating the results of growth into everyday life. These changes may threaten the stability of society if they change relative income or status positions.

Independent of relative changes, however, growth may be destabilizing if it influences social values in ways that threaten existing morals, especially the work ethic, self-discipline, or communal responsibility. Higher income and status have traditionally conferred greater control over one's life with greater ability to disregard prevailing standards of 'right behavior.' Yet even when higher national income allows everyone's income to rise, status, by its very nature, must maintain its relative scarcity.[13] So even as income gives people greater economic independence, status rankings require the same allegiance to morality.

Although status itself cannot become more plentiful, people's sense of their own status, and the power or control that is attached to it, may increase as incomes rise. At the same time, society's ability to regulate itself will diminish as the 'whip of hunger' loses its sting. Unless the whip of hunger is replaced by the compulsion to buy goods, economic growth has the potential of undermining the work ethic. But the advertising that has played such a crucial role in creating pressures to consume mass-produced goods and services has itself provoked debate about the value to society or the individual of just such advertised consumption.[14]

Concern with the relation between affluence, morality, and social order extends over many generations.[15] Yet, until 1950, the actual living standards of working people were extremely meager. Ordinary lives were dull, fatiguing, and routinized. Under these circumstances, concern with the impact on behavior of rising wages or a shorter work week attests to the oppressive nature of the economic structure that relied on the whip of hunger.

Scholars[16] tried to mitigate concern about the negative impact of growth by emphasizing the possible development of 'higher wants' such as education, cultural activities, and philanthropy. But as people showed their preference for mass culture (such as movies) over concerts or drama, and their preference for commercial recreation (such as amusement parks) over painting or playing an instrument or making handicrafts, social critics began to question the value of economic growth based on mass-produced consumer goods rather than on 'higher wants.' Ironically, since the economic growth that most benefitted the working class was based on mass production, continued growth required consumption of mass-produced goods.

Interestingly enough, economics emphasized growth as the level of affluence rose, and today most economists embrace the 'growth with freedom' criterion for evaluating economic outcomes.[17] Historically, however, some economists have argued against allowing large differences in material standards of living and against equating human welfare to money income.[18] For example, Hobson argued that as consumption incorporated more 'elements of conveniences, comforts and luxuries (not necessaries),' then problems of 'disutility or ill fare' would occur. As people or groups divert the surplus above basics for their own use rather than for social well-being, higher standards of consumption will contain 'a larger proportion of socially wasteful or injurious goods.'[19]

Today, some of this dissatisfaction with mainstream thinking still remains. Sen,[20] for example, has become the leading critic of the traditional utility approach to evaluating the standard of living. He made a major contribution to our thinking about living standards by his focus on functionings (i.e., the living conditions one achieves)[21] and capabilities (i.e., the ability to achieve functionings). Sen's philosophical approach is based on the notion that the living standard is 'a matter of the life one leads rather than of the resources and means one has to lead a life.'[22] He points out that material needs increase as the economy develops, so even if poverty is defined in terms of an absolute level of basic capabilities, the income (or commodities) required to be non-poor varies with the 'average opulence' as well as across societies.[23]

Theoretically, however, the difference between an opulence approach (i.e., measuring commodity possession) and a functionings approach (i.e., measuring the type of life people achieve) depends on the link between consumption and the social (or class) structure in determining life outcomes.[24] Whenever the socioeconomic structure primarily determines the commodities needed for a specific living condition, then the opulence and the functionings approaches become indistinguishable. This occurs when comparing a country's classes at a point in time. For comparisons over time, an update of the major structural shifts makes the opulence approach empirically equivalent to the functionings approach.

When two countries' socioeconomic structures are compared, then the opulence and functionings approaches diverge even if the link between structure, commodities, and outcomes is strong. However, the functionings approach still leaves us with the conundrum of whose value system to use for a yardstick when comparing living standards across cultures. Because of this substantial stumbling block, which is always present in any cross-cultural comparison, measurements of commodity usage may provide the least value-laden comparison of resource usage and material well-being.

The analysis and measurement of the standard of living in this book ignores these cross-cultural issues.[25] In addition, although no numerical adjustments are made to private expenditures over time to compensate for shifts in the socioeconomic structure (including externalities such as pollution or non-money transactions such as housework), these adjustments could be made.[26] In some cases (housework, traffic congestion), the externalities affect each class equally (in an absolute sense). In other cases (pollution, crime), higher income classes can buy protection. In a relative sense, therefore, their impact on a class's standard of living would decline as income rises.

Adding changes in housework to a standard of living measurement over time becomes problematic to the extent that the shift is cultural, so that the life experience of the people involved has changed. If the shift is purely economic (i.e., a replacement of one's time with market goods without changing the commodity consumed), then the shift is recorded in increased expenditures. In this case, adjustments can be made to the expenditures, which would be reflected in the standard of living index.

However, if housework is assumed to be prescribed by social rule and custom, it must be accomplished by a family according to class standards.[27] Housework is a complement, rather than a substitute, to the family's income in creating a life-style. As one moves up the class (and income) ladder, the norms governing housework change.[28] Housework hours, along with income, are assumed to be an absolute requirement in maintaining a certain standard of living. Therefore, the collapsing of housework and income into a single monetary measure would be nonsensical.[29] The importance of housework as a determinant of relative differences in living standards is an empirical question. In the United States, housework hours appear not to have contributed to important differences in the relative position of classes over time.[30]

A Relative Measure of Well-Being

If social structure dominates individual choice in determining consumption norms, specific social goals (e.g., sufficient nutrition, adequate housing, or means of transportation) replace individual choice as the appropriate yardstick for categorizing consumption as providing basics, variety, or status. Economic liberty, from the institutionalist perspective, would be measured in terms of 'social freedom,' or the opportunities available to all. Only within a structured system is the individual able to exercise liberty.[31] As long as people's options are defined by unequal material resources, the inherent tension between individual choice and social freedom will vary across class, since we must decide who is to be constrained by how much.

Individual freedom provided by choice increases with income, as higher income allows more mistakes in expenditures and more experimenting with consumption norms. This occurs in several ways. On a simple level, more money allows families to replace, discard, or simply not use items that were bought by mistake, were defective, or did not meet expectations. We can all think of purchases of food, clothing, books, knick-knacks and social outings that fall into these categories. In addition, greater freedom is obtained with increased income because expenditure mistakes made with variety or status purchases do not threaten the family's well-being as do mistakes made with spending for basics.

On a more complex level, institutions governing consumption allow more options with expenditures for variety and even more options with expenditures for status. For example, one can choose from a variety of vacations (Europe or Asia, the mountains or the seashore), a variety of types of music (classical or jazz), a variety of sports (sailing or golf, football or baseball games), a variety of types of cars (Cadillac or Porsche), and so forth. The social rules for the elite (successful entertainers, landed aristocrats) are less strict, and the public enjoys the elite's flaunting of convention, such as by their continual marrying and divorcing. Often, the disregard of rule or custom is accomplished with the expensive assistance of lawyers. In any event, the higher the class, the larger the buffer of income available to a family to help protect it from social rule and to help it through a crisis period when the family cannot fulfill social custom. In these ways, income provides freedom and control to the individual.

In contrast, expansion of social freedom allows greater functioning or achievement for all individuals. Such an approach puts greater value on the fulfillment of basics and the expansion of variety for everyone rather than the fulfillment of individual idiosyncratic choices. The evaluation of social justice and of income distribution requires a relative measure of consumption. The standard of living index developed here is intended to provide that measure.

NOTES

1. Thorstein Veblen was especially important in developing how the economy functioned within an institutional structure. See Veblen, 'Why is Economics Not an Evolutionary Science?,' *Quarterly Journal of Economics*, 12 (July 1898), pp. 373–97; Wesley C. Mitchell, ed., *What Veblen Taught: Selected Writings of Thorstein Veblen* (New York: Viking Press, 1936); and Veblen, *The Instinct of Workmanship and the State of the Industrial Arts* (New York: Viking Press, 1937). Veblen viewed the individual's personality as a reflection of the capitalist culture. He believed a person's work has a marked influence on thinking and behavior ('As he acts, so he feels and thinks,' *The Instinct*, p. 63).

2. This view of the economy, in particular, was developed by John Commons, *Institutional Economics* (New York: Macmillan, 1934).

3. Institutional economics is a holistic approach to studying the structure that shapes economic outcomes. For a discussion of the better-known institutionalists, such as Veblen, Commons, Mitchell, Kerr, and Galbraith, see Allan G. Gruchy, *Modern Economic Thought: The American Contribution* (1947; reprint edn, New York: Augustus M. Kelley, 1967). See also Charles K. Wilber with Robert S. Harrison, 'The Methodological Basis of Institutional Economics: Pattern Model, Storytelling and Holism,' *Journal of Economic Issues*, 12, 1 (March 1978), pp. 61–89; Bruce E. Kaufman, ed., *How Labor Markets Work: Reflections on Theory and Practice* by John Dunlop, Clark Kerr, Richard Lester, and Lloyd Reynolds (Lexington, MA: D.C. Heath, 1988) and Clair Brown, 'Income Distribution in an Institutional World,' in Garth Mangum and Peter Philips, eds., *Three Worlds of Labor Economics* (Armonk, NY: M.E. Sharpe, 1988), pp. 51–63. Some classics in institutional economics include Thorstein Veblen, *Absentee Ownership and Business Enterprise in Recent Times* (New York: B.W. Huebsch, 1923); John Commons, *Institutional Economics*, and *The Economics of Collective Action* (New York: Macmillan, 1950); Clark Kerr, 'The Balkanization of Labor Markets,' in E. Wight Bakke et al., *Labor Mobility and Economic Opportunity* (Cambridge, MA: Technology Press of Massachusetts Institute of Technology, 1954), pp. 92–110; Peter B. Doeringer and Michael J. Piore, *Internal Labor Markets and Manpower Analysis* (Lexington, MA: D.C. Heath, 1971).

4. See, for example, Samuel Bowles and Herbert Gintis, *Schooling in Capitalist America* (New York: Basic Books, 1976) and Michael J. Piore, 'Labor Market Stratification.'

5. The use of goods as an information system or as markers of social relations is discussed in Mary Douglas and Baron Isherwood, *The World of Goods* (New York: Basic Books, 1979). The use of goods as symbol is discussed by Mihaly Csikszentmihalyi and Eugene Rochberg-Halton, *The Meaning of Things* (Cambridge: Cambridge University Press, 1981). The importance of establishing the position of the person in the social context by economic transactions is discussed in Karl Polanyi, Conrad M. Arensberg, and Harry W. Pearson, eds., *Trade and Market in the Early Empires: Economies in History and Theory* (New York: Free Press, 1957), Chs 5, 13, 14. Consumption used for participation in validating activities is discussed in Lee Rainwater, *What Money Buys: Inequality and the Social Meanings of Income* (New York: Basic Books, 1974), Ch. 2.

6. An alternative institutional (and Marxian) analysis of income and standards of living is presented by Agnes Heller, *The Theory of Need in Marx*, translated (London: Allison & Busby, 1976).

7. Many social scientists have developed the theme of consumer satisfaction (or deprivation) as a relative measure, which is compatible with the approach developed here. Examples include: Consumption with social limits imparts a relative dimension to personal welfare (Fred Hirsch, *Social Limits to Growth*; Cambridge, MA: Harvard University Press, 1976). Income and expressed satisfaction in with life are positively correlated at a point in time in various countries but not across countries or over time in one country (Richard A. Easterlin, 'Does Economic Growth Improve the Human Lot?' in Paul A. David and Melvin W. Reder, eds, *Nations and Households in Economic Growth: Essays in Honor of Moses Abramovitz*; New York: Academic Press, 1974). Participation in the validating activities that define a full member of society imposes a relative cost that does not change over time (Lee Rainwater, 1974). Society creates needs at the same time that it allocates resources, and families require the resources of the average family in order to obtain customary living conditions and activities (Peter Townsend, *Poverty in the United Kingdom* (Harmondsworth: Penguin Books, 1979)).

8. See Gary Becker, *Human Capital* (Cambridge, MA: National Bureau of Economic Research, 1964) and T.W. Schultz, 'Investment in Human Capital,' *American Economic Review*, 51 (March 1961), pp. 1–17.

9. At least as far back as Adam Smith, economists have known that commodity requirements for specific social goals (e.g., not being 'ashamed to appear in public') depended on social norms, which were influenced by material resources. Le Play made the relationship between consumption and social structure interdependent as he emphasized the importance of families' standard of living (or material well-being) to the well-being of familial and societal relationships. The classical economists, during the second half of the nineteenth century, tied the standard of living to productivity as they emphasized the impact of consumption on efficiency. In a subsistence economy, this impact was primarily through nutrition. As economic growth accompanying industrialization allowed for a rising standard of living, classical economists such as Marshall assumed an improvement in comfort increased workers' vitality and energy (Alfred Marshall, *Principles of Economics*, 7th ed. (London: Macmillan, 1916), p. 690). The interest, then, in the standard of living was largely motivated by the desire to estimate the costs of industrial production, since wages were assumed to be determined by the standard of living, which in turn affected productivity (see Carle C. Zimmerman, *Consumption and Standards of Living* (New York: D. Van Nostrand, 1936)). The industrialization and urbanization of this period resulted in the rise of the non-farm poor, who were dependent on wage

income. Public and private income support programs were developed to deal partially with the poor, and these programs prompted interest in measuring subsistence. Scientific advancements in nutritional studies allowed the preparation of quantity budgets with a shift away from the empirical search, which had followed Engel, for 'stable' laws of consumption in order to measure the standard of living. An above-subsistence economy in the mid-twentieth century brought with it a new way of defining income adequacy and of evaluating the standard of living. As the ordinal school of utility (developed by Hicks, Robbins and Allen) replaced the material welfare school associated with Marshall and Pigou, the focus on well-being with an interpersonal concept of utility and an empirical approach was dropped. (See Robert Cooter and Peter Rappoport, 'Were the Ordinalists Wrong about Welfare Economics?' *Journal of Economic Literature*, 22 (June 1984), pp. 507–30.) Affluence brought with it an emphasis on 'individual choice,' assumed to be the way to maximize well-being.

10.   See Helen H. Lamale, 'Changes in Concepts of Income Adequacy Over the Last Century,' *American Economic Review*, 48 (May 1958), pp. 291–9. Paul H. Douglas, Curtice N. Hitchcock and Willard E. Atkins, *The Worker in Modern Economic Society* (Chicago: University of Chicago Press, 1923) summarizes 28 budgets for 1905–22.

11.   A theory of consumption based on relative income was developed by James S. Duesenberry, *Income, Saving, and the Theory of Consumer Behavior* (Cambridge, MA: Harvard University Press, 1952). Duesenberry began development of his theory of consumption by criticizing the Keynesian consumption function and rejecting two fundamental assumptions of aggregate demand theory: '(1) that every individual's consumption behavior is independent of every other individuals, and (2) that consumption relations are reversible in time.' Instead, Duesenberry developed a consumption theory that incorporated the social nature of the consumption process. His relative income hypothesis assumes that preferences are interdependent so that a family's savings rate is an increasing function of its percentile position in the income distribution, and the savings ratio is a function of the ratio of current income to the highest income previously attained.

12.   Milton Friedman, *A Theory of the Consumption Function* (Princeton, NJ: Princeton University Press, 1957). Friedman's permanent income hypothesis assumed that, for the individual consumer unit, consumption and income have permanent (i.e., reflecting lifetime streams) and transitory (i.e., reflecting random variations) components and that the transitory components are uncorrelated with permanent components and with each other. Permanent consump-

tion is hypothesized to be a constant fraction of permanent income, with the fraction depending on the interest rate, the ratio of nonhuman wealth to income, and 'other factors affecting the consumer units' tastes for current consumption versus accumulation of assets, such as the degree of uncertainty attached to the receipt of income, the consumer units' age and its composition, and objective indexes of cultural factors like race or national origin' (p. 222). Although Friedman allows race or national origin to affect consumption patterns, such 'cultural factors' play a passive role in that they affect people's 'preferences' in an unchanging way. Friedman 'found no evidence of any structural change in the behavior of consumer units in the United States with respect to spending and saving over at least the past sixty years.' (p. 227). If the social or cultural framework is fixed, then the analyst can focus exclusively on the relative price factors to account for observed changes. The permanent income hypothesis invalidated the needs-based approach to evaluating the standard of living because it invalidated the use of measured income and consumption to measure well-being. Furthermore, the permanent income hypothesis implicitly assumed that people could control the timing of their earnings stream, so that a family's earning stream was the result of rational (and freely chosen) optimization.

Empirical tests of this theory, and the related human capital theory, have been disappointing. For example, Lee Lillard, 'Inequality: Earnings vs. Human Wealth,' *American Economic Review*, 67 (March 1977), pp. 42–53, estimated inequality in human wealth (i.e., present value of lifetime earnings) for a fairly homogeneous group of men and found considerable variation. Measured variables accounted for only 10% of the variation so that individual differences in 'endowments, constraints, and abilities' accounted for most of the variation.

13. This theme is developed by Hirsch, *Social Limits to Growth*. . . .
14. See Stuart Ewen, *Captains of Consciousness* (New York: McGraw-Hill, 1976); Irving Bernstein, *The Lean Years: A History of the American Worker, 1920–1933* (Boston: Houghton Mifflin, 1960); E.P. Thompson, 'Time, Work-Discipline, and Industrial Capitalism,' *Past and Present*, 38 (Dec. 1967), pp. 56–97.
15. See Daniel Horowitz, *The Morality of Spending* (Baltimore: Johns Hopkins University Press, 1985), for a discussion of these issues during 1875–1940 in the United States.
16. See, for example, Stuart Chase, *The Tragedy of Waste* (New York: Macmillan, 1927), who also wrote for the *Contemporary Nation* (1926–9); and Robert S. Lynd and Helen M. Lynd, *Middletown: A Study in Contemporary American Culture* (New York: Harcourt,

Brace & World, 1929). In contrast, Jessica Peixotto was much more concerned about the meager standard of living of both working-class and middle-class families. She argued that their level of consumption (including mass-produced cars, household furnishings, and recreational goods) needed to be higher. See Peixotto, 'How Workers Spend a Living Wage' in *University of California Publications in Economics* (Berkeley and Los Angeles: University of California Press, 1928), and *Getting and Spending at the Professional Standard of Living* (New York: Macmillan, 1927).

17. The micro foundation can be found in utility theory and human capital theory. The most influential thinker has been Gary S. Becker, 'A Theory of the Allocation of Time,' *Economic Journal*, 75 (1965), pp. 493–517; *Human Capital*, 2nd ed. (New York: National Bureau of Economic Research, 1975); *The Economic Approach to Human Behavior* (Chicago: University of Chicago Press, 1976); 'Family Economics and Macro Behavior,' *American Economic Review*, 78 (March 1988), pp. 1–13). A thorough presentation of utility theory can be found in Angus Deaton and John Muellbauer, *Economics and Consumer Behavior* (Cambridge: Cambridge University Press, 1980).

18. Carle Zimmerman (*Consumption and Standards of Living*) reviews the major schools (Le Play, Russian, American, Classical Theory, Institutional Theory, Austrian, Hedonism, Mathematical Hedonism) up to the mid-1930s. He emphasizes that 'advancement is not always improvement' (p. 290), but that economic advancement creates a more complex culture. He was influenced especially by Le Play. For a listing of actual budget studies of wage earners, professionals and dependent families in the United States, see Faith M. Williams and Carle C. Zimmerman, *Studies of Family Living in the U.S. and Other Countries*, US Department of Agriculture Misc. Pub. 223 (1937). They list 254 studies of wage-earner families between 1869 and 1934.

19. J.A. Hobson, *Work and Welfare: A Human Valuation* (New York: Macmillan, 1914), Ch. 9. Also see E.J. Urwich, *Luxury and the Waste of Life* (London: J.M. Dent & Co., 1908); William A. Robson, *The Relation of Wealth to Waste* (New York: Macmillan, 1925); Richard Tawney, *The Acquisitive Society* (New York: Harcourt, Brace & Howe, 1920).

20. Amartya Sen, *The Standard of Living* (Cambridge: Cambridge University Press (1986); *Commodities and Capabilities* (New York: North-Holland, 1985); *Resources, Values and Development* (Cambridge, MA: Harvard University Press, 1984); *Choice, Welfare and Measurement* (Oxford: Blackwell, 1982). The approach developed in this book, compatible in spirit with Sen's functioning and capa-

bilities, is more pragmatic and less ambitious than Sen's more general model, which is based on individual outcomes within a socioeconomic structure. What may be lost in elegance is hopefully offset in execution.

21. Earlier, Tawney had lamented that the foundation of society is rights (i.e., free disposal of property and pursuit of economic self-interest) rather than functions (i.e., activities that embody and express the idea of social purpose) (*The Acquisitive Society*, pp. 8, 20).

22. Sen, *The Standard of Living*, p. 16.

23. In this way, Sen uses an absolutist approach to incorporate the relativist approach. Sen is not successful in merging the two approaches, according to Peter Townsend in 'A Sociological Approach to the Measurement of Poverty – A Rejoinder to Professor Amartya Sen,' *Oxford Economic Papers*, 37 (1985), pp. 659–68. See also Sen's Reply in *Oxford Economic Papers*, 37 (1985), pp. 669–76. The major difference between Sen and Townsend appears to be in analyzing fulfillment of social (rather than physical) needs in being non-poor. Using Sen's approach, absolute levels (as opposed to levels relative to those of others) exist for participating in social activities or retaining self-respect. I doubt, however, that these social needs can be defined in an absolute, rather than a relative, way. He discusses the innate pull between relevance and usability and between social norms and individual choice. When pressed, Sen tends to gravitate toward a focus on individual freedom, or the choices available to the individual, and on relevance, or the intellectual exploration of the complexities of the standard of living. Townsend, 'A Sociological Approach,' criticizes Sen for his emphasis on the 'minor theme of individual motivation' instead of the 'major theme of social organization' to explain poverty (p. 660). Sen implies an awareness by individuals of the conflict between their own goals and the goals of others, which is resolved in rules for 'fit and proper behavior' that allows everyone to achieve their respective goals better. Arjo Klamer, 'A Conversation with Amartya Sen,' *Journal of Economic Perspectives*, 3, 1 (Winter 1989), pp. 144–5. In the institutional model used here, individuals rarely are ever aware of their habitual following of norms. Like Sen's world, however, the resolution of daily conflict is governed by social rule and custom. Because the underlying power structure determines the institutions, however, the economic efficiency of the outcomes remains in question.

24. Although Sen sympathizes with the basic needs and opulence approaches to measuring living standards, he argues that the theoretical foundation can be either utility or functioning. In his comments in Sen, *The Standard of Living* (p. 43), Muellbauer argues

that the distinction between material characteristics and the capabilities set is unimportant as long as the relationship determining the capability set, especially for personal characteristics, is relatively universal and the variables observable. In other words, the personal characteristics and the material characteristics together determine the capabilities. This differs from my emphasis on the link between socioeconomic structure, income (commodities) and functionings that allow us to use commodities to imply (and measure) functionings within a given structure. Muellbauer explicitly recognizes these two approaches when he poses the 'fundamental problem' of what shall we attribute to the constraints households and individuals face and what to their tastes.

25.   Many authors have used a basic needs approach to deal with these issues. For an excellent survey, see Paul Streeten, et al., *First Things First* (New York: Oxford University Press, 1981). A typical example is United Nations, *Report on International Definition and Measurement of Standards and Levels of Living* (New York: United Nations, 1954), which lists a dozen components (including health, nutrition, literacy and skills, working conditions) to be measured, with priority given to eight specific items (including life expectancy at birth, school enrollment for children 5–14 years of age, literacy rate, jobs by industry and occupation, personal consumption as proportion of national income). See also Glen Sheehan and Mike Hopkins, *Basic Needs Performance* (Geneva: International Labour Office, 1979). This study estimates the effects of population growth and economic growth on basic needs performance. A basic needs approach from eastern Europe is M. Mód, ed., *The Standard of Living* (Budapest: Akadémia Kiadó, 1962).

26.   See William Nordhaus and James Tobin, 'Is Economic Growth Obsolete?' in Milton Moss, ed., *The Measurement of Economic and Social Performance* (New York: National Bureau of Economic Research, 1973). Adjustments to growth rates for changes in leisure and income distribution for OECD countries were made by Wilfred Beckerman, *Measures of Leisure, Equality and Welfare* (Paris: Organization for Economic Co-operation and Development, 1978). The idea of measuring a range of 'social indicators' to evaluate the quality of life and monitor changes was popular in the 1970s. Three reports, *Social Indicators*, were compiled by the US Government for 1973, 1976, and 1980. The latest report (US Bureau of the Census, *Social Indicators III* (Washington, DC: US Government Printing Office, 1980)) included three composite indices for socioeconomic, health, and alienation components for each country. An issue of *The Annals* ('America Enters the Eighties: Some Social Indicators,' 453 (Jan. 1981)) was devoted to analysis of the government publi-

cations with articles for each of 11 groups of social indicators (including Population and Family, Health and Nutrition, Housing and Environment, Income and Productivity, and Social Participation). As these headings indicate, this approach has much in common with the basic needs approach. Another social indicator study, which develops an aggregate index, is Jan Drewnowski and Wolf Scott, *The Level of Living Index*, UN Research Institute for Social Development, Report No. 4 (Geneva: United Nations, Sept. 1966).

27. Clair Brown, 'An Institutional Model of Wives' Work Decisions,' *Industrial Relations*, 24, 2 (Spring 1985), pp. 182–204.

28. The hours of housework are primarily determined by the number and ages of the children. See Joann Vanek, 'Keeping Busy: Time Spent in Housework, United States 1920–1970,' Ph.D. dissertation, University of Michigan, 1973, and 'Household Technology and Social Status,' *History of Technology*, 3 (1978), pp. 361–75; and Clair Vickery, 'Women's Economic Contribution to the Family,' in Ralph Smith, ed., *The Subtle Revolution: Women at Work* (Washington, DC: Urban Institute, 1979), pp. 159–200.

29. In a neoclassical model, an opportunity cost approach (i.e., foregone wages for the wife) is used to value housework to the family. Empirically, this approach results in the relative contribution remaining fairly constant across classes. An alternative approach sometimes used evaluates housework by wages paid for similar types of jobs. This results in the absolute contribution being fairly constant across classes and the relative contribution falling.

30. Amelia Preece, *Housework and American Standards of Living, 1920–1980*, Ph.D. dissertation, University of California at Berkeley, 1990.

31. John R. Commons emphasized this point in *The Economics of Collective Action*. He defined an institution as 'collective action in control, liberation, and expansion of individual action' (Introduction).

3 Consuming the Products of Mechanization, 1918

Introduction

In 1918, the US economy was showing the effects of the country's involvement in the Great War in Europe. With almost three million men in the armed forces, the civilian unemployment rate was a low 1.4%. The real gross national product grew 12.3% in 1918, and then declined at an average annual rate of 5.5% for the next three years as wartime production ended. Inflation was high. Consumer prices rose 17.4% in 1918; over the next two years, they climbed another 33.0%.[1]

Table 3.1 Income distribution, 1918

	CES sample[a]	NBER[b]
$900	3%	30%
$900–1,199	20	24
$1,200–1,499	33	18
$1,500–1,799	23	10
$1,800–2,099	13	5
$2,100–2,499	6	4
≥ $2,500	3	9
	100%	100%

[a] CES includes 12,096 families with husband-wife-children.
[b] *Source*: National Bureau of Economic Research (Wesley Mitchell, ed.), *Income in the United States: Its Amount and Distribution 1909–1919* (New York: Harcourt, Brace, 1921), Vol. 1, pp. 134–5. The distribution of personal income was estimated from upper tail of income tax returns. The distribution excludes 2.5 million soldiers, sailors and marines.

The country was urbanizing. But barely a majority (51%) of its 100 million inhabitants lived in urban areas (i.e., places with more than 2,500 people); a full third still lived on farms.[2] The urban population was disproportionately white (93%), since blacks, who still lived predominately in the South, more often lived in rural areas.

Despite the low unemployment figure, most families faced the dual hardship of a meager standard of living coupled with job insecurity. Personal consumption expenditures averaged only $580 per person in 1919 (in 1919 dollars).[3] About one-third of households received annual incomes below $900 and another one-fourth received $900–$1,199 (see table 3.1).[4] The major transformations in life-style and urban development caused by mass production of the automobile were not yet evident; only one in ten adults (21 years and older) had a car.[5] Food expenditures dominated the budget, claiming about 40% of the total; clothing and rent each claimed another 15% (see table 3.2). Families in the bottom half of the income distribution, including those headed by blacks and white laborers, did not have sufficient income to buy adequate food. Wage-earner families had adequate food, clothing, and shelter, but they did not live affluently.

Even though material standards were meager, the shift from the producer to consumer economy was basically completed by the end of World War I. Social analysts continued wrestling with the relationship between economic growth, morality, and social stability. For many centuries prevailing wisdom had been that, once material requirements were met, a higher standard of living would be translated into a more refined and cultured life-style. The problems raised by mass commercialized consumption, especially in leisure-time activities, became widely discussed. Veblen, and later the Lynds and Chase, were among the leading critics charging that economic development was resulting in conspicuous waste rather than the emergence of higher, more refined wants.[6]

Among all three white classes, everyday life was dominated by long work hours for husbands and arduous maintenance tasks at home for wives. There were few avenues of escape from this tedium, which probably explains the public's instant love affair with the movies. Family life rhythms revolved around food (preparation, meal times, and clean-up), but the meals themselves tended to be repetitive and monotonous. Clothing served functional needs, with little or no emphasis on style or aesthetics. Housing tended to be cramped, dark, and inadequately ventilated, and although most homes had cold running water, an indoor toilet, and electric lights, many remained without hot running water or an indoor bathroom, and many still used primitive wood or coal stoves for heating. Little time was available for leisure activities and families rarely went on vacations. The major recreational activity across all classes was the novelty of going to the movies.

The harshness of life is symbolized in birth and death statistics, which were to continue improving steadily over the next three decades. Life

Table 3.2 Sources of income of white urban families, 1918

	Laborer	Wage earner	Salaried
Average income	$1,037	$1,344	$2,272
Earned income	1,037	1,294	2,161
Husband	1,014	1,252	1,786
Wife	11	14	27
(amount, frequency)[a]	($101, 11.3%)	($160, 8.7%)	($304, 8.8%)
Children	12	26	343
(amount, frequency)	($140, 8.5%)	($215, 12.3%)	($739, 46.4%)
Dependents	1	1	6
(amount, frequency)	($112, 0.5%)	($269, 0.5%)	($286, 2.0%)
Average earners per family	1.2	1.21	1.57
Other income	$38	$50	$111
Garden, poultry, etc	8	11	15
(amount, frequency)	($20, 41.1%)	($24, 44.9%)	($35, 42.8%)
Gifts	21	24	46
(amount, frequency)	($28, 73.6%)	($33, 74.7%)	($64, 71.8%)
Rents and investments	2	6	23
(amount, frequency)	($38, 4.9%)	($60, 9.1%)	($105, 21.6%)
Lodgers	2	4	14
(amount, frequency)	($65, 3.7%)	($92, 4.6%)	($179, 7.7%)
Other sources	5	5	14
(amount, frequency)	($17, 30.3%)	($18, 28.6%)	($49, 28.4%)
Income minus expenditures	−$0.70	+$43.08	+$217.21
Surplus (amount, frequency)	($68, 54.0%)	($106, 69.0%)	($291, 83.0%)
Deficit (amount, frequency)	($107, 35.0%)	($122, 25.0%)	($166, 14.0%)
Zero balance (frequency)	12.0%	6.0%	3.0%
Proportion of income from earnings[b]	0.97	0.96	0.95

[a] Amounts are average for those reporting income in the category; frequency is the percentage of families reporting such income.
[b] Excludes self-employed income.
Source: Consumer Expenditure Survey, 1918.

expectancy at birth was 54.5 years for white males and 57.4 years for white females, but only 44.5 years for blacks (both sexes). Beginning life and giving birth were arduous and perilous. Many infants and mothers did not survive. Infant mortality numbered a high 10 deaths per 100 live births; the black rates were about 65% higher than the white rates. Seven mothers died out of every thousand live births. Over twice as many infants died within the first day of birth in 1918 as died within the first year of life in 1988. Diarrhea and pneumonia were leading causes of death for infants, along with congenital malformations and premature births, which continued to be the leading causes of infant death at the

Table 3.3   Budgets for urban families, 1918

Income group	Black Less than $900		Labor $900–1,200		Wage earner $1,200–1,500		Salaried $2,100–2,500	
Homeowners	NA		20.0%		24.0%		36.0%	
Auto owners	NA		9.0%		13.0%		31.0%	
Average family size	4.2		4.5		4.7		5.7	
	($)	(%)	$	%	$	%	$	%
Annual expenditures	791	100.0	1,075	100.0	1,298	100.0	2,053	100.0
Food	376	47.5	462	43.0	521	40.1	721	35.1
Clothing	105	13.3	156	14.5	207	15.9	384	18.7
Shelter	175	22.1	253	23.5	303	23.4	426	20.8
Rent	100	12.6	149	13.9	180	13.9	248	12.1
Fuel and light	47	5.9	64	6.0	74	5.7	92	4.5
Furniture and furnishings	28	3.5	40	3.7	50	3.9	86	4.2
Miscellaneous	135	17.1	202	18.8	267	20.6	522	25.4
Transportation	NA		22	2.0	32	2.5	92	4.5
Recreation and education	NA		41	3.8	59	4.5	125	6.1
Household operation	NA		26	2.4	35	2.7	66	3.2
Medical care	NA		46	4.3	59	4.5	88	4.3
Personal care	NA		11	1.0	13	1.0	18	0.9
Gifts and contributions	NA		20	1.9	25	1.9	60	2.9
Personal insurance	NA		30	2.8	37	2.9	57	2.8
Other	NA		6	0.6	8	0.6	16	0.8
Tax/gross income	NA			0.1		0.1		0.2
Expenditures/net income		99.0		100.0		97.0		90.0

end of the century. The most prevalent communicable disease in 1918 was measles (5 cases per 1,000 people), followed by diphtheria and scarlet fever (each 1 case per 1,000). In this era without antibiotics, the leading causes of adult deaths were influenza or pneumonia (2 per 1,000 people, excluding newborns) and tuberculosis (1.5 per 1,000) as well as heart disease (4 per 1,000).[7]

Income and jobs

During this period, the farm labor force was declining while the manu-facturing labor force continued to expand. At the time of the 1920 Census, most employed men (aged ten years and over) worked on farms (30%) or in traditional blue-collar jobs (48%), which were almost equally divided among skilled craftsmen, semi-skilled operatives, and unskilled laborers. Only 12% were professionals, managers, or proprietors, and the remaining 10% were clerical, sales, or service workers (see table 1.1). Employed women worked primarily as operatives (20%); clericals (19%); domestics (16.7%); or professionals (12%, usually teachers and nurses). Overall, one-quarter of the 1918 labor force worked in agriculture and another quarter worked in manufacturing. Self-employment was common, especially in agriculture, where 39% of the labor force were owner-operators and another 23% were tenant farmers. Outside of agriculture, one in five male workers were self-employed, primarily in the trade and service sectors.[8]

Husbands in the three white urban classes had annual earnings of $1,014 (laborers), $1,252 (wage earners), and $1,786 (salaried), which accounted for 80%–95% of total family income.[9] Urban black families had incomes under $900 (the lowest income group recorded). The typical laborer's family was in the second quarter of the income distribution, the wage-earner's family in the third quarter, and the salaried worker's family just below the top 10% of the income distribution. Most black families, along with farm families in general, fell into the bottom third of the income distribution.[10]

These income differences form the basis of the consumption norms that marked people's social and economic roles. Overall, salaried families spent 58% more than wage-earner families, who spent 21% more than laborer families, who spent 36% more than black families.

Sources of income

Classes were separated by how they obtained their incomes as well as by their consumption. The work patterns noted above are reflected in the earnings patterns of families by class. Employed wives were not common among any of the white classes. Laborer wives were more likely to have some earnings than salaried wives (11.3% vs 8.8%), but their earnings were only one-third as much (see table 3.2). Salaried families were likely to have an employed older child, who already earned 70% as much as the laborer husband. The typical laborer family did not have an employed child; in fact, the wife was more likely to be employed than a child. When employed, the laborer's offspring made less than 20% of the salaried offspring's earnings. In their fathers' footsteps, sons were already queued in the labor market.

Most families had sources of income other than earnings, but the values were small. For example, around 40%–45% of each class had a garden or raised poultry; the value of the food produced, however, ranged only from $20 per year for laborers to $35 for salaried. About three-quarters of each class also received gifts, with the total value ranging from $28 for laborers to $64 for salaried. All three white classes reported receiving back in gifts slightly more than the amount they had given out in gifts and contributions. This implies that families roughly followed norms of reciprocity.

Classes varied by their investment (including rental) income. One in twenty laborer families reported investment income; it amounted to only $38 per year. Over one in five salaried families reported investment income averaging $105, so even this upper-middle class did not receive much income from assets. However, the savings patterns show that the financial pressures on the salaried class were substantially less than those on the laborer class. Over 80% of the salaried class reported savings (i.e., income minus expenditures) for the year, averaging $291 for those that saved; only 54% of the laborers had savings, averaging $68. Overall, the average laborer family broke exactly even, with income equalling expenditures.

In this era, government had little direct influence on family income, either in terms of taxation or income support. In 1918, families usually paid only property tax (if they were homeowners), and poll tax (in order to vote). Taxes were 0.1% of income for the working classes and 0.2% for salaried families.

Family composition and work roles

The socially ideal family consisted of a husband, wife, and three children, a configuration consistent with the prevailing birth rate.[11] Since few people lived outside of family units, most households (90%) contained a husband and wife. In addition, one in five households contained more than one family. Overall, the average household had 5.1 persons.[12]

Young men tended to marry over three years later than young women. Their median age at first marriage was 24.6 years, compared to 21.2 for females. Divorce was rare – a stigma attached to less than 1% of the white male population (15+ years) were categorized as divorced.

By modern standards, life expectancies were low and fairly equal by sex. At birth, white males had a life expectancy of 56.3 years and white females 58.5 years. White males who were aged 20 could expect to live 45.6 more years and females 46.5 more years. Much lower life expectancy for blacks reflects their considerably lower standard of living, characterized by widespread underfeeding and inadequate medical care. At birth, black males had a life expectancy of only 47.1 years and females 46.9 years. By age 20, black men could expect 38.4 more years and black females 37.2 more years.

The impact of the large migration into the United States in the previous decades is evident both statistically and in contemporaneous policy discussions. According to the 1920 census, only 45% of the urban population was white with 'native parentage'; 29% were 'native' whites who had at least one parent born abroad; and 19% were whites who had immigrated to the United States. Only 6.8% of the urban population was non-white (with 97% being 'Negro'). Most immigrants, including 88% of urban adult male immigrants, could not speak English. However, because their children became fluent, only a small proportion of the overall adult urban population (10+ years), 9% of the men and 13% of the women, could not speak English. However, literacy was a problem for many non-whites and immigrants. Thirteen percent of the foreign-born whites and 23% of the non-whites were illiterate, as compared to a national illiteracy rate of 2% for native-born whites.

Urban school attendance was widespread in 1918, and almost 80% of children (aged 5–17 years) were in school. School attendance for white immigrant children was much lower than for the native white or black children (see table 3.12). Attendance by gender within a race group was roughly the same. However, differences in school attendance across class are more noticeable among the teenaged cohort when dropping out of school to get a job became an option – one in four immigrant teenagers (aged 14–20 years) and one in three black teenagers were in school, compared to three in seven white native teenagers.

Figures for employment in 'gainful' work, of course, are the mirror image of the school attendance statistics. Among the older teens (16–19 years), immigrants were more likely to be employed than were either native whites or blacks. Among the younger teens, blacks were more likely to be employed than native whites or immigrants (see table 3.12). At age 14, 38% of black boys and 23% of black girls were working, compared to 15% of native white boys and 5% of native white girls. Employment jumps at age 16 in many states; this was the legally approved age for leaving school. By ages 18 and 19, 84% of black men and 44% of black women, compared to 75% of white native men and 34% white native women, were employed.

Native white male employment rates do not catch up with the black male employment rate until the prime working years of ages 25–44. Then, 97% of both groups are reported as gainfully employed. White native men were more likely than black men to retire after age 65, since 39% of white men, compared to 20% of black men, were no longer working.

For women, the employment patterns differ sharply by race. Many white native women were likely to work a year or two before marriage, and one-third were employed at ages 18 and 19 years. Following marriage and childbirth, however, their employment rate would drop. Social norms dictated that wives, and certainly mothers, should not work, except under dire financial circumstances. Less than one in five native white women aged 25–44 were employed, and many of these were unmarried. One study found that the major cultural transformation in norms governing working class women's working for pay occurred between 1890 and 1920 – before this study begins.[13] Often, the wife worked when her husband was unemployed or disabled. However, employment for most women with employed husbands was still confined to years when children were not at home. In addition, wives in the salaried class did not take jobs in the early 1920s. Seldom did their husbands experience unemployment, and outside employment for the wife meant a drop in status. These norms changed later.

The white norms had little relevance for the black family. About 45% of black women aged 18–64 were employed, and this rate did not fall during the child-bearing years. Economic impoverishment and a cultural history of slavery combined to make employment of black wives and mothers more necessary and, therefore, acceptable.

Hard labor for long hours purchased only a meager material life for black and working-class families. Their actual spending patterns paint the details of a monotonous and dreary daily life.

Diet

For the typical wage-earner family, breakfast and lunch consisted mainly of bread, cereal, and home-baked goods (see table 3.4).[14] On average, a homemaker used 7.2 pounds of assorted flours and corn meal and six cups of sugar weekly. Only one meal, usually dinner, included non-grain foods and meat. The preponderance of starches and carbohydrates linked the tastiness as well as nutritional quality of meals directly to the wife's baking. Wives usually prepared three meals a day for family members, including the meals carried as bag lunches.

Table 3.4 Typical meals (servings per person for a household of five), 1918

Breakfast
2 servings home-baked muffins, biscuits, rolls or pancakes
2 slices bread (1 teaspoon sweetener other than sugar, 1 pat butter for bread)
1 Milk (6 oz)
Coffee 4 (6 oz) cups daily for parents
Six days per week, add one of the following:
   Oatmeal 3 days per week
   Bacon and sausage ⎰ daily for husband
                    ⎱ 1 day for everyone else
   Eggs 1 day per week – one egg for each child and 2 eggs for each adult
   Dry fruit 0.1 lb 1 day per week

Lunch
2 servings home-baked muffins, biscuits, and rolls
3 slices bread with 1 pat butter and 1 pat oleo daily

Table 3.4   (*cont.*)

Three days per week one of the following:
  Lunch meat 2 days
  Cheese 1 day
Vegetable soup daily
  using over the week   onion
  (each day for entire   miscellaneous vegetables ⎫
  family):   tomato   ⎬   = 0.5 cup per person
    cabbage   ⎪
    carrots   ⎭
    rice, 1 cup per person
    leftover meat bones for stock; left over from dinner
Fresh fruit 5 days (half of these apples)

Dinner
1 large potato
4.5 servings home-baked goods (muffin, biscuits, rolls)
1.5 pat butter

Meat (or substitute; 3.5 oz servings) daily
  Beef 3 days
  Other meat 3 days
  Beans/macaroni or cheese 1 day

Vegetable (0.5 cup servings) daily
  Tomato 1 day
  Cabbage 1 day
  Sweet potato 1 day
  Spinach, kale or peas 1 day
  Turnips or beets 1 day
  String beans 1 day
  Canned vegetable 1 day
Dessert: home-baked (cake, cookies, pie, etc.)[a] six days and purchased cake,
  cookies or pie 1 day

---

[a] Two cakes weekly and other baked goods could be made with 2.6 cups fat, 6.3 cups sugar, 7 eggs, 17.5 oz evaporated milk, 0.16 lb nuts as well as the flour, 0.8 lemon, and 1.4 oz cocoa.

By modern standards, the diet of a 1918 wage earner was monotonous.[15] In addition to a daily serving of potatoes, fresh vegetables were served ten times weekly and fruit (usually, apples) half as often. If the main meal included a potato and one other vegetable, then a vegetable could be served at three lunches weekly and fruit could be served five times weekly, at lunch or breakfast. Hot cereal was served three times a week and eggs once a week for breakfast, along with four servings of bread each morning. Bacon or sausage was served to everyone twice a week or, more probably, the husband ate it daily while the wife and children ate it once a week. Small amounts of salted and canned meats (two servings), cheese (one slice), nuts (0.5 ounce), and dried fruits (1.5

ounces) were available weekly for lunch for each person as a supplement to daily servings of bread and other baked goods.

If we compare the typical wage-earner family's diet to the US Bureau of Labor Statistics' 'minimum standard diet,'[16] the typical family did not consume enough milk, fruits, or vegetables; they ate slightly too much meat and sweets, and consumed just about the right amount of grain products. The minimum standard diet had 14% more fresh vegetables (by weight), 34% more fresh fruit, 33% more canned and dried vegetables and fruits, 69% more milk, and 20% more fats. The nutritional quality of actual diets declined with family incomes since grain consumption rose, and milk, vegetable, fruit, and meat consumption fell, as income fell.

Wage-earner families consumed more than adequate protein but inadequate iron and calcium,[17] which especially affected teenagers and women. Calcium deficiency reflected the low consumption of milk in most parts of the country, since the refrigeration required for the distribution of fresh milk was not yet available. In addition, niacin deficiency was a problem in the South, where it resulted in widespread pellagra before cornmeal was fortified. Families with incomes *below* that of the typical wage-earner family suffered from even more inadequate nutrition. Overall, a majority of the population consumed inadequate amounts of the B vitamins (except B_{12}) and magnesium, in addition to receiving inadequate calcium, iron, and niacin.

The nutritional standards of the period focused primarily on energy needs because many families had insufficient caloric intake.[18] The average survey diet was over 10% too low in calories for laborer families, sufficient for wage-earner families, and over 10% too high for salaried families. At least one-half of a subsample of the 1918 survey families consumed too few calories for the husband and wife to be engaged in 'moderately active work.'[19] Although no information is available on how calorie deficiencies were distributed among the surveyed family members, studies in France and England indicate that the wife reduced her food intake (and sometimes her children's intake) when food supplies were inadequate.

Caloric deficiencies were especially serious for the laborer and black families, since husbands needed 1,000 more calories daily in order to engage in strenuous physical labor.[20] In New Orleans, black families consumed more calories than white families at the same income level; they obtained one-fourth more calories per food dollar than did whites.[21] Even so, these black families would not reach the laborers' standard of 3,600 calories unless their budgets were $1,200 – far above the norm for the typical black family. Overall, two-thirds of black families sampled in New Orleans obtained less than 3,500 calories and over two-fifths obtained less than 3,000 calories.[22]

The need to consume more calories most likely accounts for the classification of alcohol under food rather than recreation. Consumption of beer and whiskey often helped provide needed calories for some laborers as well as relaxation for a broader range of people. Long after the problem arose of over-consumption of calories, and alcohol therefore lost its value as a source of calories, alcohol would remain listed under food.

Black families relied heavily on cheap foods, such as fatty meats (especially pork), molasses, and corn meal, to obtain sufficient calories; they consumed almost no fresh milk.[23] Poorer blacks' struggle to obtain an adequate diet was further hampered by their lack of refrigerators, which required them to buy food in very small quantities. But buying food frequently from the corner grocer reflected a social norm as well as a credit system. In a Philadelphia study, 80% of black families ran an account with the corner grocer and settled it each pay day. Only 10% could not get credit.[24]

Between classes, food expenditures rose only two-thirds as fast as total expenditures. The larger food budget primarily paid for additional family members.[25] However, expenditures per person did rise 10%–15% between classes. As even wage-earner families did not have fully adequate diets, nutritional inadequacies fell fairly rapidly as food expenditures rose, which allowed more vegetables, fruits, and milk. Minor increases in food expenditures translated into important nutritional differences in daily calories eaten because caloric demands were lower for the less physically demanding, higher status, occupations. The calories wives expended in housework also was higher for lower-income families whose homes lacked hot running water, central heating, or gas or electric stoves.

Most meals were eaten at home or carried to work or school. Food purchased away from home was still not considered a part of daily life, and so data on it still were not collected in the Consumer Expenditure Survey (CES). From other data, however, we know that family members did purchase snacks and drinks away from home, and that it represented a very small part of the food budget.[26] Food luxuries – 'wines, confectionery, food out of season, social entertainments'[27] – rarely, if ever, made their way into the family budget for even salaried families. Variations in affluence were marked by the variety of simple foodstuffs on the table. Luxuries were for later economic eras.

Wardrobe

Clothing played an important role in distinguishing social classes and in defining gender roles within classes.[28] Even among lower-income families, the clothing requirements of husbands and employed or school-bound children could not be compromised beyond a certain point. Clothing for public activities was still quite formal, although women's skirts were becoming shorter and men quit wearing high, starched collars. When family income was low, severe economizing seems to have focused on the wife's clothing since her public activities were more restricted. In the laborer family, about the same amount ($51–$54 per person) was spent annually on clothing for the husband and children 15 years old and over (see table 3.5). These figures indicate that, in order to function in public, an adult needed to spend at least $52 annually for clothing. The laborer's wife spent only $44 annually, almost one-fifth less than her husband spent on clothes. The wife's clothing requirements for social purposes increased with class status. Her expenditure for clothes rose relatively faster with income than did her husband's, so that in the salaried family, the wife spent only 4% less than her husband.

Table 3.5 Typical wardrobes[a]

Standard replacement	Item (longevity)	Laborer	Quantity Wage earner	Salaried
Husband				
1/3	Wool suit (3 yrs)	1.2	1.5	2.4
1/3	Summer suit (3 yrs)	0.3	3.3	0.3
2 1/2 (w/repair)	High shoes (1 yr)	1.9	2.0	2.3
5 (work)	Shirts – cotton (3 yrs)	9.3	10.5	12.6
1 (dress)	– wool (5 yrs)	1.0	1.0	1.5
	– silk (10 yrs)	0.2	0.3	1.0
1/4	Overcoat (life in years)	7.2	6.0	4.6
2	Ties (3 yrs)	5.4	6.3	8.1
	Pants – wool (5 yrs)[b]	1.5	2.0	2.5
	– cotton (3 yrs)	1.2	1.2	1.2
12 (cotton)	Socks (1 yr)			
	– cotton (1 yr)	10.5	10.5	11.3
	– wool or silk (3 yrs)	1.5	2.4	3.6
1/2	Hats – felt (life in years)	1.7	1.4	1.1
2	Straw hats and caps (2 yrs)	1.4	1.6	1.8
1/2	Sweaters and jerseys (5 yrs)	1.0	1.0	1.0
2 (overalls and trousers)	Overalls and jumpers (2 yrs)[b]	2.6	3.0	4.2
	Undershirts (2 yrs)	1.8	2.0	2.2
	Drawers (2 yrs)	1.8	2.0	2.2
5	Union suits (2 yrs)	2.4	2.8	3.4
2	Pajamas and nightshirts (3 yrs)	0.9	1.2	2.1
6 (cotton, wool)	Gloves and mittens – cotton (1 yr)	3.6	3.1	4.7
1 (leather)	– other (3 yrs)	1.2	1.8	2.7
8	Handkerchiefs (1 yr)	4.5	5.3	6.9
3 1/3	Garters, belts, suspenders	1.9	2.2	2.5
6	Collars			
1/3	Umbrellas			

Table 3.5 (*cont.*)

Standard replacement	Item (longevity)	Laborer	Quantity Wage earner	Salaried
Once	Cleaning and pressing suit			
7%	Miscellaneous			
Older boy[c]				
1/3	Wool suit (2 yrs)	1.6	2.0	2.4
1/3	Summer suit (3 yrs)	2.4	2.4	2.4
2 1/2 (w/repair)	High shoes (3 yrs)	9.0	10.8	12.3
5 (work)	Shirts – cotton (2 yrs)	6.0	7.2	8.2
1 (dress)	– wool (2 yrs)	0.5	0.5	1.0
	– silk (3 yrs)	0.1	0.5	1.0
1/4	Overcoat (3 yrs)			(missing)
2	Ties (3 yrs)	6.3	7.8	11.1
	Pants – wool (5 yrs)[d]			(missing)
	– cotton (3 yrs)			(missing)
12 (cotton)	Socks – cotton and wool (1 yr)	9.3	9.7	10.7
	– silk (3 yrs)	0.2	0.4	1.2
1/2	Hats – felt (life in years)	5.7	3.2	1.4
2	Straw hats and caps (2 yrs)	2.8	3.0	3.4
1/2	Sweaters and jerseys (3 yrs)	0.9	1.2	1.2
2 (overalls and trousers)	Overalls and jumpers (2 yrs)[d]	1.0	1.2	1.8
	Undershirts (2 yrs)	1.0	1.2	1.6
	Drawers (2 yrs)	0.8	1.0	1.6
5	Union suits (2 yrs)	2.6	3.2	3.8
2	Pajamas and nightshirts (3 yrs)	0.6	0.9	1.5
6 (cotton, wool)	Gloves and mittens – cotton (1 yr)	0.4	0.5	1.9
1 (leather)	– other (3 yrs)	1.3	1.5	2.4
8	Handkerchiefs (1 yr)	3.0	3.9	6.4
3 1/3	Garters, belts, suspenders	1.7	2.1	2.6
6	Collars			
1/3	Umbrellas			
Once	Cleaning and pressing suit			
7%	Miscellaneous			
Wife				
1	High shoes (1 yr)	1.3	1.3	1.4
1	Low shoes (1 yr)	0.4	0.5	0.6
1/3	Wool coats and cloaks (5 yrs)	1.0	1.0	1.5
1/2	Wool suits (5 yrs)	0.5	1.0	1.0[e]
2[e]	Dresses and suits			
	– cotton (1 yr)	0.44	0.44	0.6

Standard replacement	Item (longevity)	Quantity		
		Laborer	Wage earner	Salaried
1/2	– wool (5 yrs)	0.5	0.5	1.0
	– silk (5 yrs)	0.5	1.1	1.6e
1 1/2	Hats (3 yrs)	1.0	1.1	1.4
	Sweaters and jerseys – cotton, wool, and silk			
1/2	Skirts – cotton (3 yrs)	0.9	0.9	0.9
	– wool (5 yrs)	1.0	1.0	1.0
	– silk (5 yrs)	0.5	0.5	1.0
3 1/2e	Blouses and waists			
	– cotton (3 yrs)	3.3	3.6	3.9
	– wool and silk (5 yrs)	1.6	2.1	3.6e
2	Housedresses and old dresses (2 yrs)			
	– wrappers (3 yrs)	6.0	6.6	8.4
1e	Aprons (2 yrs)	1.8	2.0	2.6
	Furs and boas (life in years)	71.0	35.7	30.0
1 (muslin)	Petticoats – cotton (2 yrs)	1.4	1.6	2.0
1 (venetian or satin)	– wool or silk (10 yrs)	0.3	0.6	1.1
2	Brassieres			
2	Corsets (2 yrs)	1.6	1.8	2.2
2	Corset cover and camisoles (2 yrs)	1.6	2.0	2.4
2	Combinations and union			
2	suits – cotton (2 yrs)	2.4	3.0	4.0
1	– silk and wool (10 yrs)	0.5	1.1	1.3
	– cotton, drawers (2 yrs)	2.0	1.8	2.2
	– skirts – cotton (3 yrs)	5.4	5.4	6.0
2 1/2	Nightdresses, pajamas and kimonos – cotton (3 yrs)	3.3	3.6	5.1
8	Stockings – cotton (1 yr)	5.7	5.5	5.4
	– silk (2 yrs)	0.8	1.2	2.6
1	Gloves and mittens – cotton (1 yr)	0.2	0.2	0.3
1/2 (not kid)	kid, silk and wool (3 yrs)	1.0	1.6	2.5
8	Handkerchiefs (1 yr)	3.2	3.9	5.3
	Handbags and purses (life in years)	5.5	4.3	3.4
1/3	Umbrellas and parasols (life in years)	11.0	9.0	6.0
Once	Cleaning and pressing suit			
8 1/2%	Miscellaneous			
Older girl				
1	High shoes (1 yr)	1.7	2.0	2.2

Table 3.5   (*cont.*)

Standard replacement	Item (longevity)	Laborer	Quantity Wage earner	Salaried
1	Low shoes (3 yrs)	0.7	0.8	1.1
1/3	Wool coats and cloaks (5 yrs)	1.2	1.2	1.5
1/2	Wool suits (2 yrs)	0.2	0.4	0.4
2[f]	Dresses and suits			
	– cotton (1 yr)	1.4	1.6	1.6
	– wool (3 yrs)	0.9	1.2	1.5
	– silk (3 yrs)	0.6	0.6	1.6[f]
1 1/2	Hats (3 yrs)	2.8	3.0	4.2
	Sweaters and jerseys (3 yrs)			
	– cotton, wool, and silk	0.9	0.9	1.0
1/2	Skirts – cotton (2 yrs)	0.6	1.0	0.8
	– wool (3 yrs)	0.6	0.6	1.2
	– silk (3 yrs)	0.1	0.3	0.6
3 1/2[f]	Blouses and waists			
	– cotton (2 yrs)	2.6	3.0	4.2
	– wool and silk (5 yrs)	0.6	1.3	2.5[f]
2	Housedresses and old dresses (2 yrs)			
	– wrappers (3 yrs)	6.0	6.6	8.4
	Aprons (2 yrs)	0.4	0.4	0.6
	Furs and boas (life in years)	30.0	15.0	5.0
1 (muslin)	Petticoats – cotton (2 yrs)	1.6	2.2	3.0
1 (venetian or satin)	– wool or silk (5 yrs)	0.3	0.6	0.7
2	Brassieres			
2	Corsets (1 yr)	0.8	1.1	1.4
2	Corset cover and camisoles (2 yrs)	1.6	2.6	3.6
2	Combinations and union			
2	suits – cotton (2 yrs)	2.4	3.0	4.4
1	– silk and wool (5 yrs)	0.2	0.2	0.4
	– cotton, drawers (2 yrs)	2.4	3.9	3.4
	– skirts – cotton (3 yrs)	4.8	6.6	8.1
2 1/2	Nightdresses, pajamas and kimonos – cotton (3 yrs)	2.0	3.6	5.0
8	Stockings – cotton (1 yr)	6.0	6.3	6.3
	– silk (2 yrs)	1.8	2.8	5.2
1	Gloves and mittens – cotton (1 yr)	0.2	0.2	0.2
1/2 (not kid)	kid, silk and wool (3 yrs)	1.5	2.4	3.9
8	Handkerchiefs (1 yr)	5.0	5.3	7.4
	Handbags and purses (life in years)	5.2	3.6	2.2

Standard replacement	Item (longevity)	Laborer	Quantity Wage earner	Salaried
1/3	Umbrellas and parasols (life in years)	9.3	5.6	3.5
Once	Cleaning and pressing suit			
8 1/2%	Miscellaneous			

[a] Wardrobe is quantity purchased times longevity. Items are those with at least 20% of group purchasing. Longevity and standard replacement are determined using *Monthly Labor Review*, 'Minimum Quantity Budget Necessary to Maintain a Worker's Family of Five in Health & Decency,' June 1920, Vol. 10, No. 6, pp. 1 – 18.
[b] Work pants also include old suit pants 0.9, 1.1, 1.7 for laborer, wage earner, salaried, respectively.
[c] Some sharing since there are 1.1 (laborer), 1.1 (wage earner), 1.3 (salaried) older boys per family, with older boys present.
[d] Work pants also include old suit pants 2.4, 3.0, 3.6 for laborer, wage earner, salaried, respectively.
[e] To be made at home.
[f] To be made at home.

Clothing differences across classes for children under 15 were less marked than for older children and adults. Older daughters, looking for suitable husbands, had major clothing requirements, and their clothing expenditure rose rapidly across class. In the salaried family, the older daughter spent 20% more on clothes than the father or older son, and 28% more than the mother. These comparisons, especially for lower income families, must be made carefully, however, because family members wore each other's clothing.[29] No gender difference in clothing expenditure for boys and girls under 15 were observed, however, as they were about the same within each class.

Wool suits and high shoes were the most important clothing items for the husband, who spent one-third of his budget on them. The former was more important than the latter for status differentiation, both in quality (i.e., price) and in quantity (i.e., number purchased). Typically, the salaried husband bought a new wool suit twice as often as the laborer (1.25 vs 2.5 years). Each year, the laborer and wage earner bought two pairs of high shoes and the salaried worker bought 2.3 pairs. The price paid increased about 11% between classes for the suit and about 8% for the shoes. The quantity and quality of men's shirts also increases as one moves up the class scale. Over 90% of shirts purchased annually were cotton – 3.1 for the laborer, 3.5 for the wage earner, and 4.2 for the salaried worker. The price paid increased about 10% between classes. A silk shirt was required for major social events, and the salaried worker was more than three times as likely to buy a silk shirt as the laborer. The husband's other major clothing purchase was a wool overcoat. The salaried worker averaged one every 4.6 years, compared to 7.2 years for the laborer. The large price difference of 20% between classes indicates that the overcoat was an important status item.

The wool suit, high shoes, shirts, and overcoat accounted for around one-half of the husband's clothing budget. For other items, such as socks, handkerchiefs, and collars, the higher-status husbands bought more and higher-priced items. Ties and felt hats had greater price differences across classes, and were more important in marking status. Ties increased in average price by 13% from laborer to wage earner and 21% from wage earner to salaried. In general, the more visible the item of clothing, the more important was the price, and hence status differentiation across classes.

Wives' clothing budgets were allocated somewhat differently than their husbands'. A larger share was spent on underwear and nightwear (14% compared to 9%) and a smaller share allotted to footwear and hosiery (21% compared to 26%). The main items a wife bought were wool coats and cloaks, wool suits, dresses, high shoes, and hats; these accounted for almost one-half of her budget. The laborer's wife bought a wool coat or cloak every 5.2 years and a wool suit every 6.7 years, compared to 3.2 years and 4.1 years, respectively, for the salaried wife.

Wives primarily wore dresses or skirts and blouses. Wives of laborers and wage earners bought one inexpensive housedress each year. The salaried wife bought 1.5. Working-class wives bought a new street dress every 1.5 years and 1.5 blouses each year; the salaried wife bought a new street dress and two blouses annually. The quality of clothing varied markedly across classes; two-thirds of the dresses the laborer's wife purchased were cotton, while one-half of the dresses bought by the salaried worker's wife were silk or wool.

For wool coats, dresses, and blouses, wives paid 15%–30% more between classes. Comparable price differences for wool suits, skirts, and high shoes existed between salaried and wage-earner wives' purchases; however, the wage-earner wife spent only 8%–10% more than the laborer wife for these items.

Hats and silk stockings appear to be important status items in marking the attire of wives by classes. The salaried wife, compared to the laborer wife, had 50% more hats and three times the number of silk stockings (see table 3.5). According to a budget expert, a silk afternoon dress with silk petticoats and silk stockings were luxuries. Instead, 'a wool dress, a suit skirt with a dress waist, a Venetian cloth or sateen petticoat, and lisle or cotton stockings will supply all that is absolutely essential for health and decency.'[30] In practice, this was true for working-class wives, but for salaried wives, 'decency' demanded much more.

If we compare older daughters (15 years and up) to their mothers, we find daughters bought more clothes, but paid less per article, except for silk stockings, for which they also paid more. For longer-wearing items, this partially reflects the fact that the daughters could not have accumulated much of a clothing inventory after attaining full height. It also reflects their more active public lives since most were working or in school. The difference in quantities purchased between older daughters and their mothers increased with class. Daughters bought more high shoes, street dresses, blouses, hats, and stockings. Likewise, older sons bought more, and lower-priced, clothing than their fathers. They bought more wool suits, high shoes, caps, and ties and fewer shirts and socks.

Purchases of status items such as silk stockings, jewelry, and furs were especially important for the older children. Overall, older daughters had twice as many silk stockings as their mothers and were three times as likely to purchase watches or jewelry. Among salaried families with an older daughter, 29% bought her a watch or jewelry and 20% bought her furs or boas each year. Twenty-nine percent of older sons in salaried families also received watches or jewelry, but the average value was 15% less than for their sisters. In contrast, only 12% of the older daughters and 5% of the older sons in laborer families received watches or jewelry. Having a watch and some jewelry was the norm for professional children but fairly rare for working-class children.

Shoe repairs, shoeshines, and the cleaning, pressing and repairing of clothing accounted for about 12% of the clothing budget. These expenditures were larger for husbands than for wives across all groups. The use of the latter services rises dramatically across classes. Shoe shines were mainly a salaried class practice, with salaried husbands receiving a shoe shine at least every three months (and his son every two months). In contrast, the wage-earner husband received a shoe shine less than twice yearly (and his son almost never). Twice as many of the salaried husbands as laborers (37% vs 19%) reported cleaning expenditures of around 75% more ($4.50 vs $2.60) which indicates that laborer families generally did not use professional cleaning services. Perhaps more surprising is how little the salaried family used them. Even in professional families, the wife usually cleaned the husband's suits and starched and ironed his shirts to save money for other activities.

Typical wardrobes

Annual purchases can be translated into typical wardrobes by using standard practices of the time.[31] For example, the husband wore his summer or winter suits for 'dress up' or 'Sunday' clothes (for an unspecified period of time). The wife wore her summer dress(es) of the previous season as a house or 'everyday' dress. Work clothes and dress-up clothes were more frequently differentiated by style and materials among the higher status families; age and condition were the key criteria among the working classes.

Two main differences, then, marked the husband's clothing by class. First, the condition of everyday or work clothes was markedly different, since the salaried husband replaced his clothing more often even though he subjected it to less strenuous wear. Second, the quality of dress-up clothes was noticeably different, since the salaried worker had a silk shirt and socks to wear with his newer and more expensive wool suit, overcoat, and felt hat.

The laborer's five pairs of work pants or overalls did not permit daily changes between a weekly wash, since he had to wear pants to work on wash day. However, his nine shirts did permit daily changes. The wage earner had at least six changes of shirts and pants for work. In no class did the husband purchase enough underwear – from four sets for the laborer to six sets for the salaried workers – to permit daily changes. Either the wife did laundry more frequently than weekly, or the husbands wore some clothing for more than one day. The amount of clothing worn more than once between washings declined with class status. For the salaried husband, the only article that might not be fresh was his underwear, which was not publicly visible.

Overall, the wage-earner's clothing budget of $67 (which bought a wool suit every two years, an overcoat every six years, two pairs of high shoes every year, and sufficient work shirts for a daily change), seemed to have provided a benchmark for wardrobe adequacy. This is around 30% more than the laborer (or his older children) spent. Although the standard of a daily change of clothes is used as a benchmark, this was not the social standard in effect until after the widespread introduction of mechanical washing machines.[32] Prior to that, women starched and ironed clothes to keep them looking fresh for more than one wearing. This approach, though, was hard on clothes and made them wear out faster. So a trade-off existed between fresh-appearing and wearing out clothing faster.

Bureau of Labor Statistics (BLS) standards of adequacy placed high standards on the family's clothing, taking into account 'the physical needs of warmth, cleanliness, and comfort, but also has such regard for appearance and style as will permit the family members to appear in public, and within their rather narrow social circle, with neatness and self-respect.'[33] Wage-earner families did not pass these BLS standards. To meet BLS standards, the wage-earner husband would have had to increase his clothing budget by one-third (to $90). Husbands did not report spending $90 on clothing until the family's annual income exceeded $2,000. Although the salaried husband spent enough on clothing to achieve the BLS standards, he did not purchase enough wool and summer suits, cotton and wool shirts, high shoes, sweaters, undergarments, or pajamas. Instead, he purchased too many ties, overalls, and jumpers, and especially too many silk shirts and socks and leather gloves, which were considered luxuries by the government.

The salaried wife, like her husband when compared to the working class, had more and higher quality dress-up clothes, including a new outfit every eight months. The laborer's wife bought a new outfit only every 19 months, so that her dress-up clothes, which had to last several seasons, could be neither stylish nor in mint condition. Her undergarments were usually cotton; seldom did she wear silk stockings or petticoats. The laborer's wife probably had fairly shabby everyday clothes since she had to wear each cotton dress weekly for at least three years. Her six everyday dresses were not sufficient to allow daily changes even if she wore her dress-up clothes all day on Sunday, which was unlikely given her cooking chores for the day. In addition, her four sets of underwear would not take her through the week without an extra laundry day. Even without considering style and condition of clothing, the laborer's wife had too few pieces of clothing to take her through the week.

The wage-earner's wife barely met the standard of sufficient clothes for daily changes. She had seven housedresses to take her between washes only if she wore her dress-up clothing all day Sunday. She bought one new outfit almost every year (13 months). Her $58 clothing budget, which was 87% of her husband's budget, appears to be almost adequate if quantity alone (rather than style and condition of clothing) is the important consideration. However, the BLS standards of adequacy would have rated the clothing replacement purchases of the wage-earner's wife as inadequate. In addition, the BLS standard assumed a considerable amount of sewing at home. This does not seem to have been the practice, since the sample indicated that sewing of new articles was relatively rare. All the clothing items listed were purchased, and materials for home-made clothing were not listed separately.

The salaried wife had more than enough underwear and housedresses for daily changes. She also bought a new corset with a cover annually. However, the BLS standard provided for two new corsets with covers yearly and five new sets of underwear, which allowed for ten sets on hand. The salaried wife did not purchase a sufficient number of undergarments, wool suits, cotton dresses and hats, although she did purchase silk and kid items, which were not allowed in the standard wardrobe. Like her husband, the salaried wife considered the purchase of a few luxury accessories more important than the purchase of more basic items.

Like her mother, the laborer's older daughter did not have adequate clothing. Her five sets of underwear, four cotton or wool outfits (worn in public for two years), 1.7 pairs of high shoes, and a 2.5-year-old silk dress-up outfit were not sufficient for a job and an active social life. Although the wage-earner's older daughter had seven outfits and two pairs of high shoes, eight outfits were necessary for daily appearances in fresh clothes (with one outfit worn on washday). Also, she had only six pairs of underwear and a 20-month-old silk outfit. Her wardrobe was sufficient for a job but insufficient for an active social life. In contrast, the salaried worker's older daughter had nine cotton or wool outfits for daily public appearances, 2.2 pairs of high shoes, and eight changes of underwear. She also purchased a new silk outfit every nine months, and a pair of low shoes annually. The salaried daughter also had a fur or boa by the time she was 20 years old.

Overall, the clothing adequacy of older daughters was close to that of their mothers. The older son's clothing adequacy also tended to match his father's. (However, detailed figures cannot be given since published data do not include pants and overcoats for older sons.)

The low clothing purchases in the sample would be difficult to maintain over time. They are consistent with BLS investigations that show clothing purchases as considerably curtailed during the war.[34] Purchases of silk and decorative items were probably higher after the war for all classes. In this sample, the purchase of such luxuries was primarily for the older daughters of salaried workers. The low quantities of clothing purchased meant that clothing had to be kept in good repair for several years of at least weekly wearing. This implies that the wife did a large amount of mending and restyling. In addition, family members had to live with any shopping mistakes they made, so the purchase of new clothes or shoes was an important event. Uncomfortable, unattractive, or otherwise unsuitable clothing or shoes still had to be worn for a considerable amount of time.

Overall, for husbands, about 40% of the increased clothing expenditures between classes was used to buy higher-priced clothing and 60% was used to buy more articles of clothing. The reverse ratio was true for wives, who spent 60% of their higher clothing expenditures between classes to buy higher-priced clothing and 40% to buy more articles. So husbands spent more of their higher clothing budget to increase their clothing variety and improve the condition of clothing worn, while wives spent more to improve the status or image of their clothing.

The overall urgency for the laborer's family to increase their clothing expenditures is indicated by the fact that the clothing expenditures per person increased at a higher rate (26%) than the average expenditure rate (21%) between laborer and wage-earner families. Between wage-earner and salaried families, clothing expenditure per person increased almost as fast as total expenditure (52% vs 58%), which indicates that pressure to improve the wardrobe persisted.

Home

Housing

Housing was an important marker of class status, both by the quality of housing and the location.[35] The rate of home ownership rose rapidly across class – from 19% for laborer families to 36% for salaried families (see table 3.6A).[36] Home ownership meant better housing as well as more control and security. Living in a house rather than an apartment meant that the family had more space with larger rooms, more outside windows, and usually a yard as well as a cellar or attic. Including both renters and owners, the salaried families were 25% more likely than laborer families to live in a house than in an apartment. Although higher expenditures for housing across classes did not buy more rooms per person, they did buy better housing as well as additional rooms to accommodate more family members. For renters, the rent per room increased 12% between laborer and wage-earner families and 18% between wage-earner and salaried families.[37] The quality differences are reflected in the percentage of rooms equipped for heating (50% for laborer, 60% for salaried), the percentage with an inside water closet (61% for laborers, 84% for salaried), and the percentage with a bathroom (36% for laborer, 73% for salaried). These amenities, in turn, might differ greatly in quality. For example, the bathroom, which was the most important difference in modern amenities across classes and which was not included in the room count, might not have running hot water. The inside water closet could be shared with other families, and 'equipped for heating' could indicate the presence of a fireplace or any type of stove or it could mean central heating.

The standard for determining overcrowding was that a home averaged at least one room per person. This standard was usually met by the three white classes, but about one-half of the families fell below the standard – from 30% in Denver to 80% in St Louis.[38] The BLS space requirement for a family of five was five rooms with 660 sq ft of housing area. The standard also required one children's bedroom for each sex.

In practice if two rooms – the kitchen and living room with the dining area in one of them – were used for communal living, and if one room were the parents' bedroom, then the remaining rooms were the children's bedrooms with 1.4 (wage earner and salaried) to 1.7 (laborer) children per room. If one room were used as a dining room or as a parlor, which was recommended when older children began to receive visitors in the home, then the living room was probably adapted for sleeping purposes. The need for an extra room for social activities was most important for salaried families. However, such a use of rooms would cause cramped sleeping arrangements, since the children's bedrooms would average 2.3 people unless someone slept in the living room.

Table 3.6A   Annual shelter expenditures of white urban families, 1918

	Laborer	Wage earner	Salaried
Shelter Exp.[a]	$254	$303	$427
Rent	$150	$180	$248
Fuel and light	$64	$74	$93
Furniture and furnishings	$40	$50	$86
Home ownership	19%	24%	36%
Living in houses[b]	63%	67%	78%
Renters only[c]	81%	76%	64%
Average # of rooms total	4.5	4.9	5.6
Apartment	4.1	4.5	5.2
House	4.8	5.1	5.7
Average rent/room	$34	$38	$45
Average rent/person	$33	$38	$42
Renting house	56%	59%	68%
With bathroom	36%	55%	73%
Inside water closet	61%	72%	84%
Average # heated rooms	2.2	2.6	3.3
Family Size[d]	4.5	4.7	5.7

	Laborer		Wage earner		Salaried	
	Exp	Qty	Exp	Qty	Exp	Qty
Total fuel and light	$64	135.7m BTU	$74	154.5m BTU	$93	179.5m BTU
Coal (tons)	29.43	3.74	33.41	4.17	39.64	4.74
Gas (,000 cu ft)	13.13	23.55	16.61	29.38	23.20	38.80
Electricity (kilowatt hours)	4.23	41.67	6.92	75.69	12.05	128.24
Wood (cords)	7.29	0.72	7.75	0.80	8.06	0.81
Other	10.83		9.73		10.24	

[a] Includes homeowners in totals for fuel and light. Excludes renters (2% of sample) whose rent includes fuel and light from totals for rent and for fuel and light.
[b] Assumes all owning their own house live in houses, not in owned apartments.
[c] Information on housing quality available only for renters.
[d] Family size of laborer and wage-earner families is same for homeowners and renters. But family size for salaried families is 5.9 for renters compared to 5.7 for renters and homeowners combined.

Black families spent two-thirds as much as white laborer families on housing and three-fifths as much on furnishings. They could not economize on their energy budget, however, which was three-quarters of the white laborer's. The housing conditions of urban blacks were usually deplorable, as documented in a Philadelphia study. All but four in one hundred dwelling places were dilapidated and often unsafe. Families lived without gas and a bath, and used a toilet in the yard. They burned coal for heat and kerosene for light, and they bought these in small quantities.[39]

Using energy

Important class differences existed in the amount and convenience of the energy used in the home. Coal and wood required considerably more work to use than gas and electricity, since the wood or coal had to be stored and carried, the fire tended, and the stove cleaned. The average use of all fuel types increased by class, but the relative use of coal and wood declined and the use of gas and electricity increased. Coal was by far the most important source of energy; it provided about 70% of the energy used. Bituminous coal, the dirtiest source of heat, was also the cheapest and the most widely used. It provided 40–44% of the BTUs consumed, while accounting for only 22–24% of the fuel budget.[40] Cleaner burning anthracite coal provided 28% of the BTUs consumed while accounting for 21% of the fuel budget. Gas, the second most important fuel used, was considerably cleaner and easier to use than coal. However, it accounted for only one-fifth of the BTUs consumed and for one-fourth of the fuel budget. Wood, the third major fuel source, provided one-tenth of the BTUs consumed.

The most convenient and cleanest energy source, electricity, was not widely used, although almost one-half of non-farm dwellings had electrical services in 1920.[41] Families used it sparingly for lighting, since it was quite expensive (absorbing from 5% to 11% of the fuel budget).

Electricity use was highly sensitive to class. Wage-earner families, compared to laborer families, used their larger energy budgets primarily to buy more energy; the salaried family, compared to the wage-earner family, primarily used its larger budget to buy both more energy and easier-to-use, cleaner fuels. Overall, the wage-earner family spent 14% more on fuel and used 14% more BTUs than the laborer family. The salaried family spent 27% more on fuel than the wage-earner family but used only 16% more BTUs. The salaried family used 69% more electricity, 32% more gas, and 14% more coal than the wage-earner family. The latter used 82% more electricity, 25% more gas, and 11% more coal than the laborer family.

These averages for fuel and housing mask expenditure differences by city size and region. The variations reflect differences in fuel needs by climate, differences in the type of housing available by city size and differences in sanitation needs. In general, rent increased with city size, although large variations are found among cities of about equal size. Differential rates of home ownership and of renters who lived in houses

Table 3.6B Variations in housing by city size, 1918

City size	Small (28–61,000 population)			Medium (200–258,000 population)			Large (population >1 million)		
	Laborer	Wage earner	Salaried	Laborer	Wage earner	Salaried	Laborer	Wage earner	Salaried
Average family size	4.5	4.6	4.8	4.6	4.9	6.0	4.5	4.8	6.5
Homeowners	21%	28%	65%	11%	16%	41%	6%	11%	22%
Living in house	91%	97%	94%	45%	60%	75%	12%	11%	33%
Average # rooms: total	4.2	4.5	4.4	4.3	4.9	5.9	4.3	4.7	5.8
House	4.2	4.5	4.4	4.2	4.9	6.0	5.1	5.3	6.7
Apartment	3.5	3.3	4.5	4.3	4.9	5.6	4.2	4.6	5.3
Rentals only[a]									
Average rent	$120	$161	$311	$135	$165	$223	$176	$207	$270
per room	$29	$34	$66	$31	$33	$37	$41	$44	$47
per person	$27	$33	$59	$27	$32	$35	$39	$42	$39
With inside WC	42%	56%	64%	63%	76%	95%	91%	93%	97%
With bathroom	15%	49%	64%	30%	63%	79%	44%	61%	72%
Average # heated rooms	2.6	2.7	3.0	2.4	2.7	3.1	1.7	1.8	2.5
Fuel and light									
Expenditure	$68	$74	$118	$67	$78	$94	$63	$70	$98
Coal	$23	$27	$73	$26	$29	$28	$30	$34	$47
Gas	$5	$8	$5	$15	$21	$28	$22	$23	$33
Electricity	$7	$13	$21	$1	$3	$8	$1	$3	$5
Wood	$23	$18	$7	$11	$14	$22	$2	$1	$3
Other	$8	$8	$11	$14	$11	$9	$9	$8	$11

[a] The figures for salaried families in small cities who are renters must be used with caution since they represent a small sample.

versus apartments also affected housing expenditures and quality. For this reason, we look at three housing subsamples by city size – large metropolitan areas (New York and Chicago), mid-sized cities (Portland, Providence, and Atlanta), and small cities (Butte (Montana), Mobile (Alabama), Everett (Washington), and Pueblo (Colorado)).[42]

For each white class, the percentage of homeowners and the percentage living in houses decreased as city size grew. The average number of rooms per house increased with city size; apartments were larger in mid-sized cities than in small or large cities. Finding a suitably large apartment to rent in the large cities was a problem for many, including salaried workers' families.

Since sanitation requirements grew with city size, the percentage of renters with an inside water closet (WC) also increased with city size. In small cities, where health codes had not yet made inside water closets mandatory, the percentage of rented dwellings with WCs rose from 42% for laborer families to 64% for salaried families (see table 3.6B). In New York and Chicago, where public health laws required inside water closets, over 90% of all renters had one. Bathrooms were more sensitive than a WC to income; only 15% of laborer families in small cities had a bathroom, compared to 79% of salaried families in mid-sized cities.

Average heating expenditures were smaller in large cities because the number of heated rooms decreased with city size, primarily because apartments had fewer heated rooms than houses. (The latter were more likely to have fireplaces.) Working-class families in small cities were especially likely to heat with wood-burning fireplaces; for them, wood provided over one-half of the BTUs provided by coal. Families were more likely to use gas and less likely to use electricity and wood as city size increased. In New York and Chicago, almost no wood was used, while coal provided 70% of the BTUs consumed and gas another 25%. The fuel patterns in mid-sized cities were more diverse and varied more by class. In 1918, not all types of energy were available in all cities. For example, Butte had no gas, Pueblo had no wood, Atlanta and Portland had no anthracite, and Providence had no bituminous coal.

In mid-sized cities, each white class consumed about 20% more BTUs than the class below it. In large cities, salaried families used 35% more BTUs than wage-earner families, who used only 10% more BTUs than laborer families. Wage-earner families in all sized cities used up to twice the gas and electricity used by laborer families; however, they consumed only 2% more BTUs than laborer families. In all sized cities, salaried families used considerably more electricity than wage-earner families. However, salaried families in small cities used less than 1 million BTUs of electricity annually.

Generally, small-city families lived in houses and large-city families lived in apartments. In mid-sized cities, whether or not a family lived in

Table 3.7A Expenditures on furniture and furnishings, 1918

	Laborers		Wage earners		Salaried	
	Expenditure $	% reporting	Expenditure $	% reporting	Expenditure $	% reporting
Total	40		50		86	
Frequent purchases						
Bedding (pillows, blankets, quilts, sheets, pillowcases, spreads)	3.91	27	5.15	32	9.54	44
Napkins, tablecloths, oilcloth, towels	1.15	39	1.62	38	3.39	51
Floor coverings (carpet, matting, linoleum)	4.57	19	6.17	21	12.35	32
Window shades, screens, curtains	1.89	26	2.34	30	4.63	37
Decorative (lamps, clocks, mirrors, pictures, hatracks)	1.48	75	2.00	75	3.34	78
Dishes, glasses, flatware, washbowls	1.21	40	1.80	45	3.61	55
Kitchen utensils and cabinets	1.30	41	1.67	45	2.28	51
Brooms, brushes, mops	1.59	90	1.77	93	2.33	95
Major purchases						
Living room/dining room (chairs, tables, sofas, sideboards, desk, bookcases)	5.61	21	7.60	19	14.50	24
Bedroom (bedstead, bedspring and mattress, bureaus)	5.27	19	6.26	20	9.81	21
Stoves, ranges, heaters	4.82	25	5.16	24	7.72	29
Washtubs, washboilers, wringers, flatirons, sewing machines, etc.	0.99	21	1.17	21	1.43	21
Fireless cookers, refrigerators, carpet sweepers, washing machines	1.09	9	1.76	8	4.14	8
Other (including baby carriages)	3.32	28	3.46	32	4.49	39

Source: Royal Meeker, 'Minimum Quantity Budget Necessary to Maintain a Worker's Family of Five in Health and Decency,' *Monthly Labor Review*, X, 6, June 1920, pp. 14–15.

a house depended largely on class status – 45% of laborer families and 75% of salaried families lived in houses. The number of rooms per dwelling did not vary consistently by city size.

Like the national averages, these subsamples show families using higher income to buy higher quality housing and more rooms to house additional family members rather than more rooms per person. Families paid about the same rent per room in small and mid-sized cities; however, they paid considerably higher rent per room in New York and Chicago. Fuel and light expenditures continued to vary by class but varied little by city size. These subsamples show that local housing markets had local characteristics that were important in defining the ways in which people lived. Cost differences, however, were not significant except in the metropolitan areas.

Furnishing the home

Expenditures for furniture and furnishings were much more sensitive to class than expenditures for rent and energy. Salaried-worker families spent more than twice as much on furnishings as laborer families (see tables 3.7A and B). With higher class status, the percentage of families purchasing specific items increased slightly. The number of items and the average cost per item also increased. The most important items were living room and dining room furniture (17% of furnishings budget); bedroom furniture (11%); floor coverings (14%); bedding and linens (11%); and stoves and heaters (9%).

Standard pieces of furniture for every class – couches, chairs, tables, stoves, bedsteads and bureaus – were bought with almost the same frequency across classes. However, the proportion purchasing higher status items – sideboards and buffets, washing machines, bookcases, and writing desks – usually doubled between the laborer and salaried classes. Price differences for these items were also important. For washing machines salaried families paid 60% more than wage-earner families who paid 60% more than laborer families. These price differences reflect increasing degrees of mechanization over hand-operated machines.

Increased expenditures for furnishings across classes bought higher quality goods. Status differentiation is apparent especially in living room and dining room furniture and in floor coverings. Couches or davenports, the focal point of the living room or parlor, were an important status item, along with chairs and tables, bedsteads and bureaus. Salaried-worker families spent at least 37% more per item on these furnishings than wage-earner families. The cost differences between wage-earner and laborer families were usually smaller and more variable, ranging from 12% for bedsteads to 41% for chairs. Carpets were also an important mark of status for salaried families. They spent 41% more per

Table 3.7B   Typical furnishing – government standard

Living room	Master bedroom
Settee or davenport	Painted double bed and bureau (matching)
(wood with imitation leather)	Painted chiffon
Oak table	Two chairs
Four oak chairs	Two rag or crex rugs (3 ft × 6 ft)
Two small Axminster rugs	Sewing machine
Dining room	Children's bedroom
Oak extension table	Two white enameled bedsteads
Six plain oak chairs	White enameled crib
Oak sideboard	Painted bureau
High chair	Two chairs
Large crex or rattania rug	Two rag or crex rugs (3 ft × 6 ft)
Kitchen	
48 in. pine table with one drawer	
Painted chair	
Refrigerator	
Folding metal gokart	

Source: Meeker, 1920, pp. 14–15.

square yard of carpet than wage-earner families. The price difference between wage-earner and laborer families was only 25%. Salaried families also paid about 60% more for sideboards and bookcases and 30% more for refrigerators than wage-earner families, who paid almost 20% more for these items than laborer families.

Generally, price differences across class tended to be less for the more practical items. For example, for stoves and heaters, salaried families paid 27% more than wage-earner families, who paid 8% more than laborer families. Moving between the two working classes and between wage earners and salaried, families paid about 20% more for a sewing machine.

Higher status families bought greater comfort and convenience with higher quality bedding, cleaning equipment, and refrigerators, and more linens and dining utensils. For springs and mattresses, salaried families paid up to 40% more than wage-earner families, who paid up to 20% more than laborer families. Owning more linens and dishes meant these items were likely to be in better condition and in matched sets. In addition, more items allowed the wife greater convenience in the timing and frequency of washing. Salaried families bought more than one-third more linens as laborer families. They also spent twice as much on dishes and glassware, and 68% more on pots and pans and other kitchen utensils as laborer families. Large differences in comfort and convenience are also evident in lighting: salaried families spent twice as much[43] as laborer families for lamps, lamp chimneys, gas mantles, and electric bulbs. Finally, salaried families were more likely to own a high quality (electrical) vacuum cleaner and carpet sweeper than laborer families, who spent considerably less on their hand-pushed versions of these items.

About one-quarter of white families, in both large and small cities and across all income groups, paid for furniture and furnishings through an installment plan in 1918. The practice of buying on credit was at least as prevalent in the black community, and one-third of black urban families made installment purchases. The items most frequently purchased by installment included beds (including springs and mattresses), chairs, tables, and stoves or heaters. Black families were also likely to purchase bureaus and couches, while white families were also likely to purchase carpets and pianos, on installment credit. The 1920s were to witness sharp increases in the use of installment credit to purchase new consumer goods, especially automobiles and radios.[44]

It is hard to project the actual furnishings the salaried, wage-earner and laborer families had. According to prevailing standards, married couples purchased 'the major part of their household furniture either at or shortly after marriage.'[45] Since these families already had at least one child, it is likely that they had already acquired their basic furnishings. The rate of upgrading (replacing) or enlarging the furniture stock appears similar across classes. Similar quantities were purchased, except for the frequency of purchasing a few prized items (such as sideboards) that were a mark of class. The major class differences in furnishings were of quality.

The BLS standards for furniture indicate that houses were furnished sparingly (see table 3.7B). Families economized in this category. Annual replacement costs were calculated at 7% of the total cost of purchase.[46] This implies that the laborer's total value of furnishings was only $512 and the salaried worker's was $842. In contrast, the estimated value of the BLS standard set of furnishings was $1,297, so even the salaried family did not have the recommended furnishings. As for clothing, salaried families spent less than the government standard for furnishings, and yet they chose to buy 'non-essential' items, such as carpets, vacuum cleaners, or washing machines, which were excluded from the BLS standard.

Quantity differences in purchases across classes occurred among the less durable items, such as linens and carpeting. Families tended to economize on linens (including bedding); adequate linens were purchased only by salaried families. For example, members of laborer families received a new bath towel every 2.4 years, compared to 1.3 years for members of salaried families. Laborer families used sheets for 12 years, compared to seven years for salaried families.[47] Such heavy use, even by the salaried family, required the wife to mend the linens frequently.

Families appear to have purchased a bed each time a child left the crib. By BLS standards, each bed would have a felt mattress and bed springs, a wool blanket, a cotton comforter, a spread, a pillow for each person, in addition to linens.[48] The frequency of purchase figures indicate each bedstead had a mattress and usually a box spring (70% for laborers and 80% for wage earners and salaried). Each bed of the salaried family had a comforter, a spread, three blankets, and 0.7 pillows, with a blanket being replaced every six years. Each bed of the laborer family had 1.2 comforters or spreads, 1.9 blankets, and 0.6 pillows, with a blanket being replaced every nine years. Most laborer families had to substitute a blanket for the preferred comforter or spread; only 20% of their beds had both a comforter and a spread.

Overall, housing expenditure rose more slowly than income across classes. Expenditure on furnishings, however, rose faster than income across classes. While salaried homes provided some comfortable furnishings and some decorations, working-class families' pronounced economizing in this area resulted in woefully inadequate furnishings that did little to relieve their drab and austere living quarters.

Miscellaneous Expenditures

Most standard budgets broke expenditures into the 'big three' categories of food, clothing, and shelter, with everything else lumped under miscellaneous. These latter expenditures reflect the structure of social life – transportation, recreation, social activities, and communication – as well as the structure for daily family care – medical care, personal care, and household operations. Miscellaneous expenditures rose even more rapidly across classes than did clothing expenditures. This primarily reflects the rapid rise across classes in automobile expenditure and the more gradual climb in recreational expenditure. Automobile travel, vacations, and recreational outings provided important demarcations of status. Less visible, but more essential, expenditure for streetcar fares, household operations, and personal care accounted for a constant percentage of the budget across classes.

During the first two decades of the twentieth century, workers either walked to work or rode on streetcars, which had mostly been electrified by the turn of the century. Electric streetcars allowed the central city industrial area to draw its workforce from an area of about 12 square miles, or maybe 3.5 miles distant. After World War I, motor buses began to replace streetcars, and horse-drawn carriages had almost disappeared from urban streets.[49] Most families used streetcars for shopping and recreational excursions.[50] Working-class families, however, viewed the streetcar as a treat to be used sparingly for any travel other than to and from work. The percentage of husbands riding the streetcar to work increased by class, from 50% for laborers to 67% for salaried workers (see table 3.8). Working-class husbands economized on streetcar fares

Table 3.8 Annual miscellaneous expenditures of white urban families, 1918

	Laborer			Wage earner			Salaried		
	$201			$267			$520		
Total miscellaneous expenditures	*Distribution*	*Cost if purchased ($)*	*% reporting*	*% Distribution*	*Cost if purchased ($)*	*% reporting*	*Distribution*	*Cost if purchased ($)*	*% reporting*
Transportation	0.11			0.12			0.18		
Streetcar fares		19	86		24	89		42	91
to work		26	50		28	56		42	67
Automobiles, motorcycles, and bicycles		48	9		66	13		161	31
Travel (not vacation)		14	7		17	9		31	15
Recreation and education	0.21			0.22			0.25		
Movies		6	69		8	76		17	88
Plays and concerts, etc.		3	10		5	15		8	30
Excursion, other Amusements		5	12		6	16		10	28
Vacations[a]		15	18		22	24		45	37
Newspapers		7	93		8	96		10	98
Magazines		3	29		3	44		5	66
Books		3	9		5	14		10	26
Schools, tuition, books, etc.		6	42		7	47		16	64
Lodges, clubs, societies, etc.		10	21		11	28		14	41
Toys, sleds, carts, etc.		4	74		6	77		9	71
Music lessons		12	6		18	11		27	24
Pianos[b]		67	3		72	5		113	12
Talking machines and records		16	11		21	14		27	25
Tobacco		17	82		19	80		27	80
Household operation	0.13			0.13			0.13		
Postage		2	89		2	91		4	95
Laundry sent out		11	59		15	69		28	78

Table 3.8 (cont.)

Total miscellaneous expenditures	Laborer $201			Wage earner $267			Salaried $520		
	Distribution	Cost if purchased ($)	% reporting	% Distribution	Cost if purchased ($)	% reporting	Distribution	Cost if purchased ($)	% reporting
Cleaning supplies, soap, etc.		11	100		12	100		14	100
Tools		7	18		8	24		11	28
Telephones		11	16		15	25		20	46
Moving		8	22		9	19		13	17
Servant and day wages		13	10		19	14		40	25
Personal property insurance		4	9		5	15		6	23
Medical care	0.23			0.22			0.17		
Physician, surgeon, oculist		28	85		35	86		48	86
Medicine		9	93		10	92		14	92
Nurse		16	12		21	13		32	14
Hospital		35	8		42	10		46	14
Dentist		13	35		16	45		23	59
Eyeglasses		7	15		8	19		10	28
Accident and health insurance		16	16		15	18		21	26
Personal care	0.05			0.05			0.04		
Toilet articles and preparations		5	98		6	99		9	99
Barber		6	95		7	96		10	97
Gifts, contributions and welfare	0.09			0.095			0.10		
Church		10	65		12	72		21	80
Labor organization		12	25		14	31		18	34
Charity		2	23		4	28		7	41
Patriotic purposes		5	83		7	90		14	95
Gifts		9	40		11	53		23	66

	Laborer			Wage earner			Salaried		
Total miscellaneous expenditures	$201			$267			$520		
	Distri-bution	Cost if purchased ($)	% re-porting	% Distri-bution	Cost if purchased ($)	% re-porting	Distri-bution	Cost if purchased ($)	% re-porting
Personal insurance	0.15			0.14			0.11		
Life		35	85		43	86		64	89
Other	0.03			0.03			0.03		
Undertaker		50	3		58	3		104	4
Cemetery		15	2		17	2		35	3
Other (flowers, dog taxes, interest on loans, net loss on chickens and garden)		6	73		7	76		14	72

[a] Vacation includes transportation, lodging and all expenses while on vacation trip that involves a stay over one or more nights.
[b] Includes 'other musical instruments', purchased by 1% of the laborer families and 3% of the salaried families.

whenever possible, such as by walking to work when weather permitted, so frequency of use increased across classes. More mobility with greater convenience was an important marker of status. Overall, salaried workers paid twice the fares paid by laborers.

Working-class families' reliance on walking forced them to conduct most of their daily activities close to home. Salaried families, on the other hand, had not only more frequent access to streetcars, they experienced a vast freedom that resulted from owning an automobile. At most, one in eleven laborer families and one in eight wage-earner families owned an automobile, compared to one in three salaried families.[51] Among families which owned a car or motorcycle, the salaried family spent more than three times as much as the laborer family.

The greater sociability that accompanied increased class status was tied to mobility, especially in recreational activities. In the early part of the twentieth century, a six-day workweek left little time for family outings and recreational activities. Movies were by far the most popular recreational pastime for all classes. Although the white classes varied little in the percentage of families that went to the movies (from 69% of laborer to 88% of salaried families), the salaried family went three times as often as the laborer family. Besides attending motion pictures, entertainment consisted mainly of attending traveling shows, trolley car rides, bowling, playing and watching baseball, and swimming.[52] Cultural events were much less popular, and salaried families spent over six times as much on movies as on concerts and plays. While only 30% of salaried families attended a play or concert, this was three times the rate for laborer families.

Reading the newspaper and smoking tobacco were leisure time rituals of everyday life. Over 90% of the families reported spending an average of $7–$10 per year on newspapers, which paid for daily home delivery. Tobacco was purchased by over 80% of the families, and the expenditure for better quality rose with class. Salaried families spent 40% more on tobacco than wage-earner families, who spent only 12% more than laborer families. Smoking or chewing tobacco was associated with taking a break from work by men, sometimes sitting on the porch with friends. This ritual probably accounts for the classification of tobacco as recreational even in later years when smoking was no longer reserved for leisure time.

The two most expensive recreational items – vacations (defined as pleasure trips away from the city with an overnight stay) and musical instruments – were important status symbols. Twice as many salaried families (37%) reported going on vacation as laborer families. Salaried families also vacationed more elaborately, taking trips that cost three times as much as laborers' vacations. On average, the laborer family took an inexpensive vacation every 5.5 years and wage-earner families every 4.0 years. In addition, working-class families were much less than half as likely to have musical instruments at home than were salaried families.

The 'cultural elite' in each class – the 10%–15% of working-class families and 25%–30% of salaried families who attended plays and concerts, played music in the home, and bought books – were distinguished across classes by the amount they spent on these activities. Within the group of families buying books, salaried families bought three times as many books as laborer families. Salaried families spent twice as much as laborer families when they purchased a piano or 'talking machine' (phonograph). If they owned a phonograph, they purchased twice as many records. Since the piano and phonograph provided the major sources of music in the home, few families heard any music other than at free public concerts. Less than one-third of the salaried families had music in their homes, and even fewer provided lessons for their children.

Families were more likely to purchase magazines than books. One-third of laborer families and two-thirds of salaried families bought magazines. Even more important differences across classes are noticeable in school materials (including books, drawing (writing) instruments, and tablets) purchased for children. Such materials were bought by only one-half of laborer families with school-aged children; they were purchased by almost all salaried families with school-aged children. The quantity of school books and supplies purchased also varied by class, with salaried families spending four times as much as laborer families and three times as much as wage-earner families. Working-class family children were educationally disadvantaged, not only by having few or no books or school supplies, but also by having about one-half the toys possessed by children in salaried families.

The most important community activity was attending church. Reported attendance and average contributions increased across classes: 65% for laborer families, who contributed $0.20 weekly; 72% for wage-earner families, who contributed $0.23 weekly; and 80% for salaried families, who contributed $0.40 weekly.

For a large segment of salaried workers (40%), belonging to a lodge or club was an important part of social life. Although salaried workers were twice as likely as laborers to belong to a social club, their annual dues were not much higher ($14 vs $10). In addition, large numbers of workers belonged to labor organizations, which in many cases served primarily as insurance providers.[53] With one-fourth to one-third of working-class families belonging, membership in a labor organization was more prevalent than in a social club. In many cases, a social club, lodge, or labor organization performed the same functions which included providing sick benefits or insurance as well as social meetings. Membership was structured, of course, by class. Although one-third of salaried families belonged to a labor organization, they were more likely to belong to a social club. Generally, the annual dues for a labor organization were $12–$18, which was not much more than the dues for a social club.

Gifts to people outside the household are another indication of social integration. Salaried families were two-thirds more likely to buy gifts than laborer families. On average, salaried families spent almost as much for gifts as they contributed to church. For laborer families, church contributions were almost twice as important as gifts, and the small amount allowed in their budget for gifts indicates the harsh economizing pressures they faced. Financial constraints on gifts, clothing, and streetcar fares severely curtailed working-class families' social and community activities.

Patriotism ran high during this wartime period, and the large majority of families (from 83% of laborer to 95% of salaried families) responded to the government's appeal for contributions to help pay for the war. War contributions, which did not include the bonds or savings stamps listed under investments, ranged from an average contribution of $5 for laborer families to $14 for salaried. These contribution rates are another indication that laborer families felt much more financial pressure to carefully watch their budget and to economize wherever possible.

Outside of church and war, charitable contributions were small and were made by a minority of families – from 23% of laborer families to 41% of salaried families.

Use of the telephone greatly enhanced the social integration of the salaried class. Where the service was available, the great majority of salaried families took advantage of it. Telephone service had become a required part of their communication system. The 46% of salaried families with telephone service serves as an upper limit on the possible coverage of households. In contrast, only one-quarter of working-class households had a telephone, which was considered a luxury. Those who did have a telephone used it sparingly. Their bills were one-half to three-fourths the size of salaried families' bills. A less expensive means of communication was the postal service, which was used by almost all families. Postal expenses rose little across class. On average, laborer families spent the same on the telephone as on postage, while salaried families spent over twice as much.

Although five in six families received some doctor's care during the year, salaried families purchased considerably more, and probably better, care by spending 70% more than laborer families on doctor's visits. In addition, major class differences existed in the use of hospital care. Salaried families were 75% more likely than laborer families to go to the hospital, and their bills were one-third higher. The actual differences in hospital care were even greater by class than these budget figures indicate since some of the hospital bills were covered by health insurance policies. One-fourth of salaried families and one-sixth of laborer families had health insurance.

The condition of one's teeth, which is largely determined by dental care as one ages, was a highly visible marker of class status. Laborer families seemed to have visited the dentist only when absolutely required – only one-third of these families reported any visits to the dentist, with an annual bill of $13. Salaried families were much more likely to visit the dentist for about twice the dental work. Laborer families also economized on eye care. They were only one-half as likely as salaried families to spend money on eyeglasses. Status differentiation across class is also apparent in the amounts spent on grooming. Salaried families spent almost twice as much on the barber and on toilet articles as laborer families.

On a more practical level, all families reported expenditures for household operations, which were primarily for cleaning activities. These expenditures grew more quickly than the overall spending rate across classes, so that household operations accounted for a rising share of the budget. The diverse pattern of these expenditures across classes reflected the differences in both family life-style and the wives' housework burdens. Various soaps accounted for almost one-half of the household operations budget for laborers but less than one-quarter for salaried workers. In addition to doing the wash at home, most families sent some laundry out; six in ten laborer families did so, seven in ten wage-earner, and eight in ten salaried families. When they did send out laundry, the salaried family dispatched considerably more, spending 2.5 times as much as the laborer family. Besides having more help with the family wash, especially items that required starching and ironing, the salaried wife also had help with the heavy housework or yardwork. One-fourth of the salaried families had a helper for an average of almost one-half day weekly.[54] Only one-tenth of the laborer families hired any help; for those that did, it averaged only one-half day per month.

Finally, class status was visible in the burial ritual. Salaried families spent over twice as much as laborer families for an undertaker and cemetery services in burying their dead. Yet even the poor bought 'burial' or industrial insurance worth $150–$250 for most family members. Families paid small weekly premiums of about $0.50 for adults and $0.05 for children to the door-to-door agent. Life was harsh, and sudden death by accident or disease was an experience that most families had witnessed in their extended families or small social circles. Fear of death, coupled with dread of the 'potter's field,' compelled most families to dip into their already insufficient budgets to make the weekly insurance payments. If tragedy struck, at least the family would be spared the humiliation of not providing a decent burial for a lost spouse or child.[55]

These miscellaneous expenditures document visible differences in the daily lives of people across classes. The majority of laborer families attended church, made a $5 contribution for the war effort, and some life insurance for the husband. They received a newspaper and a monthly magazine, and the husband usually smoked tobacco. Their lives were not barren, but neither did they display the variety or freedom available to

Table 3.9 Budget standards, 1918

	Unskilled laborer				Wage earner	NWLB[b]	Government employee	Salaried
	Black	Laborer	NY	Basic[a]				
Expenditures	$791	$1,075	$1,211	$1,308	$1,298	$1,761	$1,970	$2,053
Food	376	462	612	612	521	625	694	721
Clothing	105	156	182	182	207	314	388	384
Husband	–	53	56	56	67	93	91	94
Wife	–	44	52	52	58	87	125	90
Shelter	175	253	255	275	304	345	450	426
Rent	100	149	171	171	180	220	277	248
Fuel and light	47	64	60	64	74	75	117	92
Furniture and furnishings	28	40	24	40	50	50	56	86
Miscellaneous	135	202	135	233	268	477	438	522
Transportation[c]	–	22	38	38	32	55	41	92
Recreation and education	–	41	57	57	59	85	26	125
Household operation	–	26	6	26	35	40	126	66
Medical care	–	46	25	46	59	60	73	88
Personal care	–	11	–	11	13	–	–	18
Gifts and contributions	–	20	6	20	25	32	21	60
Personal insurance	–	30	29	29	37	150[d]	103	57
Other	–	6	–	6	8	55	48[e]	16
Family size	4.2	4.5	5.0	5.0	4.7	5.0	5.0	5.7
Equivalent adult males	2.92	2.98	3.35	3.35	3.16	3.35	3.37	4.09
Adjusted expenditures (family of four)	$768	$1,005	$1,064	$1,164	$1,193	$1,591	$1,774	$1,719

[a] Basic equals value for unskilled laborer (NY) unless it is below laborer; then basic equals value for laborer.
[b] National War Labor Board's budget for minimum comfort.
[c] Includes only car fares in the budget standards, while CES data include automobile, motorcycle and bicycle expenditures.
[d] Includes savings for emergencies and invalidity.
[e] Includes gifts and tobacco.

salaried families. Laborer families travelled little, except on foot; they had few recreational outings; they usually had neither music nor a telephone in the house and they seldom bought a book or toy.

Prevailing Budget Standards

The minimum standards proposed in the first part of the twentieth century were acknowledged by their authors to be unrealistic in terms of wage-earners' incomes. In 1901 and 1909, about 40% of workers' families were estimated to have incomes insufficient to achieve the 'minimum' standard. In 1918–19, about 30% did not have incomes sufficient to cover the minimum budget.[56]

The difficulties the families below the salaried class faced as they tried to function on their meager budgets become more evident when comparing their budgets to the prevailing budget standards (see table 3.9). New York City's 1917 study[57] of the cost of living of an unskilled laborer's family of five persons estimated that $1,211 (in 1918 dollars) was required 'to maintain a normally happy and self-respecting existence' (p. 108). This is 39% higher (adjusted for family size) than the black family's budget, and 6% higher (adjusted) than the laborer's budget. The black family spent 30% less (per equivalent adult male) on food, and the laborer family spent 15% less than the New York City (NYC) standard. Blacks spent only two-thirds as much on clothing (per equivalent adult male) as allowed by the NYC standard, which included very limited wardrobes of inexpensive clothing. The white laborer spent almost as much on clothing as the NYC standard amount, but his wife and children spent considerably less.

The NYC budget standards required laborer families to economize on streetcar fares except for rides to work (12 per week), and little money was available for recreational outings. Even so, laborer families spent even less than these low amounts. Instead, they spent more than the niggardly NYC standard for furniture, cleaning supplies and laundry, and contributions. The NYC standard for medical care, especially, was too low, since the city assumed that families had access to low-cost or free government health care facilities.

In practice, poor families spent little or nothing on amusements, and few seemed to have access to low-cost medical clinics. Most of the budget of poor people was used to pay rent and buy food. One 1917 study of 377 families in New York City detailed how families economized on daily necessities such as coal, fresh food, underwear, shoes, and newspapers to live on their insufficient budgets.[58] One study estimated that poor families lost 7% on 'bad bargains' (i.e., installment buying, buying in small lots) or on rent items and paid 41% more than justified by a 10% return on market value to the landlord.[59]

Buying furniture, insurance, and sometimes men's suits and food on credit was a way of life for lower-income families. Social analysts criticized installment buying since they claimed it raised costs and lowered morale. Poor families, however, defended the practice, since otherwise they could not buy most items.[60]

The NYC budget standard was considered to be at the subsistence level. It was 2% lower than the Bellevue Hospital 'practical requirements' budget for 'decent living,' which was estimated using data from 'women who are daily meeting problems arising from poverty, and who have an exact knowledge of the needs of the typical worker's family.'[61] The main difference in the two standards was that the Bellevue budget allowed 26% more for clothing. In practice, shoes were the most imperative clothing item. Most of the poor's wardrobe consisted of cast offs and donations, usually patched.[62]

These subsistence budgets are considerably more stringent than a BLS federal government employee budget issued in 1919. Although the latter emphasizes living with 'health and decency,' it does 'not include many comforts which should be included in a proper "American standard of living" '[63] (e.g., savings, vacations, and books). The BLS budget does allow for a six-room house with a bath and running water in a low-rent neighborhood, replacement of worn-out furniture (at 6% allowance), and assistance with the laundry one day a week (at the prevailing rate of $2 per day).[64] In contrast, the NYC subsistence standard allowed only for a four-room apartment (so that the combined living room and dining room most likely also was used as a sleeping room). There was no allowance for furniture replacement (with a small replacement fund for kitchen utensils and linens) nor for a laundress. The NYC standard allowed a $500 life insurance policy, which was thought of as 'burial' insurance, compared to a $5,000 policy (which provided $300 per year) in the BLS standard. However, this more liberal standard for a government employee did not meet the BLS standard for a worker's family, which allowed a $7,500 life insurance policy, a 7% replacement allowance (rather than 6%) for furnishings, and at least one magazine in addition to the daily newspaper.[65]

Only the salaried family could match the spending in the government employee budget. But even they spent 15% less on food (per equivalent adult male), rent, and energy compared to the standard, while their expenditures were over twice as high for furnishings, transportation, recreation/education, and contributions. Wives still spent considerably less on clothing than allowed in the standard budget. As a budget expert noted,[66] 'when economies are necessary, they are made largely at the expense of the wife's wardrobe. The first baby makes a cut in the mother's clothes money, and every addition to the family cuts deeper into this item.' Accordingly, the wife's clothing expenditures are a good indicator of the pressures to economize experienced by the family. The clothing allowance for the wife in the BLS government employee budget was supposedly 'subsistence'; it should have been 30% higher to allow for more appropriate clothing for social occasions, including[67]

- two pairs of silk stockings (in addition to her cotton stockings);
- one silk dress (instead of her wool dress);
- one new georgette waist ('her only fancy blouse') every year (instead of every two years);
- one jersey-silk petticoat (in addition to cotton ones);
- one better quality winter coat (to supplement her lightweight suit);
- one new winter hat each season (instead of every other season) so that she is not 'conspicuous because her clothing is entirely out of the prevailing mode'), and
- one pair of dress shoes (in addition to her walking shoes) every other year.

The higher clothing budget would also allow the wife to have additional at-home attire (e.g., a pair of house slippers every other year, three nightgowns yearly, etc.).

This list of what the government employee budget does *not* include in the wife's clothing allowance indicates the severe budget constraints felt by even the salaried wife, who was spending 28% less on her clothing than the allowed 'subsistence' amount. Her wardrobe allowed only a limited social life. Yet, in comparison to the wage-earner and laborer wives, who spent two-thirds and one-half as much, respectively, on clothing, the salaried wife had an extensive wardrobe and faced far less severe budget constraints.

The prevailing budget standards make it clear that the wage-earner family did not have a budget sufficient to meet what were thought of as working-class standards of health and decency.[68] The wage earner spent 6% less than the National War Labor Board's (NWLB) budget for 'minimum of subsistence'[69] and was 26% less than the NWLB's budget for 'minimum comfort.' In fact, the wage-earner's budget was only 7% higher than the NYC budget for the unskilled laborer. The NWLB allowed nearly one-half again as much for clothing as the wage-earner family actually spent. Similarly, they spent less than the standard allowed on rent and energy; and significantly less on transportation, recreation, and personal insurance. In these areas, wage-earners' actual budgets looked much more like the theoretical minimums set for unskilled laborers.[70]

The NWLB standard was generally higher than other prevailing budget standards. For example, the National Industrial Conference Board's (NICB) estimate of the cost of 'maintaining a minimum but reasonable standard of living for a representative wage-earner's family' in Lawrence, Massachusetts, was about 30% less and their estimate for a 'somewhat better standard' was about 15% less.[71] The NWLB standard allowed for a better life insurance policy, more health care, and larger budgets for streetcar fares, household furnishings and cleaning supplies, and 'comforts' (tobacco, gifts, candy, and drinks). The NICB allowed for more contributions to church since Lawrence was predominantly Roman Catholic. The NWLB standard was about 10% higher than two budget standards for workers in Philadelphia.[72] The NWLB allowed more for food, household furnishings, and cleaning supplies. In addition, the Philadelphia textile workers were assumed to walk to the mill so their standards did not include car fares. However, they were allowed much more for contributions to church and labor organizations.[73]

The West Coast workers' standard budgets[74] were at the same level as the NWLB standard, although they allowed less for recreation and 'comforts' (tobacco, candy, gifts). The Peixotto budget did not even list recreation as a budget item, although it did allow a telephone, which did not appear in any other budget standard. These budgets also allowed less than the NWLB for household furnishings and cleaning supplies. Although the three budgets allowed the same amount for clothing, the rapid price increases (35%) for apparel during 1917–18[75] means that West Coast budgets actually allowed one-third more clothing to be purchased compared to the NWLB.

These budget standards indicate that even wage earners had not attained the standard of living generally considered to be adequate for healthy and decent family living. Family life was hampered by inadequate housing and energy use; social life and social integration were limited by inadequate clothing, transportation, and recreational activities; and financial security was almost nonexistent (life insurance was inadequate and families had almost no savings). It is these aspects of the family's standard of living that see marked improvement later.

These differences in consumption created economic distance between classes through the material differences in the ways these groups experienced everyday life.

Economic Distance

Simple material improvements[76] – 'facilities for personal cleanliness, more comfortable beds, larger rooms, greater variety of food, better pictures on the walls' – helped 'to raise the level of daily life above mere animal wants.' The meagerness of these sought-after improvements emphasize the reality of the statistics in this chapter. Life for blacks and, to a lesser extent, for white laborers, was bleak, monotonous, and restricted. Each additional $100 in the budget allowed a family to improve its daily existence measurably.[77] The $1,260 that separated salaried and black families represented a large array of goods that made life easier, more enjoyable, and healthier. As table 3.10 illustrates, in each group of paired classes, one-half of the larger budget was spent on more food and clothing (including for more family members). Improvements in shelter (housing, energy, and furnishings) decline in importance as a family moved up the class ladder. White laborers used almost one-third of their additional income (compared to blacks) for improved shelter. Salaried workers used only one-sixth of their income advantage over wage earners for better shelter, and instead, made major improvements (in terms of percentage increases) in other areas. For example, salaried families spent three times as much on transportation as wage-earner families (they rode streetcars 80% more often and were over twice as likely to own an automobile). They attended movies, plays, concerts, or other events about three times as often; and they were 50% more likely to take a vacation. Their high standing in the community was visible in their contributions – twice as much to the church and war effort and over twice as much to charity. Their broader social life was marked by their spending three times as much on gifts to people outside the family.

Table 3.10   Economic distance across class, 1918

	Laborer to Black		Wage earner to Laborer		Salaried to wage earner	
Net income	1.35		1.25		1.69	
Consumption expenditure	1.36	+ $284	1.21	+ $225	1.58	+ $753
Distribution of increased consumption[a]	100%	*% change*	100%	*% change*	100%	*% change*
Total food and clothing	0.47	+ 28	0.49	+ 18	0.50	+ 52
Food (per equiv. adult male)	0.24	+ 18	0.13	+ 7	0.05	+ 7
Clothing (per person)	0.15	+ 40	0.18	+ 26	0.14	+ 52
Change in family size	0.07	–	0.17	–	0.31	–
Shelter	0.30	+ 48	0.22	+ 19	0.16	+ 41
Rent	0.17	+ 49	0.13	+ 20	0.09	+ 38
Fuel and light	0.06	+ 36	0.04	+ 14	0.03	+ 27
Furnishings	0.07	+ 68	0.04	+ 25	0.05	+ 72
Miscellaneous	0.23	+ 49	0.29	+ 33	0.34	+ 95
Transportation	–		0.04	+ 41	0.08	+ 200
Recreation and education	–		0.07	+ 37	0.09	+ 119
Household operation	–		0.04	+ 30	0.04	+ 86
Medical care	–		0.05	+ 28	0.04	+ 49
Personal care	–		0.01	+ 18	0.01	+ 46
Gifts, contributions	–		0.04	+ 44	0.04	+ 108
Personal insurance	–		0.04	+ 25	0.03	+ 55
Other	–		0.01	+ 33	0.01	+ 100
Surplus	– 0.03		0.16		0.19	

[a] Percentage change = difference/original budget expenditure.

Table 3.11 Standard of living index, 1918

	Laborer benchmark			Wage earner to laborer			Salaried to wage earner			Black to laborer		
Expenditures	$1,075			$1,298			$2,053			$791		
Ratio	1.00			1.21			1.58			0.74		
Difference	$0			$223			978			($284)		
	Basics ($)	Variety ($)	Status ($)	Basics ($)	Variety ($)	Status ($)	Basics ($)	Variety ($)	Status ($)	Basics ($)	Variety ($)	Status ($)
Food and clothing												
Food	462	0	0	59	0	0	30	170	0	(86)	0	0
Clothing	156	0	0	8	18	26	B	85	92	(6)	0	0
Shelter												
Rent	149	0	0	22	9	0	B	27	41	(49)	0	0
Fuel and light	64	0	0	B	10	0	B	20	0	(17)	0	0
Furnishings	40	0	0	B	5	5	19	10	8	(12)	0	0
Miscellaneous												
Transportation	22	0	0	10	0	0	6	39	15	(66)	(1)	0
Recreation and education	41	0	0	16	2	0	B	57	9			
Household operation	26	0	0	B	9	0	B	31	0			
Medical care	46	0	0	B	13	0	B	29	0			
Personal care	11	0	0	B	2	0	B	1	35			
Gifts and contributions	20	0	0	B	1	4	B	0	5			
Personal insurance	29	1	0	B	7	0	B	20	0			
Other	6	0	0	B	0	2	B	8	0			
Subtotal	1,072	1	0	115	76	37	55	552	205	(236)	(1)	0
Proportion of total	1.00	0.00	0.00	0.52	0.34	0.17	0.06	0.56	0.21	0.83	0.00	0.00

B denotes basic standard has been met.

The Standard of Living

In meeting basics, people attempt to be fed first, clothed second, and housed third.[78] This pattern reflects the physiological requirement of food for working and then the social requirement of attire for working and shopping. Housing requirements were less related to conditions for work and required public activities. In addition, improving one's housing, as opposed to food or clothing, was a longer term economic commitment that was harder to reverse when economic hardship struck.

Improvements in living standards are characterized as basics, variety, and status. The 1918 laborer's budget is used as the benchmark for the standard of living index across classes and over time. For laborers, in 1918 the entire budget was spent on items to provide basics, since food, clothing, shelter, transportation and recreation did not meet standards of health, safety, and decency (see table 3.11). Laborer families, facing severe budget constraints, could not buy variety to reduce the drudgery of everyday life and to have active social lives. They also made no status purchases to create a distinctive social appearance.

One-half of the higher budget for wage earners (compared to laborers) was spent on improvements in basics, primarily for food (representing one-half of total improvement in basics) along with rent and recreation (see table 3.11). One-third of the higher budget was spent on improvements in variety, primarily in providing more clothing and medical care (together representing two-fifths of total variety). Wage earners were able to appropriate one-sixth of their higher budget for spending on improved status, mostly for clothing. Although the variety, and especially the status, improvements for wage-earner families were small in dollar terms, they were large in relative terms. They allowed families to purchase items that decreased the drudgery of daily chores, made leisure time and meal time more enjoyable, and added a little sparkle to an otherwise dreary life.

Salaried families used their larger budgets primarily to improve their variety over wage earners' (66% of increased expenditures); 17% of their higher expenditures was spent for improved status and only 7% was used to improve basics. As with wage-earner families, variety improvements were primarily made by having more children, which increased food and clothing expenses, and an array of recreation activities (63% of variety). Status improvements were primarily made in housing, clothing, and gift-giving (82% of status). Improvements in basics were made in food and furnishings.

A typical home economics text, written by a student of Richards, emphasized how families were compelled by consumption standards that exerted a 'civilizing' effect. The author thought that the consumption pressures were especially pronounced for the salaried workers, who 'must live up to certain conventions of dress and surroundings at peril of forfeiting the chance to earn a living.'[79]

Table 3.12   Rate of school attendance and employment – urban population, 1920

Percentage school attendance	Children 7–13 yrs	Children 14–20 yrs	Males 5–20 yrs	Females 5–20 yrs
All children	94	39		
White native – native parents	95	44		
White native – foreign parent(s)	95	37	66	66
White – foreign born	88	25		
Negro	91	33	53	55

	Native white			
Percentage engaged in gainful occupations	Native parents	Foreign parents	Foreign-born White	Foreign-born Negro
Males				
10 to 15 years	10	7	11	27
16 to 19 years	64	72	80	76
Females				
10 to 15 years	4	4	8	17
16 to 19 years	29	51	57	40

Source: Calculated from 1920 Census of Population Tables 2, 5, 26.

The fact that one-half of the wage earner's higher expenditures were spent for improved well-being indicates the harsh limitations imposed by the laborer's budget. Although wage-earner families could afford a more comfortable and diverse life-style, they still faced inadequate budgets – as indicated by the limitations placed on their purchases for medical care, furnishings, and transportation. Salaried families had greater flexibility in purchasing goods and their lives were considerably richer in material goods. The increased economic control they had over their lives is reflected in their expenditures being only 90% of their net income. They escaped the tyranny of the household budget faced by black and laborer families, who spent all of their income and whatever credit they could obtain.

NOTES

1. US Bureau of the Census, *Historical Statistics of the United States; Colonial Times to 1970*, Bicentennial Edition, Parts I and II (Washington, DC, 1975), D-3, D-9, F-31, E-13. During the wartime period (July 1914 to Nov. 1919), clothing costs of average wage earners increased 135%, which was the most of any category. Shelter costs

increased 38%, and energy costs increased 48% while food costs increased 92%. (See National Industrial Conference Board, 'Change in the Cost of Living,' Research Report No. 25, Dec. 1919.) These figures are slightly higher than those reported by the US Bureau of Labor Statistics, which also report furniture and furnishing prices increasing even faster than clothing prices (see US BLS, Bulletin 357, May 1924, p. 466).

2. The exact percentage for those living in urban areas is 51.4%; 48.6% lived in rural areas (19.0% non-farm; 29.7% farm). These and other population and labor force statistics are from *Historical Statistics*, unless otherwise noted. Only 34% of the black population lived in urban areas.

3. Frederic Dewhurst and Associates, *America's Needs and Resources* (New York: Twentieth Century Fund, 1955).

4. W.C. Mitchell, W.D. King, O.W. Knauth, F.R. Macaulay, *Income in the United States*, 2 vols (New York: NBER, 1921, 1922), see Ch. 22. Income data were not collected in the decennial census until 1940.

5. *Historical Statistics*, Q153. There were 5.6 million automobiles registered.

6. See Daniel Horowitz, *The Morality of Spending*, for a discussion of these points and their place in the development of social thought. During this period, Robson examined the influence of health, art, work, and education on human welfare. William A. Robson, *The Relation of Wealth to Welfare* (New York: Macmillan, 1925). Urwick's *Luxury and Waste of Life* argued against the consumption of goods that were not accessible to all. Hobson (*Work and Welfare*) distinguished between productive and unproductive consumption.

7. US Department of Health, Education and Welfare, *Vital Statistics of Rates in the United States*, 1940–1960, 1968, Tables 38, 44; *Historical Statistics*, Series B107–15, B136–47, B149–66. Collection of birth statistics began nationally in 1915 and covered one-third of the population.

8. Outside of agriculture, 4.6 million persons or 14% of the workforce were self-employed, primarily in trade (38%), services (31%), manufacturing (11%) and construction (10%). Women who work but are unpaid in family businesses are rarely counted as employed.

9. See Appendix for source of income figures. Families were excluded if their children did not pool income, and the principal breadwinner had to contribute 75% of family income. The CES intentionally sampled only from the broad middle of the income distribution. Only 2.7% of the sample had less than $900, compared to 30% of the population (with this low-income group over-represented by rural families). Only 2.9% of the sample had over $2,500 in 1918, compared to 8.7% of the population (see also Table 3.2).

10. There are no direct data on black family income in 1918.
11. Figures from 1920 census.
12. Although the family sizes are artificially inflated because they are only for families with a husband, wife and at least one child present, the impact on the family size across groups is probably similar. Information available on family size by family type and income in 1935 shows that husband-wife-children families average 20% more people than all families in each of the three income groups. (US BLS, Summary Volume, 1941, p. 44.)
13. Bruce A. Chadwick and C. Bradford Chappell, 'The Two-Income Family in Middletown, 1924–1978,' in Stephen J. Bahr, ed., *Economics and the Family* (Lexington, MA: Lexington Books, 1980), pp. 27–41. During 1920–4, 44% of working class and 3% of business class wives were employed at some time; during 1973–7, 48% of working class and 42% of business class wives were employed (p. 33).
14. Because food consumption data are not available by income group, only the averages for the entire sample can be studied. With an average yearly expense of $165 per equivalent adult male, these sample averages are representative of the wage-earner family, who spent $163 per equivalent adult male. The average survey family of 4.9 people (3.32 equivalent adult males) consumed around 10,050 calories daily at home (or 3,027 calories per equivalent adult male). One pound of flour (enough for 4 dozen muffins, biscuits, or rolls) and 1.25 pounds of store-bought bread supplied 29% of these calories. These calculations are based on caloric tables in Laurel Robertson, Carol Flinders, and Bronwen Godfrey, *Laurel's Kitchen* (New York: Bantam Books, 1976); Adell Davis, *Let's Eat Right to Keep Fit* (New York: Harcourt Brace & Co., 1954). These books and Irma S. Rombauer and Marian Becker, *Joy of Cooking* (Indianapolis: Bobbs-Merrill, 1964), were used to figure number of servings. All 'average servings' are hypothetical: No information on how the food was allocated within the family is available. Although food was eaten seasonally, here consumption is averaged over the entire year. Servings are *per person*, not per adult equivalent.
15. For comparison with pre-industrial standards, see Fernand Braudel, *The Structures of Everyday Life* (New York: Harper & Row, 1981). Compared to previous expenditure surveys in 1890–1 and 1901, a typical working-class family spent a much lower proportion of its budget on 'subsistence' (specifically defined as food, kerosene, and grocery store provisions) in 1917–19 (35% against 44% earlier). A similar shift occurred between the 1874–5 and 1890–1 surveys with a fall from 60% to 44% of the budget for 'subsistence'. See Commissioner of Labor, Sixth, Seventh and Eighteenth Annual

Reports (Washington, DC, 1891, 1892) (Vol. II) and 1904, respectively. The 1890–1 surveys covered workers in iron, steel, coal, freight, textiles and glass industries. See also William A. Berridge, Emma A. Winslow, and Richard A. Flinn, *Purchasing Power of the Consumer* (New York: A.W. Shaw, 1925). The average family expenditure (real dollars) was over 80% higher in 1918 than in 1901.

16. The BLS minimum standard diet calculated in 1920 was based on caloric and other nutritional needs, as well as on the food patterns of the survey families, which were adjusted 'for health reasons.' The US Department of Agriculture standard diet set even lower standards than the BLS by having 43% more fruits and vegetables, as well as less protein-rich foods, and slightly more sweets and fats. The scientific study of nutrition began around the turn of the century. The importance of vitamins was discovered in 1906. The public became more aware of the importance of nutrition during World War I when nutritional research was applied to understand the poor health of soldiers. One study in 1918 estimated that 15%–25% of children in the United States were undernourished. US BLS *How American Buying Habits Change*, 1959, pp. 108–9, 119.

17. Nutritional standards have changed over time, and now the RDA includes less protein, calcium, riboflavin, and vitamin C, and more iron and niacin. Even with the lower 1980 standards, however, the level of calcium in the average 1918 diet remains deficient; riboflavin moves to the adequate category. With the higher 1980 standard, iron becomes deficient and niacin becomes borderline inadequate. (William F. Ogburn, 'A Study of Food Costs in Various Cities,' *Monthly Labor Review*, IX, 2, Aug. 1919, pp. 20–4.) For other nutrients, we can compare the national food disappearance data (Letitia Brewster and Michael F. Jacobson, *The Changing American Diet* (Washington, DC: Centre for Science in the Public Interest, 1978)) to 1941 RDA standards. Protein, niacin, and vitamin C consumption appear to have been adequate and vitamin A intake appears to have been more than adequate. Iron and thiamin were borderline inadequate. Calcium and riboflavin were inadequate, indicating an inadequate supply of milk. Concerns about calcium deficiency were voiced at the time, and later studies show that a deficiency did exist. See Brewster and Jacobson (1978), p. 71. Nationally, niacin consumption was borderline inadequate, using 1974 standards.

18. See Royal Meeker, 'Minimum Quantity Budget Necessary to Maintain a Worker's Family of Five in Health and Decency,' *Monthly Labor Review*, X, 6, June 1920, pp. 1–18 and Ogburn (1919). A man working at moderately hard muscular work (i.e., activity which was neither sedentary nor hard physical labor) was estimated to need

3,000–3,200 calories per day. After allowing about 10% waste in food preparation, 3,400 to 3,500 was given as the caloric need per equivalent adult male for the working man's family. All the classes spent *less* than the $209.50 per man per year required in a 1914–15 study (in 1918 dollars) of 92 families to meet standards for calories (3,100), phosphorus (1.44 gr.), calcium (0.69 gr.) and iron (15 mg.). In the CES, blacks averaged only $129 per man per year, laborers $155, wage earners $165, and salaried $176. (See H.C. Sherman and L.H. Gillett, 'The Adequacy and Economy of Some City Dietaries,' The New York Association for Improving the Condition of the Poor, New York, 1917.) In this study, 76% of the families consumed less than 3,500 calories, 59% consumed less than 3,000 calories, and 53% consumed less than 0.68 grams of calcium.

Although later caloric standards varied, the 3,500 benchmark is consistent with them. The Recommended Dietary Allowances (RDA) established by the National Research Council in 1941 set 3,000 as the caloric standard for a moderately active man (aged 45), which seems conservative. A mature male weighing 154 pounds uses 3,000 calories in the following daily activities (with no moderate work): ten hours of resting and sleeping, nine hours of light work (washing clothes, shopping with light load, carpentry, cannery work, tailoring, walking), and five hours of very light work (seated and standing activities, painting trades, driving, typing, sewing and ironing). The standard for the wife, 2,500 calories, seems reasonable since 2,520 calories are used by a mature female weighing 122 pounds in the following daily activities: ten hours of resting and sleeping, six hours of very light work, five hours of light work, and three hours of moderate work (scrubbing floors, weeding and hoeing, plastering, shopping with heavy load). Calculated from National Research Council, *Recommended Dietary Allowances*, 9th revised edn (Washington, DC: National Academy of Sciences, 1980), pp. 16–30.

In the comparisons that follow, the 1941 standards are used with the 1918 weights to calculate recommended calories per equivalent adult male. If we allow the conservative recall to offset the amounts allowed for waste, then 3,300 calories per equivalent adult male for the wage-earner family of five seems reasonable. For the average survey family of 4.9 people (or 3.32 equivalent adult males), the analogous caloric requirements were 10,380 calories daily, which were only 3% higher than the calories in the average survey diet.

The laborer family needed at least 1,000 more calories per day (or 3,600 per equivalent adult male in a family of five) since the husband was engaged in more strenuous work activities. The 1941 standard for a 'very active' male was 4,500 calories, or 1,500 calories higher than for a 'moderately active' male. The 4,500 calories used here represent a daily pattern of two hours of heavy work (pick and shovel, tree felling, carrying a load uphill) plus four hours of moderate, light, and very light work activities, and ten hours of sleeping and resting. However, according to Ogburn (p. 15), five-person families with $1,000 income only averaged 2,894 calories daily per equivalent adult male, which was 12% (moderately active male occupation) to 19% (active occupation) too low. Ogburn's caloric analysis was done on a subsample of survey families in 11 localities. The average laborer family had fewer members, so the typical family was probably less deficient in caloric intake.

Five-person families with incomes of $2,000 averaged 3,535 calories per equivalent adult male (Ogburn, p. 15), so salaried-worker families had caloric intake that was 7% (active male occupation) to 17% (sedentary occupation) too high. The 1941 standard for a sedentary man was 2,500; the standard for a moderately active woman is used regardless of her husband's work. The five-person family standard is 3,030 calories per equivalent adult male (Ogburn, pp. 18–20). In addition, 22% of the subsample consumed less than 2,500 calories per equivalent adult male. If the low income (less than $900) group had been properly represented in the CES survey, the extent of underfeeding recorded would have been much higher.

19. In another study, at least one-half of the families in a Boston sample were found to consume too few calories. Only one-third consumed enough calories. Milk consumption was also seriously inadequate. Michael M. Davis, 'Food Supply in Families of Limited Means,' League for Preventive Work, Pub. 3 (Boston, 1917).

20. The extent of underfeeding among blacks is unknown, but it was certainly at least as severe as it was among white laborers.

21. Ogburn, p. 21. See also H.C. Sherman and L.H. Gillett, 'The Adequacy and Economy of Some City Dietaries,' 1917.

22. Ogburn, pp. 15, 18.

23. Ogburn, pp. 10, 22. Milk consumption was 0.03 quarts per man per day.

24. Sadie Tanner Mossell, 'The Standard of Living Among One Hundred Negro Migrant Families in Philadelphia,' *Annals of American Academy of Social and Political Science*, XCVIII, Nov. 1921, pp. 17–18. These black families were well off compared to blacks nationally. Seven in ten had incomes between $1,068 and $1,970; average family size was 3.5; the major difference in family income was the contribution of the wives' earnings. One-half of the wives worked, primarily as domestics. One-fourth had lodgers. Even 25% of these black families did not spend as much ($3.71 per adult male per week) on food as recommended.

25. Although higher income was required by a larger family size, older children also added to the family income until they left home.

26. The earlier data on food consumed away from home was gathered in 1909, when 3% of the good budgets of city families was for food and beverages purchased and consumed away from home. US BLS, *How American Buying Habits Change*, p. 111.

27. Ellen H. Richards, *The Cost of Living as Modified by Sanitary Science* (New York: John Wiley, 1899), p. 123.

28. Blacks' clothing budgets indicate that they had meager wardrobes. Black families spent only 70% as much per person on clothing as white laborer families. Thus, blacks' work clothes were no more than barely adequate and their ability to function socially severely curtailed. Because the data for black families did not include any detailed data on clothing or other categories, the analysis of consumption norms is restricted to the white classes.

29. See, for example, Mossell, 'The Standard of Living . . .,' pp. 24–5.

30. Meeker (1920), p. 10.

31. Meeker (1920). These standards were intended for the working-class family. In the current study, the same standards are used for the salaried class, overstating the quantity of clothing in the salaried wardrobes since it is likely that the salaried family retired their clothes sooner. In addition, all clothing calculations are based upon the assumption that cotton clothing lasts 3 years, wool 5 years, and silk 5 to 10 years; underwear lasts 2 years; cotton socks, gloves, and handkerchiefs last 1 year; silk socks and 'other' gloves, nightshirts, and ties last 3 years, and shoes (with repair) last 1 year. Street dresses are worn as outfits for 2 years before becoming house-dresses.

32. Mary Hinman Abel, *Successful Family Life on the Moderate Income* (Philadelphia: J.B. Lippincott & Co., 1921).

33. Meeker (1920), p. 6. He admits that a more generous wardrobe would be desirable but notes that only the clothing 'consistent with the *minimum* requirement for health and decency' was allowed (his italics).

34. Meeker (1920), p. 7.

35. Once again, the meager data for blacks do not permit a detailed analysis of their accommodation.

36. The home ownership rate of the CES sample was 27%, with home ownership lower in the South (21%) than in the North (24%). Nationally, the census reported a 44% ownership rate among non-farm households. This imbalance reflects the lower ownership rates in more urbanized areas. Including farm families, 46% of the households owned their homes in 1920; 62% of the households owned their home unencumbered. (*Historical Statistics* N238–45.)

The percentage of renters decreased with income from 87% (lowest income group) to 58.6% (highest income group), while the sample averaged 73% renters.

37. The 1918 CES collected but did not report housing expenditures for homeowners, who usually have higher imputed housing values but lower out-of-pocket expenditures than renters. For this reason, the rental data underestimate the actual increase in housing across classes.

38. Most budget standards used 1.5 persons per room as acceptable. The British census counted overcrowding at two or more persons per room. See Royal Meeker, 'What is the American Standard of Living?' *Monthly Labor Review*, IX, 1, July 1919, p. 7. These standards depend primarily on what is considered socially acceptable for sleeping – whether children need to be separated by sex or age. Most budgets experts thought that the condition of the housing was more of a problem than overcrowding for most families.

39. Mossell, pp. 26–30.

40. Meeker (1920), pp. 11–12. Calculations were made using conversions given in Putnam (1953), pp. 326, 463. The BTU consumption figures include the 'other' category since quantities are unknown. Kerosene was important for lighting. Although it was not listed separately, it probably accounted for a large proportion of the 'other' category (which also included coke, charcoal, gasoline, matches, and candles). All three groups spent about $10 on items in this residual category.

41. *Historical Statistics*, S-111.

42. Shelter (rent and utilities) is the main expenditure varying by region. The other categories had less than a 10% variation between the lower and the highest region for a given class. New York had 5.6 million people, Chicago 3.7 million, and they represented 9.6% of the population living in areas with over one million people. The mid-sized cities had 200,000–258,000 people and represented 10% of the population living in cities with 100,000–500,000 people. The small cities had 28,000–61,000 people and represented 11% of the population living in cities with 25,000–100,000 people.

43. Surprisingly, one-fourth of the families in each class did not report any expenditures directly related to lighting.

44. See Harold Wolozin, 'Use of Installment Credit by City-Worker Families in 1918,' *Monthly Labor Review*, June 1957, pp. 712–16. Martha Olney, *When Your Word is Not Enough: Racial Differences in Credit Use, 1918–1919* (Amherst, MA: University of Massachusetts, 1992) analyzes use of installment credit versus merchant credit by race.

45. Meeker (1920), p. 16.

46. Meeker (1920), pp. 14–15. The annual replacement costs, based upon the survey budgets of 100 families with annual expenditures of $1,500 to $2,100, were estimated to be $75 of the total cost of purchase ($1,297). However, these initial cost estimates are probably high since calculations of total cost of purchase for these items using the reported expenditures per article (or 10% replacement if unreported) implied that the laborer's total cost of purchase was $512 and the salaried worker's was $842. Most likely, the salaried family bought more items and the laborer family fewer than the standard list.

47. This assumes the family has one double bed for the parents and a single bed for each child, with three sheets per bed. The top sheet would become the bottom sheet, which was laundered each week. The BLS standards allowed a full weekly change of sheets, but the more conservative standards were used here because of the small number of sheets purchased by the survey families.

48. Meeker (1920), p. 14.

49. *How American Buying Habits Change*, Ch. 8.

50. Travel to school by streetcar was not common. Only 3% of laborer and 10% of salaried families paid such fares. When children did take the streetcar to school, the laborers' children spent only 13% as much on fares as the salaried workers' children. Like their fathers, the working-class children seemed to walk whenever possible in order to economize.

51. The expenditures for automobiles, motorcycles, and bicycles (not toys) are pooled in the data. Therefore, the numbers represent the maximum possible spent on automobiles and the maximum possible percentage of families owning a car. Only 15% of the sample reported expenditures on automobiles, motorcycles, or bicycles.

    In 1919, 1.65 million passenger cars were sold by the factories at the average wholesale price of $525 (BLS, *Money Disbursements of Wage Earners and Clerical Workers: 1934–36*, Bulletin 638, Ch. 2) and car production rose throughout the next decade as wholesale prices fell. After production peaked in 1929 at 4.5 million cars, it was low in the early years of the Depression. By 1935, production had recovered to a level of 3.3 million cars. (*Historical Statistics* Q148.) In contrast, 216,000 horse-drawn carriages and 342,000 horse-drawn wagons or trucks were produced in 1919. The production of horse-drawn carriages came to a halt during the following decade and only 4,000 were produced in 1929. In 1919, 470,000 bicycles were produced; in 1929, 310,000, and in 1935, 660,000. (*Historical Statistics*, pp. 296–8.)

52. *How American Buying Habits Change*, Ch. 9.

53. Labor organizations presumably include company unions as well as trade unions. If insurance payments could be separated out, they

were to be listed under insurance. Almost one-third of the 1918 sample reported payments to labor organizations. This figure is high compared to the unionization rate of 20% in 1920. Leo Wolman, *Ebb and Flow in Trade Unionism* (New York: NBER, 1936). It is likely that as many as one-third of the 1918 families, especially those in the salaried class, belonged to a labor organization in order to buy insurance. The 1918–19 sample was collected during the 1916–20 period of rapid increase in trade union membership. By 1920, mining and transportation were both 40% unionized, manufacturing and construction were 22% unionized, communications were 20% unionized, and services were 5% unionized. Wolman, pp. 16–18, App. V. There are no membership figures for labor organizations other than trade unions for 1916–20.

54. This was estimated using Simon Kuznet, *National Income and Its Composition 1919–1938* II (New York: NBER, 1941), reported annual earnings of $592 for private household workers, pp. 762, 764.

55. S.E. Thomas, 'Conditions of Living Among the Poor,' Department of Commerce and Labor, Bulletin of the Bureau of Labor, 64 (May 1906), pp. 593–698; Sadie Tanner Mossel, 'The Standard of Living . . .'

56. Dorothy S. Brady, 'Scales of Living and Wage Earners' Budgets,' *The Annals*, March 1951, pp. 32–8.

57. 'Cost of Living of Unskilled Laborer's Family, New York City, 1917' by New York City Bureau of Personal Service in Bureau of Applied Economics, Inc., *Standards of Living*, Bulletin 7, Washington, DC, 1920, pp. 102–10. This study used a combination of prevailing health standards and observed practice to set up the hypothetical budget. Here the 1917 prices are inflated to 1918 dollars by using the CPI index. *Standards of Living* reports 19 budget studies made between 1906 and 1920.

58. Committee on Home Economics, 'My Money Won't Reach . . .' (New York, April 1918).

59. See Department of Commerce and Labor, 'Conditions of Living Among the Poor,' Bureau of Labor Bulletin, 64 (May 1906), pp. 593–698. This was a study of 19 poor families in Washington, DC. All but three families had a husband with some earnings. Thirteen of the families had four to seven children. The author thought that irregularity of employment was the biggest cause of poverty.

None of the budgets showed 'expenditure of a cent' for amusement. All families paid for life insurance, often for all family members because of the dread of burial in the potter's field. Insurance premiums and other installment charges were paid weekly to the door-to-door salesmen.

60. See 'Conditions of Living Among the Poor,' and Sadie Mossell. Most furnishings purchased on the installment plan were required items like dining tables or beds. In the study of 19 poor families, one clock and one book were also purchased on installment. Many families 'rented' sewing machines by buying them on the installment plan for a while and then stopping payments.

61. 'Suggested Family Budget, Social Service Bureau of Bellevue Hospital, 1917,' in *Standards of Living*, p. 111. Another study of 75 poor families of widows with two or more children (and most with incomes between $500 and $800 in 1914) found that all families had suffered some degree of ill health as a result of insufficient income. In addition, a marked improvement in health was noted when an allowance was granted. Winifred Stuart Gibbs, *The Minimum Cost of Living* (New York: Macmillan, 1917).

62. See, for example, *Conditions of Living . . .*, pp. 608–10.

63. *Tentative Quality and Cost Budget*, US BLS, GPO (Washington, DC, 1919. See pp. 5–7. According to Horowitz, *The Morality of Spending* (Ch. 7), the 1919 government standards reflect a decline in norms for workers from wartime studies. The standards did, however, reflect a growing participation in the larger world by the working class through newspapers, transportation, and organizational life.

64. *Tentative Quantity and Cost Budget*, pp. 37–40.

65. Meeker, 1920.

66. Royal Meeker, 'What Is the American Standard of Living?' *Monthly Labor Review*, IX, 1, July 1919, pp. 6–7.

67. Meeker (1919), pp. 6–7.

68. An excellent discussion on the standard of living and the historical development of budget standards is given by Dorothy Brady in Paul H. Douglas, Curtice N. Hitchcock, and Willard E. Atkins, *The Worker in Modern Economic Society* (Chicago: University of Chicago Press, 1923), Ch. IX. In 1919, standards of subsistence were reported to cost about $1,300, health and decency $1,600, and comfort $2,260. Another important collection of institutional readings on living standards is Thomas D. Eliot, ed., *American Standard and Planes of Living* (Boston: Ginn & Co., 1931). One article reports that at least 60% of adult male workers in US cities in 1905 did not make a 'living wage,' defined as $600 annually. Abraham Epstein, 'Have American Wages Permitted an American Standard of Living?', p. 334.

69. US BLS, *Standards of Living*, p. 92. No details were given for this budget.

70. According to data collected by Oscar Ornati, *Poverty Amid Affluence* (New York: Twentieth Century Fund, 1966), Table B, men's

'low wage' (i.e., unskilled male laborer wage) in 1918–19 was 10% above 'minimum subsistence' estimates but 25%–30% below 'minimum adequacy' and 40%–45% below 'minimum comfort.'

71. 'Cost of Living Among Wage-Earners in Lawrence, MA, November, 1919,' NICB, in *Standards of Living*, pp. 81–8. The 'more liberal standard' primarily allowed higher rent and more clothing, recreation, and contributions. All budget comparisons are made in 1918 dollars.

72. 'Workingmen's Standard of Living in Philadelphia, 1918, Philadelphia Bureau of Municipal Research' and 'Suggested Budget for a Textile-Mill Worker's Family, Philadelphia, 1914' in *Standards of Living*. These budgets were estimated from standards and not from practice.

73. A 1917 study of 50 families with employed fathers in Dallas, Texas, gave budgets for these families, who spent $1,135, as well as information on budget deficits and 'moral and physical conditions' (church attendance; proximity to school, saloon, theater, and parks; housing characteristics, neighborhood amenities). Only 19% reported regular church attendance. The Commission determined $1,082 would provide 'safe normal living cost' for a family of five; $747 would provide 'lowest bare existence.' *Report of Survey Committee to the Dallas Wage Commission*, Aug. 25, 1917, Texas State Archives.

74. Jessica B. Peixotto, 'Budget Awarded in Seattle and Tacoma Street Railway Arbitration, 1917' and 'Minimum Budgetary Estimate for Pacific Coast Workers, 1917,' in *Standards of Living*.

75. Consumer Price Index (CPI), *Historical Statistics*, Series E 135–56.

76. Ellen H. Richards, *The Cost of Living as Modified by Sanitary Science* (New York: John Wiley, 1899), p. 17. Richards was concerned with drawing the line between daily comforts that 'increase uplifting tendencies of civilization' and luxuries that 'degrade the soul.' (p. 17).

77. The marginal expenditure rate for food, rent, and energy was below the average expenditure rate (i.e., the elasticity with respect to income is less than one) while the marginal expenditure rate for clothing, furnishings and miscellaneous (especially transportation, recreation, and servants) was greater than the average. The food expenditures per adult male equivalent was almost equal for the top five reported income groups (above $1,200).

78. See also the study by R.C. Chapin, *The Standard of Living Among Workingmen's Families in New York City, 1907* in Bureau of Applied Economics, *Standards of Living*, p. 148, which showed as income rose the level of underfeeding fell faster than the level of underclothing, which fell faster than the level of undersheltered.

79. Abel, *Successful Family Life*, Ch. 18, p. 215.

4 Living in the Midst of Depression, 1935

Introduction

Despite a short, severe postwar recession in the early 1920s, by 1929 disposable personal income per person was almost one-half higher than in 1919 (constant dollars). World War I had an egalitarian impact on the wage structure, but wage differentials increased during the 1920s so that the gap between high- and low-paid jobs in 1929 was almost as wide as before the war.[1] Although not everyone shared in the rising prosperity of the 1920s, it was a time of widespread optimism and comparative affluence;[2] that economic collapse lay only months ahead was literally inconceivable. The nation was as much bewildered as it was terrified by the onset of the Great Depression. By 1933, the worst of the Depression years, per capita real disposable income was almost 30% below the 1929 level.[3] As the New Deal programs went into effect over the next two years, real incomes rose. By 1935, disposable income was about 15% lower than in 1929, but around 30% higher than in 1919. Meanwhile, one in six urban families was participating in relief programs.[4]

Although these national averages indicate the overall magnitude of the economic crisis in the early 1930s, they tell us nothing about how the different segments of the population were affected. Families whose husbands were able to keep their jobs suffered relatively little economic hardship during the Depression. Full-time real earnings were only 3% lower in 1933 than in 1929. Some sectors experienced larger declines than others, however. For example, full-time earnings in manufacturing were 7% lower, while earnings in state and local government were 18% higher in 1933 than in 1929.[5] Many employed workers experienced income reductions as a result of cutbacks in average weekly work hours,[6] which declined almost 30% from 1919 to 1934–5, when the typical working week averaged 37 hours. Overall, real weekly earnings fell about 5%

between 1919 and 1934.[7] Part of the traditional wage pattern was restored as real earnings rose 2% during 1933–6: manufacturing earnings increased 11% and state and local earnings fell 2%. Overall, by 1935, real weekly earnings had returned to their 1919 level.[8]

The economic distress caused by the Depression was borne mainly by families whose heads lost their jobs and who could find, at best, intermittent work. The non-farm unemployment rate reached a peak of 38% in 1933, but it was still high (30%) in 1935. Relief families suffered great economic hardship – but their deprivation was documented primarily by photographs, not by statistics. Government data collectors confined their samples of expenditures to non-relief families, ostensibly to find out how 'normal' families were surviving the Depression, information that would be used, in turn, to set relief payments. General relief benefits varied by locality, but usually included both work and direct relief and both cash and in-kind benefits.[9] The monthly value of relief payments in 1935 was low, averaging $30–$35 (around $400 per year) for families in urban areas. For the small minority of families who could supplement relief with some private earnings,[10] monthly income was around $57 ($680 per year). General relief benefits varied greatly by state. Southern states typically paid about one-half the benefits received in northern and western states. Federal legislation prohibited discrimination by race. Nevertheless, blacks received lower benefits than whites. (For example, in May 1935, blacks in Atlanta received $19 vs $33 for whites, in Chicago $19 vs $21, and in Detroit $35 vs $40.)[11]

On average, general relief provided only 44% of the Works Progress Administration (WPA) emergency budget. Relief supplemented with earnings provided 74% of the WPA budget, or about what the typical black family had to spend. The Heller dependent budget, in which costs were the same as the WPA budget priced for San Francisco, was a 'bare bones' budget that exceeded the relief standards (but certainly not the practices) in many localities.[12]

The idea that families on relief were not 'normal' was deeply embedded in the culture, even as the path to relief remained obscure and the path back to 'normalcy' inaccessible. A wide gulf in the standard of living existed between urban families of the employed and unemployed; the lower classes, especially blacks and white laborers in our urban sample, disproportionately filled the ranks of the unemployed during the Depression. The relief rate varied widely – 60% for urban black families, 40% for laborers, 25% for craft and semi-skilled workers, and 5% for salaried workers.[13]

Income and jobs

Because of the large number of non-farm workers on relief in 1935, families with employed heads ranked higher in the income distribution in

1935 than in 1918. However, compared to all urban non-relief families in 1935, the laborer family was only in the fourth decile and the wage-earner family was in the fifth decile of the income distribution (see table 4.1).[14] As in 1918, the salaried family was just below the first decile of the income distribution for the entire population; among urban, non-relief families, it was in the eighth decile of the income distribution.[15] The relative earnings of employed wage earners to salaried workers were about the same in 1935 as in 1918.[16]

Table 4.1 Income distribution, 1935–36[a]

Annual income	All Families[b] (%)	Families receiving some relief[c] (%)	Non-relief, urban families (%)	Total urban families (estimated) (%)
Under $500	14.2	34.0	7.2	10.7
$500–750	12.9	21.88	8.3	10.6
$750–1,000	14.6	20.9	11.6	13.1
$1,000–1,250	13.2	13.5	12.9	13.5
$1,250–1,500	9.8	3.9	11.0	10.9
$1,500–1,750	8.0	2.0	9.9	8.6
$1,750–2,000	6.4	1.5	8.7	7.6
$2,000–2,500	8.4	2.2	11.6	10.2
$2,500–3,000	4.5	0.2	6.5	5.4
$3,000–5,000	5.4	–	8.1	6.7
$5,000 and over	2.6	–	4.1	3.4
Total	100.0	100.0	100.0	100.0
Proportion of population	100%	15.3%	48.2%	57.8%
Median income	$1,160	$685	$1,475	–
Average family size	3.9	4.3[d]	3.6	3.7

[a] Includes money income and inputted value of owned home. For relief families, includes inputted value of direct relief received in kind. For farm families, includes inputted value of farm-produced goods used by family.
[b] Families include households of two or more related individuals; 91.4% of the population lived in family groups.
[c] Includes all relief families, which comprised 8.9% of farm families, 19.3% of rural non-farm families, and 16.5% of urban families.
[d] Urban.
Source: National Resources Planning Board, *Family Expenditures in the United States*, June 1941, Tables 1, 2, 20, 87, 335, 362.
National Resources Committee, *Consumer Incomes in the United States*, 1938, Tables 2, 4, 7, 8.

Census data indicate that the occupational distribution for employed men changed between 1920 and 1940 because of the large influx of men into 'self-employment' after they lost their salaried jobs. The proportion of salaried professionals and managers fell from 12% to 9% while 11% of employed heads were 'self-employed professionals and managers.' The proportion of craft and operative workers fell from 30% to 29%. The proportion of laborers and service workers fell from 18% to 10% as the low end of the labor market shrank dramatically. (*Historical Statistics of the United States, Colonial Times to 1970*, p. 139). The percentage of farmers and farm laborers fell from 30% to 22%, a drop which largely reflects the relative decline in the population living on farms.[17] The data are not wholly consistent, however. A breakdown of the labor force by industry shows the proportion of workers in agriculture declining only slightly between 1920 and 1935.[18] In both years, 11% of the labor force was self-employed (non-agricultural); another 9% were farmers who owned their farms. Among wage and salaried workers, the major relative gains were in government, especially state and local, and in wholesale and retail trade. The major relative declines were in manufacturing, transportation, and utilities. As recorded by industrial payroll data, the labor force grew only 1.2% between 1918 and 1935. Meanwhile, the civilian labor force, as recorded by household surveys, grew 33.8% and the total labor force (including the armed forces) grew by 25.2%. The difference, of course, is reflected in the unemployment rate of non-farm employees: a mere 2.4% in 1918 compared to 30.2% in 1935.

The percentage of employed women working on the farm fell dramatically from 14% in 1920 to 4% in 1940. Women increasingly took clerical, service, and private household jobs.[19] Overall, women's participation rate rose slowly from 21.0% in 1920 to 25.4% in 1940.[20] The rise in participation would have been greater if the participation rate of farm women had not fallen. In addition, teenaged girls' participation rate fell sharply over this period as they increased the number of years they spent in high school. Women in their prime childbearing years (aged 20–44) surged into the labor force – nearly one-third were employed by 1940. Although wives' participation rate increased over 50%, only one in seven wives were in the labor force.[21]

Wives' higher rate of participation is reflected in the rise in the number of gainful workers per family, especially for wage-earner families (see table 4.2). However, employed wives (or older daughters) in working-class families added little ($140) to family income; employed older sons, on the other hand, added considerably (over 80% of what their fathers earned). Comparable figures for salaried families are not available; the aggregate figures indicate a similar pattern.

Black non-relief families averaged the largest number of earners even though their families were not larger. This numerical advantage was more than offset by the incredibly low wages these extra earners – usually wives – received. Typically employed as domestic servants, black wives' earnings averaged only $64 annually. Fewer than 15% of the 'subsidiary' workers in black families were older sons, who could contribute to family income almost as much as could the husbands.

Table 4.2 Sources of income of urban families, 1935

	Black	Laborer	Wage earner	Salaried
Average income[a]	$758	$1,071	$1,355	$2,260
Earned income	$742	$1,028	$1,300	$2,174
Chief earner	$692	$979	$1,215	$1,970
Subsidiary earners	$50	$49	$85	$204
freq, amount[b]	(33%, $152)	(21%, $233)	(26%, $327)	(27%, $756)
Males 16 and over	$678	$888	$1,167	NA
Females 16 and over	$64	$140	$136	NA
Average # gainful workers	1.41	1.23	1.29	1.35
Adjusted for relief	0.71	1.00	1.17	1.31
Other income	$17	$43	$55	$86
Lodgers	8	23	29	20
freq, amount	(9.3%, $86)	(1.5%, $159)	(15.7%, $185)	(8.5%, $241)
Other net rent	1	4	6	18
freq, amount	(1.1%, $91)	(4.6%, $87)	(5.7%, $105)	(7.4%, $246)
Interest and dividends	0	2	3	9
freq, amount	(5.7%, NA)	(10.0%, $20)	(11.9%, $25)	(6.4%, $141)
Pensions and Annuities	3	5	6	18
freq, amount	(6.6%, $45)	(2.8%, $179)	(2.9%, $207)	(2.9%, $612)
Gifts	2	6	7	3
freq, amount	(6.1%, $33)	(11.3%, $53)	(11.4%, $61)	(1.6%, $176)
Other sources	3	3	4	18
freq, amount	(3.5%, $8)	(3.3%, $91)	(3.7%, $108)	NA
Proportion of income adjusted for relief				
From earnings	NA	0.82	0.91	0.96
From retirement UI, Relief	NA	0.15	0.05	0.01

[a] Does not include deductions from business losses and expenses (about $3).
[b] Frequency is the percent of families reporting; amounts are average for those reporting in that category.
NA – Not available.
Source: BLS Bulletin 638, except for salaried, which is from the BLS–WPA Survey, Bulletin 648.

The number of earners varies much more across the classes when the assessment includes relief families, since the percentage of families on relief plummeted with rising class status. Overall, relief accounted for 15% of income for laborer families compared to 5% for wage earner and 0.7% for salaried.[22] Wage-earner and laborer families had about the same number of earners in 1918, which was below the number of workers in salaried families. In 1935, wage-earner families averaged 0.17 more earners than laborers and 0.14 fewer earners than salaried workers. Over half of this difference reflects the unemployment differential across classes.

Non-earned income remained unimportant for non-relief families in 1935. The Depression had, however, caused a change in the pattern of such income, with income from lodgers becoming more important and gifts becoming less important.[23] A handful of salaried families also received a few hundred dollars from rents and dividends.

The birth rate fell during the Depression, resulting in a slow shift in household composition. Average household size declined over the period from 4.34 persons in 1920 to 4.11 persons in 1930 to 3.67 persons in 1940. The average household size for the 1935 National Resources Committee (NRC) Survey was 3.9 people. Husband-wife families comprised nearly 82% of the households in 1920,[24] 76% in 1930, and 79% in 1940.[25] The decline in the number and, therefore, presence of children in the home is reflected in the elimination of the requirement that only families with a husband, wife and at least one child could be included in the survey.

Consumption norms

As mass production provided a wide array of goods to working class families, people desired variety in their meals and in their leisure time activities, and they strove for distinction in their homes and their attire. The car had greatly expanded the family's possible leisure activities and made their outings more frequent and spontaneous. With modern facilities and equipment available, expenditures for furnishings and household operations became more important in providing a structure for daily activities and in marking class position.[26]

For each of the three classes, the (nominal) earnings distribution was about the same in 1935 as in 1918, but the consumer price level, as measured by the Consumer Price Index, was 9% lower in 1935 than in 1918. The availability of certain goods, as well as the shift in relative prices and the decline in the number of children, produced quite different (and slightly higher) consumption norms in 1935 than in 1918.

The most notable improvement was in the average diet: caloric needs were met more fully and a wider array of foods was available year round. In addition, housing grew more comfortable as modern plumbing, electricity, and central heating became widespread. In 1917, only one in four dwellings had electricity service; by 1930, four in five did.[27] Instead of being a luxury, the automobile became much more commonplace, providing much greater family mobility. Radios were hardly known in 1918, but by 1935 they were present in the large majority of homes and were an important source of entertainment. The use of telephones also increased greatly. The broader availability of each of these items, previously used only by the elite, resulted in a higher standard of living and greater social integration, even though real income had risen only slightly.

The spread of these innovations to working class families had a dramatic impact on housework. Some observers believe that the period from World War I to the Depression witnessed the most important changes in patterns of housework for this century as industrial technology took over some functions and redefined standards in other functions. The changes include the switch from gas or oil to electricity for light; the switch from coal or wood to gas for cooking; the use of electricity for ironing; the use of machines to wash clothes; the introduction of bathrooms; the use of a hot water heater (gas or electric); and the switch from wood or coal stoves to electric or gas central heating. Smaller improvements include granulated soap, a variety of canned foods, and packaged cereals and mixes, and a variety of fresh fruits and vegetables all year round.[28] Even as baker's bread, canned foods, and fresh fruits and vegetables made cooking less important both in skills and time required, standards rose for cleanliness and neatness in the home and in clothing. Time needed for shopping also rose.

Social and economic analyses were focusing on Americans as consumers and producers and not just as producers.[29] Even as early as the mid-1920s, the Lynds thought that the 'manual activities of the wife in making a home' were being replaced by market goods and services so that the moneymaking activities of the husband were becoming more important. The proliferation of market goods was facilitated by installment buying, higher education for children, advertising, and the movies, so that people revised their ideas about what was essential to buy. Many new urgent occasions for spending existed, and consumption was becoming more complex as it required more time, more information, and more decision making.[30]

Even as incomes fell in the 1930s, families attempted to maintain their improvements in living standards since 1918. The nominal income group remained the same for wage earners, but total expenditures were higher in 1935 than in 1918.[31] In 1935, wage-earner families with children were spending about 9% more than their net income; in 1918 they had saved about 3% of their income (see table 4.3).[32] The higher savings rate in 1918 reflected the population's response to government appeals to buy war bonds. The negative savings rate in 1935 reflected families' optimistic buying during the mild recovery phase of the Depression. The rapid increase in unemployment from 1930 through 1933 prompted most families – even those with employed heads – to economize on expenditures because of the uncertainty of continued employment. Families paid for their budget deficits mainly by making savings account withdrawals, borrowing on installment credit (especially for automobiles), and surrendering insurance policies.

Table 4.3 Wage-earner family budgets, 1918 and 1935 (white, urban families with husband, wife, and at least one child)[a]

Income group	1918 $1,200–1,500	1918 (1934–36 prices[b]) $1,200–1,500	WPA–BLS 1935 $1,200–1,500	CES 1935 $1,200–1,500
Average annual expenditure	$1,298	$1,171	$1,461	$1,439
Average family size	4.71	–	4.25	3.53
Annual expenditures (percentage distribution)	100%	100%	100%	100%
Food (%)	40.1	33.2	34.8	32.8
Clothing (%)	15.8	14.4	9.5	9.5
Shelter (%)	24.5	28.4	27.8	28.5
Rent	14.6	16.0	16.7	17.0
Fuel and light	5.3	7.5	7.4	7.7
Furnishings	4.6	4.9	3.7	3.8
Miscellaneous (%)	19.5	24.0	27.9	29.2
Transportation	2.4	–	6.8	7.3
Recreation, education, voc.	3.8	–	5.4	5.6
Household operation	2.7	–	3.1	3.1
Medical care	4.5	–	3.8	3.7
Personal care	1.0	–	1.8	1.9
Gifts, contributions	1.7	–	4.7	2.6
Personal insurance	2.9	–	1.9	4.7
Other	0.6	–	0.3	0.3
Expenditures/net income (%)	0.97	–	1.08	1.07
Taxes (personal property and poll)	$1	–	$1	$1
Net income	$1,342	–	$1,347	$1,350

[a] Categories are slightly different than in other tables because data could not be adjusted. Estimated personal insurance moved from asset to expenditure. The items under miscellaneous were estimated from the whole sample for 1918.
[b] Using price index given in source, p. 40.
Source: BLS Bulletin 638, pp. 40, 44–5, 344–9.

Relative prices shifted dramatically as the general price level fell. The average prices of consumer goods purchased in 1935 are estimated to have fallen 5% from 1918, but food prices fell 24%; clothing, 15%; rent, 1%; and house furnishings, 4%. Meanwhile, fuel and light prices rose 29% and miscellaneous items rose 34%.[33] The food and clothing share of the wage-earner family's budget fell 12 percentage points between 1918 and 1935, with

80% of the decline reflecting lower prices.[34] This slack was taken up by rent (with utilities) and transportation, with each accounting for 5 percentage points more of the budget. Otherwise, the distribution of real expenditures for the white working class is remarkably similar between the two periods.

Even in the midst of the Depression, some social scientists were apprehensive about the impact of consumerism on the quality of life. Lynd was concerned about production for individual profit instead of consumer goals and about the continual exploitation of the consumer's desires and insecurities. He argued that the consumer had too many choices (e.g., 250 kinds of toothbrushes, 100 kinds of washing machines, 350,000 kinds of things in Macy's), and so purchases were made more or less randomly, with the hope that they would turn out all right.[35] However, few families had budgets that allowed for much experimenting or many mistakes.

Table 4.4   Budgets for urban families, 1935[a]

Income group	Black 0.4($500–$600) +0.6($600–$900)		Laborer $900–1,200		Wage earner $1,200–1,500		Salaried $2,100–2,500	
Homeowners	19.0%		24.0%		26.0%		31.0%	
Auto owners	11.0%		33.0%		43.0%		80.0%	
Average family size	3.4		3.4		3.5		3.3	
Annual expenditures	($)	(%)	($)	(%)	($)	(%)	($)	(%)
Total – Percentage distribution	697	100.0	1,165	100.0	1,439	100.0	2,285	100.0
Food	256	36.7	402	34.5	472	32.8	603	26.4
Clothing	63	9.0	102	8.8	136	9.5	231	10.1
Shelter	214	30.7	354	30.4	412	28.6	550	24.1
Rent	124	17.8	217	18.6	246	17.1	340	14.9
Fuel and light	68	9.8	99	8.5	111	7.7	137	6.0
Furniture and furnishings	22	3.2	38	3.3	55	3.8	73	3.2
Miscellaneous	164	23.5	306	26.3	419	29.1	898	39.3
Transportation	28	4.0	68	5.8	105	7.3	242	10.6
Recreation and education	34	4.9	60	5.2	80	5.6	185	8.1
Household operation	16	2.3	33	2.8	45	3.1	107	4.7
Medical care	27	3.9	42	3.6	53	3.7	103	4.5
Personal care	15	2.2	22	1.9	27	1.9	48	2.1
Gifts and contributions	16	2.3	28	2.4	37	2.6	78	3.4
Personal insurance[b]	25	3.6	50	4.3	68	4.7	126	5.5
Other	3	0.4	3	0.3	4	0.3	9	0.4
Tax/gross income	NA		$1		$1		$7	
Expenditures/net income	1.040		1.092		1.067		1.014	

[a] Revisions made, as explained elsewhere in text and tables, to make data comparable with other years.
[b] Personal insurance was estimated using the 1935–36 NRC Survey data, using information on ten groups of cities.
Source: Bulletins 638, 648.

The distribution of expenditures in 1935 varied markedly across the four classes (see table 4.4). The percentage of the budget spent on food[36] and rent declined across classes, while that spent on clothing and all miscellaneous items (except personal insurance) increased. The relative economic distance between classes was about the same in 1935 as in 1918. However, compared to 1918, families in 1935 spent more of their higher incomes on miscellaneous items, less on food and clothing, and about the same on shelter. Having a large family no longer conferred social status: Family sizes were much more similar across the three white classes, and salaried families were now smaller than wage-earner families.

Economic distance across classes was characterized primarily by a better and more refined diet, more varied and better quality clothing, a more comfortable house or apartment in a more desirable location, more automobile travel, and more recreational activities. Overall, the average wage-earner family spent about 20% more than the laborer family; on specific items, though, the gap was greater. Wage earners spent one-half more on transportation and one-third more on recreation and education, household operations, and clothing (per person). Similarly, overall, the average salaried-worker family spent about 50% more than the wage-earner family, but salaried workers spent over twice as much for transportation, recreation and education, household operations, gifts and contributions and clothing (per person). Below are details of the ways in which these budgetary differences across classes affected people's everyday lives.

Diet

At mealtime in 1935, the family sat down to a table that had a variety of appetizing dishes compared to 1918. Part of their higher food expenditures provided better nutrition as well as more variety – and part did not (see table 4.5).[37] As a result of advances by nutritional scientists studying vitamins and minerals, knowledge of the 'average' diet in 1935 is considerably richer than for 1918. Still, judging the adequacy of the 1935 diet remains problematic. In addition, cultural norms sometimes conflicted with nutritional standards and with inexpensive ways to meet these standards. The average expenditure on food was between the cost of the 'minimum-cost adequate diet' and the 'moderate-cost adequate diet' of the Bureau of Home Economics.[38] Three-fourths of white urban families (ranging from 40% in the laborer group to 98% in the salaried group) spent enough on food to purchase the 'minimum-cost adequate diet.'[39] How families in all classes chose to allot their food budgets across specific items did not necessarily result in nutritionally sound diets. For example, the leading nutritionists recommended that at least as much money be spent for milk (and cheese) and for fruits and vegetables as was spent for meat, poultry, and fish. They also recommended the use of whole grain products in place of the widely used refined products.[40] In contrast to the recommended ratios, only about 50% as much was spent on milk and 85% as much was spent on fruits and vegetables as was spent on meat, poultry, and seafood in the average 1935 diet. As a result, widespread deficiencies existed in the intake of calcium, iron, and vitamin A. Less serious deficiencies occurred in overall caloric intake and in vitamins B1 and C for white urban families.

Table 4.5   Typical meals per person, 1935[a]

Breakfast
2 servings home-baked biscuits, rolls or pancakes (1 pat butter for rolls)
2.5 slices of bread (1.5 teaspoons sweetener other than sugar; 1 pat butter for bread)
8 oz serving of milk
5 (6 oz) cups of coffee daily for parents
1 serving daily of the following
    cereal, 3 days each week/1 cold, 2 oatmeal

    bacon or sausage $\left\{ \begin{array}{l} \text{every day for husband} \\ \text{2 days each week for all others} \end{array} \right.$

    eggs, 2 days per week (1 egg for each family member)
3 days each week add one of the following
    0.5 grapefruit
    1 orange
    1 serving dry fruit
Lunch
4 slices bread
1 pat butter and 1 teaspoon mayonnaise
6 days a week lunch meat or cheese
1.5–1.6 oz serving ham per week
1.0–1.5 oz serving bologna etc. per week
1.0–1.5 oz leftover meat from dinner per week
0.4–1.5 oz canned seafood per week
slice of cheese 2 days per week
1 day per week
    1 C legumes/nuts and
    0.75 C rice
1 vegetable daily
    1.0 tomato per person per week
    0.6 C peas and string beans per week
    0.5 C celery per week
    0.6 C carrots per week
    0.7 C cabbage/week
    0.8 C lettuce per week
    0.6 C canned vegetable per week

1 fruit daily
  2 apples per week
  2 bananas per week
  2 oranges per week
  1 other fruit per week
1 serving home-baked dessert
Dinner
1 potato
2 pats butter
Meat daily
  4 oz serving beef, 3 days per week
  4 oz serving lamb, mutton, or veal per week
  4 oz serving fresh pork per week
  4 oz serving fresh poultry per week
  3.6 oz serving fresh fish per week
1 vegetable other than potato daily
  0.7 C cabbage
  0.8 C lettuce
  0.6 C carrots
  0.6 C peas and string beans
  0.4 C spinach
  0.5 C yams and sweet potatoes
  1 other fresh vegetable
1 dessert daily
  1 purchased candy per week
  2 purchased cookies, cakes and pies per week
  4 home-made desserts per week
Extra servings
  1 C noodles, twice weekly
  2–3 purchased rolls
  2 vegetables a week: 1 other fresh vegetable, 1 (5 oz) serving
    canned vegetable

---

[a] These typical meals are based upon average consumption of food (1935 survey), and so they represent the foods consumed by the urban wage-earner family. For baking or cooking, the household had 1 egg, 1.2 cup sugar, 5.7 tablespoons fats and oils, 4.9 oz evaporated milk, 0.5 onion, and 0.5 lemon per day; plus 1 oz cocoa and 1 oz peanut butter per week. (C = Cup.)

Although milk consumption increased one-fourth nationally between 1918 and 1935, calcium deficiency was widespread, even among families whose expenditures on food were liberal. This deficiency could have been offset by educational efforts and government programs that distributed milk to low-income families, as was demonstrated by the results of such programs in New York and Minneapolis.[41] These two cities had the highest milk consumption of all cities in the 1935 sample. Per capita milk consumption was about 70% above the sample average in New York for both 1918 and 1935 and was about 60% above the sample average in Minneapolis for 1935.[42] Iron deficiency declined, although it was still serious in 1935.[43]

Comparisons between 1918 and 1935 for nutrients other than calcium and iron are difficult to make because the data available for 1918 are limited. However, figures for 1935 indicate vitamin A deficiencies in 1918 as well as in 1935, since the average national consumption did not change over the period.[44] In addition, niacin consumption declined from 'borderline inadequate' in the average 1918 diet to adequate for all three classes in 1935. Consumption of riboflavin (B2) and thiamin (B1) increased from just being adequate on average in 1918 to being above adequate in 1935.

A more specific nutritional breakdown shows that the average diet for laborer families contained 10% too little calcium, 12% too little iron, and 22% too little vitamin A, along with above-adequate levels of protein, vitamins B1 and C, riboflavin, and niacin;[45] for wage-earner families, the average diet was inadequate in vitamin A (6% too little) but just adequate in calcium and iron; and for salaried families, it contained just adequate amounts of vitamin A and above-adequate levels of all other nutrients, from 210% of the standard for protein to 113% of the standard for calcium and iron.

The diets of many families were even less adequate than indicated by these averages. For example, one-half of wage-earner families consumed inadequate calcium, one-half inadequate vitamin A, two-fifths inadequate iron, one-third inadequate vitamin C, and one-quarter inadequate vitamin B1. But virtually all of wage-earner families consumed adequate protein, and 70% consumed between 1.4 and 2.0 times the standard. The dietary inadequacies of wage-earner families in 1935 reflect social norms rather than income constraints. Black families spent so little on food per equivalent adult male that they were out-spent (by 25%) by even the lowest CES income group.[46] Among the income group below the laborer, which would include our typical black family, nutritional inadequacies were widespread and serious:

- 90% consumed inadequate calcium (averaging only 69% of the standard);
- over 80% consumed inadequate iron (averaging 78% of the standard);
- over 80% consumed inadequate vitamin A (averaging 65% of the standard);
- over 60% consumed inadequate vitamin B_1 (averaging 90% of the standard);
- 75% consumed inadequate vitamin C (averaging 73% of the standard), and
- 50% consumed inadequate riboflavin (averaging the standard exactly).

By modern standards, protein is the only nutrient that was not deficient for this low-income group; only 5% had inadequate intake, and the group averages 30% above today's standard. However, whether protein consumption is deemed 'high' or 'low' is somewhat relative since such descriptions follow fluctuations in scientific judgment: by the nutritional standards of the thirties, this low-income group consumed 6% too little protein. The nutritional gap between this group and the laborer group, which spent 40% more on food, was enormous.

In contrast to those of wage-earner families, the dietary inadequacies of laborer (and even lower-income) families reflect income constraints, not eating habits. In fact, many of these groups' food choices, such as (particularly in the South) inexpensive leafy greens, sweet potatoes, less expensive cuts of meat, and self-rising flour (containing calcium), contributed greatly to their nutrition.[47]

Nutritional adequacy is not measured by level of vitamin, mineral, and protein intake alone; the number of calories consumed is also important. In 1935, caloric intake was higher than in 1918, so deficient caloric consumption was not as serious for families with employed heads as in 1918.[48] Compared to 1918, all employed workers' families now purchased a greater number of calories: laborer families' 19% caloric deficit shrank to a 6% deficit in 1935; wage-earner families' 4% surplus grew to a 16% surplus; and salaried workers' 17% surplus expanded to 30%.

Using the 1935 allowance of 3,000 calories per equivalent adult male (EAM),[49] (a figure roughly equivalent to a benchmark of 3,300 calories in 1918), on average, the three classes of employed white workers consumed adequate calories – 3,110 (laborer), 3,540 (wage earner), and 3,960 (salaried worker). However, since the laborer's average was only slightly above a standard that did not allow for waste or strenuous activity,[50] a significant proportion of this group did not consume enough calories. The group below the laborer, in which families spent 40% less on food per person, suffered seriously deficient caloric intake. On average, they consumed 2,716 calories (per EAM) but 52% consumed less than 2,700 calories per EAM, and 84% consumed less than 3,300 calories.[51] In contrast, 28% of the wage-earner families consumed between 2,700 and 3,300 calories; the average wage-earner family consumed 3,540 calories per EAM. Overall, families with unemployed workers did not have sufficient food, and probably only one-half of the laborer families had sufficient food.[52] In contrast, the majority of wage-earner families purchased enough food to allow for 16% plate and kitchen waste and spoilage.[53] On average, salaried families purchased 30%–39% more calories than needed,[54] which gave them considerable leeway in wasting food or overeating.

In addition to these nutritional and caloric alterations in the daily diet, food purchase and preparation practices changed between 1918 and

1935. The family's food purchases in the 1930s reflect a decrease in the amount of baking and food preservation done at home. The purchase of already-baked goods per capita increased by 40%, while the purchase of flour fell over 30%. Overall, the consumption of grain (equivalent, per capita) rose 5% between 1918 and 1935. The purchase of sugar, per capita, nearly doubled, suggesting that home-made desserts had become more important. The family also ate more store-bought desserts of cookies, cake, or pie, which were now served twice weekly, or four times as often as in 1918. In addition, in 1935 a serving of ready-to-eat cereal replaced one of the three weekly servings of cooked cereal. Although per capita consumption of tomatoes increased only slightly, one-half of the tomatoes were canned in 1935 compared to only one-eighth in 1918. Bottled salad dressings, mayonnaise, and soft drinks appear as separate listings for the first time in 1935. Consumption of canned fruits and vegetables (per capita) was almost four times higher than in 1918. The 1935 diet also reflects the greater availability of fresh fruits and vegetables throughout the year, allowing the family to consume a greater number as well as a greater assortment of fruits and vegetables. Improved marketing and distribution techniques and facilities increased the availability and extended the season for fresh produce.

A comparison of typical meals in 1918 and 1935 (see table 4.5)[55] shows that the consumption of bread and other grain products remained high (7.0 home-baked items and 6.5 slices of store-bought bread, per person); and one large potato per person continued to be served daily. The average person's daily ration of butter (or margarine) increased by one pat, and milk increased slightly to one full cup. The family's coffee consumption increased from four cups to five cups daily. Although the average family size was 1.3 persons smaller in 1935, the daily use of sugar was higher by one-third cup (40%); the daily use of lard and cooking oils remained the same. The average 1935 diet included more protein-rich foods than did the already protein-sufficient 1918 diet. Eggs were served for breakfast twice weekly (instead of once); breakfast meat was served three times weekly (instead of twice). Four servings of luncheon meats and two slices of cheese (instead of one) were used for lunch. The three instead of two weekly servings of fresh beef remained unchanged; however, in 1935, an animal source of protein (veal or lamb, pork, poultry or fish) was also served at dinner the other four nights of the week, so that one night was no longer meatless.[56]

Fresh vegetables (other than potatoes) were served 14 times weekly in 1935 (up from ten times) and fresh fruits were served nine times (up from five times). Canned fruit was served three times monthly, and canned vegetables twice weekly. Overall, the typical 1935 diet included 23 vegetable servings and 11 fruit servings weekly, a considerable improvement over the 19 servings of vegetables and six servings of fruit in 1918.

The typical diet included the same number of tomatoes (but fewer fresh and more canned), about the same amount of fresh snap beans and peas (but more canned), more fresh carrots, spinach, and lettuce, and more other green vegetables (both fresh and canned). The number of apples in the typical diet declined slightly, while the number of oranges increased tenfold. Oranges had become the most popular fruit. The consumption of bananas and grapefruit also increased considerably.

The 1935 diet allowed better nutrition because of the addition of fruit and more milk at breakfast and another serving of vegetables at lunch. Grain products still were a dietary mainstay, but the greater variety of foods available for lunch eliminated one serving of grains daily. Moreover, the monotony of consuming large quantities of grain products was diminished considerably through the addition of another serving weekly of eggs and meat at breakfast, a larger assortment of produce, two more servings of meat or cheese at lunch, and an extra serving weekly of meat at dinner.

The amount and variety of food purchased for meals at home varied across classes.[57] White working-class families' diets were less varied than that of the salaried families. The former ate more grains and fewer fruits, vegetables, and dairy products. White bread, grains (wheat flour, corn meal, rice, rolled oats), macaroni, lard, boiled beef, and dried legumes were the only food items the laborer family consumed in larger amounts per person than the salaried family.[58] Overall, the salaried family consumed 74% more meat, poultry, and seafood per person than the laborer family.[59] They also bought higher quality cuts and spent 112% more for them. The salaried family consumed only 8% more per person of grain products but spent 34% more; they consumed 72% more fruit and vegetables per person and spent 126% more. Fresh milk consumption was 38% higher in salaried families than in laborer families; coffee consumption was 66% higher, and soft drink consumption was over 500% higher. Salaried families consumed 31% more sugar; although they ate only 5% more of other sweeteners and prepared desserts, they spent twice as much on them. The specific foods that show the largest relative increases with income are cream, fresh grapefruit, peas, tomatoes, cakes and ice cream, lamb chops, broiling chickens, and sirloin steak.

The purchase of meals away from home – at work, on vacation, and at other times (such as dinner out) – increased rapidly with income.[60] Meals on vacation show the most sensitivity to income, with 2.5% of the laborer families spending $13 annually and 23% of the salaried families spending $23. For wage earners, meals at work accounted for 63% of the away-from-home food budget. Laborers typically packed their lunch (only one in five bought meals at work, spending $58 annually), while the salaried worker had established the practice of eating out at lunch (one-half of salaried workers spent $96 annually). All families continued to economize on snacks (or treats for children), with the pressures decreasing by class. Only two in eight laborer families reported spending for snacks ($14 annually) compared to three in eight salaried families ($35 annually). In addition, laborer families spent an average of $1.37 annually on other meals away from home, and salaried families spent almost seven times that amount.[61]

Overall, comparison of the available data for 1918 and 1935 indicates that improvements in nutrition and caloric intake resulted in adequate diets for families in the middle of the income distribution. However, the bottom 40% of the families – those with annual incomes below $1,000 – remained underfed and suffered serious nutritional deficiencies.

Wardrobe

Clothing norms changed dramatically in the generation between 1918 and 1935. Women's clothing was less ornate, less cumbersome, and more practical, especially for public activities. Men's street clothing also had become less formal and constraining, and men now spent less on hats and accessories. The need for heavy clothing to stay warm inside the home decreased as more homes were centrally heated, and the increased availability of automobile transportation lessened the amount of walking to and waiting for trolleys in cold weather. For both men and women, hats and shoes were less important status markers, but men still had regular shoe shines.

Earlier, a woman's street dress consisted of a union suit, bone corset and camisole, bloomers, petticoat, heavy, lined, wool dress, high or heavy silk stockings, and high boots. In the 1930s, appropriate street dress included a girdle-and-chemise combination, a slip, light wool dress, chiffon stockings, and pumps.[62] 'Artificial silk' (rayon), marketed in 1911, had been experiencing rapid growth since the 1920s. Sheer silk stockings became an affordable standard part of street wear after the war. They were a great improvement over the thicker version, which in 1918 were a luxury at $2 per pair, and women spent only 1%–2% of their clothing budget on stockings. Now, silk stockings accounted for a remarkable 12%–14% of the wife's clothing budget.

Clothing costs had been declining as new methods of mass-produced textiles were introduced. Men's clothing was mostly factory-made by 1920, and custom-tailoring was no longer the only way to acquire a nice suit. More ready-made children's and women's clothes were also available at fairly low prices, and the shift to factory-made clothing was almost complete.[63] Although most families reported buying yard goods and findings (trimmings) – from 59% among wage earners to 54% among salaried workers – home-produced clothing had become relatively unimportant in terms of families' overall clothing budgets, and the economic value of clothing made at home was small. Expenditures on yard goods and findings accounted for less than 3% of the total clothing budgets. Those families who bought these materials purchased enough to make the equivalent of three silk or rayon dresses for the salaried wife (or daughters) and almost four silk or rayon dresses for the laborer wife.[64]

Clothing expenditures per person (in constant dollars) generally were higher in 1935 than in 1918 (see table 4.6). The main exceptions were among white laborer and wage-earner husbands.[65] These men spent 10%–15% *less* on clothing in 1935 than in 1918, while their wives spent 10%–15% *more*. Salaried husbands spent about the same on clothing in the two surveys, while their wives spent about 20% more. Laborer husbands no longer met the meager 1918 standard of spending $50 (in 1918 dollars) on clothing, but their wives now did. The wage-earner family's clothing expenditures (including upkeep) matched the amount recommended in the Works Progress Administration (WPA) maintenance budget.[66]

Table 4.6 Annual clothing expenditures by urban families, 1935

	Black family	Laborer family	Wage-earner family	Salaried family	
Average family size	5.0	3.4	3.5	3.3	
Total clothing expenditures	$63	$102	$136	$231	
Clothing expenditures per person					
Male 18+ years	$22	$37	$43	$73[a]	
Average number per family	1.26	1.17	1.15	1.06	
Female 18+ years	$20	$38	$48	$84	
Average number per family	1.35	1.32	1.28	1.15	
Males, 12–17 years	$19	$35	$40	$76	
Females, 12–17 years	$21	$38	$48	$107	
Males, 6–11 years	$13	$25	$29	$46	
Females, 6–11 years	$11	$21	$27	$55	
Males, 2–5 years	$8	$16	$19	$39	
Females, 2–5 years	$7	$14	$18	$46	
Infants, both sexes	$4	$9	$11	$20	
Detailed expenditures (# articles purchased per person, average cost per item)					WPA maintenance standard
Males 18+ years					
Overcoat	0.07, $15.78	0.1, $18.85	0.1, $20.62	0.2, $26.41	0.3
Wool suits	0.25, $18.26	0.4, $21.83	0.4, $22.73	0.7, $26.34	0.7
Shoes (street and work)	1.27, $2.86	1.6, $3.45	1.6, $3.65	1.9, $4.36	3.0
Shirts (dress and work)	2.19, $0.89	3.0, $1.10	3.4, $1.13	4.5, $1.33	5.0
Trousers	0.60, $2.00	0.8, $2.36	0.8, $2.33	0.8, $2.70	2.0[b]
Hats and caps	0.75, $1.48	0.9, $1.85	1.0, $2.03	1.4, $2.59	1.7
Socks	7.30, $0.16	0.8, $0.20	11.7, $0.22	14.1, $0.26	10.0
Underwear	3.26, $0.50	4.4, $0.53	4.8, $0.54	6.6, $0.62	3.5
Ties	0.76, $0.36	2.1, $0.45	2.4, $0.49	3.9, $0.63	3.0

Table 4.6   (*cont.*)

	Black family		Laborer family		Wage-earner family		Salaried family		
Females 18+ years									
Shoes (street and dress)	1.30,	$2.55	1.8,	$3.11	2.0,	$3.39	2.3,	$4.30	2.0
Wool suits	0.04,	$13.99	0.1,	$10.88	0.1,	$11.78	0.1,	$14.93	3.0
Dresses and other suits	1.00,	$3.17	1.6,	$3.85	1.9,	$4.25	2.6,	$5.95	
Housedresses	1.00,	$0.87	1.3,	$1.00	1.5,	$1.06	1.7,	$1.20	3.0
Coats (including fur)	0.18,	$13.43	0.3,	$18.28	0.4,	$21.17	0.5,	$31.24	0.7
Hats	0.90,	$1.33	1.3,	$1.65	1.6,	$1.79	2.2,	$2.30	1.5
Silk stockings	4.50,	$0.57	8.3,	$0.63	9.6,	$0.67	13.6,	$0.73	2.0
Slips	1.20,	$0.67	1.5,	$0.89	1.7,	$0.99	2.0,	$1.32	1.5
Males 12–17 years									
Overcoat	0.10,	$10.78	0.1,	$12.20	0.1,	$13.64	0.3,	$16.75[c]	
Wool suits	0.40,	$12.81	0.4,	$14.63	0.5,	$15.22	1.0,	$18.06	
Trousers	1.00,	$1.45	1.7,	$2.11	1.7,	$2.20	1.7,	$2.59	
Shoes	1.60,	$2.26	3.1,	$2.43	3.1,	$2.58	3.8,	$3.13	
Shirt	2.20,	$0.69	3.5,	$0.82	3.6,	$0.86	5.1,	$1.09	
Hats and caps	0.80,	$0.79	1.2,	$0.62	0.9,	$1.01	1.0,	$1.49	
Females 12–17 years									
Shoes (street, dress, sport)	2.4,	$2.01	3.2,	$2.50	3.6,	$2.66	5.0,	$3.28	
Dresses	2.2,	$1.52	2.2,	$2.30	2.5,	$2.51	5.6,	$3.40	
Wool suits	0.1,	$9.69	0.1,	$8.69	0.2,	$9.73	0.4,	$14.62	
Coats	0.3,	$9.39	0.5,	$8.23	0.5,	$8.74	0.8,	$16.23	
Hats	0.7,	$0.99	1.0,	$1.21	1.2,	$1.33	2.6,	$1.76	
Silk stockings	3.3,	$0.47	7.2,	$0.54	8.7,	$0.57	21.2,	$0.57	
Slips	1.3,	$0.49	1.6,	$0.78	1.8,	$0.84	3.5,	$1.05	

[a] The amount spent in the 1935–36 NRC survey by husbands was $74 and by wives was $83. So the use of 1934 survey for details seems to give consistent results.

[b] The WPA maintenance standard also includes 3.5 pairs overalls.

[c] Comparable replacement rates for the older children are not available. The WPA standards were given for a boy aged 13 and a girl aged 8.

Source: Bulletins 638, 648. Calculations for all details were made from Bulletin 638 using [0.55 (< $200) + 0.45 ($200–300)] from black family expenditures unit group for blacks, ($300–400) expenditure unit group for laborers, [0.25 ($300–400) + 0.75 ($400–500)] expenditure unit groups for wage earners, and the ($700–800) expenditure unit group for salaried workers, except that the ($700 and up) expenditure unit group is used for children since it was not broken down further. These groupings result in clothing expenditures per clothing expenditure unit being 9% too high for laborers and 3% too low for salaried workers. If the laborer family figures were adjusted, they would show older males (12+) spending $2 less, older females (12+) spending $3 less and children spending $1–$2 less per person on clothing.

In contrast, black families spent only two-thirds of what the WPA considered the bare minimum. Although these families spent 8% more on clothing per person in 1935 compared to 1918 (in constant dollars), they still had insufficient clothing. Husbands spent about one-tenth and wives about one-half as much as the laborer family. These clothing allowances did not approach the funds necessary for purchasing the clothing required for most jobs or for participating in 'white' activities. Black families' inability to meet the whites' clothing standards is reflected in the Heller committee's characterization of clothing allowed in their 'dependent' budget: 'The clothing allowances frankly admit the necessity for a considerable degree of shabbiness.'[67] Yet the black family spent only 60% of the Heller dependent clothing allowance. For example, the Heller dependent budget allowed a boy aged 9–13 years only three corduroy trousers, two jeans, four shirts, and one pullover sweater for the year.[68] Yet these purchases were below the required replacement rates to have adequate clothing for the school year. In practice, the young black boy's meager clothes purchases – 0.3 wool trousers, 0.5 pair jeans, 0.5 pair overalls, 1.5 cotton shirts and 0.5 sweater, did not buy sufficient clothes to be properly dressed. Blacks economized more on children's clothing than on parents' clothing, but the degree of economizing decreased as a child's age increased. This implies that blacks did more home sewing and used more hand-me-downs than whites. Most likely, many of the hand-me-downs were from the white community, either from the employers of domestic servants or from charities. Little replacement clothing was allowed even in the Heller dependent budget, so hand-me-downs would increasingly be worn and patched.

The black family did not buy clothing for the older children to be dressed for employment as whites did. Although many black families had family members above 15 years, they spent only one-third to one-fourth what, by Heller standards, would be minimally required clothing for employment. Blacks had jobs, such as laborer (for men) or domestic servant (for women), which did not require socially presentable clothing.[69] As in 1918, blacks' lack of appropriate clothing reinforced existing patterns of segregation which, in most cities, barred blacks from white jobs, and isolated them in their own neighborhoods, except when they took a bus to work in white people's homes. The laborer family's clothing expenditures, at 18% below the WPA maintenance budget and 17% above the WPA emergency budget, were not sufficient to buy *socially* required clothing, but these outlays were enough to buy more than what was considered the minimum for physical survival. Salaried families spent 81% more on clothing than the WPA maintenance standard.

Among the very low income levels typical of most black families and some whites, status differentiation in clothing turned on its general condition – overall cleanliness and state of repair. At higher income levels, variety, quality, and level of expenditure were more important distinguishing factors. In 1935, the use of clothing to differentiate class diminished between wage-earner and laborer families,[70] but it grew between salaried and wage-earner families, especially in terms of children's clothing. Salaried families spent 75% more per person on clothing for adults and 100% more for children (under 18 years) than the wage-earner family (see table 4.6). Sex differences in clothing expenditures for younger children were more noticeable in 1935 than in 1918. Salaried families spent more on daughters under 12 years old than on sons, while laborer and wage-earner families spent slightly more on sons under 12 years than on daughters. Teenaged girls continued to spend more on clothing in 1935 than their teenaged brothers.

Overall, sons aged 12–17 years spent about the same on clothing as their fathers or older brothers, while they bought more articles of clothing that cost less per item (as in 1918). This same pattern held for daughters aged 12–17 in laborer and wage-earner families compared to their mothers. Teenaged daughters in salaried families, however, spent 27% more on clothing than their mothers spent.[71] Although they paid less per item, they bought many more items of clothing than did their mothers: over twice as many wool suits and shoes, over 50% more coats and silk stockings, and over 30% more dresses (see table 4.6, detailed expenditures). The social importance of these girls having a variety of clothing for social activities is evident in their annual purchase of five pairs of shoes, seven outfits (dresses, suits, or skirts and blouses), a coat, 21 pairs of silk stockings, and three hats or berets. Young women spent one-half more on clothes if they were employed as clerical workers and wage earners than if they only helped out at home.[72] Among white adult males in 1935, as in 1918, status differentiation – as displayed by prices paid – was most important for overcoats, hats, and ties. Salaried workers spent 28% more per article than did wage earners, who spent 9% more than did laborers. The price differences for suits, shoes, and shirts were much smaller – around 18% higher for salaried workers compared to wage earners and 4% higher for wage earners compared to laborers.

Black men paid 20%–25% less on all their major items of clothing compared to white laborers; there was no room for status differentiation by item. Across classes, white husbands divided their higher expenditures between improving status (with higher-priced clothing) and increasing variety (with more clothing) in the same way as they did in 1918. Both salaried workers and wage earners used 60% of their higher clothing expenditures to buy more articles of clothing and 40% to buy higher-priced clothing. Black husbands economized in clothing by buying lower-priced clothing (40% of savings) and by buying fewer articles of clothing (60% of savings).

Among all groups, the husband generally purchased fewer articles of clothing in 1935 than he did in 1918. His most important items were wool suits and shoes, which accounted for 36% of his clothing budget (as in 1918). His overcoat, shirts, and hats accounted for another 24% of his clothing expenditures. In general, based upon 1935 buying patterns, the black husband bought a new wool suit every four years and the laborer and wage earner every 2.5 years. Both laborers and wage earners bought a new overcoat every 7.7 years (see table 4.7A).[73] The salaried husband replaced his suits and overcoat more frequently, for he bought a new wool suit every 1.4 years and a new overcoat every 4.5 years. Black husbands bought 1.3 pairs of shoes annually; the laborer and wage earner bought 1.6 pairs, and the salaried husband bought 1.9 pairs. The salaried husband bought 50% more shirts and hats than the laborer and almost twice as many ties (see table 4.6).

Table 4.7A Wardrobe for males aged 18 and over, 1935[a]

Item(s)	Black	Laborer	Wage earner	Salaried
Wool suit (3 years)	0.8	1.1	1.5	2.0
Summer suit (3 years)	0.1	0.1	0.1	0.2
Shoes – street	0.8	1.1	1.2	1.5
work and other (1 year)	0.5	0.5	0.5	0.5
Shirts – cotton work (3 years)	3.1	3.2	3.6	3.8
dress (3 years)	3.5	5.8	6.4	9.4
Overcoat (life in years)	14.0	7.7	7.0	4.5
Ties (3 years)	2.3	6.2	7.2	11.6
Trousers – cotton (3 years)	1.0	1.2	1.3	1.1
wool and other (5 years)	1.2	2.1	2.0	2.2
Socks – cotton heavy (1 year)	2.6	4.1	3.8	4.5
cotton dress, rayon, silk, and wool (1 year)	4.7	7.7	7.8	9.7
Hat – felt (life in years)	3.3	2.3	2.0	1.4
Straw hats and caps (2 years)	0.9	1.0	1.0	1.3
Sweaters (5 years)	0.8	1.3	1.3	1.6
Jackets (5 years)	0.6	0.9	0.9	1.2
Overalls and coveralls (2 years)	1.3	1.3	1.2	1.3
Underwear suits (2 years)	1.8	2.0	2.2	2.8
Undershirts (2 years)	2.2	3.3	3.6	4.9
Undershorts and drawers (2 years)	2.4	3.5	3.8	5.5
Pajamas and nightshirts (3 years)	0.3	0.8	1.1	2.3
Gloves and mittens – work (1 year)	1.8	2.8	2.8	3.3
street (3 years)	0.2	0.6	0.7	0.9
Handkerchiefs (1 year)	3.0	4.7	4.9	7.2

[a] The assumed years of wear that were used to calculate these wardrobes are given in parentheses. For some items, the expected life of the garment, based on frequency of purchase, is given instead.
Source: Bulletins 638, 648.

The wardrobes of laborers and wage earners displayed only minor differences. Salaried wives, however, had much larger and more varied wardrobes. Among all groups, the wives' main clothing items were coats, dresses, shoes, and stockings; these accounted for 70% of her clothing budget. The major change in wives' clothing expenditures was the

Table 4.7B   Clothing for boys aged 12–17 years, 1935

Item(s)	Black	Laborer	Wage earner	Salaried
Wool suit (2 years)	0.8	0.8	0.9	2.0
Summer suit	0.06	0.1	0.1	0.3
Shoes – street (1 year)	1.6	2.2	2.3	3.1
work, canvas and other (1 year)	0.5	0.8	0.8	0.7
Shirts – cotton work (2 years)	0.6	1.2	0.9	1.0
dress (2 years)	3.8	5.8	6.2	9.1
Overcoat (3 years)	0.3	0.3	0.4	1.0
Ties (3 years)	2.4	6.1	6.3	12.3
Pants – wool (5 years)	2.3	4.2	4.0	4.2
cotton (3 years)	1.7	2.5	2.6	2.6
Socks – cotton heavy (1 year)	2.9	3.6	3.6	4.9
cotton dress (1 year)	2.6	5.3	4.9	4.3
silk, rayon and wool (3 years)	5.2	5.4	6.7	13.1
Hats – felt (life in year)	5.7	1.4	2.8	2.2
Straw hats and caps (2 years)	1.2	1.0	1.0	1.0
Sweaters and jerseys (3 years)	1.5	2.3	2.7	3.7
Jackets (3 years)	0.5	1.3	1.3	1.3
Overalls and jumpers (2 years)	0.7	0.9	0.9	0.3
Undershirts (2 years)	1.8	4.3	4.7	7.3
Drawers and undershorts (2 years)	2.0	4.6	4.9	3.9
Union suits (2 years)	1.8	1.7	1.7	1.7
Pajamas and night shirts (3 years)	0.2	1.1	1.4	4.5
Gloves and mittens				
cotton work (1 year)	0.1	0.2	0.2	0.1
other (3 years)	0.4	1.4	1.4	3.0
Handkerchiefs (1 year)	1.4	3.5	3.7	5.3

Source: Bulletins 638, 648.

dramatic rise in importance of silk stockings; the salaried wife bought 14 pairs; the wage-earner wife and the laborer wife each bought about nine pairs; and the black wife bought four pairs. In addition, wives now bought a wool suit about half as often as in 1918, so this item accounts for only 2% of their budgets in 1935. Hat styles had also become less important. Although wives bought almost 50% more hats in 1935, they bought cheaper, less fancy ones that cost about one-third less (in constant dollars).

Overall, wives bought more articles of clothing in 1935 than in 1918. The laborer and wage-earner wife bought a coat every three years and the salaried wife every two years, a replacement schedule about 60% more frequent than in 1918. Laborer and wage-earner wives bought close to two pairs of 'good' (dress or street) shoes annually; black wives bought 1.3 pairs; salaried wives bought 2.3 pairs. Wives mostly wore dresses and skirts and blouses. Wives averaged about 2.5 times as many street dresses in 1935 as in 1918. Black wives bought only one, white

Table 4.7C Wardrobe for females aged 18 years and over, 1935

Item(s)	Black	Laborer	Wage earner	Salaried
Shoes – street (1 year)	1.1	1.4	1.5	1.8
Dress and other (1 year)	0.4	0.6	0.6	0.8
Coats – wool (5 years)	0.5	0.8	1.0	1.3
Furs and fur coats (life in years)	–	100	50	20
Hats (3 years)	2.6	3.9	4.6	6.7
Sweaters and jackets (3 years)	0.5	0.5	0.6	0.8
Waists and middies				
Silk and rayon (5 years)	0.2	0.6	0.6	0.7
Cotton and others (2 years)	0.1	0.1	0.1	0.2
Street dresses and suits				
Cotton (1 year)	0.4	0.5	0.6	0.7
Silk and rayon (3 years)	1.3	2.6	3.1	4.5
Wool and other (3 years)	0.4	0.8	1.0	1.5
Housedresses (3 years)	0.7	1.4	1.6	2.0
Old dresses (2 years)	0.8	1.1	1.2	1.4
Aprons and coveralls (2 years)	1.0	1.0	0.9	0.7
Slips – cotton (2 years)	1.0	1.0	0.9	0.7
Silk and rayon (5 years)	3.2	5.2	6.1	8.2
Corsets and girdles (1 year)	0.1	0.4	0.5	0.7
Brassieres (1 year)	0.2	0.7	0.8	0.8
Union suits combinations				
Cotton and wool (2 years)	0.6	0.6	0.6	0.8
Silk and rayon (3 years)	0.4	0.7	0.8	1.2
Underwaists, shirts (3 years)	0.8	1.0	1.1	1.2
Underpanties – cotton (2 years)	0.5	0.3	0.3	0.2
Rayon (2 years)	2.6	2.9	3.2	3.5
Silk (3 years)	0.3	0.8	1.0	1.8
Nightgowns and pajamas				
Cotton (3 years)	1.3	1.9	2.2	2.6
Silk, rayon and other (3 years)	0.2	0.5	0.7	1.4
Hose – silk (2 months)	0.7	1.4	1.6	2.3
Rayon (2 months)	0.2	0.1	0.2	0.2
Cotton and wool (1 year)	0.8	0.8	0.7	0.5
Gloves – cotton (1 year)	0.2	0.3	0.4	0.5
Leather and other (3 years)	0.2	0.7	1.0	1.8
Handkerchiefs (1 year)	1.9	3.2	3.6	4.4
Handbag and purses (life in years)	4.2	2.1	1.7	1.2
Umbrellas (life in years)	20	17	14	9

Source: Bulletins 638, 648.

working-class wives averaged almost two, and salaried wives close to three new dresses. The number of skirts and blouses purchased decreased greatly as the street dress' popularity increased. Wives bought about 0.2 skirts and blouses, or about one-sixth the number purchased in 1918.

Table 4.7D   Clothing for girls aged 12–17 years, 1935

Item(s)	Black	Laborer	Wage earner	Salaried
Shoes – street (1 year)	1.8	2.2	2.3	3.0
dress and sport (1 year)	0.7	1.1	1.3	2.4
Wool coats and cloaks (5 years)	1.5	2.3	2.5	3.7
Wool suits (2 years)	0.2	0.3	0.4	0.8
Dresses and suits – cotton (1 year)	1.1	1.2	1.4	2.2
wool (3 years)	0.2	0.6	0.6	1.9
silk (3 years)	1.4	2.1	2.5	5.9
Hats (3 years)	2.1	3.1	3.7	7.9
Caps (3 years)	1.4	1.1	1.3	1.7
Sweaters and jackets – cotton, leather, wool and silk (3 years)	1.4	1.9	2.4	3.8
Skirts – wool (3 years)	0.7	1.3	1.5	2.5
Blouses, middies and waists				
cotton (2 years)	0.2	0.7	0.9	1.7
rayon and silk (5 years)	0.0	1.3	1.6	3.2
Housedresses				
old dresses (2 years)	2.1	2.5	3.5	4.4
wrappers, housedresses (3 years)	1.7	1.5	1.3	1.6
Aprons (2 years)	0.1	0.1	0.2	0.2
Slips – cotton (2 years)	1.4	1.1	1.2	1.4
wool, silk and rayon (5 years)	2.9	5.1	5.7	13.8
Brassieres (1 year)	0.3	1.0	0.9	1.5
Union suits and combinations				
cotton (2 years)	0.4	0.3	0.3	0.7
silk, rayon and wool (3 years)	0.5	1.1	1.0	1.4
Bloomers and panties (2 years)	4.6	6.0	6.6	9.2
Shirts (3 years)	0.7	1.5	1.6	1.6
Nightdresses and pajamas (3 years)	1.4	2.2	2.7	4.5
Stockings – silk (2 months)	0.6	1.1	1.4	3.5
rayon (2 months)	0.2	0.4	0.4	0.1
cotton and wool (1 year)	3.0	3.5	3.8	2.7
Gloves and mittens – cotton (1 year)	0.2	0.4	0.4	0.6
kid, silk, and wool (3 years)	0.2	1.1	1.3	2.6
Handkerchiefs (1 year)	2.2	3.5	3.6	3.9
Handbags and purses (life in years)	4	2	2	0.6
Umbrellas and parasols (life in years)	100	16	13	9

Source: Bulletins 638, 648.

Wives of laborers and wage earners bought only slightly more garments than in 1918. The types of underwear purchased changed, however, in tandem with shorter and less formal dresses: in 1935, laborer and wage-earner wives bought twice as many panties and one-half as many corsets (which now also included girdles). Wives of salaried men bought more articles of underwear (including slips, panties, and union suits) in 1918 than in 1935, since underwear garments were now simpler and women wore fewer 'specialty' garments.

The wage-earner wife used 55% of her higher (compared to the laborer wife) clothing budget to buy more articles of clothing and 45% to pay for higher-priced clothing. This division between variety and status, which now paralleled her husband's division, was the reverse of the choices made in the 1918 budget. The salaried wife had about the same division in 1935 as in 1918; in each instance, she spent 60% of her higher clothing budget on status and 40% on variety. In 1935, the wife of the salaried worker was the only adult who spent more of her higher clothing budget on status than on variety. In contrast, the black wife economized on clothing in the same ways as her husband – by buying fewer clothes (60% of savings) and by paying lower prices (40%). Her dresses, shoes, and hats cost about one-fourth less than what the white laborer's wife paid for items in these categories. These clothing budgets, which represent actual practice, continued to fall below the 'official' clothing standards published by the government. The lower the family's income, of course, the further below the government standard the family's wardrobe would fall. Certain roles would not permit economizing on clothes. For example, if a wife worked, she spent substantially more on clothing if she were a clerical worker than if she were a blue-collar worker.[74]

By the standards embodied in the WPA budgets, the husband employed at manual work would replace his winter overcoat, winter suit, summer suit, felt hat, and straw hat every three years. Each year he would buy three work shirts and two dress shirts, two pairs of work shoes and one pair of oxfords. When he was unemployed, the emergency standard allowed replacement of his overcoat every six years, his suits every five years, and his felt hat every four years (with no provisions made for a straw hat). He would buy 1.5 work shirts and one dress shirt yearly, but he would continue to purchase three pairs of shoes.[75]

The Heller clothing budgets for the wage-earner family had an implicit replacement between that used by the WPA emergency and maintenance budgets. Compared to actual practice, these standards were generous,[76] even though they were below the 1918 standards for some items. The Depression had caused clothing purchases to fall further behind prescribed social norms. Overall, the wage earner and laborer did not meet even the emergency standard for clothing. They had an insufficient number of shoes, overcoats, trousers and overalls, although they did meet this standard for suits and surpassed it for shirts, hats, and caps. Nevertheless, except in the categories of socks and underwear, they were still below the maintenance standard set for the 'manual worker of small means [whose] social requirements are simple and [whose] hard wear on dress clothes is avoided through use of specialized work garments.'[77]

Only husbands in the salaried class had wardrobes that came close to meeting the social norms of the day.[78] These men had two wool suits (no more than three years old); a pair of work and dress shoes (less than one year); an overcoat (less than five years); nine dress shirts (less than two years) and four work shirts (less than three years); a felt hat (less than a year-and-a-half); and eight sets of underwear (less than two years) (see table 4.7A). This wardrobe allowed daily changes between the weekly wash. In contrast, the laborer had only one wool suit for all-year-round wear, his work shoes and felt hat had to last over two years, and his overcoat had to last almost eight years. In order to change his shirt daily, he had to wear his one-year-old dress shirts as work shirts for two years and wear his cotton work shirts for three years. In addition, his underwear had to last for three years instead of two, in order for him to have a daily change. Such heavy usage required the laborer's wife to spend time mending to keep the clothes wearable. As in 1918, the laborer's wardrobe was older, shabbier, and less fashionable than either the wage earner's or the salaried worker's.

The WPA maintenance standards for wives allowed a new coat for spring and for winter every three years, three street dresses and three house dresses yearly, two pairs of shoes yearly, two pairs of silk stockings and six pairs of other stockings.[79] In practice, however, most wives' wardrobes did not meet even the emergency standard across all items. The laborer wife met the WPA emergency standard for winter coats (five years), and for underwear (other than girdles and corsets) – but she bought fewer dresses and more silk stockings and hats than the standard allowed. The salaried wife exceeded the WPA emergency standard in all items except non-silk stockings and corsets and girdles. She also exceeded the higher WPA maintenance standard for shoes, silk stockings, and hats. However, even she did not meet the maintenance standard for winter or spring coats, for house or street dresses, or for underwear. In order to change her clothing daily, the salaried wife had to wear the three street outfits purchased annually for everyday wear for one year after having worn them as her public outfits for one year. She would also need to wear her housedresses for two years. Her winter coat lasted 3.5 years and her spring coat five years.

In contrast, the laborer wife had to wear her 1.8 street outfits purchased annually for an additional two years after having worn them one year as her dress clothes. Her housedresses had to last three years. Her winter coat had to last five years, and her spring coat over eight years. If hats lasted two years, then the laborer wife had 2.6 hats compared to 4.4 for the salaried wife. The laborer wife's silk stockings had to last six weeks, the salaried wife's stockings less than four weeks. Such longevity requirements meant that wives from both groups occasionally wore mended stockings. If underwear lasted two years, the salaried wives had 6.4 sets, which allowed almost daily changes between the weekly wash. The laborer wife's underwear had to last for three years in order for her to have enough sets for a daily change. To keep her clothes serviceable, the laborer wife had to mend them frequently, much as she did her husband's and children's clothes. Her clothes were older, and therefore less fashionable, and of poorer quality than the salaried wife's clothing.

The amount of money spent on clothing maintenance varied by sex as well as by class. Wives spent 4% of their clothing budgets on cleaning and repairing shoes and clothes – husbands spent double that (7%–9%). Salaried husbands spent over twice as much as wage earners for clothing maintenance. Salaried wives spent more than twice as much on cleaning and repairing clothes as wage-earner wives, but their shoe repair bills were only one-third higher. Wives had their shoes repaired less frequently than husbands, indicating that they replaced them sooner or that they wore their shoes in less good condition. Wives' clothes were usually cleaned at home, while husbands' suits were cleaned commercially.

Two aspects of the 1935 clothing expenditures warrant additional comment. First, by prevailing standards neither laborer nor black families had adequate clothing for participating fully in social and community life.[80] Although the WPA maintenance level was supposed to represent the standard for unskilled manual worker families, it actually reflected the amount spent by skilled and semi-skilled wage earners. In contrast, the salaried family spent 80% more than the WPA maintenance budget. These figures confirm our observations that clothing was important in separating the salaried class from the working class and in isolating the black class.

Second, the reality and importance of social norms are dramatically illustrated by the increase in wives' expenditures for silk stockings. The advent of cheaper, mass-produced silk stockings made them no longer a luxury but a requirement for proper female attire. And the new, shorter skirts made the presence or absence of silk stockings public knowledge. That women were aware of the social importance of these stockings is clear: The laborer wife's increased clothing expenditures between 1918 and 1935 went *entirely* toward the purchase of silk stockings; the wage-earner wife's outlays for stockings accounted for *more* than the increase in her clothing expenditures; and the salaried wife spent one-half of the increase in her clothing expenditures on stockings.

Evidently, women did not feel acceptable in public without silk stockings, and there were limits to economizing on them since they could be mended but not produced at home. Although the government thought silk stockings were not a necessary part of a woman's wardrobe, as shown in the WPA budgets, the women themselves disagreed. Low-income women bought stockings before they bought another dress.

By custom, a woman was more presentable in public in an older dress with mended silk stockings than in a newer dress without silk stockings.

The necessity of silk stockings, even though they did not improve the welfare aspects of clothing, shows how powerful social norms were in setting clothing requirements, even when financial pressures were fierce.

Home

Substantial changes in housing occurred between 1918 and 1935. Homes became more comfortable, with additional plumbing and bathroom facilities, improved heating, more widespread use of electric lighting, better furnishings, and more rooms per person. Over 90% of white families' homes were equipped with a full bath and electrical service; over 80% now enjoyed hot running water (see table 4.9). By 1935, the major distinctions in housing were the presence or absence of central heating, telephone service, a mechanical refrigerator, and a washing machine. A survey conducted in 1934 described 'the typical American home' as a 'single-family dwelling, about 19 years old, of wood or frame construction containing five rooms. It is equipped with either bathtub or shower, indoor water-closet, uses electricity for lighting, and gas for cooking. For the country as a whole, reliance is placed predominantly upon heating stoves for heat, although over 31% of all dwelling units use warm-air furnaces. Coal is the principal fuel used.'[81]

The proportion of families living in houses dropped as the population shifted to larger urban areas. More families lived in rented apartments rather than in houses. The home ownership rate continued its steady increase, however. The National Housing Act of 1934 created the Federal Housing Administration (FHA) and made home financing (FHA mortgages) more readily available to large segments of the employed population. The same year, the Public Works Administration began building public housing. The Depression caused a major decline in construction, so the average age of private residential structures increased from 26.5 years (1929) to 30.2 years (1935).[82]

With these costly improvements in housing, families spent significantly more of their budgets on housing (see table 4.8).[83] Their real housing expenditures[84] per capita doubled between 1918 and 1935.[85] Housing increased from 15% to 17% of the wage-earner's budget, and fuel and light increased from 5% to 7% between the 1918 and 1935 CES surveys. Given these ownership costs, it is not surprising that many families lived in substandard housing: 16% of the dwellings were in need of major repairs; 17% were overcrowded, and 20% were unfit for use.[86] Some housing (8%) was 'shared' by families because of hard times. Over one-third of relief families averaged more than one person per room and one-tenth of them averaged over two people per room. Crowded housing was especially severe in the South, where 20% of white and 35% of black families lived in crowded dwellings.[87] A government urban housing survey noted 'the absence of sanitary plumbing on a larger scale than is commonly realized.' One-sixth of homeowners and two-sevenths of renters had neither bathtub nor shower. One-eighth of homeowners and one-fifth of renters had no indoor toilet.[88]

Table 4.8 Shelter expenditures of urban families, 1935

	Black	Laborer	Wage earner	Salaried
Total shelter expenditure	$214	$355	$412	$550
Average # rooms	3.9	4.7[a]	4.9[a]	5.5
Homeowners	19.1%	24.1%	26.4%	42.3%
Living in houses	44.1%	50.0%	51.5%	59.0%
With hot running water, inside flush toilet, and electric lights	28.0%	60.0%	70.0%[a]	90.0%
Average housing expenditure				
Total[a]	$124(154)	$217(194)	$246(218)	$340(303)[b]
Renters	$146	$211	$244[a]	$362
Owners	$188	$151	$160	$219
Owner average expenditure for[c]	$24	$65	$62	$87
Mortgage interest	$0	$0	$1	$1
Refinancing	$30	$57	$61	$79
Current taxes	$5	$1	$3	$2
Assessments	$5	$20	$28	$39
Repairs and replacements	$4	$6	$6	$11
Fuel and light	$73(68)[a]	$99	$111	$137
Coal	$30	$28	$30	$36
Gas	$4	$20	$24	$30
Electricity	$11	$23	$26	$40
Wood	$10	$2	$2	$4
Coke and briquets	$1	$6	$8	$8
Fuel oil and kerosene	$5	$5	$5	$7
Ice	$11	$10	$11	$5
Water	$4	$4	$5	$7

[a] The number in parentheses represents the 1935 totals, since the details are calculated from 1935 Survey using income groups (all occupations): 0.1 ($750–1,000) + 0.9 ($1,000–1,250) laborers; $1,250–1,500 wage earners; the blacks as in Table 4.4.
[b] Includes salaried business and professional workers only, while $303 includes all occupations in income group. Except in small cities, salaried persons spend more on housing relative to others in the $2,250–2,500 group.
[c] From 1935 Survey.
Source: The 1934–36 Survey Bulletin 638 generally used for all groups but salaried, which was generally calculated from 1935 Survey. The housing details from the 1934–36 survey usually had to be calculated from city data weighted by 0.3 (small cities) + 0.4 (medium cities) + 0.3 (large).

Table 4.9 Variations in housing by city size, 1935

	Small city			Mid-sized city			Large city		
	Laborer	Wage earner	Salaried	Laborer	Wage earner	Salaried	Laborer	Wage earner	Salaried
Average family size	3.7	3.8	4.0	3.3	3.4	3.4	3.4	3.4	3.5
Average # of rooms	4.3	4.7	5.4	4.5	4.7	5.5	4.2	4.3	4.7
Homeowners (%)	30	42	55	17	27	43	10	14	25
Living in houses (%)[a]	78	79	83	54	56	63	18	18	30
With hot running water, inside flush toilet, and electric lights (%)	65.0	73.0	81.0	60.0	66.0	93.0	77.0	89.0	96.5
Average housing expenditure total ($)	158	157	232	178	212	304	271	311	454
Renters	176	198	327	196	234	355	287	330	487
Owners	119	107	155	123	165	230	290	271	340
Owners' average expenditure for ($)									
Mortgage interest	32	38	49	49	59	92	147	135	152
Refinancing	1	–	1	1	–	–	–	1	2
Current taxes	45	47	57	46	58	84	119	96	107
Assessments	2	1	2	1	1	2	2	2	3
Repairs and replacements	27	12	20	20	37	37	13	22	60
Insurance premiums	11	7	13	5	7	9	10	14	11
Fuel and light expenditure total ($)[b]	81	91	125	93	102	135	87	84	101
Percentage distribution (%)									
Coal	0.25	0.24	0.18	0.16	0.14	0.17	0.30	0.27	0.21
Gas	0.17	0.20	0.26	0.20	0.21	0.23	0.23	0.25	0.28
Electricity	0.29	0.30	0.37	0.26	0.29	0.32	0.30	0.32	0.37
Wood	0.18	0.16	0.13	0.12	0.10	0.07	0.00	0.01	0.00
Ice	0.08	0.08	0.04	0.09	0.08	0.04	0.10	0.10	0.05
Other	0.03	0.03	0.02	0.18	0.18	0.16	0.07	0.06	0.09

[a] From Tables 15–16 of income surveys (1935) for each city separately. No distinction was made between relief and non-relief families. Data excludes business buildings and other structures not elsewhere specified; two family houses are defined as apartments.

[b] Excludes water.

Source: BLS Bulletin 638, except for salaried, which is from BLS–WPA Survey, Bulletin 648.

These figures indicate only some of the housing problems faced by low-income families. Inadequate ventilation, insufficient sunlight, poor lighting or heating, pest infestation, unsanitary conditions, and lack of privacy were not well documented.[89] People's stated desires for what they would like in a house, as compared to what they had, show the vast differences between the housing of low-income families in tenements (representative of many laborer and relief families) and of moderate income families in houses (representative of many salaried families).[90] The poorer families still wanted the basics – an outside window in all rooms, a private toilet and bath, hot running water, and central heating. Since the higher-income families already had these, they wanted more closets, more electric outlets, and more even heating of rooms.

Black families' housing was abysmal – even worse than predicted by their low incomes. Blacks living in northern cities paid higher rents than whites with the same income, but they still had less satisfactory housing. In the South, blacks paid lower rents than whites with similar incomes, but their housing was of considerably inferior quality. Outside the major northern cities, blacks were less than half as likely as whites to have the basic amenities of hot running water, inside toilet, and gas (or electricity) for cooking. The disparity was especially glaring in southern cities, where only 11% of the blacks had these facilities compared to 64% of the whites. Basic facilities for black families – accessible to two-thirds of blacks in the South but over nine-tenths elsewhere – consisted of electric lighting and cold running water. That many black families lacked electric lighting and adequate heating and refrigeration is reflected in their fuel, light, and ice budget, which was 17% less than allowed by the WPA emergency standard.[91]

Government standards for healthful housing covered many areas, including guidelines for the following:[92]

- physiological needs (standards for heating, air circulation, natural illumination, artificial lighting, noise control, and play space);
- phychological needs (standards for privacy, room for family life, access to required activities, cleanliness, housework without undue fatigue, and compatibility with mental heath);
- protection against contagion (standards for safe water supply, toilet facilities, pest control, and food preservation), and
- protection against accidents (standards for safe construction and fire prevention).

The WPA used essentially these same housing standards in setting up their maintenance budget. However, the WPA also mentioned as 'desirable': 'a respectable, non-industrial neighborhood, without traffic hazards, conveniently located with reference to schools, work, church, transportation lines, shopping area and playground, where streets are paved and there are sidewalks, gas and electricity connections.'[93]

Although these guidelines were all-encompassing, they were fairly lenient, especially with respect to housing size and amenities. For example, to meet the air circulation standard, a family of four needed only a 400 sq ft unit with 8 ft ceilings (two bedrooms of 100 sq ft each and a kitchen/living room/dining room of 200 sq ft). Adequate privacy was provided by one bedroom per two adults (aged ten years and up) or one bedroom per four children under ten years. Cleanliness required hot running water, a bathtub or shower, wash basin, and separate indoor toilet. For housework, only a laundry tub with drying facilities, a 4 cu ft icebox (for five people) and a cooking range were required. These standards appear to have been set to reflect housing standards already obtained by the majority of working-class families. In fact, laborers spent 100% of the WPA maintenance level for rent (including water) and 96% of the level for fuel and light.

Black and relief families fell far below these standards. In setting up an 'emergency level' budget, the WPA omitted from its housing standard the private tub or shower and it allowed a less desirable and less convenient neighborhood.[94] Most likely, the 25% lower 'emergency' rent guideline resulted in substandard housing. Nevertheless, black non-relief families spent only 86% of the emergency level for rent and 91% of the emergency level for fuel and light. The latter allowed coal or wood (rather than gas) for cooking and water heating, one 50-watt lamp per room, and the use of an electric iron (but no radio).[95]

The salaried family was able to buy better housing in a more desirable location and with more amenities by spending 56% more than allowed by the maintenance budget. The quality differences in housing between classes were even more striking than indicated by differences in expenditures since salaried families were two-thirds more likely to own their home than were working-class families. Home ownership resulted in lower expenditures for more spacious housing that had more of the desired features and amenities. Salaried families used about 40% more of the cleaner, more convenient fuels (gas and electricity) than wage-earner families, who used only 15% more than laborer families. Salaried families also relied much less on ice for food preservation since they were more likely to own mechanical refrigerators.

The WPA maintenance standard assumed that the family did not have a mechanical refrigerator, and so it allotted over twice as much for ice as the laborer family actually spent. The laborer family spent 5% more on fuel and 20% more on electricity than allowed in the WPA maintenance budget. (Wage-earner families spent almost 20% more on fuel and 40% more on electricity than the WPA standard.) However, because operating mechanical refrigerators cost less than buying 150 pounds of ice weekly for seven months per year, the laborer family ended up spending slightly less than the WPA standard in the combined fuel–light–ice category. This economy of operation, in addition to the convenience and improved food preservation, helps explain why the sale of refrigerators, which rose dramatically throughout the 1920s, did not decline during the Depression. In fact, refrigerator sales continued to rise slowly while the sale of electric ranges fell sharply.[96]

Furnishing the home

While amenities such as plumbing, better lighting, coal or gas heating, gas cooking, and mechanical appliances had improved considerably since 1918, furnishings remained virtually unchanged. Government standards, however, allowed a decline in the quality and quantity of furnishings for the working-class family (see tables 4.10A and 4.10B). The 1918 BLS standard included a 'wood with imitation leather' sofa and an oak table with four chairs in the living room, a dining table with six chairs and a sideboard in the dining room, and a table and chair in the kitchen. The 1935 WPA maintenance standard assumed the family had no dining room, and the living room contained no sofa and only one upholstered chair, two other chairs (one with and one without arms), and a table with a lamp and radio. The kitchen contained a table with two chairs. The family evidently dined at the kitchen or living room table by bringing in

Table 4.10A Typical furnishings – WPA maintenance standard,[a] 1935

Living room	Bedroom (master)
Upholstered chair	Bureau with mirror
Rocker or arm chair	Double bed with mattress, springs, pillows
Straight wood chair	Chair
Rug	Rug
Wood or coal stove (with venting)	
Table with lamp, radio	
Wastebasket	
Mirror	
Kitchen	Bedroom (children's)
Coal range (4 hold, oven) (with venting)	Chest of drawers
Gas plate (2 burner)	2 cots with mattresses, pillows
Portable oven	Chair
Refrigerator (ice)	Rug
Kitchen table with 2 chairs	Mirror

[a] Varied by number of children; items for family of 2 parents and 2 children given here. Also includes 4 window shades and 4 curtain rods with 8 yards of window curtain material.
Source: 'Quantity Budgets,' pp. 42–5.

Table 4.10B Expenditures for furnishings, 1935

	Blacks		Laborers		Wage earners		Salaried	
Total furnishings	$22		$38		$55		$73	
	% reporting	Average cost^a ($)	% reporting	Average cost^a ($)	% reporting	Average cost^a ($)	% reporting	Average cost^a ($)
Frequent purchases								
Cotton towels	18.1	0.83	40.0	1.48	41.6	1.63	39.0	4.64
Sheets	25.0	2.96	27.4	3.83	29.8	4.23	39.6	4.48
Pillowcases	17.0	1.29	20.9	1.67	22.3	1.75	23.3	2.44
Drapes and curtains	10.4	1.54	29.8	4.33	29.6	5.07	32.7	6.96
Kitchen utensils	12.9	0.78	22.6	2.43	25.1	1.87	72.7	3.95
Brooms, brushes, mops	64.2	1.46	66.3	1.08	63.0	1.08	70.9	0.98
Light bulbs	33.7	0.74	56.9	1.20	57.3	1.34	71.3	1.65
Major purchases^b								
Carpet	4.4	8.00	12.7	22.83	13.7	25.00	19.8	21.00
Couches, davenport	3.0	17.00	3.1	26.77	2.8	33.00	3.6	41.00
Living room suites	3.7	83.00	4.8	82.71	4.6	101.00	5.0	111.00
Bedroom suites	2.2	82.00	2.2	77.27	3.3	88.00	4.2	95.00
Dining room suites	1.6	73.00	1.4	60.00	2.1	78.00	3.3	87.00
Stoves and ranges^c	9.1	40.00	8.2	36.59	8.3	44.00	6.1	82.00
Refrigerators	0	—	2.9	166.00	5.9	155.00	8.7	177.00
Electric washing machines	0.6	115.00	6.1	59.00	6.4	62.00	4.6	75.00
Sewing machines	0.5	—	1.5	42.00	0.8	70.00	1.5	75.00
Vacuum cleaners	0	—	2.4	34.38	4.4	44.00	5.1	75.00
Ice boxes	3.1	15.00	2.9	16.55	3.0	19.00	1.5	19.00

^{a} Average cost is total amount paid by those households purchasing.
^{b} Assumes households do not buy both carpets and rugs in same year.
^{c} Assumes that households only buy one stove (hot plate) per year.
Source: Bulletin 638, except for Salaried (NRC 1935 Study, with cities and income groups merged for some categories).

sufficient chairs from other rooms. The parents' bedroom contained a double bed (with springs), a chair, and a bureau, the children's bedroom a single bed (or crib) per child, a set of drawers and a chair. The 1918 standard allowed two chairs per bedroom as well as a chiffonnier and sewing machine for the wife. Both standards allowed rugs in the bedrooms and living room; and in 1918, in the dining room as well. The 1935 standard allowed for a decline in the quality of furniture purchased; items were assumed to need replacing more frequently.[97]

Despite these standards, families did buy sofas or living room suites in the 1930s, as well as dining tables. The percentage of families purchasing a sofa or suite in 1935 varied slightly across classes – from 7% for blacks to 9% for salaried families. However, large variations existed in quality, as the salaried family bought furniture costing one-half more than the black families and one-third more than the laborer family. As in 1918, class differences were reflected more in how the family dined, and so the annual purchase of dining room suites increased across class – from 1.5% for black and laborer families to 3.3% for salaried families, who bought a suite costing about 45% more. In addition, the presence of writing desks and bookcases conferred status as symbols of literacy and culture. Frequency of purchasing bedroom suites increased across classes, but their quality differences were less than for living room and dining room furniture, presumably because they were seldom seen by outsiders. The salaried family spent only one-sixth more than blacks on bedroom furniture.

Getting Around

By 1935, travel by automobile had become a central part of American life, as car ownership rates had risen dramatically. The automobile replaced stylish clothes or new parlor furniture as the most conspicuous symbol of success.[98] Owning an automobile made people more mobile and opened up a wide range of possibilities for recreational activities and vacations. Car travel also made shopping considerably easier. Three-fourths of salaried families owned a car, and even one-third of the laborers had an auto in the midst of the Depression. Since owning a car was more expensive than riding the trolley, transportation took a much larger share of the budget (three times as much for the white working class).

The trolley still provided the basic means of travel to work, however. Eighty percent of the white working class reported trolley fares, which accounted for about one-third of their transportation budget (see table 4.11A).[99] Salaried families spent only two-thirds as much as wage-earner families on trolleys, but over three times as much on automobiles. Trolley or bus fares were generally $0.07 to $0.10, and the WPA maintenance budget allowed $53.96, or 620 rides yearly (12 weekly) to

Table 4.11A Transportation expenditures, 1935

	Blacks			Laborers			Wage earners			Salaried[a]			WPA maintenance $
	Average expenditure ($)	Average cost ($)	% reporting	Average expenditure ($)	Average cost ($)	% reporting	Average expenditure ($)	Average cost ($)	% reporting	Average expenditure ($)	Average cost ($)	% reporting	
Transportation (actual)[b]	28			68			105			242			
Details													
Total transport (estimated)[c]	27.55	34	83.5	80.37	85	96.6	101.30	105	98.8	232			
Auto[d]	7.76	78	9.9	48.41	131	37.0	64.68	151	42.8	205	281	73	
Purchase	1.24	59	2.1	11.55	170	6.8	16.82	198	8.5	96	410	23	
All operation	6.52	50	9.9	36.86	100	37.0	47.86	112	42.8	109	149	73	
Gasoline	2.82	28	9.9	20.91	56	37.0	26.85	63	42.8	57	78	73	
Other transportation	19.79			31.96			36.62			27			
Trolley	17.80	25	71.5	29.17	36	80.0	33.66	41	82.5	25			53.96

[a] Salaried households are calculated from a subgroup of cities from the 1935 NRC Survey: Chicago, Portland, Atlanta, East Central, West Central, Rocky (middle sized cities), New England, East Central (small cities).

[b] Transportation excludes all railroad, interurban bus, boat, and airplane expenses incurred during vacations, which are listed under vacations.

[c] This estimated total is a summation of the detailed expenditures, which had to be calculated using the annual unit expenditure groups.

[d] Also includes motorcycles.

Source: Bulletin 638, except for salaried. As usual, detailed expenditures are from data using annual unit expenditures (black <$200, laborers $300–400, wage earners $400–500).

work, school, or shopping.[100] Since an automobile was not included in the WPA standards, walking was assumed to provide the basic means of transportation for family members in their daily activities.

White working-class families depended on the trolley even less than assumed by the WPA. Four-fifths of these families reported trolley rides, averaging about eight rides per week for laborers and nine rides for wage earners. Probably one-quarter of the white working class owned an automobile and also rode the trolley, so that about one-third of the trolley-riding families sometimes used their own cars.[101]

Table 4.11B Automobile purchases, 1935

	Blacks	Laborers	Wage earners	Salaried
Percentage purchasing new car	0	0	2.7	6.3
Average net price$[a]	0	0	286	614
Percentage purchasing second-hand car	3.2	6.2	6.7	12.1
Average net price$[a]	106	184	231	267
Total percentage purchasing car	3.2	6.2	9.4	18.4
Average price$[a]	106	184	247	385
Percentage owning auto	11	33	43	80

[a] Price is gross purchase price minus trade-in allowance. Thus the actual price paid was higher and the discrepancy increases with class.
Source: BLS Bulletin 638, pp. 210–11. These figures are based only on the automobile, and do not include motorcycles. Salaried data here are for the $2,100–2,400 group in the 1934–36 sample rather than the $2,250–2,500 group from the NRC 1935 data set.

Although wage-earner families used the trolley only slightly more than laborer families, the automobile provided important differences in mobility between the two classes. Wage earners were about four times more likely than blacks and one-third more likely than laborers to own cars (see table 4.11B). During the survey period, blacks and laborers purchased only second-hand cars, while two in seven wage earners who purchased an auto bought a new one. Thus, wage earners tended to own nicer, more socially acceptable cars than did laborers.[102] In addition to spending one-third more than laborers for their vehicles, wage earners also could afford to drive their cars more often, since they bought 13% more gasoline.

In contrast to the white working class, black families had highly restricted mobility. Although over 70% of black families reported paying for trolley rides, they spent only $25 annually, which allowed them about six rides weekly. Only one in ten black families owned a car; and even for those families, their dilapidated automobile, costing about $100, did not provide much transportation. They spent only $28 for gasoline, or one-half of what white laborer families spent. Overall, the black family spent only 60% as much as allowed by the WPA emergency standard for transportation.

The automobile provided the salaried class with significantly more mobility, and more status, than the working class. The salaried family was about twice as likely as the working-class family to own a car. Salaried families often bought their cars new, and they could afford to pay twice as much as wage-earner families in their purchases. Even though their repair bills were lower, salaried families spent one-third more on car operations because they could afford to drive more and to keep their newer cars in better condition.

Spending Leisure Time

People still spent most of their leisure time at activities that were costless (or nearly so). Social activities centered around talking or visiting with others; leisure activities involved mainly walking, auto-riding, or idling; and intellectual activities were mainly reading newspapers or magazines and listening to the radio.[103]

The 1935 pattern for spending money on leisure and learning was similar to the 1918 pattern. Expenditure for tobacco dominated the recreation budget; moviegoing remained the primary form of paid family entertainment; and most families bought a daily newspaper (see table 4.12). The WPA maintenance budget recognized the importance of these items and allowed $20.80 for tobacco, toys and 'treats' (gum, candy, and beverages), $33.80 for motion pictures, and $10.84 for a daily newspaper.[104] The 'tobacco, toys, and treats' budget, designed to allow for 'life's more frivolous moments,'[105] was spent mainly on tobacco for the husband; only the black family spent less than $25 for tobacco. Little money (from $4 for black families to $15 for salaried) was spent on toys or music.

More families attended movies in 1935 than in 1918, and they went more frequently than before. Over three-fourths of the white classes were moviegoers (compared to one-third of the black families). All classes, however, spent less than allowed by the WPA on movies, plays, and sports events. Blacks, who were excluded from 'white' movie houses in many parts of the country, spent only one-half of what the emergency budget allotted for movies (i.e., monthly attendance); salaried families spent 70% of the movie allowance in the maintenance budget (i.e., weekly attendance). Paid attendance at plays and concerts dropped by one-half its 1918 level. Very few families attended even one paid event yearly.

White working-class families bought a daily newspaper, as was allowed in the WPA maintenance budget. Blacks felt great pressure to economize; they bought daily newspapers only half the time. In contrast, the government emergency budget cut newspapers entirely. Blacks spent almost no

Table 4.12 Recreation and education expenditures, 1935.

	Blacks			Laborers			Wage earners			Salaried			WPA maintenance ($)
	Average expenditure ($)	Average cost ($)	% reporting	Average expenditure ($)	Average cost ($)	% reporting	Average expenditure ($)	Average cost ($)	% reporting	Average expenditure ($)	Average cost ($)	% reporting	
Recreation and education (actual)	34.00			60.00			80.00			185			75.18
Details (estimated). Recreation and education	36.74			74.35			87.32			164			6.87
Recreation	30.86			65.44			75.62			122			
Education	4.77			6.34			7.35			18			
Vacation[a]	1.11			2.57			4.35			24			33.80
Movies[b]	3.93	11	35	13.38	17	77	15.92	19	82	23			
Plays and concerts	0.11	3	4	0.13	3	5	0.24	3	7	1			
Spectator sports	0.26	5	5	0.69	5	15	1.00	5	19	3			
Newspapers	5.80			11.45			12.67			16			10.84
Magazines	0.19	3	6	1.40	4	35	1.75	4	43	4			
Books borrowed	0.00	0	0	0.06	2	2.4	0.14	4	4				
Books purchased[c]	0.00	0	0	0.16	3	4.6	0.23	6	4	1			
School tuition and books	4.77	7	69	6.34	14	43	7.35	19	38	18	40	45	6.87
Sheet music and records	–		0.3	0.17	3	6	0.23	4	6	1	84	3	
Musical instruments	0.02	3	0.6	1.16	43	2.7	0.74	27	2.7	3			

Table 4.12 (cont.)

	Blacks			Laborers			Wage earners			Salaried			
	Average expenditure ($)	Average cost ($)	% reporting	Average expenditure ($)	Average cost ($)	% reporting	Average expenditure ($)	Average cost ($)	% reporting	Average expenditure ($)	Average cost ($)	% reporting	WPA maintenance ($)
Radios[d]	2.74	23	12	4.92	16	31	5.40	16	34	7	18	38	20.80
Children's play equipment	1.10	6	19	1.81	7		1.78	7	2	5			
Tobacco	14.88			24.73		26	27.97			44	51	86	
Recreation association	0.28	7	4	1.33	8	16	1.57	9	17	14	18	50	9.60[e]
Vacations	1.11			2.57			4.35			24			
Other[f]	1.56			4.05			5.98						

[a] Vacations include vacation lodging, food, and long distance public transportation.
[b] Assumes families purchasing children's admissions, also purchased adults' admissions.
[c] Not including tests or professional literature.
[d] Percentage is sum of those who purchase various types; average expenditure includes maintenance and repair on all radios as well as purchases.
[e] Includes adult clubs, other social groups.
[f] Includes pets, cameras, entertainment (except food), and athletic equipment.
Source: Bulletin 638, except for salaried.

money on other reading materials, but many of the white families bought magazines (the percentage of families increasing with class).

Radios, a rarity in 1918, were present in over 75% of homes by 1935. They provided a major source of family entertainment and nationwide communication for all classes except the lowest. Many households had more than one radio (radios cost about $16), and at least one-third of each of the white classes purchased a radio during the survey period.[106] Again, however, harsh economizing kept most black families from owning a radio: fewer than one-third had one in the home in 1935 (see table 4.12). Lack of radios, daily newspapers, and movie attendance isolated the black community from the larger community and from national events and culture. Their poverty resulted in social as well as economic exclusion.

The WPA maintenance budget (but not the emergency budget) allowed $9.60 for membership in organizations, including 'character-building' groups, school and church groups, and fraternal or ethnic (nationality) groups.[107] Black and white working-class families reported spending less than $2 for membership in recreational associations. However, about one-quarter of laborers and wage earners did belong to labor organizations, paying an average of $18 to $21 dues per year.[108]

The other item of importance in the education budget was expenditure for children's school-related needs, including books, stationery, other supplies, and gymnasium equipment. Of the 59 cities surveyed by the WPA, 55 had school systems that charged parents directly certain school-related expenses.[109] The WPA budget standards included $6.87 for school attendance (for a boy thirteen years old and a girl aged eight). Laborer and wage-earner families paid about the WPA budgeted amount for school-related expenses (see table 4.12), even though their families averaged fewer than two children. Less than a majority of working-class families actually reported such expenses, however, and for those families, the costs were considerably higher ($14–$19). Almost one-half the salaried families paid $40 for school expenses (including private school tuition). In contrast, seven out of ten black families reported school-related expenses that averaged the WPA standard amount of $7. These figures indicate the harsh economizing undertaken by black families, while working-class families (and especially salaried families) could make more money available to their children for school activities. Unfortunately, black schools suffered from lower public budgets than white schools, especially in the South, and lack of money for families to buy books for their children only reinforced this inequality.

Leisure time activities were much more mundane and repetitive in practice than in imagining. In a 1934 survey, people reported reading newspapers and magazines, listening to the radio, and going to movies as their three major leisure time activities.[110] Visiting or entertaining, reading fiction, and riding in the car were the next most common ways of passing leisure time. These activities contrasted sharply with people's desired activities. They wanted to play tennis, swim, boat, golf, camp, garden, play music, go to the theater or ice skating. Compared to their actual activities, the preferred activities were more varied, were done away from home, and cost more. They also required a more physically active and socially active life-style. In practice, people engaged in sedentary, inexpensive activities, often by themselves. They fantasized, however, about engaging in sports and other physical activities with other people that were more expensive, and more famous. As incomes rise, more people will begin to live out these fantasies.

Caring for Health

Although families used more medical care in 1935 than in 1918, medical care still took only a small amount of the budget. About 90% of families across classes reported some medical expenditures, yet they still spent less on medical care than on furnishings. Health improved, however, with dramatic decreases in major diseases, such as diphtheria and smallpox, as vaccines became available. Improved sewage disposal and water supplies resulted in far fewer cases of typhoid; and controlling insects, for example, by adding screens to doors and windows, reduced malaria. Between 1918 and 1935, malaria cases fell 40%, typhoid 30%, diphtheria 25%, and smallpox became almost nonexistent (down 91%). Syphilis, however, was even more widespread. Public health care expenditures increased rapidly during the Depression, but private expenditures fell even faster. Public expenditures rose from 10% of all personal health care expenditures in 1929 to 15% in 1935, and this trend was to continue until 1950. Although the number of physicians per person declined slightly between 1918 and 1935, the number of trained nurses was rising rapidly. The training of all medical professionals was improving during this period, and as the population became more urbanized, doctors spent less time traveling to see patients.[111]

National collection of birth and death statistics finally covered the entire population in 1933. Life expectancy rose seven years to 61.7 between the 1918 and 1935 surveys. Women lived four years longer than men, and whites still lived ten years longer than blacks. The mortality rate of everyone under 45 years old in 1935 was only one-half the 1918 rate. The maternal mortality rate had declined by one-quarter between the two survey periods. It was still quite high and would decline rapidly over the next ten years. In the mid-1930s, a woman bearing three children still faced a 1.7% chance of dying in childbirth.[112]

Measles remained the most prevalent communicable disease (6.0 cases per 1,000 people), but the number of typhoid cases (0.1 per 1,000 people) fell dramatically with public awareness of the importance of drinking only uncontaminated water and as more families had access to sanitary public water systems. Diphtheria cases (0.3 per 1,000 people) were also falling rapidly as a result of the newly discovered inoculation. Heart disease continued to rise as the leading cause of death (4.0 deaths per 1,000 people). The other leading causes of death (each 1.0 per 1,000) were cancer, which continued a rising rate, and flu or pneumonia, which accounted for only half as many deaths in 1935 as in 1918. The death rate from tuberculosis had fallen by two-thirds and from digestive tract inflammation by four-fifths since 1918, while the death rate from automobile accidents had tripled.[113]

More families now visited the dentist or bought eyeglasses.[114] One-third of the laborer families reported dental visits in 1918 – almost one-half did in 1935. One-half of the wage-earner and two-thirds of the salaried families visited the dentist in 1935, up slightly from 1918. Around one-fifth of the white working-class families and one-third of salaried families bought eyeglasses, also up slightly from 1918.

In contrast, few (14%) black families had any dental care in 1935, and even fewer (7%) bought eyeglasses. Black families spent only two-fifths as much as the white working class for doctors, but they spent almost as much as laborers on medicine. The white working class was as likely to have an office visit as a home visit by the doctor. Black families were twice as likely to report a home rather than an office visit. This reflects the black community practices that arose because few medical resources were available either to black patients or to their health care providers. Hospital care also separated the classes. Black families had almost no access to hospitals, and salaried families spent over twice as much on hospital care as the white working class. Overall, salaried families had access to much more medical care than the other classes. They spent twice as much for medical care as wage earners, who spent twice as much as blacks (see table 4.13).

The WPA maintenance budget allowed $47 for medical care and $5 for drugs and eyeglasses.[115] This is $13 more than actually spent by laborers and $3 more than spent by wage earners, excluding their reported medical expenditures of $3–$4 for accident insurance. In contrast, the salaried families spent almost twice as much as the WPA maintenance budget allowed. All families spent more than the WPA's budget of $5 for drugs and eyeglasses – from $8 for blacks to $13 for wage earners to $19 for salaried. Families varied much less across classes in their use of medicines (as indicated by the relatively low variation in expenditures) than in their use of doctor and dentist services and hospital facilities.

Poorer families had to rely at best on buying medicine off-the-shelf from the druggist or having a visiting nurse rather than seeing a doctor.

Table 4.13 Medical care expenditures, 1935

Details	Blacks			Laborers			Wage earners			Salaried			WPA maintenance ($)
	Average expenditure ($)	Average cost ($)	% purchasing	Average expenditure ($)	Average cost ($)	% purchasing	Average expenditure ($)	Average cost ($)	% purchasing	Average expenditure ($)	Average cost ($)	% purchasing	
Medical care (actual)	27.00			42.00			53.00			103			52.32
Medical care (estimated)	26.63			44.73			56.47			96			
Physician	7.57	21		17.36	42		21.14	48		33	55		
Home			35.7			40.6			40.0			60	
Office			19.2			40.3			44.0			46	
Medicine and medical appliances[a]	7.75	9	87.8	8.33	10	85.2	10.19	12	86.1	14	16	88	
Nurse	0.13			0.36			0.74			4			
Hospital and clinic[b]	0.80		3.2	4.05		9.7	5.55		11.0	11		18	
Dentist	0.63	4	13.7	7.40	16	47.0	10.93	22	50.0	20	31	64	
Eyeglasses	0.48	7	6.5	2.66	13	20.0	3.06	14	21.0	5	16	32	
Accident and health insurance	9.08	26	34.3	3.27	18	18.0	3.76	17	22.0	9	26	35	
Other medical	0.19			1.30			1.10			NA			

[a] Percentage is for those purchasing medicine alone; expenditures include medicine and medical appliances.
[b] Percentage includes percentage in private room plus percentage in ward.
Source: Bulletin 638, except for salaried.

One study found that families who were 'reasonably comfortable' in 1929 but 'poor' in 1932 had a high rate of illness.[116]

Running the Home

Household operations, although they account for only a small part of the family's budget, include expenditures that were important for distinguishing class and for determining a family's life-style. The relative importance of household operations in the overall budget increased across class – from 2.3% for black to 4.7% for salaried families. Except for cleaning supplies, families with lower incomes economized in this area by doing without (e.g., telephone service) or doing it themselves (e.g., domestic or laundry service) (see table 4.14). Black families spent two-thirds of their household operation budget on cleaning supplies, including various types of soap and paper products. Salaried families spent only one-eighth of their operation budget on supplies, since they spent four-fifths on telephone, laundry, and domestic service. Black families spent only $2 on these services, while salaried families' spending for their telephone, laundry service, and maid equalled 45% of blacks' rent bill.

Although telephone service and housework service (i.e., laundry sent out and domestic help) had a large impact on the family's social integration and the wife's workload, they were luxuries. Only 7% of black families had any telephone expenses compared to 25% of the white laborer families and 82% of the salaried families. Nevertheless, for families with a working husband, telephone usage was much more widespread in 1935 than in 1918.[117] Over 50% more laborer families reported paying for some telephone service, and they were spending over twice as much. About 80% more salaried families reported telephone expenses in 1935 compared to 1918, and they were spending over five times as much.

One in four salaried families had a domestic servant (part-time or full-time) compared to one in twelve wage earners, and one in twenty laborers.[118] Of course, black families usually provided the domestic service, and in many areas these were the only jobs available to black women.

One study of the Sears, Roebuck catalog finds a woman's 'best friend' to be a wide array of modern conveniences – electric machines (washing machine, refrigerator, electric stove) and smaller appliances (iron, vacuum cleaner, toaster, sewing machine, percolator), central heating, and modern bathrooms (bathtub, lavatory, and toilet).[119] People paid handsomely for modern, more convenient, appliances. Electric stoves cost twice as much as wood or gas stoves. An electric or gas refrigerator was an even more expensive item, costing one-half more than the electric

Table 4.14 Household operations, 1935

Details	Blacks			Laborers			Wage earners			Salaried			
	Average expenditure ($)	Average cost ($)	% purchased	Average expenditure ($)	Average cost ($)	% purchased	Average expenditure ($)	Average cost ($)	% purchased	Average expenditure ($)	Average cost ($)	% purchased	WPA maintenance ($)
Household operations (actual)	16.00			32.00			45.00			107			
Total household operations (estimated)	20.00			40.02			48.76			89			
Laundry	0.96	19	5	6.08	28	21	9.13	32	29	25			
Cleaning supplies[a]	13.26			18.57			18.37			11			18.82
Stationery and postage[b]	1.61	2	66	2.77	3	83	3.24	4	87	5			3.05[c]
Telephone	1.19	16	7	6.07	24	25	8.59	24	33	26	32	82	
Moving	0.34	4	8	0.87	8	11	1.00	9	11	1			
Domestic service[d]	0.45	38	1	1.60	36	5	3.80	45	8	21	89	24	
Property insurance	0.40	8	5	1.15	7	16	1.27	7	19	NA			
Interest on debt	1.07	12	9	2.00	18	11	2.34	22	11	NA			
Garden	0.31	2	14	0.25	3	9	0.28	4	7	NA			
Safe deposit	0.00			0.06			0.11			NA			
Other	0.41			0.54			0.63			NA			

[a] Includes matches and household paper (e.g., toilet paper, napkins).
[b] Percent is for stationery purchase.
[c] Includes 'unspecified,' such as writing materials, postage, telephone calls, twine, glue, and tacks.
[d] Sum of percentage purchasing part-time domestic service plus percentage purchasing full-time service.

Source: Bulletin 638, except for salaried. Garden expenditures are moved to here from miscellaneous to be comparable with other years.

stove and five times as much as an ice box. An electric vacuum cleaner cost one-half as much as an electric stove and ten times as much as a carpet sweeper.[120]

Although laundering remained a time-consuming and difficult task, the less formal and less cumbersome clothing styles eased the laundry chores somewhat, as did the smaller family size. In addition, washing machines operated by electricity or gasoline motors lessened the once 'savage drudgery of laundering.'[121] These machines still required a great deal of manual assistance, including wringing the clothes and changing the settings. In 1918, housewives across all classes were much more likely to send their laundry out – 59% of laborers' wives and 78% of salaried wives did so – and they spent more money for having the laundry done than in 1935. At most, 37% of wage-earner and 26% of laborer families had help with the laundry (or other housework) in 1935. Working-class wives were about twice as likely to have help in the home in 1918 as in 1935, and those with help spent almost three times as much in 1935 (constant dollars).

Housework in 1935 remained arduous, especially if the family used a wood or coal stove for cooking (supplemented by a gas plate), received no housework help, and did the laundry by hand (as the WPA budget assumed). Yet, in contrast to 1918, the WPA maintenance budget did not include an allowance for household assistance of any kind. Such help was now implicitly acknowledged to be reserved primarily for the salaried class. The maintenance budget allowances were only for cleaning supplies and 'unspecified essentials' such as writing materials, postage, telephone calls, twine, glue, and tacks.[122] The white working class spent almost exactly the WPA maintenance budget for cleaning supplies, and they spent considerably more for telephone, stationery, and postage than the meager WPA standard. Even laborer families spent almost three times as much as the maintenance standard in this area. In contrast, black families spent only as much on these communication items as was allowed for the WPA emergency standard, and they spent less than the emergency standard for cleaning supplies.

Finally, pressures to economize are clear in the figures on home gardens. Blacks were twice as likely as the white working class to have a vegetable garden, but even then, few black families (14%) had them. These class differences are more marked than the numbers indicate since only 19% of blacks (compared to 25% of the white working class) owned their own homes, and this is the group for which having a garden would be most feasible.

Looking Presentable

Expenditures for personal grooming resulted in important differences in appearance and thus in status markings. In practice, and as was expected

Table 4.15 Personal care, 1935

	Blacks			Laborers			Wage earners			Salaried			
	Average expend-iture ($)	Average cost ($)	% pur-chasing	Average expend-iture ($)	Average cost ($)	% pur-chasing	Average expend-iture ($)	Average cost ($)	% pur-chasing	Average expend-iture ($)	Average cost ($)	% pur-chasing	WPA maintenance ($)
Personal care (average)	15.00			22.00			27.00			48			24.87
Details													
Personal care (estimated)	16.93		90	26.12			29.70			47			
Barber[a]	7.85	9		12.93	13	96	15.19	20	95	24			
Toilet articles[b]	9.08	9	97	13.19	14	97	14.51	15	97	23			

[a] Percentage is for those purchasing haircuts; expenditures include all services.
[b] Percentage is for those purchasing soap; expenditure is for all toiletries.
Source: BLS Bulletin 638, except salaried.

in budget standards, families economized on personal care when their budgets were tight. This category includes family expenditures for haircuts (including hair waves for women), shaving supplies for men, and sanitary supplies for women (see table 4.15). The WPA maintenance budget allowed $25 annually for personal care and about two-thirds of that was spent for paying the barber and hairdresser. The WPA allowance reflects the wage-earner family's actual expenditures; laborers spent one-sixth less and salaried workers spent almost twice as much. The WPA maintenance standard allowed a monthly haircut for husbands (and sons 16 years and up) and a bimonthly haircut for wives (and daughters 13 years and up), with a hair wave every four months. Younger children were allowed fewer haircuts.[123] Men were allowed shaving supplies and a comb, hairbrush, and toothbrush (together totaling $1.85). Women were allowed a comb, toothbrush, some make-up and manicure supplies, a deodorant, and sanitary supplies (all totaling $2.65). The skimpiness of the WPA standard is clear in the allowance for razor blades – 40 per year. The husband was expected to shave with the same blade for nine days, a period of use almost certain to produce razor burn, nicks, cuts, and a ragged shave.

Families facing unemployment were expected to cut back on personal care, even at this minimal level. The WPA emergency standard allowed $16 for personal care (or 36% less) than the maintenance budget. This figure reflects black families' actual expenditures. Husbands had to extend their period between haircuts from one to one and a half months. Wives, on the other hand, were allowed *no* hairdressing services and were expected to cut their own hair as well as that of their daughters and younger sons (six years and under).[124] Male personal care standards were allowed to remain higher than female standards, presumably because men still had to be presentable for work or for job searching. The public appearance of housewives for shopping or socializing was not considered to be of similar importance. Husbands were expected to economize using only one-half as many razor blades as allotted in the maintenance budget (i.e., one every 18 days), thereby saving 50 cents. The wife was to use fewer hairpins and less powder (saving 30 cents) and was not to buy any nail care products (saving 20 cents). The other items, such as toilet soap and toothpaste, were already set at a minimum level for social decency and health.

Ensuring the Future

Life insurance was still considered vitally important for the working man's family, since many husbands would die before their children were grown. In practice, white families spent more on life insurance than the minimal amount in the WPA maintenance budget. In addition to the

Table 4.16 Insurance, gifts, and other, 1935

	Blacks			Laborers			Wage earners			Salaried			
	Average expend- iture ($)	Average cost ($)	% pur- chasing	Average expend- iture ($)	Average cost ($)	% pur- chasing	Average expend- iture ($)	Average cost ($)	% pur- chasing	Average expend- iture ($)	Average cost ($)	% pur- chasing	WPA maintenance ($)
Personal insurance[a]	25.00	30	84	50.00	56	89	68.00	76	89	126			46.40
Gifts etc.	16.00			28.00			37.00			78			
Other[b]	3.00			3.00			4.00			9			
Detailed expenditures													
Gifts etc. (estimated)	13.41			32.05			42.73			(75)			
Religion	8.08	9	86	13.95	18	79	15.28	20	76	24			10.40
Labor organizations[c]	0.89	16	5	4.51	18	25	5.62	21	27	NA			
Charity	0.73	2	38	1.84	4	51	2.39	4	55	8			5.00
Gifts	1.20	7	17	7.72	13	60	11.07	15	70	24	28	85	
Support of relatives[d]	2.51	28	9	4.03	32	13	8.37	54	16	19	97	19	
Funerals (other, estimated)	0.90	82	1	2.26	188	1	2.21	184	1				

[a] Mostly life insurance premiums with a small amount for annuities.

[b] Includes funerals, legal costs, and losses.

[c] Percentage in labor organization includes a very small percentage in professional organizations. Expenditures also include all vocational expenses (such as tools and uniforms, but not technical literature), which was ($0.00, $0.03, $0.05) for black, laborer, and wage-earner households.

[d] The percentage reported is percentage supporting relatives; dollar amount includes ($0.18, $0.25, $1.20) support of other persons (breakdown not available for salaried).

Source: Bulletin 638, except salaried.

industrial policies for older family members, laborers spent enough to buy a $1,300 ordinary life policy; wage earners a $2,000 policy; and salaried workers a $4,600 policy. The WPA maintenance budget allowed only an ordinary policy of $1,000 for the husband, which would remit a 'small surplus' of about $800 over funeral expenses. The wife and children were allowed small industrial or 'burial' policies that paid an aggregate lump sum of $900 for the wife and two children.[125] This sum would cover the costs of burial, which averaged $185 for working-class families reporting funeral expenses, with a nest egg of $300 left over when the wife died. The coverage allowed by the WPA maintenance standard would have cost the working-class family in our sample $43.50 per year.

Between 1918 and 1935, practice and standards had reversed. Earlier, the husband was thought to need at least a $5,000 life policy, yet none of the classes came close to achieving this level. During the Depression, the standards for life insurance fell dramatically. However, families with employed heads were able to purchase considerably more insurance than in 1918, although even the 1935 salaried family still fell short of the 1918 standard (see table 4.16).

Black families could afford little for life insurance, but they spent more than allowed by the WPA emergency standard, which included industrial policies paying about $300 each for the parents and $100 each for the children.[126] Spending one-half as much as the white laborer for personal insurance, the black family could purchase an industrial policy worth about $530,[127] plus industrial policies for the older family members. These policies would leave a small surplus after covering the meager $82 spent on funerals by black families. A 'proper burial' for black families was a much less costly ritual than for white working-class families, who spent over twice as much.

Giving

In the midst of depression, religious activities rose in importance and more families went to church than even in 1918, when churchgoing was the most important social activity. Church contributions doubled (in constant dollars). Reported church attendance ranged across class from a high of 86% for black families to 76% for wage-earner families. However, religious activities now shared with moviegoing the distinction of being the most important social activity for white families. Slightly more laborer families and fewer wage-earner families attended church compared to going to the movies, but the three white classes spent the same amount on their churches as they spent on movie tickets. In contrast, churchgoing was by far the most important social activity for black families, with 2.5 times as many families reporting church attendance as movie attendance.

In 1935, charity patterns reflected the need to help relatives and others hurt by the Depression, while in 1918, donations to charities had reflected the war effort. Although the average amount given to charities was only a few dollars, over one-half of the white families and over one-third of the black families made charitable contributions (see table 4.16). Ten to twenty percent (rising across class) made support contributions to relatives, and those families made generous donations that were almost equal to what they spent on their own family's medical care. Gifts were much more important for whites in 1935 compared to 1918; these gifts probably often represented an attempt to help a less fortunate relative. One-third to one-half more white families bought gifts in 1935 than in 1918, and they spent 45%–70% more on these gifts. Black families still could not afford to buy gifts for people outside the household; only one in six reported any gift buying and the gifts they bought cost only a few dollars.

Paying for Government

Although major social insurance programs were being legislated, the programs were not yet enacted. Government was not yet a major force in people's lives, either in collecting taxes or in providing security or services. Average taxes remained at the low 1918 level of close to $1 for white working-class citizens, who sometimes paid either personal property tax or capitation tax, depending on where they lived. Only the salaried class had enough income to pay state or federal income tax, but even they averaged only $7 in taxes. Personal property and capitation taxes were found mostly in New England and the Southern states, and the average amount of such taxes increased as city size decreased. In the WPA sample, these taxes averaged $4 when they were levied. The typical personal property tax was $2 to $3, and the typical capitation tax was $3 to $4.[128]

The CES did not include sales tax under taxes, since it was included in the price of the item. The WPA budgets give us an indication of the amounts paid in sales tax, which tended to be larger than personal property or capitation tax. It existed mainly in those cities that did not have personal or capitation taxes. The WPA maintenance budget included sales taxes of $20–$25 for Louisville, Detroit, Albuquerque, Cleveland, and San Francisco. Of the cities in the WPA survey, New York had the lowest sales tax, $6.50, for the WPA budget items because it was the only city with a sales tax that excluded all food items.[129]

Economic Security

In contrast to 1918, when blacks and the white working class were spending almost exactly their income, all classes drew upon their assets to pay bills during the Depression since their expenditures exceeded their net incomes.[130] Their ability to rely upon savings reflected both their assets and their access to credit. Black families tended to have few assets and limited credit, and so they could spend only an average of 4% more than their incomes, although they had urgent need to spend more than they made. The white working class, in contrast, spent 7% more than they made, since they had some savings and access to credit. Even the salaried class spent more than their income in 1935, while in 1918 they had a high savings rate (10%).[131]

Installment buying had grown dramatically during the 1920s. Credit buying equaled nearly one-fifth of retail sales at the end of that decade. Borrowing by the working man's family had finally become socially acceptable.[132] Black families were more likely than white families to have their savings in life insurance policies rather than savings accounts and more likely to have installment debt for purchases other than cars. Almost all families bought some life insurance (88.5% of white families and 91.3% of black families). Only a few added to savings accounts (11.6% of white and 6.1% of black), or paid off installment debt (9.2% of white and 16.4% of black).[133]

Although spending their savings decreased the family's economic security, their continued small purchases of life insurance provided some financial security against unexpected deaths. Blacks spent their savings only to pay for their insurance, while the white classes spent their savings to pay for more than insurance. In contrast, relief families depended on installment purchasing, charge accounts, and loans to finance many of their purchases of necessities. These forms of deficit financing augmented their relief payments and sporadic earnings.[134]

Dynamics of Change

Incomes became more unequal between 1918 and 1935, primarily because the lower classes bore the brunt of unemployment. Real disposable income per capita was 2% lower in 1935 than in 1918, but real expenditure was almost 20% higher for white non-relief urban families. They fell 3% for black non-relief urban families. As we have seen, important changes took place in consumption norms between 1918 and 1935 – far more families owned automobiles, almost every home had a radio (along with other electrical appliances), and women bought silk stockings and had their hair permed. These innovations were desired by all classes as they strove to appear modern and adapt to a changing economy.

As hypothesized, then, we witness innovation in consumption accompanying the low output growth, moderate expenditure growth for non-relief families, and increased inequality. Patterns of innovation, which are a signal of improvements in consumption above emulation, were similar across all classes – improved meals accounted for over one-half of innovation, better shelter accounted for one-sixth to one-half (decreasing with class), and more car ownership accounted for around one-tenth (see table 4.19). In addition, some improvement above emulation was made in personal care and personal insurance.

Families were able to pay for innovation in food, shelter, and transportation by reducing in family size (i.e., with savings on food and clothing, while emulation patterns had predicted that family size would grow). For blacks, reducing family size released up to 12% of the total budget, helping them cope with their declining real budget.[135]

All classes, except salaried, slightly reduced their real expenditures on clothing (per capita), household operations, and gifts or contributions. All classes slightly reduced their spending on medical care.

The decline in family size decreased wives' housework hours. Innovation patterns also reflect the improvements in food availability, energy, and housing amenities which helped make meal preparation, clothing care, and house cleaning easier. Changes in clothing styles, toward less formal and complicated attire (especially for females) helped reduce housewives' clothing-care chores. But changes in consumption norms, particularly the widespread purchase of automobiles, central heating, and mechanical appliances, required a costly stock of durable goods. The family's need for money income to purchase these items grew rapidly. These trends, which simultaneously made housework easier, life-styles more complex, and the family more reliant on market goods, were to continue for the next decades – forcing dramatic changes in life-styles and in women's work roles.

Prevailing Standards and Budget Norms

All families whose husbands lost their jobs suffered a substantial decline in their standard of living and experienced severe economic deprivation. But among blacks, even families with an employed head had a difficult time coping. Their limited expenditures purchased only 85% of the goods in the WPA emergency budget. In contrast, the white working class enjoyed a much higher standard of living. The laborer's budget was slightly higher than the WPA maintenance budget (see table 4.17). The wage-earner's budget fell midway between the National Industrial Conference Board (NICB) manual worker's budget and the Heller wage-earner's budget, and it was 21% above the WPA maintenance budget.[136]

The WPA maintenance budget[137] was formulated explicitly for an unskilled manual worker; it did not 'provide for a "decency and health" level which the skilled worker may hope to obtain.'[138] Specifically, the government budget makers thought a 'satisfactory American' standard of living would 'include an automobile, better housing and equipment, a more varied diet [and] preventive medical care,' as well as provision made for 'future education of the children and for economic security through saving.'[139] However, compared to the WPA emergency budget, the maintenance budget allowed a much more varied and interesting material life than allowed by the emergency budget.[140] The Heller budgets estimated 'the cost of a "decency and health" standard of living at various income levels.'[141] All three Heller standards drew upon minimum physiological requirements (as in food) or commonly accepted requirements of health and decency (as in housing), as well as average spending habits that met 'generally accepted ideas of decency and comfort.'[142] The NICB budget[143] provided 'an adequate allowance for the primary necessaries' for the wage-earner's family, and so would be expected to be lower than the Heller budget. According to the NICB, then, wage earners earned more than absolutely required by necessities and allowed them to purchase some items for social integration and personal pleasures.

Dependent or emergency budgets

The WPA emergency budget was representative of the proliferation of subsistence budgets as social workers tried to understand the actual hardships being suffered by families during the Depression and legislators debated relief levels. The Heller dependent budget, which totaled 1% higher, provides an interesting contrast to the WPA emergency budget. The Heller dependent food budget was among the lower-priced budgets that allowed adequate nutrition – eight cost more and three cost less.[144] The WPA emergency budget, which used the US Department of Agriculture (USDA) restricted diet for emergency use, cost 5% less per equivalent adult male than the Heller food budget and did not provide sufficient calories, iron, or vitamin A.[145] Four other budgets that cost about the same as, or less than, the Heller budget also did not provide adequate nutrition. Overall, the Heller Committee's conclusion that their food costs were the minimal required to provide adequate nutrition using established food habits seems reasonable.

The Heller dependent budget for clothing, also minimal relative to local relief standards, represented a 'standard and not the sums which were being actually given by relief organizations to dependent families.' Still, the Heller standard was 'only enough to prevent the family from being so poorly clothed that they would be conspicuous in their usual occupations.'[146] The Heller clothing budget was only slightly higher than the WPA clothing budget, yet Heller included garments for only one season. Overall, the other nine budgets averaged one-third higher than the Heller budget, because they provided clothes for both summer and winter, and a considerably higher clothing allowance for the husband.

Table 4.17 Budget standards, 1935

	Blacks (CES) ($)	WPA emergency ($)	Heller dependent (employed) ($)	Laborers (CES) ($)	Basics ($)	WPA maintenance ($)	NICB[a] ($)	Wage earners (CES) ($)	Heller wage earner ($)	Heller budget clerk ($)	Salaried (CES) ($)	Heller executive ($)
Expenditures	697	918	926	1,165	1,244	1,268	1,340	1,439	1,932	2,384	2,285	5,882[c]
Food	332	358	374	480	448	448	466	546	528	592	679	916
Per equivalent adult male	90	102	107	137	128	128	133	156	151	169	194	262
Clothing	72	112	119	131	139	159	157	158	174	284	288	643
Shelter	214	269	271	354	357	352	341	411	339	445	550	1,208
Rent	124	168	178	217	222	222	244	245	197	271	340	741
Fuel and light	68	82	73	99	99	99	97	111	87	91	137	226
Furniture and furnishings	22	19	20	38	36	31	–	55	55	83	73	241
Miscellaneous	164	179	162	306	300	309	404	419	719	849	898	2,423
Transportation[b]	28	45	53	68	54	54		105	289	315	242	542
Recreation and education	34	19	47	60	69	82		80	102	139	185	424
Household operation	16	21	8	33	24	23		45	34	52	107	383
Medical care	27	47	(47)[g]	42	52	52		53	61	61	103	224
Personal care	15	16	24	22	25	25		27	47	53	48	78
Gifts and contributions	16	10	11	28	27	27[h]		37	61[h]	40	78	257[h]
Personal insurance	25	21	(21)[g]	50	46	46		68	103	155	126	459[j]
Other	3	0[i]	19	3	3	0[i]		4	22	34	9	56

Table 4.17 (*cont.*)

	Blacks (CES) ($)	WPA emergency ($)	Heller dependent (employed) ($)	Laborers (CES) ($)	Basics ($)	WPA maintenance ($)	NICB[a] ($)	Wage earners (CES) ($)	Heller wage earner ($)	Heller budget clerk ($)	Salaried (CES) ($)	Heller executive ($)
Family size	3.4	4.0	4.0	3.4	4.0	4.0	4.0	3.5	5.0	5.0	3.3	4.0
Equivalent adult males	(2.84)	(3.5)	(3.5)	(2.9)	(3.5)	(3.5)	(3.26)	(3.02)	3.75	3.75[d]	(2.8)[d]	3.23
Adjusted expenditures (family of four) $[e,f,k]	782	918	994	1,273	1,244	1,268	1,368	1,535	1,760	2,170	2,417	5,190

a Includes automobile upkeep; otherwise, budget is $70 less. Also, furnishings are included under miscellaneous.

b Heller dependent budget based on family of four (husband, wife, boy 13, girl 8), with husband employed. If husband is unemployed, food, clothing, and car fare are reduced.

c Budget originally included taxes: federal ($62); state income ($21); sales ($60); and personal property ($11); taxes are not included here.

d The 'equivalent adult male' figure is slightly too high since the husband is sedentary rather than moderately active. This is offset by the higher classes' higher food wastage rate.

e The typical family of four (H–W–B13–G8) translated into 3.5 EAM (husband and wife both moderately active). This is used for all families except the Black, WPA emergency and Heller dependent, where the lower-class husbands and wives are assumed to be 'active' in their jobs and housework, and so their EAM is 3.69.

f The clothing adjustment varies slightly by age of children.

g Since family is assumed 'dependent,' they are assumed to receive medical care free at clinics and have no insurance or savings. However, the minimal amounts from WPA emergency budget have been assumed for life insurance and medical care.

h Includes union dues of $12 (WPA maintenance) or $21 (Heller wage earner) or association dues of $36 (Heller executive).

i Budget includes $2.54 for personal property and capitation taxes, taxes are not included here.

j Does not include the $200 allowed for savings for 'emergencies.'

k Adjusted for family of four for food and clothing (and other adjustments where noted).

The Heller budget is deflated by 1.11 to adjust for higher prices in San Francisco. This is the price difference cited in the WPA.

Source: See text for various sources. Taxes and savings have been excluded from budget standards. The CES figures include sales taxes, however.

The Heller and WPA budgets had the same costs for shelter, but the WPA allowance for household operation was considerably higher. The Heller budget was about average for electricity (lighting), toward the high end for gas (cooking), at the low end for coal (heating), and at the low end for house cleaning supplies.

In its allocation, the WPA budget was the most niggardly in recreation and education, which was only 40% of the Heller allotment. Heller was chosen to the norm allowed by the other subsistence budgets, one-half of which allowed budgeting for movie attendance. The Heller budget was at the low end of this group.

A close look at the Heller dependent and WPA emergency budgets leaves one wondering how relief and black families survived on their substandard incomes. Clearly, they had to forgo even necessities, and thus could not lead what was considered by white standards to be normal social and family lives. Falling below minimally acceptable social standards creates painful economic distance, since it reduces all aspects of daily life to the level of active struggle.

Maintenance or working-class budgets

The economic distance between the white working class and black families was vast, since the black families could not even maintain the WPA emergency or Heller dependent standard while white laborers reached the WPA maintenance standard,[147] and white wage earners exceeded the WPA maintenance budget by 20%. Even so, wage-earner families spent 15% less than the more liberal Heller budget for wage earners. The major difference between the WPA maintenance and the Heller wage-earner budgets was that the latter included a used car, an addition that increased the Heller transportation allotment by $235. Obviously, owning a car significantly affected what a family could do, especially during their leisure time and shopping. They were no longer constrained to the areas where they could walk or easily take a streetcar. Two-fifths of the wage-earner families in the CES survey owned a car. Their average automobile costs were $127 less than allowed by Heller, since they drove older cars than assumed by that budget.[148] However, wage-earner families drove their cars about 500 more miles than the 5,000 miles priced in the Heller budget.

Having a car allowed the family to save on the husband's car fare (trolley) to work and other car fares for shopping and outings. The Heller budget allowed only $10 for car fares while the WPA budget allowed $54 for public transportation (when the family had no car). These expenditures for car fares are consistent with the amount spent on public transportation by the CES wage-earner families.

Food costs and life insurance coverage were the other two areas where the Heller budget was more liberal than the WPA budget. In practice, the wage-earner family spent more on food in order to buy more meat and more prepared foods than provided by either budget standard, while their life insurance coverage was midway between the two standards. The Heller budget allowed almost four times as much life insurance for the husband as did the WPA, but contained to burial insurance for other family members.[149] Overall, the family's life-style met or exceeded the pragmatic WPA maintenance budget, but they were still falling short of many of the Heller standards, especially in items involving social life (transportation, recreation, clothing, personal care, gifts and contributions) as well as economic security (life insurance).

Wage-earner and lower salaried budgets

Over one-half of the difference between the Heller budgets for clerks and wage earners was allocated for more clothing and better housing and furnishings. Another quarter of the difference was spent on more life insurance, a better car, and more recreational activities. In practice, a typical salaried family's budget exceeded by 11% Heller's clerk budget, which was one-fourth larger than Heller's wage-earner budget.

The biggest improvement between Heller's wage-earner and clerk budgets was in clothing. The wife's suggested wardrobe was especially improved by her spending twice as much money. For example, the Heller budgets allowed the clerk's wife to buy a winter coat every three years, and a new silk dress, six pairs of silk stockings, and two pairs of street shoes each year. In contrast, the wage-earner's wife was allowed a winter coat every four years, a new silk dress every three years, and three pairs of silk stockings with one and one-half pairs of street shoes each year. The clerk's wife was expected to spend at least 40% more on these articles than the wage-earner's wife. In practice, the salaried family actually spent as much as the Heller clerk's budget for clothing.

The Heller clerk's family was assumed to have an occasional, glamorous social function, since the husband bought a tuxedo every ten years and the wife bought a 'dinner' dress, which cost 28% more than her afternoon silk dress, every three years. The Heller budget allowed the clerk family to take a two-week vacation in a tent (instead of the daily excursions allowed for the wage-earner family) and to entertain guests at home more often. Clerks' families went to more movies and fewer cultural or sports events than assumed by Heller. They also spent more on tobacco, newspapers, and school activities or clubs.

The Heller budgets assumed that the meals of the two families were about the same, but the clerk's family consumed fewer grain products and more fruits and increased by the husband's purchasing lunch at work instead of carrying it. The main items in both food budgets were fresh milk (two cups per person daily) and meat (five ounces per person daily), which accounted for almost 40% of the food budget. In practice, typical salaried families spent 15% more on food than budgeted by Heller.

The Heller budgets assumed that the clerk's family spent considerably more than the wage-earner's family on rent in order to have a larger place (six rooms instead of five) and a better location. Both families were assumed to have electric lights, a radio, and the same cleaning equipment (vacuum cleaner, washing machines, and iron) but the clerk's family used one-sixth more electricity. The clerk's furnishings were valued 50% more than the wage-earner's furnishings and the differential valuation between families went up with its 'showiness.' The value of linens and bedding was only one-third higher, while the value of china and glassware were almost three times higher. Although both families were budgeted a two-party telephone line, the clerk's family was also allowed toll calls and telegrams. Clerks' greater social integration and obligations were also reflected in their postage allowance – 181 letters compared to 78 for the laborer.

The Heller budgets assumed the same car expenses for the wage earner and clerk, based on buying a two-year-old low-priced model for $535. In practice, the car expenses for the salaried family were higher than in the Heller budget because the salaried family traded their cars in one year sooner and drove them about one-third more.

The wage-earner's wife was allowed no help with her housework, while the clerk's wife occasionally could send out laundry and had a cleaning service two days a year. Presumably, this service included waxing the floors since floor wax, along with aluminum cleaner, was included in cleaning supplies for clerks but not for wage earners. In practice, the typical salaried family actually spent one-third more on housing and utilities and twice as much on household operations as budgeted by Heller. In particular, they spent four times as much on domestic service and laundry sent out as the small amount budgeted by Heller.

The 'invisible' executive

Public distancing as the marker of class status became even more important for the executive (or ruling) class. This upper class is not included in our study because it was not included in the CES survey, but the Heller Committee estimated an annual executive budget[150] of $5,190 when adjusted for a family of four, which was 2.4 times the adjusted Heller clerk budget and over twice as much as the CES salaried family actually spent. The hypothesized pattern of economic distance between the executive and salaried families replicated in exaggerated form the actual pattern between salaried and working-class families.

Differences in family meals were fairly minor – higher quality meat and more fresh vegetables and fruits. The most important difference in meals was that the executive husband ate more expensive lunches at work. The executive class set themselves apart by wearing stylish clothing, owning a nice home and furnishings, driving a late model sedan, having domestic servants, and giving gifts and making contributions. Their economic position was made more secure with large life insurance policies and some savings; and their health was protected by high quality preventive care. The Heller budget assumed that the family sent laundry out, had a maid one day a week and a baby-sitter one-half day a week, and had five extra days of help a year for cleaning and gardening. The family's home, valued by Heller at $8,400, had a carrying cost three times the Heller clerk's rent for a six-room house. The executive family was assumed to have a private telephone line, a refrigerator, and small electrical appliances, and to use sterling (not plated) flatware and good china and glassware, which were worth four times as much as the clerk family's collection. The Heller budget allowed family members to have their hair styled more often and to have a large variety of clothes, including evening clothes for social events. The parents' assumed active social life included monthly attendance at a cultural event (theater, concerts, opera); entertaining guests every three weeks (16 times yearly); renting a cottage for their two-week vacation; and frequent dining out at a restaurant or hotel. The children had music lessons; the parents belonged to a club. The husband had a life insurance policy that paid $115 a month for premature death, or $16,000 for retirement. The family saved $200 a month for emergencies. By modern standards, however, this elite, material life was modest and the family economized in many areas.

Economic Distance

The most visible economic distance between blacks and whites was in housing. Blacks, segregated from whites, were housed in the most run-down part of town. Their housing was dilapidated and substandard – only one-half of the black families had flush toilets or electric lights, one-fifth had hot water, and one-sixth had gas or electric cooking or modern (i.e., hot air, hot water or steam) heating. These were all standard features in whites' housing. Thirty percent of black families still did not have running water inside their homes, and telephone service was virtually nonexistent for them.

Black families also severely economized on other basics – food, clothing, streetcar rides, and household operations – in order to spend more than the 'emergency' budget allowed for recreation, gifts, church contributions, 'burial' insurance, and furnishings and equipment. Since blacks could not hope to achieve white norms and social integration, they tried in small ways to bring some material diversity and fulfillment, along with some security, into their bleak and precarious material lives. Yet,

Table 4.18 Economic distance across groups, 1935

	Laborers to blacks			Wage earners to laborers			Salaried to wage earners		
	Ratio	Difference ($395) ($468)		Ratio	Difference ($282) ($274)		Ratio	Difference ($904) ($846)	
Relative net income	1.586			1.264			1.670		
Relative consumption expenditures	1.671			1.235			1.588		
Distribution of increased consumption	Distribution	Difference ($)	% increase	Distribution	Difference ($)	% increase	Distribution	Difference ($)	% increase
Total	100%	(468)		100%	(274)		100%	(846)	
Total food and clothing	0.393	(184)	57.7	0.383	(105)	20.9	0.266	(225)	37.0
Food (per unit)[a]	2.960	(139)	54.3	0.190	(52)	13.0	0.205	(173)	36.7
Clothing (per person)	0.083	(39)	62.8	0.104	(29)	28.0	0.130	(110)	80.9
Change in family size	0.015	(7)		0.088	(24)		-0.069	(-58)	
Shelter	0.301	(141)	65.9	0.204	(56)	15.7	0.164	(139)	33.8
Housing	0.199	(93)	75.0	0.102	(28)	12.9	0.112	(95)	38.8
Fuel, light, water	0.066	(31)	45.6	0.044	(12)	12.1	0.031	(26)	23.4
Furnishings	0.036	(17)	77.3	0.058	(16)	41.0	0.021	(18)	32.7
Miscellaneous	0.306	(143)	87.2	0.409	(112)	36.5	0.567	(480)	114.3
Transportation	0.085	(40)	142.9	0.135	(37)	54.4	0.162	(137)	130.5
Recreation, education, tobacco	0.056	(26)	76.5	0.073	(20)	33.3	0.124	(105)	129.6
Household operations	0.036	(17)	106.3	0.040	(11)	33.3	0.076	(64)	145.5
Medical care	0.032	(15)	55.6	0.040	(11)	26.2	0.059	(50)	94.3
Personal care	0.015	(7)	46.7	0.018	(3)	22.7	0.025	(21)	77.8
Gifts, contributions	0.026	(12)	100.0	0.033	(9)	32.1	0.048	(41)	110.8
Personal insurance	0.053	(25)	33.3	0.066	(18)	36.0	0.069	(58)	85.3
Other	0.002	(1)		0.004	(1)	25.0	0.005	(4)	80.0

[a] Per expenditure unit for wage earners to laborers; per person for salaried to wage earner.
Source: BLS Bulletin 638.

these black employed families were much better off than the black families living on relief.

The substandard incomes of black and relief families forced them to forgo even necessities. Their severe economic deprivation rendered the simplest daily activities, such as preparing food, providing clean clothes, and living in a safe, warm place, problematic. The economic distance created among the three white classes with employed heads was more subtle. Although it determined social and private activities, it did not preclude families in these classes from participating in normal social and family life.

White laborer families, who spent two-thirds more than black families, increased their expenditures by at least 45% across all categories (see table 4.18). The categories of food, medical care, fuel and utilities, and personal care increased the least, while expenditures for transportation, household operations, and personal insurance more than doubled.

The white laborer family spent almost exactly the amount prescribed by the WPA maintenance budget. Laborers' extra money spent on food was provided primarily by the reduced amount spent on clothes. Laborers spent almost two-thirds more on clothing than did blacks, but their wardrobes were still meager and their clothing well-worn. They felt a greater need to meet (or exceed) the nutritional content and diversity of the 'standard' diet than to meet the prevailing clothing standards. This probably reflects the reality that improving their diets would improve their health and make daily mealtimes more pleasant, while improving their wardrobes would not necessarily improve their limited social activities or rugged work lives. Improvements in these latter areas would require holding different jobs and having higher positions in the social structure – changes that, by definition, would make them no longer laborers.

One-third of laborer families owned a car, and so laborers spent more on transportation than the WPA maintenance standards, which did not allow car ownership.[151] Although their social lives were still simple, most laborer families were engaging in those activities that were the initial steps in developing the personal regimes for a more active and formalized social life.

The economic distance between wage earners and white laborers was narrow and equaled only $274. In contrast, the economic distance between salaried and wage-earner families was much broader, equaling $846. This distance was characterized by major improvements in transportation, recreation, household operations, and clothing.

Compared to the wage-earner family, the salaried family spent considerably more for a vacation and also spent considerably more for tobacco or cigarettes. In addition, salaried families went to the movies more often, bought more newspapers and magazines, and spent more on children's school activities and associations. In each of these ways, the

Table 4.19 Shifts in urban consumption norms, 1918–35[a]

Total expenditures	Realized emulation (RE)	Innovation (IN)	Disemulation	Reduced standard (RS)	Expenditure
Blacks	0	0.120	0	-0.154	-0.034
Laborers	0.037	0.205	0.035	-0.071	0.170
Wage earners	0.034	0.232	0.036	-0.075	0.190
Salaried	0.045	0.265	0.053	-0.108	0.201

Expenditure category	Blacks			Laborers			Wage earners			Salaried		
	RE	IN	RS	RE	IN	RS	RE	IN	RS	RE	IN	RS
Food per capita	0	0.063	0	0.011	0.113	0	0.007	0.133	0	0.014	0.16	0
Clothing per capita	0	0	-0.003	0	0	-0.005	0	0	-0.002	0.011	0	0
Family size	0	0	-0.124	0	0	-0.047	0	0	-0.056	0	0	-0.096
Housing	0	0.031	0	0.009	0.034	0	0.008	0.031	0	0.003	0.024	0
Fuel and light	0	0.026	0	0.002	0.020	0	0.002	0.019	0	0.002	0.016	0
Furnishing	0	0	-0.003	0.002	0.002	0	0.005	0.001	0	0.002	0.002	0
Miscellaneous	0	0	-0.024	—	—	—	—	—	—	—	—	—
Transportation	NA	NA	NA	0.004	0.022	0	0.006	0.027	0	0.006	0.024	0
Recreation and education	—	—	—	0.005	0	0	0.003	0	0	0	0	-0.005
Household operations	—	—	—	0	0	-0.005	0	0	-0.004	0.001	0.010	0
Medical care	—	—	—	0	0	-0.007	0	0	-0.005	0	0	-0.003
Personal care	—	—	—	0.001	0.007	0	0.001	0.008	0	0.002	0.005	0
Gifts and contributions	—	—	—	0	0	-0.003	0	0	-0.004	0.003	0	0
Personal insurance	—	—	—	0.003	0.007	0	0.002	0.013	0	0.001	0.023	0
Other	—	—	—	0	0	-0.004	0	0	-0.003	0	0	0

[a] Definitions are given on page 5 and formulas on pages 19–20 (footnote 5)

salaried family was more socially active and better integrated into the community than the wage-earner family. This difference was also reflected in the salaried family's much higher budgets for contributions to church and charities and for gifts.

Salaried families were also much more mobile than their wage-earner counterparts. Three-fourths of them owned an automobile, which they drove about 25% more miles (or 110 more miles monthly) than the wage-earner families with cars. Although most purchased used cars, salaried families had fairly late model vehicles (compared to wage earners), and they tended to trade them in every three years. Even though they averaged over twice as many miles by car, salaried families also rode the trolley one-third more than wage-earner families.

In addition to richer social lives and greater mobility, the salaried family also had greater security in the form of some preventive medical care, better life insurance (or retirement) policies, and the ability to pay their bills without dipping into their savings (and, in fact, increased assets from payments for homes and cars). The salaried family carried twice as much life insurance as the wage-earner family, so that the husband was covered by a policy that paid $32 a month for early death or $4,600 at age 65 (or a $40 monthly annuity at age 65).[152] As meager as these amounts were, they provided a much better death or retirement cushion than the working-class families could buy. The great majority of families had no cushion at all until the late 1930s, when the Social Security Act of 1935 went into effect.

The economic distance between the salaried class and the working class was less subtle and more public than the distance between the two divisions of the white working class or between the white working class and blacks. Although the everyday private lives of families in the lower economic classes were dramatically affected, their public lives were limited, and so the economic distance did not tend to be acted out publicly. The economic distance between the salaried class and the working (or lower) classes was much more visible as public activities became a more important part of their lives. Appearance, mobility, and social activities as well as greater security set the salaried class apart in tangible as well as symbolic ways.

The Standards of Living

The disparate impact of the Depression on whites and blacks is vividly captured in the Standard of Living Index for basics (see table 4.20). The already large gap that existed in 1918 between the black and white working classes in their ability to purchase basics widened during the Depression. Blacks improved their consumption of basics only slightly, while the white laborer basics index was over 20% higher in 1918 than in 1935.

Table 4.20 Standard of living index, 1935

Expenditure differences	Laborers (1935) to laborers (1918) ($) 264				Black to laborers ($) 468			Wage earners minus laborers ($) 274			Salaried to wage earners ($) 846		
	B 1918	B 1935	Variety	Status	Basics	Variety	Status	Basics	Variety	Status	Basics	Variety	Status
Food and Clothing													
Food	58	(21)	21	0	(124)	(21)	0	B	69	0	(11)	141	1
Clothing	(10)	(7)	0	0	(39)	0	0	15	11	8	(3)	56	42
Shelter													
Rent	23	46	0	0	(93)	0	0	5	7	16	B	48	47
Fuel and light	3	35	0	0	(31)	0	0	B	10	2	B	17	10
Furnishings	4	(4)	2	0	(14)	(2)	0	B	13	4	B	14	4
Miscellaneous													
Transportation	11	16	10	4	(26)	(10)	(4)	B	28	9	B	92	45
Medical	(6)	0	0	0	(15)	0	0	10	1	0	B	50	0
Household operations	2	(2)	8	0	(9)	(8)	0	B	0	12	B	0	62
Recreation and education	B	6	5	(1)	(21)	(5)	0	9	9	2	B	21	84
Personal care	B	10	0	0	(7)	0	0	3	1	1	B	11	10
Gifts and contributions	2	7	1	0	(11)	(1)	0	B	9	0	B	41	0
Personal insurance	2	17	4	0	(21)	(4)	0	B	18	0	B	58	0
Other	B	(3)	(2)	0	B	0	0	B	1	0	B	5	0
Subtotal	89	100	49	3	(411)	(51)	(4)	42	177	54	(14)	554	305
Proportion of total	0.34	0.38	0.19	0.01	0.88	0.11	0.01	0.15	0.65	0.20	-0.02	0.65	0.36

B denotes basic standard has been met.

Disparities in basics between the white salaried and working classes almost disappeared between 1918 and 1935 as the white working class came close to fulfilling most basic needs. Salaried families' higher living standard was evidenced mainly in variety and status components. The gap between the black and white families widened noticeably in all three components.

Among whites, a family's ability to protect its material position during the Depression increased with its class status. The variety gap between laborers and wage earners grew, and the variety and status gaps between wage earners and salaried workers grew. In relative terms, the variety gap, and especially the status gap, between salaried and working-class families continued to exceed the income gap in 1935. Salaried incomes were two-thirds higher than wage-earner incomes, but their variety consumption was three times higher and their status consumption seven times higher.

Laborers' incomes had grown sufficiently that they could now purchase a few items for variety. Still, most of their income growth was allocated to basics (0.8), and they still did not spend money on status (see table 4.20). Wage-earner and salaried families spent most of their relatively higher budgets on variety. Wage earners' higher standard of living relative to laborer families was allocated to variety (0.65), with the remainder split between basics (0.15) and status (0.20). Salaried families' also allocated 0.65 of their larger budget relative to wage-earner families to variety, and they spent the rest on status. Blacks' lower standard of living relative to laborers still was primarily in basics (0.9), with the rest reflecting reduced variety. One indicator of the improvement in living standards between 1918 and 1935 was the increasing importance of variety and comfort items and the declining importance of basics in the family's budget, and altogether, salaried families spent as much on variety and status as they did on basics. Wage earners spent 11% of their budgets on basics, and 16% on variety; laborers spent 96% of their budgets on basics.

How much higher was the standard of living in 1935 than in 1918? The answer depends on how we weigh improvements in the three components, and this differs for each class. Since all classes experienced an improvement in basics, we can say that the standard of living rose. But as we saw above, the income index and the component indices have different growth patterns. In 1935, the status index for salaried families was two-thirds higher than their 1918 level, while the variety index was one-half higher and the basics index only slightly (8%) higher. Wage earners exhibited the same trend in improvements. Overall, these indices show blacks falling further behind whites, with a slight convergence in living standards among the white classes.

Although social scientists agree that the Depression resulted in unnecessary economic loss for the nation, there is much less consensus over how to evaluate the Depression's relative impact on families. Compared to 1918, the black standard of living had deteriorated in 1935 relative to the white standard, yet the gap between the white working and salaried classes had declined, so that economic divergence by race was tempered by some convergence across white classes. In the midst of the Depression, the salaried family was spending 70% as much on variety and 28% as much on status as the laborer family was spending on basics. Although real per capita disposable income was 2.7% higher in 1935 than in 1918, the black family's income was only 1% higher, while the white working-class family's income was over 15% higher. The Depression eroded dreams of making substantial economic progress. And it made most families anxious about the future. It did not, however, have much impact on the overall standard of living of the three urban white classes with employed husbands. The burden of decline was shouldered by black families, farm families, and white families with unemployed husbands. Most of white America continued to consume the products of an increasingly sophisticated economy that allowed for an active social life and required integration into the marketplace.

NOTES

1. The period 1929–50 was another of leveling in pay: in 1929, the average income of the richest fifth was 15.5 times that of the poorest fifth; in 1951, the ratio was 9:1. Jeffrey G. Williamson and Peter H. Lindert, *American Inequality: A Macroeconomic History* (New York: Academic Press, 1980), Ch. 4.

2. The top 1% received 13% of disposable income in 1923, 19% in 1929, and 7% at the end of World War II. Charles F. Holt, 'Who Benefitted from the Prosperity of the Twenties?' *Explorations in Economic History*, 14, 3 (July 1977), pp. 277–89. The distribution of wealth followed a similar pattern, as the top 1% of adults held 31.6% of personal sector wealth in 1922, 36.3% in 1929, 28.3% in 1933, and 20.8% in 1949. Robert J. Langman, *The Share of Top Wealth-Holders in National Wealth*, National Bureau of Economic Research (Princeton, NJ: Princeton University Press, 1962), p. 24.

   About 35%–37% of non-farm families were estimated to be poor in 1929, since working class families were usually pushed into poverty if they had 'work problems' (sickness, unemployment, old age). Frank Stricker, 'Affluence for Whom? Another Look at Prosperity and the Working Classes in the 1920s,' *Labor History*, 24, 1 (Winter 1983), pp. 5–33.

3. National income figures are from the US Department of Commerce, Bureau of the Census, *Historical Statistics of the United States:*

Colonial Times to 1970, Bicentennial ed. (Washington, DC: US Department of Commerce, Bureau of the Census, 1975), Series F 9, F 26. Personal income was deflated by the wholesale price index in 1919 and the GNP price deflator for consumption expenditures thereafter.

4. Relief families comprised 8.9% of farm families, 19.3% of rural non-farm families, and 16.5% of urban families in 1935–6. US National Resources Committee, *Family Expenditures in the United States*, released by the Executive Office of the President, National Resources Planning Board (Washington, DC: US Government Printing Office, 1941), Table 20. Thirty percent of urban black households were on relief in 1933 (estimated by the ratio of urban relief black households in 1933 to urban black households in the 1930 census). Works Progress Administration (WPA), *Urban Workers on Relief: Part 1, The Occupational Characteristics of Workers on Relief in Urban Areas, May 1934*, by Gladys L. Palmer and Katherine D. Wood, Research Monograph, No. 4 (Washington, DC: Works Progress Administration, 1936), p. 6. However, the Consumer Expenditure Survey (CES) assumed one-half of blacks in urban areas were on relief. US Department of Labor, Bureau of Labor Statistics (BLS), *Money Disbursements of Wage Earners and Clerical Workers, 1934–36: Summary Volume*, by Faith M. Williams and Alice C. Hanson, Bulletin, No. 638 (Washington, DC: US Government Printing Office, 1941), p. 367. Transfer payments equaled 4% of personal income in 1935.

5. Calculations are from Census Bureau, *Historical Statistics*, using Series D 726–7, D 740, D 762.

6. Most families were forced to do some economizing, but usually in trivial ways if the head remained employed. For example, one study of skilled workers' families, one-half of whom had incomes above $2500, showed that these select families economized during the Depression by curtailing entertaining both outside and inside the home, reducing club memberships, delaying purchase of new cars or new homes, curtailing magazine subscriptions, and foregoing music and dancing lessons. Winona L. Morgan, *The Family Meets the Depression* (Minneapolis: University of Minnesota Press, 1939), pp. 22–3.

7. According to Stanley Lebergott, *Manpower in Economic Growth: The American Record Since 1800* (New York: McGraw-Hill, 1964), average real earnings when employed were about 20% higher in 1934–5 than in 1918–19. If earnings are adjusted for unemployment, then real earnings fell around 10%. However, this method spreads unemployment evenly across the workforce when, in fact, it was experienced primarily by a hard-core group, along with some reduction in hours for employed workers.

8. Unskilled male manufacturing wages were the same in 1935 as in 1920; skilled male wages were 4% higher in 1935. National Industrial Conference Board (NICB), *Wages, Hours and Employment in the United States, 1914–1936*, by M. Ada Beney (New York: National Industrial Conference Board, 1936), Ch. 3, Tables 2–4.

9. The cash component, which varied by state, increased from May 1934 through July 1935 from an average 46% to 64% of the total relief benefit. In-kind benefits were (about) 50% as food and supplies, 15% each as shelter and fuel/utilities, and 10% as clothing. In January 1935, 54% of cases received direct (cash and in-kind) relief only, 30% received work relief only, and 16% received both. Work relief payments averaged about 15% more than direct relief. Works Progress Administration, *Average General Relief Benefits, 1933–38*, by Enid Baird (Washington, DC: US Government Printing Office, 1940), pp. 6–7, 44.

10. Sixteen percent of all urban relief families with four or five persons had some private earnings.

11. Only 45% of blacks lived in urban areas, and about 60% of urban blacks lived in the South. In Cotton Belt towns, blacks averaged $10 and whites $15 monthly. In 13 cities, blacks averaged $24 and whites $29. WPA, *Relief Benefits*, pp. 18, 30.

12. Even the Heller budget exceeded the WPA budget in San Francisco by $79 when medical care and life insurance are added to the Heller budget. The Heller Committee compared 31 food standards and ten relief clothing standards and found other budget items not comparable. Heller Committee for Research in Social Economics, University of California, Berkeley, *Standards of Relief in Selected Cities of the United States, 1933* (Berkeley: University of California, June 1934).

13. Calculated from occupational distribution and Works Progress Administration, *The 1935 Relief Population in 13 Cities*, Research Bulletin, Series 1, No. 23 (Washington, DC: Works Progress Administration, December 1936), Table 7, and National Resources Committee, *Family Expenditures*, Tables 55, 360. This rate is high for urban black families with a husband present, since it includes 'broken families,' who were 23%–37% of black families, depending on the region and town size. US National Resources Committee, *Consumer Incomes in the U.S.: Their Distribution in 1935–36* (Washington, DC: US Government Printing Office, 1938), p. 73.

14. Since managers and professionals were not included in the 1934–6 CES, their consumption expenditures are taken from the 1935–6 Survey.

15. The National Industrial Conference Board (NICB) estimates were probably conservative in 1935, since they were below other earnings

estimated in 1918, and the 1934–6 income distribution was biased upward since lower-income families were not sampled. These income categories are between these two estimates and are consistent with the 1935–36 National Resources Committee median. In addition, they are consistent with the Kuznets estimates.

16. The ratio of white-collar to manual annual earnings was 2.04 in 1915, 1.48 in 1920, 1.75 in 1928, and 1.58 in 1933. Robert K. Burns, 'The Comparative Economic Position of Manual and White-Collar Employees,' *The Journal of Business*, 27, 4 (Oct. 1954), pp. 257–67.

17. The residual group is non-rural farm. Bureau of the Census, *Historical Statistics*, Series A 73–81. The migration from farms to cities that occurred during the 1920s stopped during the Depression. The percentage of the population living on farms declined from 30% in 1920 to 25% in 1930, and then fell slightly to 23% in 1940; the percentage living in urban areas rose from 51.4% in 1920 to 56.2% in 1930 and 56.5% in 1940.

18. The 1935 figures are from the US Department of Commerce, Office of Business Economics, *The National Income and Product Accounts of the U.S., 1929–1965: Statistical Tables*, a supplement to the *Survey of Current Business* (Washington, DC: US Government Printing Office, 1966).

19. The major increases occurred in clerical work (from 19% to 22%), service work (from 8% to 11%), and private household work (from 16% to 18%). The percentage in operative, craft, and laborer jobs fell by 2%, while the percentage in professional and managerial jobs rose by 2%.

20. Women aged 14–19 decreased their participation rate from 28% (1920) to 19% (1940), while women aged 20–24 increased their participation rate from 38% to 46%, and women aged 25–44 increased their participation rate from 22% to 31%. Wives' participation rate increased from 9% to 14%.

21. About 10% of the women never married (calculated from Bureau of the Census, *Historical Statistics*, Series A 160–71). These women were much more likely to be employed.

22. The adjusted figures for both relief and non-relief families were calculated using the relief percentage by occupation. In May 1935, only 14% of the relief cases had non-relief earnings. Urban relief payments averaged $34 monthly ($408 yearly) in the first half of 1935. Works Progress Administration, *Source of Income of Former Urban Relief Cases*, Research Bulletin, Series 1, No. 22 (Washington, DC: Works Progress Administration, Sept. 1936); WPA, *1935 Relief Population*; WPA, *Relief Benefits*, p. 26.

23. About 15% of the working class reported income from lodgers (including boarders) which provided over half of their 'other income.'

(In 1918, boarders were not included in income assessments.) In 1918, up to three-fourths of the white classes reported gifts, which accounted for at least 40% of their 'other income.' Gifts were received by 11% of laborers and wage earners in 1935 (and only 2% of salaried workers).

24. This figure is calculated as 94% of the number of married women (14 years and over) divided by total households, since around 94% of married couples had their own household during this period. An upper bound of 90% husband-wife households is derived from 100% of married men (14 years and over) divided by total households.

25. The percentage of one-person households in 1935 was between 7% and 8%, of two-person households, about 24%, and of three-person households, 68%. Earlier comparable figures were available only for 1900, when 5% of the households were one person, 15% were two persons, and 80% were three or more persons. Bureau of the Census, *Historical Statistics*, Series A 335–52.

26. Lance E. Davis et al., *American Economic Growth: An Economic History of the U.S.* (New York: Harper & Row, 1972), Ch. 3, 'Consumption and the Style of Life,' covers the period from mid-1800s to 1930s.

27. Ruth Schwartz Cowan, 'The "Industrial Revolution" in the Home: Household Technology and Social Change in the 20th Century,' *Technology and Culture*, 17, 1 (Jan. 1976), pp. 1–23. These changes occurred even within a city. For example, 60% of Middletown families had electricity in 1916 and 99% had it in 1925. Rural areas received electrical service later than urban areas. Robert S. Lynd and Helen M. Lynd, *Middletown: A Study in American Culture* (New York: Harcourt, Brace & World, 1929), Ch. 9.

28. Cowan, 'Household Technology'; see also Lynd and Lynd, *Middletown*, and *Middletown in Transition* (New York: Harcourt, Brace & Co., 1937), and Margaret G. Reid, *The Economics of Household Production* (New York: J. Wiley, 1934).

29. Richard Wightman Fox and T.J. Jackson Lears, eds, *The Culture of Consumption: Critical Essays in American History, 1880–1980* (New York: Pantheon, 1983).

30. Lynd and Lynd, *Middletown*, p. 168, Chs 8, 12. C. Wesley Mitchell also emphasized the complex decision making process required by housewives in *The Backward Art of Spending Money and Other Essays* (New York: McGraw-Hill, 1937).

31. The 1918 and 1935 surveys did not survey the same populations since the earlier survey included only families with a husband, wife, and at least one child. The inclusion of all families in the 1935 survey decreases the average family size by 0.7 to 0.8 persons for our three classes. Since this difference in family size affects the

composition of the budget, we first compare the 1918 and 1935 budgets for white, urban wage-earner families who had a husband, wife, and child present; 54% of the 1935 families are husband and wife with children under 16. Another 15% are husband and wife with other adults (including older children). Another 21% are husband and wife only. The remaining 10% are mixtures of adults and children. BLS, *Money Disbursements*, pp. 44–5.

32. Personal insurance payments were treated as a positive addition to assets in 1935 rather than as an expenditure (as in 1918), so reported expenditures exceeded net income by 3.3%, compared to falling 6% short of net income in 1918 (also excluding personal insurance) for wage-earner families. When personal insurance is included as an expenditure, expenditures are 97% of net income in 1918 and 109% (estimated) of net income in 1934 for families with children. The difference between total disbursements and total receipts in a family's budget is the balancing difference, which represents discrepancies in recall. Schedules were not included in the survey when the balance was more than 5% of the larger figure. BLS, *Money Disbursements*, p. 386.

33. These price changes are calculated for the goods purchased by survey families in 35 large cities (out of the 42 cities in the 1934–6 survey) and for the 92 cities in the 1918 survey. BLS, *Money Disbursements*, p. 38. Nationally, the Consumer Price Index declined 9% between 1917–19 and 1934–6. Food prices declined 39%, clothing prices 32%, and rent 1%. Calculated from Bureau of the Census, *Historical Statistics*, Series E 135–56.

34. When 1918 expenditures are calculated using 1934–6 prices, food and clothing account for 10 percentage points less of the budget in 1918. However, the share of real food expenditures in the budget rose and clothing's share fell between 1918 and 1935. Real food expenditures per person were $83 in 1918 and $113 in 1935; real clothing expenditures per person were $36 in 1918 and $33 in 1935. If we compare the budgets of wage-earner families with children to the budgets of all wage earners (the latter had 0.72 fewer persons per family), we find that the larger sample spent 2 percentage points less on food and 1 percentage point more on shelter and miscellaneous items. They also dissaved 1.7% more of their income.

35. Robert Lynd, 'The Consumer Becomes a "Problem," ' in *The Ultimate Consumer: A Study in Economic Illiteracy*, J.G. Brainerd, ed., *The Annals*, 173 (May 1934), pp. 1–6.

36. Works Progress Administration, *Quantity Budgets of Goods and Services Necessary for a Basic Maintenance Standard of Living and for Operation Under Emergency Conditions*, by Margaret Loomis

Stecker, Research Bulletin, Series 1, No. 21 (Washington, DC: Works Progress Administration, 1936), p. 17.

37. As in 1918, the diet of the sample's average family is representative of the diet of the average wage-earner family, in terms of cost. Food expenditures (per food expenditure unit) for the entire sample were 4% higher than for the white wage-earner group; the weekly expenditures per person were 5% higher. In the 1934–6 survey, detailed food data were collected by recall for the previous seven days. The data were then adjusted for seasonal differences to obtain annual averages.

38. The 'minimum-cost adequate diet' of the Bureau of Home Economics (BHE) was the same in cost as the 'emergency level diet' of the Works Progress Administration. The WPA maintenance budget, which allowed $2.15 weekly per person, allocated 32% more for food than their emergency level diet, which allowed $1.63 weekly per person. In contrast, the BHE 'moderate-cost adequate diet' cost 65% more and their emergency level diet cost 28% less than the minimum cost diet. US Department of Agriculture, Bureau of Home Economics, *Diets at Four Levels of Nutritive Content and Cost*, by Hazel K. Stiebeling and Medora M. Ward, USDA Circular, No. 296 (Washington, DC: US Government Printing Office, Nov. 1933); Works Progress Administration, *Intercity Differences in Costs of Living in March 1935, 59 Cities*, by Margaret Loomis Stecker, Research Monograph, No. 12 (Washington, DC: US Government Printing Office, 1937). In the 1935 survey, 44% of the nation's children were members of families who did not spend as much on food as recommended by the WPA maintenance budget. BLS, *Money Disbursements*, p. 85.

39. According to a Brookings study, families seemed more likely to meet nutritional goals in 1929, when families in the $800–$1,200 (in 1934–5 dollars) income range spent enough for an 'adequate diet at minimum cost.' Three-quarters of the total population did not have the required income of at least $2,400 to provide 'an adequate diet at moderate cost.' Maurice Leven, Harold Moulton, and Warburton Clark, *America's Capacity to Consume* (Washington, DC: Brookings Institution, 1934), pp. 121–4.

40. See, for example, Henry C. Sherman, *Chemistry of Food and Nutrition*, 3rd edn, rewritten and enl. (New York: Macmillan, 1927), Ch. 20.

41. BLS, *Money Disbursements*, pp. 35–6.

42. The milk distribution program brought average daily milk consumption in New York to 14 ounces per person or almost the level considered adequate by nutritionists.

43. The average diet in 1918 contained 31% too little calcium and 19% too little iron in a limited sample. William F. Ogburn, 'A Study of

Food Costs in Various Cities,' *Monthly Labor Review*, 9, 2 (Aug. 1919), p. 21.

44. Letitia Brewster and Michael F. Jacobson, *The Changing American Diet* (Washington, DC: Center for Science in the Public Interest, 1978), p. 65. The 1935 data indicate that the 1918 national disappearance data (i.e., national per capita averages based on production output) on vitamin A were not representative of actual consumption in urban areas.

45. National Research Council 1980 dietary standards are used here to analyze the 1935 diets. Protein and vitamin A standards averaged 40% higher in 1935 than in 1918; iron standards averaged 6% lower in 1935; vitamin B_1 standards averaged 15% higher in 1935; riboflavin (vitamin G) standards were 30% higher in 1935. Pellagra-preventive (niacin) standards were not given, and a serious deficiency was still found in low-income groups in the southeast (as in 1918). Vitamin A intake varied widely by region and by season.

46. Black families averaged $90 per food expenditure unit; the lowest CES income group averaged $114.

47. The weekly amount needed per person to provide an inexpensive, adequate diet, based on local practices in terms of the kinds and quantities of food purchased, varied from $1.70 for blacks in the South to $2.20 for whites in the East South Central, and $2.45 for whites in the North Atlantic. These cost variations primarily reflect different food choices, since price differences account for only 4% of the variation. US Department of Agriculture, Bureau of Home Economics, *Diets of Families of Employed Wage Earners and Clerical Workers in Cities*, by Hazel K. Stiebeling and Esther F. Phipard, USDA Circular, No. 507 (Washington, DC: US Government Printing Office, 1939), p. 83.

48. The following discussion is based on two data sources: a special study of 4,000 of CES survey families (see Bureau of Home Economics, *Diets of Families*), and a comparable analysis of diets from the 1935–6 National Resources Committee survey (see US Department of Agriculture, Bureau of Home Economics, *Family Food Consumption and Dietary Levels, 5 Regions*, by Hazel K. Stiebeling et al., USDA Miscellaneous Publication, No. 405 (Washington, DC: US Government Printing Office, 1941)). In the comparisons made in the text, laborers whose income group spent $2.20 weekly per person in the 1935–6 National Resources Committee survey are represented by the group spending $1.88–$2.49 in the special CES study; wage earners who averaged $2.60 are represented by the group spending $2.50–$3.12; and salaried workers who averaged $3.20 are represented by the group spending $3.13–$3.74. Thus, the figures in the text are high for wage-earner and salaried-worker families.

49. The 1935 allowance was 3,000 calories for a moderately active man and 2,500 for a moderately active woman. This is the same as the National Research Council's guidelines in 1941. Because of differences in the allowances for children and changes in family size, the 3,300 calories per equivalent adult male benchmark used in 1918 is equivalent to 3,050 in 1935; both are equivalent to the 1941 standards for moderately active adults. None of these caloric standards allows for waste.

50. For many laborers, a 4,000 caloric allowance would be more appropriate. This would require that the family's benchmark be around 3,300 (declining as the number of children increases).

51. The percentage breakdown of nutrient intake was given only for selected white groups, including the group below laborers (families who spent $1.25–$1.87 per person weekly) and the wage-earner group. The black family in our study fit into this group, spending only $1.73 weekly per person compared to $1.33–$2.19 in the special study. The $2.19 figure was increased by 10% to make it apply to 'active work' rather than 'moderate work' for the husband. Bureau of Home Economics, *Diets of Families.*

52. Overall, the percentage of families with inadequate nutrition would have registered about 15 percentage points higher had the CES survey included families on relief during the 1934–5 survey period, when 16.5% of urban families received some relief. When relief was at a peak, around 20% of the families in industrial cities such as Boston, Pittsburgh, Grand Rapids, Lansing, and Birmingham were on relief. Other cities, such as Minneapolis, Dallas, Houston and Memphis, had peak relief rates under 10%. Bureau of Home Economics, *Diets of Families*, Table 70.

53. 'Waste' does not include refuse or inedible material of purchased food. In 1918, 10% wastage was considered typical (Ogburn, 'A Study of Food Costs,' p. 8). In 1935, 20% was used to indicate 'considerable kitchen or plate waste of food' (Bureau of Home Economics, *Diets of Families*, p. 45). Levels of waste or spoilage above 10%–20% indicate above-normal sloppiness in food choice, preparation, and preservation, along with finicky eating at the table or over-eating.

   One study on low-income diets allowed a 5% 'safety margin' for waste. Sample menus, which used many different types of meat, were given. Ruth Okey and Emily Huntington, 'Adequate Food at Low Cost,' *The Pacific Coast Journal of Nursing*, 28, 5 (May 1932), pp. 279–83.

54. The higher figure reflects families in which the man's job was sedentary, thus reducing his need for calories. Using the 1941 allowance of 2,500 calories for a man with a sedentary job produces

an allowance of 2,850 calories per unit, which increases with the number of children.

55. Suggested menus for the low-cost food budget for one week are given in US Department of Agriculture, Bureau of Human Nutrition and Home Economics, *Helping Families Plan Food Budgets*, USDA Miscellaneous Publication, No. 662 (Washington, DC: US Government Printing Office, 1950), p. 8. In general, those menus would fit into the typical meals presented in Table 4.5.

56. Meals similar to these were found in a San Francisco study of streetcarmen's and clerks' families. The usual diet consisted of fruit and coffee for breakfast with one main dish of cereal, eggs, bacon, pancakes, or French toast. Lunch was usually a light meal of sandwiches, soup or salad, or leftovers, and sometimes included fruit. Dinner nearly always included meat and potatoes, a vegetable and/or salad, and a dessert (often fruit). Children were given milk at one meal. The families were spending more than enough for an adequate diet, but they were consuming too much meat and too little milk, citrus and tomatoes for nutritional needs. Emily H. Huntington and Mary Gorringe Luck, *Living on a Moderate Income: The Incomes and Expenditures of Street-Car Men's and Clerks' Families in the San Francisco Bay Region* (Berkeley and Los Angeles: University of California Press, 1937), pp. 60–6, 177.

57. The comparison across classes must be made on the basis of families categorized by expenditure units (expenditures divided by a standardized family size) instead of income since the 1934–6 detailed data are reported in this way. The laborer group is represented by the $200–$300 expenditure unit, which corresponds to the lower end of their income group; the salaried group is represented by the $800–$900 level, which corresponds to the higher end of their income group. The amounts reported have not been adjusted for family size within food expenditure units, which were 4.4 in the low-income group and 2.2 in the high-income group.

58. In this comparison, the laborer family is represented by the under $400 unit expenditures category, which averaged 14% lower per capita food expenditures than the laborer group; the salaried family is represented by the over $600 unit expenditure group, which averaged 11% higher per capita food expenditures than the salaried group. Therefore, the comparison exaggerates the actual differences between the two classes, since it assumes that laborer families spend only 53% per capita as much as salaried families on food consumed at home when they actually spend about 68% as much. However, the salaried class' increased purchases of food away from home offset this bias slightly.

59. BLS, *Money Disbursements*, p. 75. See also Faith M. Williams, 'Food Consumption at Different Economic Levels,' *Monthly Labor Review*, 42 (April 1936), pp. 889–94.

60. The percentage of families reporting expenditures for meals at work was 37% and for snacks was 34%. In addition, 8% reported expenditures for meals at school and 10% reported expenditures for meals on vacation. The proportion reporting expenditures for meals at work is not comparable to the 1918 figure since the latter includes all families reporting any expenditures for lunch away from home (such as a drink or a dessert), and it includes all lunches (at work, at school, or other). The 1935 figure is limited to meals at work (i.e., in a restaurant or at a lunch counter).

61. The percentage of families reporting such expenditures was not given.

62. J. Frederic Dewhurst and Associates, *America's Needs and Resources: A New Survey* (New York: Twentieth Century Fund, 1955), p. 179.

63. Dewhurst, *America's Needs*, p. 177. In the WPA budgets, government home economists assumed that the family did not own a sewing machine and that the wife mended. WPA, *Quantity Budgets*, p. 17.

64. This estimate was derived by multiplying the expenditures for materials by three, which gives the approximate retail value of ready-made clothing, and then dividing it by the average price of the wife's street dress.

65. The other exceptions were boys under six years and girls under eleven years in the working classes. There were no exceptions for the salaried class. In the 1934–6 survey, wives and husbands were included in the females 18+ and males 18+ groups, respectively. The laborer and wage-earner wife's expenditures do not seem to be biased upward by this aggregation with older daughters since females 18+ and females 12–17 have the same total expenditures. Also, for salaried families, the males 18+ total expenditures equaled the husband's expenditures in the 1935–6 National Resources Committee survey; the same comparison is true for females 18+ and wives.

66. These comparisons are based on the amounts spent by each survey group for husband, wife, boy (13 years) and girl (eight years) – the prototype family used in the WPA budgets.

67. Heller Committee for Research in Social Economics, University of California, Berkeley, *Clothing Budgets for I. Family of an Executive; II. Family of a Clerk; III. Family of a Wage Earner; IV. Dependent Families or Children, Prices for San Francisco, November 1935*, a supplement to *Quantity and Cost Budgets* (Berkeley: University of California, 1936), p. 49.

68. Heller Committee, *Clothing Budgets*, p. 23.
69. The shabbiness of their domestic servants' clothing prompted many housewives to buy uniforms for their use.
70. Young girls were an exception.
71. Since the expenditure unit category is for $700 and over rather than $700–$800, these expenditures for teenaged children are too high. However, 60% of the 73 girls aged 12–17 years in the $700 and over expenditure group were also in the $700–$800 group and another 30% were in the $800–$900 group. Of the 74 boys aged 12–17 years in the $700 and over expenditure group, 65% were in the $700–$800 group and 20% were in the $800–$900 group.
72. BLS, *Money Disbursements*, Table B-3, p. 364.
73. Black husbands averaged an overcoat every 15 years. However, many blacks lived in mild climates where overcoats were not essential.
74. BLS, *Money Disbursements*, Table B-3, p. 364.
75. WPA, *Quantity Budgets*, p. 17.
76. In San Francisco, families spent more than the national average. Streetcarmen averaged $62 on clothing and their wives spent $51. This is three-fifths more (in constant dollars) than the wage-earner spent in the CES survey and one-sixth more than his wife spent. The carman's family's clothing was characterized as simple and inexpensive, with little attempt at fashion consciousness, and worn until it was fairly shabby. The husband typically had one uniform (lasting two years), one suit (three years), a pair of extra pants, an overcoat (seven years), six shirts, and shoes lasting two years. His wife had three 'best' (street) dresses, four cotton housedresses and two hats – all lasting two years. She had three pairs of stockings, lasting six months. These families did not maintain a 'meticulous standard of personal appearance at all times,' but their clothing did permit them to engage in business and social activities without shame. Clerks' families spent one-half more on clothing. They bought higher-priced clothing and had larger wardrobes. Huntington and Luck, *Moderate Income*, pp. 66–9, 110, 177.
77. WPA, *Quantity Budgets*, p. 15.
78. The salaried husband did not quite meet the WPA maintenance standard for shoes, overcoats, shirts, and hats. He surpassed it for wool suits, ties, socks and underwear.
79. WPA, *Quantity Budgets*, p. 17.
80. The comparison of the CES budgets to the WPA standard is made by first adjusting the CES clothing budgets to be based on the standard family of husband-wife-boy (age 13)-girl (age eight). This was done by adding together the average expenditures per person in each class for each of these four types of persons.

81. 'Housing Conditions in American Cities,' *Monthly Labor Review*, 40 (March 1935), p. 724. Data are from a survey of housing in 64 cities made in early 1934. The survey was more broadly based than the CES. It included low-income and relief families as well as some high-income families.
82. Bureau of the Census, *Historical Statistics*, Series N 217.
83. For families with income of $1,200–$1,500 in 42 cities, housing costs varied by region by a factor of two. The variation for housing plus fuel, lighting and refrigeration was less – from 47% above average in New York City to 9% less in 12 Southern cities and five Pacific Coast cities. These differences reflect both variation by city size as well as by region. BLS, *Money Disbursements*, pp. 191–2.
84. Housing expenditures include rent plus repairs paid by tenants and homeowners' expenditures for taxes, insurance, repairs, refinancing charges, interest or mortgage. In addition, calculations were made (but not included in expenditure figures) for homeowners of the estimated rental value minus the expenses recorded. This net implicit rental value averaged $144 yearly for all homeowners. It would raise average housing costs by $36 yearly for blacks, laborers, and wage earners, and by $60 for salaried families. Payments on mortgage principal and costs of permanent improvements were recorded as savings. In addition, fuel, light, and refrigeration were included in housing costs when they were included in rent. BLS, *Money Disbursements*, Ch. 5.
85. Homeowners were included along with renters in the calculation of housing expenditures in the 1935 survey. Their out-of-pocket expenses (including minor repairs) were included; payments for principal and for major repairs were included under investment. Since this 'direct cost' rather than 'imputed value of rent' approach was used, housing costs for homeowners were less than for renters. If the same method of calculation were used in both years, the increase in housing expenditures would have been even higher.
86. Another 45% of the dwellings were in need of minor repairs. Overcrowding is defined as more than one person per room. 'Housing Conditions,' p. 727.
87. 'Overcrowded Housing in the United States,' *Monthly Labor Review*, 47 (July 1938), pp. 79–81.
88. US Department of Commerce, Bureau of Foreign and Domestic Commerce, *Real Property Inventory of 1934: Summary and Sixty-Four Cities Combined* (Washington, DC: US Government Printing Office, 1934).
89. For some documentation, see American Public Health Association, *Housing for Health* (Lancaster, PA: Science Press Printing Co., 1941).

90. 'What People Want in Housing,' *Monthly Labor Review*, 44 (Jan. 1937), pp. 97–100. The monthly rental for tenements averaged $20–$30. The moderate income group would live in houses costing $5,000–$10,000.

91. Refrigeration by ice cost $18.67 in the WPA emergency budget. The Heller budget made no provision for refrigeration.

92. American Public Health Association, Committee on the Hygiene of Housing, 'Basic Principles of Healthful Housing,' *American Journal of Public Health*, 28, 3 (March 1938), pp. 351–72.

93. WPA, *Quantity Budgets*, p. 28. The Heller dependent budget provided about the same housing standards. The Heller cost for housing was 28% higher than the WPA emergency budget housing costs for San Francisco.

94. They used the 'convenient guide' of 75% of the average rents of maintenance housing to calculate the emergency level rent. WPA, *Quantity Budgets*, p. 29.

95. WPA, *Quantity Budgets*, pp. 30–6. The black expenditures for rent do not include water.

96. Bureau of the Census, *Historical Statistics*, Series P 283–4.

97. The replacement ratio (i.e., the percent of total furnishings inventory value) assumed to be replaced annually was 7% in 1918 and 10% in 1935, when an 'inexpensive grade' of merchandise was assumed.

98. Faith M. Williams, 'Changes in Family Expenditures in the Post-War Period,' *Monthly Labor Review*, 47 (Nov. 1938), pp. 967–79. Earlier, the Lynds had thought one's car more important than the appearance of one's home and yard in marking position. Lynd and Lynd, *Middletown*, Ch. 9.

99. For families with incomes of $1,200–$1,500 in 42 cities, transportation costs varied from 46% below average for New York City to 30% above average for five Pacific Coast cities. Automobile expenditures varied much more than public transportation expenditures. BLS, *Money Disbursements*, p. 191.

100. The WPA standard allowed a daily round trip (306 days) to work for the man and to high school for the boy, plus an amount for other activities (shopping, recreation) equal to one-half of these two costs for the maintenance level (one-quarter for the emergency level). These costs were then adjusted downward by population size and land area to allow for walking. The final costs were 0.12 to 0.96 of the initial standard. The average adult cash fare was $0.087 in the 59 cities. The emergency trolley budget of $44.97 allowed for 517 rides yearly (ten weekly). WPA, *Intercity Differences*, pp. 73–8, 116–18.

101. Between 13% and 33% of laborers and between 27% and 45% of wage earners reported both car and trolley expenditures. This

means that 16%–41% of trolley-riding laborer families and 33%–55% of trolley-riding wage-earner families had cars.

102. Less expensive touring cars were introduced in 1908, but the price continued to drop until the early 1930s. The average wholesale value for a passenger car was $2,126 in 1908, $1,283 in 1909, $849 in 1918, and $521 in 1935 (current dollars). In 1918–19, 2.6 million cars were sold; in 1935–6, 7.0 million cars. By 1936, 24 million automobiles were registered. Bureau of the Census, *Historical Statistics*, Series Q 148–53. The price for a 'currently acceptable touring car' was $298 f.o.b. Detroit (1934–6), which is substantially less than the reported average price (Williams, 'Changes in Family Expenditures').

103. Pitirim A. Sorokin and Clarence Q. Berger, *Time-Budgets of Human Behavior* (Cambridge, MA: Harvard University Press, 1939). The activities listed each averaged between 18 minutes and 31 minutes daily in the group studied.

104. The allowances were based on 10 cents per person per week for tobacco, toys, and treats, movie attendance once per week by all family members, and a daily (including Sunday) newspaper. The emergency budget allowed only $4.83 for tobacco, toys, and treats (10 cents per person per month), $7.80 for movies (movie attendance once a month by all family members), and no newspapers. The newspaper was the only reading material allowed in the WPA budget; its cost was based on lowest cost by street purchase or carrier delivery monthly. WPA, *Quantity Budgets*.

105. WPA, *Intercity Differences*, p. 84.

106. The WPA maintenance standard allowed upkeep and operation of a radio in the furnishings and electricity budget; the emergency standard did not allow for operation of a radio.

107. Trade unions were not included; dues cost about $12 annually for unskilled manual workers. WPA, *Quantity Budgets*.

108. In 1934–5, about 3.5 million workers were members of labor unions. Union membership grew rapidly after 1935, when the Wagner Act was passed. About 3.4 million workers were also union members in 1918, and union membership grew rapidly for two years after World War I. Five million workers were union members in 1920, before the postwar recession gave employers the ability to overpower the union movement in the 1920s. Bureau of the Census, *Historical Statistics*, Series D 227, D 940–1; see also Irving Bernstein, *The Lean Years: A History of the American Worker, 1920–1933* (Boston: Houghton Mifflin Co., 1960), and Leo Wolman, *Ebb and Flow in Trade Unionism* (New York: National Bureau of Economic Research, 1936).

109. Only four-ninths of the school systems had *no* charge for textbooks and supplies, while at least one-fourth of the school systems

supplied *no* textbooks. As the amount spent for books and supplies fell by one-third between 1931 and 1934, and enrollments rose, public school systems required families to pay for some of the items previously supplied by the government. Another one-fourth supplied some textbooks, and one-eighth of the systems were not classified. WPA, *Intercity Differences*, pp. 79–81.

110. Editors of *Fortune, The Changing American Market* (Garden City, NY: Hanover House, 1955), pp. 201–2. Survey of 5,000 people by the National Recreational Association. The other four activities on the 'Top Ten' list were swimming, writing letters, reading nonfiction, and conversation.

111. Bureau of the Census, *Historical Statistics*, Series B 242–7, B 275–304.

112. Bureau of the Census, *Historical Statistics*, Series B 107–47, B 181–92.

113. Bureau of the Census, *Historical Statistics*, B 149–66, B 291–304.

114. Family requirements for medical care of all types would be expected to be greater in 1918 than in 1935 because all 1918 families included children. So the increased expenditures for dentists, eyeglasses, and doctors is even greater than indicated by these numbers.

115. The maintenance medical costs were based on a sample of 'minimum medical services required' per year per 1,000 persons (not adjusted for age or sex). The hospital services included one day per person in the cheapest pay ward. The drug budget included 2.5 non-prescription drugs and 0.5 prescription drug per person. The budget also included 2.3 doctor visits, some dental care (one-third teeth cleaning and one-fifth filling), and some professional eye care (0.025 eyeglasses per person). The costs are reduced for the emergency budget 10% (from $52 to $47) by assuming the omission of routine or even necessary nonemergency care. WPA, *Quantity Budgets*, pp. 46–8. Heller's wage-earner budget allowed 17% more than the WPA budget for routine medical and dental services. Heller Committee for Research in Social Economics, University of California, Berkeley, *Quantity and Cost Budgets for I. Family of an Executive; II. Family of a Clerk; III. Family of a Wage Earner; IV. Dependent Families or Children, Prices for San Francisco, November 1935* (Berkeley: University of California, 1936), p. 32, and WPA, *Intercity Differences*, Table 2. In practice, both the streetcarmen's and clerks' families were judged to receive only one-half to three-fourths as much medical care as was necessary to maintain health. But they received more medical care (especially for teeth and eyes) than the national average for their income class. Huntington and Luck, *Moderate Income*, pp. 82–6.

116. G. St.J. Perrott, Edgar Sydenstricker, and Selwyn D. Collins, 'Medical Care During the Depression: A Preliminary Report Upon a Survey of Wage-Earning Families in Seven Large Cities,' *Milbank Memorial Fund Quarterly*, 12, 2 (April 1934), pp. 99–114.

117. The percentage of households with a telephone actually fell from 35% in 1920 to 32% in 1934 (after peaking at 42% in 1929). Bureau of the Census, *Historical Statistics*, Series R 3. This partially reflects telephone service being widely available in rural areas and spreading slowly to some urban areas. In addition, the rapid increase in poverty from unemployment made telephone ownership impossible for families suffering job loss. The cost of toll calls (especially over longer distances) fell dramatically over the period. Bureau of the Census, *Historical Statistics*, Series R 13–16.

118. When they did hire help, salaried wives had over two to three as many days of help as the working-class wives. In the San Francisco study, household operations were easier for the clerk's wife. Clerks' homes were more likely than carmen's to have furnaces (0.8 against 0.5), electric refrigeration (0.15, against 0.05), telephones (0.8, against 0.5), domestic service (0.4, against 0.1), and commercial laundry service (0.6, against 0.4). Carmen's wives had more sewing machines and washing machines. Huntington and Luck, *Moderate Income*, p. 178.

119. David L. Cohn, *The Good Old Days* (New York: Simon & Schuster, 1940), Ch. 20.

120. Davis, *American Economic Growth*, p. 86.

121. Cohn, *Good Old Days*, p. 405.

122. The emergency budget was 90% of the maintenance budget, or $16.94 for cleaning supplies and $2.75 for unspecified essentials. WPA, *Intercity Differences*.

123. Boys 7–15 years were allowed one haircut every $1\frac{1}{2}$ months; boys 2–6 years and girls 7–12 years were allowed a bimonthly haircut; girls 2–6 years were allowed a hair cut twice a year. WPA, *Quantity Budgets*, pp. 26–7.

124. Boys aged 7–15 years were allowed a bimonthly haircut.

125. WPA, *Quantity Budgets*, p. 54, and *Intercity Differences*, pp. 85, 120. This lump sum provided about $500 for the wife and $200 for each of the children. Although the ordinary life insurance policies had lower premiums for a given benefit, the industrial policies were popular because they were paid through small weekly premiums. The Heller budget allowed life insurance only for the husband; it paid $50 a month for 20 years, or $3,800 cash. Heller Committee, *Quantity and Cost Budgets*, p. 44.

126. The total value was a little less, equaling $700. WPA, *Intercity Differences*, p. 120.

127. This exceeded the 1918 'subsistence' standard of a $500 'burial' insurance policy.
128. Of the 59 cities in the WPA study, 23 had neither property nor capitation tax, 22 cities had personal property tax, 25 cities had capitation tax, and 11 cities had both. The WPA standard budgets allowed $2.54 for taxes ($1.10 for personal property and $1.44 for capitation). WPA, *Intercity Differences*, pp. 86–7, 166, 170.
129. A sales tax, ranging from 1.0 to 3.0%, was levied in 18 of the 59 cities in the WPA study. The WPA maintenance budget included $5.14 in various expenditure categories ($2.66 in food, $1.16 in clothing, $0.94 in household operations) for sales tax; the emergency budget included $3.78 for sales tax. WPA, *Intercity Differences*, pp. 87–8, 187–8.
130. Although the CES classified life insurance as a net addition to assets, here it has been reclassified under personal insurance to be comparable with the other years.
131. These savings figures should be used only as a guide to direction of change. They are not accurate measures of actual savings.
132. See Evan Clark, *Financing the Consumer* (New York: Harper & Brothers, 1931) for a discussion of the acceptance of borrowing and of the 'mass financing' of consumption which was developing along with mass production and distribution. Clark discusses how nine-tenths of the adult population could not get a loan until the late 1920s (p. 5). Installment credit had grown from $600 million to $4,000 million in 20 years. The total volume of mass finance was $6,600 million, or equivalent to 17% of retail sales. This included $2,300 million of installment credit for autos, $1,700 million of other installment credit, and $2,600 million of credit provided by pawnbrokers, unlicensed lenders, and personal finance companies. Forty percent of total loans were to pay off previous loans (p. 13).
133. BLS, *Money Disbursements*, p. 183. However, black families were almost as likely as white working-class families (9% against 11%) to report paying interest (averaging $12 to $22 annually) on debt (see Table 4.10C).
134. One study of 75 families with average earnings of $92 per month showed about one-half of them received relief (averaging $129 per month), one-half made installment purchases, one-half had loans from finance companies, and three-fourths had credit accounts. Helen I. Clarke, 'A Study of Incomes, Emergencies, and Credit in Dependent Families,' *Family*, 12, 3 (1931), pp. 92–4.
135. The family size effect is calculated only for white families with a husband, wife and at least one child, since this was the group surveyed in 1918. Unfortunately, data were not available to make this comparison for blacks. The black family size effect is

exaggerated since it compares families with children in 1918 to all families in 1935.

136. In a 1929 Brookings study of consumption and living standards, families with income below $1,200 (in 1934–5 dollars) were classified as living at 'subsistence and poverty,' which was 42% of the 1929 population. 'Minimum comfort' required $1,200–$2,400 (36% of population); 'Moderate circumstances' required $2,400–$4,000 (14% of population); and 'Comfortable' required $4,000–$8,050 (6% of population). The top 2% were classified 'well-to-do' and 'wealthy.' Leven, Moulton, and Clark, *America's Capacity to Consume*, p. 87.

   The BLS 'Minimum quantity budget for a worker's family of five,' which cost $2,282 for ten large cities in 1922, would cost $1,898 in 1934–6 prices (excluding personal insurance). But this budget is inadequate for the mid-1930s since it does not include an auto, radio, silk stockings, or beauty parlor services. BLS, *Money Disbursements*, p. 47.

137. The WPA maintenance budget cost 10% more in New York City than the average of 53 cities. Otherwise, the cost varied from 4% less than average in 18 Southern cities to 3% more in eight East North Central cities. Average incomes varied even more, with incomes in New York City 14% above the average (42 cities) and 10% below average in 12 Southern cities. BLS, *Money Disbursements*, p. 188. The National Industrial Conference Board standard varied in cost from 104 for the East to 97.5 for the Middle West (average cost in 69 cities = 100). The variation by city size was from 104.1 for large cities (500,000+), to 98.99 for medium and small cities (25,000–500,000), to 97 for small cities (10,000–25,000). M. Ada Beney, 'Local Variations in the Cost of Living,' *Conference Board Bulletin*, 9, 12 (Dec. 10, 1935), pp. 89–95.

138. WPA, *Intercity Differences*, pp. xiii–xiv.

139. WPA, *Intercity Differences*, p. xiv. An earlier study proposed a $2,500 budget for a city family of four to meet the 'American Standard in 1929.' This translates to $2,015 (with savings) in 1934–5 dollars or $1,873 (without savings or personal insurance). 'Necessities' include modern plumbing, adequate heat, telephone, and electric lighting; newspapers and books; minimum health care; auto; and some opportunity for travel, recreation, amusement, and higher education. The author argues culture cannot flourish without physical security. Mordecai Ezekiel, *$2500 a Year: From Scarcity to Abundance* (New York: Harcourt, Brace & Co., 1936), pp. 3–4.

140. See WPA, *Quantity Budgets*. For example, the maintenance budget had one-fifth of the food dollar spent on cereals (compared to one-third in the emergency budget) and two-thirds spent on fruits,

vegetables, dairy products, and meats (compared to one-half). Clothes were less shabby and more up to date – for example, the wife's winter coat was worn only three years (compared to five) and a 'good' silk or rayon dress was purchased each year (compared to every three years). Their housing was in a more desirable neighborhood, in better condition, and was kept warm in winter. Cleaner and more convenient fuels were used.

The maintenance budget allowed a radio, a daily newspaper, and four times more tobacco, toys, and many more movie outings as well as membership in children's organizations. The men were allowed monthly haircuts (compared to every six weeks), and the women were allowed bimonthly haircuts with three hair waves a year (as opposed to doing all their own hair care).

141. Heller Committee, *Quantity and Cost Budgets*, p. 1.
142. Heller Committee, *Quantity and Cost Budgets*, p. 1. According to Horowitz, Peixotto was accepting of workers' 'pursuit of comfort.' However, she seemed to idealize the extent to which middle-class or faculty families actually pursued the 'higher life,' since in practice they spent little on education, organizations, or concerts. Daniel Horowitz, *The Morality of Spending* (Baltimore: Johns Hopkins University Press, 1985), Ch. 8. In fact, Peixotto was a sympathetic observer to all the classes she studied, and she was explicit about the economizing measures undertaken even by those with crafts or professional income levels. Her studies serve as a useful counterpoint to others' charges of profligate spending and conspicuous waste. See Jessica B. Peixotto, *Cost of Living Studies II. How Workers Spend a Living Wage: A Study of the Income and Expenditures of Eighty-Two Typographers' Families in San Francisco*, University of California Publications in Economics, 5, 3 (Berkeley and Los Angeles: University of California Press, 1929), and *Getting and Spending at the Professional Standard of Living: A Study of the Cost of Living in Academic Life* (New York: Macmillan, 1927).
143. Beney, 'Local Variations,' p. 93.
144. The prices of four others could not be compared. Nutritional standards for calories, protein, calcium, phosphorus, and iron, based on Sherman, *Chemistry of Food and Nutrition*, were used. Vitamin content was not measured.
145. Bureau of Home Economics, *Diets at Four Levels*. Their costs are lower than comparable costs reported in the WPA budget. Another 1932 USDA diet cited by Heller was developed for use by relief agencies. It was 15% below the calcium standard (0.7 gr) and slightly below the standards for calories (3,000) and phosphorus (1.2 gr). This budget was not priced.

146. Heller Committee, *Standards of Relief*, pp. 10, 15. Only one clothing budget was lower (by $2) than the Heller budget.
147. These findings show laborers reaching a higher standard than a study by Oscar Ornati, *Poverty Amid Affluence* (New York: Twentieth Century Fund, 1966), Table B. Ornati found men's 'low wage' (i.e., unskilled male laborer wage) about equal to the estimates for 'minimum subsistence' (i.e., emergency), but only 65% of the amount needed for 'minimum adequacy' (i.e., maintenance) and 45% of the amount for 'minimum comfort.'
148. Wage-earner families purchased cars 5–6 years old for $198 compared to a $535, two-year-old car in the Heller budget. They also kept their cars for six years compared to four years in the Heller budget. Their older cars resulted in higher maintenance expenses (by $10) but lower implicit depreciation charges (by $45). The family probably economized on car insurance, which was $56 a year in the Heller budget. Any garage rented ($42 yearly) in the Heller budget would be listed under Shelter in the CES. Heller Committee, *Quantity and Cost Budgets*, p. 43.
149. The WPA allowed small 'burial' policies for the whole family with a $1,000 ordinary policy for the husband. Heller allowed life insurance only for the husband that paid $50 a month for 20 years or $3,800 cash. Heller Committee, *Quantity and Cost Budgets*, p. 44.
150. Heller Committee, *Quantity and Cost Budgets*, pp. 9–23. This executive family was in the top 1%. Their consumption expenditures equaled the average for the $10,000–$15,000 income group in 1935–6. Only 0.5% of all families had income above this group, and 0.4% were in this group. National Resources Committee, *Family Expenditures*, p. 1.
151. The National Industrial Conference Board (NICB) budget provided about the same food budget but higher budgets for clothing and housing than actually spent by laborers. The NICB provided two budgets – one with and one without an automobile. If the transportation amount is calculated for one-third car ownership, then the NICB Miscellaneous amount is only $11 more than the laborers' actual miscellaneous amount (including furnishings).
152. This was less than the policy suggested by the Heller clerk budget, which would pay $75 a month between the ages of 25 and 45 and $5,750 for later death or retirement at age 65.

5 Entering the Age of Affluence, 1950

Introduction

By the end of World War II, government policies had remodeled the economic structures of daily life, most notably through programs passed in 1935 to provide some economic security (the Social Security Act)[1] and some regulation of the labor market (Fair Labor Standards Act (FLSA) and the National Labor Relations (or Wagner) Act.[2] Then followed the transformation of a depressed economy into a vigorous one fueled by wartime needs. Along with forced consumer saving and a restructuring of labor market institutions, World War II had brought economic recovery. By 1950, the United States was completing its transition to a peacetime economy, but one with enormous productive capacity relative to the Depression. Great demands were being made of the economy, both to expand its infrastructure, especially highways, schools and housing, and to help rebuild Europe. Real GNP per capita was three-fourths higher in 1950 than in 1935, and real disposable income was three-fifths higher.

The economic emancipation of women continued. Of the periods studied, that between 1935 and 1950 witnessed the largest increase in wives' labor market participation, and the increase was greatest among middle-aged women (45–64 years old). This group, whose children were grown (or at least older), had become accustomed to working during the war and did not want to return to full-time homemaking.[3] In contrast to the earlier period, the participation rate for women of prime child-rearing years (ages 25–44) increased only slightly. For younger women, aged 20–24, labor market participation actually fell as higher education became more widespread and as the birthrate rocketed. Overall, the female participation rate rose 12%, while total labor participation rate rose only 1%. Wives were replacing children as subsidiary workers. The number of workers per family, however, continued to increase across class. Salaried families were now almost equally divided between those with one worker and those with at least two workers.

Table 5.1 Budgets for urban families, 1950[a]

Income group	Black 0.2 ($1,000–2,000) +0.8 ($2,000–3,000)*		Laborer $2,000–3,000		Wage earner $3,000–4,000		Salaried $4,000–5,000	
Homeowners	27%		37%		47%		54%	
Auto owners	24%		49%		68%		78%	
Average family size	3.3		2.6		3.2		3.4	
Annual expenditures								
Amount ($) – percentage distribution (%)	2,543	100.0	2,947	100.0	3,874	100.0	4,835	100.0
Food	879	34.6	943	32.0	1,174	30.3	1,385	28.6
At home	716		747		957		1,084	
Away from home	108		157		161		227	
Alcoholic beverage	55		39		56		74	
Clothing	303	11.9	272	9.2	377	9.7	504	10.4
Shelter	576	22.7	655	22.2	796	20.5	981	20.3
Rent	270	10.6	353	12.0	404	10.4	474	9.8
Fuel and Light	132	5.2	130	4.4	156	4.0	176	3.6
Furniture and furnishings	174	6.8	172	5.8	236	6.1	331	6.8
Miscellaneous	785	30.9	1,078	36.6	1,526	39.4	1,964	40.6
Transportation	192	7.6	309	10.5	487	12.6	647	13.4
Recreation and education[b]	149	5.9	194	6.6	283	7.3	383	7.9
Household operations	94	3.7	115	3.9	145	3.7	186	3.8
Medical care	90	3.5	152	5.2	203	5.2	230	4.8
Personal care	76	3.0	63	2.1	82	2.1	97	2.0
Gifts and contributions	57	2.2	96	3.3	121	3.1	163	3.4
Personal insurance[c]	97	3.8	108	3.7	165	4.3	206	4.3
Other	30	1.2	41	1.4	40	1.0	52	1.1
Gross income ($)	2,382		2,671		3,708		4,807	
Tax $, tax/gross income (%)	72	3.0	133	5.0	219	5.9	340	7.1
Net income	2,320		2,538		3,489		4,467	
Expenditure ($), as a percentage of income	2,543	109.6	2,948	116.2	3,873	111.0	4,834	108.2

[a] Vocational expenses (union dues, work-related expenditures for tools and clothing) are excluded from expenditures and income.
[b] Includes tobacco.
[c] Personal insurance includes employee withholding for Social Security (OASDI).
* Income groups are for after-tax income.
Source: *Consumer Expenditure Survey*, 1950. Summary Volume.

As unemployment fell, job market opportunities grew for lower-class family members. The number of workers per family became more equal across classes, and earnings became more equal across non-farm occupations between 1935 and 1950 (see tables 1.1 and 1.2). The wartime economy had opened up many new job opportunities for blacks and married women and had facilitated black migration out of the rural South.[4] By 1950, black families had made substantial gains from their Depression era destitution. Improvements in their standard of living were noticeable in their diets and wardrobes, and in their car ownership. Although white families continued to improve the quality of their diets and wardrobes, their dramatic improvements occurred in car ownership (up 50% for the working class), home ownership (up 80%), better medical care, and more recreational activities (see table 5.1).

The white working class became much more integrated into community life during this decade. Although expenditures became more equal as incomes became more equal, important material differences still marked class status, despite the proclamations of many social scientists that consumption patterns no longer separated the working class from the middle (or salaried) class.[5] Almost unanimous agreement existed, however, that American families, especially working-class and minority ones, had a much higher absolute standard of living in 1950 than in 1918.[6] Their lives were easier, had more variety, and were more secure. There was less drudgery in daily activities at work and at home and more time to participate in family and social life. Instead of being forced to send children to the factory to help pay for necessities, most parents could now allow their teenaged children to remain in school, thus helping to ensure that the next generation would attain an even higher living standard. The United States was at the beginning of a remarkable quarter century of massive growth in consumerism, fueled by television advertising and facilitated by the widespread use of credit to purchase homes, cars, and furnishings.

The early 1950s were significant years in American economic history. They marked the end of a 20-year period of economic leveling.[7] The percentage of total personal income held by the top 5% of consumer units fell from 30.0% in 1929 to 26.5% in 1935–6 to 21.4% in 1950. The gains at the bottom were only slightly less dramatic, as the percentage of personal income held by the bottom 40% increased from 12.5% in 1929 to 13.3% in 1935–6 to 15.7% in 1950.[8]

Income and jobs

Since the 1930s, craft and operative jobs had increased in importance for men while farm and labor jobs had declined. Two in five household heads were operatives or craft workers. One in eight was a salaried professional or manager, and another one in eight was a service worker or laborer. Salaried professional and managerial workers headed families with average income near the eightieth percentile.[9] Black husband-wife families were centered near the fortieth percentile; wage earners were centered near the sixty-fifth percentile (see table 5.1).

Average household size continued its long-run decline, begun well before World War I, and households in 1950 had not yet started to reflect the dramatic departure from the traditional nuclear family arrangement that would come to characterize the decades following World War II. Like the two previous censuses, the 1950 census showed husband-wife families accounting for four of five households. The proportion of single-person households had begun its climb, rising from 7% in 1940 to 11% in 1950. As in 1940, one in ten families was headed by a female without a spouse. The amount of shared housing had declined since the Depression, as the percentage of married couples without their own households dropped.[10]

As the country demobilized and service men returned home, the birth rate jumped in 1946 and remained above 100 live births per 1,000 women (aged 15–44 years) until 1965.[11] The rush to begin families lowered the median age at first marriage – one year for women (to 20.3 years) and 1.5 years for men (to 22.8 years) – compared to the preceding three decades.

One legacy of the war was a rise in the number of workers per family, although the norm for husbands to provide most of the household income remained intact, and in the majority of families, husbands continued to be the only earner. When families required a second earner, however, wives began to replace children as paid workers.

For laborer families, the proportion of family members engaged in paid labor doubled from 0.27 in 1918 to 0.50 in 1950. Although fewer than one in four wives were in the labor market, one in three wives without children under six were working for pay. Women with older or grown children were now more and more likely to work, as the participation rate for women aged 45–64 years increased from 20% in 1940 to 29% in 1950. Overall, black wives were much more likely to be in the labor force (32%) than white wives (21%). The participation rate for college-aged males (20–24 years) had declined as returning service men took advantage of the GI education bill.

Weekly work hours had fallen fairly steadily since the early 1800s, but the decline between 1900 and 1940 was especially rapid. In 1900, the average workweek in non-agricultural industries was 56 hours; in 1940, it was 41 hours. The major institutional change behind the decline in hours was the passage of the Fair Labor Standards Act (FLSA), which required payment of a 50% wage premium for hours worked in excess of the 'standard' 40-hour week. After rising during World War II, the average non-agricultural working week fell back to hover between 40 and 41 hours during the 1950s. Paid vacations, holidays and sick leave spread during World War II, especially through decisions by the National War Labor Board, and afterwards, especially through negotiated contracts.[12]

Schooling had become a regular part of children's lives. Four out of five children aged 5–19 years were enrolled in school in 1950. Children were beginning school at an earlier age and staying in school longer. The proportion of five and six year olds enrolled in school rose by one-third between 1940 and 1950. In 1950, the majority (57%) of 17 year olds were high school graduates, compared to only two in five in 1935 and one in six in 1918.[13] Being a high school graduate was still fairly rare among adults (those 25 years or more), however. Only 10% of adult men and 23% of adult women had a high school diploma in 1950. Although women continued to be more likely than men to graduate from high school, they were less likely to attend or graduate from college. College graduates still comprised an elite group of only 7% of adult men and 5% of adult women in 1950.[14]

The majority of white families (around 55%) lived on earnings alone and received no unearned income.[15] Unearned income accounted for

Table 5.2 Income distribution, 1950

	All households[a]	Urban families	White families[b]	Non-white families[c]
Number (000s)	49,016	25,796	–	–
	%	%	%	%
Under $1,000	18.4	7.3	10.0	28.1
$1,000–1,999	14.2	10.4	12.2	25.3
$2,000–2,499	9.0	8.0	8.6	13.1
$2,500–2,999	8.5	8.5	8.7	10.4
$3,000–3,499	10.7	12.4	11.9	9.0
$3,500–3,999	8.1	10.1	9.4	4.5
$4,000–4,999	11.7	15.9	14.4	4.3
$5,000–6,999	11.8	16.9	15.1	3.4
$7,000–9,999	4.8	6.8	6.1	1.7
$10,000 and over	2.7	3.8	3.5	0.3
Median income	$2,990	$3,673	$3,445	$1,869
W/Non-farm earnings	$3,353	–	$3,720	$2,272
Husband/wife families	–	$3,835	–	–

[a] Households include both families (two or more related individuals) and unrelated individual(s). Families comprised 81% of households.

[b] Includes both urban and rural. Almost two-thirds of the population (64% for whites and 62% for blacks) lived in urban areas, while 86% of households were urban. The CES units had a median income of $3,724, which is only 1.4% higher than the Current Population Survey's (CPS) median income of $3,673 for urban families.

[c] See note [b].

Source: US Bureau of the Census, Current Population Survey, 'Income of Families and Persons in the United States: 1950.'

one-sixth of the family's income for laborers and one-tenth for the wage earners and salaried workers (see table 5.2). Social Security (including unemployment insurance) and veterans' payments provided the largest sources of unearned income for laborers: one in six of these families reported an annual average of $500 for Social Security and one in five families reported military allotments (including pensions) worth almost $500. Although 15% of the laborer families reported receiving interest and dividends, they averaged only about $160 annually.

In contrast, the salaried family received over 60% more in interest, dividends and profits but only about half as much in Social Security payments as laborer families. However, 30% of salaried families received

Table 5.3 Sources of income of urban families, 1950[a]

	Blacks ($)	Laborers ($)	Wage earners ($)	Salaried ($)
Income before tax	2,382	2,671	3,708	4,807
Income after tax	2,310	2,538	3,489	4,467
Implicit taxes[b]	72	133	219	340
Other money receipts	14	41	38	78
Decrease in assets	99	566	557	709
Increase in liabilities	239	346	520	681
Implicit savings[c]	−338	−912	−1,077	−1,390
Total receipts	2,661	3,491	4,604	5,934
Balance account difference	−71	−118	−151	−161
Earners per family	NA	1.31	1.39	1.40

	Laborers		Wage earners		Salaried	
	Amount ($)	*% reporting*	*Amount* ($)	*% reporting*	*Amount* ($)	*% reporting*
Wages and salary	2,079	89	3,152	95	4,035	94
Entrepreneurial	168	9	199	9	326	12
Roomers and boarders	21	7	22	7	29	7
Rents income	33	11	29	10	37	12
Interest	14	14	11	16	17	20
Dividends	11	4	17	5	21	7
Gifts	42	16	25	14	29	14
Profit from stocks	7	1	8	1	14	1
Unemployment/Social Sec.	90	18	53	13	51	13
Private pensions	19	3	9	1	11	1
Insurance	6	2	6	2	15	4
Relief	28	3	9	1	4	1
Military pay pensions	99	20	120	29	147	30
Other	44	11	39	10	57	11

[a] Laborers, wage earners and salaried include Whites only in this and all subsequent tables. Data not available for Blacks by occupation.

[b] Implicit taxes = income before tax less income after tax.

[c] Implicit savings = decrease in assets plus increase in liabilities.

Source: *Consumer Expenditure Survey*, 1950, Summary Volume, and CPR, p-60.

military allotments averaging almost $500, and this was the most important unearned income for the class.

Let us now turn to a detailed analysis of family budgets to see how material life across classes was evolving.[16]

Diet

The difference in family diets across classes continued to diminish as the quality of meals improved. The spread of the supermarket and refrigerated high-speed transportation made more foodstuffs available year-round. Families now ate more fruits and vegetables, especially fruit juices and salads, and less bread, potatoes, and cereals. Better home refrigeration made it possible to store fresh milk, and milk consumption increased by over one-half between 1935 and 1950. With the minerals, vitamins and calcium provided by the additional vegetables, fruit, and milk, nutrition improved. But families also increased their protein intake, which was already adequate for most families in 1935. By 1955, only one-tenth of the families were judged to have nutritionally poor diets, down from one-third in 1935.[17] Meals still varied somewhat by season, but improvements in variety spanned the whole year. Fresh meat was now available in summer; lettuce, tomatoes, peas, beans and oranges were available most of the year. Frozen orange juice was introduced in 1946, and consumption increased rapidly in the following decade. Many more processed foods were also available, such as canned or frozen fruits and vegetables, baking mixes, and ready-made food sold at delicatessens and bakeries. Poultry was now bought cleaned and dressed.[18]

Laborer and wage-earner families spent almost the same amount on food per capita, while salaried families spent one-tenth more and black families spent one-fourth less. However, the black family was spending 5% more on food per capita in 1950 than the laborer family had spent in 1935. Meanwhile, laborer families were spending 46% more on food per capita in 1950 than they had in 1935.

The actual improvement in meals since the mid-1930s was noticeable (see table 5.4). Typically, breakfast was based on either cooked or packaged cereal with occasional bacon and eggs. The husband probably had bacon and eggs daily. Lunch typically included two sandwiches, fresh fruit, and a fresh vegetable. Everyone also had a store-bought dessert, which they perhaps ate later as a snack. The typical dinner included meat, a potato, three rolls, a green salad every other day, a vegetable (fresh or canned), and a home-baked dessert. Sweet snacks were now commonplace – each family member averaged two soft drinks, two candy bars, and an ice cream each week (with the children probably consuming more than the parents).

Table 5.4 Typical meals, 1950

Breakfast (per person)
Husband
1.3 oz bacon with 1 egg – daily
Ready-to-eat cereal – 2 days
Cooked cereal with 0.5 oz raisins – 3 days
For everyone else
1.3 oz bacon with 1 egg – 2 days
Ready-to-eat cereal – 2 days
Cooked cereal with 1.5 oz raisins – 3 days
For everyone
3.5 servings of bread (1.5 slices of bread; 1 serving other baked good; 1 serving
home-baked good)
Jelly, jam and syrups (0.5 oz)
Butter or margarine (1 teaspoon)
1 serving of citrus (including oranges, 0.5 grapefruit, 1 canned citrus)
2 cups of coffee[a] for each adult
1 cup of milk

Lunch (per person)
2 sandwiches (4 slices of bread); 0.8 teaspoons butter or margarine; 2 oz
bologna, leftover meat or cheese
1 serving of fruit (5 fresh servings: 2 bananas,
1 melon, 1.5 apple, 0.5 strawberries, 2 canned servings)
1 serving of vegetables (0.5 cup servings: 2 of carrots, 1.5 of celery, 1 of
canned corn, 1 of cabbage, 0.5 of greens, 0.5 of beets, 0.5 of frozen vegetables)
1 purchased dessert (might be saved for snack)

Dinner (per person)
Meat (4.75 oz servings: beef – 3 days; pork – 1 day; fish – 1 day; chicken – 1
day)
1 serving starch (1–10 oz potato – 3 days; rice – 3 days; noodles – 2 days)
Fresh or canned vegetables (0.5 cup servings: 2 of canned peas; 1 of fresh snap
beans; 1 of canned snap beans; 1 of asparagus; 1 of spinach, 1 of cabbage)
Salad (1 cup serving: lettuce, tomato, cucumber, green onions with 0.8
tablespoon of dressing) – every other day
3 home-baked rolls (with 1 teaspoon butter or margarine)
6 oz milk
1 home-baked dessert

Treats
5 times weekly (1 serving ice cream; 2 candy bars; 2 8-oz soft drinks

For cooking
Per person, per week:
0.30 lb canned tomato products
0.22 lb onions
0.60 lb cream and evaporated milk
0.92 lb sugar

0.30 lb lard, shortening, oils
0.4 cup buttermilk
Plus
6 eggs per household per week

---

[a] Coffee consumption data are 1955 urban.
Source: *Consumer Expenditure Survey*, 1950, Detailed Food Data.

Consumption of the staples of earlier years – potatoes and flours – fell by about one-half between 1909–52.[19] These were partially replaced by frozen and processed products that became available only near the end of the period. Thirty-three pounds of canned fruits and juices plus four pounds of frozen juices were purchased for every 100 pounds of fresh fruits and juices. This was a five-fold increase over the decade of the 1910s. Thirty-one pounds of canned and frozen vegetables (including potatoes) were purchased in 1950, which was a two-fold increase over the 1920s decade. During the 1940s, prepared flour mixes became popular, and almost one in three housewives reported using them in 1948.[20]

The nutrition of lower-income diets improved with the mandatory enrichment of bread during the war. After 1946, enrichment of bread, flour, and cornmeal continued to be widespread, and it was eventually mandated by the majority of states.[21] The importance of the enrichment of flour for providing sufficient thiamin, riboflavin, and niacin can be seen by the percentage of nutrients contributed by flour and cereal products before and after the war. In 1935–9, flour and cereal products accounted for 28% of calories, and for 19%, 8%, and 17% of thiamin, riboflavin, and niacin, respectively; in 1947–9, these products accounted for 24% of calories, and for 34%, 16%, and 26% of thiamin, riboflavin, and niacin, respectively.[22] Changes in consumption since the 1910s also improved nutrition: families were now eating one-third more dairy products, three-fourths more leafy, green and yellow vegetables, and almost twice as many tomatoes and citrus fruits.[23]

On a less positive nutritional note, consumption of alcohol continued a climb that had begun with the repeal of Prohibition, and soft drinks grew increasingly popular during the 1940s. By 1948, the country was drinking enough of these beverages for everyone to have two 8-ounce sodas each week and for each adult to have five beers weekly (or nine beers per reported user) and 7 ounces of spirits and wine weekly (or 12 ounces per user). Smoking had increased sharply since the 1930s. In a 1949 Gallup poll, 58% of adults admitted to consuming some alcohol and 44% reported smoking an average of 17 cigarettes daily.

A government study conducted in the early 1950s estimated preparation time and cost for one day's meals, depending on the use of partially or completely prepared foods:[24]

Table 5.5 Food, 1950

	BLS standard[a]		Blacks			Laborers			Wage earners			Salaried		
	Exp. ($)	Exp. (%)	Exp. ($)	% rep.	Exp. (%)	Exp. ($)	% rep.	Exp. (%)	Exp. ($)	% rep.	Exp (%)	Exp. ($)	% rep.	Exp. (%)
Family size	4.0		3.3			2.6			3.2			3.4		
Food at home	926	88	716	97	87	747	95	83	957	98	86	1,084	99	83
Food away from home	121	12	108	66	13	157	83	17	161	88	14	227	93	17
Subtotal	1,047	100	824		100	904		100	1,118		100	1,311		100
Per person	252		206			226			280			328		
Alcoholic beverages	NA		55	52	6	39	52	4	56	64	5	74	71	5
Total	1,047		879			942			1,175			1,385		

[a] From 34-city survey, *Workers Budgets in the US*, Bulletin No. 927, US BLS, Table 6.
Source: Consumer Expenditure Survey, 1950, Summary Volume. Expenditure is average expenditure for all families.

	Cost	Preparation time
Home-prepared meals (from scratch)	$4.90	5.5 hours
Partially prepared meals (with mixes)	$5.80	3.1 hours
Ready-to-serve meals (out of a can or box)	$6.70	1.6 hours

The trend from home-prepared to partially prepared meals closely reflects the change in actual practice by homemakers, so that the availability of processed foodstuffs resulted in the cost of meals increasing only one-fifth while the preparation time fell almost one-half, or a decline of 17 hours weekly.

Family members bought more lunches at work and ate more snacks away from home than in earlier periods (see table 5.5). For the majority of workers, carrying lunch to work had given way to buying it, although differences across classes still existed – 43% of laborers, 52% of wage earners, and 68% of salaried workers bought lunch away from home. The number of eating and drinking places grew rapidly. In 1955, nearly one-fifth of the urban family's food budget was spent on meals and snacks bought at drugstores, cafeterias, coffee-shops, restaurants and candy stores. Two out of five workers bought lunch daily at in-plant cafeterias.[25] The number of meals purchased weekly away from home increased across class – from 2.6 for laborers to 5.3 for salaried workers. Overall, the percentage of the food dollar spent on food away from home varied little.[26] In actual dollars, the salaried family spent twice as much for food away from home as the black family, whose public life was much more circumscribed both because of lack of income and because of segregation.

One sign of the dramatic improvements that had been made in the quantity and quality of available foods was the new concern with obesity. As both work and daily life became less physically demanding, caloric needs dropped. Caloric consumption, though, did not fall apace – people apparently found it difficult to resist the ever-expanding array of foods available. Nutritionists agreed that Americans were consuming too many 'empty' calories in the form of sweets, and actual consumption of sweets was two-thirds higher than recommended by the Department of Agriculture.[27] The serious effects of obesity on health were still being confirmed, but by 1950 most food studies at least mentioned obesity. One study reported that 'obesity has replaced vitamin deficiency diseases as the Number One nutrition problem in the United States.' One in four adults was estimated to be obese.[28]

By 1948, only one out of five families did not purchase enough goods to consume 3,000 calories daily per person, which was the standard for being physically active. In contrast, two in five families purchased enough food for each person to eat 4,000 or more calories per day.[29] These families probably wasted food and had members who ate too much.

Laborer families were 10 percentage points behind salaried families in the percentage meeting basic nutritional requirements.[30] The 1948–9 national food survey[31] shows that the typical diet of laborers actually included 21% more meat, poultry and fish, 5% more fresh fruits and vegetables, 29% more canned fruits and vegetables, 18% more bread and 40% more coffee, but fewer sweets, than the diet suggested in the BLS city workers' budget (see table 5.6). At the same time, laborers consumed 20% fewer dairy products, flours and cereals. The city workers' budget combined practice with knowledge to describe a 'modest but adequate' standard of living.[32] This government budget expected families to use food in a less processed form and to spend a much smaller proportion of their food budgets on beverages than they actually did. The city workers' budget was much more liberal than the USDA 'low-cost' diet; the latter allowed significantly less meat and poultry, fresh fruits and vegetables, prepared grain or bakery products, and sweets, and significantly more potatoes, dairy products, and dried fruits, vegetables and nuts. The USDA moderate-cost diet was comparable to the BLS diet, except that it included more fresh and fewer canned vegetables and more dairy products.

The ways in which the laborer diet deviated from the BLS diet mirrored the way the salaried diet differed from the working class diet, except for milk. The class differences are even sharper if one looks at details – higher-class families ate more steaks and roasts, bought frozen foods, and had fancier desserts. Even in specific items, class differences are evident. For example, low-income families ate more boiled potatoes, and high-income families ate more baked potatoes.[33] Only iron and niacin show little class variation. The greatest nutritional improvement across classes was in calcium and ascorbic acid. Nationally, the greatest nutritional deficiency was in calcium, with 30% of the families consuming less than the recommended daily allowance (RDA). In addition, one in five families consumed less than the RDA for three vitamins – thiamin, niacin, and ascorbic acid.[34] The lowest income families in the CES survey (less than $1,000 income) ate far less nutritious meals than the black or white working classes. Around one-third of them consumed insufficient calories, protein, and all recorded vitamins. These poor families were at least 30% less likely than laborer families to consume adequate protein, calcium, riboflavin and ascorbic acid.

Although lack of income could result in inadequate nutrition, being in the highest income group did not ensure adequate nutrition. The highest income group ($7,500 and over), who had at least 50% more income than salaried families, was as likely as salaried families to fall short of nutritional requirements, except for Vitamin C.[35]

The 30% increase in per capita expenditures for food between the 1935 and 1950 surveys resulted in real gains in the quality of meals and their

Table 5.6 Index of food consumption, 1950

	Laborers (lbs)[a]	Blacks	Wage earners	Salaried	BLS	USDA–LC	USDA–MOD
Meat/poultry/fish	2.96	0.95	1.10	1.17	0.79	0.61	0.82
Potatoes[b]	2.06	0.99	1.05	1.00	0.96	1.26	0.98
Other fresh vegetables	2.82	0.88	1.06	1.23	0.87	0.55	1.64
Citrus	2.03	0.82	0.95	1.13	0.60	0.62	0.86
Other fresh fruits	1.46	0.86	1.14	1.21	1.39	0.34	1.28
Dried fruit/vegetables/nuts	0.29	1.03	1.00	0.90	1.34	1.72	1.31
Frozen fruit/vegetables	0.06	0.83	1.50	2.00	–	–	–
Canned fruit/vegetables	2.17	0.88	1.12	1.22	0.71	0.43	0.43
Processed dishes/soups	0.35	0.94	1.09	0.94	–	–	–
Fluid milk (qts)	3.00	0.95	1.13	1.13	1.00		
Milk equivalents (qts)	1.48	0.95	1.00	1.05	1.28	3.64	3.92
Fats and oils	0.86	0.98	1.06	1.01	1.05	0.87	⎡ 0.94
Flours	0.70	1.09	1.00	0.84	1.34	1.43	3.93
Cereal/paste	0.68	1.06	0.82	0.85	1.15	0.84	
Breads	1.77	0.99	1.12	1.08	0.82	0.95	
Other baked products	0.59	0.98	1.07	1.12	1.00	–	
Eggs (dozen)	0.54	0.89	1.06	1.17	0.80	0.78	⎣ 1.07
Sugar	0.84	1.02	1.10	0.92	1.10	0.60	1.08
Other sweets/sugar	0.38	0.89	1.18	1.24	1.13	0.74	c
Expenditures[d] (per person, per week)	$5.85	$5.51	$6.32	$6.59	$5.31	$4.39	$5.56

[a] Pounds per person per week, with the exception of milk and eggs (which are in quarts and dozens, respectively). Index was calculated using laborers' consumption.

[b] Prices in this category include sweet potatoes, although the quantities are only white potatoes.

[c] Included in above quantity.

[d] Expenditures are calculated using the prices for the foods purchased by income group comparable to laborers. Agriculture Information Bulletin No. 132, 'Food Consumption of Urban Families in the U.S.' (Oct. 1954). If prices for wage earners are used, the weekly expenditures are $6.53 for wage earners, $5.49 for BLS budget, and $5.83 for USDA moderate cost standard. If prices for salaried workers are used, salaried expenditures are $6.93 and USDA Moderate Cost Budget is $5.91. (Prices in 1948–9$.)

Source: USDA Food Consumption Surveys, 1948–9, Preliminary Report #5, USBLS Workers' Budgets in the United States Bulletin No. 927 (1948); USDA *Helping Families Plan Food Budgets*, Misc. Publications 662 (Dec. 1948).

nutritional content. The 1950 CES marks the last time improvements in nutrition occurred, except among the poor. The vast majority of families with employed workers had met basic nutritional requirements by 1950. As we shall see, further improvements in income would only increase the temptation of potentially harmful dietary choices – such as consuming too many calories and too much sugar and fat.

Wardrobe

Family members in all classes were becoming more and more fashion-conscious. Both adults and children had various types of clothing for different activities, such as school, leisure, sports, work and social events. Although wartime shortages had temporarily revived some home-sewing, little sewing was done in the home now, except for select items that became high status with the 'do-it-yourself' vogue. The appeal of synthetics, which made clothing care much easier and made clothing more durable, continued to grow. Introduced in the late 1930s, nylon became popular during and after World War II, especially for women's clothing.[36]

Clothing had become more informal as well as more specialized by activity. Increasingly, men's vests, hats, suits and ties were replaced by separates (slacks and sports jackets). As central heating and automobile travel became widespread, men wore light cotton underwear instead of heavy union suits. With greater informality, hats, gloves and handkerchiefs were no longer a part of standard public attire for women, and synthetic dresses became a wardrobe mainstay. Wives now had more clothing, especially underwear (slips and bras) and casual wear, and women continued to spend a large fraction of their clothing budget on nylon stockings.

Analysts of the clothing scene[37] observed a continuation of the trend toward greater uniformity across income groups in the types of clothing worn, except for display items (accessories and jewelry). The drive toward greater simplicity and fewer frills, which had been especially encouraged during World War II, had a long-run impact on clothing norms into the 1950s. Yet clothing was still acknowledged to have important psychological effects and to determine activities.[38]

Of the periods studied, only 1935 to 1950 witnessed a major increase in real clothing expenditures per capita. For working-class families, these expenditures climbed over 50%. Clothing's share of the total budget for white families rose only slightly, however, after declining dramatically between 1918 and 1935.[39] For the black family, clothing's share of the budget rose substantially between 1935 and 1950 as blacks made great strides toward owning the clothes needed to be socially presentable at work or in public. Black laborer families, however, still spent 10% less per person on clothing than did white laborer families (see table 5.7).

Females spent more than males on clothing, irrespective of class or age. This represents an important departure from previous surveys; wives and daughters expanded their wardrobes as the family's economic position improved. The wife's clothing budget has served as a bellwether for how

Table 5.7 Annual clothing expenditures, 1950

	Blacks[a]	Laborers	Wage earners	Salaried	City workers budget[b]
Average family size	3.3	2.6	3.2	3.4	4.0
Total clothing expenditure	$303	$272	$377	$504	$430
Expenditure per person	$92	$105	$118	$148	$108
Adjusted for 4-person family[c]	$72	$81	$100	$121	$108
Expenditure per person (if present)	($)	($)	($)	($)	($)
Male 16+ years		86	111	132	143
Female 16+ years		114	132	165	122
Males 6–16 years		59	73	86	88
Females 6–16 years		66	83	99	77
Males 2–6 years		40	53	57	
Females 2–6 years		37	51	59	
Infants under 2 years		29	33	41	
Budget breakdown					
Men and boys total	112	91	139	182	231
Outerwear	66	52	81	108	
Underwear	14	13	19	23	
Footwear	17	16	24	29	
Hats, gloves and accessories	15	10	16	22	
Women and girls total	146	137	178	242	199
Outerwear	74	67	89	121	
Underwear and nightwear	19	19	25	33	
Hosiery	21	14	17	23	
Footwear	20	21	27	35	
Hats, gloves and accessories	13	16	20	30	
Infants less than 2 years	6	5	7	8	
Clothing materials	4	7	10	13	
Clothing services	37	32	43	58	
Total clothing expenditure	303	272	377	504	

[a] More detailed data by race not available.
[b] Budget figures are from March 1946, inflated by the CPI, to 1950.
[c] Expenditures per person adjusted for family of husband, wife, boy (12), girl (8); excludes materials and services. Figure for blacks estimated using expenditure ratios by age for laborers.
Source: *Consumer Expenditure Survey*, Summary Volume and Detailed Clothing Data. Also, *Workers' Budget in the U.S., City Families and Single Persons 1946 and 1947*, BLS Bulletin No. 927.

severely the family needed to economize. As clothing requirements for the husband's work and the children's schooling were met, the wife traditionally began to spend more on her clothing. Also, as the family moved up the income ladder, teenaged daughters were allowed to

Table 5.8A Typical wardrobe – men, 1950

	Assumed years wear	Laborers		Wage earners		Salaried		BLS workers budget
		Quantity	Average cost ($)	Quantity	Average cost ($)	Quantity	Average cost ($)	Quantity
Wool suits	3	1.0	47.38	1.2	50.18	1.5	52.96	2.3
Street shoes	1	0.8	9.93	1.0	10.47	1.1	10.99	1.2
Work shoes	1	0.5	7.60	0.5	7.86	0.5	8.25	0.8
Shirts – business	2	2.6	3.25	3.2	3.37	3.8	3.52	5.8
Shirts	2	3.1	2.39	3.7	2.64	3.9	2.78	4.4
Ties	2	2.0	1.39	2.9	1.51	3.5	1.59	6.0
Trousers (wool)	5	1.8	10.10	2.5	10.74	3.0	11.29	1.8
Trousers (rayon)	3	0.5	7.15	0.7	7.44	0.7	8.00	3.0
Trousers (cotton)	3	0.7	5.11	0.8	5.43	0.7	5.69	0.9
Trousers (work)	3	1.3	3.20	1.5	3.40	1.5	3.52	1.2
Socks	1	9.2	0.43	10.2	0.45	1.1	0.49	13.5
Wool sweaters	5	0.7	6.11	0.9	6.35	1.3	6.72	1.8
Jackets	5	1.0	11.20	1.5	11.72	1.5	13.03	1.5
Undershorts	2	5.2	0.82	6.7	0.86	7.4	0.89	7.2
Light undershirts	2	3.8	0.75	5.2	0.80	5.7	0.81	6.4
Pajamas	2	0.6	3.57	0.8	3.86	0.9	3.85	1.6
Work gloves	1	1.9	0.73	2.4	0.69	2.2	0.75	4.0

	Years wear	Average cost ($)	Years wear	Average cost ($)	Years wear	Average cost ($)	Years wear
Overcoat	7.0	42.43	6.0	43.88	5.0	43.89	4.0
Hat (felt)	3.3	7.61	3.1	8.06	2.7	8.35	1.2
Watch	14.3	28.98	16.7	37.71	12.5	42.15	–

Source: Consumer Expenditure Survey, 1950, Detailed Clothing Data.

increase their clothing expenditures faster than other children in the family. The clothing standards developed by the government did not reflect this norm, however.[40] The city workers' budget still allowed slightly higher expenditures for males than for females for each age.[41]

Working-class husbands spent much less on clothing than recommended by the government budget, which assumed that the husband wore a suit and tie to work.[42] The wage-earner husband spent one-fourth less on clothing than the government standard, and even the salaried husband's clothing expenditures were 10% below the government standard.[43]

Compared to 1935, husbands in 1950 owned fewer suits and ties and more dress shirts, dress pants and jackets. They replaced their wool overcoats a little sooner but kept their felt hats a little longer. The government standard assumed that the husband bought one heavy wool suit every two years, one light wool suit every three years and five shirts and two pairs of shoes each year.[44] In practice, the salaried husband bought one suit every two years and four shirts and 1.5 pairs of shoes annually (see table 5.8A). The laborer bought one suit every three years and three shirts and 1.25 pairs of shoes annually. As meager as the white laborer's clothing purchases were, the black laborer spent almost 10% less.[45]

Clothing became a less important status marker between the salaried and working classes as the quality and availability of store-bought clothing improved. Whereas in 1935 members of salaried families spent almost twice as much on clothing as members of wage-earner families, they now spent only one-third more. Nonetheless, newer, higher-quality and less-worn clothing still distinguished a man from those in the class just beneath him. His wool overcoat was a year or two newer and his felt hat a half year newer (see table 5.8A). The salaried man, compared to the laborer, had over half as many more suits, dress shirts, dress trousers, jackets and ties. In addition, the laborer's clothing improvements did not extend to items that did not show – as in 1935, he still had a fresh change of underwear only five days per week.

Quality differences had declined sharply across classes as working-class men improved the quality of their clothing purchases. For the most visible items of clothing – suits, shirts, jackets, trousers, shoes, ties – salaried men paid only 10%–15% more than laborers (see table 5.8A). In 1935, this price difference typically was one-third greater. The main class marker was worn on the wrist: A salaried man's watch cost 50% more than a laborer's watch. Generally, higher clothing expenditures for husbands across classes paid for more outerwear and were divided three-fourths for more items (variety) and one-fourth for higher quality or prices (status). For accessories for wage earners and footwear and underwear for salaried workers, increased expenditures were split almost 50/50 between more variety and higher status.

Table 5.8B Typical wardrobe – women, 1950

	Assumed years wear	Laborers		Wage earners		Salaried		BLS workers budget
		Quantity	Average cost ($)	Quantity	Average cost ($)	Quantity	Average cost ($)	Quantity
Oxfords and Loafers	1	0.9	7.16	1.0	7.18	1.0	7.54	2.2
Pumps	1	1.0		1.1		1.4		1.5
Coats (wool)	3	1.1	45.30	1.3	45.72	1.4	47.91	1.0
Hats	1	0.7	5.39	0.8	5.25	1.0	5.70	0.9
Sweaters (wool)	3	0.9	4.43	0.9	4.33	1.4	4.70	1.5
Blouses (rayon)	3	1.5	3.82	1.9	3.65	2.3	3.88	0.5
Skirts	3	1.3	5.29	1.5	5.45	1.9	5.83	6.0
Street dresses	2	3.3	9.14	4.0	9.43	4.6	9.75	0.3
Suits	3	0.9	30.07	0.9	30.13	1.2	30.29	3.6
Housedresses (cotton)	3	2.3	3.38	2.8	3.38	2.8	3.58	8.4
Slips	4	6.0	3.16	6.6	3.24	7.6	3.47	1.4
Corsets	2	0.2	10.38	0.2	10.91	0.2	10.99	1.2
Brassieres	1	1.3	1.84	1.6	1.91	1.9	2.02	4.8
Panties (rayon)	2	4.7	0.70	5.2	0.75	5.7	0.75	
Pajamas	3	–		1.9		2.3		
Robes	3	0.5	7.15	0.5	7.91	0.6	8.14	–
Nylons	1 month	0.8	1.33	0.8	1.36	1.8	1.38	0.8

		Years wear	Average cost ($)	Years wear	Average cost ($)	Years wear	Average cost ($)	Years wear
Fur coat		100.0	–	100.0	–	50.0	–	–
Formal dress		17.0	21.05	13.0	20.83	9.0	23.29	–
Handbag		1.9	4.72	1.6	4.97	1.3	5.25	1.2
Watch		25.0	44.36	20.0	45.88	20.0	53.16	–

The high number of years of wear indicates that most females in this group did not own fur coats.
Source: Consumer Expenditure Survey, 1950, Detailed Clothing Data.

In contrast to their husbands, working-class wives spent as much on their wardrobes as recommended by the government budget. In fact, wage-earner wives spent 8% more than the government standard while laborer wives spent 7% less, and salaried wives spent 35% more. The government standard assumed that the wife bought a wool coat every two years and three street dresses and 2.2 pairs of leather shoes each year (see table 5.8B).[46] In practice, wives tended to buy fewer articles of outerwear. The wage-earner wife bought a wool coat every 2.3 years and two street dresses and 2.1 pairs of leather shoes each year. They bought more bras and panties, fewer slips and corsets, and the same number of nylons as the government standard allotted. Even the salaried wife bought fewer dresses, slips, and corsets, but more skirts, blouses, nylons, bras, panties and shoes than allowed by the government standard. One in nine salaried wives also purchased a formal dress, which was excluded from the government standard.

Wives had about the same number of street outfits and pairs of shoes as they did in 1935. As clothing became less formal, however, the number of hats owned dropped by one-half. Working-class wives could replace their wool coats a year sooner. Women were wearing less complicated and less binding underwear, and they owned more synthetic panties. Nylons were still an important part of the clothing budget, but the number owned varied less across classes than silk stockings did in 1935.

For both the husband and wife, clothing had become a less important status marker. Still, the laborer wife's wardrobe was noticeably more shabby than the wage-earner wife's. Her wool coat had to last three years, and she bought fewer than two new street dresses, one new house-dress, and two pairs of leather shoes annually. The working-class wife had more worn and lower-quality clothing than the salaried wife, who owned about one-third more clothing items. Thus, the latter was able to choose clothing more suited for various activities and to wear newer clothes. The salaried wife bought clothing items that usually cost 5%–10% more than the clothes purchased by the laborer wife. No single article of clothing for wives stood out as a status marker between classes. Even the salaried wife's watch cost only one-fifth more than the laborer wife's watch. Fur coats, which were fairly common for salaried wives in 1935, were no longer a regular part of social dress at night.

Status differences in clothes between laborer and wage-earner wives were minimal. The higher clothing budget of wage-earner wives was spent primarily on more outerwear, with nine-tenths for more items (variety) and one-tenth for quality (status). Status differences in clothes were more important between salaried and wage-earner wives, with higher quality (or price) accounting for about one-fourth of the increase in the clothing budget. Accessories had even more status difference, with 40% of the increased expenditures by salaried wives paying for higher-priced items (see table 5.8C).

Table 5.8C Typical wardrobe – boys (6–16 years), 1950

	Assumed years wear	Laborers		Wage earners		Salaried		BLS workers budget
		Quantity	Average cost ($)	Quantity	Average cost ($)	Quantity	Average cost ($)	Quantity
Wool suits	2	0.2	15.98	0.2	19.23	0.3	18.60	0.4
Light wool suits	2	0.3	13.12	0.2	15.40	0.2	17.38	0.5
Street shoes	1	2.0	5.59	2.1	5.96	2.3	6.27	3.0
Sandals and Loafers	1	0.6	3.80	0.7	3.64	0.8	3.95	–
Shirts (dress)	2	1.2	2.04	1.7	2.24	1.8	2.32	
Shirts (sport)	2	5.4	1.42	7.2	1.37	8.1	1.50	7.4
Overcoats (or fingertip coat)	3	0.4	12.66	0.4	15.33	0.4	13.48	0.6
Ties	3	1.1	0.71	1.4	0.82	1.8	0.82	4.1
Trousers (cotton)	2	1.9	3.62	2.0	3.78	2.6	4.17	2.4
Dungarees	2	4.7	2.14	5.7	2.15	6.6	2.22	1.0
Trousers (wool)	3	1.4	5.25	1.9	5.30	2.2	5.81	2.7
Socks (cotton)	1	10.9	0.34	11.9	0.35	12.7	0.37	10.5
Caps	2	1.1		1.3		1.6		
Sweaters (wool)	3	1.3	3.37	1.2	3.73	1.1	4.12	2.5
Jacket (wool)	3	0.8	8.84	0.9	9.43	1.0	9.36	0.7
Jacket (other)	2	0.4	7.52	0.6	8.13	0.7	7.82	
Undershorts	2	5.6	0.60	6.8	0.58	8.4	0.60	5.8
Undershirts	2	3.2	0.56	4.5	0.57	5.0	0.61	4.7
Pajamas	3	1.6	2.32	2.1	2.37	2.7	2.46	2.0
Gloves, mittens	2	1.0	1.25	1.0	1.36	1.4	1.36	1.2
Caps	1	0.5	1.62	0.7	1.64	0.8	1.67	0.7

Source: Consumer Expenditure Survey, 1950, Detailed Clothing Data.

The black wife, who spent 15% less than the laborer wife, had fewer and lower-quality clothes. The black wife could replace her coat and dresses even less frequently than the laborer wife, and spent considerably less on accessories. Even though black wives were able to purchase some acceptable street clothes, these had to last a long time.

Young men (aged 6–16 years) spent two-thirds of what their fathers spent on clothing and young women spent 60% of what their mothers spent (see table 5.8C). This relationship held across all three white classes.[47] Families across all classes spent less than half as much for clothing for younger children (under six years) as for their fathers, and they spent the same amount for youngsters of both sexes.

Like their fathers, older boys spent less on clothing than suggested by the government standard. Their shortfalls were also comparable to their fathers'. Older girls in wage-earner families spent 5% less than the government standard, while girls in salaried families spent 14% more than the standard.

Boys from salaried families bought more clothes than boys from working-class families – 0.5 pair more shoes, 3.5 more shirts, 3.5 more school trousers and 1.5 more dress trousers (see table 5.8C). The salaried boy's purchases fell short of the government standard in heavier clothes (by 0.1 coats, 0.2 wool suits) but exceeded the government standard in school clothes (by 2.5 cotton trousers, 1.3 shirts). For more casual non-wool items, salaried families paid only around 10% more for boys' clothes. For coats, sweaters and suits, however, they paid about one-quarter more, expenditures which match the price difference between class for husbands' clothing. Overall, status differences between classes accounted for 25%–30% of the increment in clothing budgets.

Girls from salaried families bought more clothes than girls from laborer families – 0.7 more pairs of shoes, 0.6 more coats, 0.8 more dresses, 0.8 more sweaters and 0.9 more skirts and cotton blouses. They replaced their handbags more than twice as often. For casual wear and undergarments, daughters from the three classes paid the same prices. For dresses, coats and shoes, salaried daughters paid 10%–20% more than working-class daughters (see table 5.8D). Wage-earner daughters compared to laborer daughters paid about 20% of the increased expenditures for outerwear for higher quality (or status). The proportion of the increased expenditures paying for status doubles to 40% for salaried daughters compared to wage-earner daughters. Between classes, about 40% of increased expenditures for shoes was spent for higher quality (status) (see table 5.9). For accessories, increased expenditures across classes was primarily for variety rather than status.

Overall, clothing services accounted for 12% of the families' clothing budget, and materials for sewing and knitting accounted for less than 3%.[48] Salaried families spent four-fifths more on clothing material and

Table 5.8D Typical wardrobe – girls (6–16 years), 1950

	Assumed years wear	Laborers		Wage earners		Salaried		BLS workers budget
		Quantity	Average cost ($)	Quantity	Average cost ($)	Quantity	Average cost ($)	Quantity
Shoes (oxfords)	1	1.7	4.95	1.7	5.39	1.8	5.52	3.4
Pumps	1	0.9	4.07	1.0	4.35	1.1	4.59	
Loafers	1	0.2	4.20	0.4	4.49	0.4	4.96	
Coats (heavy wool)	3	0.9	19.51	1.0	20.95	1.1	22.54	1.0
Coats (light wool)	3	0.6	14.08	0.6	14.40	0.9	14.55	1.0
Dresses (wool)	2	0.4	5.52	0.5	4.72	0.5	5.43	0.3
Dresses (cotton)	1	1.7	3.18	1.8	3.61	2.1	4.04	3.8
Dresses (rayon)	2	0.4	5.24	0.6	5.68	0.6	5.58	0.5
Hats (felt)	3	0.7	2.56	1.0	2.56	1.2	2.72	1.4
Sweaters (wool)	3	2.1	3.29	2.6	3.25	2.8	3.65	1.8
Skirts (wool)	2	1.6	3.91	2.0	3.77	2.2	4.08	1.0
Blouses (cotton)	2	1.4	2.02	2.0	1.96	2.3	2.06	1.8
Blouses (rayon)	2	0.9	2.26	0.9	2.33	1.0	2.73	0.1
Slacks	2	0.7	2.70	1.1	2.52	1.3	2.69	0.9
Slips	2	2.5	1.65	2.9	1.57	3.3	1.60	3.1
Brassieres	2	1.0	1.20	1.0	1.19	1.2	1.35	–
Panties	2	7.5	0.46	8.0	0.48	9.6	0.51	9.8
Pajamas	3	1.4	2.32	2.2	2.49	2.6	2.58	2.1
Nylons	1	1.0	1.11	0.7	1.10	0.9	1.22	–
Anklets	1	10.9	0.36	11.8	0.37	12.0	0.38	11.8
Gloves	1	0.6	1.12	0.7	1.19	0.8	1.25	0.6
Handbags	4	1.0	2.11	2.2	2.05	2.5	2.06	1.0

Source: *Consumer Expenditure Survey, 1950, Detailed Clothing Data.*

Table 5.9 Clothing: variety vs status[a] (1950 dollars)

	Laborers 1950 Annual expenditure per person ($)	Wage earners/laborers 1950			Salaried/wage earners 1950		
		Difference[b] ($)	Variety (%)	Status (%)	Difference ($)	Variety (%)	Status (%)
Husband's clothing							
Outerwear	42.02	13.25	78	22	11.96	74	26
Underwear	8.58	2.45	76	24	1.17	55	45
Footwear	11.74	2.37	73	27	1.61	54	46
Hats, gloves, ties, watches	7.10	1.60	54	46	2.22	67	33
Wife's clothing							
Outerwear	49.80	9.12	92	8	12.92	78	22
Underwear	9.72	1.74	76	24	2.31	71	29
Nylons	11.98	1.28	77	23	2.71	92	8
Shoes	13.75	1.26	96	4	3.31	74	26
Hats, gloves, and accessories	8.11	1.62	93	7	2.55	60	40
Son's clothing (6–16 years)							
Outerwear	24.91	5.87	74	26	6.14	72	28
Underwear	7.52	1.55	94	6	1.88	71	29
Footwear	13.20	1.99	66	34	2.34	59	41
Caps, gloves, ties	1.73	0.46	72	28	0.62	97	3
Daughter's clothing (6–16 years)							
Outerwear	25.08	5.18	79	21	6.76	58	42
Underwear, nightwear	6.00	1.46	88	12	1.43	75	25
Nylons, anklets	5.01	0.16	31	69	0.47	51	49
Shoes	12.64	2.61	56	44	1.85	63	37
Hats, gloves, handbags	1.79	1.07	100	0	0.54	74	26

[a] Variety reflects increase in quantity purchased (change in average number purchased per person); status reflects increase in price (change in average cost per item).

[b] Amount by which the wage-earners' adult male's (husband's) clothing expenditure exceeded the laborers' adult male's expenditure per year, etc.

Source: Clothing expenditure charts (Tables 5.6A).

services than laborer families and one-third more than wage-earner families. The government standard was 10% above the expenditures by wage-earner families and was mostly dry-cleaning for the husband (nine garments per year) and wife (eight garments) plus miscellaneous accessories equaling 3% of the clothing allowance for adults and 2% for children. Sewing materials per se were not included. In practice, dry-cleaning accounted for two-thirds of expenditures for services and materials. Shoe repair accounted for 10% of expenditures and watch repair for almost 5%. Materials for sewing and knitting were less than 20% of the combined expenditures for materials and services.

The transformation of clothing from being a central part of daily life, both as a marker of status and a housework activity, was completed by 1950. Transportation and recreation, which became more important both as daily activities and as budget items, replaced clothing as a primary marker of status. The demotion of clothing was facilitated by the continuing trend toward less formal and cumbersome clothes, and the change was made possible by the development of mass-produced high-quality, ready-to-wear clothing. These shifts in social norms to informal, ready-to-wear clothes greatly reduced the burden of caring for clothes. Clothing care was also made easier as the washing machine improved and as wardrobes grew, so that mending became less important.

At the same time that clothes became less important as a status marker, black families were catching up to minimal clothing standards, including purchasing some clothing for public activities. Class distinctions could still be made by minor differences in appearance, most notably the condition of the clothes. Now, however, one's automobile was a much more noticeable and reliable guide to class status.

Home

The urban home ownership rate hovered around 55% during the Depression; chaotic financial markets did not encourage new ownership. Home buying expanded rapidly during the 1940s, as many single-family rental units, which were subject to Federal rent control laws during the war, were sold to occupants. In 1940, 41% of dwellings in non-farm areas were owner-occupied; by 1945, 50% were owner-occupied, even though new housing construction was severely constrained by wartime regulations while temporary war housing was built by the government.[49] By 1950, two-thirds of urban housing was owner-occupied.[50]

Since the 1920s, the standard of housing had failed to keep pace with the family's income;[51] by 1950, a large, pent-up demand for housing existed. The resulting housing boom in the 1950s was sustained by federally backed loans (Veterans' Administration (VA) and Federal Housing Administration (FHA) mortgages) as well as by the use of private wartime savings. Government studies showed that owning was cheaper than renting the equivalent living space. Generally, however, families wanted to own a home in order to have control over their environment as well as have a larger, more comfortable house with modern amenities and a yard. Urban renters tended to live in apartments rather than houses, and often rentals were in the city rather than the more desirable suburbs and outlying areas.

Home ownership still differentiated classes (see table 5.10). Only one-fourth of the black working-class families owned their homes compared to over one-half of the white salaried families. But progress had been made; home ownership had grown more rapidly across all classes since the Depression than would have been predicted by emulation patterns and income growth. The home ownership rate increased by 80% for wage earners, by around 50% for blacks and laborers, and by 30% for salaried families. The potential demand for home ownership, however, was still large in all classes.

The pent-up demand for housing was reflected in the fact that expenditures (constant dollars) on housing and utilities rose dramatically less than total expenditures between 1935 and 1950.[52] Black families were the only class that substantially increased (by 43%) their real expenditures on housing and utilities between 1935 and 1950. The white working class increased such expenditures by 5%, while the salaried class actually spent 8% less on housing (constant dollars) in 1950 compared to 1935.

A significant number of laborer and black families still lived in housing that was dilapidated or had no running water. One in ten laborer families, or twice the rate for wage-earner families,[53] lived in such substandard housing (see table 5.10). Adequate plumbing facilities, including a private bath, toilet, and hot running water, also continued to separate classes. One in three laborer families, compared to one in seven salaried families, did not have full plumbing.[54] On the other hand, spaciousness, in terms of rooms per person, varied only slightly across class. The quality of housing continued to vary by region, with the South still lagging behind the rest of the country. The Southern rate of dilapidated urban housing (12%) was twice the national rate, and 18% of Southern urban units lacked a private bath or toilet, compared to the national rate of 12%. As suburban rings developed around cities, the more desirable and modern housing became located outside the city. For all classes, suburban dwellers were much more likely to be homeowners and large city dwellers to be renters (see table 5.11).[55] The large proportion of housing that lacked full plumbing or was dilapidated was one indicator of the potential demand for better housing. Shared housing also represented some unmet demand for housing. In 1950, 6% of married couples did not have their own households and 2% of families were 'secondary' (i.e., they shared housing with non-relatives).[56]

Table 5.10 Shelter expenditures, 1950

Average expenditure	Blacks			Laborers			Wage earners			Salaried			BLS standard
	Exp. ($)	% rep.	Cost ($)	Exp. ($)	% rep.	Cost ($)	Exp. ($)	% rep.	Cost ($)	Exp. ($)	% rep.	Cost ($)	
Total Shelter Cost	402			483			560			650			662
Total Housing	270			353			404			474			
Rented dwelling[a]	223	73	305[b]	252	63	394	244	53	444	246	46	492	
Owned dwelling	42	27	155	97	37	255	156	47	318	218	54	396	
adjusted for mortgage[c]			NA			280			364			440	
Other Housing[d]	4			3			5			10			
Utilities	132			130			156			176			
Owners detailed housing data													
First mortgage interest				17	41	112	39	57	144	57	63	168	
Property taxes				26	95	73	37	96	81	51	98	96	
Maintenance				36	100	97	57	100	121	82	100	152	
Painting outside					24	60		28	70		30	70	
Painting inside					38	27		42	32		46	39	
Papering					20	41		20	38		20	42	
Plumbing					15	63		20	62		20	60	
Carpentry					10	68		10	80		10	84	
Heating					10	175		10	180		15	188	
Repair (renters)	7			7			8			11			
Lodging at school	1			1			1			6	3		

	Blacks			Laborers			Wage earners			Salaried			BLS standard
Average expenditure	Exp. ($)	% rep.	Cost ($)	Exp. ($)	% rep.	Cost ($)	Exp. ($)	% rep.	Cost ($)	Exp. ($)	% rep.	Cost ($)	
Average expenditure	132			130			156			176			
Fuel/light and refrigeration													
Coal[e]					31	92		31	98		29	101	
Gas[f]					62	46		72	52		77	59	
Electricity					79	43		87	50		91	57	
Fuel oil					24	102		26	104		26	121	
Ice					13	31		8	32		6	28	
Water					42	19		53	19		59	21	
Quality of housing													
Dilapidated or no running water					10			5			3		
With private bath, toilet, hot water, not dilapidated[g]					69			81			86		

[a] Percentage renters is all non-homeowners. Rent includes fuel or utilities if included in rent. Rent also includes repair, which averaged $8 (laborers), $9 (wage earners), $11 (salaried).

[b] Cost = average expenditure ÷ percentage reporting expenditure. The percentage reporting expenditure used in this calculation exceeds that recorded in the table since those that changed from renters to owners (or owners to renters) during the year were counted as both renters and owners.

[c] Includes principal paid on mortgage. Interest was already included.

[d] Other housing includes: lodging while away at work, at school, or traveling (Volume XVIII, Summary Volume of *Consumer Expenditure Survey* 1950). Expenditure on rented vacation homes appears under recreation rather than shelter, except for blacks.

[e] Coal figures assume that a household bought only one type of coal.

[f] The percent of households using gas and electricity includes households paying for these alone and those paying for gas and electricity combined.

[g] Calculations from 1950 Census of Housing, pp. 1–16, includes all units inside SMSAs by income group. The census recorded home ownership rates at 2 to 4 percentage points higher than in *CES*.

Source: *Consumer Expenditure Survey,* 1950 Summary Volume and Detailed Housing Data, Expenditures and 'Workers' budgets in the U.S.,' Bulletin No. 927, BLS.

Table 5.11 Housing: suburb vs city, 1950 (percentage reporting by city size)

Category	Large city			Suburb			Small city		
	Laborers	Wage earners	Salaried	Laborers	Wage earners	Salaried	Laborers	Wage earners	Salaried
Homeowner	27.40	39.35	48.49	48.63	57.04	66.75	42.07	49.34	53.05
With first mortgage	13.08	23.98	31.41	19.79	33.97	41.92	14.50	28.26	34.73
Renters, pay rent	71.51	60.80	53.48	50.98	44.46	34.74	54.76	51.46	50.45
With vacation home	0.85	0.85	1.09	0.87	0.87	0.87	1.13	1.00	1.49
Repair									
Painting outside	7.70	12.95	15.99	13.48	16.12	20.59	9.22	11.90	14.07
Painting inside	11.08	17.84	22.98	17.75	27.46	33.14	17.55	19.27	24.35
Purchase heating/air	2.95	5.71	7.51	5.05	4.51	9.96	4.39	4.89	6.88

Source: Consumer Expenditure Survey, 1950, Detailed Housing Data.

Location by neighborhood is the primary determinant of housing quality – both in terms of the modern amenities as well as in terms of the desirability of the neighborhood, including such things as the amount of open space, the crime rate, noise level and public goods (schools, parks, libraries, sidewalks). These locational differences provide tangible economic distance or barriers across classes, yet are not apparent in the data collected.[57] In addition to the measures of substandard housing, the price differential can be used as a measure of the economic distance in housing across classes.

The white working class lived in units charging over one-third more rent than those occupied by black families, while salaried families paid rents that were almost one-third higher than those of the working class. The white classes had these same relative differences in homeowners' expenditures (adjusted for mortgage interest).[58] Higher-class families also kept their homes in better repair and were more likely to spend money on the appearance of their homes. For example, laborers painted the outside of their home only every ten years compared to every five to six years for salaried families. Laborers did some inside painting every six to seven years compared to every four years for salaried families. Overall, salaried families spent 2.3 times as much as laborer families on home maintenance.

The typical urban home had four to six rooms for three persons. Amenities included running water, private toilet and bath, central heating (except in the South), gas or electric stove, and mechanical refrigerator. The rent for such a home was estimated by one study to be about $38 monthly,[59] which is only 8% more than the average rent reported by wage-earner families.

The BLS included the same amenities (except for central heating) in a five-room unit in its city workers' budget (see table 5.12). A decent neighborhood was also required – one that had some open space for play, public transportation within ten blocks, and was *not* adjacent to a dump, railroad tracks, main traffic artery, or a noisy or smokey factory (see table 5.12).[60] The rent, heat and utilities for such housing was estimated to cost from $557 annually in New Orleans to $977 in Richmond, Virginia; the median for the 34 cities surveyed was $760.[61] This standard seems far above the housing most families actually could afford. Even the average salaried-class renter fell below this budget standard by 14%, and black families were 47% below. The primary difference between the two housing standards seems to be the desirability of the neighborhood. The lower expenditure (i.e., $38 monthly) reflects actual rents without any locational requirements, while the higher BLS budget reflects rents only in neighborhoods meeting specific requirements.

The two different estimates indicate that the average wage-earner family's home had sufficient amenities but that many were located in

Table 5.12   Shelter standards, 1950

Dwelling	Rented house
	Five rooms, including kitchen and bathroom
	Hot and cold water
	One window at least in each room
	Electric light in each room
	Heating to maintain 70°F
	Walking distance to food stores and elementary schools
	Neighborhood has places to play

Source: 'Workers Budgets in the US: City Families and Single Persons, 1946 and 1947' (City Workers' Budget), BLS Bulletin No. 927, p. 19.

less-than-desirable neighborhoods. Salaried families were much more likely to pass the neighborhood test, while laborer families, and especially black families, were more likely to live in units without the required amenities, as well as in unsuitable neighborhoods.

Using energy

For many families, fuel oil replaced the less desirable coal as the main energy source of heating energy between 1935 and 1950. The even more desirable energy sources – gas and electricity – were also widely used. Wood burning became more ritualistic than utilitarian.

Black and white laborer families spent considerably more per person (constant dollars) for utilities in 1950 than in 1935, while wage-earner families spent only slightly more and salaried families actually spent less. By 1950, classes seemed to diverge much less by the amount of heat and light they used; they continued to differ in the cleanliness and ease of use of their energy source (see table 5.10).

Government budget standards allowed 1,200 kilowatt-hours of electricity for lighting and appliances, 235 therms for cooking and hot water heating, 77 BTUs for heating and 9,600 cu ft of water.[62] The electricity standard allowed 3,300 watt hours daily, or the equivalent of running four 100-watt light bulbs five hours a day and having 250 watts to run electrical appliances. This equaled ten times the actual electricity usage of salaried families in 1918. The government standard for other energy usage was extremely low in comparison with earlier years. The gas standard was equal to the actual usage of laborers in 1918. The BTUs allowed for heating were equivalent to only 70% of the actual BTUs supplied by wood and coal for laborers in 1918.[63]

The reliance on gas and electricity to provide heat and light increased with the family's class status, while the reliance on coal and even fuel oil declined. Although the three white classes spent the same amount on coal, sharp class distinctions existed for electricity and gas expenditures.

Salaried families spent over 50% more on electricity and gas than laborer families. Salaried families also spent 30% more on fuel oil.

Water usage climbed by class, as did the care of lawns and use of washing machines. As mechanical refrigerators replaced ice boxes, the use of ice plummeted. Salaried families used 1.5 times as much water, but only 40% as much ice, as laborer families. The cost of electricity to run the refrigerator was less than the cost of ice for the icebox. The local ice house was fast becoming a relic of the past.

Running the home

As electric appliances became an essential part of housing, the distinction between expenditures for furnishings and operations collapsed. For example, electric refrigerators and washing machines (now including automatic) dramatically affected food preservation and clothes cleaning. These appliances changed the housewife's economic transactions, such as food shopping and use of laundry services. They also transformed the way tasks were performed in the home. Usually the changes involved both decreased drudgery for the housewife and higher standards for housework, such as cleaner clothing and fresher, more varied foods.

Real expenditures for furnishings doubled between 1935 and 1950. Equipment had become the largest category, accounting for 30%–40% of the furnishings budget (see table 5.13). Standard items included electric vacuum cleaners, toasters and irons as well as refrigerators and washing machines. Some families were also now buying the newly available deep-freeze units, clothes dryers, and automatic ironers.

Almost one-half of furniture and major household purchases in 1950 were made with installment credit. Refrigerators were most likely to be purchased with credit (54%); other likely candidates for purchase by credit were furniture (47%), televisions (44%), and washing machines (42%). The use of credit for making purchases was more important for the working classes, of which almost two-thirds reported some consumer debt, than for the salaried class, of which almost one-half reported some consumer debt.[64]

The BLS workers' standard budget included: a gas or electric stove; a mechanical refrigerator; a washing machine (probably not automatic); an ironing machine; sewing machine; vacuum cleaner; iron; toaster; waffle iron; and radio. The major appliances were expected to last 16 years. The smaller appliances, except the toaster, were expected to last considerably longer.[65] More frequent replacement rates had actually been achieved by white families in 1935, with the exception of refrigerators for laborers.

Appliance buying was at a much higher rate in 1950, partly reflecting remnants of pent-up war demand. White families did not vary in their frequency of buying stoves and refrigerators (these purchases were

Table 5.13 Furnishings expenditures, 1950

	Blacks	Laborers	Wage earners	Salaried
Average expenditures $				
Total furnishings and equipment	174	172	236	331
Household textiles	24	20	28	39
Floor coverings	7	12	18	32
Furniture	50	38	59	87
Equipment	69	73	87	115
Other housewares	25	29	44	58

Specific items	Laborers		Wage earners		Salaried	
	% reporting	Cost ($)	% reporting	Cost ($)	% reporting	Cost ($)
Sheets	36.3	2.66	41.9	2.77	49.3	2.83
Pillowcases	24.6	0.81	27.8	0.86	35.6	0.87
Turkish towels	24.7	0.80	30.5	0.83	33.4	0.91
Draperies	12.7	12.13	17.3	14.10	17.8	21.40
Curtains	23.6	10.85	29.4	12.62	33.7	15.82
Living room suite	5.4	184.70	5.7	177.65	7.4	256.01
Dining room	1.3	125.02	2.4	142.96	2.8	183.87
Dinette	5.1	69.52	7.1	91.35	7.7	93.29
Bedroom	3.9	190.05	5.2	216.67	6.3	251.88
Sofas	3.4	71.76	3.0	87.00	4.7	99.59
Wool rugs and carpets	7.4	90.14	11.9	94.45	15.6	141.86
Cotton/other fiber rug	8.8	13.41	13.9	14.17	17.7	17.01
Linoleum	18.1	20.94	19.9	21.76	19.9	27.49
Refrigerator – mechanical	13.8	224.36	12.6	235.25	14.2	259.16
Stove	10.1	129.84	10.1	152.67	10.3	173.20
Pots and pans	17.7	12.15	21.5	13.86	22.6	15.80
Vacuum (upright)	2.7	70.13	4.6	68.08	4.8	79.53
Vacuum (tank)	3.3	67.96	5.6	72.21	7.2	75.32
Brooms	57.8	3.56	64.0	4.03	64.5	4.73
Washing machine (automatic)	3.2	173.19	5.9	191.65	6.5	206.04
Washing machine (non-automatic)	6.4	96.62	7.0	103.59	7.8	121.87
Light bulbs	75.2	0.19	82.4	0.20	82.3	0.20
Sewing machine	3.4	100.47	5.4	131.47	6.9	128.63

Cost is average expenditure ÷ percentage of households purchasing.
Source: Consumer Expenditure Survey, 1950, Summary Volume and Detailed Furnishings Data.

mainly for replacement), but frequency of buying washing machines did increase with class. In 1950, one in eight white families bought a mechanical refrigerator, one in ten a stove, and one in seven (salaried) to ten (laborer) a washing machine. Although the laborer family was twice as likely to buy a non-automatic as an automatic washing machine, the wage-earner and salaried families were more likely to buy the highly coveted automatic washer. 'Blue Monday' (wash day) was finally losing its bad reputation. Automatic washers took the drudgery out of washing and allowed it to be done more frequently. Now only hanging the clothes out to dry remained a major effort.

Quality differences mattered most for washing machines, with salaried families spending over twice as much for their automatic washers as laborer families did for their non-automatics. Even when salaried families bought non-automatic washing machines, they paid one-quarter more than laborer families, in order to gain more features. The salaried family spent one-third more on a stove than the laborer family, but only one-sixth more on a refrigerator, which was the most costly appliance purchased.

Families were now spending almost as much on furniture as on household textiles ('linens') and housewares combined. Inexpensive, mass-produced furniture, using glue and metal joints as well as spray-on finishes, became widely available and allowed working-class families to furnish their homes more comfortably and stylishly. Quality differences rather than quantity differences marked class status in furniture. Over four in five salaried families now furnished their homes with matching suites of furniture in the living room and bedroom (see table 5.14). Many fewer salaried families owned dining room suites. They were more likely to have the smaller dinette sets, which cost half as much and would fit into a combined living/dining room or kitchen. One in ten salaried families appears to have had both a dining room suite and a dinette set.

In contrast to the salaried families, laborer families had less furniture and fewer stylish suites. Only four in five laborer families had a dining room or dinette suite and only three in five had a living room suite (see table 5.14).

Table 5.14 Actual furnishings, 1950 (percentage of families owning consumer durables)

	Laborers	*Wage earners*	*Salaried*
Living room suites	63	74	82
Dining room suites	31	37	44
Dinette suites	48	60	64
Bedroom suites	65	76	82
Upholstered chairs	32	40	47
Wool rugs/carpets	45	57	68
Refrigerators	64	78	83
Stoves	63	71	78
Vacuum (upright)	29	34	40
Vacuum (tank)	13	23	30
Sewing machine	35	42	51
Washing machine (automatic)	18	24	28
Washing machine (non-automatic)	36	44	47

Source: *Consumer Expenditure Survey*, 1950, Detailed Furnishings Data. No data available for blacks.

Quality differences between classes were greater for dining room and living room furniture than for bedroom or kitchen furniture. Salaried families paid 40% more than laborer families for their sofas, dining room suites, and living room suites, and they paid 30% more for dinette and bedroom suites.

Floor coverings – rugs and carpets – provided an important distinction across classes. Laborer families were only half as likely as salaried families to purchase rugs or carpets in 1950, yet they were as likely as salaried families to purchase some linoleum. Floor coverings were replaced less frequently by laborer families than by salaried families. Laborers were only two-thirds as likely to have at least one wool rug (a costly item). Salaried families spent 70% more on wool rugs than laborer families. Salaried families replaced draperies and curtains 40% more often and spent 50% more on their purchases. They also replaced linens – sheets, pillowcases, and towels – 40% more often, but price differences

Table 5.15　Furnishings standards,[a] 1950

Living room	Upholstered davenport and chair (set) (18 years)
	Chair, other (13 years)
	Table, occasional (8.5 years)
	Desk (34 years)
	Bookcase (53 years)
	Axminster rug (9 ft × 12 ft) (17 years)
Dining room and kitchen	Dinette set (50 years)
	Kitchen table (21 years)
	Kitchen cabinet (53 years)
	Kitchen chair (3 years)
	Cook stove (16 years)
	Refrigerator (16 years)
Bedroom (master)	Bed, chest, dresser (set) (21 years)
	Wool scatter rug (27 in. × 45 in.)
Bedroom (children's)	Bed with bedspring (8 years)
	Chest (21 years)
	Cot (21 years)
	Cotton scatter rug (24 in. × 48 in.)
Other	Porch furniture
	Washing machine
	Electric iron
	Toaster
	Fan
	Cooking utensils
	Brooms and mops

[a] Implied life (before replacement) is shown in parentheses if all families are assumed to own the item.
Source: 'Workers Budgets in the U.S: City Families and Single Persons, 1946 and 1947' (City Workers' Budget), BLS Bulletin No. 927, p. 19.

for linens were negligible across classes. Salaried families spent twice as much for wool blankets and 50% more for bedspreads.

In the kitchen, salaried families had more and better-quality housewares than working-class families. They paid about two-thirds more for their flatware as well as for their pots and pans. The largest price difference (90%) was observed for dish sets.

BLS workers' budget standards (see table 5.15) reflected the family's improved furnishings. Two-thirds of laborer, three-fourths of wage-earner, and four-fifths of salaried families met the BLS budget standards for furnishings, which upgraded the 1935 WPA standards considerably by adding an upholstered sofa, a desk, and bookcase in the living room; a dinette set and a kitchen cabinet in the kitchen, and a chest in the master bedroom. The quality of furnishings, and their stylishness, also became more important. Suites (i.e., matching furniture) were allowed in the living room, dining area, and master bedroom. Comfort also improved as more living room furniture was upholstered and one child was allotted a bed with bedsprings rather than a cot. In addition, the family was allowed furniture for sitting on their front porch.

The differences across classes in the household operations budget were much less pronounced in 1950 than in 1935. The major item purchased now was telephone service, which was much cheaper and more widespread than in 1935 (see table 5.16). Few families had to walk to a coin box or telephone office to make a call, since three-fourths of the families had a telephone at home. This was a remarkable change from 1935, when only one in three families had telephone service. Telephone service had finally become available to the working class, whereas, even in 1935, 80% of salaried families had telephones. Families with telephones typically paid $75 annually for local calls and $15 for long distance calls, or about double the cost of written communications. Since the telephone provided the primary means of day-to-day business and social communications, not owning this instrument resulted in a family being at least partially isolated from the community. The telephone had evolved from being a status marker into being an important part of daily life. Long distance calls, however, remained fairly rare and indicated the higher status provided by greater economic and social networks. Only one in three laborer families made long distance calls compared to over one-half of the salaried families.

Distinctions by class for help with laundry and other housework had diminished. About one-third of the white families sent their laundry out. Many more laborer families were now able to have their laundry done outside the home than in 1935. Salaried families were still much more likely than working-class families to have clothes dry cleaned. The big change for salaried families was the decline in domestic service: in 1935, one in four reported domestic help; in 1950, the rate had fallen by

Table 5.16 Household operation expenditures, 1950

	Blacks		Laborers		Wage earners		Salaried		Government standard
	Exp. ($)	% rep.	Exp. ($)	% rep.	Exp. ($)	% rep.	Exp. ($)	% rep.	Exp. ($)
Household operations	94	100	115	100	145	100	186	100	53
Selected categories									
Clothing care			24		26		32		
Maid/baby-sitter			9		14		24		
Written communications			11		14		16		
Telephone			30		39		51		11[a]
Cleaning and papers			23		30		33		35[b]

	Cost[c] ($)	% rep.	Cost ($)	% rep.	Cost ($)	% rep.	
Laundry sent out	57	34	60	34	70	37	
Dry cleaning	10	13	10	18	11	25	
Wage maid	88	7	96	10	117	13	
Baby-sitters	39	7	40	12	56	16	
Day nurseries	145	1	91	1	144	2	
Telephone/local/	42	60	45	73	49	84	
long distance	15	35	15	45	19	53	
Soap and cleaning supplies	19	89	23	92	25	95	
Paper supplies	8	73	10	82	11	85	
Postage[d]	7	95	8	97	9	97	
Stationery[e]	5	93	7	96	7	97	
Flowers for house	7	14	8	19	8	27	
Flower and lawn seeds	6	22	8	29	9	36	
Moving	30	11	41	11	41	12	7[f]

[a] Includes both written communication and telephone.
[b] In addition to cleaning and paper supplies, matches and refuse disposal are included.
[c] Cost = average expenditure ÷ percentage reporting expenditure.
[d] Expenditures are for postage and stationery combined; percentage is for postage only.
[e] See note d.
[f] Local moves only. Also, the budget allowed for 4.2% of the families to move 390 miles to another city, but the cost was not given separately. In the government's budget standard, moving expenses were included under transportation.
Source: *Consumer Expenditure Survey*, 1950, Summary Volume and Detailed Housing Data, and 'Workers' Budgets in the U.S.,' Bulletin No. 927, BLS.

one-half. Families were only slightly more likely to have a baby-sitter than a maid and salaried families were only twice as likely as laborer families to have either. When they did have a maid or baby-sitter, salaried families spent 33% more on the maid and 44% more on the baby-sitter. Day nurseries were little used by any class. Overall, the majority of white families seemed to have had some help with clothing care, house cleaning, or child care. Three in five laborer families and nine in ten salaried families reported some form of assistance (i.e., laundry sent out, dry cleaning, maid, or baby-sitter). Salaried families spent three-fourths more on housework help than laborer families.

The BLS budget standard for household operations was generally far below actual practice. The standard was outdated and reflected practices current in 1935. The operations standard did not include any assistance with laundry, house cleaning or baby-sitting. Communications were to be handled by mail, and families were allotted fewer than three telephone calls weekly, and these from a coin box. Such allowances were less than what wage earners spent on postage and writing supplies, and, of course, did not include home telephone service. The standard allowed cleaning and paper supplies at about the level purchased by wage-earner and salaried families.

Household operations became more sophisticated as housework became easier and as the family became more integrated into the community's economic and social life. The operations budget for the working class in 1935 was primarily spent on cleaning supplies. Now most working-class families had a telephone, and a majority had some form of assistance with housework.

Getting Around

During World War II, when no new cars were produced for private use and gasoline was rationed, the use of local transit soared. After the war, people resumed driving their automobiles; ridership on public transit fell by one-fourth between 1946 and 1950. By 1950, two in three people lived in urban areas. Over one-half of the population lived in a metropolitan area, and two in five metropolitan residents lived *outside* the central city.[66] Car ownership was now required for living in many areas and provided convenience in other areas. Forty million automobiles were registered in 1950, and three in five families owned a car. Four in five salaried families owned a car, as did one-half of the laborer and two-thirds of the wage-earner families. In contrast, only one-fourth of the black families owned a car, a lack which both symbolized and enforced their exclusion from white society.

Ownership of a second car was still a rare phenomenon – only 7% of families had more than one car.[67] Owning one car gave the family a new sense of private and discretionary mobility, and this new mobility rapidly became part of the structure within which the family functioned. Owning a second car gave the family much greater flexibility in transportation and increased autonomy among family members. The second car became a coveted item and a status marker. Ownership of a second car rose with

Table 5.17 Transportation expenditures, 1950

	Blacks		Laborers		Wage earners		Salaried		Government standard[a]	
									Midsize cities	Large cities
	Exp.	% rep.	Exp.	% rep.	Exp.	% rep.	Exp.	% rep.	Exp.	Exp.
Summary										
Total travel and transport	192	96	309	97	487	99	647	99	317	241
Total auto expenses	127	24	257	49	431	68	579	78		
Auto purchase (net)	76	11	136	18	229	27	321	32		
Auto operation	53	23	120	49	202	68	258	78		
Other travel and transport	63	92	52	82	56	68	68	85		
Estimated costs (using Government standards)	183		245		292		316			
	Cost[b] ($)		Cost ($)		Cost ($)		Cost ($)		Cost ($)	Cost ($)
Selected Details										
Automobile expenditures – total	529		524		634		742		(374)	(402)
Purchase (with extras)	NA		901		1,024		1,256		126	126
Net purchase (including financing and trade-in)	691		756		848		1,003			
Operating expenses – total	230		245		297		331			
Auto repairs (not covered by insurance)			127		62		66		18	18
Other transportation	68		63		67		80		(124)[c]	(134)

[a] Calculated from US BLS, *Family Budget of City Worker, October 1950*, Bulletin No. 1021, 1951, p. 3, and *Workers' Budgets in the United States: City Families and Single Persons, 1946 and 1947*, p. 38. In mid-sized cities (50 to 1,900,000), 74% were assumed to own cars; in large cities (over 1.9 million), 40% were assumed to own cars.

[b] Cost average expenditure ÷ percentage purchasing.

[c] Standards are not directly comparable to survey figures since automobile budget includes all transportation expenditures for car owners and other transportation includes all transportation expenditures for non-owners. Also, the government standard includes moving expenses of at least $7.00.

Source: *Consumer Expenditure Survey*, 1950, Summary Volume and Detailed Transportation Data.

income from less than 1% (under $3,000 income) to over 10% (over $5,000 income).[68]

The amount families could spend on transportation remained an important indicator of their standard of living. The salaried family spent one-third more on transportation than the wage-earner family, who spent three-fifths more than the black family (see table 5.17).

Many families – from one in nine black families to one in three salaried families – purchased a new or used car annually. Slightly over half of the families purchasing an automobile also traded a car. Most automobiles, including all of the used cars, were purchased for a base price and excluded extra equipment. Only three in seventeen laborers and nine in thirty-two salaried workers purchasing a car reported paying for extra equipment (see table 5.18). The ability to purchase a new car (median price of $2,120, including a $530 trade-in allowance) instead of a used car (median price of $550) increased greatly with class status. In 1950, about 20% of salaried families reported purchasing new automobiles and 10% reported purchasing used autos. About 9% of the working class reported purchasing new automobiles, and 19% reported purchasing used autos.[69] Purchasing a new car was a status marker, along with the type of car purchased. Salaried families, who spent one-fifth more than wage-earner families on their cars, bought modest or average-priced cars. The value of their cars averaged $1,255 (including extra equipment); new cars had an average wholesale price of $1,270 in 1950.[70] The quality differences between classes in car purchases decreased with class status so that white laborers spent only one-tenth more for their cars than did black families. A minority of families financed their autos – only one in four for laborers and one in three for wage earners and salaried workers.

Families who owned cars used them for different occasions and drove them varying distances. The social requirement to drive a car to various activities reflected the family's mobility, which continued to increase with the family's status. Salaried families who owned an auto spent one-fourth more on gas than wage-earner families, who spent one-seventh more than laborer families. Salaried families kept their cars in better repair, and they were much more likely to lube or wash their cars or buy new tires. Their repair bills averaged 5% of the purchase price of a 'new' car. In contrast, three in five laborers with cars reported repair bills averaging 14% of the purchase price of a 'new' car.

The usage rates and amount spent on transportation other than private automobiles did not vary significantly across the white classes. Black families relied more than white families on public transit. Most white families (seven in ten), however, still used local public transportation for some trips, especially to school or work. One in three families reported taxi fares. Very few families (2%–3%) reported traveling by plane or ship; amounts spent on these forms of travel increased with class.

Table 5.18   Transportation, detailed expenditures, 1950

	Laborers			Wage Earners			Salaried		
	Exp. ($)	% rep.	Cost[a] ($)	Exp. ($)	% rep.	Cost ($)	Exp. ($)	% rep.	Cost ($)
Auto purchase (without extras)	149.79	17	881	268.89	27	996	387.25	32	1,210
Extra equipment	3.33	3	111	7.62	6	127	14.63	9	163
Finance	3.08	4	77	10.17	9	113	10.63	11	97
Trade-in	25.39	9	282	61.43	15	410	96.25	19	507
Gasoline	48.69	46	106	78.81	65	121	112.04	75	149
Oil	4.95	45	11	8.41	64	13	10.55	73	14
Lube/wash/light repairs	3.97	37	11	7.61	55	14	10.84	64	17
New tires	6.10	15	41	10.89	26	42	13.85	30	46
Retreads	0.00	6	0	1.48	9	16	1.45	9	16
Batteries	2.64	19	14	4.24	28	15	4.87	31	16
Repairs (not covered by insurance)	38.05	30	127	28.07	45	62	34.30	52	66
Equipment	0.00	5	0	1.85	10	19	2.96	12	25
Fire insurance	0.00	0	NA	1.46	7	21	2.00	10	20
Public liability insurance	3.73	10	37	5.90	15	39	8.13	20	41
Collision insurance	1.93	4	48	3.23	4	81	3.23	7	46
Combined insurance	11.41	19	60	19.79	31	64	27.58	38	73
Registration fees	5.37	41	13	8.75	61	14	11.16	70	16
Parking	2.44	13	19	3.93	22	18	5.33	28	19
Other transportation									
Streetcar/bus/subway	31.43	70	45	32.16	72	45	36.22	72	50
Taxi	3.85	31	12	4.61	32	14	5.17	33	16
Carpool	3.24	0	NA	4.14	0	NA	4.77	0	NA
Auto share	1.44	0	NA	1.23	0	NA	1.73	0	NA
Train – first class	1.56	3	52	1.84	2	92	2.90	4	73
Train – coach	3.94	10	39	3.65	9	41	4.22	10	42
Interurban bus	3.85	14	28	2.62	10	26	2.78	9	31
Aircraft, ship, etc.	1.63	2	82	2.61	2	131	4.40	3	147
Bicycles	0.95			2.33			3.33		

[a] Cost = average expenditure ÷ percentage purchasing.
Source: Consumer Expenditure Survey, 1950, Detailed Transportation Data; NA = not available.

The BLS workers' budget allowed car ownership for three-fourths of the families in mid-sized cities and for two-fifths in large cities.[71] The family was assumed to own a six- to nine-year-old car that cost (after trade-in) about $350 in 1941, when 'cheap second-hand cars were available'.[72] The standard budget for car ownership was unrealistically low and did not allow for replacement of automobiles at 1950 prices when second-hand cars were still scarce since auto production had been halted during the war. The government allowance for automobile purchase was only $126, which was considerably less than the $370 that every laborer who owned a car spent on the purchase (net). Even blacks owning cars had an implicit auto purchase allowance one-third higher than the standard. The repair allowance was only $18 (in 1950 dollars), while laborer car owners averaged $62. The standard also allowed each car owner eight gallons of gas weekly, and insurance for only 45% of car owners (unless it was legally mandated by the state).

Public transportation allowed by the BLS budget depended on city size and car ownership. Families without cars were allowed 16 (mid-sized city) or 18 (large city) local transit rides weekly, and families with cars were allowed 3–6 local rides. Railroad trips 'for infrequent trips home to visit parents and other relatives' were also included in the budget. Thirteen percent of auto owners and 31% (mid-sized cities) to 49% (large cities) of non-automobile owners were assumed to take a yearly train trip covering 760 miles. The BLS standard for non-auto owners cost from $95 in New York City to $148 in Boston and averaged $125 across 28 cities (in 1950 dollars).

The BLS budget standard for all transportation[73] was only slightly less than the amount spent by laborer families. However, only one-half the laborer families were car owners, compared to the government standard's assumption of 74% car owners. Car ownership greatly increased transportation expenses. In the BLS workers' budget, families owning cars were allowed three times as much for transportation as families without cars, even using the BLS's unrealistically low costs for automobiles. Using the BLS's costs for car owners and non-owners to estimate transportation expenditures for each class results in blacks spending 5% more than the estimate and salaried workers spending 105% more. The disparity between actual expenditures and estimated expenditures rose with car ownership.

Mobility has always been costly and a marker of status. Widespread use of the private automobile dramatically improved the mobility of working-class people and altered forever the transportation patterns of daily life. Owning an automobile was still expensive for a married working man, however. Transportation expenditures rose to the level of housing expenses, and above the level for clothing in the family's budget.

By social norms, black families did not spend enough on transportation to be full participants in social and economic life. Their lack of mobility kept them largely confined to their own parts of the city and to specific work locations. In Southern cities, blacks and school children were assumed to be the main users of public transit. Even laborer families failed to meet the automobile ownership norms. As with three-fourths of the blacks, one-half of the white laborers spent too little on transportation to be sufficiently mobile in daily life.

For all classes below the salaried class, automobile expenses took a larger share of the transportation budget as car ownership increased between 1935 and 1950. Car ownership rose from 11% to 24% for black families, and auto expenses rose from 28% of the transportation budget in 1935 to 66% in 1950. Even though their ownership rates varied by 10 percentage points, the wage-earner and salaried classes spent almost 90% of their transportation budgets on their automobiles (the same percentage allocated to the car by salaried families in 1935). This 90% rate seems to have been an upper bound on the transportation dollars the family would spend on car travel.

Black and white working-class families had made important improvements in their transportation practices by 1950, yet the social norms for daily mobility had increased even more rapidly as the automobile allowed the building of suburban housing and the spread of shopping districts. Over the next decade, as families continued to increase their travel by car, automobile expenditures represented ever-greater portions of their budgets.

Spending Leisure Time

The Depression forced a major restructuring of the working week, which resulted in more time available for family life and leisure activities. In 1931, only 6% of industrial workers had a two-day weekend. Following passage of the Fair Labor Standards Act in 1935, the 40-hour week – eight hours, five days a week – became the norm. During the years following World War II, paid vacation days became an important part of compensation, and the yearly family vacation became a part of the normal summer pattern.

References to the possible evils of idle time and the pursuit of pleasure were now rare. The five-day workweek and higher incomes gave families both the time and money for recreational activities, and recreation became an important industry, totaling $10 billion in 1950.[74] Publishing (books, periodicals, newspapers), and motion pictures were by far the largest 'leisure time' industries, but others – such as the radio, photography, sports equipment and toys – each had sales approaching $1 billion. Among commercial entertainment, movie theaters dominated, with sales approaching $2 billion. Live theater, bowling alleys and horse racing were the only other amusement places reporting sales of over $150 million.[75] A Twentieth Century Fund study estimated that consumer needs for private recreation were being met, but that government expenditures for public recreational facilities needed to be increased 40%.[76]

During the war, four out of five families had radios, and they listened to them for entertainment (both drama and music) as well as news. By 1950, over 90% of all homes had at least one radio. Expenditures on radios had risen since their introduction in 1920, while expenditures on musical instruments and phonographs declined. Then, with the introduction of high fidelity ('hi fi'), sales of phonographs revived.

The most dramatic impact on daily life during this period, however, came with widespread introduction of television. First authorized on a commercial basis in 1941, fewer than one million households had a television set at the end of the 1940s. After the war, the Federal Communications Commission (FCC) granted licenses for stations throughout the country. One-third of households owned a television in 1950, and three-fourths by 1956.[77] Television helped to further homogenize the national culture. At the same time, television raised material aspirations by presenting programs that focused on families in affluent settings and airing commercials that urged consumers to buy a wide array of goods to become successful or fulfilled.

By 1950, leisure and recreation had become important status markers for the salaried and working classes. Affluence had brought with it the attempt to emulate the Joneses, even when at rest.[78] Partly, this reflected the fact that work and housework had both become physically less demanding. Their extra energy could now be put into recreational activities, which were often educational as well as entertaining. People had more leisure time, and they were less exhausted. In fact, people's more sedentary work lives required them to exercise in their free time to stay fit.

Recreational expenditures (including reading materials) rose rapidly with class – laborers spent 46% more than blacks; salaried spent 117% more than laborers (see table 5.19). Attending movies remained the most popular recreational activity outside the home – four in five black and nine in ten salaried families went to the movies. The proportion of black families that could afford to go to the movies had more than doubled since 1935, while the already high white rates increased slightly. Now the proportion of black and white families who went to the movies at least once was similar. How often they attended movies, however, still varied by class.

Compared to 1935, attending paid events (e.g., concerts, baseball games) other than movies increased in relative importance for white families. These events conferred status, and each class spent about one-fourth more on such events than the class beneath it.

Expenditures for leisure time activities at home were dominated by expenditures on television. Even with few laborer families owning television (TV) sets, laborers spent almost as much on TV as on movies. In 1950, TV ownership rose rapidly with class status – one-tenth of laborer, one-fourth of wage-earner, and one-third of salaried families owned a television.[79] Wage earners spent 43% more and salaried families spent 66% more for TV than for movies. Ownership of a television set was an important marker of status and social integration in cities with TV reception. Spending more on TV sets could buy a larger screen as well as a more attractive cabinet. Families purchasing television sets spent about

Table 5.19 Recreation and education, 1950

	Blacks		Laborers		Wage earners		Salaried		Government standard ($1,950)
	Exp. ($)	% rep.	Exp. ($)	% rep.	Exp. ($)	% rep.	Exp. ($)	% rep.	Exp. ($)
Total recreation and education	150	93	194	96	283	99	383	99	135
Recreation and reading	87		127		198		275		86
Admissions	25	79	30	86	39	91	48	94	
Purchase of TV, radio, musical instruments	24	30	30	28	59	38	86	46	
Newspapers, magazines, and books	19	85	28	96	34	98	41	99	
Vacations[a]	NA		9	15	15	22	25	29	
Other recreation expenses[b]	19	69	30	82	51	91	75	96	
Education	6	31	11	23	15	33	26	42	9
Tobacco	57	77	57	71	70	76	83	82	40

Detailed expenditures

	Laborers			Wage earners			Salaried		
Details	Exp. ($)	% rep.	Cost ($)	Exp. ($)	% rep.	Cost ($)	Exp. ($)	% rep.	Cost ($)
Movies	24.89	82	30	31.94	87	37	38.42	91	42
Other admissions	4.58	35	13	7.40	48	15	10.46	53	20
Doll and stuffed toys	1.48	NA	NA	2.77	NA	NA	3.18	NA	NA
Tricycles	1.60	NA	NA	2.95	NA	NA	3.90	NA	NA
Other toys	3.22	25	13	6.34	36	18	8.96	40	22
Sports goods	2.20	11	20	4.61	21	22	7.03	26	27
Fees, licenses	1.02	20	5	2.65	30	9	4.73	34	14
Records, sheet music	1.47	18	8	2.62	27	10	4.37	37	12
Cameras and equipment	2.65	31	9	4.68	45	10	8.03	55	15

Details	Exp. ($)	% rep.	Cost ($)	Exp. ($)	% rep.	Cost ($)	Exp. ($)	% rep.	Cost ($)
Dues	3.17	25	13	5.14	34	15	8.12	42	19
Other recreation	2.76	9	31	4.80	14	34	5.72	15	38
Pet food	5.59	19	29	6.96	25	28	8.93	28	32
Recreation (away from home)	3.41	15	23	6.20	22	28	9.38	29	32
Reading									
Newspapers	18.38	89	21	22.39	96	23	24.91	97	26
Magazines	5.25	58	9	7.59	70	11	10.00	78	13
Books bought	2.52	19	13	3.44	22	16	4.91	28	18
Education									
School book supplies	2.73	19	14	4.16	26	16	6.35	34	19
Tuition	5.50	8	69	6.64	12	55	12.13	17	71
Music lessons	1.51	4	38	3.89	9	43	6.34	12	53
Radios[c]	3.48	11	31	3.38	9	35	3.20	9	32
TV and TV combination[d]	20.84	8	255	42.95	15	260	59.82	27	222
TV installation	1.24	3	41	2.82	6	47	3.93	9	44
Radio/phonograph combo	2.52	16	125	4.39	24	130	6.87	30	152
Pianos	0.00	9		1.97	12	158	4.24	13	300
Vacation									
Recreation away from home	3.00	15	23	6.00	22	28	9.00	29	32
Vacation housing rent	2.00	4	50	3.00	7	43	6.00	9	67
Vacation lodging	4.00	14	28	6.00	20	30	10.00	25	40

[a] Percentage of household's spending on vacation is percentage spending for recreation away from home.

[b] Other recreation includes recreation away from home (vacations) for the black families.

[c] Average costs for radios and TVs are from data on prices.

[d] Percentage is for TV and TV combinations. Price is for TVs alone; combinations typically cost more.

Source: *Consumer Expenditure Survey*, 1950, Detailed Recreation and Detailed Education Data, and 'Workers' Budgets in the U.S.,' Bulletin No. 927, BLS.

the same amount unless they bought a 'combination' console, which cost about one-third more than the $260 for a simple television. One in five salaried families who purchased a television set in 1950 bought a combination.

White families bought many more magazines and books in 1950 in than in 1935. Their book and magazine purchases equaled about 40% (laborer) to 60% (salaried) of an annual newspaper subscription compared to 10%–30% in 1935. While fewer than 5% of working-class families bought books in 1935, one in five did in 1950. Still, magazines remained much more popular than books and were bought by three in five laborer families and four in five salaried families. The newspaper remained a part of daily life for white families and finally had become part of daily life for black families, who had doubled their frequency of buying newspapers since 1935. Most blacks could now afford a daily newspaper, so perhaps some of the 15% of black families who did not purchase newspapers did not have a family member who could read.

Compared to 1935, all families spent more money on a large array of leisure time goods and activities. Engaging in a variety of activities and owning the required equipment was becoming more important than club membership for marking status and creating social life. Compared to laborer families, salaried families spent three times as much on sporting goods and toys, bought three times as many records, and were three-fourths more likely to own a camera. Salaried families now spent as much on toys and sporting goods as on newspapers, and over one-half owned a camera. Although belonging to a civic or social club or recreation association was now less important for salaried families than in 1935, it was more important for working-class families (one-fourth to one-third were members). The dues differential across class was lower in 1950 than in 1935, but salaried families still paid 50% higher dues.

Salaried families were twice as likely to have expenses for school supplies and for tuition. Two in nine salaried families reported making average tuition payments of $71, indicating that private school enrollment was on the rise. Payments for books and supplies at public schools were down since more school districts, especially outside the South, no longer charged for books and equipment.[80] Only 31% of black families reported any expenses for school books, supplies or tuition in 1950 compared to 69% in 1935.

Blacks dramatically increased their expenditures for tobacco products relative to whites, and the white working class increased their tobacco purchases somewhat relative to the salaried class, who still had a slightly higher smoking rate. Smoking was in its heyday, and three-fourths of all families reported buying tobacco products. The amount they purchased went up slightly across classes.

The BLS workers' budget standard allowed the same constant dollar expenditure for recreation in 1950 and 1935. However, the quantities allowed in 1950 were more generous than in 1935, which raises questions about the pricing procedures used in formulating the standard. Besides the daily newspaper, families were allowed 2.7 magazines each month. Parents and the younger girl could attend the movies every three weeks, while the older boy could go every other week. The family could attend only one cultural or sports event annually (or the parents twice by themselves). An allowance was given for purchase of a radio every nine years and for repair, but television was not mentioned. Expenses for books and supplies at school were included, as well as one-half pack cigarettes daily. A small amount for all other expenses (e.g., hobbies, toys, games and parties) was also included.

In practice, white families spent considerably more on recreation than allowed in the BLS standard. Black families met the standard. All classes spent 40%–100% more on tobacco than the standard allowed. The white working class greatly expanded its budget for recreation and leisure time activities. The growth of recreation's share of the budget is an important indicator of improvement in the standard of living. Various forms of entertainment had begun to make life more interesting, and social activities were becoming a more significant part of routine patterns. Family life was also made more pleasant by outings and vacations.

Black families had to postpone expanding their recreational activities until they had met their basic needs in food, clothing, shelter and transportation. Recreation's share of their budgets lagged behind that of the white working class. In contrast, the salaried class was already spending a considerable proportion of their budget, over 8%, for leisure time activities by 1935; they increased this proportion only a small amount by 1950. Even so, their income growth had allowed them to expand their outings and vacations considerably. The path to the affluent leisure society was in full view.

Caring for Health

The quality and availability of health care and disease control rose dramatically over the first half of the twentieth century. One indicator of this improvement was the 50% decline in the infant mortality rate and the 90% decline in the maternal mortality rate. A stillbirth or death of an infant (under one year) was not a rare occurrence, however, since 2.3 stillbirths and 2.9 infant deaths occurred for every 100 live births. But the death of a child after the first year fortunately had become a rare occurrence. The cumulative death rate for children aged one through 14 years old had fallen from 1.4 per 100 children in 1918 to 0.6 in 1935 to 0.2 in 1950. By 1950, vaccines had virtually eradicated fatalities associated with the childhood diseases of diphtheria, measles, and whooping cough. The development of penicillin during World War II, and the other antibiotics that followed, provided an effective treatment of many common infections, such as pneumonia and meningitis. Deaths from influenza and pneumonia were greatly reduced (0.3 per 1,000 people in 1950). Medical breakthroughs had relegated many dreaded diseases, including typhoid and smallpox, to the history book. On the other hand, the death rates of heart disease (5.0 per 1,000 people) and cancer (1.4 per 1,000) continued to rise and were increasingly associated with industrial growth. The death rate from automobile accidents, however, were lower in the 1950s than in the 1930s.[81]

One physician termed finding a cure for tuberculosis, which was a highly contagious mass killer, the most urgent medical problem in the twentieth century. The search, which spanned over 70 years, resulted in major breakthroughs during World War II with the identification of three drugs that were effective in fighting tuberculosis. By the late 1950s, the battle against tuberculosis was won by using a combination of all three drugs to cure patients.[82]

One result of twentieth-century health improvements was longer life spans. Life expectancy at birth continued its climb, increasing by seven years between 1935 and 1950. This matched the gain posted between 1919 and 1935 but was higher than the gains that would be experienced after 1950. By 1950, the gap in life expectancy between blacks and whites had narrowed some, while the gap between men and women had widened with the decline in maternal mortality. In 1950, life expectancy at birth was 72 years for white females, 66.5 years for white males, 63 years for black females, and 59 years for black males.

Expenditures on health accounted for almost 5% of GNP. The government's share of health expenditures, which had been steadily increasing, leveled off in the 1950s at around one-fifth. Private health insurance had grown rapidly during the 1940s; by 1950, one-half of the population had some form of hospitalization insurance and one-third had some insurance covering physicians' surgical fees.[83] Among urban families in 1953, 70% had some health insurance, mainly obtained through the workplace. The variation by family income was large – from 41% (incomes under $3,000) to 80% (incomes over $5,000).[84]

Health and welfare plans in collective bargaining agreements became more widespread during World War II as wages were stabilized but employee benefits were allowed to be expanded. The 1949 decision by the President's Fact Finding Board in the Steel Industry Dispute recommended including health insurance and pensions to cover 'temporary and permanent depreciation in the human "machine".'[85]

Insurance covered only 15% of the medical expenses incurred by families; for the most part, hospital and surgery charges were reimbursed, albeit partially.[86] And so almost one in five families had outstanding health care bills.[87] This, of course, varied by class status – almost one in four working-class families owed debt on medical bills in 1952, while fewer than one in seven salaried families did.[88] Twentieth Century Fund estimated the resources required to fulfill health care needs was one-half more than the current expenditures.[89]

These national improvements in health care were reflected in black families' budgets. Over one-half of black families reported some form of health insurance, and four out of five reported direct payments for medical care. Compared to the government standard and to the usage rates of the white classes, black families still had to economize on health care costs more than was considered prudent. In contrast, three out of four wage-earner and salaried families had some health insurance and virtually all of them reported out-of-pocket medical payments. Wage earners, whose medical costs approximated the government standard, spent 125% more than blacks on health care (see table 5.20).

Group plans or insurance, which averaged $50 annually, covered hospital costs. For close to one-half of the holders, these plans also covered some part of physicians' surgical costs and laboratory tests or X-rays. Black families spent one-third of their health care budgets on group plans. White families, who were able to spend more money on health care and had better access to health care facilities, spent one-sixth of their health care budget on group plans. The three white classes averaged about $35 in direct payments for hospital expenses. Other direct payments – for physicians, eye and dental care, or drugs – all increased with class. Salaried families spent 60% more than laborer families for doctors' services and for drugs, and twice as much for eye and dental care.

The three white classes reported the same hospital usage and costs. The use of physicians at the hospital increased with class status, however. Generally, the use of physicians' services and dental care were the main class markers in health care. The use of physicians' services was expanding. Each physician now served more patients by practicing out of an office instead of making house calls. Regular dental care was not practiced by many families, and only one-third to one-half reported any visits to the dentist.

The BLS workers' budget standard assumed that families paid for 16 physicians' calls, one-fourth of them made at home. The family was expected to require a surgical procedure once every three years; one-half of the surgery was tonsillectomy, adenoidectomy and appendectomy. The wife was expected to be the greatest user of doctors' services. She was allowed six calls yearly, while the husband was allowed four calls, and the two children six together (2.7 for the boy and 3.3 for the girl). No reasons are given for why females were allowed more visits to the doctor than males. Most likely the wife's visits implicitly included pregnancy and childbirth, although the stereotypical family was not expecting to grow.

Table 5.20   Medical care, 1950

	Blacks		Laborers		Wage earners		Salaried		Government standard
	Exp. ($)	% rep.	Exp. ($)	% rep.	Exp. ($)	% rep.	Exp. ($)	% rep.	Exp. ($)
Medical care	90	91	152	96	203	99	230	99	195
Group plans, insurance	28	54	24	60	37	73	43	76	
Direct payment	62	83	128	94	166	97	187	97	
Hospital expenses			34		37		38		
Physician			33	68	47	77	53	82	
Dental			16	45	27	59	34	66	
Eye care			6	25	8	29	11	35	
Drugs			21	74	29	81	33	82	13

	Laborers			Wage earners			Salaried		
Detailed summary	Exp. ($)	% rep.	Cost ($)	Exp. ($)	% rep.	Cost ($)	Exp. ($)	% rep.	Cost ($)
Insurance									
Group hospital	9.48	29	33	14.36	38	38	15.94	39	41
Group hospital and surgery	5.94	14	42	9.46	20	47	12.59	24	52
Group medical and hospital	2.45	6	41	3.63	7	52	3.45	7	49
Combined	2.26	5	45	3.38	6	56	4.65	7	66
Disability health accident	4.51	11	41	4.84	12	40	5.83	13	45
Hospital	34.16			36.90			38.03		
Room	6.67	10	67	6.72	10	67	6.65	11	60
Physician	11.57	12	96	15.29	15	102	14.32	16	90
Nursing	0.00	0	NA	0.00	0	NA	1.29	0	NA
Other	2.44	7	35	3.54	8	44	3.44	9	38
Combined	13.48	9	150	11.35	9	126	13.62	9	151
Other Medical									
Physicians	33.33	68	49	46.70	77	61	52.69	82	64
Dental	16.50	45	37	27.13	59	46	34.55	66	52
Chiropractor	2.01	0	NA	2.28	0	NA	2.69	0	NA
Oculist (eye care)	6.27	25	25	7.66	29	26	10.68	35	31
Drugs	21.34	74	29	28.78	81	36	32.79	82	40
Appliances	1.35			1.42			1.73		
X-rays, tests	1.62	0	NA	2.29	11	21	2.50	12	21
Other	1.40			0.97			1.65		

Source: *Consumer Expenditure Survey*, 1950, Summary Volume and Detailed Medical Data, and 'Workers' Budgets in the U.S.,' Bulletin No. 927, BLS.

Unfortunately, no data are given to show use of medical care by different family members. The standard and actual practice are also hard to compare because the pricing of the standard is not broken down by categories. In practice, families' calls on physicians ranged from a low of about 2.3 calls per person for low-income families to about 6.0 calls per person for higher-income families.[90] The BLS budget standards used for health care represent the actual practice of families with a higher level of income than is assumed for other expenditure categories since, according to the BLS budget analysts, it was generally accepted that the majority of families did not receive sufficient medical and dental care.[91] The dental standard allowed the husband and girl to have their teeth cleaned once every three years and the wife and boy once every two years. The family unit was allowed one extraction annually and four fillings.[92] Little preventive dental care was done, and the need for fillings and extractions was high. The wife's teeth were assumed to require more attention than her husband's. If family members received the dental care assumed in the government standard, by age 35 a man would have had seven teeth extracted and 27 fillings; a woman would have had 11 teeth extracted and 34 fillings.

In practice, the variation in the rate of individuals' visiting the dentist was large across classes – from 23% for people in families with incomes of $2,000–$3,500 to 56% for those with incomes above $5,000.[93]

The spread of group hospital plans by 1950 represented a big step toward more adequate health care for black and working-class families. Still, black families were not able to buy sufficient physicians' services or dental and eye care. Although working-class families seemed to receive sufficient hospital care, their dental and eye care were sporadic. One in four wage-earner families reported no doctor's calls even though four out of five bought some drugs. Although medical care had improved considerably since the Depression, both in the treatment available and in access to care, families were still foregoing some essential medical care.

Looking Presentable

For the white classes, spending on personal grooming did not rise as rapidly as spending on health care. In 1935, the four classes had spent one-half as much on personal care as on medical care; in 1950, the white classes spent only two-fifths as much. Blacks, however, had dramatically increased their personal care expenditures to over 80% of their also higher medical care outlays. Black families spent one-fifth more on personal care than did laborers. Black and laborer families spent the same amount on toiletries, but blacks spent 50% more than laborers on haircuts, 'waves' (including straightening hair), manicures, and shaves (see table 5.21). Beauty parlors and barber shops often provided a center for community life, and buying their services was important enough for black families that they economized severely in other areas in order to spend as much as salaried families did for these services. This focus on appearance, both in personal care and in clothing, indicates the improved

Table 5.21 Personal care, 1950

	Blacks		Laborers		Wage earners		Salaried	
	Exp. ($)	% rep.	Exp. ($)	% rep.	Exp. ($)	% rep.	Exp. ($)	% rep.
Personal care	76	100	63	100	82	100	97	100
Toiletries	37	99	37	99	49	100	57	100
Services	39	94	26	93	33	97	40	98

Details	Laborers			Wage earners			Salaried		
	Exp. ($)	% rep.	Average cost ($)	Exp. ($)	% rep.	cost ($)	Exp. ($)	% rep.	Average cost ($)
Haircut	16.94	86	20	22.41	94	24	26.55	96	28
Permanent wave	3.79	28	14	5.03	38	13	6.25	40	16
Shampoo and set	5.03	20	25	4.69	20	23	6.21	24	26
Toilet articles	7.44	91	8	9.18	93	10	9.73	95	10
Toilet soap	4.46	64	7	5.78	74	8	6.71	82	8
Cleansing tissue	6.50	91	7	8.13	95	9	9.28	95	10
Toothpaste, etc.	4.69	75	6	6.76	84	8	8.15	87	9
Shaving soap/shampoo	1.02	27	4	1.42	35	4	1.77	41	4
Cosmetics	7.23	77	9	9.82	85	12	11.96	90	13
Combs/brushes	1.07	53	2	1.47	62	2	1.83	66	3
Razors	3.14	64	5	4.21	74	6	4.49	77	6
Sanitary napkins	1.65	28	6	2.43	36	7	3.06	40	8

Source: *Consumer Expenditure Survey*, 1950, Summary Volume and Detailed Personal Care Data.

integration of blacks into the economic community and the rise of social life in the black community as incomes climbed. It also indicates attempts by blacks to make their hair presentable by white standards.

The majority of women had professionally executed shampoos and perms or waves, for which they now paid almost one-half as much as haircuts for everyone. The appearance of one's hair still marked status among whites, and salaried families spent twice as much as laborer families both in 1935 and in 1950. Toilet articles took a larger share of the personal care budget in 1950 than in 1935, primarily as a result of most women using some make-up as a part of daily life. Cosmetics now accounted for over 10% of the personal care budget. The use of make-up increased with class status – three in four laborer wives averaged $9 on cosmetics while nine in ten salaried wives averaged $13.

The BLS workers' budget allotment for personal care coincided with laborers' actual expenditures in this area. The BLS standard was liberal in haircuts for the husband but frugal in everything else.[94] The standard assumed that the husband had his hair cut every 3.5 weeks, while the wife and daughter supposedly had haircuts every three months and the son every 5.5 weeks. The wife was assumed to visit the beauty parlor infrequently, since she was allowed only 0.6 perm, 0.8 shampoo and 2.9 fingerwaves annually. Otherwise, the family was assumed to buy shaving supplies for the husband, basic make-up (face powder, rouge and lipstick) for the wife, and dental care items for the family. But the family had to use these items carefully. The father had to make a razor blade last ten days, and he had only 11 ounces of shaving cream, 3.2 cakes of shaving soap and 1.0 ounce of after-shave lotion for the year. The wife had 2.5 ounces of face powder, 3.5 ounces of cold cream, 2.7 ounces of hand lotion and 1.9 ounces of deodorant for the year. The family shared 30 ounces of toothpaste, 20 ounces of mouthwash, and six toothbrushes over the year.[95] They were allowed one new comb annually and a new brush every other year.

The importance of personal appearance rose as family members engaged in more recreational and social activities and as the pursuit of individuality became more acceptable, although in a limited way, outside the upper class. In addition to cleanliness, make-up and hair style distinguished personal appearance and were becoming important to the working class.

Insuring and Giving

Retirement income became more important as living into retirement became more probable. In 1935, a 20-year-old white male could expect to live to be 66 years old, which precluded retiring. His black peer could expect to live to be 58 years old. In 1950, a 20-year-old white male could expect to retire at age 65–67 and die at age 70. Black males still could not expect to retire, since a 20-year-old black male could expect to die at age 64 and a 40 year old at age 67. Earlier, a husband's primary concern was providing life insurance for his family. Now, a white man needed to prepare for the more positive event that he would need income for retirement.

The majority of families – from three-fourths of the laborer to nine-tenths of the salaried – were covered by Social Security (i.e., Federal Old Age and Survivors Insurance), and so private insurance was less essential.[96] Yet most families still bought some life insurance for the husband to help pay bills in the event of his death at least during a transitional period until the family could find a new support system or greatly reduce its standard of living. Of those families who did buy private life insurance,[97] laborers bought a policy similar to the one included in the BLS budget standard, and salaried families bought a policy worth one-half more (see table 5.22). The policy purchased by blacks was about 85% of the laborers' policy, assuming that both groups made the same Social Security contributions. By 1950, the Social Security contribution rate was 1.5% on a maximum of $3,000 earnings.[98]

Table 5.22 Insurance, gifts and other, 1950

	Blacks Total exp. $	Laborers Total exp. $	Wage earners Total exp. $	Salaried Total exp. $	Government standard Total exp. $
Personal insurance	97	108	165	206	92
Gifts and contributions	57	96	121	163	68[a]
Other	30	41	40	53	36[b]

	Laborers Exp. ($)	Laborers % rep.	Laborers Average cost ($)	Wage earners Exp. ($)	Wage earners % rep.	Wage earners Average Cost ($)	Salaried Exp. ($)	Salaried % rep.	Salaried Average Cost ($)
Life endowment annuity	63	66	95	91	78	116	113	81	140
Combined life	6	6	94	6	6	98	9	6	143
Group insurance	3	12	27	5	16	31	8	20	40
Social security[c]	35	76	46	61	86	71	74	89	84
Gifts and contributions									
Contributions for support	15	9	167	22	10	224	31	13	237
Christmas gifts	33	58	58	41	69	59	55	74	75
Community chest	6	73	8	9	82	11	13	86	15
Religious	34	69	49	44	75	59	57	81	70
Other									
Interest on loans	3	8	34	4	11	34	5	12	45
Bank service charges	1	13	8	2	21	8	2	27	9
Funerals	14	12	116	8	14	59	11	16	71
Legal	5	5	110	3	7	45	4	9	40
Lost or stolen money	2	5	36	2	6	34	3	7	47
Allowance to children	4	9	43	6	15	43	12	20	58
Real estate	2	3	68	2	4	57	3	4	74
Raised food	4	17	24	4	17	24	5	18	25
Other insurance	1	2	36	1	4	33	2	5	34

[a] Cost is calculated as 2.7% of total cost of goods and services in budget standard. This equals $69 (blacks), $80 (laborers), $105 (wage earners), and $131 (salaried).
[b] This excludes the $24 for occupational expenses. The purpose of this $36 is unclear; it most likely represents an adjustment for actual expenditures for occupational expenses in the 34 cities for which the standard is priced.
[c] Social Security includes FICA and government retirement programs (e.g., railroad and federal employees).
Source: *Consumer Expenditure Survey*, 1950, Summary Volume and Detailed Data, and 'Workers' Budgets in the U.S.,' Bulletin No. 927.

Work-related expenses, such as union dues or purchase of tools or uniforms, were not reported in 1950. Instead, these expenses were deducted before recording gross income, and they were not recorded separately. This procedure makes it impossible to say anything about unions in 1950 or to make comparisons to other surveys. The implicit assumption is that any occupational expenses, including union dues, are a deadweight loss to the worker. The BLS budget standard allowed $24 (in 1950 dollars) for occupational expenses (i.e., dues to unions and special clothes or equipment) under the miscellaneous category. In pricing the budget standard in 34 cities, occupational expenses seem to be $60, however.

Outside of work-related programs, the church remained the major benefactor of contributions. Although the great majority of families still made religious contributions, their donations did not keep pace with the rise in income, and they became more equal across classes. Among families making religious contributions, laborer families contributed 1.7% of their total expenditures while salaried families contributed 1.4%. In 1935, the rate had been closer to 1% for all classes.

Charitable giving had become much more widespread since 1935, with over three-fourths of white families making contributions to the community chest. Among families making a contribution, however, their relative rate of giving had remained at the 1935 level – of about 20% of the average religious contribution.

In 1935, salaried families had spent as much for gifts to persons outside the immediate family[99] as for religious contributions. The white working class was much more restricted in their gift-giving, and gift-giving was out of the question for most black families. By 1950, a sign of affluence was the widespread practice of gift-giving by the white working class who, like the salaried class, now spent as much on gifts as on religion. Gift-giving during the holidays was practiced by over two-thirds of the white families (see table 5.22). Blacks were able to spend more for gifts in 1950 than in 1935, but their gifts and contributions still only averaged 60% of laborers' amounts.

Miscellaneous expenditures highlight important changes taking place in economic life. An increasing proportion of families were using banking services and borrowing money for purchases other than cars or houses, and more were also using a lawyer's services.[100] The use of banks and lawyers increased with class.

Signs of the complexities of modern economic life were beginning to show in these 1950 budgets. They reflected both the positive – increased integration of the working class into the society with a richer, more interesting life-style – and the negative – higher transactions costs associated with daily life. These trends would become more evident in the coming decades.

Ensuring the Future

Although the society had made no commitment to ensure that all members could participate fully in economic life, unemployment insurance and Social Security helped families with employed heads to maintain their standard of living over their lifetimes.[101] The one-third or so of families whose income fell below $2,000 had limited or no access to the labor market and so remained unaffected by these programs that had been designed to help the working class.

Families had been building up their net worth through home ownership, and those with incomes above $2,000 usually had net worths above $1,000. The majority of families with incomes below $2,000 had net worths below $1,000. By occupation, salaried families had a median net worth of $4,355; wage earner, $2,286; laborer, $892.[102]

Few families had liquid assets, which could be used in time of crisis. In 1951, the median asset holdings of the salaried class was about $900; for wage earner, $200; for laborer, $20.[103] When they were able to make investments in financial assets, the salaried class was more likely than the working class to own the riskier but higher-yield common stocks and real estate than the safer but lower-yield savings accounts and bonds.[104]

Buying on installment credit continued to be popular. For example, in 1950, 43% of department store sales were put on charge accounts and 10% were paid by installment.[105] As in 1935, all four classes spent more than they made, but they outspent their incomes at a much higher rate in 1950. Many families were drawing down their wartime savings to make purchases that had been postponed because of the war. Using savings to pay bills as a percentage of net worth declined with class – from about 25% for blacks to 15%–20% for the white working class, to 5% for salaried. Black and wage-earner families both spent 10% more than their net income. Laborer families spent a hefty 16% more than their incomes, which was twice the salaried families' rate.

Income taxes were rapidly assuming a prominent position in the family's budget. Earlier, poll taxes and property taxes had been the major form of taxation. Together, these taxes averaged less than $5 in 1935 for the working class and less than $10 for the salaried class. In 1950, families were paying 3% (blacks) to 7% (salaried) of their incomes in personal taxes, mainly income taxes (see table 5.23). Property taxes averaged 1% of income, and social security and other payroll taxes averaged another 1.5% of income. Altogether, these taxes averaged 7% to 10% of family incomes in 1950, while they averaged less than 1% of income in 1935.[106]

The growth of taxes reflected the increased role of government in providing income security and social services as the economy matured

Table 5.23   Taxes, 1950[a]

	Blacks	Laborers		Wage earners		Salaried		Government standard
	Exp.	Exp.	% rep.	Exp.	% rep.	Exp.	% rep.	
Personal taxes[b]	$72	$133	NA	$219	NA	$340	NA	$185
(% of gross income)	(3.0%)	(5.0%)		(5.9%)		(7.1%)		
Property taxes	NA	$26	35.0%	$37	45.0%	$51	53.0%	–
(% of gross income)		(1.0%)		(1.0%)		(1.1%)		
Social Security[c]	NA	$35	76.0%	$61	86.0%	$74	89.0%	$45
(% of gross income)		(1.3%)		(1.6%)		(1.5%)		

[a] Excludes sales and excise taxes, which were included in the prices paid.
[b] Includes federal, state, and local income taxes, poll taxes, and personal property taxes.
[c] Includes employee contributions to all retirement programs as well as to unemployment and disability compensation plans. The standard represents the maximum social security employee tax (1.5% on $3,000).
Source: *Consumer Expenditure Survey*, 1950, Summary Volume, and 'Workers' Budgets in the U.S.,' Bulletin No. 927, BLS.

and as the society became more affluent. More regulation of life and more provision of public goods and services became necessary to build the infrastructure, including physical plant and human development, required by the increasingly complex economy. This infrastructure both allowed economic growth and reflected the rising standard of living, as it provided or regulated, for example, health care, education, crime, transportation, parks, communications, energy, and income security. The magnitude of the government's role and the revenue required to create the structure within which the economy functions would continue to grow.

Dynamics of Change

The tremendous improvements in living standards between the Depression and the beginning of the postwar era were far-reaching. The high rate of income growth allowed families to emulate the patterns of the classes above them as well as to incorporate innovative goods and service. In the previous period of declining incomes, innovation had dominated consumption shifts, and emulation was unimportant. In 1950, about two-thirds of black and working-class expenditure growth was spent on emulation (see table 5.24). The shift to new goods and services during this period of fairly rapid innovation absorbed 40%–50% of the family's expenditure growth. Funds were released to help pay for innovation by not fully replicating the patterns of the previous period (economizing) and by reducing the size of the family.

The salaried class displayed a different pattern of change. Their lower rate of income growth resulted in relatively less emulation and more innovation. The pressure to be trendsetters and modern, i.e., buying

Table 5.24 Shifts in urban consumption norms, 1935–50[a]

Total expenditures	Realized emulation (RE)	Innovation (IN)	Dis-emulation (DE)	Reduced standard (RS)	Change in expenditures (ΔE)
Blacks	0.340	0.204	-0.108	-0.025	0.519
Laborers	0.193	0.242	-0.052	-0.128	0.306
Wage Earners	0.235	0.157	-0.073	-0.042	0.348
Salaried	0.027	0.151	-0.015	-0.006	0.171

Expenditure category	Blacks			Laborers			Wage earners			Salaried		
	RE	IN	RS	RE	IN	RS	RE	IN	RS	RE	IN	RS
Food per capita	0.095	0.061	0.000	0.054	0.085	0.000	0.056	0.028	0.000	0.004	0.015	0.000
Clothing per capita	0.042	0.028	0.000	0.026	0.022	0.000	0.034	0.001	0.000	0.000	0.007	0.000
Family size	0.000	0.000	-0.025	0.000	0.000	-0.042	0.000	0.000	-0.126	0.013	0.000	-0.042
Housing	0.032	0.000	0.000	0.009	0.000	0.000	0.008	0.000	0.000	-0.008	0.000	0.000
Fuel and light	0.015	0.000	0.000	0.000	0.000	0.000	0.001	0.000	-0.002	0.000	0.000	0.000
Furnishings	0.020	0.014	0.000	0.011	0.011	0.000	0.010	0.012	0.000	0.003	0.024	0.000
Miscellaneous												
Transportation	0.038	0.016	0.000	0.029	0.035	0.000	0.037	0.042	0.000	0.003	0.048	0.000
Recreation and education	0.024	0.016	0.000	0.017	0.016	0.000	0.024	0.017	0.000	0.004	0.012	0.000
Household operations	0.027	0.022	0.000	0.012	0.019	0.000	0.016	0.014	0.000	0.000	0.012	0.000
Medical care	0.013	0.014	0.000	0.012	0.031	0.000	0.014	0.031	0.000	0.004	0.018	0.000
Personal care	0.010	0.009	0.000	0.005	0.003	0.000	0.006	0.002	0.000	0.001	0.001	0.000
Gifts and contributions	0.011	0.000	0.000	0.010	0.006	0.000	0.015	0.000	0.000	0.003	0.002	0.000
Personal insurance	0.012	0.009	0.000	0.007	0.000	0.000	0.012	0.000	0.000	0.000	0.000	-0.003
Other	0.002	0.015	0.000	0.001	0.014	0.000	0.002	0.009	0.000	0.000	0.012	0.000

a All changes are given as a proportion of expenditures at the end of the period; therefore, ΔE = RE + IN + RS.
Source: Consumer Expenditure Survey, 1950, and BLS Bulletin 638.

fashionable items and the latest goods and services, seems to have been the primary force shaping their consumption patterns. Like wage earners, the salaried class devoted 15% of their expenditures to innovation. This, however, accounted for 88% of their increased consumption. Already near the top of the income ladder, the salaried class seemed less driven by emulation; only 15% of their expenditure growth was used to emulate past patterns. On the other hand, their rates for economizing and reduced family size were low, which indicates that they were unwilling to pay for innovation by sacrificing their past standards.

The family's absolute standard of living and income growth determine its detailed pattern of change in consumption. Blacks and laborers experienced the most innovation in food, while wage-earners and salaried families experienced the most innovation in transportation. Previously, living standards were lower and, for all classes, innovation had occurred predominately in the area of food. Innovation between 1935 and 1950 displayed a broader pattern – innovation occurred less in traditional areas, such as food and clothing, and more in inventive areas, such as transportation and medical care. It was important in food, clothing, and household operations for blacks; in food, clothing, transportation, and medical care for laborers; in food, transportation, and medical care for wage earners; in transportation and furnishings for salaried. The areas where past consumption patterns were not fully emulated across all classes were housing and utilities. The white classes also did not fully emulate past personal insurance practices; this reflects their reduced need for private insurance because of Social Security. Overall, the vast improvement in material life between 1935 and 1950 allowed families to incorporate newly introduced goods and services into past consumption practices. Thus, families could feel that they were being modern while at the same time improving their living standard by past practice.

Looking at consumption norms more broadly (see table 1.3), the proportion of the budget devoted to home life (meals at home and shelter) declined dramatically while the proportion devoted to social integration (transportation, recreation and education, gifts and contributions, food away from home) increased dramatically and the proportion spent on personal appearance increased slightly. These consumption shifts summarize well the underlying shift in social norms of a society that was becoming less home oriented as family members participated in more social and economic activities outside the home.

Economic Distance

The use of material possessions to provide status markings and thereby separate classes can be seen more clearly as variety and status purchases dominate incremental expenditures. The economic distance between

Table 5.25 Economic distance across groups, 1950

	Labourers to blacks				Wage earners to laborers				Salaried to wage earners			
	Ratio		Diff. ($)	% change[b]	Ratio		Diff. ($)	% change	Ratio		Diff. ($)	% change
Relative income	1.099		228		1.375		951		1.28		978	
Relative consumption expenditures	1.159		404		1.315		927		1.25		960	
Distribution of increased consumption	Distr.[a]	Diff.	% change[b]		Ratio	Distr.	Diff.	% change	Ratio	Distr.	Diff.	% change
Food and clothing	0.079	32	+2.7		1.375	0.365	338	+27.8	1.28	0.351	337	+21.8
Food	0.545	220			1.315	0.064	59		1.25	0.168	161	
Clothing	0.082	33				0.037	34			0.101	97	
Change in family size	−0.547	−221				0.264	245			0.082	79	
Shelter	0.196	79	+14.7			0.152	141	+21.5		0.193	185	+23.2
Housing	0.205	83	+30.7			0.055	51	+14.4		0.073	70	+17.3
Fuel and light	−0.005	−2	−1.5			0.028	26	+20.0		0.021	20	+12.8
Furnishings	−0.005	−2	−1.1			0.069	64	+37.2		0.099	95	+40.3
Miscellaneous	0.725	293	+37.3			0.483	448	+41.6		0.456	438	+28.7
Transportation	0.290	117	+60.9			0.192	178	+57.6		0.167	160	+32.8
Recreation, education, tobacco	0.111	45	+30.2			0.096	89	+45.9		0.104	100	+35.3
Household operation	0.052	21	+22.3			0.032	30	+26.1		0.043	41	+28.3
Medical care	0.153	62	+68.9			0.055	51	+33.6		0.028	27	+13.3
Personal care	−0.032	−13	−17.1			0.020	19	+30.2		0.016	15	+18.3
Gifts, contributions	0.097	39	+68.4			0.027	25	+26.0		0.044	42	+34.7
Personal insurance	0.027	11	+11.3			0.061	57	+52.8		0.043	41	+24.8
Other	0.027	11	+36.7			0.001	−1	−2.4		0.012	12	+30.0

[a] Distribution = difference/total difference in consumption expenditures.
[b] Percentage change = difference/original budget expenditure.
Source: Consumer Expenditure Survey, 1950, Summary Volume, and CPR p-60.

classes was less extreme in 1950 than in 1935, but probably more visible. World War II and migration from the South greatly improved the economic opportunities available to blacks. As a result, the distance between black families and the white working class had diminished dramatically: in 1935, white laborers spent two-thirds more than blacks; in 1950, they spent one-tenth more. In 1935, economic distance between blacks and white laborers had been especially pronounced in transport-ation, housework assistance, and income security, but the distance existed across all categories of material life. Between 1935 and 1950, improve-ments in economic distance were dominated by transportation, health, and gift-giving, although the distance was also great in the basics of food and housing (see table 5.25). In 1950, little or no economic distance between blacks and white laborers existed in energy use and furnishings, and Social Security had reduced their previous great disparity in income security. Finally, blacks distinguished themselves from the white working class by spending more on barber and beauty parlor services.

Economic distance in 1935 between salaried and wage-earner families were similar to the patterns between laborers and blacks. They were most pronounced for mobility, housework help, gift-giving and recreational activities. In 1950, the same categories, joined by furnishings, continued to provide the greatest material differences between salaried and wage-earner families. The two classes were most alike in their meals, energy use, and health care. Unlike the pattern observed between laborers and blacks, clothing, home furnishings, and personal insurance still provided salaried families with economic distance from the working class.

Within the white working class (i.e., between wage earners and laborers), improved economic distance in 1935 was most pronounced in transport-ation, home furnishings and personal insurance. This mirrored the pattern between blacks and laborers, except that furnishings replaced housework assistance. The living standards between the two working classes in 1935 were closest in food, housing and energy use. In 1950, the patterns of economic distance between laborers and wage earners had changed only slightly. Recreation joined transportation, personal insurance, and larger families in providing the greatest increase in distance; clothing joined food and housing as the categories with the least growth in distance. In the most basic categories – where they lived, what they ate, and what they wore – laborers and wage earners were becoming less distinguishable. Some dif-ferences remained, however. Wage earners drove nicer cars, engaged in more recreational activities, and had more income security.

Prevailing Standards and Budget Norms

The BLS workers' budget, described as 'the total dollars necessary to provide family health, worker efficiency, nurture of children, and social

Table 5.26 Budget standards, 1950

	Blacks (CES) ($)	BLS city worker ($)	Laborers (CES) ($)	Basics[a] ($)	BLS city worker ($)	Heller wage earner ($)	Wage earner (CES) ($)	Heller wage earner ($)	Heller white collar ($)	Salaried (CES) ($)	Heller executive ($)
Expenditures	2,543	2,986	2,947	2,578	2,714	3,055	3,874	3,346	4,672	4,834	9,787
Food	879	913	942	720	720	859	1,175	1,057	1,314	1,385	1,799
Clothing	303	372	272	289	315	289	377	340	562	504	1,379
Shelter	576	746	655	674	746	652	796	652	1,184	981	2,056
Rent[b]	270	662	353	460	662	517	404	517	938	474	1,599
Fuel and light[c]	132	*	130	130	*	*	156	*	64	176	*
Furniture and furnishings	174	84	172	84	84	135	236	135	182	331	457
Miscellaneous	785	955	1,078	895	933	1,255	1,526	1,297	1,612	1,964	4,553
Transportation	192	311	309	311	311	506	487	506	544	647	999
Recreation and education	149	133	194	129	129	157	283	157	249	383	828
Household operations	94	45	115	45	45	71	145	71	110	186	957
Medical care	90	161	152	143	143	191	203	233	248	230	462
Personal care	76	62	63	62	62	107	82	107	136	97	198
Gifts and contributions	57	85	96	60	85	60	121	60	70	163	337
Personal insurance	97	128	108	115	128	115	165	115	168	206	527
Other	30	30	41	30	30	48	40	48	87	52	245
Family size[d]	3.3	3.3	2.6	2.6	2.6	2.6	3.2	3.2	3.4	3.4	3.4
Adjusted expenditures (family of four)	2,812	3,259	3,449	3,232	3,259	3,736	4,312	3,436	4,952	5,209	10,297
Vocational expenditure[e]	–	24	–	–	24	41	–	41	0	–	0
Personal taxes[e]	72	185	133	–	185	203	219	203	398	340	1,695

[a] Basics equal the city workers' budget or the Heller wage-earner budget, whichever is less; the average of the two is used for housing (rent plus utilities).

[b] Heller housing figures are for renters in the wage-earner budget and for homeowners in the white collar and executive budgets.

[c] * indicates included in above category.

[d] Food, clothing, medical care and public school expenses were adjusted for family size to make budgets comparable.

[e] Personal taxes and vocational expenses are excluded from the total expenditures.

Source: BLS City Workers' Budget; Heller, 'Quantity and Cost Budgets for Three Income Levels, Prices for San Francisco, September 1949'; *Consumer Expenditure Survey*, 1950, Summary Volume.

participation by all members of the family,'[107] provides a benchmark standard. Based on a list of standard commodities and sources that reflected both 'scientific standards' and prevailing custom, the net BLS budget standard (adjusted for family size) was 92% of a laborer's actual budget (see table 5.26). The BLS standard was 17% more than the actual budget for blacks. However, the BLS standard did not reflect actual practice in significant ways.

Laborer families gave up buying more satisfactory housing and more complete wardrobes in order to maintain obviously important social norms in the way they furnished and ran their homes, in their leisure activities and in buying meals at work and school. The BLS standard exceeded the consumption norms of laborers in housing by 36% and in clothing by 16%. The standard fell below actual spending for furnishings and operations by over 50%, recreation (including tobacco) by 30%, and food away from home by 46% and at home by 15%. These were important categories in creating economic distance between classes.

Black families' material life also exceeded the BLS standard for household operations and furnishings, while the standards for recreation and food away from home were exactly met. Blacks' consumption of food at home was 11% below the BLS standard. Blacks exceeded the BLS standard for personal care; higher expenditures in this area were made in an effort to imitate the hair appearance of whites, with straight hair for women and short-cropped hair for men. Both black and laborer families spent one-half more on tobacco than allowed by the BLS standard.

Even more than for white laborers, BLS standards exceeded the consumption norms for blacks in housing costs (by 65%) and clothing (by 23%), as well as in medical care (79%) and transportation (by 62%). Black families, then, fell far below the BLS standard in most aspects of their material life. Even their home furnishings and equipment were probably below the standard inventory, since annual replacements were predicated upon the assumption that the couple completely furnished their home when married. This supposition reflects a middle-class bias that does not hold for subordinate classes.

Black families spent some money in ways that would provide a bit of relief from the drabness of their bleak material life – for example, tobacco for the father (with some mothers joining in), visits to the beauty parlor for the mother, and outings to movies for the children. Sometimes they spent more on these 'frills' than was sanctioned by the BLS's frugal budget. But no amount of economizing would have allowed black families to buy adequate housing, a car, and decent medical care; some small spending to promote sociability, on the other hand, ameliorated daily life.

Although working-class families were much better off in 1950 than in previous surveys, 30%–40% of workers' families were estimated to have insufficient budgets compared to the BLS standard.[108] Budget experts conceded that this standard assumed a level of housing 'still above that available to the great majority of wage-earner families and a standard of medical care not yet generally received by all groups in the population.'[109] This partially squared with the survey results – only the salaried class met the housing standard, but only the black class did not meet the medical care standard. These two areas were expected to show the greatest improvements in the coming decade. The experts didn't predict that transportation expenditures, in the form of a second car, would continue to grow rapidly.

The 1950 budget standards represented a higher plane of living than the standards used in 1935 or 1918, which had been similar. The BLS workers' budget was 37% higher in constant dollars than the NICB budget (1935) and 48% higher than the WPA maintenance budget (1935). The Heller budgets, introduced in the 1930s, established 'normative' benchmarks for wage-earner and clerk families that exceeded other standards by 20%–35%. The Heller researchers conceded that most families in these two classes did not live at these standards. Nevertheless, the Heller standards rose considerably between 1935 and 1950 (by one-quarter for wage earners and white-collar workers, by one-seventh for executives). Real living standards ascended even faster, however, so the Heller budgets were no longer normative for wage-earner families, who now spent 15% more than the Heller wage-earner budget, nor for salaried families, who spent 5% more than the Heller white-collar budget. Laborers were still catching up to the Heller wage-earner norms, which cost 8% more than the laborer families actually spent.[110]

The Heller wage-earner budget exceeded the BLS workers' budget by 14%. Food was 19% higher, furnishings and operations 60% higher, medical care 34% higher, transportation 63% higher, recreation 22% higher, and personal care 73% higher.[111] For three categories, however, the Heller budget was below the BLS standard.[112] Rent was 22% lower because it covered only rent-controlled units; life insurance was 11% lower; and clothing was 20% lower for the husband, who was assumed to wear work clothes rather than a suit to work. Clothing was the same for wife and children in the two budget standards.

The Heller wage-earner budget shed light on prevailing consumption norms and what style of living was provided by budget figures. Except for a few dollars to buy coffee at work for the husband and milk at school for the children, no other money for food away from home was included in the Heller food budget.[113] An allowance, for having 48 guests to dinner annually, was included, however. Medical care encompassed medical and hospital group-practice plans and private dental care, which allowed one annual cleaning per person. The family was allowed telephone service, but no domestic or laundry service. Automobile expenses were primarily for a new car purchased every six years, since there were few used cars available, and driven 5,000 miles annually. Public transit was used by the wife for errands twice weekly and for the children to ride to school. For the most part, recreation consisted of twice-monthly outings to the movies. There was no budget for a vacation; instead, the family was given a small allowance for making day-trips. Life insurance was a $7,000 ordinary life policy that paid $185 at the time of death plus $45 per month for 15 years if the man died young, or about $240 per month for life if the man died in middle age, after his children were grown. The Heller experts thought that the husband needed at least $3,000 more term insurance, but they did not include it because of budget constraints during a period of rapidly rising prices.[114]

The Heller Committee also priced a budget for a white-collar worker (clerical or sales, lower-level management or salaried professional). This budget cost about $5,000 for a family of four, which is consistent with the widely circulated *Fortune* magazine study that pegged the 'middle-class' range at $3,600–$6,750.[115] The Heller white-collar budget was only 3% less than the actual budget of salaried families, if they assumed that the family lived in a newly purchased home; it was 9% less if they assumed that the family lived in a rent-controlled dwelling. The Heller budget allocated the budget differently, however, than the actual practice of salaried families. It assumed that salaried families spent 40% less on furnishings and household operations than they actually did, that they gave 50% fewer gifts and contributions, that they spent 35% less on recreation and 15% less on their automobiles. At the same time, the Heller white-collar budget allocated more than was actually spent for personal appearance – one-third more for adults' clothing, one-fourth more for children's clothing, and two-fifths more for personal care.

Pent-up war demand and the surge in family formation resulted in housing prices rising rapidly, so that market prices were above FHA appraisals. Rents had also been sky-rocketing, except in some cities, such as San Francisco, that continued to control rents. The rent for a rent-controlled dwelling was only slightly higher than the actual housing costs reported by salaried families. Wage-earner families who had purchased their homes recently bought lower-cost housing that was being built outside city limits. The Heller Committee did not price outside city limits. Owner-occupiers within city limits tended to live in four-flat buildings, and these did not meet the Heller space requirements.

In the Heller budgets, white-collar and blue-collar families were assumed to have the same type of automobile since few used cars were available. However, the white-collar worker was assumed to take the trolley to work, and the blue-collar worker to drive the car while his wife used the trolley. This assumption presumably overlies another – that the white-collar worker went a short distance into town to a desk job while the blue-collar worker had to drive farther to reach the factory.

Table 5.27 Standard of living index, 1950[a]

	Laborers 1950 to laborers 1935					Blacks 1950 to laborers 1950				Wage earners 1950 to laborers				Salaried 1950 to wage earners 1950			
	Δ Exp. ($)	Basic 1935 ($)	Basic 1950 ($)	Variety ($)	Status ($)	Δ Exp. ($)	Basic ($)	Variety ($)	Status ($)	Δ Exp. ($)	Basic ($)	Variety ($)	Status ($)	Δ Exp. ($)	Basic ($)	Variety ($)	Status ($)
Food	122	B	(58)	180	0	(63)	(15)	(48)	0	233	B	161	72	210	B	38	172
Clothing	75	B	75	0	0	31	24	0	7	105	17	58	30	127	B	76	51
Housing	52	B	52	0	0	(83)	(83)	0	0	51	51	0	0	70	48	14	8
Fuel and light	(26)	B	(26)	0	0	2	2	0	0	26	B	26	0	20	B	20	0
Furnishings	96	15	12	62	7	2	B	1	1	64	B	42	22	95	B	37	58
Transportation	201	B	201	0	0	(117)	(117)	0	0	178	26	61	91	160	B	80	80
Recreation and education	88	8	6	44	30	(45)	B	(35)	(10)	89	B	57	32	100	B	53	47
Household operations	64	7	8	32	17	(21)	B	(21)	0	30	B	17	13	41	B	18	23
Medical care	90	15	66	9	0	(62)	(62)	0	0	51	B	23	28	27	B	15	12
Personal care	22	5	17	0	0	13	B	0	13	19	B	7	12	15	B	5	10
Gifts and contributions	46	0	13	6	27	(39)	(28)	(2)	(9)	25	B	6	19	42	B	0	42
Personal insurance	19	0	19	0	0	(11)	(11)	0	0	57	14	43	0	41	B	41	0
Other	35	0	24	4	7	(11)	0	(4)	(7)	(1)	B	0	(1)	12	B	4	8
Total	884	50	409	337	88	(404)	(290)	(109)	(5)	927	108	501	318	960	48	401	511
Distribution	1.00	0.06	0.46	0.38	0.10	1.00	0.72	0.27	0.01	1.00	0.12	0.54	0.34	1.00	0.05	0.42	0.53

a In 1950 dollars, Basics (1935) is the additional amount necessary to reach the basic standard in 1935; Basics (1950) is the increment above Basic (1935) spent on basics using the 1950 standard.

Source: Table 5.3 and Detailed Data Tables.

The Heller white-collar budget's allowance for ease and entertainment included husbands' lunches purchased at work (but the children still carried theirs), a cleaning service two days yearly, 68 guests for dinner yearly, three toll telephone calls monthly, one two-week vacation, outings to the theater or concert four times yearly, and to the movies twice monthly. In comparison to practice, the Heller Committee put more emphasis on appearance and adequate housing and less emphasis on making life easier, more comfortable, and entertaining.

The Heller Committee also priced a budget for the executive or managing class. This budget was twice as much as salaried families spent. The Heller executive budget assumed that the family lived in a large home in an exclusive neighborhood; they entertained outside the home as well as at home with formal dinners, bridge luncheons and cocktail parties; the children bought lunch at school; the wife had weekly cleaning help, baby-sitting, laundry services, occasional gardening help, and hired cooks and waitresses for entertaining; they purchased a new car every three years and drove it 10,000 miles yearly; the parents attended the theater, opera, or a concert monthly; and the family took a fancy two-week vacation. This active and lavish social life was much beyond the means of salaried families. Although salaried families had easier and more sociable living standards than the working class, their daily lives resembled more an 'improved' version of the working-class life-style than a 'diminished' version of the socialite executive family.

Standard of Living Index

These changes between 1935 and 1950 can be summarized by the standard of living index (see table 5.27). One-half of laborers' budget increment between 1935 and 1950 was spent on basics. As we have seen, however, the basics standard had risen, especially in transportation as well as in clothing, medical care, and housing, so that 90% of the growth in basics consumption reflected improvements made in the basic norms.

At last, laborers were able to purchase variety, especially in food, furnishings, and recreation, and variety accounted for four-tenths of their budget increment. Laborers were also able to purchase some status in recreational activities and gift-giving. Still, status accounted for only one-tenth of the budget increment.

Although blacks still lagged behind laborers, they were finally making some headway in meeting basics. Most of their lower income relative to laborers still resulted in reduced spending on basics (0.7). In 1950, black families still had not reached the 1935 basic norm for housing. They had reached the 1935 basic norm for transportation, medical care, and clothing,[116] but they still lagged significantly behind the 1950 basic norm in these categories. They met the 1950 basic norm in furnishings and home operations, recreation, and personal care. Variety accounted for one-quarter of the black budget shortfall compared to laborers, as blacks could not purchase variety in their leisure activities, diets, and home operations as white laborers did. Because blacks purchased status in their personal appearance with hair services, little of the black budget shortfall was accomplished with a decline in net status.

Wage earners spent the bulk of their budget increment over laborers on variety (0.5), and status (0.3) with only a small amount being spent on basics (0.1). The two areas where the laborer had not reached the 1950 basic norm was suitable housing and car ownership. Thus, housing and transportation accounted for most of the incremental spent on basics by wage earners. Wage-earner families made improvements in variety compared to laborers across all categories, except housing, but they especially improved their variety or comfort in meals, transportation, clothing, and leisure activities. Wage earners also used some of their higher income relative to laborers to purchase status, especially in their automobiles and their meals. Other small status purchases were made in all the other categories, except housing, and insurance.

Salaried families spent the bulk of their budget increment over wage earners on status (0.5) with variety close behind (0.4). Only 5% was spent on basics, since the wage earner had purchased all the 1950 basics except for housing. Salaried families purchased improved variety or comfort in many ways – especially with their cars, clothing, and leisure activities. Purchasing more status compared to the wage earner was important to salaried workers. Meals, especially through dining out and entertaining, was an important status category. Other categories for purchasing status markers were those where public appearances or social activities were involved – the automobile, home furnishings, clothing, leisure activities, and gifts and contributions.

The decline in family size between 1935 and 1950 allowed families below the salaried class to make important improvements in food and clothing with only small increments in their budgets. For example, laborers in 1950 would have had to spend considerably more on food and clothing to reach their higher standards if their family size had been as high as in 1935. Compared to laborer families, black and wage-earner families did not reduce their family size as much, so this was a less important source of financing improved living standards.

Between 1935 and 1950, improvements in the standard of living included basic standards that were 30% higher and significant purchases of variety and status. Laborer families were able to purchase most of the basics as well as increase their variety consumption fivefold and buy a little status. Wage-earner families doubled their consumption of variety and increased their status spending fivefold. Salaried families actually decreased their variety consumption 15% in order to increase their status spending 60%.

In general, too few basics marked the black class, improvements in variety marked the working class, and improvements in status marked the salaried class.

Conclusion

By 1950, families with employed heads were living on a high plane by historical standards. With two decades of depression and war behind them, families were in an era of personal material improvements that was to continue for two decades. Compared to the depth of the Depression, 1950 was a time of great prosperity. Real disposable income per person was three-fifths higher in 1950 than in 1935. Blacks and white laborers, who had suffered the greatest unemployment, benefited the most from the wartime recovery. Income inequality had lessened, and black families especially experienced important improvements in their standard of living.

Economic growth had produced a proliferation of the goods and services available in the marketplace, and these eradicated the dividing line between consumption and production that had occurred within the rural household. The drive to consume seemed to be increasing in relative terms even as the absolute need to consume basics was largely being met. These trends, however, were only beginning to become apparent, and they would become more obvious in later decades.

For the country generally, life was more exciting and less physically demanding. Food and clothing had become sources of variety and status, and leisure-time activities had become much more important in family life. The automobile had become a part of daily life, although the ways and the amount families used their cars varied by class. Serious congestion and pollution problems associated with the automobile were only beginning to be noticed in a few urban areas. But the car gave the family highly coveted mobility and opened up the suburbs as a desirable housing location. The pent-up war demand for housing was only beginning to be met; major expenditures and improvements in housing were not yet evident.

Consumption standards had made significant improvements in basics and variety. Within the salaried class, conspicuous consumption was becoming more important as more status markers were purchased. Economic abundance had not wiped out insufficiency and had not resulted in the avoidance of status, as some had hoped.[117] But overall, American working-class families had reached a simple yet comfortable standard of living, and black families had made a significant stride toward reaching working-class standards. Although economic distance marked these classes, the middle 70% of the families could neither be viewed as suffering economic deprivation nor accused of living profligately.

NOTES

1. The Social Security Act of 1935 provided Aid to Families with Dependent Children (often called welfare) and unemployment insurance as well as retirement income.
2. The Fair Labor Standards Act (1935) regulated hours, wages, and working conditions. It included a Federal minimum wage and required premium overtime payments. The Wagner Act (1935) established the right of workers to organize into unions and to bargain collectively with their employers. Later, the Full Employment Act of 1946 provided the basis for macroeconomic stabilization policies.
3. The 'marriage bars' against wives, present in the first half of the twentieth century, were beginning to break down. Goldin argues these bars were abandoned in the 1950s because the cost of limiting female labor supply greatly increased. Claudia Goldin, *Understanding the Gender Gap: An Economic History of American Women* (New York: Oxford University Press, 1989).
4. Only a minority (44%) of the black population lived in urban areas in 1930. In 1940, one-half (49%) lived in urban areas; in 1950, 62% did so. US Department of Commerce, Bureau of the Census, *Historical Statistics of the United States: Colonial Times to 1970*, Bicentennial ed. (Washington, DC: US Department of Commerce, Bureau of the Census, 1975), Series A 73–81.
5. See, for example, US Department of Labor, Bureau of Labor Statistics (BLS), *How American Buying Habits Change* (Washington, DC: US Government Printing Office, 1959), pp. 6–7, and Richard Parker, *The Myth of the Middle Class* (New York: Harper & Row, 1972), Chs 1, 2.
6. A comparison of 1948 with 1901 for the average worker's family is made by Witt Bowden, 'Changes in Modes of Living,' *Monthly Labor Review*, 71 (July 1950), pp. 23–30. Bowden emphasizes the decline in the hours worked per week, improvements in housing and transportation, the decline in home production for use, and the rise of public services and social insurance.

   An important study of American consumption patterns, which shows how researchers analyzed the standard of living and consumption norms in the 1950s, is Elizabeth E. Hoyt et al., *American Income and Its Use* (New York: Harper & Brothers, 1954).
7. Although not without controversy, economic historians acknowledge the period from the late 1920s to the early 1950s as one of significant economic leveling. See Jeffrey G. Williamson and Peter H. Lindert, *American Inequality: A Macroeconomic History* (New York: Academic Press, 1980), Ch. 4.

8. Selma F. Goldsmith, 'The Relation of Census Income Distribution Statistics to Other Income Data,' in National Bureau of Economic Research, Conference on Research in Income and Wealth, *An Appraisal of the 1950 Census Income Data*, Studies in Income and Wealth, 23 (Princeton, NJ: Princeton University Press, 1958), Table 7, p. 92.

9. This is the only survey year when the salaried class was not immediately below the top decile. They were about one-half decile lower in 1950 than in other years (for unexplained reasons).

10. See Clair Vickery (Brown), 'The Changing Household: Implications for Devising an Income Support Program,' *Public Policy*, 26, 2 (Spring 1978), pp. 121–51, and Bureau of the Census, *Historical Statistics*, Series A 288–319. The average population per household fell from 4.34 (1920) to 4.11 (1930) to 3.67 (1940) to 3.37 (1950), while the average family size fell from 3.76 (1940) to 3.54 (1950). In 1940, 63% of unrelated individuals and 6.8% of married couples did not have their own households. In 1950, 48% of unrelated individuals and 5.6% married couples did not.

11. The birth rate peaked in 1957 at 123 births per 1,000 women (aged 15–44). Bureau of the Census, *Historical Statistics*, Series B 5–10, A 143–57.

12. See Joseph S. Zeisel, 'The Workweek in American Industry, 1850–1956,' *Monthly Labor Review*, 81 (Jan. 1958), pp. 23–9. See Rose Theodore and John Gentry, 'Paid Vacations in Major Union Contracts, 1957,' *Monthly Labor Review*, 81 (July 1958), pp. 744–51, for a review of the number of vacation days in major collective bargaining agreements by industry. Most plans had vacation days increasing with tenure, from one week up to three weeks. In 1949, most plans had a maximum of two weeks vacation.

13. Bureau of the Census, *Historical Statistics*, Series H 599, H 442–76.

14. Bureau of the Census, *Historical Statistics*, Series H 602–47.

15. US Department of Commerce, Bureau of the Census, *Income of Families and Persons in the United States, 1950*, Current Population Reports: Consumer Income, Series P 60, No. 9 (Washington, DC: US Government Printing Office, 1952), Table 11.

16. For an excellent description and evaluation of the 1950 Consumer Expenditure Survey data, see Helen H. Lamale, *Methodology: Survey of Consumer Expenditures* (Philadelphia: University of Pennsylvania, 1959).

17. BLS, *American Buying Habits*, pp. 105–8; J. Frederic Dewhurst and Associates, *America's Needs and Resources: A New Survey* (New York: Twentieth Century Fund, 1955), Ch. 5.

18. BLS, *American Buying Habits*, pp. 105–8; Dewhurst, *America's Needs*, Ch. 5.

19. Marguerite Burke, 'Changing Food Patterns of the American People,' *National Food Situation*, No. 73 (Aug. 2, 1955), p. 14.
20. Dewhurst, *America's Needs*, Ch. 5.
21. Dewhurst, *America's Needs*, Ch. 5.
22. US Department of Agriculture (USDA), Economic Research Service, *Food Consumption, Prices, Expenditures*, supplement for 1974 to Agricultural Economic Report, No. 138 (Washington, DC: USDA, Economic Research Service, Jan. 1976), Table 39.
23. This compares US per capita consumption in 1947–9 to 1909–13. Burke, 'Changing Food Patterns,' p. 15.
24. Burke, 'Changing Food Patterns,' p. 18. A large part of the time difference was probably in baking.
25. This figure reflects 23 million lunches divided by 56 million employed non-agricultural workers (Bureau of the Census, *Historical Statistics*, Series D 17). BLS, *American Buying Habits*.
26. US Department of Agriculture, Agricultural Research Service, Home Economics Research Branch, *Food Consumption of Urban Families in the United States*, by Faith Clark et al., Agriculture Information Bulletin, No. 132 (Washington, DC: US Government Printing Office, Oct. 1954), however, reported the percentage of the food budget spent on food away from home increased with income from 12% (laborers) to 20% (salaried).
27. The low-cost adequate diet of the US Bureau of Human Nutrition and Home Economics is used for this estimate. US Department of Agriculture, Bureau of Human Nutrition and Home Economics, *Helping Families Plan Food Budgets*, USDA Miscellaneous Publication, No. 662 (Washington, DC: US Government Printing Office, 1950). In practice, blacks' and laborers' consumption of sweets was lower and wage earners' higher than average. US Department of Agriculture, Bureau of Human Nutrition and Home Economics, *Nutritive Value of Diets of Urban Families, United States, Spring 1948 and Comparison with Diets in 1942*, 1948 Food Consumption Surveys, Preliminary Report, No. 12 (Washington, DC: USDA, Bureau of Human Nutrition and Home Economics, Nov. 1949), Table 7.
28. Dewhurst, *America's Needs*, p. 164. See also Burke, 'Changing Food Patterns,' p. 20.
29. US Department of Agriculture, Bureau of Human Nutrition and Home Economics, *Nutritive Content of City Diets: Summary Report*, 1948 Food Consumption Surveys, Special Report, No. 2 (Washington, DC: USDA, Bureau of Human Nutrition and Home Economics, October 1950). Caloric consumption is calculated per adult-male equivalent. However, by my calculations, a typical laborer family would need to average 3,200 calories per equivalent

adult male (and the typical wage-earner family 3,000 calories) for the husband and wife to be 'moderately active'; the typical salaried family would need to consume 2,500 per equivalent adult male for the husband and wife to be sedentary.

30. Bureau of Human Nutrition and Home Economics, *Nutritive Content of City Diets*, Table 1. Calcium intake is adjusted to include estimated calcium in drinking water and baking powder. Without this adjustment, 42% of families would consume insufficient calcium.

31. Bureau of Human Nutrition and Home Economics, *Nutritive Value of Diets*. This survey is used because much greater detail is available by income group. Generally, the family size is smaller in the 1950 CES than in the 1948 Food Survey and the ratio of per capita food expenditure (1950 to 1948) declined across class from 1.06 (laborer) to 1.01 (wage earner) to 0.97 (salaried). The differences in food expenditures per capita across classes, therefore, are less in the CES than in the Food Survey. US Department of Agriculture, Bureau of Human Nutrition and Home Economics, *Food Consumption of Urban Families in the United States, Spring 1948*, 1948 Food Consumption Surveys, Preliminary Report, No. 5 (Washington, DC: USDA, Bureau of Human Nutrition and Home Economics, May 1949).

32. US Department of Labor, Bureau of Labor Statistics, *Workers' Budgets in the United States: City Families and Single Persons, 1946 and 1947*, Bulletin, No. 927 (Washington, DC: US Government Printing Office, 1948). Beginning in 1946, the Department of Labor priced City Workers' budgets, which were based on a list of standard commodities and sources that reflected both 'scientific standards and prevailing custom.' Initially, costs for 34 cities were included. The same standards were still in effect in 1950.

33. US Department of Agriculture, Agricultural Research Service, Household Economics Research Branch, *Household Practices in the Use of Foods, Three Cities, 1953*, by Corinne LeBovit and Faith Clark, Agriculture Information Bulletin, No. 146 (Washington, DC: US Government Printing Office, April 1956).

34. However, by 1980 RDAs, calcium, iron (especially for women), and niacin were the nutrients most lacking in the American diet in 1950. Aside from the infamous castor oil, which provided iron, no mention is made in the literature of supplements. Also, nutritionists do not discuss vitamin pills. Compared to the 1980 RDAs, the 1948 RDAs are too high for protein (by 40%), thiamine, riboflavin and ascorbic acid (each by 25%), and too low for iron (by 15%). See National Research Council, Food and Nutrition Board, *Recommended Dietary Allowances*, rev. ed. (Washington, DC: National

Academy of Sciences, National Research Council, 1948), and *Recommended Dietary Allowances*, 9th rev. ed. (Washington, DC: National Academy of Sciences, 1980).

35. Bureau of Human Nutrition and Home Economics, *Nutritive Content of City Diets*, Table 1.

36. In 1937, the fibers used in clothing were 68% cotton, 17% wool, 12% synthetic, and 3% other; in 1950, they were 62% cotton, 16% wool, and 22% synthetic. However, 4.4% of women's clothing was synthetic (mostly nylon). Dewhurst, *America's Needs*, Ch. 6. Since women refused to give up their demand for sheer hosiery during the war (David L. Cohn, *The Good Old Days* (New York: Simon & Schuster, 1940)), the shift had to be made rapidly from Japanese silk to nylon.

37. See, for example, Dewhurst, *America's Needs*, Ch. 6.

38. See the four-part study, Mary S. Ryan, *Psychological Effects of Clothing*, Cornell University Agricultural Experiment Station, Bulletin, Nos 882 (Sept. 1952), 898 (July 1953), 900 (Aug. 1953), 905 (Aug. 1954) (Ithaca, NY: Cornell University Agricultural Experiment Station).

39. Although clothing prices had fallen more than the Consumer Price Index during the 1920s and had fallen at the same rate during the Depression, clothing prices rose faster than the CPI during and after the war.

40. A study of family clothing inventories and purchases in Minneapolis–St. Paul in 1950 showed similar expenditures but even higher expenditures for the wife, and slightly lower expenditures for the husband and boy. For example, in the $2,000–$3,000 group, average clothing expenditures were: husbands ($90), wives ($137), boys ($63), girls ($65). In that study, girls and boys had the same inventory/acquisition ratio (1.6), which was fairly constant across income groups above $2,000. US Department of Agriculture, Agricultural Research Service, Household Economics Research Branch, *Family Clothing Inventories and Purchases*, by Margaret L. Brew, Roxanne R. O'Leary, and Lucille C. Dean, Agriculture Information Bulletin, No. 148 (Washington, DC: US Government Printing Office, April 1956).

41. BLS, *Workers' Budgets*.

42. In the Minneapolis study, the majority of husbands wore business suits to work only if income exceeded $4,000. In lower income groups, the majority of husbands wore work clothes. Household Economics Research Branch, *Family Clothing*.

43. One major study calculated, however, that only 28% of urban families were spending less than the City Workers' Standard for replacement and that these families needed on average to spend $100 more to reach the standard. Dewhurst, *America's Needs*, pp.

194–5. They also estimated that one-third of the families spent too little on personal care (p. 195).

44. BLS, *Workers' Budgets*, p. 5.

45. Unfortunately, detailed data on blacks' clothing are not available. This exclusion of data for blacks reflects a continuing bias whereby nonwhite, 'nontypical' families are omitted from the CES studies.

46. BLS, *Workers' Budgets*, p. 35.

47. Data for black families are not available. Also, direct comparisons to 1935 for children are not possible because the age categories are different.

48. The government standard includes clothing services within each person's clothing budget. The CES separates out services and materials from the individual's clothing.

49. Bruno A. Schiro, 'Housing Surveys in 75 Cities, 1950 and 1952,' *Monthly Labor Review*, 77 (July 1954), pp. 744–50.

50. Bureau of the Census, *Historical Statistics*, Series N 238–45.

51. Editors of *Fortune, The Changing American Market* (Garden City, NY: Hanover House, 1955).

52. As in the earlier surveys, in 1950 housing costs varied by city size, and this accounted for a large part of the variation in expenditures. Rents were lowest in the suburbs and highest in the small cities, except for laborers, whose rents were lower in small cities. Families living in the suburbs were most likely to own their home; those in large cities were least likely to do so. Differences in home ownership across classes were greatest in large cities, where salaried ownership was almost twice laborer ownership, and least in small cities, where salaried ownership was only one-fourth higher than laborer ownership. Interest payments on first mortgages and property taxes were highest in the suburbs and lowest in the large cities. This partially reflects the much newer housing in the suburbs.

53. These data are calculated using the 1950 Housing Census for units within SMSAs by income group. Figures for the black families are not available. US Department of Commerce, Bureau of the Census, *1950 Census of Housing, Volume II. Nonfarm Housing Characteristics, Part 1. United States and Divisions* (Washington, DC: US Government Printing Office, 1954), Table B-4, pp. 1–16.

54. Nationwide, 23% of housing lacked full plumbing or was dilapidated, and 8% lacked running water or was dilapidated. Bureau of the Census, *1950 Census of Housing*, pp. 1–16. According to Dewhurst, *America's Needs*, Ch. 7, housing units that were dilapidated or lacked running water needed to be replaced completely. Their count of substandard housing was slightly higher.

55. Around one-half of the working class and two-thirds of the salaried suburban dwellers were homeowners. This even exceeded the home

ownership rates of small-city residents. Rents were lower in the suburbs than in the large city, while property taxes to provide schooling and services were twice as high in the suburbs as in the large cities.

56. See Vickery (Brown), 'The Changing Household.'
57. The standard way to measure locational differences is to compare the market price of comparable housing (i.e., standardizing for differences in quality) in various neighborhoods by using micro data on residences by neighborhood.
58. No imputed rental value of own home is given for 1950, and so homeowners' expenditures include property taxes, insurance, interest payments, costs of repairs, and financing charges. The percentage of homeowners who paid interest on a first mortgage was 41% for laborers, 57% for wage earners, and 63% for salaried (data for blacks are not available).
59. Dewhurst, *America's Needs*, Ch. 7.
60. Central heating was required only in cities where the normal January temperature was at least 40°F. Otherwise, an installed heater or stove was sufficient. Units were *excluded* from the pricing if they had more than one bathroom or lots 'substantially larger than normal,' or if located in an apartment building providing telephone switchboard service, doorman or maid service. See BLS, *Workers' Budgets*, p. 19.
61. Almost two-thirds of the cities reported costs within 10% of this median. US Department of Labor, Bureau of Labor Statistics, *Family Budget of City Worker*, Bulletin, No. 1021 (Washington, DC: US Government Printing Office, October 1950), p. 1.
62. No separate price figures are given for utilities in the city workers' budget; only a combined figure for rent and utilities is given.
63. The 1950 standard allowed for 105 million BTUs annually (4.1 for electricity, 24 for gas, 77 for heating), which is one-third less than the BTUs actually consumed by wage earners in 1918.
64. US Board of Governors of the Federal Reserve System, *1952 Survey of Consumer Finances* (Washington, DC: US Government Printing Office, 1952), *Part 2, Purchases of Durable Goods and Houses in 1951 and Buying Plans for 1952*, Tables 5, 14; *Part 3, Income, Selected Investments, and Short-Term Debt of Consumers*, Tables 22, 26.
65. BLS, *Workers' Budgets*, pp. 10, 32, 33.
66. Bureau of the Census, *Historical Statistics*, Series A 276–87.
67. Bureau of the Census, *Historical Statistics*, Series Q 175–7, Q 242.
68. Board of Governors, *1952 Survey of Consumer Finances: Part 2*, Table 8.
69. Board of Governors, *1952 Survey of Consumer Finances: Part 2*, Tables 2, 3.

70. Bureau of the Census, *Historical Statistics*, Series Q 148–9.
71. Mid-sized cities encompassed 50,000 to 1.9 million people. Large cities (New York, Chicago, and Philadelphia) encompassed 1.9 million or more people. BLS, *Workers' Budgets*, p. 38. Actual car ownership rates were 38% in New York City, 43% in Philadelphia, and 54% in Chicago. Actual ownership rates in other urban areas were usually in the 65%–80% range, except in Southern cities, where the rate was usually between 40%–50%.
72. BLS, *Workers' Budgets*, pp. 21, 26. The budget analysts were concerned that inexpensive used cars were not readily available in the late 1940s. In 1946 and 1947, used automobiles were selling at about what new cars cost in 1941. Used car prices from 1941 were used in the budget, probably a product of wishful thinking (pp. 21, 26). Using the Consumer Price Index, private transportation costs rose 58% between 1941 and 1950, while public transportation costs rose 48%.
73. This is the standard for mid-sized cities, which excluded New York, Chicago, and Philadelphia ('large cities'). The standard for these cities was less because it was assumed that most people did not own cars. In practice, the average family in most cities surveyed spent 10%–20% more than the government standard, except for the South, where the figures were about one-third less because of the large black populations.
74. Dewhurst, *America's Needs*, p. 347. This represents total consumer expenditures. Recreation accounted for 4.2% of national income in 1950, up from 3.2% in 1919.
75. Dewhurst, *America's Needs*, Table 158, pp. 349–50.
76. Dewhurst, *America's Needs*, p. 376.
77. Bureau of the Census, *Historical Statistics*, Series R 93–105, pp. 792–3; BLS, *American Buying Habits*; Board of Governors, *1952 Survey of Consumer Finances: Part 2*, Tables 9, 15.
78. In the late nineteenth century, Thorstein Veblen had already analyzed the importance of leisure and of conspicuous consumption for the upper class in his *Theory of the Leisure Class* (1899; reprint ed., Boston: Houghton Mifflin, 1973).
79. Board of Governors, *1952 Survey of Consumer Finances: Part 2* showed ownership of televisions at higher levels – 10% (income $1,000–$1,999) to 54% (income $5,000–$7,499).
80. Prices collected in 34 cities in 1946 and 1947 indicated that 15 cities had no charge for books and supplies, eleven charged $5, five charged $10, and only three charged $15. Five dollars were added to this for athletic supplies, school games, clubs, and entertainment for two children.
81. BLS, *American Buying Habits*, p. 161; Census Bureau, *Historical Statistics*, Series B 136–47, 181–92; Dewhurst, *America's Needs*,

Ch. 10; HEW, *Vital Statistics of Rates in the U.S., 1940–1960*, Tables 30, 38, 44.

82. Frank, Ryan, *The Forgotten Plague* (Boston: Little, Brown & Co., 1993).

83. Bureau of the Census, *Historical Statistics*, Series B 237–47, B 276–87, B 402–8. As in the previous period, the proportion of physicians in the population remained stable while the proportion of nurses continued its upward climb. In 1918, physicians had outnumbered active nurses. By 1950, nurses outnumbered physicians almost two to one. A 1953 national survey found 57% of the population had some hospital insurance and 48% had some surgical and other medical insurance. US Congress, Joint Committee on the Economic Report, *Characteristics of the Low-Income Population and Related Federal Programs*, 84th Cong., 1st sess., 1955, Joint Committee Print (Oct. 15, 1955), pp. 148–55.

84. Congress, *Characteristics of the Low-Income Population*, pp. 148–55.

85. Walter J. Lear, 'Medical-Care Insurance for Industrial Workers,' *Monthly Labor Review*, 73 (Sept. 1951), p. 252.

86. Congress, *Characteristics of the Low-Income Population*, pp. 148–55.

87. Dewhurst, *America's Needs*, p. 332.

88. Board of Governors, *1952 Survey of Consumer Finances: Part 3*, Tables 22, 26.

89. Board of Governors, *1952 Survey of Consumer Finances: Part 3*, pp. 343–4. This excludes the 3% of current expenditures provided by philanthropy (p. 328).

90. BLS, *Workers' Budgets*, p. 14. The family was assumed to have a group hospitalization insurance plan.

91. BLS, *Workers' Budgets*, p. 15.

92. The females were assumed to have more extractions than the males, the wife more fillings than the husband, the boy more fillings than the girl.

93. Congress, *Characteristics of the Low-Income Population*, pp. 148–55.

94. Unfortunately, only the total cost for personal care was given in the government's report of prices, so laborers' expenditures for specific items cannot be compared with the standard.

95. The father was assumed to have bought a new razor and shaving brush every five years. In the government standard, the wife also had 0.5 rouge compacts, one small lipstick, one small bottle of nail polish, 120 sanitary napkins and four boxes of tissues. The family also shared 67 cakes of bath soap and 4.5 ounces of tooth powder annually.

96. Nationally, only 57% of workers were covered by Federal Old Age and Survivors Insurance (FOASI), but jobs held by minorities, women, and youth were much less likely to be covered. Bureau of the Census, *Historical Statistics*, Series H 172–85.

97. Life insurance premiums are treated here as if they pay for term insurance and create no assets. This is probably true for all classes except salaried. For them, some part of insurance should be counted as increased assets.

98. Bureau of the Census, *Historical Statistics*, Series H 172–85. The maximum contribution per worker was $45 annually. The government standard allowed $43 for Social Security. The survey figure for retirement also includes employee (but not employer) contributions to all retirement plans, such as mandatory federal programs (railroad retirement, civil service retirement), private pension plans, and mandatory state and local unemployment and disability compensation plans.

99. Gifts to family members supposedly are recorded as regular expenditures.

100. Many more families were also reporting funeral expenses, but the amount being spent was much lower in 1950 than in 1935. The data do little to illuminate the changes that were occurring in the need for funerals and in the practices associated with burials.

101. For a labor-oriented discussion of security, see Arthur J. Altmeyer, 'The Worker's Quest for Security,' *Monthly Labor Review*, 71 (July 1950), pp. 31–7. For a discussion of social welfare expenditures during this period, see Ida C. Mevrian, 'Social Welfare Expenditures in the United States, 1935–55,' *Social Security Bulletin*, 20, 10 (Oct. 1957), pp. 3–12.

102. Net worth equaled liquid assets plus homes and real estate, plus automobiles, plus stocks, minus total debt (except charge accounts). Incomes are for 1949. US Board of Governors of the Federal Reserve System, *1950 Survey of Consumer Finances* (Washington, DC: US Government Printing Office, 1950). The median is calculated by assuming a straight-line distribution of observations. The net worth of managerial and self-employed families was $16,667, which includes the value of own business. Together, the median net worth of professional and managerial families (including self-employed) was $12,205.

103. In 1951, 40% of families with incomes between $1,000 and $3,000 and 20% of families with incomes between $3,000 and $5,000 had no liquid assets. In both income groups, only 5% had liquid assets worth more than $5,000. US Board of Governors of the Federal Reserve System, *1952 Survey of Consumer Finances* (Washington, DC: US Government Printing Office, 1952), *Part 1, Consumer Expectations as to Economic Trends and Consumer Investment Preferences*, Table 2; *Part 3*, Table 12.

104. Board of Governors, *1952 Survey of Consumer Finances: Part 1*, Table 23, shows the professional and managerial class (incomes

above $5,000) equally preferring stocks and real estate (44%) to savings accounts and bonds (42%), while working-class families (incomes between $3,000 and $5,000) overwhelmingly favored savings accounts and bonds (77%) to stocks and real estate (15%).

105. US Department of Commerce, Office of Business Economics, *Business Statistics*, 1965 ed. (Washington, DC: US Government Printing Office, 1965).

106. According to national income accounts, personal taxes were 9.1% of personal income in 1950, up from 3.1% in 1935.

107. BLS, *Workers' Budgets*, p. 28. The BLS workers' budget was begun in 1946. Initially, costs for 34 cities were included, and prices were updated regularly. Budgets for a single woman were also prepared by many states to help set the minimum wage designed to keep women in 'honest professions.' These bare-bones budgets tended to be in the $1,600–1,700 range (excluding taxes, insurance, and savings) in 1949–50. US Department of Labor, Women's Bureau, *Working Women's Budgets in Thirteen States*, original ed. June 1948, rev. Dec. 1951, Bulletin, No. 226 (Washington, DC: US Government Printing Office, 1952).

A detailed presentation of a family budget standard for New York City, which builds on the BLS city worker's family budget, is given in Community Council of Greater New York, Budget Standard Service, *A Family Budget Standard* (New York: The Community Council of Greater New York, Research Department, 1955). Their cost total for the four-person family in 1954 was $4,222 (including taxes).

108. Dorothy S. Brady, 'Scales of Living and Wage Earners' Budgets,' *The Annals*, 274 (March 1951), p. 37. A study by the Franklin D. Roosevelt Foundation estimated 19% of urban households had insufficient resources to achieve an adequate level of living in 1950. This group had an average income of $2,313 and spent 40% of it on food and 19% on housing. Congress, *Characteristics of the Low-Income Population*, pp. 48–51.

109. Brady, 'Scales of Living,' p. 37.

110. These comparisons are made for budgets adjusted for four-person families.

111. The national pricing of the city workers' budget is used here rather than the San Francisco pricing in order to make adjustments for 1950 dollars. The San Francisco figures (used for the Heller budgets) are remarkably similar to the national averages. The major deviations include higher prices in San Francisco for medical care (by 28%), recreation (by 17%), and for life insurance and union dues (by 18%). Heller Committee for Research in Social Economics, University of California, Berkeley, *Quantity and Cost*

Budgets for Three Income Levels, Prices for San Francisco, September 1949 (Berkeley: University of California, 1950).

112. Heller Committee, *Quantity and Cost Budgets for Three Income Levels.*

113. Based on Heller Committee for Research in Social Economics, University of California, Berkeley, *Food for Four Income Levels, Prices for San Francisco, September 1949*, by Ruth Okey and Mary Gorringe Luck (Berkeley: University of California, 1950).

114. Heller Committee, *Quantity and Cost Budgets for Three Income Levels*, p. 77.

115. Editors of Fortune, *The Changing American Market.*

116. Although food expenditure in dollar terms was still slightly short, blacks' weekly quantities consumed were comparable to those recommended by the BLS (see table 5.6).

117. David M. Potter, *People of Plenty: Economic Abundance and American Character* (Chicago: University of Chicago Press, 1954).

6 Reaching Economic Supremacy, 1973

Introduction

The period from 1950 to 1973 was one of increasing prosperity for all classes. This generation of relative economic and political stability was sandwiched between two periods of dislocation and restructuring. Formation of a new international political order preceded it, and formation of a new international economic order followed it. Victorious in a war fought on other nations' lands, and equipped with greatly expanded productive capacity, the United States turned in the 1950s to restoring its peacetime economy with great vigor and renewed hope. Families were quickly formed, and suburban communities were almost as quickly built. The birthrate began a dramatic climb, creating a generation later dubbed 'the baby boomers.'[1]

The subperiod from the early sixties to the early seventies encompassed social upheavals: the Civil Rights Movement, the Women's Movement, and the Antiwar Movement. As a result of these protest movements, the 1960–73 subperiod showed distinctly different labor market trends and social patterns from the 1950s for the economically disadvantaged, women, and young men, even though the two subperiods shared similar trends in overall consumption norms.

The 1950s witnessed the largest increase in real expenditures of the seven decades studied as families spent their wartime savings as well as their rising real wages. Real incomes grew faster in the sixties than the fifties, but real expenditures grew more slowly as families saved more. Between 1950 and 1960, expenditures grew 45% for salaried families and almost 25% for white working-class families, yet real disposable income (per person) grew only 15%. Between 1960 and 1973, real disposable income increased an amazing 55%, a figure that was much higher than the growth rate of expenditures. Growth of output and earnings no longer determined expenditure growth across classes, as it typically had, because of the rising importance of taxes, income support programs, and private savings. The divergence between earnings and expenditures was especially noticeable for the salaried class, whose real expenditures grew less than 1% while their real income grew over 30%. 1973 was the first survey year in which expenditures fell below net income for both the working and salaried classes. Economic growth, coupled with government programs, had finally provided economic security for these classes, and their budgetary pressures lessened.

The earlier trend in the family's decreased consumption of market goods and services that were related to housework continued as the expenditures for food, clothing, and household operations declined from 44% of working-class budgets in 1950 to 29% in 1973. This trend in consumption norms reinforced women's entry into the labor market, since they could use their paychecks to buy the increasingly important items that were unrelated to their household activities.

As the economy matured and as the population became better educated, families improved their labor market status. At the upper end, husbands moved into the growing number of professional and managerial jobs; at the lower end, families left the shrinking farm sector. The farm sector provided jobs for 30% of employed heads in 1950, but a mere 4% in 1973 (see table 1.1). Professional and managerial occupations expanded from providing jobs for 12% of family heads in 1950 to providing 29% in 1973. A bare majority of employed family heads worked in blue-collar jobs, but these families had also improved their status as the husbands increased their likelihood of working as crafts or operatives (upper working class) rather than as laborers or service workers (lower working class). Jobs in clerical or sales were growing rapidly as occupations for wives and female heads.[2]

Few whites (one in ten of employed white male heads) were employed in the least desirable jobs as service workers or laborers in 1973. Four in ten white male heads had operative and craft jobs, and one in three had professional and managerial jobs.[3] The improvement in the occupational status of white families created room for black families to fill as production, craft, and clerical workers.

In earlier periods, the main economic division between black families had been between urban and rural families. Since our focus is on the urban population, this earlier bifurcation of the black population was not evident. After a massive migration, especially from the rural South to cities in the North and South, the economic lot of black families improved considerably when they found industrial jobs that allowed them to escape dire poverty on the farm. In 1930, 44% of black employed males worked on the farm, compared to 25% in 1950 and 5% in 1970. By 1973, 78% of black families lived in metropolitan areas.[4]

Table 6.1 Family budget, 1973

	Low income	Laborer	Wage earner	Salaried	Seniors
Average family size (persons)	2.76	2.90	3.17	3.47	1.62
Homeowners	37.0%	53.0%	65.0%	79.0%	63.0%
Car ownership:					
0 cars	55.0%	13.0%	7.0%	3.0%	45.0%
2+	7.0%	24.0%	35.0%	53.0%	7.0%

	Low income		Laborer		Wage earner		Salaried		Seniors	
	Avg. exp. ($)	% of total	Avg. exp. ($)	% of total	Avg. exp. ($)	% of total	Avg. exp. ($)	% of total	Avg. exp. ($)	% of total
Total expenditures	4,853	100.0	9,039	100.0	10,517	100.0	13,813	100.0	5,041	100.0
Food	1,190	24.5	1,704	18.9	1,885	17.9	2,394	17.3	1,143	22.6
Alcohol	22	0.4	78	0.9	88	0.8	127	0.9	28	0.6
Clothing	277	5.7	489	5.4	566	5.4	826	6.0	213	4.2
Shelter	1,792	36.9	2,607	28.8	3,001	28.5	3,723	27.0	1,716	33.3
Housing	1,006	20.7	1,406	15.6	1,544	14.7	1,873	13.6	841	16.7
Fuel and utilities	290	6.0	395	4.4	440	4.2	547	4.0	319	6.3
Furnishings	173	3.6	326	3.6	422	4.0	606	4.4	158	3.1
Household operations	323	6.7	480	5.3	595	5.7	697	5.0	398	7.2
Miscellaneous	1,573	32.4	4,160	46.0	4,977	47.3	6,743	48.8	1,941	39.3
Transportation	557	11.5	1,615	17.9	1,836	17.5	2,351	17.0	513	10.2
Recreation and education	317	6.5	742	8.2	906	8.6	1,322	9.6	321	6.4
Medical care	274	5.7	477	5.3	525	5.0	576	4.2	547	10.3
Personal care	77	1.6	149	1.6	186	1.8	224	1.6	106	3.5
Gifts and contributions	148	3.0	359	4.0	417	4.0	619	4.5	297	5.9
Insurance	172	3.5	725	8.0	974	9.3	1,479	10.7	90	1.8
Other	28	0.6	93	1.0	132	1.3	171	1.2	67	1.3
Gross income $	3,810		10,347		12,883		18,796		4,612	
Personal taxes $	141		1,322		1,789		3,080		76	
Taxes as percentage of gross income	3.7		12.8		13.9		16.4		1.7	
Net income $	3,669		9,025		11,094		15,716		4,536	
Expenditures $	4,853		9,039		10,517		13,813		5,051	
Expenditures as percentage of net income	132.3		100.2		94.8		87.9		111.4	

By the early 1970s, however, black families were economically divided by two new factors – the family's paid labor market position, which was the same criterion dividing white families; and by family composition, which would later become important for white families as well. In 1950, one in five black families was female-headed; by 1973, more than one in three black families were female-headed.[5] Less than one in ten white families had a female head in 1973.[6]

The employment status of black families with an employed male head had improved sufficiently between 1950 and 1973 to integrate these families into the working class. By 1973, 12% of employed black male heads were in professional, technical, or managerial jobs, although the majority were still in blue-collar occupations (47% in craft or operative and 29% in service or laborer).[7] However, the proportion of black adults with employment problems had grown. Many black families, especially female-headed, did not contain an employed adult.

Since black workers faced earnings discrimination, their gains in occupational status were not fully reflected in their earnings. By 1973, the black husband-wife family had finally reached economic parity with the white laborer family,[8] although the black husband was more likely to be employed in a skilled or semi-skilled job than in an unskilled job. Thus, for 1973, the laborer class represents the typical black husband-wife family, as well as the typical white laborer family. However, the overall economic position of urban black families must include the position of black female-headed families and black laborer families (weighted one-third and two-thirds, respectively).

Until 1973, the Consumer Expenditure Survey had provided almost no data on the economically disadvantaged. Although the BLS provided budgets for working-class families, the government did not provide official guidelines for judging whether or not a family's income was sufficient for them to be considered nonpoor until the mid-1960s. Data on low-income families in the 1973 CES and government definitions for poverty developed in the 1960s allow the creation of a 'low income' category representing the population living at the government-designated poverty threshold.

President Johnson's 'War on Poverty' was the culmination of American society's focus on the disadvantaged during the 1960s. The concern about poverty was, in turn, a spin-off of the earlier Civil Rights Movement, which acknowledged that blacks' economic disadvantage constrained them from full participation in the political and societal process. As the nation became more affluent, and as the poverty rate dropped, a political consensus supporting income support programs for the economically disadvantaged gradually developed. These programs, coupled with economic growth, were successful in halving the percentage of the population officially living in poverty from 22% in 1959 to 11% in

1973. The rate decreased from 35% to 16% for seniors (i.e., people aged 65 years and over) and from 56% to 30% for blacks.[9]

Government programs to define poverty have never included a systematic study of how families with a 'poverty threshold' income actually lived.[10] Rather, the poverty standard developed by the Social Security Administration (SSA) in the mid-1960s was based on an estimate of the minimum income level that would allow a family to purchase sufficient food. By focusing on food, the SSA poverty standard was attempting to define poverty in terms of ensuring health rather than the broader goal of ensuring social integration. Interest in poverty waned as economic growth slowed in the 1970s. Attempts to refine the definition of poverty were dropped, and the poverty thresholds were updated with the Consumer Price Index.

As longevity continued to rise, seniors were becoming a more visible and important group in the population. Between the end of World War I and 1950, life expectancy had increased ten years for men and fourteen years for women. Between 1950 and 1973, life expectancy increased another two years for men and four years for women. As a result, the percentage of the population over 64 years old was steadily increasing, from 4.7% in 1918 to 8.1% in 1950 to 10.0% in 1973.[11] We add a 'seniors' category to represent this growing group. Although the seniors category is not a distinct class, they represent the working class in retirement.

The three employed classes of laborer, wage earner, and salaried families, along with the new categories for low income and seniors, are defined by the following income groups:[12]

Laborer:	$9,200–$11,500
Wage earner:	$12,000–$13,700
Salaried:	$17,500–$20,000
Low income:	$2,025–$2,815 (1 person)
	$2,720–$3,780 (2 persons)
	$3,240–$4,600 (3 persons)
	$4,055–$5,775 (4 persons)
	$4,770–$6,340 (5 persons)
	$5,330–$7,420 (6 persons)
	$6,450–$9,170 (7 or more persons).
Seniors: (age 65+)	$3,700–$5,500

Wives' earnings provided a significant proportion of family income in 1973 as female participation in the labor force became more uniform across age groups. Female participation grew 12% in the 1950s as in the 1940s, with the largest increase among middle-aged women (45–64 years old) with grown children. Many of these women had responded to the government's pleas for help with wartime production, and many of them had resisted the government's calls to return to being full-time homemakers. In addition, mothers with children still at home began going to work in increasing numbers during the 1950s.

During the sixties, the participation rate of women grew only slightly faster than in the previous two decades. However, the participation rate of mothers rose dramatically. In 1973, one-third of mothers with young children (under six years) and one-half of mothers with older children (6–18 years) were employed. By this time, women's work roles had changed sufficiently so that the norm was for wives to have a job at least some of the time as well as to maintain their homes. But norms had not changed to release men from their obligation to be the primary earners for their families. These work roles reflected and reinforced the wage structure, where women still earned considerably less than men.

When family size increased with the high birth rates during the fifties and early sixties, the larger families required that more time be spent in maintaining the home and raising children. The rise in the participation rate of mothers and the increase in family size were in conflict in their impact on women's use of time. These trends could not be sustained without changing either women's work role or society's child-rearing practices. The conflict was partially resolved by lower birth rates from

Table 6.2 Income distribution, 1973

	All households	*Metropolitan families*	*White families*	*Black families*	*All families*
Number (000s)	69,859	37,317	48,919	5,440	55,053
Under $1,000	1.9	1.0	1.0	2.5	1.1
$1,000–1,999	4.2	1.3	1.3	5.3	1.8
$2,000–2,999	5.9	2.6	2.6	7.6	3.1
$3,000–3,999	5.5	3.7	3.5	8.4	4.1
$4,000–4,999	5.4	4.2	4.1	8.3	4.5
$5,000–5,999	5.0	4.2	4.3	7.2	4.6
$6,000–6,999	5.0	4.4	4.5	6.8	4.8
$7,000–9,999	14.6	13.5	14.6	16.9	14.9
$10,000–14,999	22.6	25.4	26.3	19.1	25.5
$15,000–24,999	22.1	28.8	27.6	14.4	26.2
$25,000 and over	7.8	11.1	10.0	3.5	9.3
Median income	$10,512	$12,961	$12,595	$7,269	$12,051
W/Non-farm earnings	$10,572	NA	$12,706	$7,338	$12,168
Husband/wife families	$13,034	NA	$13,297	$9,729	$13,028

Source: CPR P-60 and Statistical Abstract.

the mid-1960s through the mid-1970s, by the practice of sending children to preschool, and by women taking part-time jobs. However, the conflict between family life and work life would continue into the 1990s as the work place was slow to adapt to the needs of working parents.

Women and children had already switched places as the main source of secondary earnings, as children replaced paid work with formal schooling.[13] Families were generally twice as likely to report a wife working as a child working. Overall, the number of earners per family continued to grow across classes. Higher status families were able to increase their number of earners faster since their access to the labor market was better. This differential ability to add workers to the labor force increased income inequality across classes. By 1973, one-half of laborer families, two-thirds of wage-earner families, and three-fourths of salaried families had at least two earners.[14] Black wives were more likely to work than white wives, but black youths were more likely than whites to experience difficulty in finding jobs. Young white men (aged 16 through 21 years) had an employment rate of 62% compared to 46% for non-white men; young white women had an employment rate of 48% compared to 29% for non-white women.[15]

Whether or not a wife earned a paycheck had a substantial impact on the family's income. Nevertheless, wives' earnings increased only slightly as husbands' earnings rose, so the wives' earnings contributed a declining percentage of earnings across class, from one-third in laborer families to one-fourth in salaried families.[16] An income gap existed within each class between families with an employed wife and families without an employed wife, so that income differences between classes had become more blurred. The wife's earnings substantially closed the gap between husbands' earning in adjoining classes, and so a schism developed between a husband's occupation and his family's income. This schism reinforced the movement of wives into the labor force, as the appropriate money income for each class became defined by the earnings of both the husband and wife.

Living standards improved dramatically between 1950 to 1973 as real disposable income per capita rose 79%. Salaried families improved their income position relative to the working class, while incomes were slightly leveled within the working class both between white skilled and unskilled workers and between black and white working-class families.[17] Government income support programs prevented income inequality from growing for those below the working class. The poverty threshold for three-person families was about 35% of the income of the typical laborer family, which had three family members.

Increases in taxes, savings, and income support offset the divergence in income so that real expenditures across classes were only slightly less equal in 1973 than in 1950. Nationally, consumption expenditures as a percentage of personal income had fallen from 84% in 1950 to 76% in 1970, while personal taxes grew from 9% to 14% and personal savings from 6% to 7%.[18] The consumption position of laborer relative to wage-earner families remained the same with laborers' consumption equalling three-fourths of wage-earners' consumption. The consumption position of the working class relative to the salaried class fell, however, as wage-earners' consumption equalled three-fourths of salaried consumption in 1973.

The War on Poverty greatly improved Social Security and expanded programs for low-income families, such as Food Stamps, AFDC, and Medicaid. Between 1950 and 1960, government income transfer programs had declined slightly as Veterans' payments declined. The decline in Veterans' payments was more than offset by the rapid growth in Social Security after 1960, and the low-income population increasingly relied on income from the government. Retirement and income support benefits rose. In 1973, seniors received 73% of their income from pensions, and low-income families received almost 54% of their income from retirement or support programs. Nationally, transfer payments accounted for 6.6% of personal income in 1950 and 9.8% in 1970.

Personal consumption was supplemented by the rapid rise in nonwage benefits received from employers. These benefits were becoming increasingly important in determining the family's access to health care, vacation time, and retirement income. Nonwage benefits rose rapidly from 12.6% of total compensation in 1950 to 21.1% in 1970. Retirement income, both public (Social Security) and private, accounted for one-half of this increase as it rose from 2.6% (1950) to 6.4% (1970). Paid time off (i.e., holidays, vacations, and sick leave) remained the most important benefit, and it grew from 7.6% of compensation in 1950 to 10.8% in 1970. Health insurance, the other major benefit, was only beginning to become important as it reached 2.0% of compensation in 1970 (up from 0.5% in 1950).[19]

The improvements in Social Security benefits as well as the more general rise in affluence facilitated a remarkable proliferation of households as single people, both old and young, lived by themselves or with other singles. 'Primary individual' (i.e., non-family) households accounted for 11% of households in 1950 and 19% in 1970. This proliferation reflected a long-term trend in the decline of extended families as higher incomes relieved the economic pressure for seniors to live with grown children or for young adults to live with their parents. The proportion of households including an adult other than the husband or wife fell by one-half from 10% in 1950 to 5% in 1970, and the proportion of households containing more than one family fell by two-thirds, from 7% to 2%.[20] The divorce rate, which fell slightly in the fifties, rose rapidly during the sixties from 9.2 to 14.9 divorces per 1,000 married women. The decline of the extended family and the rise in divorce resulted in more households being formed, and it lowered family incomes as the

Table 6.3 Sources of income, 1973

	Poor		Laborer		Wage earner		Salaried		Seniors	
	Amount ($)	% rep.	Amount ($)	% rep.	Amount ($)	% rep.	Amount ($)	% rep.	Amount ($)	% rep.
Total gross income[a]	3,810	100.0	10,347	100.0	12,883	100.0	18,796	100.0	4,612	100
Earned income										
Wages and salary	1,301	45.8	7,934	91.4	10,524	94.9	16,334	97.4	440	22.6
Self-employed	142	8.6	437	10.7	501	10.0	491	10.7	33	5.4
Income from assets										
Rental income	31	4.3	89	6.5	59	6.8	139	9.7	94	9.2
Interest	68	36.0	253	64.9	245	73.4	293	80.1	392	70.1
Dividends	5	3.6	87	10.0	107	16.3	109	23.2	102	15.7
Retirement										
Social security Government pension	1,180	51.4	850	26.3	714	23.4	620	19.1	2,880	95.0
Social security	1,057	49.5	566	19.0	450	15.7	252	8.8	2,623	93.5
Private pensions/annuities	23	3.0	163	6.2	127	5.1	143	3.5	474	33.3
Income support										
Unemployment insurance	22	2.1	54	6.4	44	5.4	23	3.6	14	2.3
Workmen's compensation	24	1.3	39	4.1	50	4.5	85	4.0	15	1.9
Public assistance	683	27.8	54	2.3	10	1.2	26	1.4	69	4.2
Food Stamps	122	31.3	17	4.3	4	1.6	1	0.5	7	4.2
Roomers and boarders	6	1.5	5	1.2	15	1.4	8	1.2	21	1.9
Other Sources[b]	137	10.7	92	4.5	114	3.8	89	2.9	25	1.9
Gifts										
Cash	134	15.8	299	15.3	153	18.0	397	17.5	203	10.7
Furniture and equipment	43	37.5	43	43.1	50	46.5	45	45.2	15	19.5

[a] Includes income tax refunds and excludes gifts.
[b] Includes child support, alimony, royalties and scholarships.

advantage of pooling resources was passed over in favor of more privacy and control.

This period witnessed a vast expansion in education, as education expenditures by state and local governments, which accounted for 7% of GNP in 1950 and 17% in 1973, dominated the growth in government spending. This reflected both an expansion of educational services, such as public schooling for kindergarteners and more students completing high school, and an expansion in the student population as the baby boomers were educated.

Economic growth had both facilitated and depended upon the major expansion in the educational system. The heightened importance of school in children's lives and the increasing education required by employers were reflected in school enrollment rates. In 1950, 78% of children aged 5–19 years were enrolled in school grades K-12; in 1970, 88% were enrolled. Schooling was increasingly delaying entry into full-time work for many young adults. The proportion of 18–19 year olds in school was 30% in 1950 and 48% in 1970; the proportion of 20–24 year olds in school was 9% in 1950 and 22% in 1970. The educational norm for the working class had rapidly become a high school diploma. The proportion of adults who were high school graduates jumped from barely half (57%) in 1950 to a large majority (76%) in 1970 as the median years of school completed by the adult population (aged 25 or more years) increased from 9.0 years for men and 9.6 years for women in 1950 to 12.2 years for men and 12.1 years for women in 1970.[21]

Employed families spent their increasing affluence on a newer single family dwelling, often in the suburbs, and on a second car. The proportion of their budgets spent on housing and transportation rose from 23% in 1950 to 32% in 1973. The government also forced them to save more for their retirement through the mandatory Social Security payroll tax, and insurance rose from 4% of their budget in 1950 to 9% in 1973. Meanwhile, food and clothing became less important in defining life-style and status. Employed families spent 23% of their budgets on food and clothing in 1973, down from 40% in 1950.

Black husband-wife families had finally reached socially acceptable levels of consumption for food, clothing, and housing, so that they could finally increase their expenditures on transportation. Their car ownership rates grew dramatically, while expenditures for food and clothing increased slowly in the 1950s and remained steady in the 1960s. Their housing improved as expenditures rose in the 1950s, but home ownership rates did not increase until the 1960s when discrimination in credit allocation became illegal and when more residential areas became accessible to blacks.

Let us now analyze in more detail the consumption norms and living standards generated by this phenomenal income growth for the generation following World War II.

Table 6.4 Food and alcohol 1973

	Low income			Laborer			Wage-earner			Salaried			Seniors		
	Avg. exp. ($)	% rep.	Cost ($)	Avg. exp. ($)	% rep.	Cost ($)	Avg. exp. ($)	% rep.	Cost. ($)	Avg. exp. ($)	% rep.	Cost ($)	Avg. exp. ($)	% rep.	Cost ($)
Food total[a]	1,190	99.6	1,195	1,704	99.9	1,706	1,885	100.0	1,885	2,394	100.0	2,394	1,143	99.2	1,152
Food at home	1,048	98.9	1,060	1,330	99.3	1,339	1,466	100.0	1,466	1,773	99.8	1,776	1,009	99.2	1,016
Food away from home	141	72.2	196	375	94.7	396	419	96.9	432	621	98.3	632	134	73.9	181
Alcohol total	22	37.9	58	78	71.7	109	88	70.5	125	127	81.6	156	28	37.5	74
Food purchased at stores	1,030	97.9	1,053	1,286	98.9	1,300	1,419	100.0	1,419	1,703	99.8	1,706	987	97.7	1,010
Meals at restaurants	79	33.0	240	219	65.9	332	241	73.3	329	358	80.2	446	88	33.7	260
School meals purchased	16	15.4	105	29	26.1	112	36	31.6	113	48	38.8	123	2	1.5	118
Other meals purchased	32	57.6	56	102	83.3	123	115	88.8	129	209	92.9	209	39	64.4	61
Catered affairs	0	0.4	110	2	0.6	264	6	1.7	371	3	0.7	450	0	0.0	0
Meals received as pay	13	8.1	164	23	8.6	264	21	10.1	203	18	8.5	213	6	2.7	207
Alcohol (store-bought)	10	33.4	29	28	66.2	42	32	64.0	49	47	76.9	61	15	34.9	43
Alcohol at restaurants	12	18.6	65	50	47.2	107	57	49.5	114	80	64.1	125	13	13.8	93
	Avg. value (all)	% rep. (rep.)	Avg. value (rep.)	Avg. value (all)	% rep. (rep.)	Avg. value (rep.)	Avg. value (all)	% rep. (rep.)	Avg. value (rep.)	Avg. value (all)	% rep. (rep.)	Avg. value (rep.)	Avg. value (all)	% rep. (rep.)	Avg. value (rep.)
Food received without direct expense															
Value of home produced food	17	21.6	77	21	29.0	72	16	32.9	50	11	39.0	52	11	28.0	39
Value of food received from public/private welfare	21	13.9	151	5	2.8	171	1	1.4	55	0	0.5	23	0	0.8	58

[a] The food purchased with Food Stamps is included in Food total.

Diet

By 1950, nutrition no longer divided classes, as the majority of families met the recommended standards and families had diets of similar nutritional value. Between 1950 and 1973, improvements continued to be made in the variety of foods consumed and the ease of food preparation. Families also ate out more frequently. Food had become a much less important part of the family budget, as it declined from one in three dollars in the 1950 working-class budget, to only one in five dollars in the 1973 budget.

Food's share of the family budget continued to decline even though families ate more meals and snacks away from home. Grocery store bills declined even more than total food bills, since eating a meal in a cafeteria or inexpensive restaurant costs two to four times more than cooking a meal at home. As wives became employed, family members became more likely to purchase lunches at work or school rather than carry a bag lunch. In 1977, school children and adults ate at least one-fifth of their calories in meals or snacks away from home.[22]

Three meals and at least one snack were still the daily pattern for eating.[23] Families were more alike in the meals they ate at home than in any other activity. Their class differences in eating were primarily in their dining out.[24] Food expenditures per person for food prepared at home were approximately the same for families with 1976 incomes under $15,000; above $15,000, food expenditures rose with income, while the nutritional value per dollar of food actually declined.[25]

The Food Stamp Program, along with higher incomes, had improved the diets of low-income families, who now ate meals similar to those of the working class, although low-income families ate fewer meals away from home. Only one in three low-income families received Food Stamps, however.[26] For those who did, Food Stamps averaged $391 in value. Food Stamp families spent $340 more on food at the store and $302 more on food overall than families without Food Stamps, so that the Food Stamp Program significantly raised their food consumption more than an equivalent increase in income would have. Families without Food Stamps spent more on school lunches, restaurant meals, and alcohol, none of which can be purchased with Food Stamps.

The most important change in family meals since 1950 was the family's relying less on bread and potatoes as a source of calories and more on animal products and fat.[27] Families ate a larger variety of foods and they used more prepared foods. Store-bought bakery products had replaced homemade quick breads and desserts. The family's consumption of sugar and fat had become more indirect and hidden, as they bought less sugar and oils but more cakes, snacks, partially-prepared foods, and sodas at

Table 6.5 Quantities (lbs) per person per week, 1977

	Low income	Laborers	Wage earners	Salaried	BLS low	BLS moderate	BLS liberal
Milk and milk products[a]	7.41	7.57	7.81	7.86	9.00	9.50	10.26
Meat, poultry, fish	4.70	4.41	4.45	4.67	2.81	4.38	5.19
Eggs[b]	0.70	0.59	0.59	0.61	0.52	0.56	0.61
Dry beans, peas, nuts	0.33				0.35	0.22	0.22
Grain products	2.57	2.16	2.11	2.10	3.25	2.06	2.75
Citrus, tomatoes[c]	1.82	0.59	0.62	0.71	1.88	2.25	2.94
Potatoes	1.58	1.25	1.19	1.17	2.50	2.13	1.94
Other vegetables and fruit	3.88	6.42	6.65	7.50	5.63	6.25	6.94
Fats and oils	0.65	0.72	0.71	0.68	0.53	0.69	0.69
Sugar and sweets	0.85	0.92	0.87	0.80	0.69	0.85	1.06

[a] BLS standard has been converted from quarts to pounds using 1 quart to weigh 2 pounds.
[b] Eggs includes dry bean, peas and nuts for laborer, wage earner, and salaried.
[c] USDA includes only citrus fruit, no tomatoes; juices are under 'other vegetables and fruits.'
Source: USDA, *Nationwide Food Consumption Survey 1977–8*; low-income is from Preliminary Report No. 8, July 1981, 'Food Consumption and Dietary Levels of Low-Income Households, November 1977–March 1978'.

the store. Working-class families served beef four or five times weekly (rather than three times), chicken twice, pork once, and fish once. No evening meal had to rely on a meat substitute, and the portions of meat allowed were considerably larger than in 1950 (8 vs 5 ounces). Potatoes were served only twice weekly, rather than three times. Meals included one-third fewer fresh or canned vegetables, but they did include greater variety. Fresh citrus had largely been replaced with processed juice, often frozen concentrate, and the family ate 20% more fresh fruits that were not citrus.

Reliance on mixes and prepared foods had more than doubled since 1950. Prepared foods reduced the amount of time required for meal preparation without increasing the cost. A study conducted in the 1960s showed that families spent about 13% of their food dollar on processed (or convenience) foods, and their overall costs were slightly lower than if they had used only home-prepared foods.[28]

The biggest change in the mealtime activity was the change in location, as meal time, at least at lunch, became a public rather than a family activity. Although eating meals at work or school had lost its sharp class distinction after World War II for families with employed heads, important class differences still existed for eating other meals. Low-income families still could not afford as many meals out. A salaried family was 2.4 times as likely to eat in a restaurant as a low-income family. Overall, salaried families spent one-fourth of their food budget for meals outside the home; working-class families spent one-fifth, and low-income families spent only one-tenth. Snack consumption was much more similar than meals outside the home, and high-income family members spent only 1.5 times as much for snacks as low-income family members.[29] Like other aspects of family life, eating became less centered in the home and less dependent on the housewife's cooking skills.

The American diet continued its unhealthy trend toward more animal protein, more sugar and fats, and fewer flour and cereal products. In 1970, protein consumption was close to its 1918 level, but fat consumption was 22% higher and carbohydrate consumption was 18% lower. Between 1950 and 1973, the per capita consumption of meat, poultry, and fish increased by one-third, of sugars grew by one-fifth, and of flour and cereal products fell by one-sixth.[30] Sweet potatoes were less important as a source of vitamin A, while orange juice (especially frozen concentrate) was more important as a source of vitamin C. Families replaced animal fats with vegetable fats and replaced some fresh produce with some frozen fruit juice and vegetables. Overall, consumption of fresh fruits fell by one-third and of fresh vegetables by one-fifth between 1950 and 1973.[31]

The quality of diets declined between 1955 and 1965,[32] and then improved between 1965 and 1977. This partially reflects the success of the Food Stamp Program and partially reflects greater public awareness of nutrition. Improvements were made especially in consumption of vitamins A and C and calcium, which displayed an uneven path of consumption over the years and had presented nutritional problems for the nation. The consumption of these three important nutrients, after falling during the interwar period, then rising rapidly during World War II, and then falling during the years immediately following the war, had finally risen again. In the early 1970s, consumption of vitamins A and C were at their adequate pre-World War II levels, but consumption of calcium was considerably higher than its inadequate prewar level. Iron consumption had also fallen in the period following World War I and then risen during World War II and the 1960s.[33]

Generally, consumption of protein, phosphorus and vitamins A, B$_{12}$, C, thiamin, riboflavin, and niacin was above the Recommended Daily Allowance (RDA). The 1950 deficiencies in thiamin, niacin, and vitamin C had been eradicated. As in 1950, the main nutritional deficiency was in calcium, especially for women aged 15–18 and 35–64 years. Other deficiencies included iron, especially for toddlers and for women aged 12–50 years old, and vitamin B$_6$, especially for women over 14 years and men over 75 years.[34] However, these deficiencies are probably overstated, since women reported consuming only 75%–80% of the required calories and men only 85%–90%. Generally, women reported eating more nutritious foods than men, since their consumption of calcium, iron, magnesium, and vitamin B$_6$ was higher per calorie. Both sexes reported eating large quantities of protein; women consumed 40%–50% and men 60%–90% more than the RDA for protein.[35]

The diets of low-income families were even more deficient in calcium, iron, magnesium, and vitamin B_6 than the diets for the nation as a whole.[36] The problem was not that low-income families bought less nutritional foods. The nutrients per dollar's worth of food used at home declined as income rose for vitamins B_{12} and was fairly constant for calcium, iron, thiamin, riboflavin, and vitamin B_6 across lower and middle-income families. The basic problem for low-income families was insufficient food or hunger. Calories consumed increased with income in 1977 from 1,673 calories per person (families with incomes under $6,000) to 1,946 calories (families with incomes above $16,000).

The Food Stamp Program, which began in the mid-1960s, improved the nutrition of low-income families so that their nutritional inadequacies declined dramatically. Families participating in the Food Stamp Program were one-fourth more likely to consume the RDA for all nutrients than low-income families who did not receive Food Stamps.[37] Although households consumed on average more than the RDA for most nutrients (from 118% for calcium to 242% for protein), a significant percentage of households failed to meet the RDA for calcium (39%), vitamin B_6 (36%), magnesium (30%), and vitamin A (24%).

Concerns with overeating and obesity continued to dominate thinking about the national diet. For adults aged 20–44, one in six were found to

Table 6.6 Food consumption for low-income families with and without Food Stamps, 1973

| | Without Food Stamps[a] | | | With Food Stamps[b] | | |
	Avg. exp. ($)	% rep.	Cost ($)	Avg. exp. ($)	% rep.	Cost ($)
Food total	1,095	99.4	1,102	1,397	100.0	1,397
Food at home	942	98.4	957	1,282	100.0	1,282
Meals away	153	75.4	203	116	65.1	178
Meals in restaurants	89	35.2	252	58	28.1	208
School meals purchased	18	14.0	128	12	18.5	66
Other meals purchased	36	61.7	59	23	48.6	48
Meals received as pay	9	6.2	151	22	12.3	177
Alcohol total	26	38.3	67	13	37.0	36
Away from home	15	19.3	77	6	17.1	34
At home	11	34.6	31	8	30.8	24
Food and alcohol total	1,121			1,411		
Value of Food Stamps received				391	100.0	391

[a] Sample size 321.
[b] Sample size 146; expenditures include Food Stamp value.

be obese in a 1972 study.[38] Among older adults, women were twice as likely to be obese as men (26% vs 13%). Black males were the group most likely to exhibit insufficient caloric intake, and 31%–39% of them were lean. In contrast, black women were the most likely group to overeat, and between 25% and 35% of them were obese. People living in poverty were more likely than the nonpoor to have weight problems, and low-income people suffered higher rates of being both overweight and underweight.

When families sat down to meals at home, some class differences existed in the foods they ate, including the high status consumption of expensive cuts of beef, frozen vegetables and fruit juice, exotic fresh fruits, bakery products, and salads.[39] The consumption of dairy products was similar across class, while low-income families consumed more grain products than other families. Low-income families ate more potatoes, citrus fruits, and tomatoes than working-class or salaried families. Salaried and working-class families had similar consumption of potatoes, but otherwise salaried families consumed more fruits and vegetables. Altogether, salaried families consumed 14% more total fruits and vegetables than laborer families, who consumed 14% more fruits and vegetables than low-income families.

These differences in the eating habits across classes were minor in comparison with the differences between average eating habits and the government-recommended diet. The US Department of Agriculture (USDA) expected families to spend more on food than they did, and the diets in the BLS workers' budgets cost considerably more than families actually spent for food. Low-income families spent 85% as much as the USDA low-cost diet, although families receiving Food Stamps purchased food worth more than the USDA low-cost diet. Wage-earner families spent as much as allowed by the BLS low-cost diet, rather than the BLS moderate-cost diet. Salaried spent less than the BLS moderate-cost diet and only two-thirds as much as the BLS liberal diet cost.[40]

The three USDA diets divided each food dollar so that more was spent on meat, poultry, and fish and less on cereals and bakery products as incomes increased. The BLS liberal diet cost 64% more than the low-income diet and had 85% more meat, 33% more fruits and vegetables (not including potatoes), 30% more fat, and 50% more sugar, along with 33% fewer beans, 15% fewer grains, and 22% fewer potatoes. As in earlier years, the government guidelines assumed that low-income families would eat differently than the rest of the population, even though this was becoming less and less true. The USDA had devised an even more unrealistic 'economy diet,' which cost the Food Stamp allotment of $1,575, for families with incomes under $6,000. The suggested menus allowed an inexpensive cut of roast, chops, or a chicken on Sundays with nonmeat dishes, stews or casseroles for the other days.[41]

Through the years, home economists had continued their familiar refrain to families to improve their diets by including more fruits, vegetable, and milk, and to drink fewer soda pops. The problem was increasingly one of 'empty' calories, especially from snack foods such as sodas and chips instead of fruit or milk.[42] According to USDA guidelines for healthful eating, families consumed too few milk products, citrus fruits, potatoes, and grain products. If working-class families ate as suggested by the moderate cost diet, each member would drink one-fourth more milk and eat two-fifths more grain, and one-fourth more fruits and vegetables; they would eat less meat and sweets. Since low-income families had diets that were similar to the rest of the population, they also ate more meat, fat, sugar and less milk, grains, fruits, and vegetables than recommended. However, the BLS liberal diet allowed more sugar and meat, as well as more dairy products, grains, fruits, and vegetables than was consumed by salaried families.

In 1977, the American diet was declared to be more inadequate than previously thought, when the USDA made major changes in dietary goals by dramatically reducing the allowance for fat. The new goals urged a reduction in fat consumption from 42% to 30% of total calories; the reduced calories were to be replaced with calories from complex carbo-hydrates or fruits and vegetables. The new goals had suggested menus that more nearly resembled the simple diets of 1918 or 1935, which relied heavily on cereal and bread, than the richer diets in 1950 and 1973, which included meat in two or three meals daily. The new menus for a man included a breakfast of cereal with milk, toast, juice, and coffee; a lunch of macaroni salad, a vegetable, bread, and milk; a dinner of meat (alternating with fish or poultry), potato, vegetable, bread, cake, and coffee; and a snack of biscuits and juice.[43] Affluence had allowed meals to satisfy people's desire for a large variety of foods that were now easily available. Unfortunately, this outcome of economic growth did not bring progress in the form of better nutrition. Instead, people were urged to consume only the 'fruits' of progress and to forgo the fats and prepared sweets in order to return to a less rich, but healthier diet.

Wardrobe

The trends in clothing of the earlier era continued with falling relative prices and with a declining proportion of the budget for wardrobes. Clothing deprivation no longer publicly isolated even low-income families, and few households could not afford to buy acceptable clothing for school, work, and social activities. Salaried families continued to distinguish themselves from working-class families through their finer clothing. Adjusting for family size, salaried families spent one-third more on their wardrobes than working-class families (see table 6.7).

Low-income families wore less nice clothing than working-class families, but the differences were more noticeable among adults than among children. Since obvious status differences based on a lack of acceptable clothing had disappeared, clothing distinctions became more qualitative and more subtle.

The wife's appearance in public was important, and she continued to spend more than her husband on clothing as she had in 1950 (see tables 6.7A and 6.7B). Salaried wives spent 34% more than their husbands, laborer wives spent 41% more, and low-income wives spent 27% more. Synthetic stockings had made silk stockings obsolete, and so hosiery was no longer the primary reason for women spending more than their husbands. Stockings now accounted for about 7% of a woman's clothing budget. Low-income husbands especially economized on clothing. In order to purchase acceptable work clothes, laborer husbands spent twice as much as low-income husbands on pants, shirts, jackets, and shoes.

Although young women (aged 12–20 years) spent more on clothing than their brothers, except in low-income families, the differences were not as great as those between wives and husbands. The gender differences grew with class status as young women increased their spending on clothes rapidly as family income increased. Among salaried family members, young men were the least status conscious in their dressing.

Gender differences in clothes spending disappeared for children under 12 years, and families spent the same for both girls and boys. However, status differences were important for salaried children, whose clothes cost considerably more than those for working-class children.

Compared to laborer families, low-income families economized on adults' clothing but not on their children's clothing. Their purchases of children's clothing, with the possible exception of some purchases for the teenage daughter, were for basics, since growing children's clothing must be replaced. How long they could actually spend so little for the adults' clothing is uncertain, since eventually even adults must replace clothing as it becomes worn or unsuitable for public life. Compared to salaried families, working-class families economized most on the adults' and young children's clothing. Young children from low-income and working-class families spent approximately the same amount on clothes, which appears to be the minimum for social acceptance.

Young women and men spent their money on different types of clothing to distinguish themselves, and these patterns varied across classes (see table 6.7D). Working-class young women spent one-half more on shoes and hosiery than low-income daughters. Young women across all classes used accessories to distinguish themselves from the class below. These were relatively inexpensive items; together, accessories and footwear cost one-third as much as outerwear. Salaried young women distinguished themselves from working-class young women by spending

Table 6.7 Clothing–total, 1973

	Low income			Laborer			Wage earner			Salaried			Seniors		
	Avg. exp. ($)	% rep.	Cost ($)	Avg. exp. ($)	% rep.	Cost ($)	Avg. exp. ($)	% rep.	Cost ($)	Avg. exp. ($)	% rep.	Cost ($)	Avg. exp. ($)	% rep.	Cost ($)
Clothing total	276.70	97.4	284.00	489.28	99.4	492.25	566.43	99.8	567.42	825.92	99.5	830.24	212.77	97.3	218.63
Husband	46.43	46.5	99.92	141.06	80.0	176.43	171.68	88.8	193.31	244.87	95.1	257.36	60.97	57.9	105.38
Outerwear	29.77	38.1	78.10	95.31	74.4	128.11	114.74	85.3	134.49	169.95	94.1	180.60	38.67	49.4	78.23
Underwear	4.46	35.1	12.69	11.26	60.5	18.60	12.24	67.7	18.17	14.99	76.4	19.61	7.37	40.2	18.31
Footwear	8.03	31.7	25.35	23.09	59.1	39.11	28.08	67.1	41.83	37.28	76.1	48.99	8.03	29.9	26.88
Hats/accessories	4.17	19.1	21.88	11.40	45.9	24.83	16.57	51.2	32.35	22.65	67.1	33.77	6.90	21.8	31.61
Boys (2–20 years)	43.78	25.5	171.82	42.86	25.4	169.00	50.56	31.3	161.57	75.38	34.5	218.57	1.83	1.5	119.49
Outerwear	28.20	24.6	114.54	26.17	24.6	106.22	31.83	30.6	104.14	46.89	34.3	136.64	1.21	1.5	79.25
Underwear	4.69	22.7	20.66	4.85	22.9	21.12	5.42	28.7	18.90	7.94	31.0	25.60	0.19	1.1	16.35
Footwear	10.09	24.2	41.69	10.45	24.4	42.84	11.93	30.1	39.68	17.77	33.3	53.42	0.38	1.5	24.87
Hats/accessories	0.80	11.8	6.81	1.39	12.8	10.89	1.38	17.3	7.96	2.78	20.3	13.71	0.05	0.8	6.21
Wife	114.68	87.6	130.94	220.21	89.0	247.40	239.31	93.0	257.31	349.60	94.6	369.45	136.58	82.0	166.57
Outerwear	64.59	70.7	91.41	131.16	82.1	159.71	138.65	89.2	155.51	211.78	92.0	230.12	80.68	70.1	115.07
Underwear	14.03	64.2	21.84	21.80	70.5	30.90	22.79	78.3	29.10	30.62	81.6	37.51	17.47	60.5	28.86
Hosiery	11.10	67.5	16.46	17.25	73.7	23.41	18.21	81.6	22.30	25.28	86.0	29.41	10.04	64.0	15.69
Footwear	16.88	65.5	25.76	30.57	77.4	39.49	30.05	81.6	36.81	40.52	87.9	46.11	20.85	66.3	31.46
Hats/accessories	8.08	38.5	20.95	19.44	53.4	36.41	29.60	60.3	49.08	41.41	71.2	58.13	7.54	34.5	21.85
Girls (2–20 years)	48.67	28.9	168.35	47.53	25.8	183.90	55.08	28.1	198.68	96.38	36.9	261.08	0.99	0.8	129.55
Outerwear	31.64	27.4	115.45	28.80	25.0	115.18	33.73	28.0	120.58	62.76	36.4	172.43	0.60	0.8	78.87
Underwear	4.62	24.6	18.78	5.30	22.6	23.48	5.76	25.5	22.58	9.20	34.0	27.07	0.13	0.8	17.33
Hosiery	1.73	13.3	13.07	1.60	11.8	13.54	1.83	15.9	11.53	2.15	19.8	10.86	0.01	0.8	1.52
Footwear	9.35	26.6	35.21	9.62	24.6	39.06	11.40	27.4	41.53	17.79	35.4	50.32	0.20	0.8	25.96
Hats/accessories	1.31	13.9	9.45	2.20	14.3	15.47	2.36	17.1	13.75	4.49	24.3	18.50	0.05	0.4	11.75
Infants	13.58	15.6	86.90	16.93	19.9	84.96	21.33	22.6	94.58	18.81	15.1	124.73	1.15	2.7	42.94
Material, etc.	6.19	29.3	21.10	15.98	42.0	38.02	20.32	48.1	42.27	30.93	54.6	56.65	6.47	26.1	24.85
Services	3.38	21.0	16.10	4.71	31.6	14.87	8.14	38.8	20.98	9.96	45.6	21.85	4.77	30.7	15.58
Shoe repair	0.60	10.1	5.94	1.21	18.0	6.72	1.38	18.5	7.42	1.76	22.2	7.94	0.80	13.4	5.97
Alterations	1.25	12.2	10.25	2.75	17.3	15.90	4.68	25.0	18.71	5.55	31.5	17.59	3.77	20.7	18.24
Clothing rental	1.53	0.9	178.42	0.75	2.8	27.00	2.09	4.7	44.29	2.65	5.9	44.93	0.12	0.8	16.00

Table 6.7A Detailed clothing expenditures* – Husbands, 1973

	Low income				Laborer				Wage earner				Salaried				Seniors			
	Avg. exp ($)	% rep.	Quantity	Cost ($)	Avg. exp ($)	% rep.	Quantity	Cost ($)	Avg. exp ($)	% rep.	Quantity	Cost ($)	Avg. exp ($)	% rep.	Quantity	Cost ($)	Avg. exp ($)	% rep.	Quantity	Cost ($)
Coats	4	6.4	1.13	47	6	10.7	1.11	49	7	11.1	1.11	53	7	12.0	1.21	45	4	10.6	1.05	32
Jackets	4	15.5	1.28	19	5	19.1	1.26	21	7	17.5	1.34	23	7	24.1	1.33	22	3	12.2	1.14	17
Sweaters	1	6.0	1.93	11	3	13.0	1.66	12	4	15.5	1.61	14	4	18.1	1.69	13	2	11.1	1.60	10
Suits	8	10.7	1.24	54	21	16.9	1.46	84	38	16.2	1.60	80	38	24.4	1.71	88	10	7.8	1.29	99
Sports coats	2	5.6	1.08	25	9	14.6	1.37	42	17	18.9	1.30	46	17	24.6	1.37	50	5	10.0	1.11	46
Dress trousers	9	24.9	2.62	13	19	43.4	3.02	14	27	47.3	2.88	14	27	53.5	3.15	15	11	33.9	2.44	12
Casual slacks	6	19.7	2.85	10	8	28.9	2.76	10	11	31.8	2.86	11	11	32.8	2.76	11	5	17.2	2.32	13
Jeans and work pants	3	17.6	3.15	6	5	24.9	3.18	6	5	22.9	2.55	7	5	24.2	2.50	7	2	11.7	2.10	6
Dress shirts	4	21.5	2.86	6	10	39.3	3.54	7	16	44.4	3.04	7	16	55.4	3.80	7	4	19.4	2.86	7
Sport/work shirts	6	30.9	3.58	5	10	39.5	3.88	6	13	47.6	3.64	6	13	53.2	3.51	7	5	24.4	3.09	7
Undershorts	2	37.8	5.23	1	3	40.3	6.02	1	1	42.0	6.00	1	2	48.3	5.83	1	1	31.1	4.64	1
Undershirts	2	31.8	4.57	1	3	33.2	5.74	2	4	38.7	5.56	1	2	40.1	5.88	1	2	30.0	4.74	2
Socks	2	37.8	6.51	1	4	46.8	7.32	1	4	47.8	7.03	1	4	53.8	7.40	1	2	37.2	5.94	1
Street shoes	12	45.5	1.64	15	22	57.6	1.82	20	28	59.3	1.81	20	28	64.2	1.98	22	10	36.1	1.57	18
Sneakers and sport shoes	0	5.2	1.25	5	1	9.9	1.16	8	2	13.6	1.27	9	2	14.5	1.21	11	0	2.2	1.00	7
Hats	1	10.3	1.58	4	1	11.2	1.46	6	1	8.2	1.42	5	1	7.7	1.33	5	1	10.0	1.22	7
Ties	3	11.6	2.11	11	2	23.8	2.60	4	5	24.4	2.79	4	5	36.8	3.29	4	1	13.9	2.20	4
Watches	2	5.2	1.00	44	3	8.5	1.05	34	5	10.2	1.05	33	5	11.2	1.07	44	3	3.9	1.00	71
Sports clothing/swimwear	1	6.0	1.36	7	2	8.5	1.73	12	2	11.5	1.33	10	2	13.0	1.58	10	0	2.8	1.60	8
Alterations	0	6.4	2.00	2	1	7.3	3.25	3	1	9.8	3.56	3	1	13.4	2.74	4	1	9.4	1.71	3
Shoe repair	0	6.9	1.38	4	1	9.5	1.73	5	1	9.3	1.63	5	1	12.9	1.64	5	0	5.0	1.44	6
Total	79	87.1		90	147	92.8		158	160	95.1		168	212	96.5		220	82	83.3		99

* The detailed tables only include households if the relevant person (e.g., husband or young women, ages 12–20) is present. For this reason, the detailed totals are larger than the totals for all households in table 6.6.

Table 6.7B Detailed clothing expenditures – wives, 1973

	Low income				Laborer				Wage earner				Salaried				Seniors			
	Avg. exp. ($)	% rep.	Quantity	Cost ($)	Avg. exp. ($)	% rep.	Quantity	Cost ($)	Avg. exp. ($)	% rep.	Quantity	Cost ($)	Avg. exp. ($)	% rep.	Quantity	Cost ($)	Avg. exp. ($)	% rep.	Quantity	Cost ($)
Coat	9	15.2	1.39	41	16	25.3	1.21	54	12	23.7	1.16	45	21	26.6	1.23	65	12	18.8	1.25	51
Jacket	1	2.9	1.23	17	3	12.0	1.31	21	3	11.1	1.22	22	4	13.7	1.20	23	1	6.0	1.07	15
Sweater	2	12.4	1.41	9	4	20.1	1.95	11	4	21.6	2.06	9	6	25.2	2.31	11	2	17.1	1.57	9
Suit	10	23.4	1.99	22	26	40.8	2.23	28	27	40.8	2.23	30	38	51.0	2.46	31	14	28.6	1.79	27
Slacks	6	24.5	2.76	9	14	42.7	2.95	11	15	49.5	2.95	10	19	54.7	3.03	11	6	26.9	2.24	10
Jeans	1	4.2	1.63	8	2	9.7	1.97	8	2	11.1	2.03	7	1	8.3	1.82	8	0	1.3	3.33	8
Dress	17	41.7	2.62	15	35	52.6	3.05	22	30	52.1	2.77	21	45	63.4	2.87	24	36	55.1	3.46	19
Skirt	1	5.3	1.83	9	2	10.6	2.04	11	2	13.4	1.70	10	4	19.1	1.83	12	0	2.6	1.17	11
Blouse	6	30.2	3.15	6	15	52.7	3.73	7	16	58.9	3.94	7	20	64.9	4.00	8	7	33.3	2.64	8
Slip	1	13.9	2.40	3	1	15.5	1.82	5	2	17.6	1.76	5	2	19.0	1.76	5	2	15.8	2.43	5
Girdle	2	13.2	1.55	8	3	15.5	1.93	9	2	15.5	1.76	8	3	16.5	1.92	8	4	21.8	2.00	10
Bra	4	36.6	3.11	3	6	49.0	3.10	4	6	50.3	3.12	4	8	54.7	3.24	4	4	31.6	2.82	5
Panties	2	40.4	5.88	1	3	40.2	6.51	1	3	43.4	6.68	1	3	44.9	6.32	1	2	34.2	5.51	1
Nightgown/pajamas	2	21.9	1.91	5	4	29.7	2.10	6	4	33.8	2.32	5	5	35.0	1.99	7	4	28.6	2.07	6
Robe	2	14.1	1.28	10	3	17.6	1.32	13	3	15.7	1.50	13	4	22.1	1.26	13	2	17.1	1.40	10
Stockings/panty hose	10	66.2	12.65	1	15	74.2	16.37	1	15	80.7	14.62	1	21	83.0	18.10	1	9	63.7	10.58	1
Casual/dress shoes	13	54.3	2.14	11	23	68.2	2.51	13	21	65.9	2.49	13	25	72.5	2.61	13	19	65.4	2.11	14
Sandals	1	13.2	1.35	6	2	23.9	1.46	7	2	25.1	1.55	6	4	28.1	1.58	8	1	8.5	1.25	7
Sneakers/sport shoes	0	8.2	1.73	3	1	14.3	1.42	5	1	17.8	1.38	5	1	16.2	1.38	5	0	5.6	1.92	4
Hats	0	5.5	1.36	6	1	6.3	1.29	7	1	8.0	1.61	7	1	7.8	1.19	6	0	6.4	1.33	5
Handbag/purse	2	18.8	1.53	8	4	31.5	1.51	9	5	33.8	1.60	10	6	41.2	1.60	10	3	21.4	1.30	9
Watch	1	2.4	1.00	44	2	8.8	1.09	26	2	8.5	1.04	25	6	11.1	1.12	50	1	3.4	1.00	23
Costume jewelry	1	14.3	2.89	3	4	22.4	3.17	5	5	27.5	3.07	6	7	35.5	3.42	5	1	11.5	1.85	6
Non-costume jewelry	1	2.9	2.00	26	7	8.1	1.51	56	12	10.3	1.63	71	15	13.7	1.44	78	2	2.6	1.50	51
Sport clothing	1	3.8	1.06	15	2	12.1	1.34	14	3	15.2	1.23	14	4	17.8	1.46	15	1	2.1	1.60	15
Total	100	93.4		107	207	96.4		214	210	97.4		216	284	96.9		293	147	93.2		157

Table 6.7C Detailed clothing expenditures – young men, aged 12–20, 1973

	Low income				Laborer				Wage earner				Salaried			
	Avg. exp. ($)	% rep.	Quantity	Cost ($)	Avg. exp. ($)	% rep.	Quantity	Cost ($)	Avg. exp. ($)	% rep.	Quantity	Cost ($)	Avg. exp. ($)	% rep.	Quantity	Cost ($)
Coats	10	21.0	1.08	39	7	17.4	1.08	33	7	19.4	1.18	28	6	21.9	1.06	26
Jackets	4	20.2	1.13	15	9	31.7	1.28	20	6	29.2	1.36	15	9	39.3	1.40	15
Sweaters	2	18.5	1.59	7	3	18.8	1.76	8	2	12.5	1.56	8	3	22.3	1.28	9
Suits	4	11.8	1.00	31	6	9.2	1.20	53	3	4.9	1.00	59	7	11.2	1.32	47
Sports coats	1	3.4	1.00	25	5	10.6	1.48	30	4	7.6	1.27	39	5	16.1	1.08	28
Dress trousers	20	46.2	3.27	12	11	41.3	2.63	10	18	46.5	2.96	12	15	46.4	2.99	10
Casual slacks	17	52.9	4.02	7	15	51.8	3.44	8	20	50.0	4.06	9	22	60.7	3.98	9
Jeans and work pants	5	27.7	2.30	7	9	42.2	3.02	7	16	52.8	3.71	8	14	49.6	3.64	7
Dress shirts	5	24.4	3.59	6	5	33.5	2.78	5	8	45.1	3.28	5	6	41.1	2.54	5
Sport and work shirts	12	61.3	3.79	5	12	58.7	4.16	5	17	67.4	4.76	5	17	70.1	4.48	5
Undershorts	3	58.0	5.28	1	3	56.0	5.42	1	4	59.0	5.74	1	4	57.1	5.72	1
Undershirts	3	43.7	5.48	1	3	36.7	5.61	1	2	41.7	4.47	1	3	43.8	4.66	1
Pajamas	0	5.0	1.50	5	4	16.1	1.57	4	1	11.8	1.76	4	2	17.9	2.07	4
Socks	3	68.9	5.54	1	4	57.3	6.90	1	4	65.3	7.61	1	4	61.6	7.81	1
Street shoes	18	66.4	1.78	14	21	69.3	1.88	16	21	70.1	1.78	16	25	77.2	2.02	15
Sneakers and sport shoes	6	52.1	1.84	6	8	49.5	2.31	7	9	53.5	2.38	6	10	60.7	2.26	7
Hats	0	11.8	1.21	3	1	9.2	1.35	4	0	8.3	1.25	2	0	11.6	1.27	3
Gloves and mittens	0	7.6	1.11	2	1	17.4	1.79	3	1	18.1	1.50	3	1	17.0	2.18	3
Ties	0	8.4	1.10	2	1	12.4	1.74	4	0	9.7	1.29	3	1	15.2	1.65	3
Watches	1	5.0	1.00	16	3	9.6	1.00	27	2	8.3	1.00	24	3	13.4	1.03	23
Sports clothing/swimwear	1	18.5	1.23	6	3	22.9	1.54	8	2	19.4	1.86	6	3	31.3	1.57	5
Total	119	95.0		125	135	93.1		145	154	97.2		158	167	97.8		171

Table 6.7D Detailed clothing expenditures – young women, aged 12–20, 1973

	Low income				Laborer				Wage earner				Salaried			
	Avg. exp. ($)	% rep.	Quantity	Cost ($)	Avg. exp. ($)	% rep.	Quantity	Cost ($)	Avg. exp. ($)	% rep.	Quantity	Cost ($)	Avg. exp. ($)	% rep.	Quantity	Cost ($)
Coat	9	26.4	1.11	29	11	29.9	1.13	33	12	27.9	1.10	38	13	33.5	1.12	36
Jacket	2	12.5	1.06	14	5	23.4	1.38	15	5	26.4	1.35	15	8	33.0	1.43	17
Sweater	2	22.9	1.36	7	3	21.9	1.70	9	5	35.0	1.80	8	6	40.4	2.10	8
Suit	15	43.8	2.02	17	12	34.8	1.93	18	11	32.9	1.93	18	12	29.6	2.18	19
Slacks	13	54.2	2.81	9	20	68.7	3.30	9	25	73.6	3.57	10	32	75.9	4.25	10
Jeans	3	19.4	2.36	7	7	34.8	2.60	8	10	47.1	2.64	8	13	50.7	2.99	8
Dress	13	43.8	2.35	13	15	41.8	2.50	15	21	55.0	2.45	16	26	58.6	2.67	17
Skirt	2	17.4	1.84	5	2	13.4	2.04	6	2	20.7	1.52	5	3	19.7	1.63	10
Blouse	9	55.6	3.40	5	17	70.6	4.39	6	21	77.1	4.69	6	34	83.7	6.10	7
Slip	1	9.0	1.85	4	0	7.0	1.71	4	1	14.3	1.30	3	1	17.2	1.40	4
Bra	3	40.3	2.98	2	4	47.3	3.49	3	6	66.4	3.11	3	6	60.6	3.36	3
Panties	2	56.9	6.49	4	3	52.2	7.92	1	3	69.3	5.96	1	4	64.5	7.04	1
Nightgown and pajamas	1	20.1	1.76	4	3	38.3	1.79	5	3	37.9	3.26	8	5	39.4	1.97	6
Robe	0	4.9	1.14	6	2	17.9	1.11	12	1	11.4	1.00	2	2	16.7	1.09	10
Socks	1	29.9	3.26	1	2	39.8	5.99	1	2	40.0	4.32	1	3	47.3	5.31	1
Stockings	8	61.1	13.00	1	11	61.2	15.11	1	10	70.7	14.44	1	9	65.0	13.19	1
Casual and dress shoes	13	62.5	2.17	10	20	78.1	2.54	10	20	75.0	2.49	10	27	83.7	2.71	12
Sandals	2	20.8	1.53	7	2	25.9	1.29	6	2	34.3	1.31	5	3	30.5	1.21	7
Sneakers/sport shoes	2	30.6	1.48	5	2	35.3	1.55	4	3	38.6	1.89	4	4	44.3	1.67	5
Hat	0	4.9	1.00	2	0	9.0	1.22	3	1	10.0	1.07	7	1	14.3	1.07	4
Gloves/mittens	0	8.3	1.08	3	0	12.9	1.35	3	0	12.9	1.00	3	1	17.7	1.11	3
Handbags/purses	1	16.7	1.13	6	2	24.4	1.37	6	3	32.1	1.49	6	4	34.0	1.25	9
Costume jewelry	1	22.2	2.19	2	3	22.4	3.40	3	3	32.9	3.07	3	5	40.4	3.32	4
Non-Costume jewelry	2	7.6	2.09	15	4	8.5	1.35	33	10	10.7	1.47	61	1	9.4	1.26	13
Sports clothing	2	14.6	1.33	9	3	24.4	1.24	10	4	33.6	1.34	10	9	44.3	1.68	12
Total	111	86.8		128	161	94.0		171	191	97.9		195	240	95.6		251

over one-third more on their outerwear (primarily dresses, jeans, slacks, and blouses) and shoes as well as on hats and accessories. Their purchases of sports clothing also increased with class status. Salaried young men were more likely to buy suits, or sports clothing, but otherwise their wardrobes were similar to those of young working-class men.

Outerwear of both husbands and wives was marked by class. Like their sons (see table 6.7C), salaried husbands spent more on suits and sports coats to distinguish themselves from the working class. Like their daughters, the working-class wives spent more on accessories (but not on shoes) to differentiate themselves from low-income wives. Unlike their daughters, however, salaried wives spent only slightly more on accessories to distinguish themselves from the working class. Parents were less than one-half as likely to buy sports clothes as their children, and the parents' purchases varied less across classes.

Having one's clothes fit well and having well-repaired shoes imparted status. Yet few families reported paying to have shoes repaired or their clothing altered, although the percentage did increase with income from 10% of low-income to 22% of salaried families reporting shoe repair expenditures, and from 12% of low-income to 32% of salaried families reporting alteration expenditures. Services such as shoe repair and alterations accounted for only 1% of the budget, a surprisingly small number.

Clothing rental, which is primarily for men's formal wear for important occasions such as weddings, showed small but important differences across classes. One in 17 salaried families rented clothing, which was over twice the rate for laborer families. Senior and low-income families did not rent any clothing.

The percentage of families purchasing yardage and sewing notions increased across classes. The purchases were small, amounting to 5% or less of the clothing budget, and indicate that these materials were mostly for status handicraft sewing or for improved maintenance of clothing. Fewer than one-third of the low-income or senior families purchased fabric and notions (averaging $21 and $25, respectively) compared to almost one-half of the working-class families and over one-half of the salaried families (averaging $40 and $57, respectively).

Although the BLS had created new clothing standards for three budgets (lower, intermediate, and higher), the discrepancies between the BLS standard and actual practice had changed slightly since 1950.[44] Only the BLS's lower budget continued to assume erroneously that husbands would spend more than wives on clothing. The laborer wife spent considerably more than the lower budget standard, and only one-tenth less than the intermediate standard. The intermediate and higher budgets now correctly assumed wives would spend more than their husbands. Only in the salaried class did the wife spend less than the appropriate BLS standard. However, the BLS intermediate and higher standards still

Table 6.7E Detailed clothing expenditures – boys, aged 2–11, 1973

	Low income				Laborer				Wage earner				Salaried			
	Avg. exp. ($)	% rep.	Quantity	Cost ($)	Avg. exp. ($)	% rep.	Quantity	Cost ($)	Avg. exp. ($)	% rep.	Quantity	Cost ($)	Avg. exp. ($)	% rep.	Quantity	Cost ($)
Coats	6	26.6	1.29	16	4	23.0	1.08	16	4	25.4	1.08	15	7	32.8	1.11	19
Jackets	1	16.0	1.07	8	4	28.9	1.28	10	4	39.7	1.22	9	6	38.2	1.27	12
Sweaters	2	26.6	1.71	4	1	17.6	1.33	5	1	15.3	1.69	5	2	20.4	1.66	5
Suits	3	17.8	1.47	11	3	13.7	1.77	12	4	18.7	1.79	12	6	25.8	1.63	14
Dress trousers	5	32.5	2.67	6	4	25.4	2.46	6	4	30.6	2.72	5	6	36.6	2.90	6
Casual slacks	11	52.7	4.24	5	11	48.0	4.17	5	11	59.3	3.60	5	15	65.1	4.27	5
Jeans and work pants	5	30.2	3.88	4	7	40.2	3.28	5	7	49.3	3.40	4	8	47.8	3.17	5
Dress shirts	1	16.6	2.14	3	3	21.5	2.71	3	3	33.0	2.96	3	4	36.6	2.88	4
Sport/work shirts	8	56.2	4.51	3	8	58.2	4.77	3	8	61.7	4.49	3	13	69.4	5.24	4
Undershorts	3	54.4	6.97	1	3	57.8	5.34	1	2	49.3	5.60	1	3	51.6	6.45	1
Undershirts	2	37.3	5.40	1	2	37.9	5.26	1	2	31.1	5.58	1	2	38.7	5.86	1
Pajamas	1	14.8	2.16	1	3	33.2	2.11	4	4	38.3	2.22	3	4	44.6	2.27	4
Socks	3	72.2	7.15	1	3	66.8	6.82	1	3	73.2	7.71	1	4	70.4	8.10	1
Street shoes	12	75.1	1.96	8	14	73.8	1.83	9	14	78.9	1.91	9	19	84.4	2.28	10
Sneakers and sport shoes	5	63.3	1.69	4	7	68.4	1.96	4	7	77.5	2.10	4	9	72.6	2.25	5
Hats	0	14.8	1.24	2	0	16.0	1.27	2	0	11.5	1.21	2	0	14.5	1.04	2
Sports clothing/swimwear	0	10.7	1.22	4	1	21.1	1.35	5	1	23.4	1.24	3	3	38.7	1.26	5
Total	71	96.4		74	77	94.9		85	85	99.5		85	116	98.4		118

assumed that wage-earner and salaried husbands, respectively, would spend one-third more on their clothing than they actually did. As in 1950, the wage-earner wife's clothing expenditures approximated the BLS's intermediate standard, and the salaried wife spent 15% less than the higher budget standard.

The BLS standards also continued to assume erroneously that sons spent more than daughters for clothing. The standards assumed much higher purchases of clothing for boys than they actually made, except in laborer families. For girls, the standards tended to be below the actual spending. Laborer girls spent 40% more on clothing than allowed in the lower budget and only slightly less than allowed in the intermediate budget. Wage-earner daughters spent as much as allowed in the intermediate budget, and salaried daughters spent almost as much as allowed in the higher budget. For wage-earner and salaried boys, the intermediate and higher budgets were one-third too high compared to actual practice.

Since low-income families economized on the adults' clothing, the family did not meet the BLS lower budget standard for the husband or wife. The husband spent only 55% of the lower budget clothing allowance and the wife spent 86%. The boys' clothing expenditures matched the standard, and the girls' expenditures exceeded it by 27%.

Although clothes buying accounted for only 5%–6% of the family budget, clothes still provided subtle distinctions among wives and young women as well as a marker for all members of the salaried family. Lack of appropriate clothing no longer isolated children by class at school, even if this still occurred in social events. Money to pay for recreational and leisure activities provided an even more important barrier, as we shall see.

Home

Housing

The postwar housing boom, which resulted in the burgeoning development of the suburbs, had been largely financed by government-sponsored mortgages. The American Dream of owning one's home was rapidly becoming a reality for the working class; by 1973, 53% of laborer, 65% of wage-earner, and 63% of senior families were homeowners, as were 65% of all households nationwide. Salaried families also greatly expanded their home ownership, so that four out of five were homeowners (see table 6.8A). Although black laborer families had made great advances in buying homes, home ownership still distinguished white from black working-class families. Although black families with an employed husband had greatly improved their economic position, de facto housing segregation continued to keep the races spatially separated, even when black and white husbands worked in the same factory.

Table 6.8A Shelter, 1973

Homeowners[a]	Low income 37.0%			Laborer 53.0%			Wage earner 65.0%			Salaried 79.0%			Senior 63.0%		
	Avg. exp. ($)	% rep.	Cost ($)	Avg. exp. ($)	% rep.	Cost ($)	Avg. exp. ($)	% rep.	Cost ($)	Avg. exp. ($)	% rep.	Cost ($)	Avg. exp. ($)	% rep.	Cost ($)
Shelter total	1,296	97.9	1,324	1,802	99.8	1,806	1,984	100.0	1,984	2,420	100.0	2,420	1,161	97.7	1,188
Housing total	1,006	96.6	1,042	1,406	99.5	1,413	1,544	100.0	1,544	1,873	99.8	1,876	841	96.2	875
Owned dwelling total	225	37.7	596	550	57.6	955	812	68.2	1,191	1,356	82.7	1,640	377	63.2	597
Owned total + mortgage principal[b]			687			1,387			1,619			2,522			640
Rented dwelling total	779	64.5	1,209	851	52.9	1,608	722	40.0	1,803	498	29.3	1,700	463	39.5	1,174
School, college or other lodging	2	2.8	74	5	5.3	94	9	6.3	151	19	10.7	180	1	1.9	44
Fuel and utilities total	290	82.0	353	395	91.8	431	440	94.8	465	547	97.4	562	319	88.5	361
Selected details – Housing															
Homeowners															
Interest paid on first mortgage	57	10.3	557	223	35.5	627	357	48.3	740	604	66.6	907	28	7.3	382
Property tax	78	31.9	245	172	50.0	344	225	62.4	361	397	78.9	503	177	57.1	310
Property insurance	21	26.3	80	41	46.1	89	53	56.6	94	75	69.0	109	42	50.6	83
Total owned home maintenance	49	27.8	175	91	42.8	213	135	55.1	246	179	69.5	257	122	49.0	248
Interior painting	4	7.3	52	15	19.1	79	15	25.7	60	24	38.5	62	10	14.6	67
Exterior painting	9	7.3	125	11	12.9	87	12	17.3	69	19	20.3	92	22	14.2	157
Plumbing	9	11.6	77	9	12.8	73	16	20.1	80	25	24.1	106	11	16.9	67
Heating/air conditioning	2	4.5	51	6	8.1	79	8	8.7	87	16	12.7	124	6	11.9	52
Roofing, gutters	10	4.5	214	9	5.4	168	22	10.0	217	30	8.5	359	30	11.9	249
Flooring	4	4.7	94	4	4.1	108	6	5.8	107	11	8.1	141	9	3.1	286
Renters															
Small repairs cont.	6	6.1	91	8	9.2	90	16	10.9	150	10	6.5	160	2	3.2	62
Pest control	3	4.3	77	1	3.0	34	5	5.4	84	4	2.3	161	1	1.5	53
Rental repairs	5	6.9	77	12	8.5	143	8	5.4	153	5	3.6	146	3	4.6	71
Renters insurance	5	8.6	55	7	13.6	51	6	11.7	51	7	11.3	59	8	12.6	61

	Low income			Laborer			Wage earner			Salaried			Senior		
	Avg. exp. ($)	% rep.	Cost ($)	Avg. exp. ($)	% rep.	Cost ($)	Avg. exp. ($)	% rep.	Cost ($)	Avg. exp. ($)	% rep.	Cost ($)	Avg. exp. ($)	% rep.	Cost ($)
Selected details – owned dwelling															
Homeowners															
Market value	16,710			21,018			22,664			28,952			19,056		
% reporting	0.29			0.52			0.64			0.77			0.54		
Rental value	204			164			176			218			136		
Ratio	0.0122			0.0078			0.0078			0.0075			0.0071		
Home improvements	412	9.2		408	24.5		594	30.4		675	45.2		317	18.8	
Modernizing rooms	717	1.3		429	5.4		926	6.1%		773	11.3%		284	3.4%	
patio, etc.	298	2.6		230	8.1		263	12.1		404	13.9		113	7.3	
% owners carrying mortgage	28.0			67.0			74.0			85.0			12.0		
Mortgage other property (non-vacation) (% reporting)	4.0			1.9			3.1			4.2			8.0		
Expenses vacation home (% reporting)	2.4			3.6			3.5			9.2			1.9		

a Percentage of households living in owned dwelling. Some households bought or sold home during survey, so the percentage reporting owned expenses is greater than the percentage of homeowners.

b The average principal paid on mortgages is added to the interest and other expenses.

Families had eagerly been increasing their expenditures for better quality housing as they purchased sounder and more attractive housing and improved plumbing. Families lived in spacious housing, since the average number of rooms per person was 1.6–1.7 for all classes, including low income. Seniors, who often continued to live in their relatively large homes as their families shrank in size, had 2.7 rooms per person. Because of their attachment to their homes, because of the trouble and expense involved with moving, and because they could afford to pay their out-of-pocket expenses since most owners had no mortgage payments, many of the senior homeowners were large consumers of housing relative to their incomes.

Out-of-pocket expenditures for housing (i.e., mortgage payments, rent, property taxes, and maintenance) accounted for 15% of the wage-earner family's budget in 1973, up from only 10% in 1950. The other expenditures for shelter – utilities, furnishings, and operations – continued to absorb 14% of their budget. Overall shelter took 28% of employed families' budgets in 1973, up from 24% in 1950. In contrast, low-income families had to spend 37% of their budgets on shelter in 1973, while black families had spent 26% in 1950.

The financial strain felt by the different classes is indicated by their ability to meet their rent or mortgage payments versus their ability to buy additional properties. A small number of employed families (2% laborer and 4% salaried) were able to carry mortgages on other (non-vacation) homes, while an equally small number of low-income families (2%) increased their past-due rent or mortgage payments over the year. In addition, 9% of salaried families and 3%–4% of working-class families owned vacation homes.

Ownership

As expected, homeownership rates and costs both increased with class status. Because housing expenditures represent out-of-pocket expenses rather than opportunity cost (or rental value) for homeowners, these expenditures are influenced by the characteristics of financing such as the presence and age of mortgage and the interest rate. The percentage of homeowners with mortgages increased with class from 28% for low-income to 85% for salaried families. Only 12% of senior homeowners carried a mortgage. Most older homeowners had paid off their mortgages. Some low-income families owned substandard housing without a mortgage. The age of the mortgage declined with class status, since higher-class families tend to move more frequently as they upgrade their homes. Homeowners without a mortgage or with an old mortgage that covers a small percentage of the house's value had low out-of-pocket expenses relative to the rental value. Low-income and senior homeowners had only one-half of the housing costs of renters. Working-class homeowners had about three-fifths of the renters' costs, but salaried homeowners' costs were only slightly less than salaried renters' costs. Compared to the home's estimated rental value, out-of-pocket costs ranged from 24% for low-income to 63% for salaried owners, with 49% for laborer, 56% for wage earner, and 37% for senior owners.[45] Homeowners lived in better and more spacious housing, and their out-of-pocket expenses below rental value freed up income to pay some of the principal and to make home improvements, both of which added to the family's net worth. Working-class owners spent as much on housing, including principal payments and home improvements, as renters did. Low-income and senior owners still spent considerably less (by 35%) than renters. Only salaried owners, whose out-of-pocket expenses were already close to those of renters, spent considerably more (by 70%) when capital outlays are included.

The estimated value of their homes by owners is an indicator of their perceived status and quality of housing. Low-income homeowners estimated relatively high rental values. Laborer owners' estimates were one-quarter higher than low-income owners' estimates and one-tenth more than seniors' estimates. Salaried families' estimates were two-fifths more than laborer families' estimated, which were only 7% below wage-earners estimates.[46]

Renters

In 1970, one in three households rented their homes. As expected, renters tended to be young, to have one- or two-person households, and to have low incomes. Only 37% of the low-income households owned their homes. Renters were more likely to report living in less desirable neighborhoods than owners; 30% rated their neighborhoods as fair or poor (twice the rate for homeowners) and only 22% rated their neighborhood as excellent (one-half the rate for owners). However, renters were more likely to evaluate their public transportation services as adequate (75% vs 63% for homeowners). Renters were slightly more likely than owners to live in crowded housing (7% vs 5%) and to lack full plumbing (5% vs 2%) in 1974. Although two out of three renters still lived in structures with fewer then five dwellings, newer apartments often were in large structures and had swimming pools and other recreational facilities.[47]

Amenities

Housing quality improves with ownership, houses are larger than apartments and provide yards. In addition, homeownership increases a family's sense of security and control. Between 1950 and 1973, housing quality improved, however, for both owners and renters, as plumbing and central heating became standard features, even for low-income families. The percentage of housing that lacked full plumbing fell dramatically from 34% in 1950 to 3% in 1974. Fewer than 10% of working-class families did not have full plumbing in 1960, and by 1973, full plumbing was found in virtually all white working-class homes.[48]

Dilapidated housing fell from 9% of the total stock in 1950 to less than 4% in 1970. The quality and soundness of housing still varied across classes, however, and a significant proportion of families, including one in four black households, still lived in substandard dwellings (i.e., lacking running hot water or a toilet or dilapidated.) Even within a class, blacks continued to face considerable discrimination in access to decent housing. For a given income, blacks were two to four times more likely than whites to live in substandard housing. For example, for households with incomes between $3,000 and $4,000, 9% of whites and 30% of blacks lived in substandard housing in 1970. For households with incomes between $10,000 and $15,000, 2% of whites and 9% of blacks lived in substandard housing. In addition, one in five black households lived in crowded housing (i.e., more than one person per room), which was three times the rate for whites. After adjusting for income, blacks were still four times more likely than whites to live in crowded housing.[49]

Even though blacks still lagged behind whites in housing quality, their situation had improved considerably compared with the dismal conditions found in 1950, when three out of four black households lived in substandard housing. Significant improvements continued to be made in plumbing in the early 1970s for blacks, so that only 10% lacked full plumbing in 1974 compared to 17% in 1970.[50]

Central heating had become a standard feature and was found in three-fourths of working-class homes and in eight-tenths of salaried homes. Even a majority of low-income homes had central heating. Most homes were heated by gas (65%), with some homes still relying on delivered fuel oil (22%) or the more expensive electricity (10%). Only 2% of households reported having no heating system.

Once full plumbing and adequate heating had been achieved, families turned to amenities such as air-conditioning or a dishwasher, which increased comfort or reduced drudgery rather than improved health. By 1973, air-conditioning had become a coveted feature that conveyed class status. Some air-conditioning, mostly room units, was found in one in five salaried homes and in one in ten laborer homes in 1950. By 1973, air-conditioning was more widespread; 44% of laborer homes and 57% of salaried homes had some air-conditioning. However, quality varied across classes with the salaried homes twice as likely as laborer homes to have the much more desirable central units, which were quieter, easier to regulate, and cooled the entire house.

Major appliances in the home, such as washing machines, dryers, and dishwashers, continued to add features to make caring for clothes and cleaning up after meals easier. Ownership of these machines varied across classes, depending upon how long the particular machine had been available. The differences in ownership of the washing machine, which had been available for several decades, were less sharp than differences in the ownership of the dishwasher, which had been introduced more recently. A majority of families now had a washing machine but were still aspiring to buy a dishwasher. Three in five laborer families and four in five salaried families owned a washing machine, while only one in seven laborer families and three in seven salaried families owned a dishwasher.

Maintenance and insurance

Both maintenance and insurance appeared to be categories where home-owners economized when budgets were tighter. Since the housing of low-income families was often substandard and the housing for seniors was older, we would have expected their houses to require more annual maintenance. However, only three-fourths of these homeowners made repairs during the year, compared to four-fifths of laborer and nine-tenths of salaried homeowners. The amount spent on the repairs made also increased with class status; for example, repairs made by salaried homeowners cost 20% more than the repairs made by laborer home-owners. As expected, repairs made by seniors cost as much as the repairs made by wage earners.

Many low-income homeowners economized on insurance, or their houses did not qualify for insurance coverage, since 30% did not carry insurance on their houses. In contrast, almost 90% of the employed homeowners purchased insurance. The significant minority (one-seventh) of low-income homeowners who did not pay property taxes also indicates the existence of substandard housing not recorded on the tax rolls. Overall, expenditures for maintenance and insurance did not rise as rapidly as property taxes for homeowners across classes. Salaried homeowners paid 34% more for maintenance and insurance than laborer homeowners, while they paid 61% more in taxes (on homes self-estimated to be worth 38% more). With a similar pattern, laborer homeowners paid 23% more for maintenance and insurance than low-income homeowners, while they paid 44% more in taxes (on homes self-estimated to be worth 26% more).[51]

Renters were much less likely than owners to spend money on main-tenance or repairs. Only one in eight low-income or senior renter paid repair bills, which averaged under $80. We cannot tell if they economized on repairs because their landlords paid, or if they lived in inadequately maintained homes. However, the higher frequency of repairs made by one in six employed families who rented indicates the latter situation.

The employed families also paid over twice as much for their repairs as the low-income and senior renters.

Renters were not as likely to economize on insurance as on maintenance, and insurance showed class distinctions. One in seven low-income and one in three working-class and senior renters had insurance, while over one in two salaried renters carried insurance on their belongings.

Homeowners' maintenance encompassed a large array of jobs which reflected class differences, economic constraints, condition of the house as well as the adults' 'handyman' talents. Laborer families' major repair expenditure was for interior painting, while salaried and wage-earner families' major repair expenditure was for roofing. When they made repairs, salaried homeowners spent over twice as much for roofing as laborer homeowners, and one-half as much for plumbing and heating repairs. However, average expenditures for painting were more equal across classes.

Homeowners often performed many maintenance jobs, especially painting. Few employed families (3%–4%) hired outsiders to do painting, and salaried families (36%) were over twice as likely as laborer families (17%) to do some interior painting themselves. As with handicraft sewing, salaried families had more time and inclination to engage in do-it-yourself maintenance than working-class families.[52] In general, salaried homes had some interior painting every 2.5 years and exterior painting every three years, compared to laborer homes, which had some interior painting every five years and exterior painting every seven years. Low-income homeowners could not afford to paint as often, and their homes had some interior and exterior painting every 12 years.

Because of their physical limitations, senior households were much less likely than employed households to do repairs themselves. Both senior and low-income households paid for emergency work, such as plumbing, or for repair work, such as roofing and painting, that would prevent long-run structural damage. Even so, low-income families severely economized on maintenance, and their projects cost one-third less than seniors' maintenance.

Home improvements or remodeling, which are recorded as increases in family assets rather than expenditures, were made by one-fourth of low-income owners and one-half of employed owners. For all classes, modernizing of rooms, especially kitchens and bathrooms, was the most expensive improvement, and outside improvements in the garden and patio were the most frequent improvement. Salaried families spent two-thirds more than laborer families when they made improvements.

Using energy

Even though families eventually face a lower bound in how much they can reduce energy consumption through economizing efforts, utility bills

Table 6.8B Fuel and utilities detail, 1973

	Low income			Laborer			Wage earner			Salaried			Senior		
	Avg. exp. ($)	% rep.	Cost ($)	Avg. exp. ($)	% rep.	Cost ($)	Avg. exp. ($)	% rep.	Cost ($)	Avg. exp. ($)	% rep.	Cost ($)	Avg. exp. ($)	% rep.	Cost ($)
Total	290	82.0	353	395	91.8	431	440	94.8	465	547	97.4	562	319	88.5	361
Gas (piped or bottled)	82	53.3	155	99	55.2	179	93	55.9	166	118	61.5	191	80	60.5	133
Electricity	100	65.3	153	143	74.8	192	176	80.1	220	210	82.5	254	103	74.3	139
Gas/electric combined	35	15.0	231	51	17.9	284	47	15.0	312	56	16.5	339	31	14.6	214
Fuel oil/kerosene	24	10.3	234	44	15.7	278	50	18.9	265	56	17.3	320	49	19.2	258
Coal or wood	4	2.8	136	2	3.4	47	3	4.0	66	5	8.7	54	6	2.3	253
Water	15	27.6	55	19	33.1	57	25	41.6	60	33	49.0	68	17	38.3	44
Garbage	4	15.8	26	7	22.0	33	9	26.4	34	14	38.0	37	7	21.5	30
Sewer	4	13.3	29	6	13.4	44	8	19.6	41	18	20.6	87	5	16.1	32
Water/garbage/sewer	22	20.1	109	25	25.5	97	29	28.7	102	38	32.8	116	21	24.1	86
Heating system															
Central		73.0			75.0			81.0			69.0			56.0	
Other		25.0			22.0			16.0			29.0			41.0	
None		2.0			2.0			3.0			2.0			3.0	
Air conditioning															
Central		13.0			19.0			24.0			8.0			5.0	
Room		31.0			33.0			32.0			25.0			22.0	
None		56.0			48.0			43.0			67.0			73.0	

Table 6.9 House furnishings – details, 1973

	Low income			Laborer			Wage earner			Salaried			Senior		
	Avg. exp. ($)	% rep.	Cost ($)	Avg. exp. ($)	% rep.	Cost ($)	Avg. exp. ($)	% rep.	Cost ($)	Avg. exp. ($)	% rep.	Cost ($)	Avg. exp. ($)	% rep.	Cost ($)
House furnishings total	173	76.9	225	326	91.4	356	421	94.4	446	606	97.2	624	158	76.2	207
Textiles	14	51.8	28	24	69.6	35	27	74.7	36	39	80.8	49	12	50.6	23
Window coverings	5	20.3	25	16	29.2	54	20	33.2	60	30	37.8	80	9	19.9	44
Floor coverings	14	14.3	100	31	20.5	152	42	24.7	172	77	31.2	247	22	14.6	148
Furniture	58	26.1	221	112	41.3	270	151	52.3	290	219	56.8	385	49	21.8	222
Appliances	67	43.9	154	105	59.3	178	134	69.6	192	167	75.2	222	51	36.8	138
Light fixtures and lamps	3	4.9	54	5	10.0	48	5	14.0	38	7	16.5	41	2	5.7	34
Decorative items	3	10.9	29	8	15.9	50	10	21.7	45	18	30.2	59	1	6.1	18
Lawn equipment and tools	4	5.4	76	15	19.2	81	22	25.7	86	31	32.4	94	8	10.0	76
Sheets	4	26.3	15	6	36.8	17	6	38.5	16	8	49.0	17	3	21.8	13
Pillowcases	1	17.3	7	2	24.6	7	1	24.3	6	2	34.0	7	1	15.3	5
Bedspreads	3	15.0	18	4	17.9	24	4	16.4	25	7	23.6	29	1	7.9	19
Blankets and quilts	2	7.9	20	1	8.1	16	2	10.0	17	2	11.4	20	1	8.4	14
Towels	2	19.9	8	3	29.1	10	3	29.5	11	5	35.4	13	1	17.2	9
Ready-made curtains	2	13.3	16	6	18.2	33	5	22.4	22	6	21.1	27	3	11.5	27
Custom-made draperies	0	0.6	28	4	2.2	184	4	2.3	185	11	4.9	232	1	0.4	370
Ready-made draperies	2	7.5	27	4	9.7	44	6	11.7	50	9	13.9	62	3	8.8	36
Installed wall-to-wall carpet	8	1.9	405	21	5.0	425	33	8.2	402	60	13.3	447	15	5.4	278
Uninstalled wall-to-wall carpet	2	1.5	153	4	3.3	118	3	4.9	58	7	5.0	146	3	2.7	104
Rugs	4	11.3	37	6	13.9	45	7	13.3	50	10	15.6	64	4	7.3	53
Dining room	6	2.4	272	13	7.6	173	20	8.4	239	32	10.4	309	4	2.3	153
Bedroom	18	11.1	164	35	15.2	227	42	19.9	213	57	21.7	264	18	7.3	251
Living room	27	11.8	228	45	15.3	296	57	18.5	309	87	22.4	388	20	10.0	200
Sofas	10	5.6	182	14	6.0	233	21	6.5	327	29	9.0	316	6	3.1	211
Chairs	5	4.5	101	11	7.5	144	13	9.6	138	26	12.1	211	6	5.0	116
Living room suites	12	3.6	333	21	5.0	417	23	5.9	384	33	5.7	573	8	2.3	333
Outdoor furniture	0	2.8	16	2	8.2	26	5	7.9	68	7	15.3	43	1	3.4	26

	Low income			Laborer			Wage earner			Salaried			Senior		
	Avg. exp. ($)	% rep.	Cost ($)	Avg. exp. ($)	% rep.	Cost ($)	Avg. exp. ($)	% rep.	Cost ($)	Avg. exp. ($)	% rep.	Cost ($)	Avg. exp. ($)	% rep.	Cost ($)
Major appliances	46	18.6	247	74	25.4	290	90	28.3	318	115	34.7	330	40	14.6	276
Refrigerator-freezer	11	4.1	272	18	6.6	272	21	7.7	276	32	8.0	398	11	3.8	297
Freezer	7	2.4	313	6	2.3	279	8	4.2	188	8	3.8	207	5	2.3	206
Range	6	4.1	143	7	4.0	175	11	5.2	209	13	5.0	254	4	1.5	273
Built-in dishwasher	2	0.9	224	2	0.6	272	2	0.7	293	7	2.8	251	0	0.0	0
Washer	10	7.5	128	17	8.7	200	16	7.7	208	20	9.4	216	8	3.1	267
Dryer	6	4.1	137	11	7.0	160	9	5.4	161	16	8.3	186	3	1.5	184
Small appliances	15	24.8	59	20	36.8	55	32	47.9	67	34	49.0	70	9	21.5	40
Floor cleaning equipment	8	5.1	158	7	8.7	84	11	11.4	99	15	13.0	117	3	5.7	56
Sewing machines	2	2.4	105	6	4.0	141	6	6.8	138	6	3.5	166	1	1.1	117
Coffee makers	0	2.8	11	1	4.1	17	1	3.7	24	1	7.8	18	0	2.7	14
Housewares	6	18.0	33	9	24.2	37	9	28.7	30	14	34.3	42	2	10.7	18

present one more indicator of the relative economizing occurring across classes. Even though energy prices rose sharply toward the end of 1973, fuel and utilities continued to absorb only 4% of the employed families' budgets as in 1950. Low-income and senior households spent 6% of their budgets on fuel and utilities. Low-income families spent 80% as much on electricity and gas as laborer families.[53] Overall, families had more opportunity to economize on the use of electricity than on the use of gas and fuel oil, which were primarily used for heating. Water costs were about the same for low-income and working-class families; however, salaried families had 20% higher water bills, which indicates greater use of water for lawns and gardens.

Types of energy usage became more uniform across classes between 1950 and 1973, and electricity and gas represented six-sevenths of the energy expenditures for all groups except seniors, whose older homes used more fuel oil than the other groups. The use of wood or briquets for fireplaces or barbecues increased with class status; even so, only 5% of salaried families purchased briquets and 9% purchased wood.

Furnishing the home

Spending on furnishing and equipping homes did not grow as fast as other spending, and so furnishings fell from 6%–7% of the budget in 1950 to 4% in 1973. Home furnishings and equipment continued to mark class status, however, and the proportion of the budget spent on furnishings continued to rise across classes. In absolute dollars, differences in the amount spent on furnishings was immense – salaried families spent almost twice as much as laborer families, who spent almost twice as much as low-income families (see table 6.9).

The types of furnishings varied across classes, with lower-status families buying relatively more utilitarian items and higher-status families buying more decorative items. Low-income families' purchases were dominated by appliances, while employed families' largest category was furniture. One-third of the furniture spending by low-income and laborer families was for bedroom furniture, compared to one-fourth for salaried families. Salaried families were one-half more likely than laborer families to purchase living room furniture in 1973, and they bought sofas, chairs, and suites costing one-third more.

The age and the features of appliances also marked class. When buying appliances, higher-status families were more likely to purchase state-of-the-art items, such as a built-in dishwasher, while some low-income families were still having to purchase semi-automatic washing machines, which cost less than one-half as much as the more convenient automatic machines. Almost 5% of the salaried families purchased dishwashers during 1973, and over one-half of these were the more convenient and aesthetically-pleasing built-in models. In contrast, only 1% of laborer families purchased dishwashers; 3% of wage-earner families purchased dishwashers, but four-fifths were portable models.

The most frequently purchased appliances were the washing machine and refrigerator, which had become a standard part of every home. In general, low-income and working-class families purchased similar models. Salaried families bought larger and fancier refrigerators that cost almost one-half more. Few families, ranging from 20% of low-income to 10% of salaried, purchased a refrigerator without a separate freezer compartment. Like refrigerators, frequency of purchasing a washing machine increased with class status. The amount spent on a new washing machine was about the same among employed families; low-income families bought machines costing two-fifths less than those purchased by the working class.

Utilitarian housewares and textiles displayed only slight class differences, since decorative items such as draperies, wall-to-wall carpet, and wall hangings were used to mark class. One in five salaried families purchased some draperies during the year, and over one-fourth of them had their drapes custom-made. In contrast, one in nine laborer families purchased draperies, and one-sixth of these were custom-made. A few low-income families purchased some inexpensive ready-made drapes, which cost only three-fifths as much as the ready-made drapes purchased by laborer families. For carpeting, class differentiation was in the frequency of purchases and in whether or not the carpet was installed professionally. Families paid three times more for professionally installed wall-to-wall carpet than for uninstalled carpet. One in five salaried families purchased some wall-to-wall carpeting during the year, and three-fourths of them had it professionally installed. Only one in twelve laborer families purchased wall-to-wall carpeting, and three-fifths of them had it professionally installed. Very few low-income families purchased carpeting during the year.

Running the home

The share of the budget devoted to household operations rose from 4% in 1950 to 5%–6% in 1973 for employed families. These expenditures had become less discretionary as housekeeping supplies, telephone services, and baby-sitting[54] rose in importance both in the budget and as a social norm. Clothes cleaning services, maid service, and postage and stationery became less important. As a result, families were less able to economize on household operations, which took a larger share (7%) of the low-income and senior family's budget. Telephone service and housekeeping supplies together accounted for 65% of the wage-earner family's household operating budget in 1973, compared to only 48% in 1950.

Table 6.10 Household operations, 1973

	Low income			Laborer			Wage earner			Salaried			Senior		
	Avg. exp. ($)	% rep.	Cost ($)	Avg. exp. ($)	% rep.	Cost ($)	Avg. exp. ($)	% rep.	Cost ($)	Avg. exp. ($)	% rep.	Cost ($)	Avg. exp. ($)	% rep.	Cost ($)
Total including housekeeping supplies[a]	323			480			595			697			398		
Household operations (without supplies)	233	94.4	247	338	99.4	340	404	99.5	406	495	100.0	495	303	98.9	307
Clothing care	64	64.9	98	88	78.4	112	81	81.1	100	91	84.2	109	43	73.2	59
Maid/baby-sitter	35	15.4	229	37	21.7	168	67	29.5	227	109	32.2	338	27	16.1	168
Telephone service	112	77.3	145	174	93.8	185	195	97.0	201	216	99.1	218	120	90.8	132
Housekeeping supplies	90			137			191			202			95		
Selected details															
Laundry sent out	5	5.4	96	7	7.2	96	6	6.1	90	11	9.9	114	11	12.3	88
Dry cleaning sent out	31	46.3	67	52	64.6	80	50	69.6	71	65	75.2	86	17	55.6	31
Coin-operated machines	27	35.3	77	29	35.9	82	26	33.7	76	16	25.1	62	15	34.5	43
Maid	12	6.0	201	11	6.9	157	20	9.1	225	40	11.8	341	0	16.1	168
Baby-sitter	23	9.6	241	26	15.2	169	47	22.6	207	69	23.2	296	0	0.0	0
Child care	3	0.9	299	2	0.7	303	3	1.2	242	0	0.3	107	0	0.4	61
Telephone/local	83	75.6	110	112	92.5	121	125	96.2	130	132	98.4	134	87	90.4	96
Telephone/long distance	27	58.7	45	58	82.4	71	66	86.9	76	81	92.9	87	32	75.1	42
Elderly care	1	1.1	123	0	0.4	61	5	0.9	550	1	0.2	546	59	4.6	1,291
Flowers and house plants	0	0.0	0	0	0.5	28	0	0.5	28	0	1.0	27	0	0.0	0
Lawn care service	5	12.6	41	9	12.3	77	10	14.0	70	15	17.7	83	18	26.1	70
Fertilizer and pesticides	2	19.5	10	5	32.9	14	7	44.2	16	11	56.2	20	5	41.8	12
Major appliance repair	4	12.8	30	7	20.8	32	7	24.3	29	11	32.3	33	7	19.5	35
Minor appliance repair	1	4.5	17	2	8.5	24	3	13.8	22	4	17.6	22	2	12.7	13
Recreational goods repair	0	0.8	15	1	1.2	48	2	2.8	85	1	3.1	40	1	1.5	83
Moving	2	3.6	52	5	3.7	128	9	4.0	229	13	3.1	411	13	4.6	285

[a] Data on housekeeping supplies were collected in a separate diary survey, and information on percentage reporting is not available.

Having home telephone service had become required for economic and social life; by 1973, the telephone was universally owned by employed families. Even three-fourths of low-income families managed to pay for telephone service. The proportion of families making long distance calls doubled between 1950 and 1973, and long distance calls declined as a marker of status. Even so, one in five laborer families and two in five low-income families still did not pay for any long distance calls.

With a wide array of specialized cleaning and paper products available, families could spend a surprisingly large amount of money on supplies. Low-income families economized in this area and spent only two-thirds as much as labor families. With limits on how many cleaning supplies could be stored and used, class differences in expenditure narrowed as salaried families spent only 5% more than wage-earner families.

As the washer and dryer became standard household items, actual practices for clothing care became more alike across classes, and so the proportion of the budget spent on clothing care decreased with class status. Some class differences remained, however, as salaried families spent more on dry cleaning and low-income families spent more doing their laundry at the laundromat. Fewer than one in ten families sent out laundry, although one in three had sent out laundry in 1950. More families were now buying clothes that required dry cleaning, and the use of dry-cleaning services had become widespread as class differences had lessened. Now two-thirds of working-class and three-fourths of salaried families sent out dry cleaning. Even one-half of low-income families had some clothes dry cleaned.

The relative use of maids and baby-sitters switched places between 1950 and 1973, as the proportion of wage-earner and salaried families having maid service decreased slightly between 1950 and 1973, as the use of baby-sitters increased markedly across all classes as more wives became employed. Almost one in six of labor families and one in four of salaried families had a baby-sitter. Even one in ten low-income families had a sitter, whom they paid $20 monthly. Differences in maid service were dramatic across employed classes, both in the percentage of families hiring a maid as well as in how many hours the maid worked. Overall, the salaried family paid almost four times as much for maid service as the laborer family in 1973, compared to less than three times as much in 1950. Low-income families' maid service was similar to the infrequent use of maids by laborer families; one in sixteen low-income families had a maid costing $16 per month.

Many seniors used services to compensate for their physical problems, and they were more likely to send out laundry or to have a maid than salaried families. Because of health problems, one in twenty senior households paid for expensive elderly care, which cost $1,300 annually. This accounted for 15% of services' household operations budgets. If this type of care were not required, senior households would allocate the same 6.7% of their budgets for household operations as low-income families. For seniors who require this type of care, however, household operations would potentially absorb one-third of their budgets. Of course, this was not possible, and so these families had to use their assets to pay for elder care.

Lawns replaced flowers, as the custom of buying flowers for the home diminished between 1950 and 1973. Only 1% of salaried families bought flowers or house plants in 1973, while 27% had bought flowers in 1950. Paying someone to mow the lawn was seldom done in 1950. It became more common in 1973 as lawns became more widespread. Even 12% of low-income and laborer as well as 18% of salaried and 26% of senior families at least occasionally paid someone to mow the yard.

The repair of major and minor appliances reflected the ownership of appliances, and these repairs increased with class, from 13% of low-income to 32% of salaried families paying to repair a major appliance, such as a washing machine. Overall, repairs absorbed 2% of the family's household operations budget.

Moving expenses, the final category in the operations budget, were incurred by only 4% of households. For families who moved, their moving costs, like their number and value of possessions, increased with class status. Moving costs for low-income families were only one-half of the costs for labor families. Moving costs for salaried families, who were more likely to move to another city, were over three times those for laborer families.

Getting Around

Car ownership had become even more vital to participation in economic, social, and political life in 1973 than in 1950. Mobility had created even more economic distance between the low-income and employed households. The 45% of low-income families without a car were strictly limited in their mobility and were largely confined to their neighborhoods. Their frugality in their use of transportation, including their low car ownership rate, reduced their transportation expenditures to only 12% of their budgets. In contrast, working-class and salaried families spent 18% of their budgets on transportation.

Virtually every working-class family owned at least one car by 1973. 'A car for every driver' had become the family's new aspiration as access to and reliance on public transportation simultaneously declined. For suburban families, access to public transportation was often nonexistent. Even when public transportation was available, many people preferred the convenience of driving to work or shop or chauffeur the children to various activities. The city bus systems were used primarily by the poor, seniors, and school-aged children. Fewer than one in six employed families reported using any public transportation.

Without access to good public transportation, lack of an automobile for each adult meant serious limitations in mobility. Ownership of more than one car, rather than ownership of the first car, became the major difference in transportation between the working and salaried classes. In 1973, laborer families owned an average of 1.2 cars, while salaried families owned an average of 1.7 cars, and low-income an average of 0.5 cars. Over one-half of salaried families, but only one-fourth of laborer families, owned two or more cars. Employed families owning automobiles spent about $300 on gasoline and oil per car, which allowed them to drive about 9,300 miles per year,[55] regardless of class. A family's mobility, therefore, was determined primarily by the number of automobiles they owned. On this basis, salaried families were one-third more mobile than working-class families and three times more mobile than lower income families.

Low-income households were twice as likely to use public transportation, and only half as likely to have an automobile as working-class families. Only 45% of low-income households had an automobile, although another 10% had access to someone else's car. Seven percent had the luxury of owning more than one car. At the other end of the spectrum, over one in five low-income families reported spending no money on transportation.

Low-income users of public transit were much less likely to have a car available than working-class families, yet they still spent only 54% as much on public transit. Many of them did not need transportation to go to work since they were not in the labor force. The use of buses to go to work or to school varied little across classes. Few families (3%–4%) relied on buses to take their children to school; slightly more (7%–10%) took public transit to work. Low-income families were over three times more likely than laborer families and over five times more likely than salaried families to use public transit for leisure time activities or shopping. Seniors, who did not have jobs or children in school, had fewer transportation needs. Their public transit usage and car ownership patterns were similar to those of low-income households.

The percentage of families purchasing a car in 1973 was high. Usually, an older car was replaced with a newer used car. However, salaried families were much more likely than working-class families to be driving a new car. Almost one in five salaried families purchased a new car in 1973, compared to one in eight working-class families. Among families purchasing vehicles, 42% of salaried families, and 15% of low-income families, bought a new car. Typically, the salaried family's primary car averaged 2.5 years old; its secondary car averaged five years old. The working-class family's primary car averaged four years old; their secondary car, if they were among the fortunate group owning one, would

Table 6.11 Transportation, 1973

	Low income			Laborer			Wage earner			Salaried			Senior		
Number of vehicles	Avg. exp. ($)	% rep.	Cost ($)	Avg. exp. ($)	% rep.	Cost ($)	Avg. exp. ($)	% rep.	Cost ($)	Avg. exp. ($)	% rep.	Cost ($)	Avg. exp. ($)	% rep.	Cost ($)
0		55.0			13.0			7.0			3.0			45.0	
1		38.0			63.0			58.0			44.0			48.0	
2+		7.0			24.0			35.0			53.0			7.0	
Average # vehicles[a]		0.5			1.2			1.4			1.7			0.6	
Transportation total	557	78.40	711	1,615	98.40	1,641	1,836	99.70	1,843	2,355	99.80	2,351	513	82.40	623
Auto expenses total	511	54.8	933	1,541	94.0	1,640	1,770	96.5	1,834	2,282	99.1	2,262	480	59.8	803
Auto purchase	233	23.8	979	766	52.3	1,466	875	56.5	1,550	1,834	63.1	1,157	188	10.3	1,817
Gas and oil	137	53.1	257	357	93.0	384	414	95.3	434	502	98.4	494	116	58.2	199
Insurance	47	31.5	150	162	74.4	218	185	78.8	235	286	77.1	221	74	51.0	145
Repair/maintenance	73	47.1	156	203	88.0	231	232	92.3	252	317	95.3	302	79	56.3	141
Fees/charges	19	46.0	42	49	82.0	60	60	86.0	69	89	92.2	82	22	56.7	39
Other transport total	46	31.3	145	74	21.2	348	66	18.8	352	374	24.0	90	33	29.0	114
Motorcycle	3	1.9	152	26	6.2	430	25	6.6	372	407	10.2	42	1	0.4	321
Public transit	39	29.1	135	40	16.2	249	31	12.4	248	232	15.1	35	27	27.6	97
Trips away from home	4	3.2	119	7	3.7	176	11	6.1	175	172	7.6	13	5	2.3	227
Auto lease	2	3.0	59	3	4.8	68	4	4.5	82	120	5.4	6	1	2.3	27
Selected details															
Vehicle cost[b]	195	15.6	1,246	686	32.7	2,095	742	34.3	2,166	2,581	40.7	1,051	107	6.1	1,740
New vehicle	76	2.4	3,226	415	12.0	3,472	438	12.8	3,436	3,534	18.2	643	41	1.5	2,654
Used vehicle	119	13.7	866	271	22.0	1,231	304	22.9	1,326	1,624	25.1	408	66	4.6	1,436
Financing cost	38	13.7	277	81	37.4	216	133	42.8	311	226	47.0	106	81	5.7	1,415
Liability insurance	11	9.2	118	24	15.1	158	28	14.9	189	205	10.6	22	15	15.7	98
Combined insurance	34	21.6	158	129	58.8	220	151	65.9	229	281	67.6	190	55	34.5	159
Oil change/lube	5	29.8	17	13	62.6	21	15	64.9	24	29	72.6	21	7	41.4	18
Tune ups	5	17.6	31	18	46.0	39	21	50.2	43	52	61.2	32	9	23.4	38
Tires	20	27.2	74	50	55.3	91	63	59.4	106	115	63.1	72	18	28.0	66

	Low income			Laborer			Wage earner			Salaried			Senior		
	Avg. exp. ($)	% rep.	Cost ($)	Avg. exp. ($)	% rep.	Cost ($)	Avg. exp. ($)	% rep.	Cost ($)	Avg. exp. ($)	% rep.	Cost ($)	Avg. exp. ($)	% rep.	Cost ($)
Batteries	4	16.7	25	8	25.5	31	9	29.0	32	10	32.4	31	5	17.2	27
Repairs	37	36.0	102	108	68.1	158	118	77.1	153	158	81.5	194	39	43.7	89
Registration fees	16	42.6	37	37	79.2	47	43	84.3	51	57	90.3	63	17	54.4	32
Inspection fees	1	21.6	4	2	37.7	6	3	42.7	6	4	40.4	9	1	21.5	6
Driver's license	1	23.3	6	3	41.2	7	4	49.3	7	4	58.2	7	2	29.1	5
Parking	1	4.9	16	6	17.0	33	9	20.6	42	15	28.8	53	1	6.1	23
Transit/work	9	7.1	129	27	10.4	260	20	6.5	310	27	9.0	298	4	3.4	113
Transit/school	4	3.9	97	4	3.1	117	3	3.5	72	4	3.6	100	0	0.4	78
Transit/other	26	23.3	113	10	7.1	135	8	6.3	130	4	4.5	100	23	25.7	88
Train/bus	1	2.6	30	1	1.7	42	0	0.7	12	1	1.0	62	1	1.1	87
Plane	1	0.9	140	5	2.1	267	7	3.7	187	10	3.5	274	1	0.8	67

[a] Calculated assuming families owning 2+ cars average 2.3 cars.
[b] Costs exclude trade-in values.

average seven years old. The low-income family who was fortunate enough to own a car would typically be driving a ten-year-old used car.[56] Even though families owned older cars, the incidence of financing cars with loans was high. Among families owning cars, over 40% of working-class and 30% of low-income families had an outstanding car loan.

Salaried families would buy pricier new cars than working-class families, but their out-of-pocket expenses would be only slightly higher because they would be trading-in a lower mileage car of greater value. The value of salaried families' newly-purchased used cars was one-third higher than the value of used cars purchased by laborer families. Low-income families purchased used cars costing one-third less than those purchased by laborer families. The values of used cars sold by families had an even greater variance across classes. Salaried families sold their used cars for one-half more than laborer families, who sold their used cars for over twice as much as low-income families.

Although spending for car maintenance increased with class, the differences were small among employed families. Low-income car owners were about one-half as likely to replace tires or have tune-ups than employed families. They were about three-fourths as likely to carry insurance. One-third of low-income car owners drove without insurance, which exposed them (and other drivers) to financial risk. When low-income car owners purchased insurance, one-third carried only liability insurance, since this was often the only insurance required by state law. In contrast, over 80% of salaried and working-class car owners carried insurance and fewer than one in five purchased only liability.

Spending Leisure Time

Commentators began to wonder why leisure hours were not rising more rapidly after two decades of impressive economic growth uninterrupted by a major recession. In fact, the entrance of wives into the labor force reduced their average leisure time by 13 hours. Housewives had eight hours more leisure than their husbands; when wives were employed, they had four fewer hours.[57] Total housework hours for all family members dropped when wives became employed, since employed wives have fewer and older children; however, when these hours were adjusted by number and age of children, housework hours dropped by less than 10%.[58] Nationally, as family size and the birth rate fell between 1965 and 1976, wives' housework hours declined by about 12%. At the same time, husbands became more involved in housework as they increased their time by 8%.[59]

Even though families had not increased their time for leisure, they had dramatically increased their spending for recreation and educational activities. This major improvement in resources available for recreation indicates the reduced financial constraints felt by families in 1973 compared to 1950. Spending for leisure time increased faster than income increased, so that recreation spending was a larger part of the employed families' budgets in 1973 compared to 1950. Recreational spending also continued to mark status. Salaried families spent 9.6% of their budgets on recreation and educational activities. In contrast, laborer families spent 8.2%, but this exceeded the 7.9% spent by salaried families in 1950.

As leisure activities became more varied, more likely to require spending money, and more likely to require special clothes and equipment, the distinction between educational and recreational activities became more clear-cut. Earlier, major leisure activities such as reading or learning to play the piano could be viewed as partly educational and partly recreational. But as moviegoing, and then television watching, became the paramount leisure activity, recreational activities became divorced from educational activities. Education became viewed as a formal process that occurred in schools. In addition, as jobs and housekeeping became less physically demanding, adults engaged more in sports activities to get exercise. Increasingly, leisure activities became recreational only and were characterized as passive or active.

Once television ownership became widespread, watching television dominated leisure activities. Although only one-third of households owned a television set in 1950, by 1962, 90% of households owned at least one television set. In 1938 (before television), people had selected reading as their favorite leisure activity, followed by going to the movies. In 1954, households with a television set had their sets turned on an average of 4.8 hours. Daily hours with the TV on grew steadily to reach 6.2 hours in 1972.[60] Of their average 38 hours of weekly leisure, adults spent almost one-half (18 hours) watching television in 1975. The second most popular form of leisure was socializing with friends (eight hours). Although large percentages of people in all classes watched television as a favorite evening pastime, this decreased with income and education and increased with age.[61]

Ownership of leisure equipment other than television had also grown. Audio equipment, including cassettes and stereo component systems not available in 1950, as well as phonographs had become quite popular. Over one-half of laborer and two-thirds of salaried families bought cassettes or records during 1973, and they spent the same amount. Meanwhile, almost no families paid for pianos, which had been a popular item to buy on the installment plan in 1950. The high status item was separate stereo components, which cost about $200 and was purchased by 9% of salaried families, 5% of laborers, and 1% of low-income households.

Purchases of toys no longer marked status, but purchases of sporting equipment did. One in three salaried families reported paying an average

Table 6.12 Recreation and education, 1973

	Low income			Laborer			Wage earner			Salaried			Senior		
	Avg. exp. ($)	% rep.	Cost ($)	Avg. exp. ($)	% rep.	Cost ($)	Avg. exp. ($)	% rep.	Cost ($)	Avg. exp. ($)	% rep.	Cost ($)	Avg. exp. ($)	% rep.	Cost ($)
Total recreation and education	317	90.4	350	742	99.3	748	906	99.5	911	1,322	99.8	1,325	321	94.6	339
Recreation and reading	205	84.2	243	554	98.9	560	693	99.1	699	996	99.7	1,000	261	91.6	285
Membership fees	4	17.6	24	16	37.8	42	21	42.7	48	44	55.6	78	10	39.8	26
Admissions	16	39.0	42	47	70.9	67	66	77.8	85	79	84.9	93	11	28.7	37
TV/audio equipment	37	22.5	163	86	36.5	235	104	44.1	235	98	46.4	211	36	14.2	254
Newspapers, magazines, and books	23	61.9	38	41	87.1	47	52	92.3	57	71	96.2	74	26	78.5	34
Recreational vehicles	10	1.7	560	50	10.5	473	66	10.8	607	123	17.5	702	3	3.1	102
Vacations	61	31.9	192	192	64.4	298	232	68.7	338	363	81.6	445	151	48.7	311
Education	28	10.7	260	44	18.1	241	72	29.5	243	148	39.0	378	2	2.3	86
Tobacco	84	45.8	184	145	61.0	237	142	61.9	229	179	66.9	267	58	30.3	191
Selected details															
Country clubs/swimming pools	0	0.9	54	3	1.7	159	4	3.1	111	12	9.0	131	0	0.0	0
Social/fraternal organisations	2	12.4	17	8	24.2	34	12	28.3	43	25	38.3	65	7	30.3	23
Civic organizations	2	8.4	18	5	19.6	24	5	21.2	24	7	27.2	26	3	17.6	19
Theatre/concert subscriptions	0	0.8	39	1	2.4	32	1	2.5	47	1	2.5	50	1	2.8	38
Season tickets for sports events	0	0.2	12	1	1.6	91	2	1.7	91	2	2.6	82	0	0.0	0
Single admissions – movies, sports, etc.	16	39.0	41	45	70.9	63	64	77.8	82	76	84.9	89	10	28.7	34
Black and white TV	8	7.9	103	9	8.0	115	9	8.6	101	7	8.0	91	4	2.7	143
Color TV (all types)	12	2.8	414	45	10.8	420	56	13.9	400	47	10.8	440	28	5.8	475
Radio	1	5.8	25	4	10.9	37	5	13.8	33	7	16.5	44	1	3.4	32
Phonograph	11	5.8	183	9	5.7	165	11	7.2	159	8	6.9	113	0	0.4	59
Tape recorder	2	3.9	46	4	5.6	70	4	4.9	74	6	6.6	85	0	0.4	43
Separate stereo components	2	1.3	152	10	4.8	208	15	6.6	229	18	9.0	197	3	1.1	269
Other sound equipment	1	2.4	54	4	2.5	143	5	3.7	129	5	4.9	104	0	0.4	10
Records/tapes/cassettes	6	29.1	22	19	52.5	35	23	60.0	38	24	68.6	35	2	9.2	20
Piano	1	0.4	288	1	0.2	551	6	1.0	610	3	0.5	561	0	0.0	0
Other musical instruments	8	3.6	211	8	4.4	182	6	5.0	120	13	6.8	195	0	0.8	25
Photographic equipment	2	6.2	38	9	12.7	70	8	14.2	57	12	17.3	69	1	1.1	130

	Low income			Laborer			Wage earner			Salaried			Senior		
	Avg. exp. ($)	% rep.	Cost ($)	Avg. exp. ($)	% rep.	Cost ($)	Avg. exp. ($)	% rep.	Cost ($)	Avg. exp. ($)	% rep.	Cost ($)	Avg. exp. ($)	% rep.	Cost ($)
Film (including developing costs)	6	27.6	21	19	62.4	31	25	72.2	35	34	80.6	42	4	19.5	18
Toys	6	8.6	73	7	10.7	69	13	16.6	77	12	17.5	70	NA	NA	NA
Bicycles	5	6.6	79	12	14.9	83	13	16.1	83	21	20.5	104	NA	NA	NA
Playground equipment	0	1.7	17	1	2.3	24	0	2.3	21	1	3.8	34	NA	NA	NA
Major camping equipment	1	1.1	68	2	5.1	48	3	6.5	39	4	9.0	47	1	0.8	73
Swimming pool	1	0.4	182	2	2.1	87	2	3.1	56	4	2.1	181	0	0.0	0
Pool table	0	0.4	22	3	1.1	283	2	1.0	228	2	1.4	157	0	0.0	0
Sporting goods	3	8.1	31	9	17.3	55	17	24.3	70	28	32.2	86	1	5.0	29
Lessons (golf, swimming, dancing, etc.)	2	3.4	62	4	8.3	47	11	14.3	74	20	25.1	78	0	1.1	17
Pets and pet supplies (except food)	1	0.9	121	1	3.1	43	5	5.8	87	7	6.6	106	1	1.9	40
Veterinarian/kennel expenses	1	2.1	38	2	5.3	34	2	4.9	35	3	6.5	48	0	0.8	16
Cable TV	6	9.2	69	9	13.3	71	8	11.2	74	7	12.3	61	7	10.7	61
Newspaper subscriptions	9	35.3	24	13	51.0	26	16	59.4	28	23	70.4	32	15	58.6	25
Magazine subscriptions	2	18.4	10	6	40.6	14	7	49.7	14	11	63.4	18	4	37.5	11
Book or record club subscriptions	1	3.4	33	3	10.7	31	5	14.9	32	8	18.5	41	0	0.4	36
Encyclopedias/other sets of books	4	1.7	252	3	2.9	115	3	3.0	111	4	5.4	79	0	0.4	16
Nonsub. books/newspapers/magazines	8	40.0	19	16	65.9	24	21	69.6	30	25	76.1	33	7	37.5	20
Boats	1	0.9	136	12	4.3	286	15	3.7	403	39	8.7	445	1	1.1	64
Trailers/campers	0	0.2	26	9	4.7	189	16	5.8	276	49	7.6	637	2	1.5	148
Self-propelled campers	6	0.4	1,495	19	1.1	1,715	29	1.7	1,673	15	1.7	892	0	0.0	0
Domestic vacations	38	30.6	125	151	62.0	244	179	65.7	272	287	78.3	366	111	45.6	244
Foreign vacations	23	4.1	564	40	6.6	609	53	9.6	554	76	12.1	630	40	7.3	548
Vacation expenses by category															
Transportation/travel	28	27.8	102	72	62.0	117	86	66.8	128	123	78.7	157	62	43.3	143
Automobile	9	19.1	49	32	55.2	58	41	62.9	65	58	74.7	78	13	29.1	44
Plane	13	5.8	230	35	14.9	237	40	13.5	295	56	19.6	284	40	13.8	291
Train/Bus	4	9.0	46	4	6.9	54	2	4.2	56	4	5.5	68	7	12.6	55
Food	15	21.2	69	41	53.0	78	52	61.5	85	91	75.2	121	28	36.8	77
Alcohol	1	4.7	25	5	23.1	24	7	26.0	25	10	38.3	26	2	3.1	50

Table 6.12 (cont.)

	Low income			Laborer			Wage earner			Salaried			Senior		
	Avg. exp. ($)	% rep.	Cost ($)	Avg. exp. ($)	% rep.	Cost ($)	Avg. exp. ($)	% rep.	Cost ($)	Avg. exp. ($)	% rep.	Cost ($)	Avg. exp. ($)	% rep.	Cost ($)
Motels and lodging	9	8.8	105	30	32.6	90	42	41.8	100	53	55.3	96	26	14.9	177
All-expense trips	3	2.8	105	26	6.8	383	24	7.7	309	50	9.9	510	25	4.6	549
Entertainment/admissions	2	7.3	21	6	24.4	25	9	29.0	30	14	39.0	35	1	8.4	14
Sport fees	0	1.9	10	2	8.9	19	2	8.4	26	6	17.3	37	0	1.1	9
Other expenses (souvenirs/misc.)	3	9.2	34	9	22.6	39	11	27.3	41	14	37.8	37	7	12.6	54
Vacation homes[a]	2	2.4	90	20	3.6	553	11	3.5	304	96	9.2	1,042	7	1.9	346
Education expenditures															
Tuition	25	6.9	360	34	11.8	287	58	21.9	264	106	27.9	379	2	1.1	146
Private	20	3.6	542	20	5.7	350	40	10.8	369	70	14.6	479	1	1.1	105
Nursery/kindergarten	1	1.1	139	3	1.3	202	4	3.1	136	5	2.9	163	0	0.0	0
Elementary/high school	5	1.7	289	3	2.1	164	12	2.6	445	22	6.2	349	1	0.4	170
College	13	0.6	2,033	12	1.4	806	22	3.7	599	38	3.1	1,232	0	0.4	133
Other postsecondary	0	0.4	52	2	1.3	159	2	2.3	90	5	3.6	128	0	0.4	11
Public	5	3.9	127	14	6.5	217	18	12.2	145	36	16.5	219	0	0.4	123
College	4	2.6	166	14	4.3	312	16	7.3	218	30	11.8	253	0	0.4	123
Other postsecondary	1	0.4	121	0	0.8	26	1	1.7	34	3	2.3	115	0	0.0	0
School books/supplies	3	7.9	37	6	12.3	51	11	20.1	54	22	28.4	76	0	1.5	20
Elementary/high school	1	4.7	17	2	5.3	32	2	8.2	27	5	11.8	41	0	0.4	2
College	2	3.0	68	4	5.3	73	6	9.1	70	15	14.2	106	0	0.8	31
Other postsecondary	0	0.4	13	1	3.0	26	2	3.8	55	2	5.2	33	0	0.4	16

a Vacation homes are not included in the recreation totals since these expenses are included under assets.

of $86 for sports equipment, compared to one in six laborer families paying $55. Many of these items, such as exercise equipment, had been developed since 1950.

Taking lessons, such as golf or dancing, cost only slightly less than sports equipment and also created class distinctions. One in four salaried families took lessons compared to one in twelve laborer families. 'Taking lessons' had been less varied and less widespread in 1950, when the only lessons recorded were for the piano. The proportion of families taking piano lessons in 1950 was one-half the proportion taking all lessons in 1973.

Taking photographs of family events and vacations had become part of family custom in employed families, with three-fifths of laborer and four-fifths of salaried families buying and processing film. The frequency for laborer families had doubled since 1950. Few low-income families, however, could afford photography, and only one-fourth of them purchased any film.

Only slightly more than one-half of the families reported going on outings in 1972. The large majority (over 80%) of these families attended outdoor sports events or went bicycling. A majority also reported engaging in golf, swimming, attending outdoor plays or concerts, and picnicking. When families did participate in outdoor activities, their activities were sharply divided by class. Higher-income families were more likely to engage in outdoor sports, and comprised most of the sailors and golfers. Middle-income families comprised most of those going camping and hiking, or visiting zoos, amusement parks, and sports events. Lower-income families were much less likely to engage in outdoor activities. When they did, they picked activities that incurred few extra expenses, such as going for drives and picnics, or that had a payoff, such as hunting or fishing.[62]

In 1973, families used their increased incomes to purchase a wide array of leisure activities outside the home. No longer was the recreational budget dominated by expenditures for movies, reading, and watching television, which had fallen from 40% of the family's recreational budget in 1950 to 15% of the salaried recreational budget and 20% of the working-class recreational budget in 1973. Vacations had become the single largest expense for employed families as well as the major status marker for leisure activities across families. In 1973, vacations absorbed one-quarter of their recreational budget.[63] Two-thirds of working-class families and four-fifths of salaried families took a vacation in 1973. For low-income families, vacation expenditures ranked second to tobacco expenses although one in three low-income families took a vacation. Even though only one-half of seniors went on vacation, vacations accounted for almost one-half of the senior's otherwise meager recreation budget.

Although taking a vacation had become the norm for employed families, the type of vacation one took marked status. One in eight salaried families had a foreign vacation, and one in twenty traveled by air. Salaried families were twice as likely as laborer families to go on a foreign vacation and were one-third more likely than laborer families to travel by plane. One in eleven salaried families could visit their own vacation homes, which was almost three times the rate for working-class families. While on vacation, salaried families were one-fourth more likely than laborer families to attend events that charged admission, such as amusement parks or zoos, or to buy souvenirs. Four-fifths of salaried families going on vacation paid for lodging (including all-expense trips), compared to three-fifths of laborer families, who were almost as likely to go camping or to stay with relatives or friends as they were to stay in a motel. Salaried families averaged $200 for the high status items of commercial lodging, all-expense trips, vacation home upkeep; working-class families spent $75, and low-income families spent $14 for these items. Vacations were still a luxury for low-income families. Of those who did go on vacation, fewer than two-fifths paid for lodging.

Seniors were as likely as working-class families to go by aircraft, and they were over twice as likely to go by bus or train. Once on vacation, seniors were less than one-half as likely as laborer families to attend a paid event, and three-fourths as likely to buy a souvenir. However, seniors spent 40% more than the laborer family when they bought a souvenir. Many seniors probably took vacations to visit friends or relatives, since only 40% reported paying for lodging while on vacation.

Memberships in social and civic clubs reflected the improved life-style and increased sociability of the population. Between 1950 and 1973, working-class families increased their membership rate to emulate the 1950 salaried rate, and salaried families increased their membership rate by one-third. However, membership continued to account for only 2% of the family's recreation budget. The type of organization still varied by class, with the salaried class much more likely to belong to a country club or swimming pool than the working class.

A significant minority of families (11% of working-class and 18% of salaried families) now owned recreational vehicles, which had been reserved for a small elite in 1950. The expenses associated with owning a recreational vehicle were at least 60% higher than the cost of a vacation for employed families. Families owning boats and campers spent over one-half of the typical recreation budget just on their recreational vehicles.

Tobacco

The recreation budgets include tobacco expenses, and these changed in important ways. Fewer families reported buying tobacco products in 1973 compared to 1950, and the national smoking rate fell with increased knowledge and concern about the health hazards associated with smoking, especially after the issuance of the Surgeon General's report. Fortunately, the health warning also undermined smoking as a marker of status, and the smoking rate across employed families became more similar. Earlier social norms had pressured men to smoke and women to refrain from smoking; the gap between male and female patterns was closing as men reduced their smoking rates and women increased theirs. Although smoking had been declared a health hazard, the population found it difficult to quit, and over 60% of employed households continued to have at least one smoker. More than one-half of the low-income families did not buy tobacco, which reflects both their financial constraint and their higher likelihood of being female-headed. Seniors also were less likely to smoke, which reflected the increasing popularity of smoking over the previous decades until more recent health concerns caused the rate to fall. For low-income families, the habit of smoking increased their financial pressures. Smoking cost them more than the average spending for furnishings or for gifts and contributions. The smoking habit cost the low-income family almost as much as a coveted vacation. In addition, tobacco expenditures by low-income families, seniors, and laborers who smoked averaged as much as one-sixth of the food budget. Of course, the financial pressure caused by smoking decreased as income rose.

Education

Although the proportion of families with children declined between 1950 and 1973, the importance of educational expenses in the recreation/education budget had risen dramatically for wage earners and salaried workers as they sent their children to college in increasing numbers. In 1950, employed families were twice as likely to spend money for school books and supplies as for tuition. In 1973, the proportion reporting expenditures for books and tuition were almost equal. This reflected a decline in the practice of public schools, especially in the South, to charge for school books, and an increase in the proportion of families sending children to post-secondary schools.

Between 1950 and 1973, the differences in educational expenditures between salaried and laborer families widened both in the likelihood of paying tuition and in the amount paid. Also, the types of schools attended varied by class. Laborer families' largest tuition expenses were for public college (reported by 4.3%) and for private college (1.4%). In contrast, salaried families were over twice as likely to have a child attending private college and almost three times as likely to have a child attending public college. Salaried children attended more elite private colleges than laborer children, and their parents paid over 50% more in tuition. In the elementary or high school grades, salaried families were three times as likely to have a child in private school as a laborer family. They paid over twice as much tuition, which indicates they were more likely to be sending their children to non-parochial schools.

A few adults (1% of the working-class families and 3% of the salaried families) took classes that were paid for by their employers. The value of the educational subsidy was low, averaging only $135 for working-class families and $245 for salaried families. In contrast, a few families received educational subsidies, such as college fellowships, that were high in value. These subsidies did not reflect family need, since subsidies worth over $900 were received by 4% of salaried families and by 2% of working-class families.

Recreation and education had become a larger part of the family's budget and more important in defining the family's life-style. Accordingly, leisure and learning activities were important markers of class and these activities created different experiences for families by class. For children particularly, the accumulation of these experiences, which built skills, knowledge, and networks, created a widening gulf between classes over time.

Caring for Health

As access to health care continued to improve in the postwar era, health care patterns became much more similar across classes. The most significant improvement since 1950 in health care access was for seniors, with some important improvements also for lower-income and working-class families. The percentage of the population covered by some type of health care plan rose from one-half in 1950 to four-fifths in 1973. Two-thirds of the population had employer-provided health insurance; another one-third had Medicare, and one-twelfth had Medicaid. There was still room for more insurance coverage, since one-half of the population did not have insurance covering doctor's care outside the hospital. As a result of the increasing use of employer-paid insurance to pay for health care costs, the share of the family's budget devoted to health care fell between 1950 and 1973, and the share decreased with class status in 1973. However, Americans were spending a rising proportion of national income on health care – from 5% of GNP in 1950 to 8% in 1973 – partly as a result of the growth in employer-sponsored health care plans and in government-sponsored health care for seniors (Medicare) and the poor (Medicaid). Medicare paid 12% of personal health care, public assistance paid 11%, and private insurance paid 63%.[64] Part of the rise, however, reflected only price increases, as the prices of health care rose much more rapidly than prices generally.

Nine in ten seniors were covered by Medicare, and 60% of those with Medicare also had some form of private insurance (see table 6.13A). The average Medicare payment per enrollee was $202 for hospital care and $108 for medical care, which is 2.6 times what the seniors paid directly for hospital care and physicians services.[65] Only 5% of seniors did not report expenditures for insurance.

Six of eleven low-income households were covered by Medicare or private insurance, and this group was equally likely to have Medicare or private insurance or both, as well as some free services. Another one in nine low-income families received only free health care from public or private welfare services (usually Medicaid). The remaining one-third of low-income families had neither insurance nor free care[66] (see tables 6.13B–C). For the one in seven low-income families who received free medical services, the value was high ($464). Four percent of low-income families also received medical care worth an average of $163 paid by others, probably relatives. For the families with some free services or insurance, the free medical care was worth 40 percent of their out-of-pocket expenses. Without it, the medical care received by low-income families would have been even less adequate.

By 1973, frequency of health care insurance coverage was 68% for laborers and 72% for salaried.[67] The coverage had improved for laborer families and was slightly lower for wage-earner and salaried families. In 1973, because of Medicare and Medicaid, low-income households were as likely as laborer households to have some health care provided through insurance or without fee. Two out of three low-income and laborer families had some health insurance or free care, but the value of medical care for these low-income families was only 70% of the value of care received by laborer families. This is in marked contrast to 1950 when health insurance separated classes by providing access to health care.[68]

Frequency of hospital care increased with class status in 1973, from 15% for low-income families to 21% for laborers to 25% for salaried families, although hospital care did not separate classes in 1950. Average out-of-pocket hospital cost declined with class status, except for low-income families, who were much less likely to receive hospital care if they were not covered by insurance or receive care free of charge at the county hospital. Higher-status families had better insurance coverage, so their out-of-pocket costs were less. Because information is available only for out-of-pocket expenses and not for total costs, we cannot compare the actual hospital costs.[69]

Seniors appear to experience a low incidence of hospital care, given their age. On average, seniors and laborer families received some hospital care every five years. In contrast, salaried families received some hospital care every four years, and low-income families every seven years.

Frequency of physician's care, eye care, and dental care divided classes, since seeing the doctor and dentist increased with class status. Between 1950 and 1973, the percentage of families seeing a doctor declined for

Table 6.13A Medical care details 1973

	Low income			Laborer			Wage earner			Salaried			Senior		
	Avg. exp. ($)	% rep.	Cost ($)	Avg. exp. ($)	% rep.	Cost ($)	Avg. exp. ($)	% rep.	Cost ($)	Avg. exp. ($)	% rep.	Cost ($)	Avg. exp. ($)	% rep.	Cost ($)
Medical care total	274			477			525			576			547		
Medical care excluding non-prescription drugs[a]	230	79.4	290	414	94.3	439	454	96.5	470	506	97.7	518	479	98.9	485
Insurance	92	56.0	165	141	62.0	227	167	65.0	257	146	65.3	224	186	95.0	196
Hospital	32	14.8	214	82	21.3	384	59	22.0	269	59	25.3	231	72	20.3	356
Physician	54	58.0	93	131	83.7	157	166	89.5	186	242	92.2	262	86	82.0	104
Other medical (excluding non-prescription drugs)	53	58.0	91	61	68.4	89	61	78.7	77	60	78.9	76	135	78.2	173
Non-prescription drugs	44			62			71			70			68		
Insurance															
Private insurance	58	35.3	163	126	57.6	218	158	62.6	252	141	64.5	218	100	61.3	163
Medicare	34	37.9	90	15	14.3	106	9	11.4	83	6	6.6	87	86	89.3	96
Hospital															
Hospital – physician	16	11.6	138	49	17.1	287	30	18.0	169	38	20.1	191	31	17.2	182
Hospital – other	16	10.3	153	33	12.8	254	29	14.2	205	20	14.2	141	41	13.0	315
Physicians															
MDs	25	49.3	51	53	67.6	78	68	73.6	92	81	76.9	105	38	65.9	58
Eye care doctor	12	22.5	52	23	33.9	67	25	37.1	67	34	45.8	75	18	37.5	48
Dentist	17	16.7	99	54	49.5	109	72	57.2	126	125	65.3	192	25	31.8	80
Other doctor	1	1.5	42	2	3.3	52	2	3.5	51	2	3.3	52	4	4.6	88
Other Medical															
Nursing services	0	0.0	0	1	0.5	255	2	0.2	900	0	0.3	30	15	0.4	3,830
Nursing homes	1	0.2	258	0	0.0	0	0	0.3	133	0	0.0	0	13	1.1	1,122
X-rays/lab tests	5	11.8	39	6	23.3	26	7	28.5	23	7	28.8	23	5	17.2	30
Prescriptions	42	56.3	74	47	63.9	73	48	76.6	62	49	74.2	66	86	75.1	114
Non-prescription drugs	44	NA	NA	63	NA	NA	71	NA	NA	70	NA	NA	67	NA	NA
Appliances	2	1.9	112	2	1.4	137	0	1.4	25	1	1.9	27	5	3.4	155
Miscellaneous	4	7.1	54	5	10.0	45	4	9.3	45	3	9.4	34	12	15.3	77

[a] Data on non-prescription drugs were collected in a separate diary survey and information on percentage reporting is not available.

Table 6.13B Medical care expenditures by insurance coverage,[a] 1973

	Insurance			Hospital care			Doctors			Other care[b]			Total medical care[c]		
	Avg. exp. ($)	% rep.	Cost ($)	Avg. exp. ($)	% rep.	Cost ($)	Avg. exp. ($)	% rep.	Cost ($)	Avg. exp. ($)	% rep.	Cost ($)	Avg. exp. ($)	% rep.	Cost ($)
Low income (n = 467)															
With insurance (67%)	136	82.5	165	36	19.4	187	58	65.7	88	68	67.9	100	414	100.0	414
Without insurance (33%)	–	–	–	22	5.3	425	46	42.1	109	21	37.5	57	90	53.9	166
Laborers (828)															
With insurance (68%)	208	91.6	227	88	20.4	430	136	86.6	157	69	73.6	94	595	100.0	595
Without insurance (32%)	–	–	–	69	23.1	300	121	77.6	156	43	57.5	74	233	84.3	277
Wage earners (572)															
With insurance (71%)	236	91.9	257	58	23.5	246	166	90.9	183	67	80.0	84	593	100.0	593
Without insurance (29%)	–	–	–	63	18.6	341	167	86.2	193	45	75.4	59	274	88.6	310
Salaried (577)															
With insurance (72%)	205	91.3	224	61	27.8	219	246	93.5	263	67	82.1	82	632	100.0	632
Without insurance (28%)	–	–	–	53	18.9	278	231	89.0	259	40	70.7	56	323	92.1	350
Seniors (261)															
With insurance (96%)	194	99.2	196	73	20.4	360	86	82.8	104	140	79.2	177	508	100.0	508
Without insurance (4%)	–	–	–	47	18.2	259	69	63.6	43	23	54.5	43	140	72.7	193

[a] With insurance also includes those with premiums or cost of services provided by others.
[b] Includes nursing services, lab tests, and prescriptions; excludes non-prescription drugs.
[c] Total includes all out-of-pocket expenses, including insurance, plus value of services or insurance paid by others.

Table 6.13C Value of medical care paid for by others, 1973

	Average value ($)	% rep.	Cost ($)	% paid by welfare or private charity	Average value ($)	Insurance premiums % rep.	Cost ($)
Low income	72	17.7	404	91.7	6	4.70	133
Laborer	47	7.2	654	93.4	16	8.30	192
Wage earner	22	9.8	228	90.2	24	10.00	241
Salaried	8	6.9	108	85.1	30	10.60	283
Senior	11	5.4	206	45.9	2	3.10	67

wage-earner and salaried families. Still, the probability of receiving care by a medical doctor in 1973 increased across class from one-half for low-income families to two-thirds for laborer and senior families to three-fourths for salaried families. Although most seniors had hospital coverage through Medicare, many had no other coverage. Overall, one in three senior households reported no doctor's visits, even though only one in four did not purchase any prescription drugs. The number of doctor's visits per family increased with class status, as indicated by average costs, which were one-third higher for salaried and one-third less for low-income compared to laborer families.

Few employers provided insurance covering dental or eye care or prescription drugs, and these were also not covered by Medicare. For these items, expenditures provide a good indicator of value of care received. The probability of laborer families' visiting the dentist increased from 1950 to 1973, when one-half of the families received some care. Still, one-third of salaried families were still receiving no preventive dental care, and they did not visit the dentist during 1973. However, salaried families who did visit the dentist purchased twice as expensive services as laborer, senior, or low-income families. Non-emergency dental care appeared to be expendable and not purchased by low-income families, since only one in six visited the dentist during the year.

Access to eye care had improved greatly between 1950 and 1973, yet still less than one-half of the salaried families received eye care. Although the incidence of wearing eyeglasses increases with age, only three in eight senior households received eye care, which is the same proportion as for wage-earner families. Even fewer (two in nine) low-income families had eye care, which indicates that financial constraints prevented some of them from receiving glasses or having their prescriptions updated.

Comparisons of families with and without insurance (including access to free medical care) can provide an indicator of how much care seems to be affected by insurance (see table 6.13C). Generally, employed families with insurance were more likely to visit the doctor. However, out-of-pocket expenses per family member were similar for employed families with and without insurance, since many of the insured families did not have doctor's visits reimbursed. Insured families spent 50%–70% more on prescription drugs than uninsured families. Since the purchase of prescription drugs should not be affected by insurance coverage, this may reflect access to doctors to obtain prescriptions.

We would expect hospital care in particular to be affected by insurance coverage. This is true for wage-earner and salaried families, who are one-third more likely to have hospital care and pay 20%–30% less out-of-pocket if they are insured. However, for laborer families, the insured are less likely than the uninsured to have hospital care and they pay more out-of-pocket for the care they receive. This indicates that laborer families have much less comprehensive insurance coverage than wage-earner and salaried families.

Overall, employed families with insurance paid twice as much out-of-pocket for health care as those without any insurance. We can safely assume that the insured received more than twice the actual care since the expenses paid for by insurance are not shown. Being part of a health care program appears to make families more conscientious about receiving medical care, while it increases their access and their willingness to pay. This pattern of health care use between families with and without coverage is even more pronounced for low-income families. Without any insurance or free care, and facing severe financial pressures, uninsured low-income families received much less care, with one-fourth as many receiving hospital care and three-fifths as many receiving a physician's care or prescription drugs as families with insurance or access to free care. Low-income families without subsidized care spent only 30% as much on health care as low-income families with subsidized care. Since low-income families are under severe financial constraints, even those with subsidized health care economized on incurring any health care expenses. Insured low-income families spent 60% as much as insured working-class families on health care.

People's awareness of their own health status reflected significant class differences in health. In 1973, one-half of whites reported themselves to be in 'excellent' health, compared to one-third of nonwhites. People in higher (over $15,000) income families were twice as likely to report being in excellent health as people from low-income families (under $5,000), or 61% compared with 32%.[70]

BLS budgets for lower and intermediate standards assumed that a family had an insurance policy purchased through the husband's employer for hospital and surgical expenses; only the higher standard allowed for major medical insurance. The cost to the family depended upon how much of the policy was paid by the employer.[71]

In practice, some families did not have any medical insurance, and some families in the working class had major medical as well as hospital insurance. Senior households clearly had better health care coverage than younger families because of their hospital insurance with Medicare. Although their incomes were substantially below the incomes of employed households, their Medicare coverage resulted in their access to health care being similar. Overall, the majority of employed families and seniors had adequate health care. But the 30% of employed or low-income families without any health insurance did not have adequate access to health care and protection from the possibility of major illnesses. Unfortunately, the problem of health care coverage was going to worsen for non-seniors.

Looking Presentable

Personal care spending expanded from basic purchases of haircuts and toiletries, to include more of the fancier hair salon services, such as shampoos and sets and perms for women. Meanwhile, toiletries took a much smaller share of the personal care budget, as it declined from 60% to 40% for employed families. Altogether, household spending on personal care became a less important part of the budget as it decreased from 2.1% in 1950 to 1.6% in 1973 for employed families. Women were now spending twice as much on hair services as men, which reversed the patterns in the previous surveys. In addition, one in nine women in employed families reported spending money on wigs and hairpieces. In 1973, women were one-half as likely to purchase a wig as they had been to pay for a shampoo and set in 1950.

Electric appliances, which were rare in 1950, were popular and imparted status in 1973 (see table 6.14). Salaried families spent 3% of their personal care budgets on a wide array of electric gadgets, especially hair dryers, shavers, and hair curlers. Across classes, the most popular electric item was the hair dryer, which was purchased in 1973 by 3% of low-income families and 9% of salaried families. The use of a hair dryer allowed women more flexibility in washing their hair, since they did not have to wait for it to dry before leaving the house. Although they were purchased by few families, electric curlers (or hair setters) were highly desirable status markers. Salaried women were twice as likely as laborer women to purchase electric curlers. The hair dryer, along with electric curlers, made hair styling easier while allowing women to style their hair in a variety of ways.

Low-income households economized severely on personal care spending in 1973. They spent three-fifths of the BLS standard and only one-half as much as laborer families. Low-income families economized both on toiletries and hair salon services. This is in contrast to 1950, when black families spent one-half more on hair services than laborer families and an equal amount on toiletries. Low-income families were much less likely to go to the barber shop or beauty parlor than employed families. When low-income women did go to the beauty parlor, they spent only two-thirds as much as laborer women.

These trends reflect the increased importance of professional hair services for women in the working class as well as salaried families, and the larger array of toiletries bought by employed families in 1973 compared to 1950. Working-class families' ability to purchase a variety of toiletries and hair services is one more indicator of their increased affluence.

Table 6.14 Personal care 1973

	Low income			Laborer			Wage earner			Salaried			Seniors		
	Avg. exp. ($)	% rep.	Cost ($)	Avg. exp. ($)	% rep.	Cost ($)	Avg. exp. ($)	% rep.	Cost ($)	Avg. exp. ($)	% rep.	Cost ($)	Avg. exp. ($)	% rep.	Cost ($)
Personal care total	77			149			186			224			106		
Selected details															
Personal care (w/o toiletries)	48	69.6	68	91	83.0	109	99	89.5	110	140	92.9	151	78	84.7	92
Hair salon services/males	16	42.0	38	29	62.7	46	35	73.1	47	44	78.2	56	19	53.3	35
Hair salon services/females	28	35.1	78	55	48.3	115	57	53.0	108	86	63.1	136	56	56.3	100
Male hairpieces	0	0.0	0	0	0.2	8	0	0.2	30	0	0.7	13	0	0.4	4
Female hairpieces/wigs	3	10.5	24	3	11.2	25	2	9.4	23	4	13.7	26	2	6.9	28
Hair dryers	0	2.8	13	1	6.5	19	1	7.3	20	2	9.4	19	0	0.0	0
Electric shavers	0	1.7	28	1	4.0	21	1	3.5	21	1	5.4	26	1	4.2	20
Electric hair setters	0	1.7	18	0	2.2	17	0	2.8	15	1	4.3	20	0	0.4	21
Electric toothbrush sets	0	0.4	11	0	1.0	11	0	1.7	10	0	2.3	17	0	0.0	0
Other electric personal care items	0	1.7	17	1	5.9	17	2	9.8	19	3	11.3	22	0	1.1	34
Toiletries and sundries[a]	29			58			88			84			28		

[a] Data from diary survey; percentage reporting not available.

Giving

The sense of social obligation to go to church or give to charities had deteriorated, and the proportion of employed families who made contributions to churches or charities declined between 1950 and 1973. The act of making charitable gifts had taken on class distinctions between 1950 and 1973, as the proportion of salaried families contributing to charity declined slightly and the proportion of working class declined noticeably. At the same time, the size of the contributions made increased. Overall, gifts and contributions rose from 3% of the family's budget in 1950 to 4% in 1973. Families were now more likely to give gifts to relatives and friends rather than to donate money to charities and churches (see table 6.15).

Employed families, who had spent slightly more for religion than for gifts in 1950, spent almost twice as much for gifts as for church in 1973. Salaried families' religious contributions continued to be 40% higher than laborer families' contributions.

Gift-giving had become a part of social life, even for laborer families. Only one in five laborer families, and one in nine salaried families did not buy any gifts in 1973. Clothing was the most popular gift item, and cash was the most valuable gift given. Salaried families were more likely than others to have family members rely upon them to help pay the bills. One in ten salaried families paid an average of $100 per month to help support relatives; the likelihood and the size of payments declined with class status. Gifts of cash were made by over one-third of working-class families and two-fifths of salaried families, and salaried families averaged one-fourth more for their cash gifts. However, seniors made more and larger cash gifts than salaried families, so that one-half seniors spent $248 on cash gifts. All classes reported receiving more than giving in cash gifts. Although this is unlikely, the relative differences reported in receiving and giving across classes is reasonable, ranging from 18% for low-income to 80% for wage earners.

Low-income families economized on gift buying, and they still gave more money to church and charity than they spent on gifts. Only about one-half of low-income families bought gifts or gave to their religious organization. Even fewer, three in ten, made contributions to a charity. However, those who made charitable contributions felt strongly about giving and made sizable contributions that averaged even more than the contributions made by salaried families.

Seniors preferred cash gifts over actual presents that required shopping and more cumbersome shipping, and seniors spent only one-half as much as working-class families on clothing presents, which was their preferred gift when they went shopping for presents.

Table 6.15 Gifts and contributions, 1973

	Low income			Laborer			Wage earner			Salaried			Seniors		
	Avg. exp. ($)	% rep.	Cost ($)	Avg. exp. ($)	% rep.	Cost ($)	Avg. exp. ($)	% rep.	Cost ($)	Avg. exp. ($)	% rep.	Cost ($)	Avg. exp. ($)	% rep.	Cost ($)
Gifts/Contributions Total[a]	148	74.7	198	359	93.4	384	417	96.7	431	619	98.1	631	297	91.2	326
Gifts	61	55.9	110	208	81.4	255	228	86.5	263	356	88.7	402	177	73.6	241
Expenses for persons outside household[b]	6	2.1	274	11	2.5	439	15	3.1	485	25	5.9	421	2	1.9	86
Contributions	81	57.6	140	140	79.3	177	174	85.5	203	238	91.2	261	118	81.6	144
Cash gifts for support	5	1.9	279	47	7.2	652	62	7.9	789	121	10.1	1,204	3	1.9	133
Other gifts (cash, financial assets)	23	19.7	117	55	36.6	149	60	37.6	160	85	43.0	198	122	49.0	248
Gifts of appliances, equipment and tools	1	4.5	23	5	14.3	32	6	19.6	31	9	24.8	37	5	9.2	55
Gifts of housewares and linens	3	16.9	19	9	30.6	28	9	35.8	25	12	39.2	31	7	27.2	27
Gifts of clothing	18	40.5	43	47	65.1	72	48	68.7	70	63	76.3	82	26	48.3	55
Gifts of recreation	4	12.4	29	20	28.9	68	22	34.1	65	34	39.9	86	12	21.8	54
Contributions to charities	29	29.8	98	30	63.2	48	35	72.4	49	62	82.3	75	20	59.4	34
Contributions to church/religious organizations	50	48.6	102	106	57.6	183	136	62.6	217	170	66.4	256	91	67.0	136
Contributions to educational organizations	0	1.5	16	2	4.5	46	1	5.8	24	3	7.6	39	3	6.5	48
Political contributions	0	0.9	36	2	3.1	58	1	3.7	14	2	8.0	29	1	3.8	18

a Excludes gifts of food and all gifts under $15.00.
b Medical expenses, education expenses and miscellaneous expenses for persons outside the consumer unit.

Political contributions marked class status and indicated active participation in the electoral process. Salaried families were over twice as likely as working-class families to make political contributions. Even so, only one in twelve salaried families made a political contribution. This is the same proportion that made a contribution to an educational organization, and these latter contributions showed less sharp class distinctions.

Just as the growth of gifts and contributions in the family's budget indicate the increase in discretionary income, the small amount spent by low-income families, equal to only 3% of their small budgets, indicates the severe economic constraints they faced. Seniors, on the other hand, spent 6% of their budgets on gifts and contributions, even though the proportion making gifts and charitable contributions was lower than for employed families. Like employed families, seniors spent 50% more on gifts than on contributions. Aging seemed to make seniors more conscious of religion, and the proportion of seniors making contributions to religious organizations (67%) exceeded that of the working class.

Miscellaneous

Miscellaneous expenses were primarily for finance charges (interest on consumer loans excluding vehicles and homes), occupational expenses, and real estate charges (see table 6.16). As in 1950, these miscellaneous charges accounted for 1% of the family's budget. In 1973, interest and banking charges exceeded funeral expenses, which reversed the situation in 1950. The use of checking accounts had become widespread. Employed families were at least twice as likely to have bank service charges in 1973 as in 1950, and the class differences were lessened. From 54% laborer to 66% salaried families paid for banking services of about equal value.

Financing consumer purchases other than automobiles had become more accessible to employed families as the use of credit cards spread, and replaced installment loans. Class differences had vanished or possibly reversed. In 1950, one in eight salaried families had consumer loans, which was twice the frequency for laborer families. In 1973, almost one in three working-class families paid finance charges, and salaried families were slightly less likely to pay finance charges. However, the amount of interest paid increased with class. Even one-in-six low-income families incurred finance charges, although the value of these charges was considerably below those of the laborer families. Seniors exhibited the most restraint in using credit cards to finance consumer purchases. They were one-third as likely as low-income families to pay any finance charges, and their charges were 30% less.

The proportion of households, ranging from 25% of laborer to 32% of salaried families, with a union or association member mirrored the national unionized rate of 29% of the non-agricultural workforce.[72]

Table 6.16 Other expenditures, 1973

	Low income			Laborer			Wage earner			Salaried			Seniors		
	Avg. exp. ($)	% rep.	Cost ($)	Avg. exp. ($)	% rep.	Cost ($)	Avg. exp. ($)	% rep.	Cost ($)	Avg. exp. ($)	% rep.	Cost ($)	Avg. exp. ($)	% rep.	Cost ($)
Total other expenditures	28	46.3	61	93	74.8	125	132	80.0	165	171	81.3	211	67	53.3	126
Finance charges[a]	12	17.8	68	32	29.7	108	40	31.8	126	40	28.8	138	3	6.5	49
Total bank service charges	4	27.6	15	11	54.0	21	14	62.8	22	16	66.0	24	5	43.7	11
Funerals	1	0.9	118	1	0.4	283	0	0.5	62	0	0.3	111	10	0.8	1,268
Legal/accounting fees	2	0.9	244	5	4.1	118	6	4.9	119	12	4.0	301	35	1.9	1,825
Total expenses on other real estate[b]	4	3.0	150	19	7.7	247	37	10.3	361	26	10.2	259	11	3.8	285
Total occupational expenses	1	9.9	6	18	42.8	43	26	49.0	51	63	56.2	112	0	6.9	3
Checking account/bank service charges	4	19.7	18	10	44.2	23	12	53.0	23	14	52.9	27	3	18.4	16
Safe deposit box charges	1	10.7	6	1	16.5	8	1	18.9	7	2	24.6	8	2	33.7	6
Legal fees	0	0.2	8	1	3.0	19	1	2.8	18	1	2.6	49	0	1.1	27
Accounting fees	2	0.6	323	4	1.4	295	5	2.3	233	11	1.9	563	35	1.5	2,261
Non-pleasure trips	3	7.5	42	6	11.0	58	9	11.5	74	13	15.4	85	3	5.4	57
Unions dues	0	3.0	2	6	25.5	22	8	29.7	28	14	32.4	42	0	0.4	0
Other occupational expenses	0	7.1	4	4	21.3	21	6	24.7	23	23	32.2	71	0	6.5	2.92

[a] Excludes mortgage and vehicle finance charges.
[b] Unimproved land, house under construction, and second homes not used as vacation homes. In 1950, these expenses for vacation homes were included here. For 1973, such expenses are grouped under vacation homes in table 6.12.

Employed families had negligible funeral or burial expenses during 1973. A few seniors and low-income families paid for funerals or burials during the year. The value paid for funerals averaged $1,268 for seniors, but only $118 for low-income families. A few employed families paid for upkeep on cemetery lots. This is in sharp contrast to 1950, when over 15% of employed families reported some funeral expenses. Funerals were apparently becoming less important for class status, and families did not seem as preoccupied with making sure that appropriate burial arrangements could be purchased or that burial sites of ancestors were maintained.

In 1973, employed families used even fewer professional services than they had in 1950. Employed families, especially salaried, were less likely to have a family lawyer, and such services no longer marked class status. Although one in eleven salaried families had legal fees in 1950, fewer than one in thirty did in 1973. Some of the lawyer's tax duties had been taken over by an accountant, and a few (2%) employed families paid accounting fees. Even so, salaried families were less likely to hire a lawyer or accountant in 1973 than a laborer family was to have a lawyer in 1950.

Ensuring the Future

As the economy matured and as family income provided many consumption opportunities beyond buying basics, economic security became an important and attainable goal for employed families. Many workers gained security through workplace benefits, including increased sick leave and vacation days, private pensions to supplement the mandated Federal Social Security program, and health insurance. Protection of some income in the event of job loss or injury had also improved for employed families since unemployment insurance and workers' compensation had been greatly expanded by most states during the 1950s and 1960s. Social Security payments and coverage, including hospital insurance, had also been improved since 1950.

One-half of the differences in insurance expenditures for the employed classes, and two-thirds of the difference between laborer and low-income families, however, reflected mandatory Social Security contributions rather than improved pensions or life insurance. The ability to insure income in the event of early death or disability continued to mark classes, and the proportion of families having various types of insurance policies and the value of those policies increased with class status. The majority of employed families continued to buy life insurance, but families were less likely to use life insurance as a savings instrument and they were more likely to buy term life than in 1950. Quite a few salaried families bought term life insurance to supplement their life insurance that provided a cash reserve.

A major indication of the improvement in the economic security of employed families, and of the decrease in the daily financial pressures they faced, is that employed families' income finally met or exceeded expenditures in 1973 as spending rates (i.e., expenditures divided by net income) fell.[73] In 1973, salaried families spent 88% of their net incomes, compared to 108% in 1950. Even laborer families' did not spend more than their incomes, compared to a spending rate of 116% in 1950. Greater economic security through savings had become a new way to mark class.

Increases in life expectancy, along with the provision of retirement income, meant that many husbands would enjoy a period of comfortable retirement. Between 1918 and 1973, the expected age at death for 20 year olds increased five years for white males (from age 65.6 to 71.0) and 12 years for white females (from age 66.5 to 78.1). Starting from a lower life expectancy, blacks closed some of the racial gap. For 20 year olds, life expectancy increased from age 58.4 to 65.7 for black males and from age 57.2 to 73.5 for black females. At age 40, white men could expect three years of retirement (if they retired at age 67) in 1918, and eight years of retirement (if they retired at age 65) in 1973.[74] As the probability of early death from accidents and disease decreased, the need for life insurance to provide an income to the family in case of the husband's pre-retirement death diminished dramatically. Meanwhile, the need for retirement income for both spouses was increasing.

Government programs

Taxes, and the government programs they financed, had become first noticeable in the family's budget in 1950, and their importance increased rapidly as the government became the major provider of economic security for workers' families when they were retired or unemployed or injured. The government also provided economic security, albeit at a lower level, for families whose employment history did not entitle them to the government programs for workers. Aid to Families With Dependent Children (AFDC), Food Stamps, and Medicaid formed the bulk of support for these families.

Since class has been defined by wage-earning ability and stability, the observations that the frequency of receiving Unemployment Insurance (UI) and the total amount received, which indicates length of unemployment, decreased with class are not surprising. Laborer families were three-fourths more likely than salaried families to have a family member in the UI line. In contrast, employed families were similar in their frequency of receiving workers' compensation (or disability insurance, DI) but the amount they received during the year increased with class.[75]

Compared to 1950, families in 1973 were more likely to be receiving wage income and income from assets and less likely to be receiving military benefits. The frequency of having self-employed income remained about 10% for employed families, but self-employment income was a smaller proportion of the family's total income in 1973 compared to 1950. The proportion of gross income represented by wages decreased for the working class and increased for the salaried class over the period. Between 1950 and 1973, pension and UI income, rather than military benefits, became a more important source of income for employed families. In 1973, laborer families received 9% of their incomes from pensions and UI, while salaried families received only 3% from these sources.

Seniors, of course, relied on their pensions provided through the Social Security program, which accounted for 57% of their income in 1973. In addition, about one-half of the low-income households collected some Social Security benefits. The seniors who fell into the low-income group differed from the typical seniors in two important respects, which reflects their labor market history and corresponding lower incomes. Low-income seniors received three-fourths the Social Security benefits received by the typical senior, and they were less than one-fifth as likely to receive a private pension that paid only one-half the benefits. For the average senior household, private pensions accounted for 10% of their gross income.

Low-income families included two major groups, seniors and families with little work history. The latter group had weak attachment to the labor market because of low wages, chronic unemployment, health problems, and/or family responsibilities as single mothers. Overall, five in eleven low-income households reported wages and one in three reported Food Stamps and public assistance. For those low-income families receiving Food Stamps and public assistance, their benefits provided three-fourths of their income.

Taxes and insurance

The average present tax rate doubled between 1950 and 1973, and it increased more (2.6 times) for laborer families than for salaried families (2.3 times). However, if payroll taxes for Social Security[76] are included (see table 6.17), the overall tax rate increased by the same proportions across classes. Overall, laborers paid 19% of their income for income, payroll, and property taxes, compared to 23% for salaried families. Personal taxes accounted for 70% of the combined taxes for employed families, and the progressivity of the income tax continued to be offset somewhat by the more proportional payroll and property taxes.

Assets

Improvements in the assets augmented the family's economic security. Employed families were four times more likely to receive some interest

Table 6.17 Personal insurance, 1973

	Low income			Laborer			Wage earner			Salaried			Seniors		
	Avg. exp. ($)	% rep.	Cost ($)	Avg. exp. ($)	% rep.	Cost ($)	Avg. exp. ($)	% rep.	Cost ($)	Avg. exp. ($)	% rep.	Cost ($)	Avg. exp. ($)	% rep.	Cost ($)
Personal insurance total	172	62.1	277	725	95.9	756	974	97.9	995	1,479	98.8	1,497	89.84	63.2	142.15
Total life/disability insurance	77	44.3	173	190	77.2	246	250	83.0	301	375	91.2	412	62.64	56.7	110.46
Social security[a]	73	37.5	195	447	87.1	514	564	91.1	619	816	95.0	859	20.93	16.5	127.04
Private pensions	2	0.6	343	20	7.1	276	29	8.7	328	42	10.2	414	0.10	0.4	25.00
Other insurance[b]	20	8.1	243	68	15.9	428	132	22.4	590	245	29.3	838	6.18	69.0	89.56
Details															
Life insurance[c]	64	36.4	176	145	62.0	235	191	68.5	278	277	79.7	348	48.11	44.8	107.32
Term life insurance[d]	9	7.9	110	33	25.0	133	35	29.4	118	67	41.9	160	7.54	8.8	85.61
Accident/disability insurance	2	4.3	51	5	8.1	66	9	11.0	81	13	17.7	71	3.98	9.2	43.25
Income insurance	1	0.9	103	5	4.5	102	11	7.0	160	14	9.0	159	2.39	1.5	156.00
Other life insurance	1	1.5	44	1	2.2	58	4	4.0	105	4	2.8	135	0.61	1.5	40.00

[a] Includes FICA and government retirement programs (e.g., railroad and Federal government employees).
[b] Includes personal liability insurance, credit card insurance, other non-health insurance (e.g., burial insurance), and other insurances items deducted from pay.
[c] Life, endowments, or combination with cash benefits life insurance.
[d] No cash reserve.

Table 6.18 Taxes, 1973

	Low income			Laborer			Wage earner			Salaried			Seniors		
	Avg. exp. ($)	% rep.	Cost ($)	Avg. exp. ($)	% rep.	Cost ($)	Avg. exp. ($)	% rep.	Cost ($)	Avg. exp. ($)	% rep.	Cost ($)	Avg. exp. ($)	% rep.	Cost ($)
Total taxes	290	67.0	433	1,948	99.4	1,960	2,587	99.8	2,592	4,300	100.0	4,300	266	77.4	344
Percentage of income	7.6			18.8			20.1			22.9			5.8		
Property taxes	76	33.4	229	179	52.4	342	234	65.0	360	404	80.2	503	169	57.5	295
Social Security tax[a]	73	37.5	195	447	87.1	514	564	91.1	619	816	95.0	859	21	16.5	127
Personal taxes	141	45.4	311	1,322	96.7	1,366	1,789	99.0	1,808	3,080	99.7	3,091	76	37.9	201
Federal income tax	67	38.8	173	876	95.9	914	1,215	98.6	1,232	2,237	99.7	2,244	37	28.7	130
State/local tax	11	28.1	38	158	78.3	202	217	80.4	270	382	84.6	451	2	20.3	11
Personal property tax	3	5.1	58	8	12.1	69	11	15.6	68	14	14.6	98	4	8.8	40

[a] Includes FICA and government retirement programs.

Table 6.19 Net changes in assets, 1973

	Low income			Laborer			Wage earner			Salaried			Seniors		
	Amount ($)	% rep.	Avg. chg[a] ($)	Amount ($)	% rep.	Avg. chg[a] ($)	Amount ($)	% rep.	Avg. chg[a] ($)	Amount ($)	% rep.	Avg. chg[a] ($)	Amount ($)	% rep.	Avg. chg[a] ($)
Net change in assets	(183)	50.3	(67)	456	79.0	1,493	551	85.5	1,892	1,739	90.3	2,971	33.86	67.4	123.73
Net change in checking/savings accounts	(27)	32.8	(82)	169	56.2	302	260	60.3	431	(7)	65.3	(11)	206.00	50.6	407.31
Purchase price of home	178	0.9	20,750	1,003	5.0	20,265	1,345	5.8	23,319	2,509	7.8	32,168	275.67	1.5	17,987.50
Home improvements total	38	9.2	412	100	24.5	408	181	30.4	594	306	45.2	675	59.53	18.8	317.10
Net change in assets of own farm/business	78	1.3	6,077	18	2.1	870	48	2.3	2,097	339	3.6	9,316	8.36	0.8	1,091.00
Net change in US Savings Bonds	(6)	1.7	(356)	8	10.3	75	14	15.7	90	46	20.3	225	−41.38	3.4	−1,200.00
Net change in other securities	19	1.5	1,289	(15)	3.6	(410)	66	7.3	899	270	13.3	2,023	−32.70	2.3	−1,422.33
Sale of autos or other vehicles	(21)	7.9	(270)	(112)	18.5	(607)	(132)	18.7	(703)	(202)	22.2	(909)	−14.56	5.7	−253.33
Sale of furnishings/equipment/other belongings	(4)	3.4	(118)	(7)	4.3	(152)	(16)	5.6	(284)	(10)	7.3	(144)	−15.03	4.2	−356.73
Net change in other assets	(30)	13.5	(225)	(5)	20.4	(24)	95	17.8	532	110	14.6	752	−72.42	12.6	−572.78

	Low income			Laborer			Wage earner			Salaried			Seniors		
	Amount ($)	% rep.	Avg. Chg[b] ($)	Amount ($)	% rep	Avg. Chg[b] ($)	Amount ($)	% rep.	Avg. Chg[b] ($)	Amount ($)	% rep.	Avg. Chg[b] ($)	Amount ($)	% rep.	Avg. Chg[b] ($)
Net change in liabilities	149	42.6	350	723	74.9	966	1,067	81.1	1,316	944	86.5	1,092	49.57	23.0	215.63
Reduction of mortgage principal	(136)	10.3	(1,326)	(228)	35.3	(645)	(278)	48.1	(578)	(685)	66.0	(1,038)	−25.94	7.3	−356.32
Mortgage principal balance at year end	187	1.3	14,565	734	4.6	15,995	1,106	6.5	17,100	1,355	5.9	22,997	60.33	1.1	5248.33
Net change in principal of vehicle loans	14	14.83	91	101	40.6	249	125	44.8	280	99	51.0	195	−2.75	4.6	−59.92
Net change in amounts on installment debt (credit cards)	83	31.0	268	91	49.4	184	89	49.7	178	103	48.5	212	21.96	15.7	139.80

	Low income			Laborer			Wage earner			Salaried			Seniors		
	Amount ($)	% rep.	Avg. Chg[a] ($)	Amount ($)	% rep.	Avg. Chg[a] ($)	Amount ($)	% rep.	Avg. Chg[a] ($)	Amount ($)	% rep.	Avg. Chg[a] ($)	Amount ($)	% rep.	Avg. Chg[a] ($)
Total market value	1,485	51.6	2,878	5,322	84.2	6,322	6,763	88.8	7,615	7,844	92.9	8,444	8,161.08	75.5	10,812.40
Amount in savings acct	1,175	36.4	3,228	2,988	63.5	4,703	3,645	73.4	4,964	4,029	77.3	5,213	6,083.38	63.6	9,564.83
Amount in checking acct	178	33.6	531	336	66.3	506	347	74.7	464	513	83.7	612	414.26	55.6	745.66
Market value of US Savings Bonds	43	5.4	808	308	19.7	1,564	279	27.6	1,009	509	36.4	1,398	272.03	9.6	2,840.00
Market value of securities	89	2.6	3,450	1,691	10.9	15,560	2,492	18.0	13,842	2,793	29.5	9,481	1,391.42	14.2	9,815.16

[a] Average change in asset value for reporting households.

[b] Average change in liability value for reporting households.

[c] Average market value of asset at year-end for reporting households.

income in 1973 than in 1950. Only one-tenth as many employed families received rental income as interest. However, the value of rental income was much higher than for interest for those receiving it, since it usually came from another property rather than from renting out part of one's own home. Although from two-thirds of laborer to four-fifths of salaried families received some income from assets, only 3% of employed families' gross income came from assets (up from 2% in 1950). The assets themselves, rather than the income they generated, made the families more economically secure.

Families decreased their net assets by an amount equal to almost one-third of their gross incomes in 1950, as many of them spent wartime savings. In 1973, the situation had reversed dramatically. Employed families increased their net worth by an amount equal to 4% of gross income for working-class families and 9% for salaried families.

The major savings instruments were savings accounts and securities. These liquid holdings separated classes. Salaried families' liquid assets averaged one-half more than laborer families' holdings. Low-income families had only 28% of the liquid assets of laborer families. Seniors had larger liquid assets than salaried families, and they still did not draw down their net worth. Seniors were risk-averse and held higher balances in their savings accounts, but held fewer securities than salaried families. The majority of employed families and seniors had checking accounts and savings accounts, and families tended to hold 10%–15% as much in their checking account as in their savings account. Only one in three low-income families had savings accounts or checking accounts, however, and few of the low-income families without bank accounts had any liquid assets. In 1973, low-income families decreased their net worth by an amount equal to 5% of income.

A sizable number of families (5% of low income, 20% of laborer and 36% of salaried) still held savings bonds. Although only 10% of seniors held savings bonds, the value of their holdings was over $2,800, which was about twice the value held by employed families. A handful of low-income and senior households cashed in some of their savings bonds during the year, while employed families added to their holdings.

Families were increasingly reliant on credit cards. One in three low-income families and one in two employed families increased their credit card debt during the year, and the increase averaged $200 for working-class families. One in three low-income families used their credit cards to increase their purchasing power an additional $268, which was the highest of all the groups. Only one in six seniors added to their credit card debt.

As was discussed earlier, a family's major asset was its house, whose value increased with class status. Not only did the family's home shape daily life, it also provided security as the family's last asset to be drawn upon in case of financial need. If problems in the labor market eventually required a family to sell its home and move to cheaper quarters, the transition to a lower class could be cushioned and delayed by drawing upon the assets in the house.

Purchases of more expensive homes or home improvements were the ways that families increased their home values. For laborer families, 5% purchased a home worth $20,000 and 25% spent $400 improving their homes. For salaried families, 8% purchased a home worth $32,000 more and 45% spent $675 on home improvements.

A small group of working class families (2%) and salaried families (4%) reported a net increase in the value of a family business (including farms). This added a substantial amount to the assets for salaried families ($9,300), but the amount for laborer families was fairly small ($870).

Overall, salaried families were more secure than working-class families because their budgets were a smaller proportion of their net incomes, they were less likely to experience unemployment, and they held higher liquid and real assets. Upon retirement, salaried families were more likely to supplement their Social Security checks with a private pension check. Low-income families, who never had much economic security provided through employment, relied mostly on various government programs for whatever security they offered. However, employer-provided health care and government-provided pensions supplemented the income gap in creating a vast security gap between those with and without access to decent jobs.

Dynamics of Change

Economic growth allowed strong expenditure growth, and employed families were able to emulate the consumption practices of higher income groups while also modernizing their consumption to include innovative goods and improvements in housing, automobiles, and leisure activities. In order to achieve emulation and include innovation in these preferred and more modern areas, families were willing to reduce their standard consumption in the more basic area of food as well as to forgo emulating the standards of earlier eras in traditional markers of status – clothing, furnishing, personal care, and contributions (see table 6.20). Altogether, employed families were willing to give up over 40% of expected emulation. Declines in expected family sizes also released money to increase per capita consumption. Higher incomes increased economic security, as employed families' budgets no longer surpassed their incomes. Improvements in retirement security were required, and provided, by the government as it raised both Social Security benefits and payroll deductions.

As expected, the ability of a class to replicate emulation norms and adopt innovative norms depended upon the growth rate of expenditures.

Table 6.20 Shifts in urban consumption norms, 1950–73

	Realized emulation (RE)	Innovation (IN)	Dis-emulation	Reduced standard (RS)	Change in expenditures (ΔE)
Total expenditures[a]					
Laborers	0.44	0.18	-0.13	-0.02	0.60
Wage earners	0.33	0.16	-0.06	-0.06	0.42
Salaried	0.37	0.17	-0.18	-0.03	0.51

	Laborers				Wage earners				Salaried			
	ΔE	RE	IN	RS	ΔE	RE	IN	RS	ΔE	RE	IN	RS
Expenditure category												
Food (per capita)	-0.15	0.00	0.00	-0.15	-0.15	0.00	0.00	-0.15	-0.11	0.00	0.00	-0.11
Clothing (per capita)	0.01	0.01	0.00	0.00	-0.07	0.00	0.00	-0.07	0.00	0.00	0.00	0.00
Housing	0.94	0.44	0.51	0.00	0.87	0.42	0.44	0.00	0.93	0.54	0.39	0.00
Fuel/utilities	0.71	0.42	0.29	0.00	0.59	0.31	0.28	0.00	0.75	0.38	0.37	0.00
Furnishings	0.43	0.43	0.00	0.00	0.35	0.35	0.00	0.00	0.38	0.38	0.00	0.00
Miscellaneous												
Transportation	1.85	1.31	0.55	0.00	1.06	0.73	0.32	0.00	0.98	0.72	0.26	0.00
Recreation and education	1.23	1.13	0.11	0.00	0.87	0.68	0.19	0.00	1.02	0.60	0.42	0.00
Household operations	1.11	0.86	0.24	0.00	1.07	0.89	0.18	0.00	0.89	0.89	0.00	0.00
Medical care per capita	0.15	0.15	0.00	0.00	0.07	0.07	0.00	0.00	0.01	0.01	0.00	0.00
Personal care per capita	0.13	0.13	0.00	0.00	0.23	0.23	0.00	0.00	0.23	0.23	0.00	0.00
Gifts and contributions	0.97	0.97	0.00	0.00	0.82	0.82	0.00	0.00	1.00	1.00	0.00	0.00
Personal insurance	1.90	1.21	0.69	0.00	1.56	0.85	0.70	0.00	2.11	1.18	0.93	0.00
Other	-0.02	0.00	0.00	-0.02	0.43	0.43	0.00	0.00	0.43	0.43	0.00	0.00
Family size	0.12	0.12	0.00	0.00	-0.01	0.00	0.00	-0.01	0.02	0.02	0.00	0.00

[a] ΔE = RE + IN + RS.

All three employed classes used 16%–18% of their base expenditure level to achieve innovation. With the largest growth in expenditures, laborers were able to achieve the highest degree of realized emulation and innovation, while reducing food consumption 15%. In contrast, wage-earner families, whose expenditure growth was only two-thirds that of laborer families, had to reduce clothing consumption by 7% as well as food consumption by 15%, in order to achieve slightly lower rates of innovation and emulation. Salaried families, with an expenditure growth rate between that of laborers and wage earners, were able to achieve their innovation with an 11% reduction in food and a slightly lower rate of emulation than achieved by wage-earner families.

Overall, as expenditure growth slows, innovations take a larger share of increases in spending. Consumption norms continued to dictate that families maintain their relative position through innovation, even at the expense of maintaining standards in the traditional areas of food and, then, clothing. Innovations in consumption norms, however, varied by class. The importance of innovations in housing, household operations, and transportation declined with class status while the importance of innovations in recreation increased with class status. Besides reducing previous norms for food and clothing, families varied in how they curtailed their emulation in other areas. Willingness to forgo emulation in furnishings diminished with class status while foregoing emulation of charitable and gift giving increased with status. In addition, salaried families were willing to reduce emulation of household operations, while working-class families were innovating in this area, especially with telephone services. These trends molded economic distance, where lower-class families sought to close the gap in mobility, housing quality, and communications, while higher-class families widened the gap in leisure time pursuits.

Economic Distance

Employed classes differentiated themselves in varying ways. Although their higher incomes allowed them to increase their spending in all categories, laborer families especially distanced themselves from low-income families by improving their mobility with ownership of one or two automobiles. The life-style of laborer families was also distinguished from low-income families by more active social and recreational lives supported by relatively high spending on recreation, gift-giving, and cars, as well as by more security provided by insurance. Overall, laborer families' expenditures were almost twice as large as expenditures of low-income families, but they spent almost three times as much on transportation, four times as much on insurance, and over twice as much on recreation and gifts (see table 6.1).

Table 6.21 Economic distance across groups, 1973

	Laborers to low income			Wage earners to laborers			Salaried to wage earners		
	Ratio	Difference ($)		Ratio	Difference ($)		Ratio	Difference ($)	
Relative net income	2.460	5,356		1.229	2,069		1.417	4,622	
Relative expenditures	1.863	4,187		1.163	1,478		1.313	3,296	
Distribution of increased consumption									
	Distribution	Difference ($)	% change	Distribution	Difference ($)	% change	Distribution	Difference ($)	% change
Food and clothing	0.187	783	52.6	0.181	268	11.8	0.245	808	31.8
Food, alcohol	0.136	571	47.1	0.129	191	10.7	0.166	548	27.8
Food	0.123	515	43.3	0.122	181	10.6	0.154	509	27.0
Alcohol	0.013	56	256.9	0.007	10	13.2	0.012	39	44.4
Clothing	0.051	213	76.8	0.052	77	15.8	0.079	259	45.8
Shelter	0.157	659	44.9	0.188	278	13.1	0.188	621	25.8
Housing	0.096	400	39.8	0.093	137	9.8	0.100	330	21.3
Fuel and utilities	0.025	106	36.4	0.030	45	11.4	0.032	107	24.3
Furnishings	0.037	153	88.7	0.065	96	29.5	0.056	184	43.7
Miscellaneous	0.656	2,745	144.8	0.630	931	20.1	0.567	1,868	33.5
Household operations	0.037	157	48.4	0.078	115	24.0	0.031	101	17.1
Transportation	0.253	1,058	189.9	0.150	221	13.7	0.156	515	28.1
Recreation/education	0.102	425	134.3	0.111	164	22.1	0.126	416	45.9
Medical care	0.048	203	74.0	0.032	48	10.0	0.016	51	9.8
Personal care	0.017	72	93.9	0.025	37	25.1	0.011	38	20.3
Gifts/contributions	0.050	211	142.8	0.039	58	16.1	0.061	202	48.5
Insurance	0.132	553	321.9	0.169	249	34.4	0.153	505	51.8
Other	0.016	65	232.0	0.026	39	41.4	0.012	39	29.7
Total	1.000	4,187		1.000	1,478		1.000	3,230	

Since laborer families had achieved the mobility provided by automobile ownership, wage-earner families distanced themselves from laborer families by creating more comfortable home lives and richer social lives. They improved their homes through relatively high expenditures on furnishings and household operations. Their social lives included more entertainment at home as well as more social outings supported by their relatively high expenditures on personal care and recreation. Greater security through insurance also distinguished wage-earner families from laborer families. Overall, the upper working class spent one-sixth more than the lower working class, but their expenditures for furnishings, household operations, recreation, personal care, and insurance were at least one-fourth higher.

Economic distance between the salaried and the working class primarily was achieved by an even richer and more active social life with relatively high expenditures for clothing, furnishings, recreation, and gifts. Again, security also created economic distance. Overall, salaried families spent 30% more than wage-earner families, but their expenditures for clothing, furnishings, recreation, and gifts were almost 50% higher.

In 1973, the economic distance between the working class and the lower class was defined by mobility and the beginnings of a more active social life. Within the working class, economic distance was defined primarily by improvements in shelter that allowed a better home life and continued improvements in social life. Economic distance between the salaried and the working class was defined by more public display as well as a richer and more active social life. Across all classes, security helped define economic distance. These differences in economic distance are reflected in expenditures for shelter, transportation, recreation, and insurance, which account for over 60% of the increase in income across classes. However, families differ in their allocations of higher income across these four major categories. Overall, laborer families, compared to low-income families, spent 25% of their higher income on transportation plus 16% on shelter (see table 6.21) Wage-earner families, compared to laborer families, spent 19% of their higher income on shelter plus 15% on transportation. Salaried families, compared to wage-earner families, also spent 19% of their higher income on shelter and 15% on transportation plus 13% on recreation.

Budget Standards

In the postwar era, family budgets changed fairly rapidly to incorporate innovative goods and services, and the BLS standards were slow to subsume these changes. Those devising standards clung to their emphasis on the traditional goods of food, clothing, and, to a lesser extent, shelter, to mark well-being. They continued wistfully to assume that wives would be full-time homemakers, families would use public transit rather than buy a second car, and parents and children would dress up for their daily activities of school, work, and shopping. They also added the unrealistic assumption in 1967 that adults would not smoke cigarettes because of the reports that smoking was hazardous to health. They continued to assume that families furnished their homes when married, so that they required only limited replacement of items.

Two major trends explain the divergence between BLS standards and consumption norms. First, families' reliance on food and clothing to provide them with variety and status was being supplanted by purchases of more modern recreational goods and cars. As we have already seen, families had become fairly homogeneous in their food and clothing practices. Higher incomes were now being used to buy a second car, go on vacation, and buy electronic entertainment gear as well as to increase financial security with insurance and savings. Second, wives were taking paid jobs so that the family could afford to buy the market goods and services that could not be produced or augmented at home. At the same time, wives' employment increased work-related expenditures for commuting, child care, clothes and dry cleaning, and Social Security.

For these reasons, the BLS lower budget standard is modified, based on the practices of laborer families, before it is used as the benchmark for basics.[77] The adjustments increased the BLS lower budget by 7%.

For clothing, the basics standard was reduced for the husband and children and increased for the wife. The standard for the husband, who is assumed to wear casual clothes rather than a suit to work, was reduced by 37%. The standard for the wife, who is assumed to be employed rather than a full-time homemaker, was increased by 5%. The standard for the boy was reduced 25% and for the girl was reduced 4%.[78]

Basics for transportation were increased to allow 90% rather than 55% of families to own a car. The standard for basic housing was increased to permit ownership, and one-half of families are assumed to be homeowners. Personal care was adjusted to reflect one-quarter fewer haircuts for men and more beauty salon services for women.

Basics for household operations were increased to allow local telephone service for all families, some dry cleaning for work clothes, some expenses for baby-sitting and child care, some repairs for appliances and equipment, and some purchases of yard supplies.

Basics for recreation were increased to allow a simple vacation every two years. The family is assumed to travel by car, train, or bus, and to stay in an inexpensive motel, so that the vacation costs ($120) reflect those of laborer families.

The laborer family's budget exceeded the BLS lower budget[79] by 30% and they spent more on all items (see table 6.22). However, the laborer family spent over twice the BLS lower budget allowance for transportation and recreation, and spent only slightly more for food and medical care. The wage-earner family's expenditures were 8% more than the BLS intermediate budget, yet they spent considerably less than the intermediate standard for food, clothing, and shelter. Instead, the wage-earner family spent 75% more than the standard on transportation and recreation. Salaried families' expenditures showed a similar pattern compared to the BLS higher budget.

Overall, the BLS standards lagged behind practice in how quickly working-class families bought innovative goods and services, while they passed up fancy wardrobes and banking services. A clothes dryer, dishwasher, and waste disposal were included in only the higher BLS budget. Window air conditioners, and no central systems, were included in twice as many areas for the higher as the moderate BLS budgets; no air-conditioning was allowed in the lower BLS budget. Only a few families were assumed to have a color television set in the higher BLS budget (and only a black and white television set in the moderate and lower budgets.) Even after reducing the BLS budget standards for clothing and personal care, wage-earner families still spent 15% less than the intermediate clothing standard, and salaried families spent almost 25% less than the BLS higher standards for clothing and personal care. Without these adjustments, the gap between standards and practice would become a gulf.

Families spent more on transportation than suggested by the BLS standards, which did not allow a second car even for the higher budget. The BLS lower standard assumed that between 50% and 100% of families, depending on their location, owned an automobile that was six years old when purchased and ten years old when scrapped. The BLS moderate standard assumed that between 80% and 100% of families owned an automobile that was two years old when purchased and six years old when traded in. The BLS higher budget assumed that all families owned an automobile that was either new (60%) or two years old (40%) when purchased and four or six years old when traded in.

All classes except salaried spent more than the BLS standards for recreation. A large part of the difference is accounted for by vacation expenses and by cigarette purchases, which were not allowed in the government standards, although a majority of families still had a smoker. Only the higher budget allowed lodging expenses while on vacation, since lower and moderate income families were assumed to stay with family, friends, or camp out.[80] However, 11% of low-income families (one-third of those taking vacations), 39% of laborer families (three-fifths of those taking vacations), 49% of wage-earner families (seven-tenths of those taking vacations), and 65% of salaried families (eight-tenths of those taking vacations) spent money for vacation lodging[81] (see table 6.12).

Excluding vacations and cigarettes, laborer families still spent 70% more than the BLS lower budget allowed for recreation and education,

Table 6.22 Budget standards, 1973

	BLS dependency budget	(CES) low income	BLS lower budget (Basics)	(CES) Laborer	BLS intermediate budget	(CES) Wage earner	BLS higher budget	(CES) Salaried	BLS retired budget	(CES) Senior
Annual expenditure $	4,359	4,853	6,674	9,039	9,742	10,517	13,838	13,813	4,938	5,040
Average family size	2.76	2.76	2.90	2.90	3.17	3.17	3.47	3.47	1.62	1.62
Food $[a]	1,333[b]	1,212	1,750	1,782	2,522	1,973	3,487	2,521	1,295	1,171
Clothing $[a]	431	277	478	489	663	566	1,061	826	244	213
Shelter $	1,664	1,792	2,094	2,607	2,948	3,001	4,386	3,723	1,839[c]	1,716
Housing + fuel/utilities	1,261	1,296	1,576	1,802	2,223	1,984	3,204	2,420	–	1,161
Furnishings	159	173	159	326	356	422	662	606	–	158
Household operations	244	323	359	480	369[d]	595	520[d]	697	–	398
Miscellaneous $	931	1,573	2,352	4,160	3,609	4,977	4,904	6,743	1,560	1,941
Transportation	190[e]	557	713	1,615	1,014	1,836	1,315	2,351	462[f]	513
Recreation/education[g]	316	317	361	742	516	906	854	1,322	277	321
Medical care[a]	63[h]	274	478	477	526	525	600	576	369[i]	547
Personal care[a]	116	77	122	149	187	186	291	224	126	106
Gifts/contributions	183	148	183	359	323	417	593	619	326	297
Insurance	0[j]	172	402[k]	725	837	974	914	1,479	–	90
Other	63	28	93	93	206	132	337	171	–[l]	67

	BLS dependency budget	(CES) low income	BLS lower budget (Basics)	(CES) Laborer	BLS intermediate budget	(CES) Wage earner	BLS higher budget	(CES) Salaried	BLS retired budget	(CES) Senior
Expenditures adjusted for four persons $	6,317	7,033	9,206	10,138	10,163	11,368	14,669	14,446	5,414[m]	5,537[b]
Personal taxes $	—	141	724	1,322	1,607	1,789	3,080	3,080	9	76

[a] The categories for food, clothing, medical care, and personal care are adjusted for family size.

[b] USDA Economy Food Budget is used.

[c] Housing for seniors includes shelter, fuel and utilities.

[d] Repairs on appliances and recreational goods are not included in operations; they remain in furnishings and recreation, respectively. They were moved for the lower budget.

[e] Public transportation only is used, with no car ownership. If one-half to two-thirds of families are assumed to own an automobile, depending on the size of the metropolitan area, transportation costs rise to $563.

[f] Seniors are allowed 25%–60% car ownership, according to city size.

[g] For the BLS lower budget, a bi-annual vacation is allowed, and includes expenses for food, lodging, and travel by car, bus, or train. The dependency budget allows the same bi-annual vacation without lodging. The BLS intermediate and higher budgets are not adjusted, and expenditures for vacations are under food, travel, and lodging. For seniors, recreation also includes miscellaneous expenses.

[h] This covers non-prescription drugs. Medical care is assumed to be provided. Otherwise, the cost would be $455 for the family of 2.76 people. Adjustment does not include Social Security tax Y.

[i] Includes items not covered by medicare (drugs, dental care, eye examinations and glasses).

[j] This assumes no payroll taxes are collected.

[k] This assumes full coverage, under Social Security, so the maximum amount for FICA and DI is given.

[l] Miscellaneous is included under recreation for seniors.

[m] Budget adjusted for two people.

which included a radio, black and white television set, and some movie tickets. Wage-earner families spent about the same amount as the BLS intermediate budget, which added a phonograph (not hi-fi), records, and other musical instruments. The BLS higher budget standard allowed liberal spending for recreational goods and activities, and salaried families spent only 90% as much as the standard for recreation and education (excluding tobacco and vacations).

Although low-income families spent as much on recreation and education as allowed by the BLS lower budget, they spent one-fourth of it for smoking, which was not allowed by the standard. Excluding tobacco and vacations, they spent only 70% as much as the lower budget standard. Low-income families economized on many recreational and educational items, in order to pay for tobacco and vacations. Excluding tobacco, seniors spent as much for recreation and education as allowed by the intermediate budget. However, in order to spend one-half of it for vacations, they economized on other leisure activities and goods.

As the population was relying increasingly on television for its news and entertainment, people were reading much less than hoped by the BLS budget makers. All classes spent considerably less on newspapers, books, and magazines than assumed by the BLS budgets, ranging from 37% for low-income families to 64% for wage earners and salaried families. Total expenditures on education, including books, supplies, and fees, however, displayed a class bias. Lower income and laborer families spent less than two-thirds of the relevant BLS budgets for education, while wage-earner families spent slightly more and salaried families spent 90% more.

The dependency budget

Low-income families, whose incomes approximated the poverty level by definition, spent 78% of the BLS lower budget.[82] They fell below the BLS standard for food and clothing, but they met or exceeded the BLS standard for housing, transportation, and recreation. Since low-income families have only sporadic employment,[83] they pay little into Social Security, and so they spent considerably less on insurance.

The inability of low-income families to purchase basics reflected their lack of social integration, especially in the labor market. The lack of a steady job simultaneously explained their low incomes and how they coped with insufficient income to provide the grooming, lunches, and transportation needed for employment. Many low-income families spent their incomes to meet norms that did not include steady employment. Although their budgets required them to live in low-rent areas, their recreational, housing and transportation budgets allowed them to be integrated into their social class and lead fairly active social lives within their neighborhoods. One in six belonged to a club or organization, and they owned entertainment equipment, such as televisions, sound systems, and cameras, and many read newspapers and magazines.

Their budgets confined them to their neighborhoods in ways other than housing options. Their clothing was shabby. If they owned an automobile, as 45% did, it was often not reliable and sometimes not insured or registered. Since poor families often relied upon public clinics, how much health care they received usually depended upon the proximity of a clinic. The adequacy of their diet depended upon receiving Food Stamps. As might be expected, poor families had developed consumption norms that fit their limited incomes. These norms, based upon a neighborhood social life, did not allow integration into the larger community, which required steady employment.

Judging whether families have sufficient incomes to purchase basics depends upon their expected social roles. If the adults are expected to be employed, then the family's incomes needs are greater than if the adults are dependent upon the state and are not expected to be employed. The basics calculated here, based upon the BLS lower budget, assume that adults are employed. A dependency budget, for families who rely upon income from the State rather than from employment, was estimated from the BLS lower budget with some adjustments,[84] including free medical care (except for nonprescription drugs) and no payroll taxes. The dependency budget of $4,359 was 10% below expenditures of low-income families. However, 40% of the low-income families were 'working poor' who paid payroll taxes and did not have access to free medical care. Their standard should be the BLS lower budget. Excluding medical care and insurance, low-income families spent only 2.6% more than the dependency budget.

Standard of Living Index

The substantial improvement in living standards achieved between 1950 and 1973 is reflected in the Standard of Living Index comparing laborers in 1973 and in 1950 (see table 6.23). Laborer families dramatically improved their housing by finally meeting, and surpassing, the 1950 basics as well as the improved 1973 basics. They also experienced significant improvements in household operations, recreation, and transportation, as the basics for these categories had risen with the growing intricacy of the economy. As we have seen, home temperature control and plumbing requirements had improved; basic telephone service was widespread; life and disability insurance had become more important and Social Security costs had risen with benefits; basic home equipment included a colored television and audio equipment; and more families required a second car for basic transportation to work and shopping.

Table 6.23 Standard of living index,[a] 1973

	Laborer 1973–laborer 1950					Low income 1973–laborer 1973				Wage earner 1973–laborer 1973				Salaried 1973–wage earner 1973			
	Δ exp. ($)	B50 ($)	B73 ($)	Variety ($)	Status ($)	Δ exp. ($)	B73 ($)	Variety ($)	Status ($)	Δ exp. ($)	B73 ($)	Variety ($)	Status ($)	Δ exp. ($)	B73 ($)	Variety ($)	Status ($)
Food	(100)	B	313[a]	(107)	(306)	(570)	(538)	10	(42)	191	B	125	66	548	B	233	315
Clothing	52	–	(28)[a]	6	74	(212)	(144)	(41)	(27)	77	B	72	5	260	B	131	129
Housing	848	353	270	43	182	(506)	(280)	(43)	(183)	182	B	71	111	436	B	179	257
Furnishings	99	B	48	14	36	(153)	B	(101)	(52)	96	B	70	26	184	B	97	87
Household operations	252	B	270	(12)	(6)	(157)	(36)	(87)	(34)	115	B	60	55	102	B	19	83
Transportation	1,049	B	143	489	417	(1,058)	(156)	(744)	(158)	221	B	96	125	515	B	275	240
Recreation and education	411	B	140	(54)	325	(425)	(44)	(305)	(76)	164	B	139	25	416	B	189	227
Medical care	106	25	81	0	0	(203)	(203)	0	0	48	1	14	33	51	B	23	28
Personal care	32	B	7[a]	0	25	(72)	(47)	0	(25)	37	B	37	0	38	B	13	25
Gifts/contributions	177	B	21	(6)	162	(211)	(35)	(122)	(54)	58	B	30	28	202	B	68	134
Personal insurance	526	37	211	7	271	(553)	(374)	(84)	(95)	249	B + 117	54	78	505	B + 252	70	183
Other	(2)	B	B	1	(3)	(65)	(65)	0	0	39	0	17	22	39	B	3	36
Total	3,450	415	1,476	381	1,177	(4,185)	(1,922)	(1,517)	(746)	1,477	118	785	574	3,296	252	1,300	1,744
Distribution	1.00	0.12	0.43	0.11	0.34	1.00	0.46	0.36	0.18	1.00	0.08	0.53	0.39	1.00	0.08	0.39	0.53

[a] Includes changes in the basic standard (family size 2.6) for food ($132), clothing (– $77), and personal care (– $6) in addition to the improvements in basics shown under B73.

Besides incorporating the higher basics, the living standard of laborer families also allowed more variety and status in transportation, as most families had two cars. Surprisingly, laborer families spent little of their higher incomes on variety in any area except transportation and to pay for more children. Instead, they dramatically increased their status in housing, recreation, and gifts, while they decreased it on food. They could afford to drive more and better cars, live in nicer homes, stay in a motel while on vacation, and spend more money for nicer presents in 1973 than in 1950, while they frequented fast food restaurants and reduced the cost of eating out. Improvements in basics allowed the social and economic integration into modern life, which was shaped by complex transportation, communication, and financial systems, and population growth. Many of these improvements, which absorbed 55% of the increase in the laborer family's budget, were probably taken for granted. In some instances, such as long commutes on congested streets, the higher material quality of life had not improved living standards. Improvements in status, however, made laborer families more cosmopolitan and modern, and it was probably these improvements that they relished the most. Overall, laborer families spent only 11% of their income growth on variety, and 34% on status.

Wage-earner families spent their higher budget increment over the laborer's budget more on improvements in variety than in status. They improved their variety in furnishings, recreation, and insurance, and paid for more children. Wage earners' homes had more furnishings, appliances, and televisions; they went out to the movies more often and took more vacations; and their children were more likely to attend college. However, they often paid less for home furnishings such as rugs and window shades than those purchased by laborer families. Wage-earner families were willing to sacrifice quality in order to purchase the variety of goods they wanted.

Wage-earner families improved their status in household operations, housing, and transportation. Even though they purchased fewer housekeeping supplies, they paid more for those they bought, which indicates that they were buying specialized items that performed better for a specific purpose or that took care of special items. Compared to laborers, wage-earner families drove nicer cars, lived in better neighborhoods, and had more insurance coverage to protect their life-style.

The increase in the standard of living for salaried families above the wage-earner standard was marked primarily by improvements in status (53%). Four-tenths of their increase in budget was spent on improving variety. Salaried families extended the status trends of wage-earner families in housing, household operations, transportation, and insurance. In addition, they purchased status by dining out in better restaurants and purchasing more expensive ready-made foods, by wearing more stylish clothing, by going on more lavish vacations, and by giving more expensive gifts. Although the improved standard of living of wage-earner families over laborer families was accomplished through both 'more' and 'better,' salaried families achieved their higher standard of living over wage-earner families primarily through 'better.'

Households with incomes near the poverty threshold met only the basic standard for furnishings in 1973. They did not meet the standards in any other area. Because laborer families were able to consume considerably more than basics, one-half of the difference in income between laborer and low-income families was absorbed by forgoing variety (0.4) and status (0.1). One-half, however, still had to come from a decline in basics. Low-income families had to pass up the variety and status provided by automobiles, as well as the variety and status provided by housing located in a decent neighborhood, modern furnishings, and leisure-time activities. They did not consume even the basics in transportation, housing, recreation, or food.

If low-income families are dependent on government welfare payments rather than earned income, then the basic standard should be the lower dependency budget. In that case, low-income families met the basics for housing, household operations, transportation, and recreation.

In 1973, the divisive Vietnam War was winding down. Although the war had created national soul-searching about the American role in global politics, the nation had reason to be proud of its economic accomplishments. Since World War II, the living standard of all classes had risen dramatically, and the plight of the poorest had been improved considerably. The economic security of seniors had also been ameliorated. In addition, great strides had been made in reducing discrimination against blacks and women, and they continued to become more integrated into the labor market. Concern about the future was focused primarily on politics, not economics. Everyone expected that children could look forward to living better than their parents, discrimination would continue to decline, and the lot of the economically disadvantaged would improve. The economic chaos caused by the sudden OPEC price increase and embargo in fall 1973 was seen as a temporary problem rather than as part of a major realignment of the world economy that would slam the brakes on America's rapidly advancing standard of living.

NOTES

1. The birthrate peaked in the late 1950s before dropping back to prewar levels in the mid-1960s. The 'baby boomers' were born between 1946 and 1962.

2. Family heads were still designated as male by the Census Bureau, whenever possible. Women could qualify as family head only when no adult male was present. Few white families did not have an adult male present, but this was no longer true for black families.
3. Bureau of the Census, *Current Population Report*, P-20, No. 258, Table 21. Another 14% were divided between clerical and sales jobs. These figures exclude the 18% of white male heads who were unemployed or not in the labor force and the 5% who worked on farms.
4. Michael Reich, *Racial Inequality* (Princeton, NJ: Princeton University Press, 1981), pp. 63, 24. In 1973, one-half of Blacks still lived in the South.
5. Black female-headed families had a median income in 1973 of $4,225. Only 43% of the black female heads were employed during the year; the majority (51%) were not in the labor force and the remainder (6%) were unemployed. One-half of the employed black female heads had service jobs, including work as maids, and one-fourth had clerical jobs. Bureau of the Census, *Current Population Report*, P-20, No. 33, Tables 4, 7, 9, and P-60, No. 9, Tables 8, 9.
6. White female-headed families had a median income of $6,560. Bureau of the Census *Current Population Report*, P-60, No. 97, Table 25.
7. Bureau of the Census, *Current Population Report*, P-20, No. 258, Table 21. These figures exclude the 24% of black heads who were unemployed or not in the labor force and the 3% who were farmers or farm workers. In 1950, black men employed in non-farm jobs were almost exclusively in service or laborer occupations (52%) or in craft or operative occupations (41%). Reich, p. 24.
8. Black husband-wife families had a median income equal to 95% of the median income for families headed by a laborer or service worker, of which one-fifth were non-white. Bureau of the Census, *Current Population Report*, P-60, No. 97, Tables, 25, 41, 45.
9. Bureau of the Census, *Current Population Report*, P-60, No. 98, 1975, Table 1. The composition of the families of persons in poverty changed dramatically during this period. In 1959, 70% lived in male-headed families, 18% lived in female-headed families, and 12% lived alone or with non-relatives. In 1973, the comparable breakdown is 44%, 36%, and 20%.
10. See Mollie Orshansky, 'Counting the Poor: Another Look at the Poverty Profile,' *Social Security Bulletin* 28 (Jan. 1965): 3–29; Orshansky, 'Who's Who Among the Poor: A Demographic View of Poverty,' *Social Security Bulletin* 28 (July 1965): 3–31; Bureau of the Census, 'Revision in the Poverty Statistics,' *Current Population Report*, P-23, No. 97 (1975).

11. Seven out of ten seniors lived in families rather than alone. Seniors living alone had a median income of $2,725, and these individuals represented 42% of the senior households. *Current Population Report*, P-60, No. 97, Table 25; *CPR* P-60, No. 96, Table 7; *Historical Statistics*, Series B 107–17, A29–42.

12. Urban households, both black and white, with complete income reporting are included in these groups. Seniors included households who had a head aged 65 years or older. In 1973, the median income for families headed by laborers and service workers was $10,300, by craft workers and operatives was $12,800, and by professional and managerial salaried workers was $18,700. The median income for senior families was $6,426. *CPR*, P-60, No. 97, Tables 4, 25. Poor families include households with incomes from 0.9 to 1.25 times the government's 'poverty' thresholds. Since the CES oversampled poor one-person households, the one-household sample was reduced by random selection to reflect the national distribution of low income households. *CPR*, P-60, No. 98, Table A-2. The sample sizes are laborer (828), wage earner (572), salaried (577), seniors (267), and low income (467).

13. Louise A. Tilly and Joan W. Scott, *Women, Work, and Family*, (New York: Holt, Rinehart & Winston, 1978) also found this switch in work roles between mothers and children in England and France after World War II. In the United States, this trend of mature women working more and their children working less had occurred earlier and was more pronounced for black than for white families. But the source of this was the labor market problems of black youths as well as their remaining in school longer.

14. Fifty percent of laborer wives and 62% of salaried wives were employed. Black wives had a participation rate of 51% compared to 38% for white wives: *CPR*, P-60, No. 97.

15. The racial differences are even more dramatic if only teenagers are compared. Black wives had a participation rate of 51% compared to 38% for white wives.

16. The husband's median earnings were estimated to be $7,550 (laborer), $9,800 (wage earner), and $13,500 (salaried), and the wife's median earnings given the husband's earnings were $3,709, $3,950, and $4,005, respectively. *CPR*, P-60, No. 97, Tables 39–40.

17. Labor families received an average income equal for the thirty-seventh percentile for all metropolitan families (although it equaled the median for all households) (see table 6.2). Wage-earner families averaged incomes equal to the median for all metropolitan families, while salaried families averaged incomes equal to the seventieth percentile.

18. US Department of Commerce, *National Income Accounts*, various issues.
19. Colien Hefferan, 'Employee Benefits,' *Family Economics Review*, No. 1, 1985, pp. 6–14.
20. In 1950, primary households were composed almost entirely of one-person households. In 1970, 10% had more than one unrelated adult. Married couples accounted for 78% of households in 1950 and 71% in 1970, and female-headed households for 9.4% in 1950 and 10.8% in 1970. *Historical Statistics*, A 288–319 and B 216–20.
21. *Historical Statistics*, Series H599, H442–76.
22. These groups include males aged 6 through 50 years and females aged 6 through 34 years. Robert L. Rizek and Elizabeth M. Jackson, 'Current Food Consumption Practices and Nutrient Sources in the American Diet,' US Department of Agriculture, June 1980, Table III.
23. Rizek and Jackson, 'Current Food Consumption . . . ,' p. 98.
24. The income elasticity for food at home was 0.17 and for food away from home was 0.84 in the 1973 CES. Larry E. Salathe, 'Household Expenditure Patterns in the United States,' US Department of Agriculture, Economics, Statistics, and Cooperatives Service, Technical Bulletin No. 1603, April 1979. Another study using the 1973 CES found that the probability a household will eat away from home rises with income; once a household has decided to eat out, income does not affect food expenditures, except for higher income households. J. Lee and M. G. Brown, 'Food Expenditures At Home and Away From Home in the United States – A Switching Regression Analysis,' *Review of Economics and Statistics*, 142–7, 1986.
25. US Department of Agriculture, *Money Value of Food Used by Households in the United States, Spring 1977*, Nationwide Food Consumption Survey 1977–78, Preliminary Report No. 1, Aug. 1979, p. 8.
26. Nationally, 8.2% of the population received Food Stamps in 1973.
27. The popularity of French fries at hamburger stands actually resulted in an increase in national per capita consumption of potatoes between 1950 and 1973.
28. Table reproduced in George J. Mountney, *Poultry Products Technology* (Westport, CN: The AVI Publishing Co. Inc., 1966), p. 210. Overall, the home prepared or fresh foods cost 2% more to duplicate the convenience foods than to buy them directly. This varied by food group with fruits and vegetables 40% more expensive to duplicate, meat 14% less expensive, and bakery products 32% less expensive.
29. The highest income group had 20% of meals out and the lowest income group had 10%, and the highest income group spent over

three times as much per family member as the lowest income group. *Money Value of Food*, pp. 4, 10.

30. CES data.

31. US Department of Agriculture, *Food Consumption, Prices, and Expenditures*, Supplement for 1974 to Agricultural Economic Report No. 138, Jan. 1976, Tables 1, 39. National intake data show protein consumption increasing 6% between 1950 and 1970, fat consumption increasing 8%, and carbohydrate consumption decreasing by 6%. *Historical Statistics*, Series B 448–52.

32. Between 1955 and 1965, food expenditures per capita increased, but the national proportion with good diets fell from 60% to 50% while the proportion with bad diets rose from 15% to 21%. US Department of Agriculture, 'Nutrient Levels in Food Used by Households in the United States, Spring 1977,' *Nationwide Food Consumption Survey, 1977–78*, Preliminary Report No. 3, Jan. 1981; US Department of Agriculture, 'Dietary Evaluation of Food Used in Households in the United States,' Household Food Consumption Survey, 1955, Report No. 16, Nov. 1961; US Congress, House of Representatives, 'Nutritive Quality of Diets, USA,' 1968 (Summary of the 1965 Survey).

33. US Congress, 'Nutritive Quality of Diets, USA,' 1968; *Food Consumption, Prices, and Expenditures*, p. 84; *Historical Statistics*, B 448–52.

34. US Department of Agriculture, *Food and Nutrient Intakes of Individuals in One Day in the United States, Spring 1977* (Sept. 1980), p. 24. For the groups listed, the average intake of the nutrient was below 70% of the 1980 RDA. In addition, calcium intake was below 90% of the RDA for females above age eight years; magnesium intake was below 90% of the RDA for all persons above age eight years; and vitamin B6 intake was below 90% of the RDA for all males above age 18 years and females above eight years.

35. The survey was based on a 24-hour dietary recall of the day preceding the interview. USDA, *Food and Nutrient Intakes*, p. 84, Tables 3.6; USDA, *Food Consumption, Prices, and Expenditures*, Table 39.

36. USDA 'Nutritive Level of Food . . .' The average household's consumption of calcium and vitamin B6 was 125% of the RDA with one-third of the households consuming too little calcium and vitamin B6. Consumption of calcium, magnesium, and vitamin B6 rose with income until income reached $16,000; iron consumption was higher, and fairly uniform, for families with incomes above $6,000. *Food and Nutrient Intakes*, Tables 3.5, 3.6.

37. Among low-income households, 48% of Food Stamp participants met the RDA in all nutrients compared to 38% for non-participants

in 1977–8. The biggest differences were in vitamins A, B6, B12, C, and thiamin. The differences are even more striking for people living in the central city, where 51% of the participants compared to 39% of the nonparticipants met the RDA in all nutrients. Non-metropolitan households showed no nutritional differences by status in the Food Stamp Program. US Department of Agriculture, 'Food Consumption and Dietary Levels of Low-Income House-holds, Nov. 1977–Mar. 1978,' *Nationwide Food Consumption Survey 1977–78*, Preliminary Report No. 8, Tables 9, 10. In 1965, 36% of families with incomes below $3,000 had diets that supplied less than two-thirds of the RDA for at least one nutrient. US Congress, 'Nutritive Quality of Diets, USA,' 1968 and USDA *Food Consumption, Prices, and Expenditures*, p. 84.

Between 1948 and 1974, the RDA was reduced for protein, calcium, riboflavin, niacin, and vitamin C along with vitamin A for children and women. The RDA for iron was increased for women and children but reduced for men. The caloric requirements in 1974 were equivalent to the 1948 requirements for a sedentary woman and to the average of the 1948 requirements for a sedentary and physically active man. In 1968, RDA for six more nutrients were added (vitamins E, B6, B12, phosphorus, iodine, and magnesium). Only minor modifications were made in 1980, except for higher vitamin C, iodine and vitamin B6 requirements. National Research Council, *Recommended Dietary Allowances*, Washington, DC, various dates.

38. US Department of Health, Education, and Welfare, *Anthropometric and Clinical Findings*, 'Preliminary Findings of the First Health and Nutrition Examination Survey: US, 1971–72,' Publication No. (HRA) 75-1229. Definitions of lean and obese were based on the triceps skinfold measurement.

39. Income elasticities were high (i.e., > 0.39) for roast beef, steak, lamb, turkey, yogurt, fresh fruit (other than apples, oranges, bananas), lettuce, frozen fruit juice, frozen vegetables, vegetable juice, candy and chewing gum, sodas other than cola, prepared snack foods, alcohol, and fresh cakes. Income elasticities were highly negative (i.e., < 0.14 or < −0.14) for prepared baby foods, organ meats, chicken, flour and prepared mixes, rice and pasta, sugar, white bread. The income elasticity for white potatoes was −0.07. Larry E. Salathe, 'Household Expenditure Patterns in the United States.'

40. The USDA estimated that four-person families with incomes between $6,000 to $9,000 could afford the USDA 'low-cost' diet (costing $2,440); with $9,000 to $15,000, the 'moderate-cost' diet ($3,183); and with incomes above $15,000, the 'liberal' diet ($4,020). Incomes are in 1974 dollars and food costs are for Autumn 1973.

The USDA food budgets were based on food prepared at home. The BLS food budgets adjusted the USDA food budgets to include food away from home. Betty Peterkin, 'Food Plans and Family Budgeting,' *Family Economics Review*, Spring 1975, pp. 9–10; and Jean Brackett, 'Urban Family Budgets Updated to Autumn 1973,' *Monthly Labor Review*, Aug. 1974, p. 57.

41. Cynthia Cromwell and Bernice McGeary, 'Economic Meals for a Month,' *Family Economics Review*, Fall 1975, p. 11.

42. See, for example, Constance Ward, 'Better Diets Possible by Shifting Expenditure Pattern,' *Family Economics Review*, December 1970.

43. The amounts of food included 3 cups grains, 12 pieces bread, $1\frac{1}{2}$ cups milk, 1 cup juice, 1 cup vegetables, 1 small potato, 2T sweetening and 3T margarine. Betty B. Peterkin, 'The Dietary Goals and Food on the Table,' *Family Economics Review*, Spring 1978, pp. 11, 21.

44. US BLS, *Three Standards of Living for an Urban Family of Four Persons, Spring 1967*, Bulletin No. 1570–5, Washington, DC, 1969. The standards issued for 1973 did not list individual clothing standards by age and sex, so these were calculated from the 1967 standards using the CPI. Another calculation of clothing costs by USDA was based on actual expenditure patterns for income groups defined on the basis of their spending sufficient money to meet USDA food plans at three income levels (economy, low cost, and moderate). Compared to the BLS standards, the USDA low-cost clothing budget was about 11% higher for males and 32% higher for females; the USDA moderate budget was about 33% higher for all groups. Wives not in the labor force were estimated to spend about the same on clothing as their husbands, while employed wives were calculated to spend more than their husbands (34% more for the moderate budget and 14% more for the low cost budget.) Girls, especially teenaged, were calculated to spend 25%–40% more than boys on clothing. Teenaged boys spent almost as much as their fathers, and teenaged girls spent almost as much as their employed mothers.

45. Rental values should implicitly include forgone interest on principal paid. However, owners reap inflationary gains, and so at least part of the forgone interest is seldom seen as a cost. Rapid inflation of housing prices, however, will cause a wide divergence in out-of-pocket costs by age of owner.

46. The estimated rental values compared to the estimated market price are high (15%) for low-income and low (8%) for senior owners. Employed owners reported average estimated rental value equal to 9% of estimated market value.

47. In 1970, three in four families with a male head under 25 years and two in three one-person households were renters. More than half the renters consisted of households with one or two persons. Lucie

G. Krassa, 'Rental Housing in the United States,' *Family Economics Review*, Winter 1974, p. 11, and US Bureau of the Census, *1974 Annual Housing Survey*, Series H150, Part A.

48. US Bureau of the Census, *1950 Census of Housing*, Vol. 1; *1974 Annual Housing Survey*, Series H 150, Part A.

49. US Bureau of the Census, *1970 Census of Housing*, Vol. 1, Part 1; Office of Management and Budget, *Social Indicators, 1973*, US Government Office, Washington, DC, 1973, Table 6.6.

50. US Bureau of the Census, *1950 Census of Housing, 1970 Census of Housing*, and *1974 Annual Housing Survey*.

51. Percentages were calculated using average expenditures divided by percent homeowners.

52. Salaried owners were only slightly more likely than laborer owners to do some exterior painting (23% against 21%), but they were much more likely to make plumbing repairs (18% against 12%). This most likely indicates their larger number of bathrooms and more complex devices such as hot tubs or Jacuzzis.

53. This comparison is between families who paid these bills. However, one-fifth of low-income families had their utility bills included in rent, which made their utility expenses appear smaller than the actual value.

54. Although child care expenses are recorded separately from baby-sitting, fewer than 1% of families reported having a child in a child care center. Such expenses for school-age children are recorded under education.

55. Gasoline cost 3.03¢ per mile and oil cost 0.19¢ per mile. *Statistical Abstract, 1975*, Table 957.

56. The buying patterns are consistent with the following scenario: The average salaried family bought a new vehicle every five years, and the working-class family every eight years. On average, the salaried family bought a used vehicle three years old and drove it for four years; the working-class family's bought a five-year-old used car and drove it for four years. The low-income family rarely bought a new car; they bought a seven- to eight-year-old used car and drove it for seven years.

57. John P. Robinson, 'Changes in America's Use of Time, 1965–1975,' Communication Research Center, Cleveland State University, 1977.

58. Clair Brown, 'An Institutional Model of Wives' Work Decisions,' *Industrial Relations*, 24, 2, Spring 1985, p. 189. These figures use 1968 data.

59. Clair Brown, 'Women's Economic Contribution to the Family,' in Ralph Smith, ed., *The Subtle Revolution*, Washington, DC: The Urban Institute, 1979, p. 194.

60. Bureau of the Census, *Social Indicators*, 1973, Table 7.8.

61. Bureau of the Census, *Social Indicators, 1976*, 1977, Tables 10.1, 10.4, 10.5.
62. Ibid.
63. The 1973 vacation data did not have the same limitations as the 1950 vacation data. Expenses for automobile and other travel associated with vacations are itemized under vacation travel (rather than in the transportation category). Food and lodging are treated in a similar manner. Vacation home expenses include maintenance and repairs, taxes, insurance, and utilities.
64. *Social Security Bulletin*, various issues.
65. *Statistical Abstract*, 1975, p. 298.
66. Nationally, 36% of the poor did not have a health plan (Medicaid, Medicare, or private insurance).
67. Nationally, 70% of all workers had insurance for hospital/surgical care, and 67% for regular medical care; 33% had major medical. Medium to large employers provided almost universal coverage (95%–97%); 90%–93% provided medical coverage; 72%–92% provided major medical; 10%–12% provided dental coverage. *Social Security Bulletin*, various issues.
68. Although the CES data show 65% salaried families and 56% low-income families having some insurance coverage, other data show 1970 hospital coverage to resemble the much broader range of coverage in 1950, from 40% for low-income (under $3,000) families to 90% for high-income (over $15,000) families. Marjorie S. Mueller, 'Private Health Insurance in 1971,' *Social Security Bulletin*, February 1973, and *Social Indicators*, 1973, Table 1.28.
69. Private insurance covered 40% of personal care expenditures, including 75% of hospital costs and 49% of physician services in 1973. *Social Security Bulletin* 38(2), February 1975.
70. Public Health Service, *Health, United States, 1975*.
71. The assumption made in calculating the budgets was that 30% of the families paid the full cost of the insurance, 26% paid half cost, and 44% paid zero cost. US Bureau of Labor Statistics, *Three Standards of Living for an Urban Family of Four Persons, Spring 1967*, Bulletin 1570–5, 1969, pp. 44–5, 64.
72. Bernard and Susan Rifkin, *American Labor Sourcebook* (New York: McGraw Hill, 1979), pp. 2–60.
73. The CES data are not a good source for absolute saving rates, because they calculate savings as a residual and do not have controls to check savings against more reliable data. However, they can be used to indicate changes over time in the proportion of the family's net income that is not earmarked for spending.
74. *Historical Statistics*, Series B 118–19, and *Statistical Abstract, 1976*, Table 87.

75. UI shows less variation since it has a floor and a ceiling on benefits that keep weekly payments within a narrow range. This is less true of disability payments.

76. Withholding includes both retirement (FICA) and hospital insurance (Medicare), as well as government retirement programs for Federal government employees and railroad workers. The Social Security payroll tax rose from 1.5% on the first $3,000 of earnings in 1950 to 5.85% on $10,800, and the proportion of the workforce covered rose from 57% to 82%.

77. The BLS lower budget allowed a higher standard of living than the BLS City Workers' budget used in 1950 for basics. For example, some food away from home is allowed in the former but not the latter. Therefore, the 1973 basics were higher than the 1950 basics before the adjustments mentioned here were made.

78. The new standard reflects spending by members of laborer families. Boys' and girls' expenditures are on average of the two age groups. These same relative reductions were also made in the BLS intermediate and higher budgets. The dependency budget does not increase the wife's expenditures.

79. Scientifically determined standards of adequacy were used for food-at-home and shelter components; for other components, data on actual spending patterns from 1960–1 CES with statistical procedure (quantity–income–elasticity technique) were used to estimate when families stop buying 'more' and start buying 'better.' The budgets were priced directly in 1969; price updates have been done since 1969 with the CPI. See 'Bureau of Labor Statistics Family Budget Program,' *The Measure of Poverty*, Technical Paper IV, US Department of Health, Education, and Welfare, 1977. Other sources include: Department of Labor, Bureau of Labor Statistics, 'Three Standards of Living for an Urban Family of Four Persons, Spring 1967' Bulletin 1570–5, 1969; 'Three Budgets for an Urban Family of Four Persons, 1969–70,' Supplement to Bulletin 1570–5, 1972; 'Three Budgets for a Retired Couple in Urban Areas of the United States, 1967–68,' Bulletin 1570–6, 1970; 'Three Budgets for a Retired Couple in Urban Areas of the United States,' Supplement to Bulletin 1570–6, 1971.

80. Expenses for lodging, transportation, and food while on vacation are included under their respective categories. The lower BLS standard was adjusted to allow a bi-annual inexpensive vacation. Together, vacations and tobacco account for about 40% of the CES family budgets. Because of its fixed-cost nature, tobacco as a proportion of the recreation budget declined in importance with class, from 26% for low income to 14% for salaried families. A luxury, vacations as a proportion of the recreation budget rose in

importance with class, from 19% for low-income to 27% for salaried families.

81. This includes those paying for lodging or for all-expense trips.

82. This uses the unadjusted BLS lower budget standards for shelter (all renters), transportation (lower car ownership), and recreation (no lodging on vacation).

83. For our low-income household, 54% reported no wage or salary income (excludes self-employed). In 1973, 38% of poor families had no earners. *CPR*, P-68, No. 98 (Jan. 1975).

84. Food uses the USDA economy plan; housing assumes only renters (no home ownership); transportation assumes only public transportation and no car ownership; and recreation includes a vacation without lodging; household operations assumes everyone has basic phone service.

7 Living With Technological Change and Economic Stagnation, 1988

Introduction

Expectations that the standard of living would continue its rapid rise across all classes had become the norm. The rate of economic growth achieved during the three decades following World War II, however, was difficult to maintain. When expectations continued to be disappointed, especially for low-income and working-class families, people found themselves feeling less well off than might be indicated by their actual living standards. In 1973, the country still had hopes of eradicating poverty and of children attaining a better education and a higher standard of living than their parents. The United States did not question that its economy would continue to dominate the world economy, and its citizens consume a disproportionate share of the world's resources, even in the presence of the control by the Organization of Petroleum Exporting Countries (OPEC) of world oil prices. In addition, the country felt an obligation to maintain world-wide economic order and to aid developing economies. A burgeoning Federal budget deficit helped to mask some of these changes as lower taxes were not matched by lower spending. Social conflict over the income distribution grew steadily. By the 1990s, middle- and lower-income groups were voicing widespread discontent about both economic performance and fairness. In 1993, the Reagan/Bush economic program was replaced by the Clinton program, which promised to reduce the deficit by higher taxes on 'the rich,' to provide universal health care coverage, and to provide more high-skill jobs.

Low growth rates, coupled with related problems such as pollution, congestion, and crime, placed real constraints on the country's ability to maintain large and growing defense and social programs as well as a continually rising standard of living in terms of smaller households, increased homeownership, more automobiles per family, and a burgeoning array of leisure time pursuit. Families attempted, with some success, to overcome these constraints by increasing labor force participation, especially through wives' working, and by increasing their net liabilities. The national participation rate rose from 61% in 1973 to 66% in 1988 even as the proportion of seniors working declined. Expenditures as a percentage of income rose between 1973 and 1988, while net borrowing also rose. In addition, the government borrowed to finance a growing proportion of its budget, and the country increased its indebtedness to the rest of the world through trade.

Mediocre economic performance, especially in productivity growth, between the early 1970s and the late 1980s meant that family incomes did not grow as rapidly as in the previous survey period. The increased strength of our trading partners, especially Germany and Japan, and the decreased willingness of the people to pay for government services, coupled with an extraordinary rise in military and civilian demands upon the government, resulted in the United States incurring large trade deficits and large Federal government deficits. Monetary policy was used to keep inflation in check. High interest rates constrained private investment in research and development and real capital, while output in key manufacturing sectors such as automobiles, steel, and consumer electronics, declined as imports captured market share. Unprecedented government deficits swallowed up puny personal savings. Private investment was channelled into highly profitable mergers and leveraged buyouts and away from investment in research, development, and capital equipment. The productivity rate of the economy slowed dramatically and real wages stagnated or declined.

Average real hourly wages fell 11% between 1973 and 1988, and weekly wages fell even further (17%).[1] Many families offset this decline by increasing the wife's participation. But even as consumption norms were requiring families to have two incomes, the growth of families with only one adult was increasing. Families had watched their median incomes (constant dollars) almost double between 1950 and 1973, but increase only 7% between 1973 and 1988 (see table 1.1).

One-third of families belonged to the salaried class and another one-third to the wage-earner class. The laborer class continued to account for only one-seventh of families. Laborer families' incomes remained only slightly higher than that of farmers and fell behind relative to wage earners. Meanwhile, wage-earner families' income fell further behind the income of the growing number of families headed by clerical and sales workers.

Table 7.1A Family budgets, 1988

	Poor		Laborer		Wage earner		Salaried		Seniors	
	(CES)	% of total	(CES)	% of total	(CES)	% of total	(CES)	% of total	(CES)	% of total
Annual expenditure	$14,363	100.0%	$25,508	100.0%	$32,781	100.0%	$44,624	100.0%	$18,091	100.0%
Average family size	3.04		2.63		2.91		3.11		1.83	
Homeowners	34%		52%		69%		84%		77%	
Without vehicle	47%		16%		11%		9%		21%	
With 2 + vehicles	16%		34%		42%		56%		23%	
Food and alcohol	$3,070	21.4%	$3,925	15.4%	$4,609	14.1%	$5,541	12.4%	$3,081	17.0%
Away from home	13.7%		26.6%		28.4%		29.9%		20.8%	
Clothing	$610	4.2%	$1,172	4.6%	$1,526	4.7%	$2,121	4.8%	$600	3.3%
Shelter $	5,001	34.8	7,757	30.4	9,162	27.9	12,282	27.5	5,446	30.1
Housing	2,682	18.7	4,496	17.6	5,071	15.5	6,918	15.5	2,512	13.9
Fuel and utilities	947	6.6	1,110	4.4	1,318	4.0	1,586	3.6	1,209	6.7
Furnishings	334	2.3	680	2.7	972	3.0	1,639	3.7	528	2.9
Household operations	1,039	7.2	1,470	5.8	1,801	5.5	2,139	4.8	1,197	6.6
Miscellaneous $	5,682	39.6	12,654	49.6	17,483	53.3	24,681	55.3	8,964	49.5
Transportation	2,108	14.7	4,486	17.6	6,496	19.8	7,576	17.0	2,637	14.6
Recreation and education	1,377	9.8	2,352	9.3	3,058	9.3	5,155	11.6	1,396	8.3
Medical care	775	5.4	1,002	3.9	1,177	3.6	1,389	3.1	2,268	12.5
Personal care	205	1.4	373	1.5	437	1.3	604	1.4	306	1.7
Gifts and contributions	505	3.5	1,683	6.6	2,223	6.8	3,316	7.4	1,383	7.6
Insurance	373	2.6	2,204	8.6	3,395	10.4	5,414	12.1	433	2.4
Other	339	2.4	555	2.2	697	2.1	1,227	2.7	540	3.0
Personal taxes, taxes/gross Y $	185	2.9	1,748	7.2	3,119	9.2	5,311	10.0	441	2.7
Expenditure, exp./net income $/%	14,363	234.9	25,508	113.5	32,781	106.1	44,624	93.7	18,091	113.6
Family income after taxes $	6,115		22,484		30,903		47,613		15,926	
Family income before taxes $[a]	6,300		24,232		34,022		52,924		16,367	

[a] Family incomes are adjusted to equal income after taxes plus personal taxes.

Table 7.1B   Employer provided benefits, 1950–88

	1950	1973	1988
Total compensation ($ million)	155,339	812,839	2,907,664
	100.0%	100.0%	100.0%
Total wages and salaries (%)	94.7	87.1	83.5
Estimated pay for time not worked	7.6	10.7	12.0
Non-wage and salary compensation (%)	5.3	12.9	16.5
Employer contributions to social insurance[a]			
Private	2.1	4.3	5.4
Government	0.8	2.5	3.2
Private pension, profit sharing	1.1	2.6	1.7
Group health insurance	0.5	2.3	4.6
Other[b]	0.8	1.2	1.6
Total benefits (non-wage compensation and paid time off) (%):	12.9	23.6	28.5

[a] Social insurance includes payroll taxes for OASDHI, state and Federal UI, RR and UI, government employee UI and retirement, military medical insurance, publicly administered workers' compensation.
[b] Other is primarily private workers' compensation and life insurance.
Sources: For 1950 and 1973, *National Income Product Accounts of the U.S., 1929–1982*, Tables 6.4B, 6.5B, 6.12, 6.13. For 1988, *Survey of Current Business*, Vol. 69, No. 7, Tables 6.4B, 6.5B, 6.12, 6.13

Fringe benefits were rising more rapidly than wages, which meant that employers' labor costs were rising faster than wages. Paid time off, payroll taxes, pensions, and health insurance rose from absorbing 13% of total compensation in 1950 to absorbing 24% in 1973 and 29% in 1988 (see table 7.1B). Health insurance costs doubled from 2.3% (1973) to 4.6% (1988) of total compensation. As various benefits competed in employers' stringent budgets, many private pension plans were scaled back, and pensions fell from 2.6% to 1.7% of total compensation. The most expensive fringe benefit, paid time off, accounted for 12% of total compensation in 1988, while employer payroll taxes for social security, unemployment insurance, and worker's compensation accounted for 9%.[2]

The distribution of income

The slow-down in economic growth and in wage growth seemed to intensify the struggle over income distribution as well as popular opposition to taxes. As people's expectations for rising living standards crumbled, they became less willing to pay for public services and income support for the poor in their attempt to protect their consumption of private goods and services. In addition, families tried to work more hours; leisure was seen as expendable when incomes were declining or not meeting expected increases. The ongoing conflict in the labor market over distribution of income was resolved during this period of slow productivity growth in favor of slowly rising earnings for college graduates and declining earnings for high school graduates and dropouts. The economic distance between the working and salaried classes widened, and the laborer class found its opportunities and living standards shrinking.

Deep divisions within the society by race and ethnicity became visible as the economic plight of minorities worsened. The economic and social segregation of the underclass increased, and the chasm between the haves and the have-nots widened. Disenchanted with the results of the War on Poverty programs, threatened by mediocre performance of the domestic economy, overwhelmed by massive Federal government and trade deficits, and mindful that other countries' economies were closing the gap, Americans turned inward in an effort to protect what they had. From the vantage point of the late 1980s, 1973 appeared to be the end of a golden era of high economic performance and social if not political cohesiveness.

Real per capita disposable income rose only 25% between 1973 and 1988, after rising 56% between 1960 and 1973.[3] Economically, the post-1973 period resembled the 1950s, when real disposable income per capita had risen only 14% during the decade. However, the 1950s had followed two decades of enormous hardships from depression and international war; families were relieved to have a stable economy and a chance to spend their wartime savings.

The post-1973 period was different, since families hoped to combine a peacetime economy with continued high levels of economic and wage growth. Because of President Reagan's defense build-up, however, defense accounted for as large a part (6%) of GNP in 1988 as it had in 1973 at the end of the Vietnam conflict. Tax cuts under Reagan required that the growth in defense and social programs be paid through budget deficits. Consumers were not asked to reduce their spending in order to pay for rising Federal expenditures, and so consumption rose from 62% of GNP in 1973 to 66% in 1988. Personal savings fell from 8.2% of disposable income in 1973 to 4.2% in 1988. Taxes as a share of personal income remained fairly constant and absorbed about 19% of income in both 1973 and 1988. Meanwhile, taxpayer revolts at local and state levels resulted in holding the line on rising government expenditures, since state and local governments do not have the ability to finance operating deficits. Overall, state and local governments' share of GNP fell slightly from 13% in 1973 to 12% in 1988.[4]

Social welfare expenditures (constant dollars, excluding education) rose 45% between 1973 and 1988 to average $2,301 for every man, woman, and child in 1988. Transfer payments had increased from 9.8% of personal income in 1973 to 14.4% in 1988. Yet poverty rates had remained stubbornly resistant to falling below the 11% rate of 1973, after being halved during the heady social policy days of the 1960s. Reliance on economic growth to 'trickle down' to low-income families as the rising tide lifted all ships no longer seemed to hold. The economic expansion of the 1980s created many new jobs, but the job expansion was disproportionately at the lower end of the wage spectrum. Earnings became more unequal as the earnings of high school dropouts fell 7% and the earnings of college graduates rose 8% between 1978 and 1987.[5]

This increase in earnings inequality resulted in the poverty rate increasing during the 1980s, even as output grew. A rise of 1% in GNP during 1983–9 raised incomes of families in the bottom quintile by $30 and of families in the top quintile by $473. Economic growth had been more widely shared in 1963–9, when a rise of 1% in GNP raised incomes of families in the bottom quintile by $70 and in the top quintile by $348.[6]

Even as the labor market was signaling the need for young people to stay in school longer and to obtain more technical skills,[7] their response was divided along gender and race lines. The percentage of young men (18–21 years old) attending college rose slightly from 34% in 1973 to 37% in 1988, while the percentage for young women increased substantially from 28% to 42%. The gender differences were especially conspicuous by race. The percentage of young black males (18–21 years old) attending college fell from 22% in 1973 to 21% in 1988, while the percentage of young black females attending college doubled from 17% to 34%.[8]

The education level of the population continued its increase, and the percentage attending college grew. In 1988, 41% of men had some college and another 36% were high school graduates; in 1970, only 25% had some college and another 30% were high school graduates. Women were as likely to have at least a high school diploma as men in both 1970 and 1988. Far behind men in attending college prior to World War II, they had made great strides in closing the gap and, as we saw above, young women had surpassed young men in college attendance. The proportion of women with some college was 34% in 1988, twice the 1973 rate. Although the rates for beginning college had risen, many college students (over 40% of males and 50% of females) dropped out before graduation.

The growing disparity in earnings by education and the improvements in Social Security benefits for seniors are reflected in the following income ranges for the three employed classes, senior and poor households:

Laborer:	$21,300–$26,600 (average $24,232)[9]
Wage earner:	$31,400–$36,000 (average $34,022)
Salaried:	$49,400–$56,900 (average $52,924)
Seniors:	$20,000–$24,000 (couple) $8,200–$9,800 (individual) } (average $16,367)

Poor: households below poverty thresholds[10] for single person ($6,155), two-person family ($7,958), three persons ($9,435), four persons ($12,092), five persons ($14,305), six persons ($16,149), seven persons ($18,248), eight persons ($20,279), nine or more persons ($24,133); median $6,300.

Working-class families fell in their relative income position. In 1973, laborer families were centered in the middle of the income distribution; in 1988, they were centered at the 45th percentile (see table 7.2). Wage-earner families fell even further in their relative income position. In 1988, they were centered at the 60th percentile, down from their position at the 70th percentile in 1973. Salaried families maintained their relative income position. By definition, poverty thresholds remain constant in real terms, although the relative position of those at the poverty threshold may shift within the income distribution. Since laborer families witnessed a decline in their real incomes between 1973 and 1988, the poverty threshold as a proportion of laborer family income rose from 0.34 in 1973 to 0.37 in 1988.

In real dollars, income for laborer families fell 9%, income for wage-earner families rose 13%, income for salaried families rose 21%, and income for seniors rose 42%. If the value of health insurance were included as income, incomes for employed families and seniors would have risen accordingly.

Table 7.2 Income distribution, 1988

	All households	Metropolitan families	White families	Black families
Number (000s)	92,830	50,573	56,492	7,409
Under $5,000	6.2	3.8	3.0	11.9
$5,000–9,999	10.8	6.1	5.5	15.4
$10,000–14,999	10.3	8.2	8.1	13.6
$15,000–24,999	18.6	16.3	17.7	19.7
$25,000–34,999	16.0	16.2	17.4	13.4
$35,000–49,999	17.3	20.2	21.0	13.3
$50,000–74,999	13.4	18.2	17.6	9.3
$75,000–99,999	4.2	6.3	5.6	2.0
$100,000 and over	3.2	4.7	4.2	1.3
	100.0	100.0	100.0	100.0
Median income	$27,225	$34,841	$33,915	$19,329
W/non-farm earnings	$27,280	NA	$34,127	$19,360
Husband/wife families	$36,436	NA	$36,840	$30,385

Numbers in % except where indicated.
Source: *CPR* P-60 No. 172.

Inequality increased across employed classes (see table 7.1A). Laborer incomes fell from 80% of wage-earner incomes in 1973 to 66% in 1988. Wage-earner incomes fell from 69% of salaried incomes in 1973 to 64% in 1988. Families sought to maintain their relative living standard, and their increases in spending partially offset the increased dispersions in income. Wage-earner families were able to maintain their 1988 expenditures at three-fourths of the level of salaried families, as in 1973. However, laborer families slipped in their standard of living relative to wage earners, although not by as much as the decline in their relative income. Surprisingly, poor families spent 58% as much as laborer families by spending considerably more than their reported incomes. The quality of the income data in 1988 is questionable as the proportion of unreported income appears to have grown considerably in the 1980s.

In 1988, virtually all jobs were legally covered by Social Security or a government retirement program. Not all employers obeyed the law, however, and some people were paid off-the-books. A Department of Labor study estimates that the underground economy exceeded $500 billion in 1992, or 10% of the reported economy.[11] Among the CES sample, the proportion of families who reported paying Social Security taxes exactly equaled the proportion reporting earnings in each group. This implies off-the-book earnings, i.e., those paid without payroll taxes or income taxes being withheld, were not reported in the CES.

Off-the-book earnings in both legal and illegal activities accounted for 21% of spending for a small sample of AFDC mothers, while AFDC and Food Stamp benefits covered 57% of actual spending. The remaining 22% of their spending was covered by money from relatives and friends.[12] Off-the-book earnings and money from others would help explain why expenditures are so much higher than income for the poor in our sample. The differences in expenditures as a proportion of earnings in 1973 and 1988 for low-income groups are remarkable, however. In 1988, the discrepancy between income and expenditures grew as reported incomes fell. For households with incomes below $5,000, expenditures averaged 4.6 times income.[13] Households in the bottom 20% of the income distribution spent twice as much as their reported incomes. This is consistent with the relationship between expenditures and welfare benefits of the AFDC mothers cited above. Households in the next 20% spent three-tenths more than their reported incomes. The two groups of lowest income households (below $5,000; between $5,000 and $10,000) both averaged about $11,000 in expenditures, which indicates that this is a norm for the lowest sustainable budget. As we will see, this expenditure level is close to the level of the dependency budget.

In the 1972–3 CES, expenditures were closer to reported incomes. The bottom 20% spent one-half more than their reported income; the lowest

10% had expenditures twice their income, and the next 10% had expenditures 1.3 times their income.[14]

Earnings accounted for only 45% of poor families' income (see table 7.3). Another 20% was provided by Social Security. In contrast, 89%–96% of employed families' income was earned. For seniors, pensions (two-thirds Social Security and one-third private) accounted for 58% of income. Earnings and interest from savings were their next largest sources of income.

Household composition and work roles

The translation of income into a standard of living depends upon who is sharing the income and life-style. As we saw in the previous chapter, the fragmentation of families and the proliferation of single-person households constrain the growth of living standards since people forgo economies of scale in shelter and transportation in order to purchase privacy and control. Purchasing privacy by buying a bigger house is apparent when comparing families, but purchasing privacy becomes hidden when it is done through setting up more households. Yet the costs associated with maintaining more and smaller households is real and one that people control through their family formation.

Even as income growth slowed, the fragmentation of the family accelerated, and single-person households and single-mother families dramatically increased their relative importance between 1970 and 1990. By 1988, one in four households were single people (up from one in six in 1973). This trend reflected the rising age at first marriage, which had increased by three years for both men and women between 1970 and 1990, and the rising divorce rate, which had tripled the number of divorced people per 1,000 married persons from 47 in 1970 to 142 in 1990.[15] Adults were spending more of their years living alone before marriage, after becoming divorced, and in retirement after the death of a spouse.[16] In 1990, households averaged 2.6 people, or 0.5 fewer than in 1973. The family size of all three classes of employed families decreased by 0.3 persons between 1973 and 1988. However, poor families increased in average size from 2.76 people in 1973 to 3.04 people in 1988.

Between 1940 and 1970, the proportion of families headed by single mothers had hovered near 10%, but the formation of families headed by single mothers grew dramatically during the next two decades to account for 16.5% of families as the divorce rate climbed and as more women, especially black, had children outside marriage. The rapid rise in families headed by single mothers made it more difficult for economic growth to reduce poverty, since families are much more likely to be poor without the resources of two parents. In 1988, 38% of the poor lived in single-mother families, up from 29% in 1973.[17]

Table 7.3 Sources of income, 1988

	Poor		Laborer		Wage earner		Salaried		Senior	
	Amount ($)	% rep.	Amount ($)	% rep.	Amount ($)	% rep.	Amount ($)	% rep.	Amount ($)	% rep.
Total family income[a]	6,144	100.0	24,037	100.0	33,756	100.0	52,631	100.0	16,289	100.0
Earnings	2,739	55.1	21,366	95.5	32,078	99.3	50,462	99.9	1,994	27.2
Income from non-farm business	118	6.0	703	10.4	1,378	9.2	2,835	16.9	163	4.9
Income other than earnings	3,405	74.1	2,671	51.9	1,678	54.3	2,169	62.3	14,295	98.8
Income from boarders	4	0.2	44	1.7	40	1.4	40	0.8	52	1.4
Dividends, royalties, etc.	15	1.1	110	6.8	66	6.2	304	12.7	190	10.9
Interest on savings account	26	8.7	277	30.8	253	37.4	400	46.9	1,057	48.6
Rental income	(4)	0.9	16	2.2	7	3.3	106	5.5	63	2.6
Net amount from sale of stock	0	0.0	117	1.1	44	1.1	257	1.8	29	0.5
Pensions/Social Security	1,206	26.4	703	8.7	361	4.9	245	4.0	9,463	97.8
Amount received from pensions	98	3.2	717	8.7	493	5.9	488	6.1	3,171	57.5
Alimony/child support	157	9.7	372	8.2	167	6.9	271	5.9	106	2.4
Food Stamps	593	35.4	28	1.3	3	0.3	6	0.4	12	1.9
Unemployment compensation	76	4.3	112	5.7	126	6.3	72	5.1	1	0.2
Public assistance or welfare	919	23.7	74	1.5	3	0.4	0	0.0	11	0.9
Suppsec checks	231	10.9	59	1.2	23	0.9	17	1.3	92	3.7
Lump sum payments	239	2.5	340	6.2	118	5.2	459	3.5	129	4.1
Receipts excluded from income	245	4.6	353	10.8	142	12.6	497	11.5	156	10.4
Other money income	22	1.5	37	1.7	4	1.0	132	4.1	0	0.0

[a] This income figure is calculated to equal earnings plus income other than earnings.

Many wives went to work to offset the stagnation of their husband's earning power rather than to take advantage of improvements in their labor market opportunities, as had been the case in the 1950–73 period.[18] By 1988, female participation rates had finally passed the 50% mark, and almost three-fourths of women aged 20–45 years old, including those with school-aged children (over six years old), were in the labor market. The most significant change was in the employment of wives with young children (under six years old). A majority (57%) worked in 1988, compared to only one in three in 1973.[19] The social norm had finally completed its transition from having mothers of young children stay at home to having them work at least part-time. Among teenagers, girls were as likely to work as boys, whose participation had declined from 62% in 1973 to 57% in 1988.

As we have seen, the labor market in 1988 presented considerably diminished opportunities compared to the 1973 labor market in terms of wages paid and job vacancies. For working-class families, 1988 is the first survey year since 1935 that the number of earners declined – from 1.5 in 1973 to 1.3 in 1988 for laborers and from 1.8 to 1.6 for wage earners. Salaried families were able to expand their advantageous access to jobs, and their average numbers of workers rose from 2.1 in 1973 to 2.2 in 1988 (see table 1.2).

Consumption patterns

Families could not increase their living standards as rapidly as they had in the previous two decades,[20] yet innovations resulting from applications of micro-electronics presented the consumer with significant improvements in a wide array of goods, such as automobiles, home appliances, audio-visual equipment, and telecommunications. Expenditures on medical care exploded from 8% of GNP in 1973 to 11% in 1988, partially because of expensive investments in innovative big-ticket equipment for diagnosis and treatment. Still, access to health care did not improve, and a large number of people still received limited or no health care. The budget patterns studied here diverge from the national expenditure pattern because employed families, who usually received health care through insurance or Medicare, spent only a small fraction (4%) of their budgets on health care. Seniors spent 12.5% of their budgets on health care.

With slow income growth, families reduced relative expenditures for the traditional goods of food and clothing in order to buy new or improved goods and services, especially in transportation and recreation. The proportion of homeowners remained at 64% in both 1973 and 1988. Nationally, consumer expenditures for transportation and housing maintained the same share in 1988 as in 1973, and recreation's share rose slightly.[21]

For the wage earner, food took a declining share of the budget (from 19% in 1973 to 14% in 1988), and clothing fell from 5.4% to 4.7%. The other traditional category, housing, rose from 15% to 16%. Spending for mobility and leisure time continued to rise, and transportation and recreation rose from 26% of the budget in 1973 to 29% in 1988.

Spending on information and communication became much more important as it expanded from buying telephone service and television sets to purchasing electronic audio-visual equipment, cable television service, and computers. From 1918 to 1988, we witnessed families incorporating technology into their lives in ways that dramatically change the ways they live and the ways they are economically separated from each other. In 1918, families were still in an age of physical subsistence, provided by food and clothing and shelter, but they were entering an age of mobility, provided by the automobile. In the current period, we see families entering an age of information and communication, which requires electronic hardware and the knowledge to use it. Exactly how the electronic revolution will affect everyday life remains to unfold, but we can anticipate that the impact will be at least as great as the revolution brought by the automobile.

Diet

The dramatic decline in food's share of the budget that occurred in the previous decades had come to an end. Families could no longer depend on a relatively shrinking food budget to release money to spend on more discretionary items. However, food expenditures themselves had become more discretionary as families paid for the convenience and social experience provided by eating away from home. Having meals and snacks away from home continued to increase in importance as a part of daily life. The proportion of families eating out increased considerably between 1973 and 1988 – from 66% to 88% for laborer families, from 80% to 94% for salaried, and from 34% to 71% for seniors (see tables 6.4, 7.4). Even 55% of poor families ate out sometimes. compared to 33% of low-income families in 1973. As eating some meals out had become the social norm, differences in the proportion of families dining out had diminished. The frequency and the quality of restaurant meals still separated classes, however. For those families who did have restaurant meals, poor families spent only three-fifths as much as laborer families, and salaried families spent two-fifths more than laborer families. Eating and drinking at home still consumed most of the food and alcohol budgets – from 86% for poor families to 73% for working-class families and 70% for salaried families.

Even as families had more restaurant meals, children were eating fewer school-prepared meals. This most likely reflects the children's preferences

Table 7.4 Food and alcohol expenditures[a], 1988

	Poor			Laborer			Wage earner			Salaried			Senior		
	Avg. exp. ($)	% rep.	Cost ($)	Avg. exp. ($)	% rep.	Cost ($)	Avg. exp. ($)	% rep.	Cost ($)	Avg. exp. ($)	% rep.	Cost ($)	Avg. exp. ($)	% rep.	Cost ($)
Food and alcohol[b]	3,070	99.3	3,091	3,925	100.0	3,925	4,609	100.0	4,609	5,541	100.0	5,541	3,081	99.3	3,103
Total food and alcohol at home	2,647	98.8	2,680	2,882	99.8	2,888	3,300	99.8	3,306	3,885	99.9	3,889	2,440	99.3	2,456
Total food and alcohol away from home[b]	422	62.1	679	1,043	93.0	1,122	1,309	94.1	1,391	1,656	97.8	1,694	640	76.8	833
Food	2,947	99.3	2,969	3,616	100.0	3,616	4,225	100.0	4,225	5,119	100.0	5,119	2,963	99.3	2,983
Food at home	2,578	98.6	2,614	2,736	99.6	2,747	3,145	99.7	3,153	3,680	99.7	3,692	2,364	99.1	2,385
Food away from home[c]	369	61.3	602	880	92.4	952	1,080	93.8	1,152	1,440	97.3	1,479	598	74.9	799
Alcohol	109	29.8	365	283	60.6	467	307	62.1	494	356	71.5	498	109	32.9	332
Total alcohol at home	69	24.3	283	146	49.1	298	155	50.4	308	205	61.5	333	75	23.9	315
Alcohol away from home[c]	40	13.8	287	137	37.3	367	152	39.2	387	151	50.6	299	34	12.8	265
Food and alcohol on out of town trips[d]	14	2.4	120	26	5.9	96	77	7.5	218	65	8.2	170	8	2.8	65
Selected details															
Food and non-alcoholic beverages from grocery store	2,421	97.8	2,475	2,491	99.1	2,512	2,863	99.6	2,873	3,391	99.4	3,410	2,225	99.1	2,244
Food and non-alcoholic beverages from convenience/specialty store	157	27.4	575	245	38.2	642	282	41.7	676	288	43.5	663	140	29.2	478
Dining at restaurants (no alcohol)	280	55.2	508	744	88.2	843	881	89.4	985	1,182	94.1	1,256	464	71.1	653
School meals	28	7.4	373	46	15.6	294	77	21.0	366	78	23.7	328	5	1.7	313
Food and board including school	24	1.3	1,880	25	1.5	1,724	33	1.8	1,850	21	2.8	744	2	0.2	1,188
Catered affairs	9	0.5	343	23	1.2	415	54	1.7	696	100	3.1	518	104	5.7	394
Meals provided as pay	29	2.2	1,274	42	4.2	998	36	3.5	1,035	59	1.8	3,266	22	0.7	3,240
Beer and wine for home use	56	22.9	244	120	47.3	254	124	48.2	256	158	60.2	263	42	18.9	224
Other alcohol for home use	13	6.8	195	26	13.8	191	32	13.8	230	46	21.5	216	33	11.2	292
Alcohol at restaurants	40	13.8	287	137	37.3	367	152	39.2	387	151	50.6	299	34	12.8	265

[a] Figures are for annual average expenditures, quarterly percentage reporting, and implicit annual costs.

[b] Includes food and alcohol on non-vacation out of town trips.

[c] Excludes food on non-vacation out of town trips.

[d] Non-vacation trips (excludes vacations and trips to relatives and friends).

Table 7.5A Food quantities (lbs) and unit prices (weekly)[a]

	Low income[b]			Laborer			Wage earner			Salaried		
	Avg. exp. ($)	Quant.	Unit price ($)	Avg. exp. ($)	Quant.	Unit price ($)	Avg. exp. ($)	Quant.	Unit price ($)	Avg. exp. ($)	Quant.	Unit price ($)
Food and alcohol total	60.22			91.47			102.38			124.07		
Food and alcohol at home	45.22			65.09			67.65			75.79		
Dairy	5.44	15.41	0.42	7.76	21.57	0.43	8.58	23.62	0.42	9.30	25.00	0.44
Protein	16.59	11.48	1.50	22.87	14.39	1.74	23.43	13.82	1.81	24.65	13.09	2.02
Fruits, vegetables	8.92	18.84	0.51	13.29	25.88	0.56	13.57	26.23	0.55	16.39	29.90	0.58
Grains	7.38	7.06	1.16	10.83	8.74	1.33	11.46	8.73	1.40	12.60	8.71	1.50
Fats, Oils	1.48	1.69	1.01	1.78	1.87	1.06	1.81	1.78	1.10	2.13	1.78	1.24
Miscellaneous[c]	6.39	5.44	2.15	9.20	8.56	1.77	9.27	9.67	0.90	11.20	10.82	1.56
Food away total (% of total)	14.80	(24.6%)		26.38	(28.8%)		34.73	(33.9%)		48.28	(38.9%)	
Size[d]	2.15			2.59			2.64			2.65		

[a] This table was calculated from the 1987–88 Nationwide Food Consumption Survey tapes by Don Rose. His assistance, plus extremely helpful advice from Suzanne Murphy, greatly improved the food section. The converted prices and quantities were used for all categories except grains. Quantities are in pounds.

[b] Low income includes households with incomes in the range of 0.9 to 1.1 times the poverty threshold.

[c] This is mostly sugar; also includes alcohol.

[d] Household size includes those present for meals at home, adjusted to adult equivalency.

for bag lunches over school lunches, even though their parents had less time to prepare bag lunches as they rushed to work.

The most luxurious item recorded in the food budgets was catered affairs. Like any luxury, a catered affair was expensive and rare. However, many more employed families reported having a catered affair in 1988 than in 1973, ranging from 1.2% of laborer families to 3.1% of salaried families. Surprisingly, seniors were the group most likely to host a catered affair, and one in seventeen seniors had one in 1988. The cost of this lavish event, which displayed a large variance, averaged over $2,000, which is over one-half of the average family's yearly food costs.

Variation by class

The National Food Consumption Survey of 1987–8 is used to compare food consumption across classes.[22] In the types of foods eaten at home, miscellaneous (mostly sugar products and alcohol) displayed the greatest variation across classes and grains the least variation (see table 7.5). Along with miscellaneous products, consumption of dairy products and fruits and vegetables increased with class status, while consumption of protein products and fats and oil decreased with class status.

Salaried families ate meals that included fairly large amounts of dairy products and fruits and vegetables as well as protein and sugar. Laborer and wage-earner families had very similar diets, which included more protein, fewer fruits and vegetables, and less sugar and dairy products

Table 7.5B Quantities (per equivalent adult), benchmarked to laborers (lbs)

	Low income	*Wage earner*	*Salaried*
Dairy	0.86	1.07	1.13
Protein	0.96	0.94	0.89
Fruits, vegetables	0.88	0.99	1.13
Grains	0.97	0.98	0.96
Fats, oils	1.10	0.93	0.92
Miscellaneous	0.76	1.11	1.23

Table 7.5C Prices benchmarked to laborers ($)

	Low income	*Wage earner*	*Salaried*
Dairy	0.98	0.98	1.02
Protein	0.86	1.04	1.16
Fruits, vegetables	0.91	0.98	1.04
Grains	0.83	1.05	1.13
Fats, oils	0.95	1.04	1.17
Miscellaneous	1.19	0.92	0.88
Expenditures per equivalent adult	0.79	1.10	1.33

than salaried families. Low-income families consumed less than working-class families of all food groups except fats and oils, which they used to compensate for their lower supply of calories from dairy and sugar products. Fats or oils supplied 20% more calories to low-income families than salaried families. Although salaried families did well nutritionally by consuming more fruits and vegetables and less fat and protein than working-class families, they still relied too much on sugar and too little on grains for their calories.

Price differences across classes were the greatest for protein and grain products and the lowest for dairy products. As salaried families were cutting down on protein, they were eating more expensive types. Although families were similar in the amount of grain they ate, salaried families were buying expensive products, and low-income families were economizing by buying inexpensive bakery products. In contrast, low-income families purchased expensive sweets and miscellaneous products; this was the only food group whose price declined with class status.

The Food Stamp Program did not increase poor families' consumption of food in 1988 as it had in 1973 for low-income families. Even though poor Food Stamp recipients received an average of $1,675 in Food Stamps, they spent only four-fifths as much on food as poor families who did not receive Food Stamps. The two groups spent almost an identical amount at the grocery store; but Food Stamp families spent 88% of their food budgets at the grocery store and non-Food Stamp families spent only 72% (see table 7.6). The families without Food Stamps ate out more and drank more alcohol, and these two activities could not be purchased with Food Stamps. Among poor families using Food Stamps, 43% spent an average of $263 on restaurant meals and 23% spent $266 on alcohol. In contrast, among poor families without Food Stamps, 62% spent an average of $594 on restaurant meals and 33% spent $432 on alcohol.

Why the Food Stamp Program appeared to increase the food expenditures for and improve the diets of poor families in 1973 but not in 1988 is unclear. The proportion of families receiving Food Stamps rose from 8.2% in 1973 to 9.8% in 1988, which reflects the rise in the poverty rate. Important changes were made in the program, however, which might have affected its impact on people's food buying. The requirement that eligible families receive Food Stamps equal in value to the USDA Thrifty Food Plan with their contribution determined by their income was changed. Since 1979, families pay no money and they receive Food Stamps equal to the difference between the Thrifty Food Plan and their former contribution. The net value of their Food Stamps did not change, and families can now spend their former Food Stamp contribution in any way they choose. Food Stamp families spent enough to purchase the Thrifty Food Plan, but that plan does not allow the 12% that low-income families spent on food away from home and alcohol.

Table 7.6 Food expenditures with and without Food Stamps, 1988

	Poor with Food Stamps			Poor without Food Stamps		
	Avg. exp. ($)	% rep.	Cost ($)	Avg. exp. ($)	% rep.	Cost ($)
Food and non-alcoholic beverage from grocery store	2,414.47	97.76	2,469.90	2,437.85	98.08	2,485.57
Food and non-alcoholic beverage from convenience specialty store	111.47	22.44	496.73	179.24	29.03	617.40
Food at home, total	2,525.94	98.18	2,572.85	2,630.04	99.00	2,656.57
Food on out of town trips	11.34	6.17	183.82	76.87	18.28	420.51
Food prepared by CU on out of town trips	2.18	1.12	194.50	12.95	5.61	230.99
Dining out at rest. (no alcohol)	112.21	42.64	263.18	366.81	61.75	594.01
School meals	12.71	4.63	274.55	36.54	9.14	399.76
Food away from home, total	138.45	47.69	290.33	546.08	68.66	795.30
Food/board including school	10.38	0.28	3,702.00	36.94	1.84	2,004.17
Catered affairs	0.81	0.28	290.00	8.52	0.69	1,232.89
Meals provided as pay	9.53	1.54	617.45	20.40	2.46	830.12
Food/alcohol away from home, total	20.72	2.10	985.07	65.87	4.84	1,361.27
Beer/wine for home use	39.30	18.79	209.13	70.60	25.27	279.40
Other alcohol for home use	5.03	3.51	143.36	17.81	8.83	201.67
Alcohol at home, total	44.33	19.21	230.72	88.41	26.88	328.90
Alcoholic beverage purchased on trips	0.62	1.12	55.50	6.75	5.76	117.09
Alcohol at restaurants	15.80	6.87	229.96	48.18	17.59	273.96
Alcohol away from home, total	16.43	7.85	209.14	54.93	20.20	271.93
Food/alcohol at home, total	2,570.27	98.32	2,614.27	2,718.46	99.23	2,739.50
Food/alcohol away, total	154.87	49.09	315.50	601.01	69.82	860.86
Food total	2,685.11	98.60	2,723.31	3,241.99	99.85	3,246.98
Alcohol total	60.76	22.86	265.77	143.34	33.18	432.02
Food and alcohol total	2,745.87	98.60	2,784.93	3,385.34	99.85	3,390.00

The USDA revised its food plans in 1983 to reflect actual eating patterns as well as the changes made in the Recommended Dietary Allowances (RDA) in 1980.[23] In developing the Thrifty Food Plan based on actual dietary practices, the USDA identified several problem areas: too little consumption of calcium, iron, folic acid, zinc, and magnesium, and too much consumption of fats, sugars, and sodium. Women especially suffered from inadequate nutrients and men especially suffered from too much fat and cholesterol. Compared to the Thrifty Food Plan, poor households were eating one-third too few grain products, three-fifths too much protein, and one-third too much sugar.[24]

The nutritional problems of the 1970s – too much protein, junk food, and sodas – continued into the 1990s. People were eating too much fat, sugar, and salt and too few grains. In 1988, per capita consumption of animal products increased to a record high of 187 pounds. Although people had been following the advice to switch from animal fat to vegetable fat, they had been less successful in decreasing total fat consumption, which had increased 27% from 1967 to 1988. The increased consumption of a large variety of fresh fruits and vegetables improved diets; unfortunately, per capita consumption of sugars also increased. As a result of the high consumption of empty calories from fat and sugar, being overweight and deficient in iron, calcium and several other nutrients remained the main nutritional concerns.[25]

These nutritional patterns of underconsumption of nutrients and overconsumption of fat and salt were observed at all income levels, not just the low end. One study found that only 22% of adults consumed two-thirds of the RDA for 15 nutrients and only 14% consumed less than 30% of their calories from fat, as recommended. Only a very small fraction (2%) had diets that met both the two-thirds RDA and 30% fat tests. Low nutritional and high fat diets characterized all income groups. Because women tended to focus on limiting calories, they did worse than men in meeting the RDA but better on restricting fat consumption. Conversely, men were more likely than women to consume required nutrients but less likely to limit their fat intake.[26]

These data do not include nutrients provided through vitamin pills or other supplements. Taking supplements offsets some of the differences between women and men in consuming nutrients, since 41% of women and 31% of men took supplements in 1986. Nationally, 36% of adults (over 17 years) and 43% of children (2–6 years) took supplements. Taking supplements increases with income and education,[27] and people who take supplements tend to eat more nutritious than average diets.[28]

On average, the population's consumption of nutrients appears high. But the variation among people is large, so that the average is not a good indicator of the actual proportion of people falling way below standards. The average nutrient intake did not fall below two-thirds of the RDA for any of the 15 nutrients for either men or women, and the average intake was over 100% of the RDA for all nutrients except magnesium, zinc, calcium, and vitamins B$_6$ and E, plus iron for women. However, at least 40% of women consumed less than two-thirds of the RDA for calcium, iron, magnesium, zinc, and vitamin E, and at least 40% of men consumed less than two-thirds of the RDA for magnesium, zinc, and vitamin A.[29]

Wardrobe

Clothing had lost much of its importance as a marker of status by 1973, and the distinctions that existed were primarily between women and girls in salaried and working-class families and between adults in low-income and laborer families. By 1988, clothing had returned to being used to mark class with more noticeable distinctions between the salaried and working classes and between poor and laborer families. As working-class children spent more on their clothes, children from poor families fell behind laborer families in trying to wear similar clothing and keep up appearances. Among employed families, clothing differences between girls narrowed slightly while salaried teenaged boys joined their sisters in spending more money on clothes to differentiate themselves from working-class peers. Salaried husbands, who dressed only slightly better than working-class husbands in 1973, dramatically improved their wardrobes compared to laborer husbands in 1988. Even salaried wives, who already wore considerably nicer clothes than working-class wives in 1973, widened the gap in appearance.

Between 1973 and 1988, families spent a slightly smaller proportion of their budgets on clothing as they shifted money to other areas, such as recreation, transportation, and security. Compared to these areas, clothing remained a traditional item that had witnessed few changes even as its production was revolutionized and its relative price falling.

Poor families economized even more on clothing in 1988 than low income had in 1973. In 1973, economizing on clothing by low-income adults had allowed their children, except teenage girls, to come close to purchasing clothes similar to their classmates from laborer families. This was no longer true in 1988. Even though poor women economized even further, boys spent 65% and girls spent 57% of that spent by classmates from laborer families.[30] Poor women spent only two-fifths as much as laborer wives in 1988, while they had spent one-half as much in 1973. Poor men, whose clothing needs are largely defined by their jobs, spent slightly over one-half as much as laborer husbands on clothing, in both 1973 and 1988 (see tables 6.7 and 7.7A).

Women continued to spend more than men on clothing, and the differential grew for the employed classes. In 1988, laborer wives spent 86% more than their husbands, salaried wives 46% more than their husbands. As in earlier years, the gender differences between children were less pronounced than those between adults. For poor and laborer families, girls increased their purchases for clothes relative to their brothers; for wage-earner and salaried families, boys increased their purchases of clothes and partially caught up with their sisters' purchases.

Salaried men distinguished themselves from working-class men by wearing suits or sports coats to work more often. Salaried men wore the same priced suit as the wage earner, but their sports coats were one-third more expensive. The salaried man's suits and sports coats were newer, since they were purchased more than twice as often. Poor men, who bought suits one-half as often as working-class men, purchased suits that cost almost 20% less. Although fewer than 1% of poor men purchased sports coats in any quarter, those who did indulged themselves with a

Table 7.7A Clothing totals,[a] 1988

	Poor			Laborer			Wage earner			Salaried			Senior		
	Avg. exp. ($)	% rep.	Cost ($)	Avg. exp. ($)	% rep.	Cost ($)	Avg. exp. ($)	% rep.	Cost ($)	Avg. exp. ($)	% rep.	Cost ($)	Avg. exp. ($)	% rep.	Cost ($)
Clothing totals[a]	610	72.8	180	1,172	81.9	307	1,526	84.2	389	2,121	86.6	526	600	80.0	161
Men	116	24.2	103	270	48.1	121	356	54.9	139	571	65.1	188	126	26.8	101
Boys	79	18.9	90	78	17.2	97	117	21.4	117	132	23.1	123	12	4.7	53
Women	226	44.2	110	503	63.9	169	612	68.5	192	834	73.1	245	305	60.0	109
Girls	88	19.6	97	104	19.6	115	133	24.0	119	171	25.0	147	23	5.9	84
Infants	56	14.4	83	60	16.4	78	83	22.4	79	82	21.9	81	20	11.4	38
Other and services	45	12.7	75	157	31.8	106	225	37.4	129	330	47.9	148	114	16.4	149
Selected details[b]															
Men	160	32.2	87	296	56.2	112	340	61.0	120	493	67.5	157	171	40.3	91
Boys	165	53.0	67	255	63.1	87	306	71.9	91	376	74.1	109			
Women	203	49.2	88	526	74.8	151	596	77.8	164	748	78.9	204	308	64.9	102
Girls	188	55.8	72	327	67.1	105	339	69.3	105	451	78.1	124			
Infants	308			407			428			455					
Other and services[a]															
Materials	4	2.7	32	8	5.0	34	12	31.3	39	20	7.8	54	8	4.5	36
Watch	8	3.4	53	21	7.2	62	38	50.4	74	32	9.8	71	11	4.7	50
Jewelry	22	5.8	82	102	15.8	139	143	83.5	171	242	25.6	203	78	5.9	285
Shoe repair	1	1.9	14	4	5.8	14	3	25.2	12	6	7.5	16	2	3.6	9
Rental	2	0.6	67	8	2.4	69	4	6.1	60	4	1.3	58	1	0.2	100
Alterations/repairs	2	2.0	19	5	5.1	22	5	27.4	17	9	8.6	22	4	3.8	24
Watch/jewelry repairs	1	1.8	18	3	4.4	17	11	27.4	39	6	5.2	26	6	3.3	41

[a] Average annual expenditures per consumer unit with percentage reporting quarterly, so annualized cost is based on quarterly percentage purchasing.
[b] Average annual expenditures per person (including those not purchasing) with percentage reporting quarterly and implicit annual cost.

Table 7.7B Clothing for men,[a] 1988

	Poor			Laborer			Wage earner			Salaried			Senior		
	Avg. exp. ($)	% rep.	Cost ($)	Avg. exp. ($)	% rep.	Cost ($)	Avg. exp. ($)	% rep.	Cost ($)	Avg. exp. ($)	% rep.	Cost ($)	Avg. exp. ($)	% rep.	Cost ($)
Total	160.00	32.2	87.12	296.00	56.2	111.80	340.00	61.0	119.53	493.00	67.5	156.87	171.00	40.3	90.77
Suit	13.97	1.5	201.39	32.88	2.9	241.90	30.56	2.7	244.48	74.90	6.4	252.39	24.88	2.5	217.75
Sports coat	4.54	1.0	98.10	7.08	2.1	72.97	15.54	4.2	79.69	25.77	5.4	101.93	4.85	1.1	95.49
Coat	16.95	5.5	66.63	32.20	7.7	90.14	25.82	8.3	67.06	37.58	9.8	82.40	22.05	8.2	57.88
Underwear	5.50	8.1	14.56	10.03	12.8	16.89	8.94	13.2	14.54	11.17	15.9	15.06	6.94	9.0	16.56
Hose	4.88	9.5	11.00	7.47	14.2	11.31	7.86	14.3	11.83	11.33	18.4	13.22	5.05	8.4	12.82
Pajamas	1.49	1.7	18.44	4.71	2.9	34.62	2.68	2.3	25.56	5.37	3.5	32.59	0.99	1.1	19.47
Accessories	4.00	4.6	18.52	8.22	10.1	17.49	15.00	13.2	24.38	16.29	15.3	22.80	5.99	7.6	16.86
Sweater	8.37	4.7	38.10	13.49	7.3	39.46	21.09	8.2	55.50	35.06	11.7	64.45	9.27	4.1	48.66
Active sportswear	7.19	4.1	38.06	15.31	8.7	37.91	14.78	9.2	34.36	21.86	12.1	38.62	3.61	3.3	23.69
Shirt	25.12	15.5	34.85	46.23	26.4	37.55	58.55	28.2	44.53	83.69	35.0	51.28	27.01	15.3	37.98
Pants	35.58	17.5	43.75	59.14	29.4	43.15	69.85	31.5	47.52	86.86	34.1	54.69	28.27	14.7	41.23
Shoes	3.02	3.2	20.08	5.47	6.3	18.79	8.63	7.8	23.65	8.59	8.3	22.32	2.76	3.0	19.73
Uniform	2.45	1.0	52.97	3.34	1.5	47.76	3.69	1.9	40.96	3.88	1.7	50.48	0.86	1.1	16.93
Other	1.06	0.2	138.03	0.56	0.8	16.13	0.53	0.6	17.77	0.60	0.7	18.16	0.00	0.0	0.00
Footwear	25.46	16.4	33.36	46.41	19.6	50.86	56.44	22.0	55.07	70.09	24.9	60.44	28.14	13.4	45.23

[a] Figures are for average expenditures, quarterly percentage reporting, and implicit costs.

Table 7.7C Clothing for women,[a] 1988

	Poor			Laborer			Wage earner			Salaried			Senior		
	Avg. exp. ($)	% rep.	Cost ($)	Avg. exp. ($)	% rep.	Cost ($)	Avg. exp. ($)	% rep.	Cost ($)	Avg. exp. ($)	% rep.	Cost ($)	Avg. exp. ($)	% rep.	Cost ($)
Total	203	49.2	88	526	74.8	151	596	77.8	164	748	78.9	204	308	64.9	102
Coat	18	6.4	61	51	9.2	120	51	11.4	96	103	13.8	160	38	8.4	96
Dress	31	10.6	62	92	21.2	93	88	24.7	77	102	25.8	85	45	14.4	66
Sports coat	1	1.2	23	5	2.5	48	6	2.8	46	12	3.5	75	1	0.8	38
Sweater	18	8.8	45	36	15.8	49	52	20.3	54	69	24.7	60	22	11.1	43
Blouse	22	16.0	30	53	30.5	37	68	32.2	45	77	35.3	47	39	22.9	36
Skirt	7	6.4	25	23	13.3	36	23	14.1	36	30	17.7	36	11	7.9	29
Pants	22	13.6	35	42	23.8	38	52	25.4	44	54	28.1	41	19	12.9	32
Shoes	4	4.2	18	9	8.9	22	11	9.8	24	20	13.6	31	4	5.1	19
Active sportswear	7	4.5	33	15	11.0	30	28	13.0	47	28	16.5	37	8	4.3	38
Nightgown/pajamas	6	6.9	20	16	11.4	30	20	13.1	32	26	18.2	31	15	11.4	29
Underwear	11	13.1	18	22	22.2	21	21	21.5	21	30	26.1	24	15	15.8	20
Hose	11	21.0	11	30	40.0	16	34	40.8	18	41	45.4	19	13	26.8	11
Suit	8	2.0	90	35	5.8	128	32	5.2	132	37	6.8	117	16	4.1	81
Accessories	7	8.3	17	22	19.8	24	26	18.7	30	32	23.2	29	17	12.8	28
Footwear	26	19.5	29	67	31.5	46	76	34.2	48	80	38.0	45	45	25.9	37
Uniform	2	1.8	21	4	2.6	31	6	3.0	44	7	2.6	62	1	0.8	37
Other	0	0.2	51	2	0.8	62	1	1.1	18	0	0.5	14	0	0.2	2

[a] Figures are for average annual expenditures, quarterly percentage reporting, and implicit annual costs.

version that cost almost as much as those purchased by salaried men (see table 7.7B).

The biggest expenditures for men were for trousers and shirts. Although trousers did not mark class, shirts did. Working-class men bought shirts twice as often as poor men, and salaried men bought shirts one-third more often than working-class men. The prices paid for shirts increased with class status, so that salaried men bought shirts that cost almost one-half more than the shirts purchased by poor men. Poor men purchased trousers one-half as frequently as working-class men and salaried men bought trousers more frequently than working-class men but they paid similar prices.

Like the men, poor women bought the wardrobe staples, coats and dresses in this case, only one-half as often as working-class women (see table 7.7C). Poor women were also only one-half as likely to purchase skirts or pants. The severe economizing done by poor women on their wardrobes is indicated by the fact that only one-fifth purchased stockings in any quarter. Poor women bought stockings only one-half as often as laborer wives, and they purchased only two-thirds as many. Among the employed wives, higher quality coats marked status, but quality of dresses varied little. The frequency of purchases for pants and blouses increased with class status among employed wives, and the prices paid for blouses increased much more than the prices paid for pants. The frequency of purchase for shoes, and especially accessories, rose across the employed classes while the price remained fairly stable. Overall, coats and blouses were the items that marked status for women.

The economizing on clothes by poor women is further reflected by the fact that they spent a scant one-seventh more on their clothing than their daughters, while women in the employed classes spent two-thirds more than their daughters. The staples in a girl's wardrobe were blouses, skirts and pants, dresses, and footwear. These items averaged two-thirds of a girl's clothing purchases (see table 7.7E). Like their mothers, girls used blouses to mark status. Salaried daughters paid one-fourth more for their blouses than laborer daughters. In contrast to their own pattern in 1973, accessories were not an important status item. Frequency of purchasing, but not prices paid, for underwear and skirts also increased with class status for employed families. Poor daughters purchased blouses, skirts, and underwear two-thirds as often as working-class daughters. Economizing on shoe purchases was more difficult, and poor daughters purchased shoes only 20% less often.

Although brothers spent 10%–30% less on their wardrobes than their sisters, boys' expenditures matched their fathers' in poor families and they spent 85% as much in working-class families. Only in salaried families did fathers spend considerably more (30%) than their sons for clothing. Status differences in clothing across classes was more for boys

Table 7.7D Clothing for boys[a] (2–16 years), 1988

	Poor			Laborer			Wage earner			Salaried		
	Avg. exp. ($)	% rep.	Cost ($)	Avg. exp. ($)	% rep.	Cost ($)	Avg. exp. ($)	% rep.	Cost ($)	Avg. exp. ($)	% rep.	Cost ($)
Total	165	53.0	67	255	63.1	87	306	71.9	92	376	74.1	109
Coat	16	7.1	47	25	11.9	45	24	12.9	39	46	15.5	63
Sweater	8	6.0	29	11	7.1	33	25	14.1	39	18	13.0	30
Shirt	24	20.5	25	46	28.3	35	40	27.4	32	56	37.2	32
Underwear	9	14.1	14	9	15.2	12	12	22.1	11	16	27.6	12
Pajamas	2	2.5	14	6	6.0	23	5	7.2	14	8	10.5	16
Hose	5	14.2	7	9	19.6	10	8	24.0	7	12	29.3	9
Accessories	2	4.2	10	5	10.7	10	4	10.3	8	6	14.2	9
Suit	6	3.2	43	4	2.7	30	5	4.6	24	16	6.3	55
Pants	45	27.0	36	64	32.7	42	73	35.0	45	85	46.0	40
Shoes	8	8.7	21	14	14.9	21	19	17.9	22	24	18.4	28
Uniform	5	6.1	16	15	13.1	25	22	18.6	25	28	23.4	25
Other	0	0.1	9	2	1.5	24	1	2.3	9	1	1.7	9
Footwear	36	29.9	26	44	36.3	26	70	44.1	34	62	41.4	32

[a] Figures are for annual average expenditures quarterly percentage reporting, and implicit annual costs.

Table 7.7E Clothing for girls[a] (2–16 years), 1988

	Poor			Laborer			Wage-earner			Salaried		
	Avg. exp. ($)	% rep.	Cost ($)	Avg. exp. ($)	% rep.	Cost ($)	Avg. exp. ($)	% rep.	Cost ($)	Avg. exp. ($)	% rep.	Cost ($)
Total	188	55.8	72	327	67.1	105	339	69.3	105	451	78.1	124
Coat	18	10.0	39	45	15.1	64	25	15.2	36	37	17.5	45
Dress	27	16.4	36	39	22.6	37	34	22.0	34	46	26.8	37
Blouse	34	22.5	32	53	30.6	37	68	37.8	39	86	40.2	46
Skirt and pants	34	21.1	34	62	30.9	43	68	35.1	41	78	37.4	45
Shoes	11	11.1	22	19	12.9	32	15	15.2	21	24	24.8	21
Active sportswear	8	6.2	28	15	13.7	23	21	22.0	21	38	27.2	30
Underwear	11	18.3	13	20	27.1	16	23	31.4	16	34	38.2	19
Hose	5	17.4	6	11	28.3	8	12	31.1	8	17	33.7	11
Accessories	3	7.4	9	8	14.9	12	10	17.6	13	10	19.5	11
Uniform	2	1.6	26	3	2.6	28	9	4.4	45	10	6.5	34
Other	0	0.6	10	3	2.3	31	3	4.4	14	2	3.3	14
Footwear	34	31.8	23	49	42.3	25	49	38.2	28	69	47.2	32

[a] Figures are for annual average expenditures, quarterly percentage reporting, and implicit annual costs.

Table 7.7F Clothing for infants,[a] 1988

	Poor			Laborer			Wage-earner			Salaried		
	Avg. exp. ($)	% rep.	Cost ($)	Avg. exp. ($)	% rep.	Cost ($)	Avg. exp. ($)	% rep.	Cost ($)	Avg. exp. ($)	% rep.	Cost ($)
Total	308			407			428			455		
Coat	14	8.5	36	16	8.3	42	42	22.1	41	24	16.8	30
Dress	47	29.6	34	107	41.0	56	76	43.4	37	66	42.1	34
Diapers/underwear	218	59.3	79	243	63.2	82	228	63.1	78	285	63.2	97
Nightgown/pajamas	8	12.2	13	19	15.3	27	25	27.0	20	21	29.5	16
Playwear	14	18.9	16	18	22.9	17	34	36.1	20	33	28.4	25
Other	4	5.6	16	3	2.8	24	12	7.4	35	20	11.6	37
Accessories	0	0.4	0	0	0.7	2	0	2.5	2	0	0.0	0
Socks	3	5.6	11	1	3.5	5	11	9.8	24	6	7.4	19

[a] Figures are for average expenditures, quarterly percentage reporting, and implicit annual costs.

than for girls in 1988, which is a reversal of the pattern in previous surveys. Pants, shirts, and shoes were the mainstay in a boy's wardrobe. These items accounted for two-thirds of a boy's clothing purchases (see table 7.7D).

Boys from salaried families, compared to their peers from working-class families, improved their wardrobes through more frequent purchases, rather than through more expensive purchases, of shirts, pants, and underwear and socks. Like their sisters, boys did not rely on accessories to mark status. However, salaried boys were much more likely than working-class boys to own a suit, and their suits were twice as expensive. School and recreation events also divided the classes; one-fourth of salaried boys and one-eighth of laborer boys purchased uniforms each quarter.

Poor boys lagged behind their working-class peers in their clothing purchases. They bought shirts, footwear, and pants 70%–80% as often, and they paid 30% less for shirts and 20% less for pants.

Overall, poor families economized severely on their wardrobes, so that they had to wear worn clothes and had to forgo wearing a variety of clothes. In contrast, salaried families had ample clothes in good condition. They owned a large array of clothes so they could appear well-dressed at many types of occasions. These wardrobe discrepancies reflected social obligations across classes while they helped erect and maintain the invisible boundary around various social and recreational activities through requiring a specific outfit.

Home

Housing

As employed families spent an increasing proportion (16%) of their budgets on housing, this became even more central to marking class and defining economic distance. The price of housing rose more rapidly than the general price level during the 1980s, so those who owned their homes reaped a capital gain while those who were not homeowners found it more difficult to buy their first house. Housing expenditures and quality of housing vary by one's age as well as by class, with middle-aged and older people living in better houses that cost less to carry than the houses for younger people. Overall, wage-earner, salaried, and especially senior families were more likely to own their homes in 1988 than in 1973; laborer families did not increase their ownership rate. Poor families were almost as likely to own their home in 1988 as low-income families in 1973 (see tables 6.1, 7.1A).[31]

Among poor families, renters paid $2,758 and homeowners had out-of-pocket expenses of $2,954 for housing. Rent often includes some of

Table 7.8A Housing expenditures, 1988

	Poor			Laborer			Wage earner			Salaried			Senior		
	Avg. exp. ($)	% rep.	Cost ($)	Avg. exp. ($)	% rep.	Cost ($)	Avg. exp. ($)	% rep.	Cost ($)	Avg. exp. ($)	% rep.	Cost ($)	Avg. exp. ($)	% rep.	Cost ($)
Shelter total	2,682	94.4	2,841	4,496	100.0	4,496	5,071	100.0	5,071	6,918	100.0	6,918	2,512	84.5	2,972
Owned dwelling total	847	28.7	2,954	2,248	55.3	4,062	3,337	71.2	4,684	5,665	86.5	6,551	1,618	58.8	2,753
Owned dwelling total + reduction of principal	985	28.7	3,435	2,588	55.3	4,677	3,834	71.2	5,381	6,507	86.5	7,525	1,706	58.8	2,902
Property taxes and other assessments	211	7.4	2,871	400	13.6	2,941	499	14.4	3,473	954	20.5	4,654	635	24.1	2,634
Repairs and maintenance	99	10.9	906	236	29.3	806	220	37.4	590	341	48.0	710	541	34.2	1,584
Insurance	70	9.7	722	102	18.0	566	153	27.6	554	251	34.2	733	172	19.6	875
Ground rent	24	1.7	1,455	66	3.0	2,169	27	1.2	2,229	12	0.6	2,174	62	3.1	2,013
Rented dwelling total	1,812	65.7	2,758	2,217	48.6	4,563	1,675	32.0	5,237	1,149	17.4	6,607	882	22.4	3,942
Total rent	1,800	65.7	2,739	2,185	48.5	4,502	1,641	31.8	5,160	1,124	17.0	6,591	863	22.0	3,916
Tenants insurance	5	1.0	472	10	3.5	291	15	3.4	444	10	2.8	374	8	2.4	321
Repairs and maintenance	8	2.4	322	23	3.0	743	19	3.2	599	14	2.2	648	11	1.4	841
Other shelter total (renters and owners)	22	1.2	1,799	31	2.6	1,204	60	3.4	1,748	104	4.2	2,485	11	1.8	630
Selected details[a]															
Homeowners															
Reduction of mortgage principal	138	16.3	182	340	37.4	195	497	56.1	190	842	72.8	248	88	10.9	172
Mortgage/financing, except interest	443	16.5	576	1,442	38.0	815	2,438	57.0	917	4,103	73.6	1,196	207	11.0	403
Closing costs	8	0.2	845	65	0.6	2,354	153	1.5	2,199	278	1.6	3,826	8	0.2	962
Other selling charges	0	0.0		30	0.2	3,199	0	0.0		0	0.0	0	0	0.0	0
Total selling expenses	42	0.2	4,593	82	0.3	6,642	31	0.3	2,361	7	0.1	1,373	0	0.0	0
Penalty charges on spec. or lump sum mortgage	0	0.0	0	0	0.0	0	0	0.0	0	0	0.0	0	0	0.0	0
Mortgage interest, etc.	393	16.3	2,412	1,265	37.4	3,381	2,254	56.1	4,016	3,818	72.8	5,247	200	10.9	1,825
Special assessment	1	0.1	159	0	0.2	45	0	0.0		5	1.2	84	6	0.9	158
Property taxes	210	7.3	2,895	400	13.5	2,967	499	14.4	3,473	949	19.9	4,760	628	23.7	2,646
Repair and maintenance[a]															
Plumbing/water heater	1	0.4	31	0	0.2	40	0	0.2	45	0	0.1	6	0	0.0	0
Electric/heater/air conditioner	0	0.1	46	0	0.1	18	0	0.1	39	0	0.0	0	0	0.0	0
Paint/wallpaper contractor supplies	27	0.8	744	22	3.5	137	19	4.2	97	68	4.9	297	118	5.8	436
Plumbing/heating contractor	14	1.6	197	21	4.8	94	19	5.5	75	25	6.9	76	27	8.2	72
Materials for outdoor remodel	9	1.6	141	21	5.4	83	51	6.8	161	39	6.7	124	59	8.4	151

	Poor			Laborer			Wage earner			Salaried			Senior		
	Avg. exp. ($)	% rep.	Cost ($)	Avg. exp. ($)	% rep.	Cost ($)	Avg. exp. ($)	% rep.	Cost ($)	Avg. exp. ($)	% rep.	Cost ($)	Avg. exp. ($)	% rep.	Cost ($)
Roofing/gutters contractor costs	8	0.4	416	33	3.1	231	13	3.3	87	21	3.7	123	123	5.6	468
Other services	24	1.8	287	104	5.9	374	54	6.9	169	84	11.3	160	159	10.6	322
Service contract garb. disp., etc.	1	0.1	96	1	0.2	76	1	0.4	35	4	1.6	59	2	0.7	48
Paint/wallpaper supplies	4	1.4	57	10	3.6	59	34	7.9	91	32	7.9	86	17	4.8	77
Paint/wallpaper equipment	0	1.4	6	1	3.6	6	4	7.9	10	3	7.9	9	2	4.8	8
Outdoor supplies/materials	2	0.3	27	5	0.8	138	3	1.1	52	9	1.7	119	10	1.2	180
Roofing/gutters supplies/materials	2	0.2	172	0	0.1	6	2	0.7	67	8	1.0	181	11	1.0	223
Outdoor patio	0	0.2	4	0	0.1	6	0	0.6	13	2	0.3	143	1	0.9	23
Misc. construction materials	4	0.9	83	9	1.9	106	5	1.5	73	16	4.8	70	3	1.7	41
Hard flooring	0	0.1	60	1	0.3	77	4	0.7	128	12	1.1	227	6	1.7	0
Plumbing/water heat supplies materials	1	0.5	42	4	1.2	78	4	2.0	48	6	2.7	50	1	1.7	78
Elec./heat/air-condit. supplies materials	2	0.3	120	2	0.8	61	4	1.1	80	8	1.9	89	1	0.3	86
Landscaping	0	0.0	0	1	0.3	77	2	0.2	275	4	0.6	167	2	0.3	118
Fire/extended insurance	4	1.3	271	8	2.2	316	5	1.6	296	3	0.7	431	14	2.2	603
Homeowners insurance	66	8.6	711	94	16.7	523	148	26.9	510	248	34.1	673	157	17.8	820
Renters															
Rent received as pay	13	0.9	1,412	11	0.6	1,836	6	0.4	1,602	15	0.4	3,316	2	0.2	1,200
Rent including parking fees	1,786	65.7	2,719	2,174	48.5	4,480	1,635	31.8	5,141	1,109	17.0	6,504	861	22.0	3,906
Repair and maintenance															
Termite pest control renter	0	0.0	0	0	0.0	0	0	0.0	0	0	0.0	0	0	0.0	0
Materials for addition renter	0	0.0	0	4	0.1	1,202	0	0.1	43	5	0.1	927	0	0.0	0
Services – renter	6	1.1	108	17	1.5	248	13	1.5	185	5	0.4	223	8	1.0	159
Service contract garb. disp. etc. renter	0	0.0	0	0	0.1	17	1	0.3	51	0	0.0	0	0	0.0	0
Wallpaper supplies renter	1	0.7	30	1	0.7	28	3	0.6	101	3	1.1	63	0	0.2	56
Hard flooring renter	1	0.0	300	0	0.1	62	0	0.0	0	0	0.0	0	0	0.0	0
Misc. construction materials – enter	0	0.3	21	0	0.5	25	1	0.3	87	0	0.1	6	0	0.3	20
Outdoor repair supplies etc. – renter	0	0.0	0	0	0.1	20	1	0.4	72	1	0.6	51	3	0.2	386
Paint and wallpaper equip. renter	0	0.7	3	0	0.7	3	0	0.6	11	0	1.1	7	0	0.2	6
Outdoor patio renter	0	0.0	0	0	0.0	0	0	0.0	0	0	0.0	0	0	0.0	0
Lodging away from home	9	1.0	181	17	2.2	169	37	2.8	280	52	3.3	343	11	1.8	135
Housing for someone at school	14	0.4	3,081	14	0.7	2,082	23	1.2	1,900	52	1.9	2,764	0	0.0	0

[a] Figures are for annual average expenditures, quarterly percentage reporting, and implicit annual costs.

the utilities, and so renters had considerably lower fuel and utility bills than homeowners. Together, poor renters paid an average of 22% less than poor homeowners for housing, fuel, and utilities. For rent, fuel, and utilities, laborer renters paid 55% more than poor renters (see tables 7.8A, 7.9).

Status was marked by the type of home as well as by the location, size, and age. Living in a detached single-family dwelling rose with class status, from 44% of poor to 53% of laborer to 78% of salaried families (see table 7.8B). Only one in nine salaried families lived in an apartment, while two in five poor families did. Salaried families typically had three bedrooms and 1.6 baths, while laborers had 2.5 bedrooms and 1.3 baths.

One in five employed families lived in housing that was less than eight years old. Poor or senior families were much less likely to live in newer

Table 7.8B   Housing characteristics, 1988

	Poor	*Laborer*	*Wage earner*	*Salaried*	*Senior*
Type of housing %					
Single family	44	53	64	78	65
Townhouse, duplex	11	11	11	9	7
Apartment	39	30	20	11	19
Mobile Home	5	5	3	1	7
Number of bedrooms	2.4	2.5	2.7	3.0	2.5
Number of bathrooms	1.2	1.3	1.4	1.6	0.12
Air-conditioning %	47	65	68	69	66
Central	21	38	41	48	38
Heating %					
Central forced air	48	55	59	61	66
Type: Gas	59	56	61	57	64
Electric	23	29	25	23	16
Fuel oil	12	10	9	15	13
Coal, wood, bottled gas	2	3	3	3	2
Other	4	2	2	2	5
Swimming pool %	5	13	11	13	6
Rental value of owned home $	440	497	551	670	474
Top code > = $1,000 %	7	7	11	19	6
Own %	34	52	69	84	77
With mortgage %	17	38	57	73	11
Without mortgage %	17	14	12	11	66
Rent %	66	48	31	16	23
Without payment %	3	–	–	–	–
Government subsidized %	8	–	–	–	1
Age of dwelling %					
< = 8 Years	13	19	20	22	8
Built before 1950	38	29	25	20	35
Percentage reporting age	52	71	82	89	81

dwellings, and they were much more likely to live in housing built before 1950. Amenities such as air-conditioning or swimming pools were often available in the newer apartment complexes. For this reason, 5% of poor and 13% of laborers had a swimming pool. 13% of salaried families also reported having a swimming pool, but theirs was usually a private pool.

Although air-conditioning imparted less status than in 1973, central air-conditioning continued to separate the classes. One-half of salaried homes had central air, while two-fifths of laborer and one-fifth of poor homes did. Families were more alike in how they heated their homes, and a majority had the preferred central forced air system (see table 7.8B).

The price of energy rose rapidly as a result of international oil price shocks throughout the 1970s and 1980s. This meant higher energy bills for everyone, but utility bills did not rise faster than overall spending on shelter for employed families. For working-class families, furnishings' share of the shelter budget declined, and they shifted the funds to improve housing. Salaried families spent less of their budgets on operations and energy than the working class, and they increased their discretionary expenditures on furnishing and equipping their homes. Seniors paid the same share of their shelter budget for operations and furnishings as working-class families paid, but energy accounted for a 50% higher share for the seniors, who had larger homes and lower mortgage costs.

Homeowners

The great majority (66%) of senior homeowners fully owned their homes. Only 11% of seniors were still paying off a home mortgage. This made seniors' cost of carrying their homes very low, since few homeowners had monthly mortgage payments. This was true to a lesser extent of poor homeowners, since one-half of them fully owned their homes. These low carrying costs help explain how some poor families could afford to own homes with relatively high rental values, and why many seniors remained in their relatively large homes. One in six poor families had a mortgage, up from only one in ten low-income families in 1973. This improved access to home financing partially reflects government regulations to prevent banks from red-lining certain neighborhoods.

The large majority of employed families financed their homes through mortgage loans, which they were still paying off. The ability to carry a high mortgage determined the type of house a family could buy. For salaried homeowners, 87% were paying mortgages; laborer homeowners were one-fifth less likely to be carrying a mortgage. Overall, salaried homeowners paid 70% more than laborer families for mortgage payments, while laborers paid 95% more than poor families and nine times as much as seniors. Poor families were only one-half as likely as laborer families to own their own homes.

Overall, the rental value of salaried houses was one-third higher than the rental value of laborer homes, which was 13% higher than the rental value for poor homes, and 5% higher than the rental value for senior homes.[32] For all groups, the imputed rental value was significantly higher than the out-of-pocket expenditures, which includes interest, taxes, repairs and maintenance, and insurance. Homeowners' out-of-pocket expenditures are especially inadequate indicators of housing consumption for senior and poor families, since they represent only 37% and 48%, respectively, of the rental value. The discrepancy was less for employed families, ranging from 71% for wage-earner to 81% for salaried families.[33] These comparisons indicate that homeowners' expenditures overstate the differences across classes of housing consumption.[34]

Employed homeowners did repair and maintenance work on their homes about every two years, seniors every two years and three months, and poor families every three years. Painting and wallpapering was done most frequently, and accounted for one-fourth of all repair expenses. Seniors spent one-fourth of their maintenance bills for roof and gutter work.

The type of repair and maintenance work and the amount spent varied less by class than in 1973. When families did make repairs, the costs were actually lower for the employed classes than for poor and senior families. This reflects that low-income and senior households lived in houses that were less well-maintained and older, respectively, and so their repair and maintenance needs were more costly. Poor families probably waited until essential repairs could no longer be delayed, and they therefore cost more. The salaried class was distinguished in small ways, such as by their maintenance of hardwood floors and outdoor patios.

Poor homeowners were only three-fourths as likely to carry insurance on their homes as wage-earner and salaried families, and the difference had widened since 1973. However, poor homeowners were as likely to pay property taxes, which is another indication that little of their housing was substandard.

Renters

Expenditures for rent were much more equal across class than expenditures in general. Poor families spent relatively more and salaried families spent relatively less on their rents than on other items. Although the salaried family budget exceeded the laborer family budget by 75%, their rent was less than 50% higher. Poor-family budgets were about one-half those of laborer families, but their rents were three-fifths as high. Although seniors had budgets that were only seven-tenths as large as the laborer family budget, they spent almost nine-tenths as much on rent. This is not surprising, since seniors represent retired working-class families, who rent comparable but smaller apartments. Few renters reported maintenance expenditures, and the differences across class were smaller in 1988 than in 1973.

Using energy

Energy use was no longer a marker of class by 1988. The use of electricity and gas had become universal, and the use of wood and coal became almost nonexistent. Electricity and gas made heating and cooling homes cleaner and easier. However, as electricity and gas accounted for almost 95% of energy bills, families found it more difficult to economize in this area. Fuel oil, which was used for heating in older homes, was the only other major source of fuel. Wood, coal, and bottled gas now accounted for less than 2% of the energy budget. Energy bills now depended primarily on home size rather than on type of energy used. Since owners lived in larger homes than renters, their energy bills were one-half to three-fourths higher than renters. The fuel usage and costs of poor families were more similar to that of working-class families in 1988 than in 1973, but the difference in patterns between salaried and working-class families remained. Poor families spent 95% as much as laborer families on energy, while salaried families spent 30% more than laborer families in 1988. Poor families used as much gas as laborer families, and they economized only slightly on electricity.

Bills for water and garbage were the same for poor and laborer families and 20% higher for salaried families. Differences in water bills primarily reflected watering gardens, and this increased with status across employed families. Garbage bills indicate that salaried and senior families paid for more garbage cans than working-class families.

Furnishing the home

Although furnishings and equipment account for only a small proportion of the budget, this is an area where families use discretionary spending to make life more comfortable and interesting and their homes more pleasant. Families continued to spend an increasing proportion of their higher income to furnish and equip their homes, and the divergence across classes had grown so much that by 1988 salaried families spent 4% of their budgets on furnishings compared to 3% for laborer families (see table 7.1). Buying new equipment and furniture was a status marker for families; at the same time, it indicates the financial pressures the family faced. Some shifts reflected changes in fashion, such as increased purchases for lamps and decorative items and fewer purchases of carpets and rugs. Some shifts reflected innovations in technology, such as first purchases of microwaves and of modular wall units and no need to

Table 7.9 Fuel and utilities expenditures, [a] 1988

	Poor			Laborer			Wage earner			Salaried			Senior		
	Avg. exp. ($)	% rep.	Cost ($)	Avg. exp. ($)	% rep.	Cost ($)	Avg. exp. ($)	% rep.	Cost ($)	Avg. exp. ($)	% rep.	Cost ($)	Avg. exp. ($)	% rep.	Cost ($)
Fuel and utilities total	947	83.3	1,137	1,110	91.9	1,208	1,318	94.6	1,393	1,586	97.0	1,635	1,209	91.3	1,324
Fuel	825	82.8	996	957	91.8	1,043	1,120	94.6	1,184	1,323	96.5	1,370	1,021	91.3	1,118
Owner fuel	425	32.8	1,293	642	49.3	1,304	865	66.4	1,303	1,186	82.2	1,443	890	74.7	1,190
Renter fuel	400	50.1	798	315	42.8	736	255	28.6	889	137	15.3	895	132	16.8	785
Utilities	123	40.4	304	153	49.5	309	198	58.5	339	263	70.2	375	188	64.4	292
Owner utilities	85	25.0	339	117	37.5	313	172	50.7	340	248	65.1	381	171	59.2	290
Renter utilities	38	15.5	245	35	12.0	297	26	7.9	325	15	5.2	291	17	5.4	309
Selected details[a]															
Fuel oil	35	2.6	1,356	42	3.9	1,084	52	4.9	1,048	79	8.1	967	88	8.1	1,081
Bottled gas	12	1.8	669	16	2.8	576	7	1.8	389	8	3.0	278	12	2.8	446
Coal	0	0.0	472	3	0.4	790	2	0.4	595	0	0.0	0	2	0.3	544
Electricity	535	81.4	657	641	90.9	705	746	93.1	802	909	96.3	944	578	90.7	638
Natural gas	235	47.5	495	245	50.7	484	306	58.2	526	313	57.4	546	333	59.7	558
Wood	7	1.7	434	10	2.2	450	6	2.3	266	13	2.6	518	8	1.7	466
Water/sewage	96	38.3	250	119	46.4	256	158	54.9	288	204	65.7	310	140	61.1	230
Trash/garbage	27	22.6	119	34	28.9	117	39	32.3	122	59	39.8	148	47	32.7	143
Septic tank	0	0.1	428	0	0.1	520	1	0.2	300	1	0.2	403	1	0.3	260

[a] Figures are for average expenditures, quarterly percentage reporting, and implicit annual costs.

replace the previously purchased dishwasher. Overall, the shift of expenditures from the more standard textiles and floor coverings to the more discretionary appliances and furniture indicates that families were feeling less financial pressure as they made more discretionary purchases of modern goods (see table 7.10).

This trend becomes more noticeable as we move up the income ladder. Salaried families spent two and one-half times as much as laborer families on furniture and equipment, even though their total shelter budgets were only one and one-half times as large. Salaried families spent three to eight times as much as laborer families on the purchases of living room and dining room furniture, carpets, and refrigerators. On less showy items, such as bathroom linens, bedroom furniture, washers and dryers, and kitchen utensils, they spent only one-half more. As would be expected, the prices paid by salaried families compared to the working classes were the most divergent for those items that were showier. For example, salaried families paid 2.5 times as much for new slipcovers, but they paid the same amount for bedroom linens, as wage-earner families. They were 50% more likely to replace window coverings, but they did not pay more than working-class families. Salaried families paid considerably more for their carpeting and living room furniture but less for their bedroom furniture than wage-earner families. Wage-earner families paid more for their bedroom and dining room furniture than laborer families, but paid the same for their living room chairs and tables as laborer families. No class spent much money on table settings and serving dishes. Instead, they opted for utilitarian items rather than silver flatware and china.

Although poor families spent relatively large proportions of their furnishing budgets for standard items such as bathroom linens and refrigerators, they also spent relatively large proportions on discretionary items such as dining room furniture, decorative items, and microwave ovens by economizing on rugs and carpets, bedroom furniture, patio furniture and yard equipment, and modular wall units.

Running the home

As families continued to increase their total hours in the labor market, they continued to simplify their lives at home. As they spent less time on housekeeping, they spent less (in constant dollars) on housekeeping products. They also bought clothes that were easier to care for and did not require dry cleaning. Few families bothered to have items repaired. However, almost one in five employed families paid for some child care.

Telephone service continued to dominate household operation expenses. Telephone bills accounted for 30%–40% of families' household operations expenses in 1988, and the use of telephone service had become less divergent across classes. Overall, telephone bills for salaried families

Table 7.10 Household furnishings expenditures[a], 1988

	Poor			Laborer			Wage earner			Salaried			Senior		
	Avg. exp. ($)	% rep.	Cost ($)	Avg. exp. ($)	% rep.	Cost ($)	Avg. exp. ($)	% rep.	Cost ($)	Avg. exp. ($)	% rep.	Cost ($)	Avg. exp. ($)	% rep.	Cost ($)
Total furnishings	334	34.2	209	680	52.4	279	972	58.3	358	1,639	67.1	524	528	42.0	270
Furniture	115	8.9	279	268	14.8	389	418	16.2	553	723	22.6	686	169	9.3	388
Textiles	23	14.6	34	45	23.5	41	79	29.5	58	89	32.0	60	34	19.6	38
Window coverings	13	3.2	87	26	4.7	118	47	6.0	169	60	9.1	142	41	3.6	249
Floor coverings	2	1.1	41	9	3.2	58	22	2.7	175	35	3.9	192	7	1.7	86
Equipment/machinery	108	10.6	218	211	18.7	243	274	21.1	279	477	29.4	348	205	15.9	277
Other items	61	13.8	9	95	25.4	80	105	27.1	83	213	36.2	126	56	17.0	71
Kitchen/serving ware	12	7.4	34	26	14.1	40	26	13.7	41	43	18.8	49	15	9.7	33
Selected details															
Slipcovers, etc.	0	0.4	20	1	1.3	20	2	1.8	21	0	1.6	51	0	0.3	16
Sewing material for slipcovers	5	3.2	32	1	6.6	25	16	8.0	43	12	8.9	43	12	8.5	30
Other linens	0	0.4	15	1	0.6	27	1	0.7	32	2	0.3	32	2	1.0	43
Bathroom linens	5	5.1	21	9	8.3	23	16	10.1	35	6	9.4	32	6	5.7	22
Bedroom linens	11	5.8	41	24	10.0	53	42	12.9	70	11	15.1	71	11	5.7	41
Kitchen/dining room linens	1	1.8	12	2	3.3	14	2	3.5	13	3	3.6	16	3	3.5	22
Venetian blinds	1	0.9	25	10	2.8	75	15	3.2	103	21	4.9	94	12	2.1	126
Curtains/drapes	12	2.7	93	16	3.3	105	32	4.3	160	38	6.1	134	29	2.4	258
Roomsize rugs	2	0.9	37	6	2.4	49	10	2.0	111	16	3.5	99	6	1.4	92
Non-installed wall-to-wall carpeting	1	0.2	47	3	0.9	75	12	0.7	341	19	0.6	732	1	0.3	62
Mattress and springs	12	1.2	223	44	2.4	384	91	3.0	652	74	4.3	367	41	2.4	368
Other bedroom furniture	14	2.2	129	38	3.0	269	84	4.3	419	68	5.2	280	3	0.7	99
Sofas	21	1.8	255	45	2.4	391	76	2.3	697	197	4.8	883	64	1.7	798
Living room chairs	18	1.7	236	38	2.7	298	28	2.2	270	66	3.5	412	30	1.6	409
Living room tables	15	1.6	213	19	2.4	174	25	2.9	186	37	2.8	286	3	0.9	86
Kitchen/dining room furniture	16	1.9	190	18	2.1	186	68	2.6	555	140	4.9	611	7	0.7	229

	Poor			Laborer			Wage earner			Salaried			Senior		
	Avg. exp. ($)	% rep.	Cost ($)	Avg. exp. ($)	% rep.	Cost ($)	Avg. exp. ($)	% rep.	Cost ($)	Avg. exp. ($)	% rep.	Cost ($)	Avg. exp. ($)	% rep.	Cost ($)
Infants furniture	4	1.3	70	4	0.9	88	5	1.3	84	14	2.6	120	1	0.3	57
Patio/porch/outdoor furniture	3	0.9	76	11	2.6	87	6	2.6	53	27	3.8	154	4	1.9	40
Modular wall unit/shelves	10	1.6	127	48	3.2	316	32	3.3	211	86	4.6	403	15	1.7	188
Office furniture for home	2	0.3	145	4	0.8	116	3	1.0	67	12	1.5	184	0	0.0	0
Lawn mowing and yard equipment	10	1.1	191	26	2.4	230	33	3.2	222	64	6.0	228	15	2.6	128
Power tools	2	0.6	62	10	2.5	87	7	2.5	58	29	5.4	115	16	1.2	291
Electric floor cleaning equipment	8	1.3	137	34	2.4	304	26	3.1	183	37	3.9	202	9	1.4	142
Sewing machines	3	0.3	192	4	0.5	204	3	0.5	129	13	0.8	361	0	0.0	0
Small electric kitchen appliances	6	4.4	27	17	9.0	41	20	9.5	46	24	13.4	39	14	9.3	32
Portable heating/cooling equipment	0	0.0	0	0	0.0	0	0	0.0	0	0	0.0	0	0	0.0	0
Purchase/installation of refrigerator/freezer	27	1.6	362	34	1.7	436	72	2.5	610	112	3.1	770	66	2.4	589
Purchase/installation of clothes washer	18	1.1	353	27	1.9	307	32	2.0	350	48	2.5	416	23	1.4	362
Purchase/installation of clothes dryer	7	0.6	253	20	1.7	254	21	1.9	246	23	1.4	347	14	0.9	343
Stove/oven	6	0.7	198	13	1.1	257	30	1.5	435	45	1.7	577	10	0.9	249
Microwave oven	11	1.2	200	13	1.9	144	21	2.6	176	23	2.5	199	18	1.9	208
Purchase/installation of dishwasher	0	0.0	58	1	0.1	350	0	0.0	0	3	0.1	505	3	0.2	382
Purchase/installation of window air-conditioning	8	0.5	342	4	0.3	241	6	0.8	157	20	0.7	634	8	0.5	339
Other household appliances	3	0.9	76	9	1.6	116	2	1.1	41	7	1.6	100	7	0.7	221
Lamps	5	1.8	63	16	4.4	78	11	3.3	72	16	4.5	79	8	2.4	69
Other decorative items	29	6.2	101	39	14.0	60	52	15.0	74	121	23.2	112	31	7.1	94

Table 7.10 (cont.)

	Poor			Laborer			Wage earner			Salaried			Senior		
	Avg. exp. ($)	% rep.	Cost ($)	Avg. exp. ($)	% rep.	Cost ($)	Avg. exp. ($)	% rep.	Cost ($)	Avg. exp. ($)	% rep.	Cost ($)	Avg. exp. ($)	% rep.	Cost ($)
Telephone accessories	4	2.9	31	11	4.6	53	14	5.5	55	26	6.7	85	3	2.2	31
Telephone answering machine	3	0.5	118	5	1.5	77	5	1.1	96	11	2.6	96	1	0.2	103
Calculators	2	0.9	36	2	2.1	23	4	2.8	28	3	2.9	22	1	0.5	55
Typewriters	1	0.2	93	8	0.8	224	8	0.8	219	10	0.9	237	1	0.2	152
Furniture rental	9	1.5	606	5	0.9	585	3	0.4	673	1	0.3	357	0	0.2	4
Infants equipment	3	0.9	62	1	0.7	41	4	1.7	45	6	2.3	53	1	0.9	21
Outdoor equipment	1	0.3	87	4	1.1	70	3	0.8	74	13	1.9	149	7	1.2	124
Clocks	4	1.3	73	3	1.8	32	3	1.4	49	4	2.1	41	3	2.4	27
Plastic dinnerware	1	0.8	28	2	2.2	15	1	1.8	14	1	1.8	18	1	1.4	13
China/other dinnerware	4	2.4	36	6	3.3	41	8	3.7	47	14	4.5	66	4	2.2	37
Stainless steel, silver, flatware	1	1.4	22	5	1.6	70	2	1.5	32	7	2.6	61	1	0.7	30
Glassware	2	2.7	14	5	4.3	26	4	3.4	23	6	5.9	23	2	1.7	30
Silver serving pieces	0	0.0	0	0	0.2	14	1	0.2	84	0	0.1	45	0	0.2	23
Non-silver serving pieces	1	0.5	34	1	1.4	22	2	1.2	33	3	2.0	29	0	0.7	14
Non-electric cookware	3	2.6	23	7	5.2	28	9	5.0	37	11	7.1	33	6	4.2	32

[a] Figures are for annual average expenditures, quarterly percentage reporting, and implicit annual costs.

averaged only 10% more than for working-class families, and this primarily reflects out-of-town calls. One in seven poor families had to forgo telephone service in 1988, down from one in four low-income families in 1973. Poor families with telephones spent only 10% less on service than laborer families (see table 7.11).

Purchases of dry cleaning and domestic help became more divergent across classes between 1973 and 1988 as the use of such services declined across classes. As better job opportunities had become available for women, especially black women, their employment as baby-sitters and maids continued to decline. Day care, which was used very little in 1973, was as popular as baby-sitting in 1988, and housecleaning services increasingly replaced maid service. When job commitments required the parents to find child care for pre-schoolers, low-income and laborer families were more likely to rely on relatives than higher income families.[35] Still, only one in five wage-earner and salaried families paid for any form of child care, and one in ten laborer families and one in twenty poor families did.

Use of housekeeping services increased with class status, so that salaried families were three times as likely to employ such services as laborer families. However, all families, except salaried, were only one-half as likely to use a maid or housekeeping services in 1988 as in 1973. Less than 4% of working-class families bought housekeeping services, compared to 10% of salaried families. Although families were twice as likely to pay for gardening services as for housekeeping services in 1988, the use of gardening services had declined from 1973, especially for poor and working-class families. One in six salaried families paid for gardening help in 1988, and this was twice the ratio for laborer families. Although seniors economized on telephone service, they were still more likely to have housekeeping and gardening services than salaried families. Even so, the difference in domestic help between salaried and senior households had almost disappeared by 1988. Although seniors were relatively better off in 1988 than in 1973, the proportion with domestic help had fallen from one in six to one in nine, and more seniors were left with cleaning chores that were physically difficult to do.

Most families now did their laundry at home, and going to the laundromat declined markedly. Use of cleaning services, both self-service and commercial, accounted for most of the clothing care purchased. Although 70% of low-income families paid for some cleaning, they were over twice as likely to use coin-operated machines as to drop it off. The use of commercial dry cleaning increased with class status, as families switched from self-service to commercial service. Laborer families used commercial cleaning services only slightly more than they used self-service. In contrast, salaried families were over four times more likely to use commercial than self-service, and only 10% of them did not pay for commercial cleaning.

Table 7.11 Household operations expenditures,[a] 1988

	Poor			Laborer			Wage earner			Salaried			Senior		
	Avg. exp. ($)	% rep.	Cost ($)	Avg. exp. ($)	% rep.	Cost ($)	Avg. exp. ($)	% rep.	Cost ($)	Avg. exp. ($)	% rep.	Cost ($)	Avg. exp. ($)	% rep.	Cost ($)
Total household operations	1,038			1,470			1,800			2,139			1,197		
Services	821			1,158			1,404			1,580			912		
Baby-sitting, etc.	84	5.6	1,483	202	11.9	1,699	362	19.7	1,833	379	18.7	2,031	148	11.3	1,301
Clothing care	130	69.8	186	177	82.4	215	191	81.8	233	202	95.3	212	57	48.9	117
Telephone/postage	527			677			729			807			506		
Other services	81	19.0	91	103	26.2	84	122	24.7	106	193	32.8	126	201	38.4	112
Products total	217			312			397			559			285		
Selected details															
Baby-sitting, homecare	30	3.1	979	87	7.5	1,161	158	12.2	1,295	82	8.2	997	16	0.5	3,176
Housekeeping service	21	2.2	939	32	3.2	976	29	4.2	701	75	9.5	788	99	10.2	965
Care for invalids/disabled in the home	7	0.5	1,414	4	0.4	1,007	1	0.1	1,400	39	0.7	5,833	30	1.2	2,458
Daycare	26	2.4	1,064	79	5.0	1,564	173	10.7	1,609	183	9.5	1,935	3	0.5	525
Clothing cleaning (includes dry) coin-operated	92	57.1	162	88	49.9	177	56	30.9	182	35	20.1	175	22	25.7	87
Clothing cleaning (includes dry) non-coin	38	25.4	148	89	58.0	153	135	66.3	203	166	90.5	184	35	36.0	97
Telephone	438	85.7	511	553	96.7	572	593	98.7	601	646	98.7	655	373	96.9	385
Postage/stationery	89			124			136			161			133		
Non-clothing dry cleaning (non-coin operated)	1	0.7	18	2	1.8	21	1	2.0	12	1	2.2	11	2	1.6	23
Non-clothing dry cleaning (coin-operated)	6	11.5	12	8	13.2	13	6	8.4	15	4	5.6	14	3	9.3	7
Gardening, lawn care	18	4.5	84	21	8.1	57	22	10.0	47	51	16.3	67	81	21.8	79
Moving, storage	16	1.8	189	28	3.7	164	22	3.3	144	45	4.0	240	7	1.2	121
Appliance repair	11	2.9	79	13	3.5	77	22	6.0	79	18	5.5	69	27	6.6	89
Rental/repair of tools, lawn equipment	1	0.7	35	2	1.5	28	4	1.7	52	14	4.1	72	10	2.8	79
Miscellaneous home services	12	1.8	145	15	3.2	104	14	3.6	80	31	4.5	150	14	4.3	71
Management, upkeep, security	0	0.0	0	0	0.0	0	0	0.0	0	0	0.0	0	0	0.0	0
TV and radio (non-auto) repair	7	1.8	91	9	2.4	75	11	3.5	67	18	3.9	98	21	5.2	86
Computer repair	0	0.0	62	1	0.2	128	2	0.1	345	1	0.6	37	0	0.0	0
Furniture repair, reupholstery	9	0.7	272	4	1.3	62	19	1.9	222	11	2.3	100	36	1.6	499

	Poor			Laborer			Wage earner			Salaried			Senior		
	Avg. exp. ($)	% rep.	Cost ($)	Avg. exp. ($)	% rep.	Cost ($)	Avg. exp. ($)	% rep.	Cost ($)	Avg. exp. ($)	% rep.	Cost ($)	Avg. exp. ($)	% rep.	Cost ($)
Repair of personal care appliances	0	0.1	34	0	0.2	39	0	0.3	20	0	0.3	0	0	0.7	0
Landscaping supplies, non-owner	0	0.0	0	0	0.3	115	0	0.3	143	0	0.1	32	0	0.0	0
Landscaping supplies, owner	0	0.0	0	1	0.3	361	2	0.2	1,280	4	0.6	777	2	0.3	550
Non-power tools	2	1.8	138	9	5.3	174	14	5.4	261	24	7.4	325	5	2.8	195
Fresh flowers, plants	15	10.7	142	37	24.8	149	57	30.3	190	112	35.5	317	26	19.7	130
Closet, storage items	1	0.7	107	3	2.0	168	1	1.3	107	5	2.1	226	1	1.0	123
Water softener	1	0.3	181	1	0.7	203	4	1.7	252	8	2.3	351	2	0.7	258
Rental of household equipment	5	1.0	477	1	0.3	344	1	0.3	240	1	0.3	155	0	0.2	80
Rental of non-business office equipment	0	0.0	108	0	0.1	100	0	0.1	40	0	0.0	0	0	0.3	32
Laundry/cleaning supplies	97			109			132			146			89		
Other household products	96			150			184			259			160		

[a] Figures are for annual average expenditures, quarterly percentage reporting, and implicit annual costs.

Buying flowers and plants is a discretionary purchase to make the home environment more pleasant. Only a minority of any class bought flowers, and the number increased with class. Over one in three salaried families and one in four laborer families purchased flowers or plants, although the salaried families paid over twice as much as the laborer families. Only one in nine poor families purchased flowers or plants, and they paid as much as the laborer families for their purchases.

Child care became a growing part of the budget, and cleaning supplies and clothing care dwindled in importance, at the same time that parents were working more. Families had less time for housework, yet they felt too financially pressed to spend more money to save time. Divergence in ability to pay for help with housecleaning and gardening and to pay for dry-cleaning created class differences in the availability of leisure time. As these housework services became more divergent across class between 1973 and 1988, access to free time became more important as a marker of class status. Meanwhile, telephone service no longer created economic distance. Although telephones helped to integrate the society with an omnipresent communications system, other communications systems linked to computers were simultaneously segregating the society in new ways, as we shall see.

Getting Around

Families were willing to devote an even larger proportion of their budgets to owning and maintaining their cars and trucks in 1988 compared to 1973.[36] Transportation absorbed an increased proportion of the family's total budget, as automobiles absorbed an increasing proportion of the transportation budget. Only salaried families did not improve their car ownership rates between 1973 and 1988. Mobility of the working class and poor had improved as the working class acquired more second cars and the poor acquired more first cars. Owning at least two cars was now a reality for 34% laborer and 42% wage-earner families. Finally a majority (53%) of poor families owned at least one car, compared to a minority (45%) of low-income families in 1973 (see table 7.12). Another 13% of poor families had some access to a car, and so two out of three poor families had car-related expenses. A lucky one in six poor families owned two or more vehicles. At the other extreme, however, one in five poor families still did not spend any money on transportation, so their mobility was usually restricted to the neighborhood or they depended on friends and relatives for rides.

The majority of employed vehicle owners was paying off financing loans, ranging from 57% of laborer to 74% of salaried families. Only 28% of poor vehicle owners were able to carry financing. Most seniors owned their cars, and only one in six owners was making car payments. Seniors were much more likely to own a car in 1988 than in 1973, as the

Table 7.12 Transportation expenditures,[a] 1988

	Poor Avg. exp. ($)	Poor % rep.	Poor Cost ($)	Laborer Avg. exp. ($)	Laborer % rep.	Laborer Cost ($)	Wage earner Avg. exp. ($)	Wage earner % rep.	Wage earner Cost ($)	Salaried Avg. exp. ($)	Salaried % rep.	Salaried Cost ($)	Senior Avg. exp. ($)	Senior % rep.	Senior Cost ($)
Transportation total	2,108	81.0	2,602	4,486	98.6	4,552	6,496	99.8	6,508	7,576	99.8	7,589	2,637	89.2	2,957
Vehicle expenditures	2,025	66.1	3,065	4,408	95.1	4,634	6,412	98.9	6,486	7,498	99.6	7,528	2,611	82.1	3,182
Auto purchase	671	15.9	4,222	1,436	37.9	3,790	2,618	45.0	5,820	2,758	50.2	5,495	1,118	13.2	8,481
Finance charges	67	12.8	523	221	34.7	637	283	41.8	677	383	48.0	798	45	11.6	384
Used car – net outlay	374	4.3	1,866	580	4.8	2,576	1,079	4.8	4,853	893	4.0	4,762	429	1.9	4,825
New car – net outlay	230	0.4	12,621	643	1.4	9,788	1,257	2.0	13,728	1,482	2.5	12,932	645	0.9	15,945
Other vehicle purchase	395	3.6	2,376	892	15.8	1,209	1,198	21.1	1,216	1,650	23.5	1,508	202	1.7	2,495
Trucks and vans – finance charges	17	2.7	1,226	96	14.7	653	123	18.7	1,334	197	22.1	1,819	14	2.0	3,011
New trucks and vans – net outlay	228	0.3	16,710	446	0.8	12,054	551	0.7	15,799	992	1.6	13,601	97	0.2	12,031
Used truck/van – net outlay	141	0.9	3,434	300	1.8	3,614	488	2.2	4,669	406	1.5	6,001	91	0.3	5,622
Gas/oil	493	63.4	778	862	93.1	926	1,051	97.0	1,084	1,197	97.9	1,223	469	80.9	580
Repair/maintenance	213	38.0	120	523	60.8	184	575	62.2	198	661	63.4	224	298	57.4	111
Insurance	200	20.4	210	532	50.0	228	680	53.4	273	870	55.0	339	431	33.7	275
Rental	9	0.8	265	60	3.6	361	128	5.6	486	198	6.5	654	6	1.0	128
Fees, charges	44	22.2	42	101	46.7	46	161	53.2	65	161	59.0	59	86	33.8	55
Other transport	84		81	81		86	86		81	81			27		
Trips away from home, train/bus	1	0.2	88	0	0.2	47	0	0.0	0	1	0.3	83	2	0.4	82
Number of vehicles (% distribution)															
0	47			16			11			9			21		
1	37			50			47			35			56		
2	12			27			31			36			19		
3	3			5			9			14			3		
4 or more	1			2			2			6			1		
Average number	0.8			1.3			1.4			1.7			1.1		

[a] Figures are for annual average expenditures, quarterly percentage reporting, and implicit annual costs.

ownership rate increased from 55% to 79%. In contrast, employed families actually decreased their ownership rates slightly, as 4% of them gave up driving and relied on public transit. Most likely, these families lived in dense urban areas where congestion had made driving or parking a car increasingly inconvenient.

Among employed families, status was marked by the type and age of vehicles purchased rather than by the number of automobiles owned. Salaried families bought a brand new vehicle every five years, while wage-earner families waited for eight years and laborer families for ten years. Salaried families also bought a used car every four years, so that on average they owned a new car that was 2.5 years old and a used car that was seven years old. Working-class families' second car was a used car replaced every three years, since it was eight to ten years old when purchased. Seniors with automobiles replaced them every six years, and they bought used cars 70% of the time. When poor families purchased a car, they bought an older used car, but they replaced it every three years, as did employed families. The value of the used cars purchased varied across class; poor families bought cars that cost seven-tenths as much as those purchased by laborer families, whose used car cost only one-half as much as those bought by wage-earner and salaried families.[37]

As with housing, poor families had partially closed the transportation gap between themselves and laborer families since 1973, while the gap between laborer families and wage-earner and salaried families widened. Poor families spent almost one-half (up from one-third for low-income families in 1973) as much on automobiles as did laborer families, and wage-earner families spent almost one-half more (up from one-seventh) than laborer families.

Owning an automobile was the main determinant of a family's mobility. Although the appearance, comfort, and performance of the family car varied across classes, actual differences in mobility were much less, as indicated by the family's purchases of gasoline. Poor car drivers bought 84% as much gasoline as laborer car owners, who bought 85% as much as salaried car owners.

Poor families were still much more likely to drive uninsured than were employed families. Although we cannot know with certainty how many families were driving without car insurance, poor owners were two-thirds as likely as employed owners to purchase any form of insurance.[38] Registration of at least two cars appeared to be universal among employed families and 70% of poor car owners paid to register their cars.

Although the frequency of maintenance did not vary much among car owners, the amount spent on repair and routine maintenance did. Salaried car owners spent one-fifth more than laborer car owners on maintaining their cars, while poor car owners spent only two-thirds as much as laborers.

As families became more dependent upon their automobiles, the use of public transit became more marked by class. Poor families were by far the heaviest users of public transit in 1988, while in 1973 laborer families had spent as much on public transit and seniors were as likely to report some use of public transit as low-income families. Laborer families had the most noticeable decline in their relative expenditures on public transit, which fell to only 72% of the amount spent by poor families. The proportion of laborer families who regularly used public transit dropped from about one in six (1973) to one in eight (1988). The proportion of seniors who regularly used public transit fell by 60%. Like wage-earner and salaried families, only one in ten senior families continued to use public transit, but the cost to seniors was considerably lower since they paid reduced fares. The majority of seniors had abandoned public transit, however, and instead drove their cars. Even within public transit, class differences existed. The poor primarily used buses while the employed classes primarily used the more modern and more desirable subways.

Spending Leisure Time

Spending on recreation and education zipped ahead, even as tobacco's share of the recreation and education budget fell by one-half.[39] Spending for leisure and learning burgeoned, especially for poor and senior households, although they pursued dissimilar activities. Poor families dramatically increased their educational expenditures, while seniors especially increased their spending on electronic equipment, admissions, and reading. Employed families increased their educational spending more than their recreational spending. However, to keep abreast of high-tech offerings, employed families boosted their spending for electronic equipment. Many salaried families also purchased big-ticket items, campers and boats (see tables 7.13A, 6.12).

Commentators' concern with the public's waning interest in reading was reflected in an overall decline in the frequency of book buying, either at the store or through a book club. The daily newspaper, which required less concentration or reading skill than books, became the predominant reading material. Patterns of buying newspapers and magazines became more similar as the proportion of families purchasing newspapers rose substantially to three-fourths of all families, except the poor, and as the proportion of wage-earner and salaried families subscribing to magazines dropped. As the proportion of families purchasing books fell, book buying became a marker of class status. This reversed the patterns observed in 1973, when families had similar patterns of buying books, but purchases of newspapers and magazines marked class status.

Vacations continued to dominate the family's recreational budget and to be a primary marker of class status. Vacation spending grew less

Table 7.13A Recreation and education expenditures[a] summary, 1988

	Poor			Laborer			Wage earner			Salaried			Senior		
	Avg. exp. ($)	% rep.	Cost ($)	Avg. exp. ($)	% rep.	Cost ($)	Avg. exp. ($)	% rep.	Cost ($)	Avg. exp. ($)	% rep.	Cost ($)	Avg. exp. ($)	% rep.	Cost ($)
Recreation and education total	1,375	100.0		2,488	100.0		3,188	100.0		5,253	100.0		1,431	100.0	
Recreation total	1,101	100.0	401	2,258	100.0	248	2,868	100.0	240	4,434	100.0	500	1,411	100.0	500
Education total	274	14.7		229	19.8		319	28.5		818	35.1		20	2.8	155
Reading total	67	52.7	128	136	81.4	167	172	85.9	200	234	92.0	255	154	83.6	185
Recreational vehicles total	39	0.1	8,384	41	0.9	949	101	0.7	2,909	461	2.1	4,668	6	0.2	776
Sports equipment total	23	6.4	76	83	17.5	102	113	22.9	105	172	28.9	128	19	5.9	70
Tobacco total	240	45.7	526	265	42.1	631	262	41.6	631	295	41.4	713	145	25.3	573
Electronics total	232	47.7	104	416	73.3	122	491	79.1	133	710	87.7	174	271	57.1	102
Admissions/fees total	85	31.6	268	214	63.9	335	303	74.0	409	441	78.7	560	117	42.9	272
Other miscellaneous total	135	35.3	82	300	63.3	101	393	71.4	118	568	78.0	156	130	38.9	72
Vacations total	279	13.3	378	804	31.1	444	1,033	37.1	500	1,553	43.4	638	568	22.1	435

[a] Figures are for average annual expenditures, quarterly percentage reporting, and implicit annual costs.

quickly than other recreational spending, but taking vacations became even more widespread and class differences in vacation practices diminished. The class marker now appeared to be the number of vacations taken more than the type of vacation, except for salaried families, who distinguished themselves by both more and better vacations. Employed and senior families spent one-third of their recreation (excluding tobacco) budgets on their vacations. Only poor families were unable to spend much of their recreation budget (21%) on vacations; but even the poor were more likely to take a vacation in 1988 than the low-income families were in 1973.

Salaried families now went on two vacations per year.[40] Over four in ten laborer and seven in ten wage-earner families took more than one vacation per year. Seniors took an annual vacation, and six in ten poor families had an annual vacation. Salaried families especially distinguished themselves by the type of vacations they took, since their trips cost 45% more than laborers' trips. In particular, they spent more on food and lodging. Poor, wage-earner, and senior families spent within 15% of what the laborer family spent. Salaried families paid for lodging one-half of the time, compared to one-fourth the time for poor and four-tenths the time for employed families.

Employed families who went on vacation were most likely to go by car. One-fourth to one-fifth employed or senior families went by plane; even one-sixth of the poor flew. While on vacation, one-third of employed families paid for special outings to paid events. This is one area where the poor economized, and one-fifth paid for entertainment while on vacation.

Salaried families were less likely to own a vacation home or to maintain a recreational vehicle in 1988 than in 1973. Those with boats and campers incurred large expenses, however, and salaried spending on recreational vehicles continued to absorb 9% of the recreational and education budget. Working-class families decreased their spending on campers and boats from 7% of the budget in 1973 to 3% in 1988. As we will see, families were willing to give up the more traditional campers and boats in order to equip their homes with a wide array of electronics, many of them only recently available. This change in spending switched some leisure-time activities from the outdoors to inside the home.

The proportion of families maintaining a vacation home declined except for seniors, who were over twice as likely to have a vacation home in 1988 as in 1973. The proportion of families with vacation homes had become more equal across classes, but the costs of the homes remained unequal. Salaried families still spent three times more than working-class families to carry their vacation homes.

Buying television and audio equipment already absorbed 7% to 18% of the recreation budget in 1973. Dire marketing predictions of a saturated market for consumer electronics were unfounded. Instead, major

Table 7.13B Recreation expenditures,[a] 1988

	Poor			Laborer			Wage earner			Salaried			Senior		
	Avg. exp. ($)	% rep.	Cost ($)	Avg. exp. ($)	% rep.	Cost ($)	Avg. exp. ($)	% rep.	Cost ($)	Avg. exp. ($)	% rep.	Cost ($)	Avg. exp. ($)	% rep.	Cost ($)
Recreation total	1,101	100.0		2,258	100.0		2,868	100.0		4,434	100.0		1,411	100.0	
Reading total	67	52.7	128	136	81.4	167	172	85.9	200	234	92.0	255	154	83.6	185
Newspaper	36	44.3	82	59	70.9	84	69	75.7	92	96	83.7	114	88	77.0	114
Magazines/periodicals	14	19.0	73	38	40.4	94	45	46.4	98	61	54.1	114	41	35.6	114
Books from clubs	2	1.7	104	9	6.0	148	14	9.8	148	16	12.3	129	10	6.9	146
Other books (not book club)	15	10.5	31	30	25.0	26	43	31.0	29	61	42.3	31	16	15.2	22
Encyclopedias/reference books	1	0.3	52	5	1.6	67	4	1.0	79	5	2.0	57	1	0.7	41
Recreational vehicles total	39	0.1	8,384	41	0.9	949	101	0.7	2,909	461	2.1	4,668	6	0.2	776
Outboard motor	0	0.0	0	0	0.1	150	1	0.1	276	0	0.1	26	0	0.0	0
Boat without motor/trailer	2	0.1	670	5	0.3	397	9	0.2	981	36	0.6	1,387	0	0.0	0
Motorized camper	38	0.1	16,309	3	0.1	448	90	0.4	5,168	132	0.1	25,751	0	0.0	0
Boat with motor	0	0.0	0	25	0.3	2,045	0	0.0	0	276	0.8	7,597	6	0.2	773
Boat rental	0	0.0	0	0	0.0	0	0	0.0	0	7	0.1	1,288	0	0.0	0
Camper/RV rental	0	0.0	0	1	0.1	258	1	0.1	275	1	0.3	49	0	0.0	0
Sports equipment total	23	6.4	76	83	17.5	102	113	22.9	105	172	28.9	128	19	5.9	70
Athletic gear, gametables, etc.	7	3.1	48	44	10.2	92	40	11.8	72	69	17.7	84	14	3.6	84
Bicycles	6	1.3	103	9	2.1	96	24	3.3	156	25	3.2	165	0	0.5	15
Camping equipment	1	0.4	65	2	0.9	40	3	1.6	45	8	2.7	68	0	0.3	33
Hunting and fishing equipment	4	1.1	68	11	3.0	79	20	4.9	88	24	5.5	96	2	0.7	53
Winter sports equipment	2	0.3	182	8	0.8	229	11	1.6	155	14	1.7	176	2	0.3	114
Water/miscellaneous sports equipment	2	0.8	46	8	2.2	75	11	4.2	55	29	4.2	148	0	0.2	46
Rental/repair of sports equipment	1	0.2	49	1	0.7	37	4	1.7	48	2	1.2	43	0	0.3	18
Tobacco total	240	45.7	526	265	42.1	631	262	41.6	631	295	41.4	713	145	25.3	573
Cigarettes	231	42.7	539	253	39.8	635	254	39.5	643	276	38.4	719	131	22.3	588
Other tobacco products	10	4.5	220	12	4.2	295	9	3.6	243	19	5.5	353	14	4.8	282
Electronics total	232	47.7	104	416	73.3	122	491	79.1	133	710	87.7	174	271	57.1	102
Black and white TV	1	0.4	60	1	0.5	65	1	0.3	100	2	0.8	65	1	0.2	140
Color console/large screen TV	11	0.6	395	11	0.6	408	24	0.9	553	54	1.1	1,038	43	1.2	758
Color TV – portable	37	2.5	320	47	2.8	362	57	3.2	383	89	3.9	489	28	1.9	313

	Poor			Laborer			Wage earner			Salaried			Senior		
	Avg. exp. ($)	% rep.	Cost ($)	Avg. exp. ($)	% rep.	Cost ($)	Avg. exp. ($)	% rep.	Cost ($)	Avg. exp. ($)	% rep.	Cost ($)	Avg. exp. ($)	% rep.	Cost ($)
VCR, video disk player, video camera	29	1.6	385	34	2.2	332	75	3.6	442	99	4.1	515	25	1.2	442
Video cassettes/tapes	3	2.0	34	11	8.1	30	19	10.7	37	24	14.5	36	10	4.7	45
Video games hardware/software	10	2.3	97	26	4.4	130	23	5.0	99	34	7.1	103	6	1.0	134
Radios	4	2.0	40	7	3.3	46	8	3.5	50	15	4.2	75	2	1.0	36
Phonographs	1	0.1	119	3	0.1	434	0	0.1	46	2	0.3	152	0	0.0	0
Tape recorders/players	2	0.4	95	6	1.4	93	4	1.9	43	8	2.2	81	1	0.3	38
Sound components/systems	10	0.9	251	56	2.0	603	24	1.6	324	62	3.0	442	8	0.3	473
Accessories/sound equipment	1	0.3	43	3	0.9	80	4	1.4	64	10	1.9	113	0	0.3	7
Records, tapes from club	2	1.5	127	5	3.8	132	8	4.6	168	5	3.7	129	1	1.2	97
Records, tapes, needles	12	10.2	115	27	21.3	129	33	23.1	144	48	30.2	159	5	5.9	77
Rental of video cassettes	11	7.8	139	27	22.0	123	38	26.1	145	45	29.7	152	3	2.9	88
Rental of VCR, radio, etc.	3	1.4	42	3	1.4	52	0	0.7	14	1	0.7	20	0	0.2	3
Rental of TV	4	0.8	536	1	0.3	398	2	0.3	633	0	0.1	28	0	0.0	0
Cable TV/community antenna	92	32.1	286	146	51.6	284	171	57.7	297	211	64.3	328	140	49.5	282
Admissions/fees total	85	31.6	268	214	63.9	335	303	74.0	409	441	78.7	560	117	42.9	272
Country clubs	26	7.5	352	49	18.2	267	78	23.2	337	121	31.5	382	57	23.0	250
Fees for participant sports	13	4.9	271	59	17.2	340	68	21.2	323	96	24.5	389	25	6.7	373
Admissions	24	21.6	113	58	40.7	144	76	46.5	163	103	50.7	202	21	13.3	155
Admissions to sports events	6	4.2	143	11	9.6	117	22	12.3	176	35	16.1	218	6	3.1	188
Recreational lessons	15	3.1	469	37	7.4	497	59	12.7	463	87	16.3	534	8	1.4	550
Other/miscellaneous total	135	35.3	82	300	63.3	102	393	71.4	118	568	78.0	156	130	38.9	72
Toys, games, tricycles	74	17.3	92	132	28.3	101	180	32.7	118	221	37.3	127	46	13.3	74
Playground equipment	0	0.0	13	1	0.6	51	2	0.7	50	11	1.3	180	1	0.2	180
Musical instruments/accessories	8	1.3	142	15	3.8	86	16	2.8	122	47	6.1	163	8	1.2	144
Film	8	14.0	57	20	33.0	59	23	40.4	58	37	49.2	76	9	19.6	49
Photographic equipment	3	0.9	64	15	2.8	117	20	3.3	131	36	4.5	172	12	0.9	304
Film processing	10	11.0	89	26	28.4	92	30	32.6	93	50	43.9	114	9	13.7	62
Pets/pet supplies	15	8.4	174	30	15.7	189	47	19.6	240	64	22.5	283	8	7.3	112
Pet services	3	1.6	204	10	5.0	190	15	5.6	275	22	8.5	256	5	2.8	190
Vet services	9	3.5	59	34	9.9	73	42	12.0	74	55	15.2	78	20	6.6	64

Table 7.13B (*cont.*)

	Poor			Laborer			Wage earner			Salaried			Senior		
	Avg. exp. ($)	% rep.	Cost ($)	Avg. exp. ($)	% rep.	Cost ($)	Avg. exp. ($)	% rep.	Cost ($)	Avg. exp. ($)	% rep.	Cost ($)	Avg. exp. ($)	% rep.	Cost ($)
Rental/repair of musical instruments	1	0.3	54	2	0.9	35	1	0.5	58	3	1.4	37	0	0.0	0
Rental/repair of photographic equipment	0	0.0	29	0	0.0	0	0	0.1	110	0	0.1	33	0	0.0	0
Vacations	279	13.3	378	804	31.1	444	1,033	37.1	500	1,553	43.4	638	568	22.1	435
Entertainment	18.00	0.03	133	48.00	0.10	101	76.00	0.12	137	100.00	0.14	152	39.00	0.06	148
Fees for participant sports	5	1.8	54	12	6.3	40	26	8.1	69	37	10.8	74	3	2.9	
Admissions	9	4.7	41	21	13.5	34	33	15.2	47	39	17.6	48	25	7.8	
Other entertainment	5	3.5	28	15	10.6	30	17	12.8	28	23	14.4	35	11	5.9	
Transportation	89		0	252		0	281		0	446		0	167		0
Vehicle expenses	44	14.1	67	92	31.9	62	113	37.1	65	183	43.7	90	47	19.5	51
Gasoline	42	14.0	64	75	31.1	52	99	36.5	58	138	42.5	70	42	18.8	48
Motor oil	0	1.0	4	1	1.9	6	1	2.7	6	1	2.1	8	0	0.9	5
Tolls	1	3.3	8	3	7.8	9	4	9.1	9	6	12.5	10	2	5.1	6
Other transportation	45			160			168			263			121		
Airline fares	36	2.1	364	151	8.2	396	151	7.9		242	10.9	475	92	4.4	446
Intercity train	2	0.1	227	2	0.6	77	3	0.7	100	12	0.6	451	3	0.5	136
Intercity bus	7	1.1	133	2	1.4	35	10	0.9	228	3	0.9	83	5	1.4	85
Ship	0	0.0	0	1	0.3	71	0	0.1	50	2	0.2	236	17	0.5	703
Local transit/taxi	1	0.4	44	3	1.3	57	4	1.5	53	3	2.5	30	3	1.0	57
Food	72	13.3	116	197	31.1	136	272	37.1	157	366	43.4	181	123	22.1	120
Lodging	40	3.5	244	117	12.0	208	211	16.2	279	296	21.2	299	92	8.2	242
Package trips	15	0.6	550	30	1.5	442	25	1.3	405	82	2.1	826	26	1.0	538
Vacation homes[b]	47	1.5		25	2.8		39	3.9		167	5.9		85	4.3	

[a] Figures are for average annual expenditures, quarterly percentage reporting, and implicit annual costs.

[b] Vacation homes are not included in the totals for vacations or recreation.

innovations – video players and cameras, video games, and compact discs – resulted in electronics equipment taking an even larger share of the recreation budget. By 1988, families were as likely to purchase VCRs as to buy televisions.[41] The family's ability to buy these coveted and costly new items became markers of class status. The new electronic equipment competed with older activities, especially movies, for both leisure time and dollars. Overall, the proportion of the recreational budget spent on admissions fell by the same amount as the electronics budgets rose for all families.

These electronic innovations reversed the earlier trend of families spending more of their leisure time outside the home as they went to movies and other paid events. Now, families began reducing their leisure time activities outside the home in order to watch videos as well as television, play video games, and listen to their compact disc players, which were rendering their record and tape collections obsolete. As cable television became the standard, families were able to watch a much wider array of television programs, including music television (MTV) for the teenagers and news and home shopping for the adults. In 1973, only about one-tenth of families received cable. In 1988, 50%–65% of employed families and seniors had cable service. Only poor families had been left behind.

How well one's home was equipped with the latest in electronic gear replaced recreational outings as a primary marker of class. Spending leisure time at home no longer necessarily meant a family was economizing on recreational spending, and the leisure-time activities at home had become very different across classes. As class status increased, families were less likely to rely on network television and more likely to watch cable television, rent movies, and listen to their sound systems.

Compared to working-class families, poor families economized severely on vacations and paid events in order to purchase electronic equipment. Even so, poor families spent only one-half as much on electronic equipment. They were three-fourths as likely to purchase a VCR or camera, one-half as likely to purchase a video game, and two-fifths as likely to purchase a sound system as laborer families. However, poor families had a long way to go to catch up to laborer families in ownership and use of VCRs, since they were only one-fourth as likely to buy video tapes and one-third as likely to rent a movie. Poor families were more likely to purchase records or tapes than rent a video, while employed families were as likely to rent a video as to purchase recorded music.

Families were still more likely to go out to the movies than to rent a video, but subscribing to cable television was more popular than either moviegoing or video rentals. Although class status was marked by all three of these activities, families were most similar in their probability of watching cable television and were least similar in their renting of video movies, which was still novel. Fewer than one in twelve poor families rented a movie, while one-third had cable television and two-ninths went to the movies. In contrast, almost one-third of salaried families rented videos, two-thirds watched cable, and one-half went to the movies. For families who did participate in these activities, cost (or frequency) differences existed by class. Laborer moviegoers spent one-fourth more than poor moviegoers, and salaried two-fifths more than laborer moviegoers. Salaried families who rented videos spent one-quarter more than laborer families. Salaried cable subscribers were more likely to subscribe to premium cable service, and so they paid 15% more for cable than laborer families.

Salaried families were much more likely to purchase specialized equipment for sports activities than the working class, who spent much more than poor families. Purchases of bicycles and hunting or fishing equipment displayed fewer class differences, with low-income and laborer families both economizing on these items compared to wage-earner and salaried families. Spending on toys and games, which exceeded spending on equipment, also separated the classes.

Both club fees and admissions to paid events displayed class characteristics in participation rates and in prices paid. All families were less likely to belong to a social or civic organization in 1988 than in 1973. Membership in a club was no longer the social norm even for salaried families in 1988. Only one-third of salaried families belonged to an organization, which was below the membership rate of laborer families in 1973. By 1988, only one-fifth of laborer families belonged to organizations.

When families left their television sets, they were more likely to engage in active rather than passive sports activities. Employed families were up to twice as likely to pay to participate in a sport, such as swimming or golf, as to attend a sports event, and one in five employed families participated in a sport in a season. Furthermore, wage-earner and salaried families were as likely to pay for recreational lessons as to attend a sports event.

Tobacco

The major improvements in buying college education and in spending more to enhance leisure activities were largely achieved by the salutary act of quitting or at least cutting back on smoking cigarettes. Working-class families spent only 60% as much on tobacco (constant dollars) in 1988 as in 1974. Nationally, men sharply decreased their smoking rate from 43% in 1974 to 31% in 1987, while women decreased their rate from 31% to 26%.[42] Employed families reduced their smoking rate from over 60% to 42%. This trend is universally viewed as representing an improvement in health and living standards. However, poor families maintained the same proportion of smokers (46%) as low-income families in 1973, so that poor families were more likely to smoke than employed families in 1988. Even seniors reduced their smoking rate from 30% in 1973 to 25% in 1988. After much public pressure and education on the hazards of smoking, no smoking had replaced the previous norm of smoking as expected behavior. However, a substantial minority of families still needed to kick the habit. The economic incentives were enormous, since working-class smokers spent more money on cigarettes than working-class families spent on admissions and electronic equipment.

Education

In 1988, sending a family member to college was no longer the marker of class status that it had been even as recently as 1973. Laborer and poor families made substantial increases in expenditures for college as they sacrificed to improve their job opportunities (see table 7.13C). Poor families' share of the recreation and education budget spent on college tuition and books was 14% in 1988, compared to only 6% for low-income families in 1973. Some poor families' willingness to economize severely on clothing, transportation, and recreation was probably motivated by their desire to return to college or to send their children to college. Almost as many poor families had a member attending college as working-class families, although salaried families were still much more likely to have a child in college than working-class families. The proportion of laborer and wage-earner families paying college tuition was the same in 1988, while in 1973 wage-earner families were almost twice as likely to have a member in college. Overall, the proportion of families with a member attending college doubled for poor families, increased by over one-half for laborer families, decreased for wage-earner families, and remained constant for salaried families.[43] As we saw earlier in the chapter, the gains in college going were achieved almost entirely by women.

Although the American dream of sending a child to college was being achieved by a growing minority and becoming less of a class marker, the type and cost of the college still divided classes. Salaried families also distinguished themselves by sending their children to private elementary and secondary schools.

Computers, which had been revolutionizing the workplace, also made it into the home as educational and recreation equipment. Computers were a big-ticket item, and so even though only one in eight salaried families purchased one in 1988, they accounted for 2% of the recreation and education budget. The proportion of families purchasing computers and software varied sharply by class, with salaried families over twice as likely as laborer and poor families only one-half as laborer families likely to purchase a computer. Computers in the home not only marked status,

Table 7.13C Education expenditures[a] details, 1988

	Poor			Laborer			Wage earner			Salaried			Senior		
	Avg. exp. ($)	% rep.	Cost ($)	Avg. exp. ($)	% rep.	Cost ($)	Avg. exp. ($)	% rep.	Cost ($)	Avg. exp. ($)	% rep.	Cost ($)	Avg. exp. ($)	% rep.	Cost ($)
Education total	274	14.7	401	229	19.8	248	319	28.5	240	818	35.1	500	20	2.8	155
School books/supplies, college	24	3.5	149	19	3.0	134	23	3.9	128	34	5.5	133	0	0.0	0
School books/supplies, elementary/high school	7	4.5	34	5	3.8	28	6	4.4	29	8	3.3	50	1	0.5	35
School books/supplies, daycare/other	1	0.6	42	1	0.9	31	8	1.3	139	4	1.6	59	0	0.2	10
College tuition	169	3.6	1,022	100	4.6	466	144	4.6	678	470	7.7	1,312	8	0.3	501
Elementary/high school tuition	33	1.2	574	32	1.7	422	45	2.4	395	165	6.9	511	7	0.3	429
Other school tuition	12	0.5	519	3	0.6	107	12	1.4	188	19	1.9	219	0	0.0	0
Other school expenditure including rental	9	2.3	85	12	3.6	71	17	5.5	64	28	7.2	83	0	0.2	26
Computers, non-business	17	0.6	579	49	1.2	885	52	1.8	628	76	2.7	608	2	0.3	129
Computer software, non-business	2	0.6	64	8	1.7	100	12	2.99	85	14	3.5	88	2	0.5	76

[a] Figures are for annual average expenditures, quarterly percentage reporting, and implicit annualized costs.

they also indicated if the parents were computer literate in their jobs and they provided the children an advantage in school.

Caring for Health[44]

Even though life expectancy did not continue to rise as dramatically in the second half of the century as in the first half, slow improvements were made as advancements in health care continued to decrease the death rates from major diseases. In 1988, life expectancy at birth was 75 years, or 3.6 years higher than in 1973. Men could expect to live seven years less than women, and blacks could expect to live four years less than whites.[45]

The death rate from heart disease (4 per 1,000 people), the leading cause of death, was lower than in 1970, but the death rate from cancer (2 per 1,000), the second major cause of death, had risen. Another major cause of death, automobile accidents, had continued to fall, partially because the highway speed limit was reduced to 55 mph and many states required passengers to wear seatbelts. Changes in the other causes of death were not as remarkable, since medical advances in the first half of the century had already reduced the deaths of children and young adults. Both infant and maternal mortality rates had fallen to less than half of their 1970 rates. A woman bearing two children faced a 0.017% chance of dying in childbirth. A newborn faced a 0.010% chance of dying during the first year of life. The only major killer of young adults waiting for a cure was AIDS, which had been unknown in 1973. In 1989, AIDS primarily killed men aged 25–44 years. For them, AIDS was the second major cause of death (following accidents) with a death rate of 0.4 per 1,000 men.

The high death rates for young men that were not related to health problems posed serious questions to the society, if not to the medical profession. Younger men, aged 15–24 years, suffered high death rates from automobile accidents (0.5 per 1,000 men) and from homicides (0.3 per 1,000 men). The death rate from suicide for young adult males aged 15–44 years was a high 0.2 per 1,000 men.

Health care expenditures continued to absorb an increasing share of national income even as they absorbed a declining share of employed families' budgets. In 1988, the nation spent 11% of GNP on health care; by 1992, health care would absorb 14%. The government paid 40% of health care spending, and individuals (including their insurance plans) paid for 60%. Spending for retired people (Medicare) accounted for 18% and for the needy (Medicaid) for 11% of all health care.

Health care coverage, thanks to the Medicare program, remained universal for seniors. The changes for the employed and poor were more complex. Since 1973, health insurance provided by employers had increased in its coverage, so that more workers had insurance and workers with private insurance had more services covered. However, during the 1980s, coverage of lower wage workers declined. While the great majority of workers, who had improved insurance, were better off, some workers became worse off because they had no insurance.

Comparisons of 1988 with 1973 are difficult to make because of data limitations, but some overall generalizations can be made. Three-fourths of the population had health insurance (private and Medicare) in both 1973 and 1988, but Medicare accounted for a larger percentage in 1988 than in 1973 (14% and 11%, respectively). In 1973, 8% of the population received Medicaid and were under 65 years, so that about 15%–20% of the population was not covered. In 1988, 7% of the population was covered by Medicaid and 3% by other government programs, so that 13% of the population did not have any health care plan.[46] Because private health insurance is tied to employment, the health plans of many families change with their employment status. For this reason, the proportion of people with some health care coverage during 1988 was thought to be as high as 93%.[47]

In 1987, one-half of the uninsured were employed at least part of the year.[48] One-third were poor. One-fifth were children under 15 years old, and one-third were single adults without children. The age group most likely (25%) to have no health care coverage was young adults aged 18–24 years. Young adults, who are in transition from school to work, are no longer eligible for coverage on a parent's policy and are often students with only part-time jobs.

In 1988, 44% of the poor received Medicaid. Some poor received Medicare or had private insurance. About 36% of the poor were estimated not to have health care coverage, the same uninsured rate estimated for the poor in 1974.[49]

In 1989, three-fourths of seniors had private insurance in addition to Medicare. One in six had Medicare only. The remaining one in ten received Medicaid, with and without Medicare. Only 1% of seniors were not covered by any type of health plan.[50]

Most important for our spending comparison between 1973 and 1988 is that households' out-of-pocket spending for health care was a declining share of the total (from 35% in 1973 to 24% in 1988), so that their increased consumption of health care is not recorded in the 1988 family budgets. The government's share of health care spending rose only slightly from 38% to 40%. Private insurance's share, however, rose from 26% in 1973 to 33% in 1988. Improvements in insurance benefits were reflected in the growth of insurance's share of privately-paid care from 40% in 1973 to 57% in 1988. Private insurance paid for 87% of hospital care (up from 74% in 1973) and 71% of physician services (up from 48% in 1973). In 1988, households paid one-fourth of the private insurance premiums and business paid three-fourths.[51]

As insurance coverage expanded to encompass more services, and as premium costs soared, employers modified their health care plans to share more of the costs with employees. Fully-paid premiums were offered in 1988 to only 51% of workers in firms with more than 100 employees, compare to 72% in 1980. Other employers paid from 75% to 90% of the premium, depending upon the type of plan.[52] Even though more workers were paying part of the premium, employees in firms with 100 or more employees had good health insurance coverage in 1988. Medical insurance was provided to 92%, and hospital/surgical to 90%. A dental plan was provided to 66% of employees, and vision care to 32%.[53]

Over this period, the consumption of health care increased for seniors and children relative to adults under 65 years old. In 1972, seniors received 2.7 times as much health care per person as other adults; in 1987, they received 3.5 times as much care. Children almost kept up with seniors in their increased consumption of health care, although they received only a fraction (0.14) as much care per person.[54]

Of the 64% poor with health care coverage, 45% relied on Medicaid only, 25% had Medicaid plus insurance (Medicare or private insurance), and 30% had insurance only.[55] Poor families spent 6% of their budget on health care. The CES senior's budget showed extensive health care coverage. Besides being covered by Medicare for hospital care, 86% paid for the medical insurance to cover professional fees, and 82% paid for private insurance, including commercial Medicare supplements[56] (see table 7.14). Direct payments and Medicare payments per senior are expected to continue growing as seniors age, since the costs of health care for older seniors (over 74 years old) is higher than for younger seniors (65–74 years old). Direct health care spending (per person) for older senior households was 40% higher than for younger senior households in 1984. Older seniors were 0.4 of the senior population in 1970, but they were closer to 0.5 in 1990.[57]

Insurance was 43% of seniors' health care budget. Seniors' payments for insurance had grown rapidly since 1973 and were now their largest health care category. Dubious commercial supplements to Medicare accounted for almost one-quarter of their insurance payments.[58] Drugs, both prescription and over-the-counter, accounted for 20% of seniors' health care spending in 1988, down from 28% in 1973. Direct payment for hospital and physicians' services absorbed 28% of their health care spending.

Employed families spent about one-third of their health care budgets on insurance. If we assume one-half of employed families with employer-sponsored health insurance received paid-in-full insurance premiums, wage-earner and salaried families were universally covered and only 5% of laborer families lacked health coverage. Employed families spent only 3%–4% of their family budgets on health care in 1988. As spending on hospitals and physicians became a smaller part of working-class health

Table 7.14 Medical care expenditures[a] 1988

	Poor			Laborer			Wage earner			Salaried			Senior		
	Avg. exp. ($)	% rep.	Cost ($)	Avg. exp. ($)	% rep.	Cost ($)	Avg. exp. ($)	% rep.	Cost ($)	Avg. exp. ($)	% rep.	Cost ($)	Avg. exp. ($)	% rep.	Cost ($)
Total medical care	775			1,002			1,177			1,389			2,268		
Insurance	241	32.9	679	349	49.5	451	396	51.6	711	412	54.5	699	986	94.6	965
Hospital	80	4.5	380	85	5.0	370	67	6.2	235	121	4.0	647	195	7.3	576
Convalescent/nursing home	27	0.3	9,195	0	0.1	500	0	0.0	0	13	0.5	2,988	28	0.9	3,255
Professional services	151	27.2	119	307	46.8	141	386	53.8	154	514	58.0	190	430	56.6	163
Drugs, tests, equipment, supplies	275			259			328			330			629		
Selected details															
Insurance															
Commercial health insurance	70	9.7	675	163	23.8	635	185	28.3	605	158	24.2	606	159	16.8	876
Blue Cross or Blue Shield	58	6.4	836	79	10.6	692	95	10.0	880	106	12.7	772	207	24.0	799
HMO	23	2.9	739	56	9.7	538	67	9.0	685	73	11.5	590	47	8.8	492
Medicare	60	17.7	338	12	3.7	332	8	2.5	334	11	3.3	326	354	85.6	413
Commerical Medicare supplement	30	5.0	562	39	10.2	353	41	10.5	361	63	12.2	483	219	25.6	793
Hospital room	49	2.9	358	51	3.4	319	44	3.6	258	74	2.2	708	121	4.8	537
Hospital service other than room	31	3.9	173	34	4.8	154	24	5.4	94	47	2.9	351	74	6.4	248
Professional services															
Physician services	65	19.9	70	141	32.6	93	196	38.2	110	206	40.4	110	194	40.7	103
Dental services	58	7.9	157	118	18.9	134	135	22.5	129	243	28.5	183	151	17.8	182
Eye care	12	3.1	85	17	7.1	50	24	8.2	64	25	7.6	70	33	10.6	68
Other practitioners	3	1.2	60	28	3.1	193	18	3.5	112	23	4.0	125	31	8.0	84
Nursing services	1	0.1	206	0	0.1	53	0	0.1	33	9	1.0	198	5	0.9	124
Other medical care services	11	1.2	209	4	1.5	55	12	2.7	96	7	2.1	71	15	2.1	157
Other services															
Laboratory tests and X-rays	17	3.4	109	17	7.1	52	20	7.1	59	31	7.1	94	18	7.8	51
Prescription drugs	106	29.0	79	102	41.0	54	134	46.1	63	117	46.5	54	380	64.9	126
Eyeglasses and contact lenses	14	3.3	94	51	8.7	125	52	10.3	109	49	8.8	119	41	8.8	100
Medical equipment	2	1.1	40	1	0.5	41	16	2.7	127	33	2.7	265	17	3.6	100
Rental of medical equipment	0	0.0	0	1	0.2	67	1	0.6	46	0	0.4	10	1	0.9	22
Non-prescription drugs	93			76			86			74			83		
Topicals, dressings	43			11			19			25			88		

[a] Figures are for annual average expenditures, quarterly percentage reporting, and implicit costs.

care budgets, insurance payments became a larger part. Salaried families had a spending pattern similar to working-class families, except that they spent a larger proportion (0.37) of their budget on professional services and a smaller proportion (0.30) on insurance.

The distribution of the family's health care expenses indicates that poor families were much less likely to receive professional care. Poor families were one-half as likely to visit the doctor or to have X-rays or laboratory tests as working-class families. Instead, they often had to treat some problems with remedies purchased at the drugstore. Poor families spent one-fifth of their health care budgets on professional services and one-quarter on drugs. In contrast, laborer families spent one-third of their larger budgets on professional services and one-sixth on drugs. Although poor families were only two-thirds as likely as working-class families to purchase prescription drugs, their prescriptions cost one-half more, since they were less likely to be covered by insurance. Poor families spent almost as much on non-prescription as on prescription drugs, while employed families spent considerably less. Low-income families' heavier reliance on over-the-counter remedies in place of visits to the doctor is indicated by their spending one-quarter more on non-prescription drugs and four times more on first aid supplies than laborer families. As expected, seniors had a greater number of ailments, and two out of three filed prescriptions in any quarter, compared to less than one-half of employed families. Seniors were almost one-half more likely to be in the hospital than laborer families, and their stay cost over one-half more. Nationally, Medicare paid 4.2 times seniors' direct payments for hospital and physicians services (per person) in 1988.[59]

Doctors' visits did not separate the employed classes. Instead, dental care marked class status, with salaried families one-half more likely to visit the dentist than laborer families, and laborer families twice as likely to visit the dentist as poor families. Few poor families received eye care, and they were only two-fifths as likely to visit an eye care professional as employed families.

A very small number of senior, salaried, and poor families was paying for nursing home care for a family member. For these families, the financial burden was extremely high and exceeded the cost of a hospital stay.

Seniors with incomes below $10,000 spent only one-half as much for hospital care and professional services as seniors with average incomes. Even so, health care spending equaled one-fifth of income for low-income seniors. Compared to the average poor household, poor seniors spent one-half more for hospital and professional services.

These expenditure data indicate that employed families, who were mostly insured, received adequate health care as long as they kept their jobs. Only those few employed families that did not have health insurance were at risk of not receiving adequate health care if they had a serious illness or accident. Typical seniors appeared to be receiving health care at least comparable to the insured employee families. Their insurance costs seemed to be higher than necessary as a result of some seniors buying supplemental health insurance policies of dubious value. One in twelve seniors incurred large bills averaging almost $3,000 for hospital stays or nursing home care, and their income and asset level indicate that they could handle this financial demand.

Poor families' health care depended upon whether or not they qualified for Medicaid or Medicare or had employer-sponsored insurance. For those who did, their health care costs and usage appear similar to those of laborer families. Those without coverage clearly could not afford to purchase sufficient health services.

Medicare had accomplished its goal of providing adequate health care to seniors. The nation needed to turn its attention to providing at least equivalent care to children and young adults, who would benefit over time from increased investment in providing them with health care.

Looking Presentable

As personal appearance regained some of its former significance, spending on haircuts, toiletries, cosmetics, and sundries kept up with total expenditure growth. Seniors were the only group that spent considerably less of their budgets on personal care in 1988 compared to 1973, and this drop reflected a dramatic decline in their purchases of personal care supplies. Most likely, this reflects a more relaxed life-style and casual grooming (see table 7.15).

Women still went to the beauty parlor less than men went to the barber shop, but the difference had decreased substantially since 1973 as more women and fewer men paid to have their hair cut.[60] For salaried families, three-fourths of the men and two-thirds of the women had haircuts quarterly. Husbands and wives in laborer families had almost three haircuts yearly, while poor adults did not even average two haircuts per year.

When they did go to the beauty parlor, women continued to pay substantially more than men to have their hair done. However, the cost differentials had narrowed substantially since 1973 for employed families. Women appeared to be having their hair cut professionally more often without paying for fancier services such as permanents or coloring. Overall, paying to have one's hair cut and set professionally had declined as a marker of class, but salaried wives continued to pay for fancier services.

Giving

Gift-giving continued its dramatic ascent. Gifts and contributions almost doubled their share (to 7%) of the employed families' budgets between

Table 7.15 Personal care expenditures,[a] 1988

	Poor			Laborer			Wage earner			Salaried			Senior		
	Avg. exp. ($)	% rep.	Cost ($)	Avg. exp. ($)	% rep.	Cost ($)	Avg. exp. ($)	% rep.	Cost ($)	Avg. exp. ($)	% rep.	Cost ($)	Avg. exp. ($)	% rep.	Cost ($)
Personal care total	205			373			437			604			306		
Personal care (excluding supplies)	135	57.6	235	208	80.4	259	248	87.3	284	324	89.9	361	216	81.0	267
Electrical personal care appliances	2	2.3	18	5	5.2	23	10	6.7	32	11	6.8	36	2	1.6	31
Beauty services (haircuts)	86	36.2	237	128	54.1	237	141	62.9	225	190	68.3	278	163	62.5	261
Barber services (haircuts)	47	39.4	120	74	59.3	124	95	69.9	136	119	77.0	154	50	51.9	96
Wigs and hairpieces	0	0.4	25	1	0.4	53	2	0.7	57	4	0.4	204	1	0.7	28
Personal care supplies[b]	70		164	164			189			279			90		

[a] Figures are for annual average expenditures, quarterly percentage reporting, and implicit annual costs.

[b] Data on supplies were collected in a diary survey and percentage reporting is not available.

Table 7.16 Gifts and contributions, 1988

	Poor			Laborer			Wage earner			Salaried			Senior		
	Avg. exp. ($)	% rep.	Cost ($)	Avg. exp. ($)	% rep.	Cost ($)	Avg. exp. ($)	% rep.	Cost ($)	Avg. exp. ($)	% rep.	Cost ($)	Avg. exp. ($)	% rep.	Cost ($)
Gift and contributions total	505	29.9	1,689	1,683	57.5	2,925	2,223	64.6	3,439	3,316	68.2	4,860	1,384	61.2	2,261
Non-cash gifts	369		1,382	1,382		1,796	1,796		2,810	2,810					
Clothing	153	11.8	280	656	28.5	495	807	31.8	544	1,005	36.3	594	267	25.3	315
Appliances, equipment, tools	5	1.1	100	17	4.4	85	37	5.1	157	70	7.5	201	20	3.2	135
Furniture	4	0.8	93	5	1.7	69	14	2.1	150	23	3.3	151	34	2.4	303
Housewares, linens	7	2.6	59	24	6.7	77	33	7.9	88	37	11.1	71	17	8.0	45
Recreation	183	6.2	632	636	20.1	678	835	22.9	784	1,563	29.7	1,131	438	17.9	524
Miscellaneous	16	5.3	66	43	13.8	67	70	17.0	88	112	18.2	132	26	11.1	51
Cash gifts or contributions outside CU[a]	136	16.7	811	301	33.2	905	427	40.1	1,064	506	43.9	1,151	533	42.2	1,262
Gifts in form of cash, bonds, gifts	6	1.7	74	17	3.2	117	29	4.8	132	23	4.9	100	11	5.8	193
Contributions to education organization	2	0.3	111	0	0.8	7	1	2.2	10	4	2.7	30	0	1.0	14
Contributions to charities	10	2.9	78	6	7.5	78	14	12.0	26	29	12.2	51	5	8.7	53
Contributions to religious organization	20	5.7	75	45	7.8	124	68	10.6	137	90	9.7	199	14	11.2	122
Contributions to political organization	0	0.3	16	1	0.8	15	1	2.1	6	1	2.0	11	1	1.4	8
Cash contributions for support	9	0.6	1,449	40	1.6	2,507	52	1.8	2,911	90	1.7	5,372	100	0.2	100

[a] Figures are for annual average expenditures, quarterly percentage reporting, and implicit annual costs.

1973 and 1988. Non-cash gifts grew more rapidly than cash gifts, as present became a part of social life. Employed families' non-cash gifts were only 25%–30% of gifts and contributions in 1973, but were 80%–85% in 1988 (see table 7.16). Two out of three employed families had at least one gift-giving occasion each quarter. The frequency for poor families was only one-half as often.

Families were much less likely to make cash gifts or contributions in 1988 than in 1973, when cash gifts were 30% and contributions were 40% of all working-class gifts and contributions. Unfortunately, the data on contributions were incomplete, and so we cannot make realistic comparisons across classes on religious, charitable, and political contributions as we did in 1973. The proportion of families making cash gifts or contributions each quarter increased with class status in 1988 from only one in six poor families to one in three laborer families to four in nine salaried families. The differences across classes were narrower in 1973.

Across all classes, the favorite gifts were clothing and recreational items. Class differences existed, however. For example, in a single season, 28% laborer and 36% salaried families gave clothing gifts, and the salaried families spent one-fifth more. Price distinctions were even greater for gifts of recreational items, which were given by 20% of laborer and 30% of salaried families in a single season with salaried families spending two-thirds more.

Other Spending

Miscellaneous spending, which was primarily for bank and legal fees and funeral expenses in 1973, grew in the families' budgets from 1% in 1973 to 2%–3% in 1988 as the category became dominated by transactions costs for real estate. Poor families spent 45% and salaried families spent 64% on real estate transactions (see table 7.17).

Although finance charges on unpaid balances on charge cards were reported by only 15% of employed families and 6% of poor and senior families, those paying such charges paid a sizable amount, averaging $468 for laborer families, $529 for salaried families, and $250 for poor and senior families. Working-class families spent one-sixth of the miscellaneous budget on bank and finance charges and another three-tenths for legal and accountant fees. The use of lawyers and accountants had expanded considerably since 1973, when only 5% of employed families paid for legal or accounting services during the year. In 1988, 5% of working-class and salaried families paid for legal services each quarter, and the bills paid did not reflect class. However, the use of accountants, often to file income tax statements, increased with class status from 2.6% of poor to 6.2% of laborer to 9.4% of salaried families.

Table 7.17 Other expenditures,[a] 1988

	Poor			Laborer			Wage earner			Salaried			Senior		
	Avg. exp. ($)	% rep.	Cost ($)	Avg. exp. ($)	% rep.	Cost ($)	Avg. exp. ($)	% rep.	Cost ($)	Avg. exp. ($)	% rep.	Cost ($)	Avg. exp. ($)	% rep.	Cost ($)
Total	339	29.1	1,166	555	66.0	841	697	71.1	981	1,227	72.2	1,698	540	37.0	1,459
Selected details															
Finance charges (credit cards)	15	5.9	225	61	13.0	468	72	16.4	437	80	15.1	529	17	6.3	243
Safety deposit box	2	2.5	89	3	3.0	114	8	6.2	125	6	6.4	95	11	9.5	115
Checking account charges	11	15.0	72	31	39.2	80	33	38.6	86	30	34.6	88	7	8.7	77
Legal fees	28	2.4	249	117	5.3	475	190	4.8	856	107	4.6	501	24	2.4	215
Accountant fees	21	2.6	174	28	6.2	96	38	7.1	115	61	9.4	140	26	6.4	88
Funeral and burial	67	1.7	869	36	2.0	373	18	3.7	106	19	3.3	121	214	5.0	916
Cemetery plots, vaults	22	0.9	546	11	0.8	302	22	1.7	278	7	1.7	96	59	4.3	294
Real estate expenses	154	1.9	1,734	223	6.2	772	219	6.1	774	783	8.3	2,036	172	4.3	854
Occupational expenses	7	2.3	321	13	6.4	198	37	9.6	384	51	10.5	486	2	1.5	100
Non-pleasure trips	12	5.8	44	32	14.1	48	61	19.0	69	83	20.5	87	8	6.8	25

[a] Figures are for annual average expenditures, quarterly percentage reporting, and implicit annual costs.

Funeral expenses were not as low as in 1973. Five percent of senior and 2% of poor families had funeral expenses each quarter that averaged about $5,500. Although 2%–4% of employed families had expenditures related to funerals, their relatively low spending indicates that they were making partial payments either towards expenses for a relative, toward upkeep of a grave, or toward future burial expenses.

Ensuring the Future

As incomes grew more slowly than expected and as unemployment rates remained stubbornly high, employed families felt less secure even when their own position was improving. Slow economic growth and family instability, coupled with a large influx of both legal and illegal immigrants in the 1980s, put pressure on government programs for the poor. The aging population also increased the proportion of the Federal budget absorbed by Medicare payments and Social Security benefits. Public social welfare programs (excluding education) rose from 11.4% of national income in 1970 to 16.7% in 1988. Meanwhile, public education programs fell from 6.1% of national income in 1970 to 5.5% in 1988.[61]

The feeling of increased financial pressures and decreased economic security is reflected in spending and saving behavior, with expenditures rising faster than incomes and in the value of liquid assets declining. The laborer budget, which equaled net income in 1973, exceeded income in 1988 by 14%. Even wage-earner families spent 6% more than income in 1988, after spending 5% less in 1973. The only class reporting expenditures below income in 1988 was the salaried, whose budgets equaled 94% of net income (and 88% in 1973). Seniors increased their spending rate slightly from 111% to 114% (see table 7.1).

Personal insurance

Like health insurance, retirement insurance (both government and private) had undergone significant changes since 1973 that worsened coverage for some, improved coverage for many, and required more cost-sharing between employers and workers. Overall, the personal insurance share of employed family budgets rose two percentage points between 1973 and 1988 to equal 9%–12%. This largely reflects a substantial contribution to the popular individual retirement plans as well as private pensions, and a smaller increase in Social Security payments[62] coupled with a major decline in life insurance payments. Payments for retirement (public and private) were only 60% of personal insurance for wage-earner families in 1973; by 1988, retirement plans absorbed 89% of personal insurance (see table 7.18).

Table 7.18 Personal insurance, 1988

	Poor			Laborer			Wage earner			Salaried			Senior		
	Avg. exp. ($)	% rep.	Cost ($)	Avg. exp. ($)	% rep.	Cost ($)	Avg. exp. ($)	% rep.	Cost ($)	Avg. exp. ($)	% rep.	Cost ($)	Avg. exp. ($)	% rep.	Cost ($)
Personal insurance total	373			2,204			3,395			5,414			433		
Insurance	126	22.5	561	238	42.1	565	377	53.1	710	465	55.5	837	236	32.4	730
Retirement[a]	247	54.3	454	1,967	95.6	2,058	3,018	99.4	3,035	4,949	99.9	4,955	197	27.2	725
Selected details															
Life insurance, endowment, annuities	125	22.2	562	229	41.1	557	366	52.1	703	446	54.4	820	224	31.0	723
Other non-health insurance[b]	1	0.8	185	8	3.0	280	11	3.7	284	19	3.7	509	12	2.8	439
Social Security deductions	217	54.2	401	1,631	95.5	1,707	2,437	99.3	2,455	3,786	99.9	3,791	159	26.5	600
Government retirement	1	0.9	155	33	3.8	873	108	7.0	1,540	174	8.0	2,173	2	0.2	1,086
Railroad retirement	0	0.1	230	1	0.2	411	20	1.0	1,968	7	0.1	6,451	0	0.0	0
Individual retirement plan	25	1.3	1,905	192	8.7	2,221	279	15.2	1,837	542	24.8	2,190	32	2.0	1,571
Private pensions	2	0.6	349	110	10.2	1,078	174	11.1	1,564	439	18.1	4,231	4	0.7	615

[a] All retirement data annualized.

[b] Includes personal liability insurance, burial insurance, and other insurance items deducted from pay.

Private pensions have been an important employee benefit, and private industry contributions to pensions and savings plans were two-thirds as large as contributions to Social Security in 1987. Private pensions are paid largely by employers, and so coverage rates are important in indicating the economic security provided to families. In both the early 1970s and late 1980s, 45% of the work force belonged to a private pension program.[63] The nature of the plans changed between 1973 and 1988, largely in response to Federal regulation, in order to improve the likelihood that employees would actually receive a private pension as well as to limit pension cost increases. Defined-benefit plans, which were completely employer funded for 94% of participants in 1987, stagnated because of the possibly large liability they posed for employers; defined-contribution plans, which were completely funded for 70% of participants, gained in favor as a way to limit future liability for the company while increasing the contribution paid by the worker.[64]

For workers who remain with one employer for a working life, a defined-contribution plan fully-paid by the employer might be preferred to a defined-benefit plan to which the employee contributes. This latter type of plan, which represents the type usually negotiated in union contracts, combines Social Security with a private pension plan to replace a large and defined part of the employee's earnings. However, employees who work for several employers are penalized by this type of plan; many workers ended up not receiving any pension benefits from their employers with defined-benefit plans. This class of employee, which disproportionately includes women and minorities, would prefer a defined-contribution plan that they carry with them. However, defined-contribution plans may end up providing less income security for retirement because workers can, and do, withdraw money (minus a penalty) from them before retirement. Defined-contribution plans tend to function more like individual pension plans, such as Individual Retirement Accounts (IRAs) and Keogh plans, which have grown dramatically since the late 1970s in response to tax regulations. These plans add to family savings, but they add to retirement income only if families resist the temptation to make early withdrawals. Meanwhile, retirement plans have become an increasing share of household savings.[65]

These changes in private pension plans are reflected in the family budgets. The proportion of wage-earner families contributing to private pensions increased from 9% in 1973 to 11% in 1988, with an additional 15% contributing to an individual plan. The shift from defined-benefit to defined-contribution seems to be greatest for salaried employees and least for wage earners. The employer's contribution in defined-contribution plans often depends upon how much the employee opts to contribute. Salaried families made higher payments to pension plans than working-class families, and their pension payments were four times those of laborer families in 1988, up from 1.5 times in 1973. Rather than buy security with life insurance, families now were using individual retirement plans, which had tax advantages and which could also be cashed out if necessary. Individual retirement plans, which were not even listed in 1973, separated classes in 1988, when 9% of laborer families and 25% of salaried families paid an average of $2,200 into an individual retirement plan. This represented almost 10% of average income for laborers.

The norms governing life insurance had changed, and employees were much less likely to buy insurance above the basic amount provided by their employers.[66] One-half of employed families bought life insurance, but the value was modest since the cost was only a fraction of their contributions to private retirement plans. As workers expected to live many years into retirement and as families had more income protection with both parents working, income security meant planning for retirement rather than planning for an unexpected early death. The switch from buying life insurance to contributing to retirement plans reflects these fundamental changes in life expectancy and work roles.

Taxes

Nationally, Federal, state, and local taxes as a proportion of personal income were only slightly higher in 1988 (27.9%) than in 1973 (27.2%). This was a legacy of the Reagan tax cuts in the early 1980s. If payroll taxes are included, then taxes as a proportion of personal income declined slightly from 34.1% in 1973 to 33.7% in 1988.[67] Although tax rates were not higher, the rate of spending by the Federal government had escalated, and so the Federal budget deficit grew at an alarming rate during the 1980s.

The taxes reported in the CES, which exclude sales and excise taxes, are lower than these national rates, which include taxes from all sources, including business. Even so, the CES reported higher and more progressive tax rates (personal, payroll, and property) in 1973 than in 1988. The salaried tax rate was 19% in 1988 and 23% in 1973. The working-class tax rate was 16%–18% in 1988 compared to 19%–20% in 1973. Poor families had a tax rate of 10% on reported income in 1988, and low-income families an 8% tax rate in 1973 (see table 7.19). Taxes had become less progressive as they relied more on payroll taxes and less on personal income taxes. In 1988, personal taxes were one-half, and payroll taxes two-fifths, of the taxes paid by employed families.

Assets

The median net worth of households nationally was $35,752 ($9,840 excluding home equity) in 1988.[68] Own homes were the most important

Table 7.19 Taxes, 1988

	Poor			Laborer			Wage earner			Salaried			Senior		
	Avg. exp. ($)	% rep.	Cost ($)	Avg. exp. ($)	% rep.	Cost ($)	Avg. exp. ($)	% rep.	Cost ($)	Avg. exp. ($)	% rep.	Cost ($)	Avg. exp. ($)	% rep.	Cost ($)
Total personal taxes	185	21.3	870	1,747.96	61.1	2,861	3,119	68.8	4,531	5,311	72.2	7,352	441	28.7	1,533
Federal income tax	19	23.8		1,185.00	69.4		2,231	79.3		3,998	79.8		257	27.0	
State/local tax	39	16.5		387.00	53.6		699	66.6		1,096	67.7		74	19.0	
Personal property	9	3.5		24.00	10.8		39	10.2		52	9.5		30	7.5	
Other taxes	8	1.2		25.00	4.2		20	3.5		22	3.0		25	4.9	
Property taxes	210	7.3	2,895	400	13.5	2,967	499	14.4	3,473	949	19.9	4,760	628	23.7	2,646
Social Security tax	217	54.3	400.55	1,631	95.5	1,707	2,437	99.3	2,455	3,786	99.9	3,791	159	26.5	600
Total taxes	613			3,779			6,055			10,051			1,235		
Percentage of income	9.7			15.6			17.8			19.0			7.5		

Table 7.20 Market value of liquid assets,[a] 1988

	Poor			Laborer			Wage earner			Salaried			Senior		
	Amount ($)	% rep.	Avg. value ($)	Amount ($)	% rep.	Avg. value ($)	Amount ($)	% rep.	Avg. value ($)	Amount ($)	% rep.	Avg. value ($)	Amount ($)	% rep.	Avg. value ($)
Checking account	115	20.6	556	121	19.4	624	247	20.3	1,217	388	20.4	1,902	636	20.1	3,109
Savings account	135	21.2	636	437	19.2	2,276	1,049	20.6	15,092	2,155	20.1	10,720	2,981	18.2	16,379
Market value of stocks	140	0.7	19,037	562	2.4	22,998	414	4.7	8,866	1,478	7.3	20,397	801	4.1	19,625
US Savings Bonds	7	22.4	29	41	20.3	204	118	23.0	512	118	21.3	553	149	22.8	653
Total	396			1,161			1,827			4,138			4,566		

[a] Amount equals asset holdings for group and average value is given for those households owning the asset.

asset, accounting for 43% of net worth. Three-fourths of households had an interest-bearing account worth $3,494 (median); these accounts were 14% of their net worth in 1988. Other financial assets, including bonds, stocks, and IRAs, were 16% of net worth.

Families in the third quintile, which includes laborer families, had a median net worth of $28,044 ($8,418 excluding home equity). Families in the top quintile, which includes salaried families, had a median net worth of $111,770 ($40,688 excluding home equity). The top quintile was three times as likely as the third quintile to own bonds or money market funds or to have an IRA or Keogh account and over 2.5 times as likely to own stocks. Homes and cars represented 52% of the net worth for the third quintile but only 42% for the top quintile.

Unfortunately, assets in the 1988 CES were underreported, and so the data cannot be compared to those gathered in previous surveys. For example, four in ten working-class households reported paying for a checking account, and others had 'free' accounts. But only one in five reported the amount they had in a checking account. Nationally, 83% of households reported having a checking account. In the CES, 19% of laborers had savings accounts with average value $2,276 and 2% had stocks with average value $22,998. Nationwide, 77% of the third quintile had savings-type accounts with average value $15,966 and 16% had stocks with average value $17,818 (see table 7.20).

The median net worth nationally for senior households was $73,471 ($23,856 excluding home equity). Seniors had 30% of their net worth in interest-bearing assets, and 43% in their home or cars. The typical senior household analyzed in this study would fall in the second quintile, and seniors in this quintile had a median net worth of $76,050 ($28,168 excluding home equity.) Even seniors in the lowest quintile had a median net worth of $25,220 ($3,536 excluding home equity).

Laborer families (third quintile) in the 1988 national data had liquid assets with an average value 60% higher than the liquid assets of laborer families in the 1973 CES (constant dollars). More families had savings accounts (64% in 1973 and 77% in 1988) worth one-fourth more. More families held stocks (11% in 1973 and 16% in 1988), but the average value was 40% lower. Seniors also improved their liquid asset holdings, since their median net worth (excluding home equity) was 30% higher in 1988 than their average value of liquid assets in 1973.[69]

Dynamics of Change

As earnings failed to continue their rapid upward climb, families sought to augment income through more hours of employment, especially for wives. As we have already noted, family income fell for laborer families and increased for wage-earner and salaried families. Because spending

Table 7.21 Shifts in consumption norms, 1973–88

	Change in expenditures (ΔE)	Realized emmulation (RE)	Dis-emulation	Reduced standard (RS)	Innovation (IN)
Total expenditures					
Laborers	0.09	0.00	−0.05	−0.06	0.15
Wage earners	0.21	0.02	−0.07	−0.05	0.23
Salaried	0.27	0.03	−0.07	−0.05	0.28

	Laborers				Wage earners				Salaried			
	ΔE	RE	RS	IN	ΔE	RE	RS	IN	ΔE	RE	RS	IN
Food (per capita)	0.07	0.00	0.00	0.07	0.12	0.00	0.00	0.12	0.08	0.00	0.00	0.08
Clothing (per capita)	0.08	0.00	0.00	0.31	0.68	0.01	0.00	0.67	0.64	0.01	0.00	0.63
Shelter	0.05	0.00	0.00	0.05	0.08	0.00	0.00	0.08	0.21	0.00	0.00	0.21
Fuel and utilities	−0.16	0.00	−0.16	0.00	−0.10	0.00	−0.10	0.00	−0.13	0.00	−0.13	0.00
Furnishings	0.06	0.00	0.00	0.06	0.17	0.04	0.00	0.13	0.37	0.03	−0.13	0.34
Household operations	0.44	0.00	0.00	0.44	0.42	0.00	0.00	0.42	0.44	0.00	0.00	0.44
Miscellaneous												
Transportation	0.06	0.00	0.00	0.06	0.35	0.06	0.00	0.29	0.23	0.05	0.00	0.18
Recreation and education	0.35	0.00	0.00	0.35	0.44	0.01	0.00	0.42	0.66	0.10	0.00	0.56
Medical care per capita	−0.29	0.00	−0.29	0.00	−0.25	0.00	−0.25	0.00	−0.17	0.00	−0.17	0.00
Personal care per capita	0.13	0.00	0.00	0.13	0.05	0.00	0.00	0.05	0.23	0.03	0.00	0.20
Gifts and contributions	0.76	0.08	0.00	0.69	1.00	0.19	0.00	0.82	1.01	0.20	0.00	0.81
Insurance	0.08	0.00	0.00	0.08	0.24	0.00	0.00	0.24	0.30	0.00	0.00	0.30
Other	0.79	0.00	0.00	0.79	0.59	0.00	0.00	0.59	1.15	0.00	0.00	1.15
Family size	−0.10	0.00	−0.10	0.00	0.01	0.02	−0.07	0.05	0.01	0.05	−0.07	0.05

rates were lower in 1973 than in 1988, emulation of 1973 consumption patterns would have required families to reduce their consumption in many areas, including shelter, household operations, and food (per capita.) Instead, families increased their spending rate rather than reduce their consumption standards. Overall, expenditures rose faster than incomes and innovation exceeded the increase in expenditures (see table 7.21). The difference was financed by reduced savings and a smaller family size along with employer-provided health insurance covering more health care expenses and energy-saving advances in fuel and utilities.

Compared to the previous period, the improvements achieved in consumption norms between 1973 and 1988 were disappointing. Families in the three employed classes, however, continued modernizing their consumption to include innovative goods and services in recreation and leisure time activities. Judged independently of expectations, noticeable improvements were made in recreation, gift-giving, transportation, clothing, and household operations. These improved norms are related to active social lives and activities outside the home. Even household operations had become part of social life, since 60% is devoted to child care and telephone service. Their social activities included giving more and better gifts. They improved their appearance as they spent more on their wardrobes, after having reduced their clothing purchases to very low levels in 1973. Wage earners, and to a lesser extent salaried workers, also displayed large innovations in their automotive norms. Salaried families were the only class to spend considerable sums on innovation in shelter and furnishings, which contributed to a more active social life at home.

The slow growth in income resulted in very little emulation (0%–3%), which increased with expenditure growth, and a high reduction in standards (5%–6%), which was fairly constant across the employed classes. Innovation, which was high even for such slow income growth, rose with expenditure growth rather than remaining constant across classes. Outside the family's budget, additional improvements in medical care were paid by employer-sponsored health insurance. Meanwhile, employed families were required to pay more Social Security taxes in order to protect the national retirement fund. Their own financial security declined, however, as their spending rate increased and their liquid assets fell.

Economic Distance

Economic distance in 1988 was created in ways similar to the patterns for 1973. Although laborers had incomes 3.9 times poor incomes, their expenditures were only 1.8 times as high (see table 7.22). The expenditure difference would have increased by 6% if family size differences were

Table 7.22 Economic distance across groups, 1988

	Laborers to low income			Wage earners to laborers			Salaried to wage earners			Laborers to seniors		
	Ratio	Difference ($)		Ratio	Difference ($)		Ratio	Difference ($)		Ratio	Difference ($)	
Relative net income	3.912	17,893		1.404	9,719		1.559	18,875		1.476	7,748	
Relative expenditures	1.753	10,812		1.302	7,606		1.361	11,844		1.392	7,084	
Distribution of increased consumption	Distribution	Difference ($)	% change	Distribution	Difference ($)	% change	Distribution	Difference ($)	% change	Distribution	Difference ($)	% change
	1.000			1.000			1.000			1.000		
Food and clothing	0.100	1,083	29.4	0.180	1,372	28.8	0.129	1,527	24.9	0.153	1,083	29.4
Food	0.079	855	27.9	0.090	684	17.4	0.079	932	20.2	0.119	844	27.4
Clothing	0.021	228	37.5	0.090	688	82.1	0.050	595	39.0	0.034	239	39.8
Shelter	0.255	2,756	55.1	0.185	1,405	18.1	0.263	3,120	34.0	0.326	2,311	42.4
Housing	0.168	1,815	67.7	0.076	575	12.8	0.156	1,846	36.4	0.280	1,985	79.0
Fuel and utilities	0.015	163	17.2	0.027	208	18.7	0.023	268	20.3	-0.014	(99)	-8.2
Furnishings	0.032	347	103.8	0.038	292	42.9	0.056	667	68.6	0.021	152	28.8
Household operations	0.040	432	41.6	0.043	330	22.5	0.029	339	18.8	0.039	273	22.8
Miscellaneous	0.645	6,973	122.7	0.635	4,829	38.2	0.608	7,197	41.2	0.521	3,690	41.2
Transportation	0.220	2,378	112.8	0.264	2,010	44.8	0.091	1,080	16.6	0.261	1,849	70.1
Recreation and education	0.090	975	70.8	0.093	706	30.0	0.177	2,097	68.6	0.135	956	68.5
Medical care	0.021	227	29.3	0.023	176	17.5	0.018	212	18.0	-0.179	(1,267)	-55.8
Personal care	0.015	167	81.5	0.008	65	17.3	0.014	166	38.1	0.009	66	21.6
Gifts and contributions	0.109	1,178	233.3	0.071	540	32.1	0.092	1,093	49.2	0.042	300	21.7
Insurance	0.169	1,832	491.6	0.157	1,191	54.0	0.170	2,019	59.5	0.205	1,771	408.7
Other	0.020	215	63.5	0.019	142	25.7	0.045	530	76.0	0.002	15	2.7
Family size adjustment	-0.058	(628)		0.086	653		0.045	533		0.386	2,735	

included. Laborer families distanced themselves from poor families through the mobility provided by reliable automobiles. Laborer families also spent considerably more furnishing their homes, giving gifts, and making donations. Spending on traditional categories – food, clothing, fuel and utilities, household operations, and medical care – was fairly similar between laborers and the poor and created little economic distance.

Within the working class, wage earners spent 30% more than laborers, and over one-fourth of this was to support a larger family. Wage-earner families distanced themselves from laborer families through their purchases of showy items for appearances – better and more automobiles, clothing, and home furnishings. In contrast, their housing, energy use, and food, along with their spending on personal care and medical care, created little economic distance. Salaried families spent 40% more than wage-earner families, and only one-eighth was used to support a larger family. As in 1973, salaried families distanced themselves from wage-earner families through their richer and more varied social lives made possible through their spending on recreation and education, furnishings, and gifts and contributions. In contrast, their spending on automobiles, as well as utilities, household operations, and food created much less economic distance. Spending on medical care was similar across employed classes since insurance was usually provided by the employer.

Differences in security, including the family's spending rate and the ownership of liquid assets, is another important way that families were divided economically and were affected in their daily lives and decisions. For all classes, higher spending on insurance provided some additional security to ensure the economic distance could be maintained.

Although laborer families spent 40% more than seniors, differences in family size accounted for this. However, laborer and senior families spent their money in dissimilar ways as a result of differences in their life cycle. Laborer families spent much more than seniors on transportation and recreation to support a more active social life. Laborers also had larger insurance payments, especially for withholding for Social Security. Advanced age brought seniors lower housing costs, since many owned their homes outright, along with more medical problems and bills.

As in the previous years, higher spending translated into differences in appearances, everyday activities, and economic security across classes. In some important and fundamental consumption, such as diets, medical care, and energy use, families had similar patterns. As families became more similar in their consumption of these traditional items, they distinguished themselves through the consumption of more modern products and services, especially in leisure time activities.

Budget Standards

Interest in budget standards continued to decline, and by the 1980s the BLS budget standards were dropped. Their usefulness was undermined because the basket of goods and services was based on 1960 CES, and only prices had been updated using the CPI since 1969. The decision to drop the BLS standards rather than update them using the 1973 CES was made during the Reagan presidency, which did not want the government to provide data that allowed comparisons of inequality or economic need. The Reagan economists assumed that people were making optimal decisions based upon their preferences that resulted in disparate outcomes in living standards. Those with higher incomes were making more human capital investments, were working more, and were more capable – all valid reasons for their higher incomes. To publish differences in material living standards might give the erroneous impression that the government thought these differences were socially undesirable. However, we will continue to use the BLS standards as a benchmark by updating it with the CPI.

Based upon actual practice of laborer families, basics for 1988 were revised in several categories to reflect shifts in social norms in personal appearance, in communication, and in use of hi-tech equipment and services. Attention to appearance in terms of clothing appropriate to the situation and more haircuts resulted in increasing clothing basics back to the BLS clothing standards, and personal care basics back to the BLS personal care standards. Both of these basics had been reduced in 1973 because of more casual grooming norms. Basics in household operations were increased to permit more telephone service, including long distance calls, and more child care services. Basics in medical care assumed a health care plan that included both hospital care and physician services; one-half of the families contributed to the cost of the premium. Based upon the actual practice of laborer families, recreation was increased to allow a vacation every year, instead of every two years; to permit ownership of a color television; to allow ownership of a VCR with tape rentals by 10% of families; and cable TV service by 50% of families. Personal insurance basics, which are the mandated payroll taxes, included the increases in Social Security payroll taxes.

Transportation basics remained the same as in 1973 – 90% car ownership combined with public transportation. The lower BLS standard's automobile costs, which are still used for basics, are based on the purchasing a six-year-old used car and keeping it for four years; the average car is eight years old.[70]

The dependency standard was modified to allow ownership of a color television and to allow more local telephone service. Transportation remained only by public transit with no car ownership allowed.

Even with the improvement in basics and a diminished real income, laborer families' standard of living advanced even farther above basics in 1988 than it had in 1973. The laborer family's budget was 1.4 times the BLS lower budget standard in 1988. Their living standard was even 6% above the BLS intermediate budget standard (see table 7.23). Laborers' consumption remained close to basics for food, housing and utilities, medical care, and personal care. Their consumption was considerably above basics, and emphasized variety and status, transportation, furnishings, recreation and education, and gifts in order to support an active social life and a wide array of leisure time pursuits.

As in 1973, a dependency standard was estimated for families who are dependent on income support payments and are not working.[71] The needs of working poor, however, should be judged using the basics standard. Poor families spent 30% more than the dependency standard in 1988. If medical care and insurance are excluded since the dependency standard assumes the medical care and no Social Security withholding, poor households spent 20% more than the dependency standard in 1988. They spent considerably more on transportation, because 53% owned at least one vehicle, and poor families owned an average of 0.8 cars. Poor households' spending on transportation exceeded even the basic standard by 12%, since their cars were newer than the assumed eight-year-old car.

If transportation, along with medical care and insurance, is excluded from the budget, then poor households spent only 5% more than the dependency budget. For food, furnishings, and gifts, their budgets matched the dependency standard. The poor economized on clothing, personal care, and housing, spending $623 less than allotted in the dependency standard, in order to spend $1,023 more on recreation, education, and household operations. Their consumption of these latter items matched the basic standard rather than the dependency standard. Poor households obviously put great value on transportation, recreation, education, and household operations, which allowed a more active social life than assumed by the dependency budget. For some families, these expenditures, especially for education, might be used as a step toward employment and away from dependency. For others, these expenditures are probably seen as providing some stimulation and variety in an otherwise dreary life.

A survey of 25 welfare mothers in 1988 in a midwestern city[72] found that they spent two-thirds more than they received for AFDC benefits and Food Stamps. Their budgets were slightly lower than the dependency budget, but their rent and utility bills were 9% higher. Their food budget was similar to the dependency standard. Food accounted for 30% and rent and utilities for 37% of the total budget for these AFDC families. Compared to the CES poor renters, who had slightly smaller families, these AFDC families spent almost one-fourth more for rent and utilities.

Table 7.23 Budget standards, 1988[a]

	1988 BLS dependency budget ($)	Low income (CES) ($)	1988 BLS lower budget (Basics) ($)	Laborer (CES) ($)	1988 BLS intermediate budget ($)	Wage earner (CES) ($)	1988 BLS higher budget ($)	Salaried (CES) ($)	BLS intermediate budget (Retired) ($)	Seniors (CES) ($)
Annual expenditure	11,139	14,363	17,738	25,508	24,555	32,781	34,262	44,624	10,871	18,091
Average family size	3.04	3.04	2.63	2.63	2.91	2.91	3.11	3.11	1.83	1.83
Food	3,084[b]	3,070	3,754	3,925	5,373	4,609	7,239	5,541	1,855	3,081
Clothing	808	610	914	1,172	1,063	1,526	1,661	2,121	268	600
Shelter	4,862	5,001	6,301	7,757	8,447	9,162	12,443	12,282	5,315	5,446
Housing + fuel/utilities	3,947	3,629	4,933	5,606	6,958	6,389	10,029	8,504	–	3,721
Furnishings	314	334	314	680	702	972	1,305	1,639	–	528
Household operations	602	1,039	1,055	1,470	787	1,801	1,109	2,139	–	1,197
Miscellaneous	2,385	5,681	6,768	12,654	9,672	17,483	12,919	24,681	3,433	8,964
Transportation	395[c]	2,108	1,881	4,486	2,675	6,496	3,469	7,576	1,207	2,637
Recreation and education	791	1,377	1,276	2,352	1,113	3,058	1,799	5,155	409	1,396
Medical care	190[d]	775	852	1,002	1,571	1,177	1,750	1,389	755	2,268
Personal care	312	205	332	373	419	437	637	604	193	306
Gifts and contributions	487	505	487	1,683	860	2,223	1,579	3,316	868	1,383
Insurance	0	373	1,631	2,204	2,349	3,395	2,565	5,414	–	433
Other	210	339	309	555	685	697	1,121	1,227	–	540
Personal taxes		185	1,929	1,748	4,282	3,119	8,206	5,311	24	441

[a] BLS budgets are based upon the BLS budgets used in 1973 (table 6.22) with prices updated using the CPI modifications to BLS lower budget and dependency budget.
[b] Used USDA Thrifty Food Budget.
[c] Public transportation only is used. If 55% of families are allowed to own an automobile, then transportation costs rise to $1,485.
[d] This covers non-prescription drugs and supplies. Medical care is assumed to be provided, otherwise the cost would be $1,631.

The field-worker reported that one-half of the families lived in 'very bad' neighborhoods with monthly rents between $180 and $265 (average $2,670 annually), which is slightly below the rent in the dependency standard or the rent ($2,788) paid by the CES poor.[73] The monthly rent in 'average' neighborhoods was $325 to $425 (average $4,500 annually), which compares to the rent ($4,563) paid by laborer families.

These families economized in a variety of ways. One-sixth owned a reliable car; one-third did not own a telephone; and one-third spent nothing on entertainment. All families had a color television, and one-third had VCRs. These budgets show that the major decision of how much to spend on the apartment determines how much is left for items other than food and rent. The total budgets are similar to the dependency budget, which was meant to be applicable to AFDC families.

Since no adjustments have been made to the BLS intermediate and higher budgets, they represent consumption norms from the early 1960s. Wage-earner families lived slightly above the BLS intermediate budget standard in 1973; by 1988, their spending was one-third above the intermediate standard and equaled the BLS higher budget. Salaried families matched the BLS higher budget standard in 1973, but in 1988 salaried families spent 30% more than the higher standard. When new budget standards are once again devised for urban classes, they will reflect new consumption norms that incorporate higher standards of living as well as innovative goods and services.

Standard of living index

The standard of living for laborer families began at a high level that covered improvements in basics for food, clothing, household operations, recreation, personal care, and Social Security withholding. Expenditures had increased only modestly for laborer families between 1973 and 1988, and laborers spent 66% of the increment for status. The improvements in basics between 1973 and 1988 absorbed 1% of the increase in real expenditures, and improvements in variety the remaining 5% (see table 7.24).

Laborer families had especially increased their status in their wardrobes, gift-giving, and recreational activities. At the same time, they decreased their variety in these areas. Families gave more expensive recreational gifts and made fewer donations. The status of the husband's clothing increased as he bought better clothes; to a lesser extent the wife also bought more expensive clothing. Husbands and wives also decreased their clothing variety as they purchased fewer but nicer articles of clothing.

While laborer families were decreasing variety in gifts, recreation, and clothing, they were increasing their variety in their purchases of automobiles, furnishings, and food. They also reduced their variety in insurance policies.

Table 7.24 Standard of living index, 1988

	Laborer 1988 less laborer 1973					Poor 1988 less laborer 1988				Wage earner 1988 less low income 1988				Salaried 1988 less wage earner 1988			
	DE ($)	B73 ($)	B88a ($)	Variety ($)	Status ($)	DE ($)	B88 ($)	Variety ($)	Status ($)	DE ($)	B88 ($)	Variety ($)	Status ($)	DE ($)	B88 ($)	Variety ($)	Status ($)
Food	134	B	(233)	62	37	(855)	(684)	(102)	(69)	684	B	518	166	932	B	382	550
Clothing	366	B	126	(165)	405	(562)	(304)	(186)	(72)	354	B	246	108	595	B	424	171
Shelter																	
Housing + fuel/utilities	127	B	139	6	6	(1,977)	B	(128)	(545)	783	B	266	517	2,114	B	719	1,395
Furnishings	38	B	B	227	(190)	(347)	B	(237)	(109)	292	B	126	167	667	B	486	181
Household operations	447	B	290	1	156	(432)	B	(270)	(162)	330	B	101	229	339	B	97	241
Miscellaneous	1,576	B	335	(639)	1,881	(6,588)	(1,837)	(3,543)	(1,207)	4,159	B	2,597	1,563	6,383	B	2,736	3,646
Transportation	267	B	B	321	(55)	(2,378)	B	(2,261)	(117)	2,010	B	718	1,292	1,080	B	677	403
Recreation and education	608	B	428	(58)	238	(974)	B	(375)	(599)	706	B	232	474	2,097	B	471	1,626
Medical care	(551)	B	(703)	(116)	267	(227)	(77)	(36)	(114)	176	B	119	56	212	B	4	208
Personal care	9	B	34	50	(75)	(167)	(127)	(38)	(2)	65	B	61	4	166	B	51	115
Gifts and contributions	727	B	B	(340)	1,067	(1,178)	B	(768)	(410)	540	B	1,989	(1,449)	1,093	B	38	1,055
Personal insurance[b]	273	B	440	(317)	150	(1,832)	(1,414)	(409)	(8)	1,191	B+806	196	189	2,019	B+1,349	375	295
Other	244	B	B	474	(230)	(215)	B	(463)	248	142	B	45	98	530	B	216	314
Total	2,688	0	521	145	1,778	(11,145)	(3,910)	(5,274)	(1,959)	7,272	806	4,617	1,851	11,844	1,349	3,940	6,554
Distribution	1.00	0.00	0.19	0.05	0.66	1.00	0.35	0.47	0.18	1.00	0.11	0.63	0.25	1.00	0.11	0.33	0.55

a Includes changes in the basic standard (family size 2.9) for food ($152), clothing ($220), personal care ($62), and medical care (−$559) in addition to the improvements in basics shown under B88.

b The basic for personal insurance is the mandatory payroll tax for Social Security and DI, thus the basic standard increases with earnings.

Wage-earner families spent 30% more than laborers, and salaried families spent 36% more than wage earners in 1988. Salaried families continued to spend relatively more on status and wage earners relatively more on variety as in previous years. Because of the increase in the earnings that were subject to Social Security withholding, both wage-earner and salaried families spent 11% of their increased budgets on basics for insurance.

Wage-earner families substantially increased their variety and status over laborers in transportation, as they purchased more and better automobiles. Wage-earner families also bought considerably more variety than laborer families in food and gifts and more status in housing (but less status in gifts). Wage-earner families purchased as much variety in 1988 as salaried families did in 1973, and they spent almost as much for status as for variety in 1988.

Salaried families substantially increased their variety and status over wage earners in housing, as they purchased larger homes in better locations, and in recreation, as they took more vacations and purchased a wider array of goods and services to enrich their leisure time. While on vacation, salaried families were more likely than wage-earner families to attend paid events, such as amusement parks, and were more likely to stay in a motel. At home, salaried families had more and better athletic gear; more and higher quality color televisions, VCRs, and sound components; more video games; more tapes and records; more newspapers and books; more and better toys and games; and more musical instruments. Salaried families were more likely to subscribe to cable and to pay for premium services. They owned more boats and had better campers. They purchased more and better automobiles. They bought higher priced tickets when they attended paid events. To record their active family life, they had more film processed. Overall, salaried families' purchases of status equaled 80% of laborers' basics. Salaried purchases of variety equaled laborers' basics in 1950.

Compared to laborer families, wage-earner families had more active social lives. They took more vacations and owned a wider array of recreational goods, especially sports equipment, VCRs, and toys and games. They were more likely to belong to a club, take sports lessons, and subscribe to cable television. But the recreational spending between wage-earner and laborer families was much more similar than the large gulf that existed between wage-earner and salaried families.

While the employed classes were increasing their purchases of variety and status across the board, poor working families did not meet basics in several important categories, including food, clothing, and housing. However, they met or surpassed the basics in transportation as well as in several categories that are thought of as less important – furnishings, recreation and education, and gifts and contributions. For a dependent family, basics were met in food and household operations, and were almost met in housing.

Poor families' budgets, compared to laborer families, resulted in their consuming considerably less variety in transportation because of less car ownership and less variety in gift-giving. Their main decline in the consumption of status compared to laborers was in housing and recreational activities. Compared to laborer families, poor families lived in run-down neighborhoods. They took fewer vacations, but they spent more on their vacations because of their higher transportation costs, which reflects the need to use transportation other than an unreliable (or nonexistent) car. At home, they bought less and cheaper audio equipment, rented fewer videos, bought fewer tapes, records, toys or games, and were less likely to have cable television service. They were less likely to attend paid sports or cultural events or have sports lessons than laborer families. Their meager budgets translated into limited social activities. Poor families had to entertain themselves without spending much, or any, money.

Surprisingly, poor families paid higher college tuition than laborer families, even though laborer families were more likely to have someone in college. Among employed classes, the frequency of college tuition increased with class status. Laborer and wage-earner families were almost equal in the frequency of paying for college tuition, but wage-earner families were more likely to have a child in private K-12 school than laborers. Salaried families were more likely than wage earners to be paying tuition for college and K-12 private school.

As expected, the frequency of buying a computer increased with class status across all classes. Traveling on vacation, having cable TV and an array of books and newspapers, and participating in a variety of recreational activities made families more integrated into the society and better prepared their children to function as adults in an increasingly complex and global economy. But having a computer in the home was perhaps an even more important tool of integration for the family and of preparation for the children.

Computers are becoming as influential as television was in shaping family life and cultural values. The impact of computers differs significantly from the homogenizing impact of television, which played to a passive audience. Computers empower by providing access to information and by serving as a communication device. A computer at home, which is an indication of computers being used in the school as well as at work, helps children with their school work. Computer literacy is rewarded in the workplace.[74] Although computers are becoming a part of everyday life in many families and at work, many children are still not computer literate and many have never touched a keyboard or mouse. With the rapid expansion of information and communication services that rely upon owning and using computers, this form of economic distance is destined to become an important force in segregating and isolating families and their children, just as housing, education, recreation, and transportation traditionally have.

NOTES

1. *Statistical Abstract* of the United States, various years.
2. 'Employee Benefits and the Tax Base,' Alicia H. Arunell, *New England Economic Review*, Jan.–Feb. 1984. Colien Heferan, 'Employee Benefits,' *Family Economics Review* No. 1, 1985, p. 7.
3. Real GNP (per capita) rose 70% between 1950 and 1973 and 26% between 1973 and 1988. US Department of Commerce, *Current Survey of Business.*
4. *Survey of Current Business.* Federal, state, and local government receipts were the same (39% of national income) in both years.
5. Lawrence Katz and Kevin Murphy, 'Change in Relative Wages: 1963–87: Supply and Demand Factors,' NBER Working Paper No. 3927, 1992.
6. Rebecca Blank, 'Why Were Poverty Rates so High in the 1980s?' NBER Working Paper No. 3878, 1992.
7. Commission on the Skills of the American Workforce, *America's Choice: High Skills or Low Wages* (Rochester, NY: National Center on Education and the Economy, 1990); Ray Marshall and Marc Tucker, *Thinking for a Living: Work Skills and the Future of the American Economy* (New York: Basic Books, 1992).
8. *CPR*, P-20, various issues.
9. The median family income nationally was $27,225 with an average family size of 2.6, 1.4 earners, 2.0 vehicles, 0.7 children, and 0.2 seniors. *CPR*, P-20, #447. In the 1988 CES data, several important variables were top-coded. Top codes included: $100,000 for earnings, financial accounts, asset variables, taxes; $200,000 for market value or sale of owned home, medical and physician services; $1,000 for rent of dwelling, rental equivalence of owned housing, lodging away from home.
10. Slightly lower thresholds are used for households headed by persons over 64 years old. Since expenditures of households in the bottom decile are similar to expenditures of households in the second decile, differentiation among low-income families by the amount of reported income is not meaningful. For this reason, the definition of the low-income group was changed in 1988 to include all households below the poverty threshold in the poor class. In 1973, only households with incomes close to the poverty threshold were included in the low-income group.

11. Gregory Schoepfle, *The Underground Economy in the U.S.*, US Department of Labor, Office of International Economic Affairs, 1992.
12. Christopher Jencks and Kathryn Edin, 'The Real Welfare Problem,' *The American Prospect*, Winter 1990, p. 34.
13. Income includes the value of in-kind and money benefits from government programs. BLS, *Consumer Expenditure Survey, 1988–89*, Bull. 2383, 1991.
14. BLS, *Consumer Expenditure Survey: Integrated Diary and Interview Survey Data, 1972–73*, Bull. 1992, 1978. The growth in underreported income was somewhat masked by demographic changes. Households in the bottom 20% were more likely to be seniors, who had smaller families and were more likely to be spending assets, in 1973 than in 1988. Households in the bottom 20th percentile had 1.5 persons (with 0.6 seniors) in 1973 and 1.9 persons (with 0.4 seniors) in 1988.
15. *CPR*, P-20, various issues. Families are 71% of households in 1988, and only 43% of households had three or more persons.
16. This trend in families toward single-person households is reflected in our employed classes, where 29% of laborer, 18% of wage-earner, and 10% of salaried families have only one person.
17. Bureau of the Census, *CPR*, P-60, various issues.
18. Female participation on the basis of wages would have declined, rather than increased, between 1973 and 1980. Brown, C., 'An Institutional Model of Wives' Work Decisions,' *Industrial Relations*, 24, 2, Spring 1985, pp. 182–204.
19. US BLS, *Handbook of Labor Statistics*, Aug. 1989. Wives with children aged six and older had a participation rate of 73%. Women aged 45–64 had a participation rate of 57%.
20. Published CES data for 1992 indicates that 1988 and 1992 expenditure patterns for the household in the middle of the income distribution (slightly below that for laborers) were similar, with three exceptions. Shelter accounted for 17% of the budget in 1988 and 19% in 1992; health care accounted for 4.7% of the budget in 1988 and 6.4% in 1992; transportation accounted for 23% of the budget in 1988 and 21% in 1992. Both average expenditure and income (constant dollars) were about the same in the two years.
21. US Department of Commerce, *Survey of Current Business*, various issues.
22. This survey shows families spending an even higher proportion of their food budgets on food away from home and a wider variation among employed classes in eating out.
23. Compared to 1974 RDA, the 1980 RDA increased for iodine and vitamins C and B6, with slight decreases in protein for some groups and lower caloric levels for teens.

24. Richard L. Kerr, et al., 'USDA 1983 Thrifty Food Plan,' *Family Economics Review*, No. 1, 1984, pp. 18–33. The major changes in the RDA included increases in ascorbic acid and vitamin B6. Dietary practices were based on the 1977–8 National Food Consumption Survey. The quality of the 1987–8 National Food Consumption Survey is debated because of the low response rate.

25. Judith Jones Putman, 'Food Consumption, Prices, and Expenditures, 1967–88,' USDA Economic Research Service, Statistical Bulletin No. 804, May 1990.

26. Suzanne Murphy, et al., 'Demographic and Economic Factors Associated with Dietary Quality for Adults in the 1987–88 National Food Consumption Survey,' *Journal of the American Dietetic Association*, 92, 11, Nov. 1992, pp. 1352–7. The quality of the 1987–8 National Food Consumption Survey is debated because of the low response rate.

27. US National Center for Health Statistics, 'Advance Data for Vital and Health Statistics,' No. 174.

28. Suzanne Murphy, discussion with author.

29. Ibid. and USDA, Human Nutrition Service, 'Nationwide Food Consumption Survey 1987–88: Food and Nutrition Intakes, One Day,' NFCS Report I–1, 1992.

30. The comparisons between 1973 and 1988 for children are not exact, since the data are available for 2–11 year olds and 12–20 year olds in 1973, but only for 2–16 year olds in 1988. Men and women include all people over 20 years old in 1973 and over 16 in 1988.

31. Katherine S. Newman in *Declining Fortunes: the Withering of the American Dream* (New York: Basic Books, 1993) argues that the expectation that each generation would exceed that standard of living of their parents had been crushed. The fall of home ownership rates for young household heads (under age 35 years old, p. 30) is her most important symbol of the withering of the American dream. However, she reports home ownership rates for households rather than families, and so the rate is not adjusted for the rise of single-person households and the decline in households with children.

32. The CES added an imputed rental value for homeowners in order to improve the CPI for housing. This was not available in 1973, when the rental value was estimated by owners and its quality was questionable. Unfortunately, the rental value has a top-code of $1,000 monthly, which affected 7% of laborer and poor families and 19% of salaried families. For this reason, the divergence in housing values is greater than the averages given here.

33. The discrepancy is decreased if the full mortgage payment, including principal, is included. Out-of-pocket expenses then equal 0.39

(seniors), 0.55 (poor), 0.78 (laborer), 0.81 (wage earner), 0.94 (salaried) of the rental value.

34.   For example, the ratio of poor to laborer rental values was 0.89 and the ratio of CES housing expenditures was 0.62; the comparable ratios for salaried to laborer was 1.35 for rental values and 1.61 for CES housing expenditures; the comparable ratios for senior to laborer was 0.95 for rental values and 0.52 for CES housing expenditures.

35.   In 1986, 45% of families with income under $30,000 and employed mothers used nonrelatives for child care for preschoolers; over 60% of families with incomes above $30,000 used nonrelatives for care. US Bureau of the Census, *CPR*, Series P-70, No. 20, July 1990.

36.   The terms 'car' or 'automobile' will be used in the text to include automobiles, pickup trucks, utility vehicles, and minivans, since they all are used to provide personal transportation for the family. The CES lists trucks, utility vehicles, and minivans under 'other vehicles.'

37.   The price paid for new cars is difficult to compare across classes because only the net cost after trade-in is recorded. Since higher class families trade in later model cars, their net outlay is reduced.

38.   The three employed classes reported 60% of car owners paying for insurance in any given quarter, compared to 38% poor owners, and 43% senior owners. The quarterly data do not allow us to estimate with confidence how many families purchased insurance over the year.

39.   A study using the 1986 CES found that families with college-educated heads spent nearly twice as much on recreation than those without college experience, although their total budgets were only 60% higher. John Robinson, 'The Time Squeeze,' *American Demographics*, Feb. 1990, p. 25.

40.   Implied annual frequencies are 4.66 times the reported quarterly frequencies.

41.   Actual comparisons of the percentage buying equipment and supplies in 1988 with 1973 are not possible, since the data are for annual purchases in 1973 and quarterly purchases in 1988.

42.   The rates are for adults over age 21; *Statistical Abstract*.

43.   The 1988 figures are annualized, in order to compare them to 1973, by assuming that tuition is paid every other quarter by families with a member in college.

44.   My thinking about, and knowledge of, health care issues has benefited from discussions with Ruth Given and her guidance in using the data.

45.   *Statistical Abstract 1992*, Table 103.

46.   These figures are compiled from *Social Security Bulletin* (various issues), *Statistical Abstract of the United States* (various issues);

National Center for Health Statistics, Characteristics of Persons with and Without Health Care Coverage: United States, 1989, Advance Data, No. 201, 1991; and Richard Kronick, 'Health Insurance, 1979–1989: The Frayed Connection Between Employment and Insurance,' *Inquiry*, Winter 1991, pp. 318–32.

47. The SIPP data for 1986 found 84% of the population with private health insurance, compared to the CPS figure of 76% for 1987. Some analysts argue that the CPS data reflect current status rather than coverage over the past year. See 'Health Insurance Coverage, 1986–88,' *CPR*, Series P-70, No. 17, 1990.

48. One-half of the employed uninsured had small employers with fewer than 25 employees. 'Data Watch,' *Health Affairs*, Summer 1989, pp. 102–10.

49. National Center for Health Statistics, Characteristics of Persons With and Without Health Care Coverage: United States, 1989, *Advance Data*, No. 201, 1991.

50. National Center for Health Statistics, Health, United States, 1990, DHHS Pub. No. (PHS) 91–1232, 1991.

51. *Social Security Bulletin*, various issues.

52. These figures are for individual coverage. Only 32% received fully-paid premiums for family coverage, down from 51% in 1980. In 1988, the employer paid an average of 90% of the premium for individual coverage and 75% for family coverage in conventional plans and HMOs. 'DataWatch,' *Health Affairs*, various issues; and Thomas P. Burke and Rita S. Jain, 'Trends in Employer-provided Health Care Benefits,' *Monthly Labor Review*, Feb. 1991, pp. 24–30.

53. *BLS*, 'Employee Benefits in Medium and Large Firms, 1989,' Bulletin 2363.

54. US Health Care Financing Administration, *Health Care Financing Review*, Fall 1989, 11, 1, and *Social Security Bulletin*, May 1973.

55. These estimates combine the national data with the CES data. The information collected on health care expenditures in the CES was different in 1973 and 1988, so that we have less information on the insurance coverage in 1988 from the CES.

56. This group includes 54% paying for private insurance and 28% paying for supplemental insurance.

57. Beth Harrison, 'Spending Patterns of Older Persons Revealed in Expenditure Survey,' *Monthly Labor Review*, Oct. 1986.

58. These programs have come under increasing scrutiny as analysts question how much value they are to seniors, who perhaps are pressured to purchase dubious policies. See, for example, Thomas Rice, Nelda McCall, and James M. Boismier, 'The Effectiveness of Consumer Choice in the Medicare Supplemental Health Insurance Market,' *Health Services Review*, 26, 2 (June 1991), pp. 223–46.

59. *Statistical Abstract of the United States*, 1991, p. 96.
60. The 1988 figures for percentage reporting are quarterly and the 1973 figures are annual. Annual figures for 1988 would probably be slightly higher than the quarterly figures.
61. *Statistical Abstract.*
62. By 1988, the Social Security payroll tax was 7.51% on base earnings of $45,000.
63. John A. Turner and Daniel Beller, *Trends in Pensions*, GPO, 1990, p. 357.
64. The percentages for wholly paid plans is for employees in firms with more than 100 employees. The passage of the Employee Retirement Income Security Act (ERISA) in 1974 hastened the shift to defined-contribution plans and away from defined-benefit plans. Bradley R. Braden, 'Increases in Employer Costs for Employee Benefits Dampen Dramatically,' *Monthly Labor Review*, July 1988, pp. 3–7.
65. This section is based on Teresa Ghilarducci, *Labor's Capital: The Economics and Politics of Private Pensions* (Cambridge, MA: MIT Press), 1992, as well as on conversations with the author.
66. In 1988, 92% of employees in firms with over 100 employees had a basic life insurance plan paid entirely by the employer. BLS, *Employee Benefits in Medium and Large Firms*, various issues.
67. *Statistical Abstract of the United States*, various issues.
68. All net worth data are Bureau of the Census, 'Household Wealth and Asset Ownership: 1988,' *CPR*, Series P-70, No. 22.
69. The figures to calculate the average value of liquid assets for seniors in the second quintile were not available, and so the (lower) median figure is used.
70. No BLS budget standard had allowed more than one car. The differences in the BLS standards were the proportion owning one car and the age of the car. The moderate transportation standard allows 95% ownership of a newer car, which is two years old when purchased and kept for four years. The higher standard allows 100% car ownership; when purchased, 60% of the cars are new and 40% are two years old. All cars are kept four years.
71. A budget for AFDC families was calculated for California by Consumers Union of U.S., Inc., 'Sold Short: The Actual Cost of a Minimum Adequate Living Standard Compared to AFDC Levels in California,' June 1992. Rent was set at the HUD Fair Market Rent for 'recently occupied adequate quality rental units' at the 45th percentile. This value, which is close to the median rental value (i.e., set at the 50th percentile) seems unreasonably high, since poor households would be expected to rent at the 10th to 20th percentile (depending on the percentage of households in poverty.) The BLS had used the average of the lower third of rents for five-room units

in setting up their lower budget. Depending on the city, rent accounts for at least 50% (and often over 60%) of the Consumers Union budgets for three-person families. Excluding rent, the three-person budget is about $473 monthly, which is only 80% of our 1988 dependency budget (also without rent).

72. Christopher Jencks and Kathryn Edin, 'The Real Welfare Problem,' *The American Prospect*, Winter 1990, pp. 31–50.

73. The Jenck's rent figures do not include utilities. The CES figures include utilities that are paid as part of the rent, which is why the CES utility figures are lower than the Jenck's utility figures. The rent allowed in the dependency standard is at the upper end of the AFDC rents in 'very bad' neighborhoods; the rents in 'average' neighborhoods are one-quarter to two-thirds higher than the rent in the dependency standard.

74. Alan B. Krueger, 'How Computers Have Changed the Wage Structure: Evidence from Microdata, 1984–89,' NBER Working Paper No. 3858, 1991.

8 Conclusion

Introduction

Economic growth has improved living standards in ways not dreamed of in 1918. Working-class families have been able to attain high levels of living as basics evolved to include car ownership, home ownership, a multiplicity of equipment for entertainment and recreation, and an annual vacation. Their consumption grew to include purchases of variety and then status as the importance of social life expanded and home life shrank as a proportion of the family's budget. This transformation in consumption norms, from a focus on home life to a focus on social life, is reflected in the economic distance created across classes, which use resources to separate and distinguish themselves from the classes beneath them.

Consumption Norms and Economic Distance

In 1918, American families' daily lives were filled with hard physical work both on the job and at home. After a long working week, laborer husbands brought home only enough money to buy some, but not all, basics; their wives spent 69% of their budgets on home life (food and shelter) (see figures 8.1, 8.2). Laborer families also spent a significant proportion (20%) of the budget on presentability (clothing, personal care, and medical care).

Meager budgets provided little relief from the drudgery and monotony of everyday life. People stayed home except to go to work, school, or shopping, and their main social activity was going to church. How well a family ate and dressed was largely determined by the wife's cooking and sewing skills, as well as her ability to shop wisely and stretch a dollar.

Distribution of the Wage Earner's Family Budget

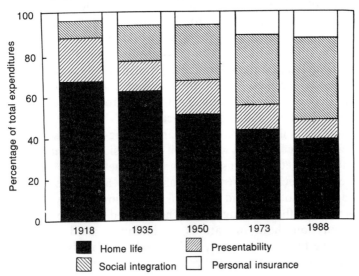

Percentage of homeowners: 1918, 24%; 1935, 26%; 1950, 47%; 1973, 65%; 1988, 71%
Average family size: 1918, 4.7; 1935, 3.5; 1950, 3.2; 1973, 3.17; 1988, 2.91.

Figure 8.1 Distribution of wage earner's family budget

Wage–earner family expenditures

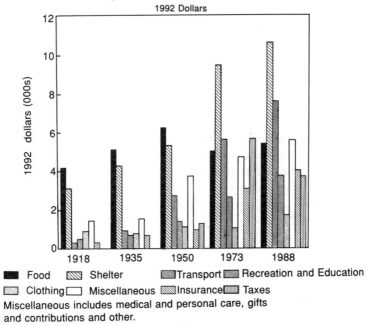

Miscellaneous includes medical and personal care, gifts
and contributions and other.

Figure 8.2 Wage-earner family expenditures

Black families suffered enormously compared to the white working class, as they often went hungry and wore rags. Their budgets were one-third below the level required for them to buy the basics, and their poverty kept them isolated from the white working class.

Although the automobile had been mass produced for almost a decade, World War I interrupted the salaried class's rush to buy a car. Only one in three salaried families owned the coveted car in 1918, but this proportion was to grow dramatically as the automobile changed the landscape and the daily habits of Americans.

Salaried husbands lives' were easier than working-class husbands' lives because their white-collar jobs were much less physically demanding, and they were not completely exhausted when they came home in the evening. Their higher paychecks allowed their families to buy some relief from drudgery and monotony, and this was the primary way they were distinguished from the working class. The salaried wife spent considerably more on household operations, including a maid and laundry service, to make her chores easier, and the salaried family spent money to create a social life that included recreational activities.

In 1935, our next survey year, families were suffering through the economic uncertainty of the Depression, even when their own living standards had been little affected because the husband had been fortunate enough to keep his job. Although home life activities still dominated the budget, families were now spending more money on their social lives as their work lives became physically easier. The share of the budget going to home life diminished slightly in order to make room for more spending on social integration, including purchases for recreation, education, and transportation, and of gifts or donations. Social life includes both presentability and integration (or 'fitting in'), yet families felt that their spending for appearance was already fairly adequate and did not have to rise as rapidly as their overall spending. So spending on social life shifted from being mostly for presentability and became more oriented towards participating in activities.

Work hours had been reduced by the Depression, and mass production and automation helped reduce the physical demands of work. Housework became physically easier with smaller families and housing amenities, including plumbing, indoor hot water, electric and gas heating systems, and appliances like the refrigerator and washing machine. Although both paid work and housework would continue to become less physically exhausting, the improvements experienced between 1918 and 1950 were perhaps the most welcome because they finally allowed the family to use their time off for leisure activities rather than merely for recovering in order to return to their tasks. At last, working-class families could have some social activities other than going to church and buy some goods other than tobacco to enhance leisure time.

Unemployment provided the main economic distance between families during the Depression, but these families were kept hidden by the data collectors. Employed families created economic distance amongst themselves by purchasing a rich social life, more mobility, varying recreational activities, and by easing the drudgery of housework for the wife. Four out of five salaried families now had an automobile, while only a minority of working-class families could afford a car. Salaried families improved their living standards compared to working-class families by spending considerably more on recreation and household operations.

Within the working class, wage-earner families improved their living standard over laborer families by subtle improvements across all categories. The greatest economic distance was created by ownership of an automobile.

Black families, who were forced to bear a disproportionate share of the unemployment, continued to suffer economically. Those who were unemployed lived in dire poverty. Those with jobs had not improved their living standard compared to 1918, and their budgets allowed them to purchase less than two-thirds of basics. They remained hungry, poorly clothed, poorly sheltered, and economically isolated.

After World War II, families were considerably better off economically. Their Depression-provoked anxiety had been replaced by optimism for the future. Many families had savings that had accumulated as they bought War Bonds both because they were patriotic and because they found few goods at the store to buy.

Car production had been halted by the war, but when peace came, families rushed to dealers to buy cars as they rolled off the line. Finally, working-class America had wheels; one-half of laborer and seven-tenths of wage-earner families owned an automobile. The proportion of the budget devoted to home life continued to shrink while social integration blossomed to assume a share of the budget as large as the share of food at home or shelter. Spending on presentability maintained its share of the budget. Shelter's share of the budget declined, after having jumped in 1935, as families had been forced by a wartime moratorium on residential construction to put off house buying plans. The rush to buy new government-financed housing in the suburbs was only beginning to show up in the data. In 1950, only a bare majority of salaried families had attained the American dream of owning a home.

Blacks were considerably better off after the war, which opened new labor market opportunities to them. The war hastened their migration out of the rural South – first to the urban South and then to the urban North to the rapidly growing factory jobs, especially in automobile-related industries. Blacks' budgets in 1950 were sufficient to cover 1935 basics, but their budgets fell 13% short of the higher 1950 basics.

The war had halted any major transformations in consumption norms. In 1950, salaried families spent their higher income relative to wage-earner families in subtle ways and increased spending across all categories by 13%–40%. As usual, they spent money on recreation, transportation, furnishings, and gifts to create a varied and active social life both at home and in public.

Within the working class, wage-earner families were finally able to mimic salaried families in the ways they used to create economic distance. Wage earners could spend their higher income relative to laborers on recreation and transportation to begin creating a more active and varied social life outside the home.

In earlier times, shelter and diet formed economic distance across classes. The addition of social life, first in public and then at home, to create economic distance across classes was becoming an important force in consumption norms.

By 1973, dramatic economic growth fueled by the war on poverty and the Vietnam War magnified the trends of expanded spending for social life and growth of home ownership. Prodigious improvements in housing had been achieved – working-class families finally achieved the American Dream of paying a mortgage monthly on their own home rather than paying rent. Owned homes were typically larger and newer with more amenities and a yard. Perhaps more importantly, home ownership gave families a sense of control and security.

Home ownership did not halt the movement of activities to the public areas or facilitate a more intense focus on home life for long. Wives gave birth to more children for a decade, and then their rush to paid work resumed and child-bearing fell. Eventually, their homes, filled with modern amenities, lay empty during weekdays; adults were at work and children were at school. Fewer meals were eaten at home, where people mostly watched television, slept, and prepared to return to work or school during the working week.

Presentability was a smaller part of the budget (12%) in 1973, but social life continued its expansion since spending for social integration absorbed 35% of the working-class budget. Spending on home life shrank to 45% of the budget, even though families had augmented their spending on housing as they became homeowners. Shelter had become the largest budget category, but its growth was offset by the decline in spending for food to eat at home.

Transportation had expanded to become the second largest budget category as the second car was becoming a required part of life to accommodate the shopping and commuting needs of the two-paycheck family. With both the husband and wife working, the family's time pressures rose along with their paid work hours. Leisure time declined, especially for employed wives. Time spent shopping expanded as the assortment of stores along with the goods and services offered multiplied. Only the salaried class could afford two cars as a norm, however, and the working class still struggled toward that goal.

The War on Poverty had reduced, but not eradicated, poverty by 1973. Black husband–wife families had finally made it into the working class, but black single-mother families, which were rapidly increasing in number, usually lived in poverty. Black families had become bifurcated by their family composition.

Families living at the poverty threshold did not have sufficient budgets to purchase the basics for employed families. However, their budgets allowed them to purchase the dependency basics, except for clothing. Many low-income families preferred to spend money on an automobile, so they would not have to rely on public transportation or friends, rather than spend money on appearance (clothing and personal care). For the 45% car owners, their cars made life easier and integrated them into their social stratum, but owning a car was costly and forced them to cut back severely in other areas. Still, low-income families spent considerably less than laborer families on transportation, as well as recreation and gifts.

In 1973, economic distance within the working class had shrunk to the lowest point witnessed in this book. Wage earners had budgets only 16% higher than laborers' budgets. Wage earners favored spending the increment to create economic distance from laborers by making home life easier and more pleasant with spending on furnishings and household operations, by improving appearance with more haircuts and perms, and by having more active social lives through paying for recreational admissions and vacations.

Salaried families continued to spend their higher incomes relative to wage earners on recreation, gifts, and clothes as their social activities separated them from working-class families. Higher spending on home furnishings also allowed them to bring part of their social lives into the home. Salaried families augmented spending on housing and household operations at a much lower rate, however, in improving their living standard over wage earners. Ownership of the proper equipment and clothing for a particular activity, both at home and in public, and taking vacations had become markers of class status.

The period following 1973 brought disillusionment to Americans, who had begun to believe that they could control the economy, improve the lot of the disadvantaged, and maintain ascending living standards for employed families. When these expectations were not met, and when income growth lagged, social conflict over income distribution surfaced.[1] The steady and impressive economic improvements of the previous period left Americans unprepared for the challenges imposed by an increasingly interconnected world economy that was largely the result of US policies. With high and unmet expectations, both developed and developing countries made claims for a larger share of resources and improvements in living standards.

By 1988, the shifting of the budget from home life to social life had noticeably slowed down. Families allocated their budgets in a remarkably similar fashion to 1973. Home ownership edged upward for wage-earner and salaried families, and the favored minority of working-class families owning more than one car expanded. But families increased their spending rates in order to improve their consumption norms in an attempt to meet unrealistic expectations based on the past. Technological innovations, especially those based on the applications of microelectronics to communication and audio-visual equipment as well as personal computers, provided the major source for ameliorated living standards between 1973 and 1988.

Over the years, miscellaneous expenditures, which are primarily transactions costs (banking and legal services, finance charges, real estate fees), rose steadily.[2] These transaction costs represented the expenses imposed by an increasingly complex and more regulated economy. Although required for economic functioning, their value added to the standard of living was neither visible nor obvious.

Economic distance between salaried and wage-earner families displayed the same pattern in 1988 as in the previous two surveys. Salaried families spent their higher budgets relative to wage earners on recreation and furnishings as they bought modern electronic equipment. Similarly, wage earners distanced themselves from laborers through purchases of modern electronic equipment. Surprisingly, wage-earner families also distanced themselves from laborer families by spending considerably more on clothing.

The 1973 poverty rate of 11.1% turned out to be the lowest rate achieved by the United States. After falling steadily in response to income support programs enacted in the 1960s to help the disadvantaged, the poverty rate rose after 1973 to a peak of 15.2% in 1983 before falling to 13.1% in 1988. The heightened inequality of the 1980s still generated poverty rates below those of the years prior to the 1960s. Poor families' standard of living rose during the 1980s because their expenditures rose much more rapidly than their reported incomes.[3]

Both poor families and seniors made gains relative to employed families between 1973 and 1988, but the source of their gains was not the same. Seniors had considerably higher living standards in 1988 than in 1973 because Social Security benefits expanded and are indexed for inflation. Seniors' budgets, which were only slightly higher than the BLS Retired Intermediate Budget in 1973, were 77% higher than the BLS budget in 1988. In retirement, seniors spent only 56% of what laborer families spent in 1973. In 1988, seniors spent 72% as much as laborer families, who had additional financial obligations with growing children and home mortgages. Seniors were likely to own their homes without mortgages, and they had much higher assets than middle-aged, working-class families. Although they spent more on medical care than employed families, they had access to basic medical care through the Medicare program. Employed families who did not have employer-sponsored insurance were left to hope that no one in their family would require hospitalization or ongoing doctor's care.

Poor families in 1988 were typically better off than families at the poverty threshold in 1973 because of the substantial increase in unreported income, especially for the lowest income families. In 1973, families at the poverty threshold were significantly better off than the average poor family. In 1988, the relationship between repeated income and expenditures had disintegrated for poor families so that reported income was no longer a reliable indicator of the family's actual consumption.

The poverty threshold, which had been constructed assuming families would spend one-third of their budgets on food, reflected consumption norms of the 1960s when food absorbed a larger part of the budget. By 1973, low-income families spent only one-fourth of their budgets on food; in 1988, only one-fifth. Although few commentators express confidence in the poverty thresholds as being up to date in defining minimum material requirements, no attempt has been made to calculate new thresholds. What light does the data presented here shed on the adequacy of the official poverty thresholds? The dependency budget standard developed in this book for non-employed families in 1973 and 1988 indicate that the poverty thresholds are not too low. In fact, poor families in 1988 spent 21% more than the dependency standard. However, compared to the dependency standard, poor families economized on housing and appearance (clothing and haircuts) in order to reach or exceed the working-class basics for transportation, recreation, and household operations. Their standard of living, at least in their social integration, had improved considerably between 1973 and 1988. As is often the case, the actual consumption practices of families diverged from the patterns advocated by the experts. In order for poor families to consume the dependency standard for housing and clothing, they would have to forgo part of their spending for cars and recreational activities and increase their spending for appearance and housing, or else they require considerably higher incomes to entice them to spend more for housing and appearance.

Laborer families experienced a substantial decline in their living standard relative to the poor between 1973 and 1988. At the same time, laborer families fell behind wage-earner families as the economic distance within the working class expanded back toward a more common historical relationship after falling to an atypically low level in 1973. Laborer families were feeling squeezed by diminished job opportunities and a living standard that was not keeping up with the other employed classes. Meanwhile, the economic distance that protected them from poverty was shrinking.

The economic security of families steadily improved from the Depression until the 1980s. After falling since the Depression, spending rates for employed families rose in the 1980s; after rising since the Depression, the real value of liquid assets fell. Only the economic security of seniors had continued to improve in the 1980s. As the United States borrowed against the future to maintain and improve current living standards, the country incurred massive Federal government debts and trade deficits while investments in plant and equipment languished. Low savings and investment reinforced the slow growth of income and productivity, and Americans found themselves in a vicious cycle.

Even though many families were disappointed by the slow economic growth of the 1980s, the economic growth of the previous seventy years had brought phenomenal improvements in the daily lives of people. Instead of revolving around physically demanding work, life was filled with a variety of stimulating activities using an array of goods. Advances in medical care had dramatically reduced the tragic experiences of losing a child and had prolonged the years of life so that most adults would enjoy a period of retirement. Complaints of physical exhaustion were replaced with complaints of pressure to do too many things in too little time. The array of options in how to spend one's time, coupled with the time required to comply with complex consumption norms, generated widespread feelings of stress. The transformation of consumption norms was accomplished through a process of emulation and innovation coupled with economizing and lowering the savings rate as families attempted both to replicate past practices and to incorporate new goods and services into their consumption patterns.

We leave our families in 1988 facing a more complex and rapidly changing world and experiencing vastly different life-styles than in 1918. The age and cause of death encompasses as well as symbolizes the improvements made in living standards. A person born in 1988 could look forward to 20 more years of life, living almost 40% longer, than a person born in 1918. Death of a young parent or child was an occurrence in 1918 that few families escaped. Working for 40 years and then retiring only became an expected part of life in the second half of the century.[4]

The process of birth had become much less traumatic as it became less dangerous. Infant and maternal mortality rates in 1989 were one-tenth the 1918 rates. Doctors' knowledge and the tools available to them had also improved the life chances of children and young adults. A one year old in 1989 was only one-twentieth as likely as a one year old in 1919 to die before age 14 or before age 24 years old. In 1919, before antibiotics and immunizations, 12 in 1,000 one-year-olds would not live to celebrate

Table 8.1 Life and death figures, 1918–89

	Fetal mortality (per 1,000 live births)	Infant mortality	Maternal mortality	Life expectancy at birth			Cumulative death rates (per 1,000 population)			Death rate (per 1,000 population)[d]					
				Total	M	F	<45 years	1-44 years	1-24 years	Heart disease	Cancer	Flu and pneumonia	Accidents	DPM	TB
1919[a]	NA	87	7.4	55	53	56	124	33	17	3.5	0.8	2.2	0.6	0.2	1.3
1935	36	56	5.8	62	60	64	80	19	9	4.3	1.1	1.0	0.8	0.1	0.6
1950	19	29	0.8	68	66	71	42	9	3	5.1	1.4	0.3	0.6	0.0	0.2
1973[b]	12	18	0.2	71	68	75	29	7	2	4.9	1.7	0.3	0.6	–	0.0
1989[c]	7	10	0.1	75	72	83	12	3	1	3.8	2.0	0.3	0.4	–	0.0

[a] 1919 figures are given instead of 1918 since they are more consistent with historical trends.
[b] Cumulative death rates are for 1970.
[c] Life expectancy figures are given for 1988 to be consistent with text.
[d] DPM covers diphtheria, whooping cough, and measles; TB is tuberculosis; accident covers all types including automobile and industrial.
Source: Historical Statistics, B 107-115, B 136-146, B 181-192, and Statistical Abstract, 1992 and 1976.

their fourteenth birthday and 17 in 1,000 would not live to their twenty-fourth birthday. In 1989, 1 in 1,000 one-year-olds would not live to their twenty-fourth birthday (see table 8.1).

Compared to the MD of 1918, who often carried all the tools of his trade in a physician's black bag, the MD in 1989 used an impressive array of medicines, procedures, and equipment for diagnosing and treating medical problems. Some killers, such as tuberculosis, typhoid, diphtheria, and whooping cough, along with other dreaded diseases that often left debilitating aftereffects, such as polio, scarlet fever, and measles, had almost vanished in the US. Other diseases, such as influenza and pneumonia, had dwindled to become a threat only to those already weakened by infirmity or age. In 1919, heart disease, influenza or pneumonia, and tuberculosis were the three leading causes of disease. In addition, occurrences of measles (4.7 per 10,000 people), diphtheria (1.0 per 1,000), scarlet fever (0.9 per 10,000), smallpox (0.8 per 10,000), and typhoid (0.5 per 10,000) were common. By 1989, heart disease and cancer were the leading causes of death. The death rates of flu and pneumonia had fallen by 86% and of tuberculosis by almost 100%. Reported cases of diphtheria, scarlet fever, and smallpox could be counted on one hand. The most virulent, and spreading, communicable disease in 1989 was AIDS.

The transformation of the cause of accidents symbolizes the complexity of the economic changes being made. In 1989, one was more likely to be in a fatal accident while riding in a car rather than working on a job, and the probability of surviving an accident had been considerably improved since 1918. The death rate from accidents rose between 1918 and 1935 as automobile accidents became more common. As work became more automated and as the medical profession's ability to treat trauma improved, industrial accidents fell more rapidly than automobile accidents, and the total accident rate began to fall in the second half of the century. With improvements in car safety, the death rate from automobile accidents finally began to fall. By 1989, the death rate from accidents was only 60% of the 1919 rate.

Emulation and Innovation

As hypothesized in Chapter 2, periods of slow or declining income growth would be the most disruptive to consumption norms. Families would not be able to buy innovative goods and services and to emulate past practices without sufficient income growth. In addition, the pressure to innovate would intensify as the economy matured and variety and status became a larger part of consumption. Disruption in consumption norms occurred especially between 1918 and 1935, which is the survey period with the most remarkable discontinuity in consumption norms and the only period with a decline in national income (see figure 8.3).

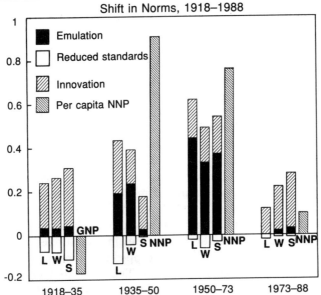

Shift in Norms, 1918–1988

Changes between reference years for laborer (L), wage earner (W) and salaried (S) families.
Changes for per capita Net National Product are also shown, except the 1918–35 changes is for GNP.

Figure 8.3 Shift in norms, 1918–1988

Economic distance increased at both ends of the income spectrum – between the working class and blacks and between the salaried class and the working class. Working-class families reduced their family size and reduced their consumption in clothing, household operations, and gifts in order to buy innovation in food, housing, utilities, and transportation. At the same time, only one-fifth of emulation (the imitation of traditional patterns) was realized.

The other period of disruption in consumption norms occurring during slow, but not negative, national income growth, was 1973–88. Families once again reduced their family size and spent some savings, but this time they reduced their standards in only one area – utilities – in order to purchase innovation in gifts, recreation, clothing, and household operations. Emulation of previous norms was almost nonexistent.

During the period with the highest national growth rate, 1935–50, less innovation occurred than during the low or negative growth eras. After expanding in the previous period, economic distance shrank at both ends of the income distribution. Laborer families tried to offset their loss of economic distance from blacks by reducing their family size and utilities in order to exceed the other classes in innovation, especially in food and transportation. Since salaried families experienced the slowest budget growth across the classes, they had to spend most of their budget increment on innovation in order to appear modern. In contrast, working-class families experienced faster growing budgets and so were able to purchase innovation as well as some emulation.

The other era of high national income growth, 1950–73, witnessed much more emulation and slightly less innovation with less reduction in standards than in the preceding high growth era. Families purchased innovations in housing and utilities, transportation, household operations, and recreation. Overall, families witnessed the least disruption to consumption norms of any period surveyed, and this period is remembered nostalgically as the golden era of attaining new heights in living standards.

Veblen's theory of emulation seemed to hold only when incomes grew sufficiently rapidly in an economy of mostly basic consumption. When incomes grow slowly, families will purchase innovations rather than emulate, and consumption norms are disrupted. This process of innovation at the expense of emulation intensifies in a mature economy. When some older practices are modified or dropped and some new practices are added, families seem to feel less well off. They tend to overvalue the lost emulation and undervalue the innovations, which they take for granted.

Basics, Variety, and Status

The transformation of consumption norms encompassed substantial improvements in basics for working-class families from 1918 to 1973, especially between 1950 and 1973, when homeownership, car ownership, and a biannual vacation became an expected part of working-class life (see figure 8.4 and table 8.2). After purchasing basics, families mainly purchased variety through 1950. In 1973, family spending turned toward status purchases. In 1950, laborers spent 12% of their budgets on variety and 2% on status; salaried families spent 25% on variety and 18% on status. By 1988, laborers spent 11% on variety and 21% on status; salaried families spent 25% on variety and 31% on status.

During the 70 years surveyed, laborer families progressed from a situation of spending 100% of their budgets on basics in 1918 to spending 32% on variety and status in 1988. Still, laborers' ability to purchase variety and status in 1988 did not match that of salaried families in 1935. In 1988, laborer families purchased only one-third as much variety and status as salaried families. Laborer families spent some of their savings to augment their status purchases between 1973 and 1988, when they experienced a decline in real income. Even without a decline in real income, wage-earner families also spent some of their savings in order to expand their purchases of status. The working class must have felt enormous social pressure to purchase status in order to keep up appearances. The meeting of basics, or the achievement of absolute social norms, did not mitigate the coercion to purchase variety and status, or the achievement of relative social norms. If anything, the attainment of basics seemed only to intensify social conflict over who would be able to buy variety and status.

Table 8.2 Standard of living index, 1918–88

		Basics	*Variety*	*Status*	*Income*
1918	Laborer	0.45	0.00	0.00	0.31
	Wage earner	0.50	0.03	0.01	0.40
	Salaried	0.51	0.25	0.09	0.67
1935	Laborer	0.54	0.02	0.00	0.37
	Wage earner	0.56	0.11	0.02	0.46
	Salaried	0.56	0.38	0.15	0.77
1950	Laborer	0.69	0.10	0.02	0.52
	Wage earner	0.72	0.23	0.11	0.72
	Salaried	0.73	0.33	0.24	0.92
1973	Laborer	0.98	0.17	0.21	1.10
	Wage earner	1.00	0.27	0.29	1.35
	Salaried	1.04	0.46	0.55	1.97
1988	Laborer	1.00	0.17	0.31	1.00
	Wage earner	1.05	0.44	0.42	1.52
	Salaried	1.13	0.66	0.80	2.39

Benchmark for basics, variety and status is 1988 laborer basics in 1992 dollars ($20,321). Benchmark for income is laborers' income for 1988 in 1992 dollars ($28,661).

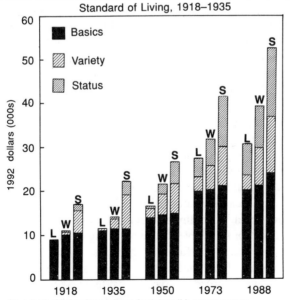

Standard of living breakdown for labor (L), wage earner (W) and salaried (S) families for 1918–35.

Figure 8.4 Standard of living, 1918–1935

Salaried families' consumption included all the basics in 1918. Wage-earner families were also able to buy the basics in all categories except food and transportation, and basic consumption in these two categories was attained in 1935. In 1918, laborer families did not meet basic requirements in any major category – food, clothing, housing, transportation, and recreation and education.[5] They made great strides in 1935 when they purchased basics in food, clothing, transportation, and recreation and education. They would not consume basics in all categories until 1973, when they finally bought basics in housing.

Salaried families attained basic transportation that allowed car ownership in 1935; wage earners attained basic car transportation in 1950 and laborers in 1973. Salaried families met the housing basics that allowed home ownership in 1950, and working-class families attained basic home ownership in 1973. Overall, 1973 was a watershed year in that working-class families had finally achieved consumption above basics in all categories. This achievement presupposed that families were covered by an employer-sponsored health insurance plan. Families without this important benefit could be denied basic medical care. Even those with health insurance had to worry about losing the insurance if they became unemployed.

Even though blacks' economic position had improved considerably by 1950, they met or exceeded basics in only four unimportant categories – furnishings, energy, household operations, recreation, personal care, and gifts. Their segregation from the white community allowed them to create their own criteria for consumption norms. They focused on less costly areas where extra spending could make life more pleasant and foster a social life – making their homes nicer inside and more presentable, having their hair styled, going to the movies, and giving gifts.

In 1973, after a decade of the war on poverty, families living at the government-defined poverty threshold consumed sufficient food only if they participated in the Food Stamp Program. They received basic health care only if they were eligible for Medicaid. They economized on personal appearances and did not purchase the basics in clothing or haircuts. They had to rely on public transportation.

By 1988, poor families were substantially better off in many ways, but their housing situation had deteriorated. Their budgets allowed them sufficient food and car transportation. They were able to consume above the dependency level, and almost reach the basic level, in recreation and household operations. They still were frugal in their purchases for personal appearance. Poor families, however, were no longer living in acceptable housing. This contributed to the already difficult lives they led, since many were forced to live in unsafe areas with inferior schools. At the extreme, they were living on the streets as the phenomenon of homelessness reappeared, reminiscent of the Depression. Just like the Depression, the homeless are not represented in expenditure data in 1988.

For many immigrants from developing countries, being poor in the United States provides an enormous improvement in the standard of living along with the opportunity for their children to be educated. These improvements in living standards are hidden and are not recorded in the standard of living index, which compares living standards over time by US norms.

In the 1960s and early 1970s, as basics were being met by laborer families in all categories, the economic growth and the ensuing high standard of living appeared to facilitate the development of a social consensus to distribute income in a more equal manner and to shorten work hours. As income growth slowed after 1973, these goals were quickly replaced by the objective of increasing private spending, which led to the tax revolt in California in the mid-1970s. The tax revolt quickly spread to the rest of the country. The public's demand to lower taxes successfully diverted resources from public to private spending. As families spent more on private goods and services to obtain variety and status, public problems such as environmental degradation, homelessness, and crime worsened. Even as traffic congestion lengthened commuting times and added to air pollution, the public resisted using public transportation. The societal and market bias against public goods and in favor of private goods was in full force.[6] Within their private spheres, employed families were experiencing a rising standard of living; outside their homes, however, the quality of life was rapidly deteriorating in many ways.

Where We Stand

At the end of the 1980s, the public was voicing discontent about the nation's economic fortunes. The incorrect perception that private living standards were falling and children were not living as well as their parents was widespread.[7] However, our income and expenditure data show that families generally continued to do better than families of the same class in 1973, and considerably better than in 1950. Only laborers did not do better in 1989 than in 1973, but they did not do worse. Laborers did considerably better than in 1950. The findings of a Congressional Budget Office (CBO) study are consistent with these conclusions. The CBO found that baby boomers, those born between 1946 and 1964, had both higher real median income and household wealth in 1989 than their parents had at a comparable age.[8] The financial improvement reflects both the higher educational achievement of the boomers[9] along with the increase in labor market participation of women. There are forces at work that might explain this rising discontent. Here we will consider three possible sources of discontent: Higher income provides improvements only in variety and status, not basics; the public standard of living declines; and conflict arises over distribution of resources, both within the US and across the global economy.

With employed families spending one-third to over one-half of their incomes on variety and status, the question arises – what are variety and status buying in terms of quality of life, as opposed to a standard of living?

What are the forces that propel families to purchase variety and status in recreational goods even though they dread to leave their homes during the day because of smog and at night because of crime? Feeling powerless to influence public problems that significantly undermined their own standard of living, people have turned inward to focus on their private consumption. Disillusioned with society's ability to tackle social problems, much less solve them, families have withdrawn to their private lives and sought solace in consumption of variety and status. For many people, the demands in their private lives of going to work and taking care of family deplete their time and energy. Yet social pressure to maintain consumption norms prevents them from expanding leisure time or focusing on social problems.

The economic distance generated through purchases of basics in an earlier period resulted in substantial differences in the way people lived and in their well-being. The standard of living and the quality of life were almost congruent, and economic growth produced noticeable improvements in both. Economic distance created during the present time through purchases of variety and status result in only subtle differences among classes in the way people live and in their well-being. In a more mature economy and crowded society, the standard of living and the quality of life coincide less and less. Yet people yearned to augment their variety and status in private consumption between 1973 and 1988. This longing does not seem to have diminished in the 1990s, the decade when the popular home shopping stations became the 'fifth' network on television.

The tax revolt was only one sign of the ensuing conflict over income distribution. Several forces had converged to heighten the conflict. Expectations were not met as the growth of the economy abated; poverty appeared to be more costly to eradicate as the two-parent family declined; and government programs seemed to have provided most people with the basics. President Reagan reinforced this belief that no one was denied the 'necessities of life,' even though the poverty rate for children was growing as he spoke. If absolute needs were met, people apparently reasoned, then fighting over the distribution of relative wants seemed justifiable (if self-serving). Between 1973 and 1988, social concerns about poverty and equity ebbed and individual concerns about making and spending money blossomed. Flaunting one's money and status spending were in vogue, and we see that this permeated consumption norms across the income spectrum. We left our American families at this point in history.

A Final Evaluation

The question that engendered this inquiry remains: Why are Americans driven to seek an ever-higher material standard of living, instead of a more leisurely life style and a higher quality of life? Although the complete answer should also include the political, cultural, and social forces at work, the analysis presented here allows us to discuss the economic basis for this behavior. Several economic dimensions appear to be important.

- Fulfillment of basics by the great majority of the US population has generated and justified public competition for consumption of variety and status. Rather than reducing the drive to use goods and services to create economic distance, affluence has intensified the desire to distinguish oneself by status and to buy an ever more varied set of consumption bundles.
- Economic growth has added to basic consumption in two ways: First, consumption that supports complex economic and social transactions has increased, for example, the need for car transportation, for telephone services, for banking services, and for cable television. With the development of computer and interactive multimedia for information dissemination and for financial and knowledge transactions, the basic requirement for taking part in such transactions will change dramatically and will necessitate purchase of the requisite commodities.
- Innovation has become increasingly important in the latter part of the twentieth century as introduction of new goods and services has speeded up. Family incomes have not grown sufficiently to allow both innovation and emulation of traditional consumption norms. Consumers have opted for innovation at the expense of traditional emulation, and this disruption of consumption norms seems to cause families to undervalue the improvements made in their standard of living.
- The American perception that the period 1950–73 should serve as a benchmark for judging the future has resulted in unrealistic expectations. This period was extraordinary in the improvements achieved in living standards across classes. Unrealistic, unmet expectations have supported the quest to improve material standards of living ever since.
- Social welfare programs set up for those at the bottom of the income distribution dramatically diminished the economic distance between the lower working class and those receiving welfare. The shorter distance increased class conflict and undermined public support for

welfare programs, as the lower working class felt threatened by a closing of the economic distance between themselves and the poor.

The strength of these economic forces in the United States should not be underestimated. In the past two decades, wages have stagnated, but American families have maintained or improved living standards by increasing total paid work hours and by reducing savings. Neither of these techniques is without a hidden cost to the family and neither can be sustained as a method to improve living standards. Continued wage stagnation will eventually translate into stagnation of living standards.

In the absence of a major transformation of social values, our class conflicts over income and what it buys can be expected to intensify. Instead of a diminished materialistic drive, we might experience an even more dedicated quest for an ever higher standard of living. Americans will no doubt remain focused on acquiring private goods to impart status, rather than directing our nation's resources to resolve social problems – even as these problems undermine our own quality of life.

Looking ahead

Evaluation of American standards of living in the 1990s depends on whether one has a worldwide perspective or a national perspective. From a global perspective, the United States enjoys the highest private standard of living in terms of housing, automobile use, recreational activities, food, clothing, and energy use. Americans continue to use a disproportionate amount of the world's resources. Private medical care is excellent, but costly for employers and a large drain on the economy. Social Security provides an unparalleled system of income and medical care for seniors, but it relies on a transfer of income from employed people to retired people that will be difficult to sustain when the baby boomers retire. The higher education system is world class, but the K-12 system lags behind those of other developed countries in terms of graduation rates and test scores. Social services for the poor also lag behind those in many western European countries. To some extent this gap reflects the emphasis on individual choice and liberty in the United States, which results in more lenient immigration policies, for both legal and illegal immigrants, and in more social acceptance of individual decisions that have an adverse social impact, such as the substantial increase in single-mother families.

From a national perspective, we Americans seem unaware of our disproportionate use of the world's resources. Instead, we are more concerned about our ability to maintain a high and growing standard of living. We are especially troubled by the slow economic growth of the 1980s and the debt we have amassed at the Federal level and in world trade. Although concerned about public education, Americans are uncertain how to improve it. Although troubled about the dissolution of the family, we are uncertain how to halt it. We Americans take great pride in our military superiority and our role in the downfall of the USSR. We also take pride in being a world leader in advancing equal rights for women.

Two major forces that affect living standards in substantial but opposite ways are still evolving – globalization and computerization. The US economy and society have had to adjust to intense competitive pressures as the world economy has become more open and interconnected. As the Cold War has collapsed into many localized wars, the United States is re-examining its military role. As American wage-earner jobs are disappearing with the movement of capital abroad or the importing of foreign-made manufacturing goods, the United States is reevaluating its need to protect its semi-skilled and skilled labor market. As the number of immigrants swells, the United States is reevaluating its role as a haven for refugees and those seeking a better life.

From a national perspective, the inclination to protect labor markets and living standards seems reasonable; from a global perspective, a protectionist approach seems selfish and harmful. Some researchers predict that revitalizing productivity and income growth will expand domestic jobs sufficiently and will make the United States competitive internationally. Economic theory does not point to this conclusion, however. The formation of a worldwide market economy should lead to a convergence of wages and living standards, as capital moves to take advantage of lower wages and as workers move to take advantage of higher wages. The importance of domestic markets and domestic resources fades as the world provides an expanding marketplace. Americans benefit in the short run as consumers of less expensive goods, but we are penalized in the long run when real wages decline. Without institutions that regulate these flows and protect the structure of domestic labor markets, living standards in the developed world will decline, or stagnate at best, until living standards in the developing world have caught up. How the United States evaluates this situation depends upon whether the welfare of the world's population or the welfare of US citizens is foremost.

Regulating immigration is an important variable in this evaluation. Although immigrants from developing countries usually raise their consumption standards instantaneously by coming to the United States, from a national perspective, large-scale immigration of less-educated people simultaneously results in an increase in the poverty population with a lower standard of living. In addition, the increased supply of less-educated workers puts downward pressure on wages in the low end of the labor market. This reinforces earnings inequality and undermines the ability of the US to achieve the goal of restructuring and upgrading its labor market to provide primarily high wage, high skill jobs.

Although many individual immigrants improve their lives, the American standard of living declines. The country correctly perceives this overall decline as detrimental to the 'American way of life' predicated on the living standards and socioeconomic roles of wage-earner families. A large, and growing, proportion of the population that has lower living standards and less education and skills will change the American way of life. If other advanced economies absorb immigrants more slowly, the US standard of living will fall relative to Western Europe and Japan. How this change in the US relative standard of living will affect the American global standing depends on the complex interaction of domestic and international policies of the US and its trading partners.

The other major force still evolving is computerization, which simultaneously changes the skills used at work and opens new consumption worlds in communication and recreation. Some economists predict that computerization will restore US productivity growth and provide high skill, high wage domestic jobs. To do this, technological innovation must provide the United States with a comparative advantage in innovative products that will stop the decline in living standards generated by the globalization process. As consumers, Americans can look forward to living standards that expand to incorporate a wide array of modern communication devices and multimedia home entertainment systems. As employees, however, Americans do not seem better situated than foreigners to provide the various levels of skilled labor in designing, developing, manufacturing, and servicing these new goods and services.

Even so, the development of these new goods and services should provide a boost to economic growth both in the United States and worldwide. If this is the case, then we would expect American standards of living to gradually increase to incorporate the innovative goods and services. At the same time, further improvements in income and living standards will be constrained by the pressures of global competition. Constrained expenditure growth in the United States should continue the modifications in consumption norms that occurred between 1973 and 1988, when slow growth resulted in innovation with almost no emulation and in the expansion of variety, and especially status, purchases.

Worldwide economic development, coupled with the number one problem of population growth, will force serious attention to environmental degradation. Congestion and environmental problems may force the American people to broaden their focus from fixation on private standards of living, which reflect relative standing in the community, to broader concern with the public standard of living, which is shared by all. If so, the concepts developed here – economic distance and the division of the standard of living into basics, variety, and status, along with the dynamics of emulation and innovation – will have to be expanded to include environmental conditions and the global economic situation. The path of the United States and the rest of the world in using the world's resources, including its people's energy and talents, is at a crucial crossroads. Our ability to protect our private living standards and enhance the public living standard, while we participate in the development and preservation of the world economy, remains to be tested.

NOTES

1. Frank Levy, *Dollars and Dreams* (New York: W. W. Norton, 1988), documents how the slower income and productivity growth, combined with demographic trends, has changed the American income distribution. Overall, the position of the elderly has improved, the position of children has deteriorated, and sons face a lower earnings profile than their fathers. Paul Krugman, *The Age of Diminished Expectations* (Cambridge, MA: MIT Press, 1990), explores the macroeconomic foundations of the decline in income and productivity growth and the role that United States economic policy played.

2. Funeral expenses and occupational expenses are also included in miscellaneous. Over the years, these two categories declined substantially in their importance. On the theoretical development of transactions costs, see Oliver Williamson, *The Economic Institutions of Capitalism* (New York: Free Press, 1985).

3. David M. Cutler and Lawrence F. Katz in 'Rising Inequality? Changes in the Distribution of Income and consumption in the 1980s,' paper presented to the AEA meetings, January 1992, present data that shows the lowest quintile in the family income distribution had a higher share of consumption in 1973 than in 1960 or during the 1980s and that their share of consumption continued to fall during the 1980s, largely as a result of their relative increase in family size. Cutler and Katz also estimated the 1989 poverty rates based on consumption were 18% for children under 18 years old and 5% for seniors (over 65 years old).

4. This and the following data on life expectancy and death rates are from *Historical Statistics* and *Statistical Abstract of the United States*, various issues. Death rates should be used with caution since they are not adjusted for comparability.

5. Employed families met basics in medical care provided they had a major medical health insurance policy sponsored by their employer.

6. J. K. Galbraith, *The Affluent Society*, 4th edition (Boston: Houghton Mifflin, 1984).

7. See, for example, Katherine S. Newman, *Declining Fortunes: The Withering of the American Dream* (New York: Basic Books, 1993).

8. Congress of the United States, Congressional Budget Office, *Baby Boomers in Retirement: An Early Perspective*, Washington, DC, 1993. The parents of the baby boomers are defined to be people aged 55–74 in 1989. Two notable exceptions to the average improvement in the economic situation of the baby boomers are those without a high school degree and those who are unmarried with children. In general, the financial position of the older baby boomers, those born before 1955, was even more improved than that of the younger boomers born after 1955. However, real wealth of the older boomers who are not homeowners fell.

9. One of every four boomers had completed four years of college by 1989.

Appendix

Data sources for American Standards of Living 1918–1988

The principles used to structure the data collection are discussed here. Three main topics are covered – why data were organized along occupation or class lines, how income by occupation was calculated, and how the years studies were chosen. Finally, the handling of specific problems of consistency within the CES data and the quality of the CES data are briefly mentioned.

The Classes and Other Groups Analyzed

The main source of household budget data for this study is the Consumer Expenditure Surveys (CES), which have been made periodically by the Bureau of Labor Statistics as the basis for weighing the Consumer Price Index (CPI). Because the CPI was devised to reflect cost of living increases for the urban working class, the CES was not meant to represent the US population. Over the years, the definition of which households to include varied as the demographics of the workforce changed and as policy concerns shifted. As a result of the lack of consistency of the Surveys and the lack of national representation, these Surveys have been used only peripherally in studies of changes in consumption and living standards over time, although they are one of the largest and most complete sources of data on household expenditures available.

In this study, the creation of three stylized urban classes with employed heads (lower (unskilled) working class; upper (semi-skilled and skilled) working class; salaried and middle class (salaried professional and lower and middle manager class)) allows the CES to be used as the primary data source. The working class is divided into a lower and upper segment, which reflects skills and economic vulnerability. Preferably, the upper segment could have been further divided into semi-skilled (or production workers) and skilled (or craft workers), but limitations of sample size prevented this. In addition, the upper working class has traditionally been protected by unionization, which has also tended to decrease the wage differential between skilled and semi-skilled workers and to provide some mobility from semi-skilled to skilled jobs. Although in the earlier periods many male clerical workers were generally in the salaried class, clerical workers are excluded because this occupation undergoes a transformation from a managerial to a staff position that is increasingly filled by women workers.

Because the self-employed and high-level management are not included in the earlier CES surveys, and because the sample size for these groups is small when they are included, the upper middle class (self-employed professionals and salaried high-level management) is not included in this study. Whenever available, other studies such as Peixotto's study of executive families in 1935, are compared to the salaried class included in this study.

With households analyzed by their position in the labor market (i.e., class), rather than by their position in the income distribution, the means of earning a living is coupled with living standards. This approach is consistent with the empirical issues under study; i.e., the economic distance across classes and the relationship between work roles, living standards, and economic growth. Business cycle differences (i.e., temporary unemployment) are incorporated into the analysis through the impact on the median income of the occupations. Changes in family composition and demographics are also incorporated in the analysis as these trends become part of the classes themselves. As is noted in the chapters, the position of the classes in the income distribution and the relative size of the classes vary somewhat over the periods studied.

In addition to the traditional classes based on labor market position, urban black families are included because of the disadvantaged position of blacks as the primary minority group and because of the segregation of blacks in the labor market. The labor market position of blacks changes as blacks have job opportunities opened to them during World War II and following the Civil Rights Movement in the 1960s. At the same time, the family composition of blacks changes so that a substantial proportion of them are no longer headed by an employed male. In the 1973 and 1988 chapters, the black class is bifurcated into husband–wife families, whose husband has now reached working-class status, and into single-parent families, who form an important segment of the poor population.

Changes in the design of the CES and the sampled population have occurred, especially since 1972–3, as the government recognized uses of the data for purposes other than construction of the CPI. With better data on demographic and income groups available, two groups – the poor and the elderly – are added to the analysis in 1973 because of their importance in policy issues. These two groups are defined by income. The government's official poverty benchmarks are used to identify poor urban households, and the median income for urban households headed by a person over 65 years old is used to identify the typical group for the elderly.

Income Calculations

In order to analyze representative families in each class, an income range centered around the median income for the occupations in that class had to be calculated. This entailed a cum rome estimation procedure in 1918 and 1935; in the latter years, the Current Population Survey could be used to assign income to class.

The income of the occupational classes for **1917–19** was estimated from a variety of sources (1918$ given). The earnings for laborers were derived from the wages for laborer and non-union manufacturing reported by Douglas ($21.20–$21.50) and for unskilled males in 25 industries reported by the National Industrial Conference Board (NICB, $21.88) and for non-domestic service by Kuznets ($949). The earnings for wage earners were derived from the weekly wages for union manufacturing and building trades reported by Douglas ($1,266–$1,290) and for skilled and semi-skilled males by the NICB ($28.63). The earnings for salaried workers were derived from the earnings of lower-level salaried and clerical workers in manufacturing reported by Douglas ($1,765) and by the BLS for clerical employees in manufacturing and railroads ($1,697) and by Kuznets for salaried managers ($1,766). The figure ($778) for salaried professionals reported by Kuznets included mostly teachers and ministers, and so was not used.

These earnings were compared to the estimated provided by Lebergott for full-time manufacturing ($1,107 yearly), Coomb for unskilled male laborer ($21.69 hourly), NBER male manufacturing wages ($1,097 yearly), BLS for building trades ($1,260), and in vehicles ($1,249), and Kuznets for annual earnings for production workers in manufacturing ($1,015), mining ($1,024), construction ($1,072), and transportation ($1,502). The earnings figures used conform to the 1.3 skill differential between laborers and the semi-skilled and skilled workers in manufacturing reported in 1920 by NICB.

Earnings for low-income workers, especially immigrants and blacks, are represented by the annual earnings in curative ($519), domestics ($592), and laundry ($715), as reported by Kuznets. This, coupled with extrapolations from 1935 non-relief earnings, puts black families in the lowest income group (<$900) in 1918.

These earnings figures for the employed husband are transposed into family income figures using the ratio of earnings to total family income from the CES.

The relative position of the occupational classes in the income distribution is estimated from the NBER estimates of the national income distribution, which was based upon income tax returns. This distribution was estimated by fitting the tail of the income distribution, since incomes had to be reported only if in excess of $1,000 for single persons and $2,000 for married couples.

For **1935**, the national survey on 300,000 households compiled by the National Resources Committee as a Federal Works Project in 1935–6 provided information on the income distribution by occupation. The median income (1935$) for non-relief families was $2,485 for salaried businessmen, $2,100 for salaried professionals, and $1,175 for wage earners. The latter occupational group was not broken down further by skill level. The NICB reported semi-skilled male workers in manufacturing earned $24.98 weekly ($0.665 hourly for 37.7 hours) and unskilled workers earned $18.32 weekly ($0.495 hourly for 37.0 hours). These full-time earnings were adjusted downward by a factor of 0.12 for short-term unemployment. This factor, which equaled the total non-farm unemployment rate of 30% in 1935 minus the relief rate of 18% for non-farm families, was assumed to represent the unemployment experienced by the typical non-relief worker. These earnings were then adjusted by the ratio of husband's earnings to family income, using the CES data, to arrive at family income by class.

For blacks, the median family income for non-relief urban black families in the Southern and North Central cities was $678. This covered 87% of all urban blacks.

The Years Chosen

CES data are available for two periods preceding 1917, and comparable studies are available for other years during the 1918 to 1986 period. My study begins in 1918, so that the CES data from 1901 and from 1888–90 are not included for two primary reasons. First, the earlier data had serious comparability problems. The 1888 data were from nine selected industries, which produced dutiable products, in the United States and Europe. The 1901 survey included only the larger industrial areas and had an earnings ceiling of $1,200. In both studies, the salaried class was excluded. In addition, national data for defining the correct income by occupation were not available, and making such an estimation would have been even more problematic than it was for 1917–18.

For the other survey years, the **Current Population Report** is used to calculate the median income for urban households by occupation of head. For blacks, the CPS is also the source for the median income for urban husband–wife families. The CPS is the source for the median income for households headed by someone 65 years or older. The income benchmarks used to define urban poor households are those defined by the Federal government by family size.

Second, the year 1918 provided a good beginning point for economic reasons. The process of urbanization and the industrial transformation of the economy was well under way, yet the life-style of the working class had not yet been affected by the most important product of mass production – the automobile, which would come to dominate manufacturing production as well as consume a large proportion of the family budget. Ford's mass production of the automobile began only within the decade preceding the 1917–19 survey, and production and consumption of the car was to become increasingly important in the growth of both the economy and the family's budget over the next three decades.

Within the period studied (1918–86), several surveys were excluded. Two wartime studies (1941–2 and 1944) were undertaken to provide data for wage and price controls. But the regulated war economy did not provide a good period for comparing living standards across classes, since basic goods were rationed and consumers had forced savings.

Studies of farm families have also been excluded, since this is a study of the living standards of families dependent on selling their labor in the marketplace. The living standards of farm families were typically dependent on producing for own use and on selling crops rather than on wage labor. A comparison between the living standards of white farm and laborer families and of black farm and urban families in 1918 would be especially interesting. However, it is beyond the scope of this study.

How the periods used in this study serve as markers of important turning points is discussed in the text. The CES was also collected in 1960–1, but that survey is not included in this study since the period did not provide a benchmark for a turning point, as was true of the other survey periods. An earlier paper ('Consumption Norms, Work Roles, and Economic Growth, 1918–80' in Brown and Pechman, eds) included 1960 in the analysis, and the 1960 data showed that the trends apparent in 1950 continued. The culmination of strong economic growth and income support programs are seen in the 1973 data, which marks the end of the high growth period before the impact of sharply higher energy prices and a more interdependent world economy.

The final survey year, 1988, presents the most recent data available. The CES is now collected on an ongoing basis so that this study could be updated continuously.

Other Considerations

The CES changed both its inclusion of households and its categorization of goods and services over the surveys. The characteristics of the sample are noted in the text, and some comparisons are made for the different samples used. In 1935, since the CES excluded salaried workers other than low-level clerical workers, the NRC sample is used as the data source for the salaried class. The NRC data are also used to derive the details for the other classes, since the details are available in the CES only by 'expenditure unit' (i.e., total expenditure divided by a measure of equivalent adults) and not by income. Since the NRC data are published only by city, a national figure is calculated using nationally-representative weights for the cities.

Data were collected on an annual basis in most circumstances through 1973. When the CES began to be collected continually, data were collected on a quarterly basis, as in 1988. The procedures used to adjust the data for annual comparisons are noted in the text.

The categorization of goods and services are adjusted in the study so that the various categories do not change across the surveys. The most important categories that have discrepancies in the CES are noted in the text. In general, for users of the CES data, comparisons of the reported details with the actual data will reveal whenever specific items have been moved in order to make the data comparable across years.

The use of the CES to study living standards over time has required many adjustments and the use of outside data, whenever possible. Comparisons are made to other data sources, such as national expenditure data or other survey data, in order to check the reliability of the data. Other references (such as Helen Lamale, *Methodology: Survey of Consumer Expenditures,* 1959) that discuss the reliability of the data are also mentioned. Generally, the expenditure data seem to provide a good measure of the actual consumption of most items. One exception is alcohol. The figures for savings, which sometimes are calculated in the CES as the difference between reported income and reported expenditures and sometimes as the net increase in assets, are not a reliable source for savings data. However, trends in expenditures as a proportion of income can be used as a relative measure of financial pressure or security across classes and across time.

Sources

For budget data

For 1918 (blacks), *Monthly Labor Review*, Vol. 9, No. 2; for 1918 (whites), *Cost of Living in the United States*, Bureau of Labor Statistics,

Bulletin No. 357, May 1924. In 1935, for all classes except salaried, *Money Disbursements of Wage Earners and Clerical Workers 1934–36: Summary Volume*, BLS Bulletin No. 638. For salaried families in 1935, *Study of Consumer Purchases*, BLS Bulletins No. 643–649. For 1950, *Study of Consumer Expenditures, Incomes, and Savings* (18 volumes), tabulated by the Wharton School of Finance and Commerce for the BLS, 1957. For 1973, the 1973 CES interview and diary public use tapes, and *Consumer Expenditure Survey Series: Interview Survey, 1972–73*. (BLS Bulletin No. 1985, Aug. 1978.) For 1988, the 1988 CES interview and diary public use tapes, and *Consumer Expenditure Survey, 1988–1989*, US Department of Labor, Bureau of Labor Statistics, Bulletin 2354.

For earnings

Paul Douglas, *Real Wages in the United States, 1890 to 1926*, 1930; National Industrial Conference Board, *Economic Almanac for 1950 and Wages, Hours, and Employment in the United States, 1914–1936*; Simon Kuznets, *National Income and Its Composition, 1918–1938*, vols. 1 and 2, 1941; Bureau of Labor Statistics, *History of Wages in the United States From Colonial Times to 1928*, revision of Bulletin No. 499 with Supplement, 1929–1933, and *Employment and Earnings, United States, 1909–1971*, Bulletin 1312–8; Stanley Lebergott, *Manpower in Economic Growth*, 1964; Whitney Coombs, *The Wages of Unskilled Labor in the United States, 1890–1924*, 1926.

For income distribution

NBER (King, Knauth, and Macaulay), *Income in the United States: Its Amount and Distribution, 1909–1919*, Vol. 1, 1921; National Resources Committee, *Consumer Incomes in the United States*, 1938 and *Family Expenditures in the United States*, 1941; Bureau of Labor Statistics, *Income of Families and Persons in the United States*, Series P-60, 1950, 1973, and 1988.

Index